Java 2 Developer's Handbook

Java™ 2 Developer's Handbook™

Philip Heller and Simon Roberts

SYBEX®

San Francisco • Paris • Düsseldorf •Soest • London

Associate Publisher: Amy Romanoff
Contracts and Licensing Manager: Kristine Plachy
Acquisitions & Developmental Editor: Maureen Adams
Editor: Marilyn Smith
Project Editor: Raquel Baker
Technical Editors: Tim Russel and Matthew Fiedler
Book Designer: Kris Warrenburg
Graphic Illustrator: Tony Jonick
Electronic Publishing Specialists: Kate Kaminski and
Cyndy Johnsen
Production Coordinator: Rebecca Rider
Indexer: Ted Laux
Companion CD: Ginger Warner
Cover Designer: Design Site
Cover Illustrator: Daniel Bowman

Screen reproductions produced with Collage Complete.

Collage Complete is a trademark of Inner Media Inc.

SYBEX is a registered trademark of SYBEX Inc.

Developer's Handbook is a trademark of SYBEX Inc.

TRADEMARKS: SYBEX has attempted throughout this book to distinguish proprietary trademarks from descriptive terms by following the capitalization style used by the manufacturer.

The CD Interface music is from GIRA Sound AURIA Music Library © GIRA Sound 1996.

The author and publisher have made their best efforts to prepare this book, and the content is based upon final release software whenever possible. Portions of the manuscript may be based upon pre-release versions supplied by software manufacturer(s). The author and the publisher make no representation or warranties of any kind with regard to the completeness or accuracy of the contents herein and accept no liability of any kind including but not limited to performance, merchantability, fitness for any particular purpose, or any losses or damages of any kind caused or alleged to be caused directly or indirectly from this book.

Library of Congress Card Number: 98-85540
ISBN: 0-7821-2179-9

Manufactured in the United States of America

10 9 8 7 6 5 4 3

ACKNOWLEDGMENTS

We would like to thank Tom McGinn, Mike Ernest, Josh Krasnegor, James Casaletto, Charlotte Jordan, Georgianna Meagher, and Mike Bridwell for their support. Russel Taylor, Devon Tuck, Tim Lindholm, and Urs Eberle were generous with their knowledge and explanations.

We would also like to thank Suzanne Rotondo, Maureen Adams, Kim Crowder, and Krista Reid-McLaughlin, developmental editors; Laura Arendal, managing editor; Raquel Baker, project editor; and Marilyn Smith, editor. We appreciate their infinite patience with our narrative voices and their fine editing. Big thanks to Tim Russell and Matthew Fiedler, technical editors, for sending our manuscript through the technical wringer. Thanks also to Rebecca Rider, production coordinator, for her proofreading and organizational skills, and to Kate Kaminski, electronic publishing specialist, for her expert and speedy book layout.

Special thanks to Emily Roberts for striking the perfect pose with that enormous pastry (see `javadevhdbk\ch06\Emily.gif` on the CD-ROM).

CONTENTS AT A GLANCE

TABLE OF CONTENTS

PART III   The New APIs

Appendix

INTRODUCTION

Because this is an introduction, let us take a moment to introduce ourselves. Here we are together: the authors, the readers, and the book.

First the authors. One of us lives on the West Coast, and one recently moved to the U.S. from England. We bring a broad perspective, and not just because of geography. We are Java instructors by trade. Between us, we have taught Sun's Java classes to more than 1,000 students.

We have said, "Welcome to class, please turn to page 1 of your tutorial." Time after time, someone in the back of the room has said, "Yes, yes, we all know this already. How do I connect an applet to a database via TCP/IP?" During lab exercises, we have said, "Please do the lab on page 33." Time after time, someone has said, "I did that one last time. Now I'm writing my own layout manager, and it isn't working. What have I done wrong?"

In other words, we have been exposed to real-world uses of Java. Vicariously, we have accompanied more than 1,000 Java students through their learning processes and experiences. When they got stuck, we were asked about it. Where the classroom theory broke down, we were told about it—in no uncertain terms.

We have explored the dark and dusty corners of Java, armed only with flashlights, feather dusters, the API pages, and the source code. We are here to tell you what we found.

We originally wrote this book to describe revision 1.1 of the Java Developer's Kit (JDK). When we heard that Java 2 was coming, we thought it would be a good idea to revise the book. We have made extensive changes, so you will learn about the modern tools that are available to you. However, we have not changed the book's fundamental philosophy, which is to go far beyond describing the Java toolkit. We want to tell you how to use the tools.

So much for who we are. Who are you? That is, who did we write this book for? What assumptions have we made about you?

We assume that you have already been through your first Java book or your first Java class. You understand the theory. You know the syntax of the language.

You know about objects. You know most of the basics of most of the packages. You are comfortable with looking up class and method descriptions in the API documentation. You have written applets and applications. You are moving beyond the well-lit regions of Java into the dark and the dusty, and you would like some guidance for your journey.

If the previous paragraph describes you, then this is the book for you. This is the book that plunges right in. No introductory chapters on the history of the Internet. No discourse on object polymorphism. The name James Gosling is not mentioned even once in this book. Oops—well, only once.

So much for introductions. We are delighted to make your acquaintance. Now that we all know one another a bit better, we would like to make you aware of a few details concerning this book.

What This Book Contains

We kept a number of principles in mind when we wrote this book. Foremost, every chapter begins with a review of the relevant background material, then gets into the meat of the topic. If you're confident about the basics, you can skip right to the second or third section.

We have strong feelings about sample code. We have tried our best to keep it relevant. For example, in the chapter on threads, the sample code is intended to teach you about how threads interact, not to impress you with how clever we are. Reading lengthy source code is difficult, and we have kept the samples as small as possible. However, in the real world, it sometimes takes a lot of lines to make a program robust. The code in this book is as terse as possible but as long as necessary.

The Organization of the Book

This book is divided into three parts:

- The first part, The Basics (Chapters 1 through 5), discusses such issues as the Java environment, applets and applications, components, layout managers, and portability. Although the topics are basic, the discussions are broad and deep.

- The second part, Advanced Topics (Chapters 6 through 14), discusses images, threads, animation, files and streams, networking, database access, distributed objects, and content and protocol handlers.

- The third part, The New APIs (Chapters 15 through 18), examines functionality that is new or enhanced in release 1.2 of the JDK. This part covers Java Foundation Classes (JFC) components, the 2D API, Java Beans, and security.

The book also has an appendix that contains a collection of answers to frequently asked questions.

Conventions

This book uses various conventions to present information in as readable a manner as possible. Tips, Notes, and Warnings, shown here, appear throughout the text in order to call attention to specific highlights.

TIP

This is a tip. Tips contain specific programming techniques.

NOTE

This is a note. Notes contain important side discussions.

WARNING

This is a warning. Warnings call attention to bugs, design omissions, and other trouble spots.

This book takes advantage of several font styles. **Bold font** in text indicates something that the user types. A monospaced font is used for program code, URLs, and file and directory names.

The CD-ROM

All of the source code and class files for the sample programs discussed in this book can be found on the CD-ROM. Wherever we could, we implemented our sample code as applets and included simple web pages so you can run them as is. Sometimes this strategy is not possible; some operations, especially those relating to the network and the file system, may be executed only by applications. These can still be invoked right off the CD-ROM.

The CD-ROM has a directory called javadevhdbk, which has one subdirectory for each chapter of the book that contains code. The applications can be run by command-line invocation. The applets, of course, require a browser. Each applet has a simple `html` file whose name closely resembles the name of the applet subclass. We recommend using the Applet Viewer to browse the applets.

You'll also find a new kind of sample program, called *labs*, on the CD-ROM. The source for the labs is not discussed in the book (though it is provided for interest's sake on the CD-ROM). With these labs, learning happens not from reading the sources but from executing the applets. For example, there is a lab for Chapter 4, which covers layout managers, called `GridBagLab`. The only way to develop an intuitive grasp of how to use the `GridBag` layout manager is to create a lot of layouts that mix and match the myriad possible combinations of values of the grid bag constraints. One way to create all these combinations is to write a lot of code. However, with `GridBagLab`, you need only use the user interface to select constraint values, click a button, and see the result. Experience and intuition are developed in much less time. The labs are educational toys.

Revisions and corrections to the CD-ROM can be found at the publisher's web site at `http://www.Sybex.com`.

Together, the book and the CD-ROM will guide you along the path to developing robust, platform-independent Java programs. We, the authors, are pleased and excited with how the book has turned out. We wish you a fruitful and pleasant learning experience.

PART I

The Basics

CHAPTER

ONE

1

Java Ecology

- Java's networking support

- Java class loading and initialization

- Java's security mechanisms

- Java's threads

- Java's colors, fonts, and component support

- GUI component layout

Java programs run on a virtual machine that is implemented on a real platform. A Java program runs with considerable support from its environment.

We begin this book with an examination of Java's environmental issues, including networking, classes, security, the file system, properties, multithreading, and screen display. A programmer who has a clear understanding of this material will have an easier time developing code and will understand how the Java Developer's Kit (JDK) works.

Java and the Network

The most obvious component of Java's environment is the network. Applets exist on the Internet or on intranets. Java includes the following networking support:

- There are classes that enable applets and applications to communicate across the network using the UDP or TCP/IP protocols.
- Java's class loader is designed to facilitate network operation.
- Java's security mechanisms are designed to protect against infiltration through the network.
- Many of the functional restrictions imposed on applets are intended to prevent them from exhibiting inappropriate network behavior.

In order to create robust networking applets and applications, it is important to understand the functionality provided by Java's networking classes, as well as the limitations imposed by Java's security model. Chapter 10 explores Java's networking capabilities, and Chapter 18 explains Java's security support.

Java Classes

Every line of executable Java code belongs to one class definition or another. Java uses classes to represent everything: buttons, applets, URLs, files, and even classes themselves. Here we will discuss how classes are loaded and the role that class loading plays in Java's security mechanism.

Class Loading

Consider the simplest applet imaginable:

```
public class SimplestApplet extends java.applet.Applet
{
}
```

This code clearly does absolutely nothing, but it is valuable to study the process by which it comes to do absolutely nothing. First, being an applet, it must be mentioned in an HTML page so that a browser can download and execute it:

```
. . .
<APPLET CODE=SimplestApplet.class WIDTH=200 HEIGHT=150>
</APPLET>
. . .
```

Eventually, a user will browse to this page, which will be parsed by the browser's HTML interpreter. The APPLET tag tells the browser that a Java class must be loaded.

By default (since there is no CODEBASE tag), the browser looks for the applet in the same directory where it found the HTML page. What the browser is looking for is a file named SimplestApplet.class. If the browser finds this file, it loads the applet class.

Now the applet definition file undergoes a thorough security check. A theorem prover, known as the bytecode verifier, decides whether or not the class definition meets its safety criteria. For example, every opcode must be valid and must be followed by the proper number of valid arguments. Access restrictions must be honored. There cannot be any operand stack overflows or underflows.

> **NOTE**
>
> The Java compiler converts Java source code to platform-independent *bytecode*, which can be thought of as machine language for the Java Virtual Machine (JVM). Just like machine language for actual hardware, bytecode is a series of instructions. Each instruction consists of an operation code, or *opcode*, followed by some number of operands.

Once the bytecode verifier has given its approval, the Java runtime environment within the browser must build an internal representation of the SimplestApplet class. Since every Java class (except Object) is an extension of some other class, building this internal representation requires two steps:

- A representation of the superclass must be created, if one does not already exist. Unless the superclass is Object, this process is recursive.

- The new data and functionality contributed by the subclass must be represented.

   The second step is easy: The class loader simply loads the SimplestApplet class from the network. Before this can be accomplished, the first step is to represent the superclass, which is Applet. Assuming the browser's Java runtime does not yet have a representation for class Applet, that class must be loaded. But Applet extends Panel, which extends Container, which extends Component; so every one of those classes must be loaded as well. This raises the question of where Java looks for classes to load. Java uses the following search strategy for finding class definitions:

- The Java runtime system's own set of class definitions is searched.
- If the class is not found, other locations on the local file system are searched, as specified by the class path.
- If the class is still not found, the remote web server is searched.

   Java utilizes this three-part search strategy as a method of security and time efficiency. The following sections describe each of these sources of class definitions.

The Core Java API

Every Java runtime environment has its own copy of the standard JDK classes. Some vendors keep these files in plain sight; others obscure them. Typically, the files are zipped together, although they are not compressed. Wherever and however the classes may appear, every runtime knows how to find its own system classes.

   This strategy ensures that frequently used class files are close at hand. For example, every Java program needs the definition of Object, and every Java program with a GUI (graphical user interface) needs the definition of Component. More obscure classes (LineNumberInputStream, for instance) are rarely required, but when they are loaded, it is important that their definitions are the correct standard version of the class.

The Class Path Classes

If a desired class file is not found in the system repository, the runtime next searches elsewhere on the local machine. If the environment variable CLASSPATH is set, all the directories listed there are searched in order of appearance. CLASSPATH is a list of path names, separated by semicolons on DOS platforms, and colons on other platforms. If CLASSPATH is not set, only the current working directory is searched.

The following command sets CLASSPATH on a Unix machine:

```
setenv CLASSPATH /w/x/java/classes:/y/z/morejava/classes
```

The following command does the same on a DOS machine:

```
SET CLASSPATH=C:\w\x\java\classes;C:\y\z\morejava\classes
```

Remote Classes

If a class required by an applet is not found on the local machine, the next place to search is the web server. (If a class required by an application is not found locally, however, there is no web server, and the search fails.) This search strategy ensures that remote classes, which are less trustworthy and take longer to load than local classes, are used only when no local version is available.

By default, the class file is expected to reside in the same directory where the browser found the web page. This can be overridden by the optional CODEBASE tag. For details on CODEBASE and on the location of packages, refer to Chapter 5.

It is also possible to store remote applet classes in Java Archive (JAR) files. (A JAR file is a container file, compatible with zip formats.) This approach offers several advantages, especially when applet code involves more than one class file:

- A single JAR file is easier to install and administer than multiple class files.

- All class files in the JAR file can be downloaded to a client browser in a single operation. With multiple class files and no JAR, every file transfer requires its own connection.

- A JAR file can be digitally signed with a private key. If a browser detects an applet from a trusted source, then the ordinary security restrictions can be relaxed. At the browser's discretion, for example, a trusted applet might be permitted to read or write the local file system.

Chapter 2 explains how to modify an APPLET tag to specify a JAR file, and Chapter 18 describes signing JAR files.

Static Initialization

After a class is loaded and has passed the bytecode verifier's checks, storage is allocated for any static variables that the class may declare. If a static declaration includes any initialization statements, the initialization is also performed at this time. For example, if a class had this declaration:

```
static int rev = 6;
```

then space would be allocated for the int and initialized to 6.

The Java compiler permits blocks of code in a class to be static. The code has no method name, no parameters, and no return value; it is simply a block of static code within a class. For example, a class definition might begin like this:

```
class MyClass extends MyOtherClass
{
    int             i, j;
    static double   d = 123.456;

    static
    {
        System.out.println("MyClass was just loaded.");
        d = d * 2.1;
    }
        . . .
}
```

There may be more than one static code block within a class definition. Static variable initialization and the static code blocks are executed in their order of appearance in the class definition. Like static methods, static code blocks may only refer to static variables within their own class.

Static code blocks look strange, they are hard to read, and many programmers are unfamiliar with them. They always execute, whether or not the execution is ever needed. This adds up to a maintenance risk, so you should use static blocks only when there is a compelling reason to do so. Their benefit is that they run early—as early as possible.

The most common use of static blocks is in classes that contain native methods. Native methods make calls to dynamically loaded libraries, and there is a great performance advantage to having the library fully loaded by the time any native call is made. To ensure this, classes with native methods have static blocks, which invoke the System.loadLibrary() call.

Another legitimate use of static code in a class is to initialize static variables that will be used by static methods of the class. Clearly, such initialization cannot be performed in a constructor, since it is possible that no constructor will ever be called. If the initialization is simple, it can be performed on the declaration line:

```
public class SimpleStatic
{
    static int i = 4;
    . . .
}
```

Some initialization, however, requires execution of code that is more complicated than the literal assignment shown above. The following code fragment shows how to use a static block to perform an initialization that involves catching an exception:

```
public class SimpleStatic2
{
    static Socket sock;
    static boolean sockOK = false;
    . . .
    static
    {
        try
        {
            sock = new Socket("dragonfly", 8765);
            sockOK = true;
        }
        catch (IOException x) { }
    }
    . . .
}
```

Java's Security Support

Java has a number of mechanisms to protect clients from attacks by rogue applets. We have already mentioned the bytecode verifier, which protects Java runtime environments against loading disreputable class files. A good Java compiler is not capable of generating opcodes that violate the bytecode verifier's criteria, but bytecode also can be generated by an attacker.

The following sections describe a few other security mechanisms. See Chapter 18 for a detailed discussion of Java's security support.

Browsers and Security Managers

Java applets have less access to resources on the client machine than do applications. This is not an inherent trait of applets, but rather a browser imposition.

Every browser constructs an instance of the SecurityManager class. Before attempting certain operations, such as file or socket access, the various JDK classes that encapsulate the operations must get permission from the security manager. The security manager grants or denies access to a wide range of functionality. File system access and network access are the two major categories of functionality that it controls.

It has often been said that applets may not read or write from the local or the remote file system. This is not strictly accurate. The truth is that nearly all Java-enabled browsers have security managers that do not allow applets to read or write locally or remotely. The limitation is a business decision on the part of the browser vendor, not a limitation inherent in the nature of applets. There is general consensus, however, as to what applets should and should not be allowed to do. Most browsers, including all Netscape Navigator products so far, implement security managers. These security managers do not let applets read or write locally or remotely, do not let applets be TCP/IP servers, and do not let applets be TCP/IP clients unless the server is the machine that served the applet itself.

Spoofing Protection

In addition to the bytecode verifier and the security manager, the class-loading mechanism described earlier in this chapter is an additional line of defense; it protects against a kind of attack known as *spoofing*.

Spoofing involves creating a class of the same name as a standard class, in the hope that the counterfeit class will be loaded instead of the genuine one. Classes that control access to sensitive resources are candidates for spoofing. In Java, the SecurityManager class is a prime target for spoofing. As we shall see, the class-loading algorithm makes SecurityManager (and every other standard JDK class) spoof-proof.

The attacker creates an applet as bait, and includes it in an enticing web page on a server. The attacker also creates a spoofing SecurityManager.class file, which grants permission to read and write anywhere. The applet, the counterfeit `SecurityManager.class` file, and the web page are all placed in the same directory on a server. The attacker hopes that the counterfeit version of `SecurityManager` will be downloaded and used in place of the authentic version.

The attack fails because the counterfeit class never gets loaded. When the browser realizes that it needs to load the `SecurityManager` class, it looks first in its own repository of classes. It finds `SecurityManager` there, so no further searching is required. The counterfeit version is ignored.

Java and File Systems

Applets ordinarily are not allowed to access the local file system, but applications may do so. The variety of path name and permission conventions presents problems that single-platform programs do not need to deal with. Unix uses a forward slash as a path separator and supports a moderate variety of permissions. Windows 95/98 uses a backslash, requires a drive letter and a colon for absolute path names, and supports limited permissions.

The `java.io.File` class encapsulates access to the local conventions, enabling Java applications to use the file system in a platform-independent manner. In particular, path separator and permission issues are hidden from the programmer. The `FileDialog` class presents users with a platform-independent file-selection dialog box. Chapter 9 goes into more detail about Java and file systems.

Java Properties

Java programs have no way to read environment variables from the local machine. This is to be expected, since not all platforms support environment variables. Java offers an alternative means of specifying environmental information, called *properties*.

Java properties resemble X resources. Applets read properties and property values from a table provided by the browser. Applications may get properties from a file or from the command line. Due to security issues, applets have restricted access to properties on the local machine. Chapter 5 goes into more detail about the uses and limitations of properties.

Java's Thread Support

Since the Java environment is multithreaded, programmers are offered access to Java's threads to create multithreaded applications and applets.

Some implementations of Java use the thread-support mechanisms of the underlying machine; others build their own thread support from scratch. Different platforms offer a variety of thread-support mechanisms. The result is that thread behavior varies noticeably from one platform to another. The major difference is that some implementations are time-sliced, and others are not. Writing successful, portable Java multithreaded programs requires an understanding of the different models and an ability to create code that is robust in all cases. Chapter 7 addresses these issues.

Java Screen Displays

As a programmer, you know how important the screen display is to users. We will discuss the various aspects of the screen display in detail in later chapters. Here, we will take a quick look at colors, fonts, and GUI components.

Java's Color Model

Java's color model supports 24-bit color with 8 bits for alpha (opacity), providing a palette with more than 16 million colors. However, since very few machines running Java today have hardware capable of supporting that many colors, the runtime system must convert requested colors to colors that the system can actually produce.

There are three ways to map colors:

- Use a very expensive computer that can actually support all the colors.
- Map requested colors to the closest available color. Under this scheme, many distinct combinations of red, green, and blue intensities map to the same color on the underlying platform.
- Create dither patterns to fool the eye.

You can run the `TrueColors` applet on the CD-ROM to see how Java colors are rendered on your machine. The source is `javadevhdbk\ch01\TrueColors.java`, and the applet resides in `javadevhdbk\ch01\truecolors.html`. The applet displays three squares, each 256×256 pixels. The square on the left contains every color that can be created by mixing various intensities of red and green, leaving out blue. Red intensity varies from zero at the top to full intensity at the bottom. Green varies from zero at the left to full intensity at the right. The square in the middle mixes green with blue, and the square on the right mixes blue with red.

Chapter 6 discusses color models in more detail.

Java's Font Support

Like colors, fonts vary from platform to platform. Java ports are supposed to support Helvetica, Times-Roman, Courier, and Dialog fonts; but they are free to map them to whatever actual font they please.

NOTE   As of release 1.1 of the JDK, the Helvetica font family is called SansSerif, Times-Roman is called Serif, and Courier is called Monospaced.

Java uses the `java.awt.Font` class to encapsulate font behavior and mapping. The constructor for `Font` builds an instance of the object and also requests the underlying windowing system to build the font itself. By and large, fonts tend to stay cached within their windowing system for as long as possible, so there is not much of a penalty for multiple constructions of identical fonts. For example, consider an applet that calls the following constructor many times:

```
Font bigfont = new Font("Serif", Font.ITALIC, 55);
```

The first time this code is executed, an instance of `Font` is built, which takes practically no time at all. Additionally, the windowing system is requested to make a 55-point italic Helvetica, which could be time-consuming, especially on X platforms. The next time the constructor is called, a new object is built, but the request to the windowing system returns almost immediately because a 55-point italic Helvetica is already present.

The `Font` class has methods to retrieve an instance's family, style, and size, but they are not generally useful. What is returned is not the true family, style, or size as implemented in the windowing system, but only the requested values that were passed into the Font constructor.

Chapter 5 examines font issues in more detail.

Component Layout

Even more than colors and fonts, GUI components (such as buttons and textfields) show great variety from platform to platform. This creates a component layout problem. An OK button might be 50 pixels wide on one platform and 56 pixels wide on another. A program would need to take into account every possible button size (and scrollbar size, textfield size, and so on) to create an aesthetic layout. In the worst case, components or vital screen regions could be obscured by components that turned out bigger than anticipated.

Java solves this problem by allowing layout decisions to be deferred until the components are created. Java encapsulates the task of precise layout into various layout manager classes. Instead of telling components precisely where to go, the programmer decides on a layout policy and constructs combinations of layout managers to implement that policy. Chapter 4 discusses these complexities in detail.

Components and Peers

The new Java Foundation Classes (JFC) components, introduced with JDK 1.2, maintain a consistent cross-platform look and feel. However, the older Abstract Windowing Toolkit (AWT) components borrow their appearance and behavior from the underlying machine.

A Java component—a button, for example—is no more than an object, an instance of some class. The java.awt package conceals a complicated mechanism for enabling a component to represent itself on the window system of the local computer. The java.awt.Toolkit class is the intermediary between the component subclasses, such as Button, and the underlying windowing system. The class is abstract. Part of the job of porting Java to a new platform is to create a subclass of Toolkit that is appropriate for the target machine.

When a toolkit is created, Java checks the value of the property awt.toolkit. This value is the name of the subclass of Toolkit for the local machine. Subsequently, all activity that requires the creation of something (components, images, fonts, and so on) on the local windowing system works by making calls to the toolkit.

Consider the example of a button. At the moment when the button is added to its container, the toolkit is asked to construct an instance of some class that implements the ButtonPeer interface. A ButtonPeer is not much more than a bundle of native calls to a platform-specific library called awt, which interacts with the local windowing system. Every Java platform has its own local version of ButtonPeer. On a Motif system, the Motif subclass of Toolkit creates a Motif implementor of ButtonPeer, which interacts with the Motif version of the awt library, which in turn interacts with the X server on the local machine. Similarly, on a Windows platform, the Windows subclass of Toolkit creates a Windows implementor of ButtonPeer, which interacts with the Windows version of the awt library, which in turn interacts with Windows 95/98 on the local machine.

It is certainly not necessary to understand all the details of the peer mechanism to write good Java code, but it is instructive. Knowing a bit about peers will help you to understand why Java operates the way it does. Modifying or subclassing at the level of peers is, by and large, the job of those who port Java to new platforms. Applet and application programmers work one level higher, with the various subclasses of java.awt.Component. However, even at that level, references to peers are commonly seen in the API documentation and in the Java source code.

Chapter 3 discusses how to create custom components that behave like standard components, without coding on the peer level. Chapter 15 discusses the new suite of JFC components that operate without peers and offer a platform-independent look and feel.

Summary

Modern computer programs run in a rich environment that includes GUIs, heterogeneous networks, the Internet, security threats, and many other features. These environmental features are so much a part of today's computing landscape that we take them for granted. Java has been designed with today's environment in mind. Successful Java programming requires an understanding of how to use the tools that Java provides for communicating within modern computing environments.

The next chapter gives an overview of the main components of Java applets and applications, providing a foundation for the information presented in the rest of this book.

CHAPTER
TWO

Applets and Applications

- Browser and applet methods

- Applet communications

- Restrictions on applets

- Application loading

- Applications and peers

- Display update mechanisms

As a Java programmer, you can create Java applets or Java applications. This chapter reviews the construction and characteristics of both types of Java programs—first applets, then applications. The final section discusses Java's drawing mechanisms for painting and updating the screen display, which apply to both applets and applications.

An Overview of Applets

Every applet is a subclass of the `java.applet.Applet` class. Thus, every applet inherits a large amount of functionality from `Applet`, and also from the superclasses of `Applet`: `java.awt.Component`, `java.awt.Container`, and `java.awt .Panel`. Figure 2.1 shows the applet inheritance hierarchy.

FIGURE 2.1:

Applet class hierarchy

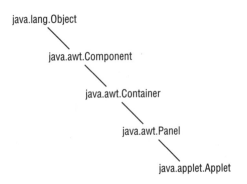

```
java.lang.Object
    java.awt.Component
        java.awt.Container
            java.awt.Panel
                java.applet.Applet
```

Applet Construction

Applets are displayed in browsers, which is what makes them different from applications. A browser constructs and manages an applet when, in the course of parsing an HTML file, it encounters the <APPLET> tag.

The <APPLET> and <PARAM> Tags

The format for the <APPLET> tag is:

```
<APPLET CODE=AppletClass.class WIDTH=width HEIGHT=height [optional
tags] >
```

```
[ <PARAM NAME=ParamName VALUE=ParamValue> ]
[ alternate HTML ]
</APPLET>
```

Everything within square brackets is optional. There may be any number of `<PARAM>` tags. The optional tags are listed below. If used, they must appear within the first set of angle brackets.

ALIGN=alignment   Specifies the alignment for the applet on its HTML page. Possible values for `alignment` are `left`, `right`, `top`, `texttop`, `middle`, `absmiddle`, `baseline`, `bottom`, and `absbottom`.

ALT=alternateMessage   Specifies that `alternateMessage` should be displayed on the HTML page. This tag is for browsers that can parse the `<APPLET>` tag but are not Java-enabled; the alternate message is displayed in place of the applet.

ARCHIVE=archive   Specifies a JAR file containing Java class files. For added security, the JAR file may contain a digital signature. To specify multiple JAR files, delimit their names with commas and surround the entire list with double quotation marks, as in `ARCHIVE="a.jar, b.jar, c.jar"`.

CODEBASE=URL   Specifies that the applet bytecode file is to be found in the directory specified by `URL`. This directory does not necessarily need to be on the same machine where the HTML file resides. It this tag is missing, the codebase directory is assumed to be the directory where the HTML file resides.

NAME=appletName   Specifies a name for the applet. Other applets on the same page may use this name for communicating with this applet.

HSPACE=spacing   Specifies the number of empty pixels to the left and right of the applet.

VSPACE=spacing   Specifies the number of empty pixels above and below the applet.

MAYSCRIPT=boolean   Specifies whether the applet may interact with Javascript code. This tag is recognized by only Netscape Navigator browsers. The `boolean` parameter should be either `true` or `false`.

An applet may read the value of any parameter by calling the following method:

```
String getParameter(String paramName);
```

If `paramName` appears in a `<PARAM>` tag on the applet's page, then this method returns the parameter's value as a string. If `paramName` does not appear on the applet's page, the return value is `null`.

TIP

The `<PARAM>` tags are especially useful for web pages that change periodically. For example, consider an applet that draws a weather map with geographical regions color-coded by mean temperature over the past 24 hours. This applet could receive the raw temperature data via `<PARAM>` tags. Every day, a script could read the raw data from a file and emit an up-to-date HTML page with the current date. When the script writes the `<PARAM>` tag portion of the HTML page, it inserts the raw temperature data. The result is a changing web page with a stable applet.

The `<OBJECT>` Tag

There is a proposed extension to HTML 3.2 that supports a general way to describe objects. One kind of object that can be described is a *serialized applet*. Serialization is described in Chapter 12. For now, you just need to be aware that, by convention, serialization results in a file with a `.ser` filename extension. The proposed extension is the `<OBJECT>` tag, which has the following attributes:

DATA   A URL that identifies the object. For a serialized applet, the URL would point to a `.ser` file.

TYPE   The MIME type of the object indicated by the DATA attribute.

CLASSID   Like DATA, but it references an object that is guaranteed to be on the local server.

CODETYPE   Like TYPE; used when all objects are local.

The following HTML code is an example of the `<OBJECT>` tag:

```
<OBJECT
    WIDTH=500 HEIGHT=50
    DATA=purplecup_ltd/commercial_products/BondTradeApplet.ser
```

```
        TYPE = application/x-java-serialized-object>
</OBJECT>
```

The Applet Class Instance

An applet's life cycle begins when a browser visits the applet's web page. The first part of this process is described in the previous chapter, in the discussion of class loading. Here, we continue the story at the point after the applet's class has been loaded.

Having loaded the class, the browser creates an instance of the applet class. It does this simply by calling the applet's constructor. From this moment on, the applet instance is passive. In other words, it does nothing spontaneously. It simply reacts to method calls made by the browser.

The Applet's Peer

After constructing the applet, the browser allocates space for the applet within its viewing area on the screen. At this point, a very important thing happens: the applet is given a *peer*. Peers are mentioned later in this chapter in the context of applications, and they are discussed in detail in Chapter 6. For now, suffice it to say that a peer is a component's connection to the local, platform-specific, underlying windowing system. Java components receive much of their functionality by recruiting the facilities of the local windowing system.

Browser Method Calls to Applets

In the next step in the life cycle, the browser sends several startup method calls to the applet. Each of these methods is inherited from the `java.applet.Applet` superclass. The inherited versions do nothing; programmers may override any of them to give the applet its desired character. It is important to note that by the time these methods are called, the applet has been completely constructed and has been given its peer.

The init() Method

The first call that the browser makes to the applet is `init()`. This is the only startup method that is called only once, so this is where the applet should perform one-time initialization. Functionality performed in init() commonly includes the following:

- Creating the applet's GUI
- Reading values from <PARAM> tags
- Loading off-screen images from external files
- Loading audio clips from external files

Instance variables may be initialized in init(), or they may be initialized on their declaration lines. From the standpoint of maintenance, it is generally better to initialize them in the init() method so that everything is initialized in one place.

The start() and stop() Methods

The next method called by the browser is start(). The name is a bit ambiguous, since it does not make clear what it is that should be started. The start() method works in partnership with the stop() method.

After the initial start() call, the browser calls stop() whenever the user browses away from the applet, and calls start() again when the user browses back to the applet. This terminology is vague, and different browsers make the calls under different circumstances. As a general rule, stop() is called when the browser displays a new web page or when it becomes iconified; start() is called when the browser returns to the applet's page or when it becomes de-iconified.

NOTE   It may come as a surprise to some readers that an applet's code is not deallocated when its page is left behind. The rationale is that the page may be visited again in the future and it would be a shame to have to reload the applet in this case. Moreover, in this situation the user would reasonably expect the applet to be in the same state it was left in, and not initialized. Thus browsers cache applets in memory.

In general, there are three activities that an applet should suspend in the stop() method and resume in the start() method:

- Animation, because there is no benefit in wasting cycles on an animation that cannot be seen.

- Sound, because it would confuse the user to play sound for a different page than the one being viewed. Iconified programs of any kind should not play sounds.

- General background thread processing, because the thread would be doing work for a page other than the one currently being viewed. This would steal resources that should be available to the current page.

The paint(Graphics g) Method

The paint(Graphics g) method, like start(), is called both at startup time and subsequently at the browser's discretion. The paint() method is passed an instance of the Graphics class. Every instance of Graphics is dedicated to drawing on a component's region of the screen or on an off-screen image. The instance passed into paint() draws on the applet's pixels.

After the initial call, the browser calls paint() whenever it needs the applet to render itself. The circumstances that cause this to happen are browser-specific. Most often, the cause is damage repair. When the applet's portion of the browser is covered by another window and then becomes exposed again, the applet's exposed pixels must be rendered somehow in order to maintain the illusion that the screen is a three-dimensional desktop.

Some browsers, including Netscape Navigator, use a *backing store* strategy for damage repair; these browsers always cache their current appearance in an off-screen image. When part or all of the browser becomes exposed, the damage is repaired by rendering the backing store cache onto the screen. With this strategy, it is never necessary to repair damage by asking the applet to paint() itself. Browsers that use a backing store pay a memory penalty but are able to repair damage very quickly.

Other browsers, including the Applet Viewer, require the applet to repair its own damage. When this happens, paint() is called, but the Graphics parameter is a bit different from the one passed into the initial paint() call. Every instance of Graphics has a clip rectangle that defines the portion of the drawable area within which drawing operations have an effect. Methods such as Graphics.drawLine() and Graphics.fillRect() do not modify pixels outside this clip rectangle. When the Applet Viewer calls paint() in order to repair damage, it sets the clip rectangle of the Graphics parameter to be the smallest rectangle that encompasses all of the damaged area. This setting minimizes the number of screen pixels that must be updated.

NOTE   The clip rectangle can be modified programmatically. Chapter 8, which discusses animation, shows an example of when and how to do this.

The destroy() Method

The browser is supposed to call destroy() when it no longer needs the applet. Because the browser caches the applet even when the applet's page is no longer displayed, many browsers rarely call destroy().

The destroy() method is the applet's opportunity to release any non-memory resources it might have, such as threads and network connections.

Applet Context Methods

The applet method getAppletContext() returns an object that implements the AppletContext interface. This object has methods that give details about the applet's environment. The following are the methods of the AppletContext interface:

Applet getApplet(String name)   Returns a handle to the named applet. An applet receives its name via the NAME=appletName tag.

Enumeration getApplets()   Returns an enumeration of applets that were loaded by the same class loader as the current applet.

AudioClip getAudioClip(URL soundFileUrl)   Returns an audio clip object. The soundFileUrl parameter should specify a sound file in the .au format. This method returns immediately; actual loading of the file occurs when the data is needed.

AudioClip newAudioClip(URL soundFileUrl)   Returns an audio clip object. The soundFileUrl parameter should specify a sound file in the .au format. In contrast to getAudioClip(), this method loads the sound data immediately.

Image getImage(URL imageFileUrl)   Returns an image. The imageFileUrl parameter should specify an image file in the .gif, .jpg, or .xbm format.

void showDocument(URL documentUrl)   Requests the browser to display the HTML page specified by the documentUrl parameter.

void showDocument(URL documentUrl, String where)   Requests the same as the previous method, but the `where` parameter specifies where in the browser the new page should be displayed relative to the current page's frame. The options for `where` are "_self", which uses the current page's frame; "_parent", which uses the parent frame of the current page's frame; "_top", which uses the top-level frame; and "_blank", which uses a new, unnamed top-level window. If any other string is used, the new document is shown in a new top-level window whose name is the `where` string.

void showStatus(String message)   Displays `message` on the browser's status line. This method should not be relied on for communicating important information to the user because other subsystems of the browser may overwrite the status line at any time.

Inter-Applet Communication

The getApplet() and getApplets() methods of AppletContext are used for inter-applet communication. The returned values are references to applet objects, and they may be sent method calls just like any other object.

Browsers impose restrictions on applet communication. For example, 2.x versions of Netscape Navigator require that communicating applets reside on the same page. Netscape Navigator 3.0 is more restrictive: In order for two applets to communicate, they must share the same codebase, and their <ARCHIVE> and <MAYSCRIPT> tags, if present, must be identical.

As an example, consider two applets that meet their browser's communication requirements. The first applet's name (as specified by the NAME=appletName tag) is victim. The second applet could use the following code to draw a red diagonal line across the first applet:

```
Applet otherApplet = getAppletContext().getApplet();
if (otherApplet != null)
{
    int x = otherApplet.size().width;
    int y = otherApplet.size().height;
    Graphics g = otherApplet.getGraphics();
    g.setColor(Color.red);
    g.drawLine(0, 0, x, y);
}
```

Applet Restrictions

There are many restrictions on an applet's behavior. This is to be expected—an applet is, in a sense, a stranger borrowing the host machine's CPU and display. Some of these restrictions are inherent in the implementation of Java, and some are imposed by the browser through its instance of the SecurityManager class. (Some security FAQs are presented in the Appendix.)

The following are four general categories of applet restrictions:

- An applet's access to both the local and the remote file system is restricted. Most older browsers simply forbid all such access. Newer browsers honor *signed applets*, which come from trusted sources and may be permitted file system access. Signed applets are discussed in detail in Chapter 18.

- An applet class (or any other class) that was loaded from the network may not make native calls. Remote classes also may not execute local commands via the exec() method of the java.lang.Runtime class. However, there is no restriction on classes that are used by the applet but loaded locally, such as Object or Component.

- An applet may not be a network socket server, and may be a socket client, only if the server machine is one that served the applet's web page. (Servers, clients, and sockets are discussed in detail in Chapter 10.)

- An applet may display a frame, but the frame displays a warning message. The text and coloring of this message vary from browser to browser.

An Overview of Applications

An application is a program that happens to have been written in Java. It runs without a browser, a security manager, or an applet context. Compared to an applet, there is so little going on in an application's environment that there is not much to say on the general topic of applications. This section will just touch on a few of the relevant issues.

Application Startup

An application is invoked from the command line by typing:

java *classname*

For example, to invoke class `TelescopeController`, residing in file `Telescope-Controller.class`, as an application, you would enter:

java TelescopeController

Note that you should not type the `.class` extension.

The command starts up a Java runtime environment and tells its class loader to load the named class from somewhere in the CLASSPATH. Once the class is loaded, a call is made to the class's `main()` method, whose signature must be:

```
public static void main(String[])
```

Clearly, `main()` must be public so that the runtime will have permission to call it. The `void` return type just means that a Java program, unlike a C or C++ program, does not return a value to the command line from which it was invoked. (A value still can be returned by calling `System.exit()`.)

The `static` designation requires some explanation. In Java, a static variable is associated with its class rather than with an individual instance of the class; thus, a static variable may be read or written before any instances of the class are constructed. A method may be designated as static if it only accesses static variables and methods within its own class. In other words, a static method cannot access nonstatic variables or methods. Thus, a static method also is associated with the class, rather than with any instance of the class, and may be called before any instances of the class have been constructed.

Applications usually have GUIs, which means that a frame must be constructed. It is common practice to subclass `java.awt.Frame` and to put the `main()` method in the Frame subclass. The result is code similar to the following:

```
public class MyApplication extends Frame
{
    // Instance variable declarations here.

    public static void main(String args[])
    {
        MyApplication that;
        that = new MyApplication();
        that.show();
    }

    // Constructor and many other methods follow.
}
```

The idea here is that on entry into main(), there is no instance of the MyApplication class. In programs with this structure, the first job of the main() method is to construct an instance of the class.

An alternate structure would be something like the following:

```
public class Launcher
{
    public static void main(String args[])
    {
        MyApplication that;
        that = new MyApplication();
        that.show();
    }
}


public class MyApplication extends Frame
{
    // Data and code omitted.
}
```

There is very little difference between these two approaches. The second way is cleaner, but requires one extra class definition.

TIP

If you are developing a large application that requires many classes, it's helpful to give every important class its own main() method. These methods are never invoked during normal execution of the program—they are only used for testing. Each of the main() methods constructs an instance of the class and invokes methods on the instance, checking return values and instance variable values. All methods and instance variables are accessible to main(), even those that are declared private. This test strategy can be used with applets as well as with applications. If a class both extends java.awt.Applet and has its own main() method, then it is both an applet (when invoked by a browser) and an application (when invoked from a command line).

Peer Creation

Applications generally have an easier life than applets. They have access to the file system and the network, and may invoke native methods. There is, however, a drawback to being an application.

An applet resides in a browser. The browser will not invoke the applet's init() method until the applet has a peer. As long as an applet performs all of its initialization in its init() method, there is no danger that operations relying on the peer will fail. An application has no such luxury.

Most application initialization activities do not require a peer, but a very important one does. Empty off-screen images are created by the createImage(int width, int height) method of the Component class. If the component has a peer, an empty image is returned; if the component has no peer, the call returns null. The code below, which appears reasonable, will fail.

```
import java.awt.*;
public class ImageNoPeer extends Frame
{
    Image     im;

    public static void main(String args[])
    {
        ImageNoPeer that = new ImageNoPeer();
        that.show();
    }

    public ImageNoPeer()
    {
        resize(500, 300);
        im = createImage(500, 300);
        Graphics g = im.getGraphics();              // Crash!  im is null
        // Various operations involving g
    }
}
```

Until the instance of the Frame subclass ImageNoPeer has a peer, the createImage() call will fail. The time to make the call is after the peer is created. This happens during the course of the show() call, when the addNotify() method is invoked. An easy way to create images safely is to override addNotify() and call createImage() after calling the superclass's addNotify() method, as shown here:

```
import java.awt.*;
public class ImageWithPeer extends Frame
{
    Image     im;

    public static void main(String args[])
```

```
    {
        ImageWithPeer that = new ImageWithPeer();
        that.show();
    }

    public ImageWithPeer()
    {
        resize(500, 300);
    }

    public void addNotify()
    {
        super.addNotify();
        im = createImage(500, 300);
        Graphics g = im.getGraphics();          // No problem
        // Various operations involving g
    }
}
```

Display Updates

It is important to understand Java's drawing mechanisms for painting and updating the display, especially if you are developing applets and applications that frequently modify their display. First, we will review the interaction of Java's drawing methods, and then we will discuss your design choices for programs that frequently modify their display in response to user events.

The Drawing Methods Calling Structure

The Component methods repaint(), update(), and paint() are the heart of Java's drawing mechanism. Understanding how these methods interact is essential to creating robust, maintainable code. Figure 2.2 shows the calling structure of these three methods.

Every component has a background and a foreground color. The update() method clears the component to its background color, then sets the graphic object's drawing color to be the foreground color, and finally calls paint().

FIGURE 2.2:

Calling structure of
repaint(), update(), and
paint()

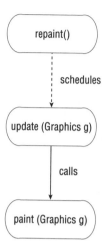

The important point about the calling structure is that repaint() does not call update(). It *schedules* update(), which is very different. The first time a call is made to a component's repaint(), a request is made for a thread to call update() in the near future (in 100 milliseconds, by default; see Chapter 5 for information on how to modify the default). Subsequently, repaint() checks to see whether an update is pending—that is, whether repaint() has previously been called, and called within the 100 milliseconds, so that the call to update() has not yet been made. If indeed there is an update pending, repaint() just returns. If no update is pending, then one is scheduled.

The result is that update() is never called more than 10 times per second, no matter how many calls are made to repaint(). Consider a large application or applet that handles a large number of events. Every event (mouse click, mouse movement, component action, and so on) could result in a screen change. By calling repaint() rather than paint(), the program does not need to worry about falling behind in its painting duties.

Display Updating Design Choices

There are three design choices for a program that frequently modifies its display in response to user events:

- The event handlers can call getGraphics() to obtain a Graphics object that is dedicated to the screen; the handlers can then make their own graphics calls to draw directly.

- The event handlers can set instance variables to reflect the current state of the program; the handlers can then call `paint()`, which reads the values of those instance variables and modifies the screen appropriately.

- The event handlers can set instance variables to reflect the current state of the program; the handlers can then call `repaint()`, rather than `paint()`, to modify the screen.

Using `paint()` is slower than using `repaint()`, which eliminates intermediate `paint()` calls. But unlike calling `getGraphics()`, where event handlers draw directly to the screen, using `repaint()` imposes an intermediate step: The program's state must be encoded in instance variables, which are interpreted by the `paint()` method. For a small applet or application, this can be a burden. However, for a program that is of any significant size or that must be maintained over time, the extra effort is well worth the gains.

It is significantly easier to fix a display bug or to add a display feature if the display code is centralized rather than scattered. The instance variables always dictate what the screen is supposed to look like so if the screen is wrong, either the instance variables are being set to the wrong values (in the event handlers), or they are being interpreted incorrectly (in `paint()`).

Using `repaint()` has two other advantages. First, we have observed that some browsers may call `paint()` at any moment; should this happen, any drawing that was performed by methods other than `paint()` will be lost. This problem can be avoided with the `repaint()`/`paint()` scheme. Second, printing components is considerably easier if all painting is centralized in a single method.

This design strategy can be called the "always call `repaint()`" rule. For most programming tasks, the extra effort required pays off handsomely in terms of performance and maintainability.

Summary

This chapter has reviewed some of the issues related to Java applets and applications, and the differences between them. The remainder of this book presents detailed information and techniques for developing fully functional, robust, maintainable applets and applications. In the next chapter, we will focus on custom components.

CHAPTER

THREE

3

Custom Components

- Event delegation and listeners

- Custom component design strategies

- A component for a new kind of data

- A three-way component

- Validating textfields

Java's AWT (Abstract Windowing Toolkit) provides a small but reasonable set of user interface components. The JFC (Java Foundation Classes), which were introduced with release 2, substantially extend the toolkit (the new JFC components are discussed in Chapter 15). However, you still may find that the standard set of components do not provide the functionality you need for certain applications. In such cases, you will need to develop your own custom components.

A major consideration in the development of custom components is the handling of events. This chapter begins with a quick review of event delegation, and then focuses on three alternative strategies for creating custom components, along with criteria for selecting the most appropriate strategy for your situation. We'll develop three examples of custom components based on each of the design strategies.

The Event Delegation Model

The event delegation model is based on the concept of the *event listener*. An event listener is an object that receives notification when a GUI event takes place. There are ten categories of GUI events, each represented by a different class, and there is almost a one-to-one correspondence between event types and listener types (the correspondence breaks down in the case of mouse events, as explained later in the chapter). The event class hierarchy is shown in Figure 3.1.

At the top of the hierarchy is the event object class. EventObject is perhaps an inelegant class name, but the name Event was already taken by the java.awt.Event class, which is deprecated. The EventObject superclass is intended to be the parent of all imaginable event types. AWT events (those that are triggered by the components of the AWT) are only one subset of all possible event types; AWT events are represented by subclasses of java.awt.AWTEvent. Other families of events include Bean events and application-specific events. The subclasses of java.awt.AWTEvent belong to the java.awt.event package.

NOTE   This book is based on the event delegation model introduced with Java release 1.1. The older 1.0 propagation model, in which events ripple outward through the containment hierarchy, has been deprecated.

FIGURE 3.1:

The event class hierarchy

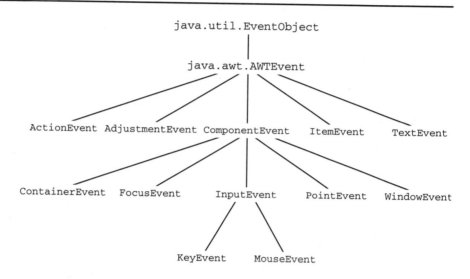

All classes belong to java.awt.event package unless otherwise noted.

All event subclasses inherit the getSource() method from EventObject. This method returns the object that originated the event. For the AWTEvent subclasses, getSource() returns the component in which user input took place.

Listener Interfaces and Methods

When a user stimulates a GUI component with a key or with the mouse, a method call is made to all objects that have registered with the component as listeners for the type of event that took place. The method has a parameter whose type is one of the subclasses of java.awt.AWTEvent. Additional information about what occurred can be obtained by making method calls on the event.

For example, the key event category is represented by the KeyEvent class. When a user triggers a key event by pressing a keyboard key while the mouse is in a canvas, the system creates an instance of java.awt.event.KeyEvent and calls key-Pressed() on all of the canvas's key listeners, passing the key event as a parameter. Any implementation of keyPressed() that is interested in the event's data—for instance, to discover which key was pressed—can call getKeyCode() on the key event.

In order to be eligible to become a listener for a certain type of event, an object must implement an interface that corresponds to the event type of interest. For any event type *XXX*, the name of the corresponding listener interface is *xxx*Listener. To register an object as an *xxx* listener of a particular component, call the component's add*xxx*Listener() method, passing the listener as the method argument.

> **NOTE**   There are two listener interfaces that handle mouse events: **MouseListener** and **MouseMotionListener**. A mouse listener is notified when a mouse button is used, or when the mouse cursor enters or leaves a component. A mouse-motion listener is notified when the mouse is moved or dragged.

The various listener interface types, interface methods, and add methods are listed in Table 3.1.

TABLE 3.1:   Listener Interfaces

Interface	Interface Methods	Add Method
ActionListener	actionPerformed(ActionEvent)	addActionListener()
AdjustmentListener	adjustmentValueChanged(Adjust-mentEvent)	addAdjustment-Listener()
ComponentListener	componentHidden(ComponentEvent) componentMoved(ComponentEvent) componentResized (ComponentEvent) componentShown (ComponentEvent)	addComponent-Listener()
ContainerListener	componentAdded(ContainerEvent) componentRemoved(ContainerEvent)	addContainer-Listener()
FocusListener	focusGained(FocusEvent) focusLost(FocusEvent)	addFocusListener()
ItemListener	itemStateChanged(ItemEvent)	addItemListener()
KeyListener	keyPressed(KeyEvent) keyReleased(KeyEvent) keyTyped(KeyEvent)	addKeyListener()

Continued on next page

TABLE 3.1 CONTINUED: Listener Interfaces

Interface	Interface Methods	Add Method
MouseListener	mouseClicked(MouseEvent) mouseEntered(MouseEvent) mouseExited(MouseEvent) mousePressed(MouseEvent) mouseReleased(MouseEvent)	addMouseListener()
MouseMotionListener	mouseDragged(MouseEvent) mouseMoved(MouseEvent)	addMouseMotion- Listener()
TextListener	textValueChanged(TextEvent)	addTextListener()
WindowListener	windowActivated(WindowEvent) windowClosed(WindowEvent) windowClosing(WindowEvent) windowDeactivated(WindowEvent) windowDeiconified(WindowEvent) windowIconified(WindowEvent) windowOpened(WindowEvent)	addWindowListener()

Explicit Event Enabling

As an alternative to delegating a component's events, you can use another technique called *explicit event enabling*. Components have a method called enable-Events(), which can be invoked to detect events before listeners are notified. The argument to the enableEvents() call is an int value that specifies the type or types of events to be enabled; constants for these values are defined in the AWTEvent class.

When a component has explicitly enabled events of type *xxx*, an *xxx* event causes a call to the component's process*xxx*Event(*xxx*event) method. By default, these methods notify all of the component's registered event listeners. Component subclasses can override the process*xxx*Event() methods to perform desired event processing.

For example, to explicitly enable action events, a subclass of Button can call enableEvents(AWTEvent.ACTION_EVENT_MASK) in its constructor and override processActionEvent(ActionEvent). To explicitly enable both key and action events, a subclass of TextField can call enableEvents(AWTEvent.KEY_EVENT_MASK |

AWTEvent.ACTION_EVENT_MASK) in its constructor and override both processAction-Event(ActionEvent) and processKeyEvent(KeyEvent).

In all cases, the subclass version of the method should call the superclass version, so that registered listeners will be notified. A processKeyEvent() method, for example, should look something like this:

```
public void processKeyEvent(KeyEvent e) {
   // Subclass-specific processing goes here.
   super.processKeyEvent(e);
}
```

As you will see later in this chapter, explicit event enabling provides custom components with a convenient mechanism for handling events.

Strategies for Designing Custom Components

The decision to create a custom component class should not be undertaken lightly. By far, the most important GUI design consideration is user convenience, and user convenience is usually best served by providing the smallest possible learning curve. A standard component that does an adequate job can be preferable to a custom component that does a spectacular job, because users already know how to use the standard version.

However, you may still encounter situations where no standard component will be adequate. In these cases, once you have decided to create a custom component class, you have three options:

- You can subclass Component and have the subclass take care of all painting and event handling. The result is a completely new look and feel.

- You can subclass Container and populate the subclass with standard components. These will interact with each other to provide higher-level behavior. The result is an aggregation of preexisting components.

- You can subclass one of the noncontainer components such as Button or Checkbox. The subclass will enhance the inherited behavior.

Each of these approaches has its pros and cons. When judging an approach, the primary consideration is ease of mastery. Users should be able to quickly figure out how to use a new component, and the component should assist users in doing productive work. Any feature of a component that is difficult to understand or difficult to use should be considered a serious liability.

Component Class Subclassing

In general, components designed with the first strategy—subclassing Component—will be the most difficult for the user to master. Because the look and the feel are completely new, the user has no experience with similar components to suggest how to interact with this new one.

Because the user will need to learn how to use this new component, its use should be as intuitive as possible. Thus, the component should match the user's mental image of the data to be entered as closely as possible. Subclassing Component works best when the user's job is to enter a new kind of data, which is not well represented as text, a checkbox state, or a scrollbar position.

As an example of creating a custom component using this method, we'll develop a new component for entering a value in polar coordinates (see the "Subclassing Component: The Polar Component" section later in this chapter).

Aggregation

The second strategy—aggregation—is most likely to result in a component that the user will be able to learn to use easily. Everything the container contains is already well known. Only the interactions among the subcomponents within the container are new. Since users already know how to use checkboxes, textfields, and scrollbars, there is little for them to learn.

By using this approach, you take advantage of all the expensive usability research that has been done over the years to refine the subcomponents. This strategy is useful when a component must combine both input and output functionality or when you want to offer multiple input paradigms.

As an example of using the aggregation strategy, we'll develop a custom component that offers three options for entering a numeric value. The example includes a choice of checkboxes, a textfield, or a scrollbar for inputting a value (see the "Aggregation: The ThreeWay Component" section later in this chapter).

Standard Component Subclassing

The third strategy provides a familiar look with a new feel. When you subclass a component, the user sees something familiar and approaches it with the expectation that it will behave like its standard superclass. Users will need some education so that they realize that this is not the case.

This strategy works best when you must restrict the set of valid inputs to a component. As an example, we'll develop two versions of a validating textfield component (see the "Subclassing a Standard Component: Validating Textfields" section later in this chapter).

Design Considerations

Before deciding on a design strategy—subclassing Component, aggregating in a container, or subclassing a primitive component—there are two questions that you need to consider:

- How should the component display its value?
- How should the user specify new values?

Once these look-and-feel issues are decided, the best subclassing strategy will generally be obvious. At this point, the following list of issues can help you to organize your thoughts and make well-founded design decisions:

- How can the programmer modify the component's appearance?
- What limits should be set on the component's possible values?
- How should the value be stored, set, and retrieved?
- What events should the component send? Will custom event types and listener interfaces be required?
- Will the component behave properly in a multithreaded environment?
- Will the component behave properly if it is resized?

As we work through the examples of custom components in this chapter, you will see that the answers to these questions provide the basis for a sound design plan.

Subclassing Component: The Polar Component

The first example is a component called `Polar`, which is used for inputting a point in polar coordinates. Polar coordinates describe a point in terms of its distance from the origin (usually called ρ, or rho for radius) and the angle it makes with the right-pointing horizontal (usually called θ, or theta).

NOTE

Polar coordinates are an alternative way of using two numbers to describe a point in a two-dimensional space. It is easy to translate between the polar (ρ, θ) coordinates and the familiar (x,y) coordinates of rectangular Cartesian space: $x = \rho \cos \theta$; $y = \rho \sin \theta$.

Polar's Look-and-Feel Issues

As you learned in the previous section, before you can develop a custom component, you need to consider how the user should see and use the component.

Displaying Values

The first consideration is appearance: How should the component display its value? Because the component is to represent a point in 2-D space, the only reasonable choice is a square region or a squarish rectangle. It is not necessary to force the component to be perfectly square, but neither dimension should be particularly narrow. We can decide somewhat arbitrarily that the component will declare its minimum and preferred size to be 50×50 pixels (minimum and preferred size are of concern to layout managers, which are the subject of the next chapter). As with other components, the minimum and preferred size of a `Polar` component are likely to be overruled by the prevailing layout manager.

As for what is to be drawn in the component's region, the appearance should match as closely as possible the picture in the user's mind's eye. Probably, the user's mental picture is a textbook illustration: a pair of axes with a dot superimposed, possibly with an arrow from the origin to the dot, as shown in Figure 3.2.

FIGURE 3.2:

Mental picture of polar coordinates

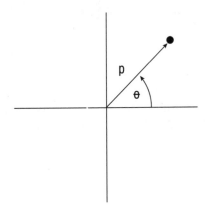

The Polar component should resemble Figure 3.2 as closely as possible. However, in practice ease-of-use considerations will suggest some modifications and compromises. The current point should certainly be represented by a circular dot. In practice, rendering an arrowhead at the tip of the line would produce visual clutter and obscure the dot, so there will not be an arrowhead.

The user should be cued that this device operates in the polar domain and not the Cartesian, so drawing a circle would be preferable to drawing a rectangle. If there is to be a circle, where should it go? If we draw a ring that passes through the current point, the user will receive additional feedback about the distance from the center. The result is shown in Figure 3.3, which is a screenshot of the finished product. Note how the ring cues the value of rho, while the line cues the value of theta.

FIGURE 3.3:

The Polar component

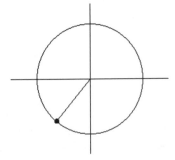

Specifying Values

How should the user specify new values? The `Polar` component clearly wants to be clicked.

The simplest interface lets the user "grab the ring" by holding down the mouse button anywhere inside the component. The current point and the ring will jump to the mouse cursor location. Subsequently, as long as the mouse button is down, the value will track the mouse. When the user releases the mouse button, the value ceases tracking. As long as the user is dragging the mouse, the dot, the line, and the ring will be rendered in (arbitrarily) blue, so the component can tell the user, "I'm listening." At times when the component is not responding to the mouse (which is almost always), it will be rendered in black. Because the axes never change and do not communicate information about the current value, they will be rendered in their own constant color. Proliferation of colors is dangerous because a GUI with too many colors is confusing. Therefore, it is best to take a conservative approach and draw the axes in gray.

This process gives satisfactory graphical feedback. Because numerical feedback is also required, the values of rho and theta will be displayed in the upper-left corner of the component.

Choosing a Subclassing Strategy

Now that we have defined a look and a feel, it is time to choose a subclassing strategy. Clearly, there are no standard components that render a ring or an arrow, so aggregation and simple subclassing are out of the question. To create the `Polar` component, we will need to subclass `Component` and write all the rendering and event-handling code from scratch:

```
public class Polar extends Component
```

Polar's Design Issues

We can now continue developing the `Polar` component by addressing the design issues: modifying the component's appearance, limiting values, handling value input, handling events, and providing for multithreading and resizing behavior.

Modifying the Component's Appearance

How can the programmer modify the component's appearance? Consider those aspects of the appearance that are susceptible to change. The numeric value display comes to mind—you may want to disable it or modify its font. You should also be able to change the drawing colors and the component's background color. For the most part, the programmer can be given control over these aspects with no extra effort.

Every component has a background color, a foreground color, and a font. When a component is told to repaint(), the GUI thread will eventually call the component's update() method; update() clears the component using the background color, sets the current color to the foreground color, and calls paint(). So, if the paint() method assumes that the component has been cleared using some appropriate background color, you can change a Polar component's background by calling its setBackground() method. Since this method is inherited from the Component class, programmers have nothing extra to learn.

Similarly, it is reasonable for you to expect that the ring, dot, and ray will be rendered using the foreground color. With this arrangement, you can simply call setForeground() to change the rendering color.

If the paint() code does not explicitly set the font used to render the textual value, i, the value will default to the component's own font. Thus, you can control this font by calling setFont() on the component.

The only conditions that cannot be modified by using the component's inherited methods are the color of the display during dragging and the presence or absence of the textual feedback. For such modification, two public methods are needed: setDragColor() and setShowText().

Limiting the Value

Next, we need to consider the component's ability to put limits on its value. Theta is inherently constrained to the range 0 to 360 degrees.

Rho, on the other hand, needs limits. There needs to be a maximum value for rho, represented by a ring that fills the component; this dictates a scale for translating distance in pixels into values for rho. This maximum is to be provided as an argument to the Polar component's constructor, and it is stored in an instance variable called maxRho. In theory, the maxRho value should correspond to a ring whose diameter (in pixels) is the lesser of the component's width and its height. In practice, a ring that grazes the boundary of the component is unsightly, so maxRho will actually correspond to a ring that is 10 percent smaller than the smaller dimension of the component.

There are many points within the Polar component—especially near the corners—that represent illegal values because rho would be greater than maxRho.

When the user drags through these regions, the ring should refuse to follow; it should instead remain at its maximum legal size.

Storing, Setting, and Retrieving Values

The next issue is how the value should be stored, set, and retrieved. Rho and theta should be represented by floats or doubles. Doubles are more convenient because the component will need to make numerous calls to the trigonometric methods of the Math class, which uses doubles. Programmers who use the Polar class will be likely to do trigonometric operations on the results and will likewise prefer values that are doubles. An auxiliary class called PolarPoint will be defined to encapsulate doubles for rho and theta.

NOTE

If you use the Polar class, remember that all of Java's trigonometric functions deal in radians. For conversion to and from degrees, the Math class defines a static final double called PI.

The PolarPoint class definition follows. The source code for the PolarPoint class appears on the accompanying CD-ROM in the file javadevhdbk\ch03\ PolarPoint.java. The bytecode file, PolarPoint.class, can be found in the same directory.

LIST 3.1   *PolarPoint.java*

```
/*
 *  The PolarPoint class describes a point in polar coordinates.  Used
    by the Polar component class for storing its value.
 */

public class PolarPoint
{
    private double          rho;
    private double          theta;


    public PolarPoint(double rho, double theta)
    {
        this.rho = rho;
        this.theta = theta;
    }


    public PolarPoint(PolarPoint p)
```

```
{
    this.rho = p.getRho();
    this.theta = p.getTheta();
}

public double getRho()              { return rho; }
public void setRho(double rho)      { this.rho = rho; }
public double getTheta()            { return theta; }
public void setTheta(double theta)  { this.theta = theta; }

public String toString()
{
    return "RHO = " + rho + " ... THETA = " + theta;
}
}
```

This class stores rho and theta as private doubles, with public accessor and mutator methods. The nomenclature of the accessors and mutators (or *getters* and *setters*) is in keeping with the Beans naming discipline. (See Chapter 17 for more information about the Beans naming conventions.)

Now the Polar class can be given a private instance variable called value, of type PolarPoint, and public methods to get and set the value. These methods will be called getPolarValue() and setPolarValue(), again in keeping with the Beans naming convention. Setting the value should force a repaint, so that the component's appearance will reflect its new value. The paint() method can assume that value is valid; it also assumes the validity of a scale factor called unitsPerPixel, which correlates rho units to screen pixels, and of a boolean called dragging, which tells whether a mouse drag is in progress. The paint() method looks like this:

```
public void paint(Graphics g)
{
    int        radiusPix;
    int        centerX;
    int        centerY;
    Dimension  size;

    radiusPix = (int)(value.getRho() / unitsPerPixel);
    size = getSize();
    centerX = size.width / 2;
```

```
    centerY = size.height / 2;
    int ulx = centerX - radiusPix;
    int uly = centerY - radiusPix;

    // Draw axes in light gray.
    g.setColor(Color.lightGray);
    g.drawLine(centerX, 0, centerX, size.height);
    g.drawLine(0, centerY, size.width, centerY);

    // Draw label string in upper-left corner.
    g.setColor(getForeground());
    if (showTextValue)
    {
        g.drawString((value.getRho() + ", " + value.getTheta()),
                    5, size.height-5);
    }

    // If dragging, subsequent drawing will use the drag color.
    if (dragging)
    {
        g.setColor(dragColor);
    }

    // Draw ring.
    g.drawOval(ulx, uly, 2*radiusPix, 2*radiusPix);

    // Draw dot.
    int arrowTipX = centerX +
                    (int)(radiusPix * Math.cos(value.getTheta()));
    int arrowTipY = centerY -
                    (int)(radiusPix * Math.sin(value.getTheta()));
    g.fillOval(arrowTipX-3, arrowTipY-3, 7, 7);

    // Draw line from center to dot, space permitting.
    if (radiusPix > 5)
    {
        g.drawLine(centerX, centerY, arrowTipX, arrowTipY);
    }
}
```

The Mouse and MouseMotion event handlers have the job of updating the value and dragging instance variables. The Polar class will serve as its own MouseListener and MouseMotionListener. The code fragment below lists the event-handling portion of the class. Note that the class declaration has been modified to declare implementation of the two listener interfaces.

```java
public class Polar extends Component
                    implements MouseListener, MouseMotionListener
{
    private PolarPoint        value;
    private double            maxRho;
    private double            unitsPerPixel;
    private boolean           dragging = false;
    private Color             dragColor = Color.blue;
    private boolean           showTextValue = true;

    public void mousePressed(MouseEvent e)
    {
        value = xyToPolar(e.getX(), e.getY());
        repaint();
    }

    public void mouseDragged(MouseEvent e)
    {
        dragging = true;
        value = xyToPolar(e.getX(), e.getY());
        repaint();
    }

    public void mouseReleased(MouseEvent e)
    {
        dragging = false;
        value = xyToPolar(e.getX(), e.getY());
        repaint();
    }

    private PolarPoint xyToPolar(int x, int y)
    {
        double        newRho;
        double        newTheta;
```

```
        int deltaX = x - getSize().width/2;
        int deltaY = getSize().height/2 - y;
        double deltaLen = Math.sqrt(deltaX*deltaX + deltaY*deltaY);
        double rho = unitsPerPixel * deltaLen;
        rho = Math.min(rho, maxRho);
        double theta = Math.atan2(deltaY, deltaX);
        while (theta < 0.0)
            theta += 2*Math.PI;

        return new PolarPoint(rho, theta);
    }

    public void mouseClicked(MouseEvent e)      { }
    public void mouseMoved(MouseEvent e)        { }
    public void mouseEntered(MouseEvent e)      { }
    public void mouseExited(MouseEvent e)       { }
}
```

The xyToPolar() method converts pixel coordinates to polar coordinates, returning an instance of PolarPoint. The four empty methods at the end are present so that the two interfaces will be completely implemented.

So far, the new component class has an appearance and a value, both of which are appropriately adjusted when a user provides mouse input. Now it is time to consider event handling.

Handling Events

The next issue is the kind of event that the Polar component will send out when activated by a user.

It would be convenient if the custom component could send one of the standard event types. The type that comes to mind is the Adjustment event, since a Polar component is a kind of round two-dimensional scrollbar. Unfortunately, Adjustment events are not quite adequate because the AdjustmentEvent class has a getValue() method that returns an int, and the value of a Polar component is a PolarPoint.

Since there is no truly appropriate event type, we must invent one: PolarEvent. The listing for the PolarEvent class follows.

LIST 3.2   *PolarEvent.java*

```java
import java.awt.AWTEvent;

public class PolarEvent extends AWTEvent
{
    private PolarPoint      polarValue;

    public PolarEvent(Polar source, PolarPoint p)
    {
        super(source, RESERVED_ID_MAX+1);
        polarValue = p;
    }

    public PolarPoint getPolarValue()      { return polarValue; }
    public void setPolarValue(PolarPoint p) { polarValue = p; }
}
```

In the first line of the constructor, the second parameter passed to the super-class constructor is the ID for the event. Values up to and including AWTEvent .RESERVED_ID_MAX should not be used by programmers creating new event classes.

The PolarEvent class is simple, but inventing a new event type requires more work. First, there must be a listener interface. It seems natural to call this interface PolarListener. The interface will have a single method, called polarValueChanged(), whose argument will be an instance of PolarEvent. The listing for the Polar-Listener interface follows.

LIST 3.3   *PolarListener.java*

```java
public interface PolarListener extends java.util.EventListener
{
    public void polarValueChanged(PolarEvent pe);
}
```

Now any object that wants to receive notification from a polar component can implement the PolarListener interface and provide a polarValueChanged() method.

The `Polar` class will need to provide `addPolarListener()` and `removePolar-Listener()` methods. An easy way to keep track of listeners is with a vector. We give the `Polar` class a vector instance variable called `listeners`, as shown in the code fragment below.

```
public class Polar extends Component
                    implements MouseListener, MouseMotionListener
{
    private Vector listeners = new Vector();

    public void addPolarListener(PolarListener listener)
    {
        if (!listeners.contains(listener))
            listeners.addElement(listener);
    }

    public void removePolarListener(PolarListener listener)
    {
        listeners.removeElement(listener);
    }


    . . .

}
```

When the mouse is clicked or dragged, the event handlers (which already update the value and call `repaint()`) should also notify all listeners. They do so by calling the method listed below, which constructs an instance of `PolarEvent` and then calls `polarValueChanged()` on all registered `Polar` listeners.

```
private void notifyListeners()
{
    // Clone vector of listeners in case a listener's
    // polarValueChanged modifies the original vector.
    Vector copyOfListeners = (Vector)(listeners.clone());

    // Create a Polar event that encapsulates the current value.
    PolarPoint pp = new PolarPoint(value);
    PolarEvent event = new PolarEvent(this, pp);

    // Notify each listener.
```

```
Enumeration enum = copyOfListeners.elements();
while (enum.hasMoreElements())
{
    PolarListener listener = (PolarListener)enum.nextElement();
    listener.polarValueChanged(event);
}
}
```

Notice that notification is performed by cloning the vector of listeners and working from the clone rather than from the original. The reason for this will be made clear in the next section.

So far, we have examined the issues of how the new component class handles its value and appearance, and how it notifies its listeners. These are the central issues, and considering them will result in a class that behaves well under most circumstances. The remaining two considerations have to do with how the class behaves in stressful environments: multithreading and resizing.

Behaving in a Multithreading Environment

The first stressful consideration is multithreading. A multithreaded situation is always a potential threat to shared data (data that might simultaneously be accessed by two different threads). In our example, there are two pieces of shared data that need to be considered:

- The single `PolarEvent` that is sent as an argument to all `Polar` listeners. This object contains a reference to a `PolarPoint` that reflects the current value.

- The vector of listeners. `Polar` listeners can register and unregister with a `Polar` component asynchronously.

The `PolarEvent` is created and written by the `Polar` class and read by the registered listeners. The danger is that one of the listeners could corrupt the event. This is a general hazard of the event propagation model. By convention, the problem is solved by alerting programmers of listener methods that could present a threat. Listener methods that need to modify events should copy the events and modify the copies, leaving the originals alone. Since this is good practice in general, it is not really necessary to take further precautions.

The vector of listeners, on the other hand, requires special attention. This vector is traversed when a user modifies the component, so that listeners can be notified.

The main danger is that a listener's `polarValueChanged()` method might deregister the listener from the component's listener list. If this were to happen, traversal of the vector would be corrupted. It is also conceivable that independent threads could register or deregister other listeners, again corrupting traversal of the vector. The safest solution is to clone the vector of listeners and notify by traversing the clone rather than traversing the original.

NOTE   All methods of the `Vector` class that modify the internal data are synchronized, so there is no danger that the vector might be corrupted at times other than event notification.

Behaving during Resizing

The final question is what to do when the component resizes. It has already been decided that the constructor should specify a maximum value for rho, which will define a scale conversion factor from rho's units to pixels. This conversion factor will be consulted whenever the value changes, so it should be stored as an instance variable.

Appropriate variable naming is always important, but this is a case where it is doubly so. If the conversion factor is called `conversionFactor`, future developers who maintain this code will need to work out for themselves whether converting from pixels to units requires multiplying or dividing by `conversionFactor`. A mistake here could introduce a very subtle bug. It is much better to eliminate all possible confusion by calling the instance variable either `pixelsPerUnit` or `unitsPerPixel`. Here, `unitsPerPixel` is used because the example converts from pixels to units, and this entails multiplication rather than division. Multiplication is commutative, so there is no possibility that in the future somebody will introduce a maintenance bug by getting the operands in the wrong order.

When the component resizes, `unitsPerPixel` is recomputed:

```
private void adjustScale(int w, int h)
{
    unitsPerPixel = 2.0 * maxRho / Math.min(w, h);
    unitsPerPixel *= 1.1;
}
```

Multiplying by 1.1 ensures that when the component represents the maximum allowable rho, the ring occupies only about 90 percent of the entire component, and will never get so close to the edges that the component is difficult to read or use.

```java
public void setBounds(int x, int y, int w, int h)
{
    adjustScale(w, h);
    super. setBounds(x, y, w, h);
}
```

The Polar Component Class and Test Applet

The full Polar class listing follows. This listing is included on the CD-ROM in javadevhdbk\ch03\Polar.java.

LIST 3.4   *Polar.java*

```java
import  java.awt.*;
import  java.awt.event.*;
import  java.util.*;


/*
 *  Our home-made component for specifying a point in polar
 *  coordinates.  Gives constant graphical and textual feedback
 *  of its current value.  Posts a PolarEvent to all Polar listeners
 *  when the mouse is dragged or released.
 */

public class Polar extends Component
                implements MouseListener, MouseMotionListener
{
    private Vector              listeners = new Vector();
    private PolarPoint          value;
    private double              maxRho;
    private double              unitsPerPixel;
    private boolean             dragging = false;
    private Color               dragColor = Color.blue;
    private boolean             showTextValue = true;


    public Polar()
    {
        this(100.0, 0.0, 100.0);
    }
```

```
public Polar(double initRho, double initTheta, double maxRho)
{
  value = new PolarPoint(initRho, initTheta);
  this.maxRho = maxRho;
  setBackground(Color.white);

  addMouseListener(this);
  addMouseMotionListener(this);
}


public void setDragColor(Color c)
{
    dragColor = c;
}


public void setShowText(boolean b)
{
    showTextValue = b;
}


public void setValue(PolarPoint newValue)
{
    value = newValue;
    repaint();
}


public PolarPoint getValue()
{
    return value;
}


public void addPolarListener(PolarListener listener)
{
    if (!listeners.contains(listener))
        listeners.addElement(listener);
}
```

```java
public void removePolarListener(PolarListener listener)
{
    listeners.removeElement(listener);
}


private void notifyListeners()
{
    // Clone vector of listeners in case a listener's
    // polarValueChanged modifies the original vector.
    Vector copyOfListeners = (Vector)(listeners.clone());

    // Create a Polar event that encapsulates the current value.
    PolarPoint pp = new PolarPoint(value);
    PolarEvent event = new PolarEvent(this, pp);

    // Notify each listener.
    Enumeration enum = copyOfListeners.elements();
    while (enum.hasMoreElements())
    {
        PolarListener listener = (PolarListener)enum.nextElement();
        listener.polarValueChanged(event);
    }
}


/*
 *  Adjust scale so that the largest permissible value takes up
 *  not quite the entire component.
 */
private void adjustScale(int w, int h)
{
    unitsPerPixel = 2.0 * maxRho / Math.min(w, h);
    unitsPerPixel *= 1.1;
}


/*
 *  When the component resizes, we need to adjust our scale.
 *  Note that we do not need to override setSize(), because
 *  setSize() calls setBounds().
 */
```

```java
public void setBounds(int x, int y, int w, int h)
{
    adjustScale(w, h);
    super.setBounds(x, y, w, h);
}


public void paint(Graphics g)
{
    int         radiusPix;
    int         centerX;
    int         centerY;
    Dimension   size;

    radiusPix = (int)(value.getRho() / unitsPerPixel);
    size = getSize();
    centerX = size.width / 2;
    centerY = size.height / 2;
    int ulx = centerX - radiusPix;
    int uly = centerY - radiusPix;

    // Draw axes in light gray.
    g.setColor(Color.lightGray);
    g.drawLine(centerX, 0, centerX, size.height);
    g.drawLine(0, centerY, size.width, centerY);

    // Draw label string in upper-left corner.
    g.setColor(getForeground());
    if (showTextValue)
    {
        g.drawString((value.getRho() + ", " + value.getTheta()),
                     5, size.height-5);
    }

    // If dragging, subsequent drawing will use the drag color.
    if (dragging)
    {
        g.setColor(dragColor);
    }
```

```
        // Draw ring.
        g.drawOval(ulx, uly, 2*radiusPix, 2*radiusPix);

        // Draw dot.
        int arrowTipX = centerX +
                        (int)(radiusPix * Math.cos(value.getTheta()));
        int arrowTipY = centerY -
                        (int)(radiusPix * Math.sin(value.getTheta()));
        g.fillOval(arrowTipX-3, arrowTipY-3, 7, 7);

        // Draw line from center to dot, space permitting.
        if (radiusPix > 5)
        {
            g.drawLine(centerX, centerY, arrowTipX, arrowTipY);
        }
    }


    public void mousePressed(MouseEvent e)
    {
        value = xyToPolar(e.getX(), e.getY());
        repaint();
    }


    public void mouseDragged(MouseEvent e)
    {
        dragging = true;
        value = xyToPolar(e.getX(), e.getY());
        repaint();
        notifyListeners();
    }


    public void mouseReleased(MouseEvent e)
    {
        dragging = false;
        value = xyToPolar(e.getX(), e.getY());
        repaint();
        notifyListeners();
    }
```

```
private PolarPoint xyToPolar(int x, int y)
{
    double      newRho;
    double      newTheta;

    int deltaX = x - getSize().width/2;
    int deltaY = getSize().height/2 - y;
    double deltaLen = Math.sqrt(deltaX*deltaX + deltaY*deltaY);
    double rho = unitsPerPixel * deltaLen;
    rho = Math.min(rho, maxRho);
    double theta = Math.atan2(deltaY, deltaX);
    while (theta < 0.0)
        theta += 2*Math.PI;

    return new PolarPoint(rho, theta);
}


public void mouseClicked(MouseEvent e)      { }
public void mouseMoved(MouseEvent e)        { }
public void mouseEntered(MouseEvent e)      { }
public void mouseExited(MouseEvent e)       { }


public Dimension getMinimumSize()
{
    return getPreferredSize();
}


public Dimension getPreferredSize()
{
    return new Dimension(50, 50);
}
}
```

The Polar component class may now be used like any other component. Figure 3.4 shows a simple applet that contains a Polar component and a textfield.

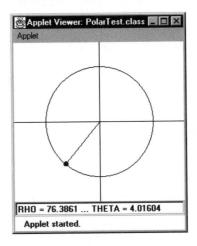

The source code for the `PolarTest` program follows. This listing is also included on the CD-ROM in javadevhdbk\ch03\PolarTest.java (the bytecode is in PolarTest.class).

LIST 3.5 *PolarTest.java*

```java
import   java.awt.*;
import   java.applet.Applet;


public class PolarTest extends Applet implements PolarListener
{
    private TextField        tf;

    public void init()
    {
        setLayout(new BorderLayout());

        Polar polar = new Polar();
        polar.setShowText(true);
        polar.addPolarListener(this);
        add(polar, BorderLayout.CENTER);
        tf = new TextField("RHO = 0.0   ...    THETA = 0.0");
        tf.setEditable(false);
        add(tf, BorderLayout.SOUTH);
    }
```

```
public void polarValueChanged(PolarEvent e)
    {
        tf.setText(e.getPolarValue().toString());
    }
}
```

Aggregation: The ThreeWay Component

Sometimes absolute precision is required when specifying a number; other times a fair approximation is good enough. The Polar component we described in the previous section is inherently imprecise, because it receives freehand input and its resolution is limited to radius increments of one pixel.

 The next example offers users a choice of three different levels of precision for entering an int: the complete accuracy of a textfield, the moderate accuracy of a scrollbar, and the vagueness of a set of radio buttons. The less accurate components will be easier to use. The resulting component will be called a ThreeWay.

The ThreeWay class goes a few steps beyond the traditional numeric scrollbar coupled with a nearby label or read-only textfield to reflect its value. We want three ways to write a number *and* three ways to read one. Again, the design issues listed earlier in the "Design Considerations" section provide a way in which to move through the process.

ThreeWay's Look-and-Feel Issues

Because it uses familiar elements, the decisions of how to display the component and how to specify its values are easier to make for the ThreeWay component than for the Polar component.

Displaying Values

First, we need to consider how the ThreeWay component should display its value. Of the three elements—scrollbar, textfield, and set of radio button checkboxes—the visually dominant one is the scrollbar. The textfield goes to the right of the scrollbar to conserve screen space. Above the scrollbar is a row of five radio checkboxes.

If the component's value is at or near its minimum, the leftmost radio button will be selected, and this button is to be positioned above the left end of the scrollbar, which, of course, is the slider position that represents the scrollbar's own minimum value. The rightmost radio button is positioned above the extreme right-hand position of the scrollbar, and it is selected if the component's value is at or near its maximum. The three radio buttons in the middle designate values that are approximately the half and quarter marks of the component's range. Simply stated, every subcomponent will do its best to reflect the ThreeWay component's current value. Figure 3.5 shows a ThreeWay component.

NOTE   The screenshot shown in Figure 3.5 comes from a Windows 95 machine. Note that scrollbar and checkbox appearances vary greatly from platform to platform.

FIGURE 3.5:

The ThreeWay component

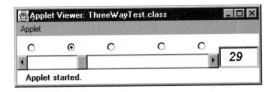

Scrollbar Cautions

On Motif platforms such as Sun workstations, the triangular arrow buttons of a scrollbar can grow without bounds. A very tall horizontal scrollbar will have very tall arrow buttons, and the buttons are equilateral triangles, so the width will be about 0.9 times the height. This encroaches on space that would otherwise be available to the slider. A tall scrollbar, no matter how wide it might be, could be useless because its slider's range is only a few pixels, and so it is important to restrict a horizontal scrollbar's vertical growth.

On Windows platforms, the scrollbar arrows are well-behaved. They lie inside rectangular boxes, and while the boxes grow taller, the arrows do not. A tall scrollbar has tall, narrow buttons that contain small triangles.

Specifying Values

With the manner in which the ThreeWay component will display its value established, it is now time to decide how users should interact with the new component. In this example, the answer is simple: Users should manipulate the scrollbar, the textfield, and the checkboxes in the expected way.

Choosing a Subclassing Strategy

Next, we need to decide on a subclassing strategy. In this case, the best approach has been obvious from the outset: We will subclass Container and populate it with standard subcomponents. This is the aggregation strategy, which allows users to interact with familiar devices. The programming task benefits from object reuse; the main task is to get the subcomponents to interact properly with each other, and there is more to this than may be immediately obvious. The components will be referenced by instance variables called textfield, scrollbar, and checkboxes[].

ThreeWay's Design Issues

Now we can move on to the remaining design issues, which guide us through the development of the custom component.

Modifying the Component's Appearance

Let's consider programmatically modifying the component's appearance. As with the previous example of the Polar class, the setForeground(), setBackground(), and setFont() methods can be made available to clients.

There is a bit of work to be done to support setForeground() and setBackground(). Because panels are likely to be used to lay out ThreeWay's subcomponents, there will be a modest containment hierarchy, and any intermediate panels will need to have their foreground and background colors set. Consider setForeground(), which must be overridden. One could simply call setForeground() on everything, component by component, but this would introduce a maintenance risk. Somebody could change the containment structure, introduce a new subpanel, and forget to modify setForeground() accordingly. Hence, a recursive algorithm will be used to call setForeground() on all components within the ThreeWay panel:

```
public void setForeground(Color color)
{
    super.setForeground(color);
```

```
        setForegndRecursive(this, color);
    }

    private void setForegndRecursive(Container parent, Color color)
    {
        Component children[] = parent.getComponents();
        for (int i=0; i<children.length; i++)
        {
            children[i].setForeground(color);
            if (children[i] instanceof Container)
            {
                setForegndRecursive((Container)children[i], color);
            }
        }
    }
```

We do much the same thing for the overridden setBackground() method. There is no need to go this far for setFont(), because the only child that actually uses this font is the textfield.

Limiting the Value

Next, we need to consider how to limit input values. The ThreeWay class is not so different from the Scrollbar class; certainly there should be an upper limit and a lower limit.

In the constructor for Scrollbar, the initial value appears before the minimum value, which comes before the maximum. This is the order maintained in Three-Way's constructor. The constructor's calling sequence is ThreeWay(int value, int minValue, int maxValue).

Storing, Setting, and Retrieving Values

The next issues are storing, setting, and retrieving the component's value. Storing and retrieving the value are simple. There is a private instance variable called value and a public accessor called getValue():

```
    private int     value;
            . . .
    public int getValue()
    {
        return(value);
    }
```

Setting the value requires updating the visible subcomponents. Setting the scrollbar and textfield values is easy. For the checkboxes, a float instance variable called `spreadPerRadio` is needed to help decide which checkbox is to be turned on. Because there are five checkboxes, the computation of `spreadPerRadio` (performed in the constructor) is:

```
spreadPerRadio = (float)(maxValue-minValue) / 4.0f;
```

The methods to revise the visible components are as follows:

```
private void reviseScrollbar()
{
    scrollbar.setValue(value);
}

private void reviseTextfield()
{
    textfield.setText((new Integer(value)).toString());
}

private void reviseRadios()
{
    float f = (value - minValue) / spreadPerRadio;
    int nth = Math.round(f);
    if (nth < 0)
    {
        nth = 0;
    }
    else if (nth > 4)
    {
        nth = 4;
    }

    cbgroup.setSelectedCheckbox(checkboxes[nth]);
}
```

Handling Events

Next to be addressed is the question of event handling. When any of the subcomponents is activated, the `ThreeWay` component should fire some kind of event to its listeners. With the `Polar` component of the previous example, we needed to invent a new event type (along with a new listener interface) because the `Adjustment` event was not quite appropriate. In this case, however, the Adjustment event will do the job perfectly, so it will not be necessary to develop a custom event type.

However, the Container class, from which ThreeWay inherits, does not provide support for adding, removing, or notifying Adjustment listeners. We need to write this support explicitly, much as we added support for adding, removing, or notifying Polar listeners to the Polar component.

The ThreeWay class's event support code is shown here. It is nearly identical to the event support for the Polar class; the only difference is that Adjustment events are sent rather than Polar events.

```java
public void addAdjustmentListener(AdjustmentListener listener)
{
    if (!listeners.contains(listener))
        listeners.addElement(listener);
}


public void removeAdjustmentListener(AdjustmentListener listener)
{
    listeners.removeElement(listener);
}


private void notifyListeners()
{
    AdjustmentListener  listener;

    AdjustmentEvent event = new AdjustmentEvent(this,
        AWTEvent.RESERVED_ID_MAX+1,
        AdjustmentEvent.ADJUSTMENT_VALUE_CHANGED,
        value);
    Vector copyOfListeners = (Vector)(listeners.clone());
    Enumeration enum = copyOfListeners.elements();
    while (enum.hasMoreElements())
    {
        listener = (AdjustmentListener)enum.nextElement();
        listener.adjustmentValueChanged(event);
    }
}
```

When input occurs in any of the components, the other components need to be updated to reflect the new value. The code that supports this behavior is shown here. The only unusual part of the code is the ActionPerformed() method, which is called when the user presses the Enter key in the textfield. Since nonnumerical input is meaningless, the code makes sure that the input is valid and restores the old value if the input does not represent a positive integer.

```
private void reviseScrollbar()
{
    bar.setValue(value);
}


private void reviseTextfield()
{
    textfield.setText((new Integer(value)).toString());
}


private void reviseRadios()
{
    float f = (value - minValue) / spreadPerRadio;
    int nth = Math.round(f);
    if (nth < 0)
    {
        nth = 0;
    }
    else if (nth > 4)
    {
        nth = 4;
    }

    cbgroup.setSelectedCheckbox(checkboxes[nth]);
}


//
// Called when the scrollbar is moved.
//
public synchronized void adjustmentValueChanged(AdjustmentEvent e)
{
    value = e.getValue();
```

```
        reviseRadios();
        reviseTextfield();
        notifyListeners();
    }


    //
    // Called when one of the checkboxes is clicked.
    //
    public synchronized void itemStateChanged(ItemEvent e)
    {
        // Only react to selected checkbox.
        if (e.getStateChange() != ItemEvent.SELECTED)
            return;

        // Determine new value.
        int newValue = minValue;
        for (int i=0; i<checkboxes.length; i++)
        {
            if (e.getSource() == checkboxes[i])
                break;
            newValue += spreadPerRadio;
        }

        value = newValue;
        reviseTextfield();
        reviseScrollbar();
        notifyListeners();
    }


    //
    // Called when the user hits ENTER in the textfield.
    //
    public synchronized void actionPerformed(ActionEvent e)
    {
        // Only accept valid numeric input.
        int     newValue = 0;
        try
        {
            newValue = Integer.parseInt(textfield.getText());
        }
        catch (NumberFormatException x)
        {
```

```
        textfield.setText("" + value);
        return;
    }

    // Normalize to within bounds.
    newValue = Math.min(newValue, maxValue);
    newValue = Math.max(newValue, minValue);

    value = newValue;
    reviseScrollbar();
    reviseRadios();
    reviseTextfield();
    notifyListeners();
}
```

Our final considerations are how the ThreeWay component behaves when it is stressed by multithreading or by resizing.

Behaving in a Multithreading Environment

The ThreeWay component, like the Polar component, clones its vector of listeners and notifies via the clone, rather than via the original. Aside from the listeners vector, there is no other data that is subject to modification (and hence corruption) from external objects, so multithreading will not present any problems.

Behaving during Resizing

What should be done when the component resizes? The Polar class had to adjust its scale factor. Here, there is no comparable internal state to revise. The scrollbar has an internal scale factor, but the Scrollbar class takes care of it automatically. Our only responsibility is to ensure that the layout looks reasonable no matter how the ThreeWay component is resized. This means we do not need to override setSize(), but we must build a robust containment hierarchy in our constructor.

As mentioned at the beginning of this section, scrollbars should be constrained in the vertical direction. On the other hand, when the ThreeWay component grows horizontally, all the new pixels should be given to the scrollbar; the textfield is always wide enough, and there is no benefit in making it any wider. This suggests a border layout manager, with the scrollbar occupying the South region. On the other hand, we need to align a row of checkboxes above the scrollbar, and this suggests a grid layout with two rows of one column. As usual, there are probably several feasible solutions. Here, the checkboxes are put in a panel (called cboxPanel), and the cboxPanel is placed above the scrollbar in a 2×1 grid. (See Chapter 4 for more information about layout managers and how they constrain components.)

The cboxPanel uses a grid bag layout manager to keep the checkboxes centered in the bottoms of their cells. So far, we have the structure shown in Figure 3.6, which introduces a new informal notation. Each container is labeled reasonably close to its upper-left corner. The label's format is *name @ position u layout*, where:

- *name* is the container instance variable handle.
- *position* is its position within its own container (for example, N for north in a border or 2,1 for column 2, row 1 in a grid).
- *u* stands for uses.
- *layout* is the type of layout manager used by the container (B for border, G for grid, F for flow, GB for grid bag, or C for card).

Noncontainer components are labeled near the center, if at all.

FIGURE 3.6:

Containment of
cboxSbarPanel

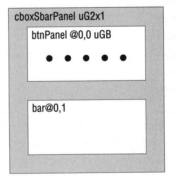

The cboxSbarPanel will ensure that the checkboxes stay above the scrollbar. The checkboxes will be put at South of some other panel, whose only job is to constrain cboxSbarPanel from vertical growth. This new panel is called restrictor-Panel and it contains only the single child.

The restrictorPanel is put at Center of the ThreeWay so that it can grow in both directions. Horizontal growth will be passed to cboxSbarPanel. In the case of vertical growth, restrictorPanel will grow taller, but btnSbarPanel will not; btnSbar-Panel will stick to the bottom of restrictorPanel. This produces the structure shown in Figure 3.7.

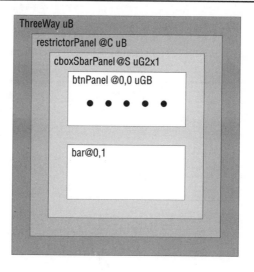

The textfield should go at East, to restrict its horizontal. But it would also be convenient if it could go at South, so that it is horizontally aligned with the scrollbar. An extra panel, called tfPanel, is needed. If tfPanel had to contain several components, a grid bag layout manager might be in order; however, in this simple case, a border with the textfield inside tfPanel at South is sufficient. This completes our design of the ThreeWay component's containment hierarchy, which is shown in Figure 3.8.

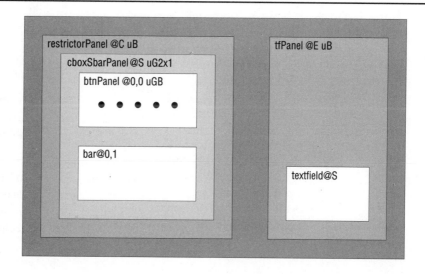

The ThreeWay Component and Test Applet

Here is the full listing of ThreeWay. The code also appears on the CD-ROM, in javadevhdbk\ch03\ThreeWay.java and javadevhdbk\ch03\ThreeWay.class.

LIST 3.6	*ThreeWay.java*

```java
import java.awt.*;
import java.awt.event.*;
import java.util.*;


public class ThreeWay
    extends Container
    implements ActionListener, AdjustmentListener,
               ItemListener, Adjustable
{
    private Vector          listeners = new Vector();
    private Scrollbar       bar;
    private TextField       textfield;
    private CheckboxGroup   cbgroup;
    private Checkbox        checkboxes[];
    private int             minValue;
    private int             maxValue;
    private int             value;
    private float           spreadPerRadio;

    public ThreeWay(int value, int minValue, int maxValue)
    {
        this.minValue = minValue;
        this.maxValue = maxValue;
        this.value = value;

        setLayout(new BorderLayout());

        // Build and add textfield.
        Panel tfPanel = new Panel();
        tfPanel.setLayout(new BorderLayout());
        textfield = new TextField("   " + value);
        textfield.addActionListener(this);
        tfPanel.add(textfield, BorderLayout.SOUTH);
        add(tfPanel, BorderLayout.EAST);
```

```java
    // Build and add checkboxes.
    Panel cboxPanel = new Panel();
    GridBagLayout gbl = new GridBagLayout();
    cboxPanel.setLayout(gbl);
    GridBagConstraints gbc = new GridBagConstraints();
    gbc.gridwidth = gbc.gridheight = 1;
    gbc.weightx = gbc.weighty = 1;
    gbc.gridy = 0;
    gbc.fill = GridBagConstraints.NONE;
    gbc.anchor = GridBagConstraints.SOUTH;
    checkboxes = new Checkbox[5];
    cbgroup = new CheckboxGroup();
    for (int i=0; i<5; i++)
    {
        checkboxes[i] = new Checkbox("", (i==0), cbgroup);
        checkboxes[i].addItemListener(this);
        gbc.gridx = i;
        if (i > 2)
            gbc.anchor = GridBagConstraints.SOUTHEAST;
        gbl.setConstraints(checkboxes[i], gbc);
        cboxPanel.add(checkboxes[i]);
    }
    spreadPerRadio = (float)(maxValue-minValue) / 4.0f;

    // Build and add scrollbar.
    Panel cboxSbarPanel = new Panel();
    cboxSbarPanel.setLayout(new GridLayout(2, 1));
    cboxSbarPanel.add(cboxPanel);
    bar = new Scrollbar(Scrollbar.HORIZONTAL, value, 0,
                        minValue, maxValue);
    bar.addAdjustmentListener(this);
    cboxSbarPanel.add(bar);
    Panel restrictorPanel = new Panel();
    restrictorPanel.setLayout(new BorderLayout());
    restrictorPanel.add(cboxSbarPanel, BorderLayout.SOUTH);
    add(restrictorPanel, BorderLayout.CENTER);

    // Make all subordinate components reflect current value.
    reviseScrollbar();
    reviseTextfield();
    reviseRadios();
}
```

```java
public int getValue()
{
    return value;
}


public synchronized void setValue(int newValue)
{
    value = newValue;
    reviseScrollbar();
    reviseTextfield();
    reviseRadios();
    notifyListeners();
}


public void addAdjustmentListener(AdjustmentListener listener)
{
    if (!listeners.contains(listener))
        listeners.addElement(listener);
}


public void removeAdjustmentListener(AdjustmentListener listener)
{
    listeners.removeElement(listener);
}


private void notifyListeners()
{
    AdjustmentListener  listener;

    AdjustmentEvent event = new AdjustmentEvent(this, 0, 0, value);
    Vector copyOfListeners = (Vector)(listeners.clone());
    Enumeration enum = copyOfListeners.elements();
    while (enum.hasMoreElements())
    {
        listener = (AdjustmentListener)enum.nextElement();
        listener.adjustmentValueChanged(event);
    }
}
```

```
private void reviseScrollbar()
{
    bar.setValue(value);
}


private void reviseTextfield()
{
    textfield.setText((new Integer(value)).toString());
}


private void reviseRadios()
{
    float f = (value - minValue) / spreadPerRadio;
    int nth = Math.round(f);
    if (nth < 0)
    {
        nth = 0;
    }
    else if (nth > 4)
    {
        nth = 4;
    }

    cbgroup.setSelectedCheckbox(checkboxes[nth]);
}


//
//  Called when the scrollbar is moved.
//
public synchronized void adjustmentValueChanged(AdjustmentEvent e)
{
    value = e.getValue();
    reviseRadios();
    reviseTextfield();
    notifyListeners();
}


//
// Called when one of the checkboxes is clicked.
//
```

```java
public synchronized void itemStateChanged(ItemEvent e)
{
    // Only react to selected checkbox.
    if (e.getStateChange() != ItemEvent.SELECTED)
        return;

    // Determine new value.
    int newValue = minValue;
    for (int i=0; i<checkboxes.length; i++)
    {
        if (e.getSource() == checkboxes[i])
            break;
        newValue += spreadPerRadio;
    }

    value = newValue;
    reviseTextfield();
    reviseScrollbar();
    notifyListeners();
}


//
// Called when the user hits ENTER in the textfield.
//
public synchronized void actionPerformed(ActionEvent e)
{
    // Only accept valid numeric input.
    int     newValue = 0;
    try
    {
        newValue = Integer.parseInt(textfield.getText());
    }
    catch (NumberFormatException x)
    {
        textfield.setText("" + value);
        return;
    }

    // Normalize to within bounds.
    newValue = Math.min(newValue, maxValue);
    newValue = Math.max(newValue, minValue);
```

```
        value = newValue;
        reviseScrollbar();
        reviseRadios();
        notifyListeners();
    }



    /*
     *  Set background color of everything by setting it on this
     *  container and recursively on all children.
     */
    public void setBackground(Color color)
    {
        super.setBackground(color);
        setBackgndRecursive(this, color);
    }



    private void setBackgndRecursive(Container parent, Color color)
    {
        Component children[] = parent.getComponents();
        for (int i=0; i<children.length; i++)
        {
            children[i].setBackground(color);
            if (children[i] instanceof Container)
            {
                setBackgndRecursive((Container)children[i], color);
            }
        }
    }



    /*
     *  Set foreground color of everything by setting it on this
     *  container and recursively on all children.
     */
    public void setForeground(Color color)
    {
        super.setForeground(color);
        setForegndRecursive(this, color);
    }
```

```java
    private void setForegndRecursive(Container parent, Color color)
    {
        Component children[] = parent.getComponents();
        for (int i=0; i<children.length; i++)
        {
            children[i].setForeground(color);
            if (children[i] instanceof Container)
            {
                setForegndRecursive((Container)children[i], color);
            }
        }
    }


    public void setFont(Font font)
    {
        textfield.setFont(font);
    }


    //
    // Methods of interface Adjustable.
    //
    public int  getBlockIncrement() { return (int)spreadPerRadio;    }
    public int  getMaximum()        { return maxValue;               }
    public int  getMinimum()        { return minValue;               }
    public int  getOrientation()    { return Scrollbar.HORIZONTAL;   }
    public int  getUnitIncrement()  { return bar.getUnitIncrement(); }
    public int  getVisibleAmount()  { return bar.getVisibleAmount(); }
    public void setBlockIncrement(int b)   { }
    public void setMaximum(int m)          { }
    public void setMinimum(int m)          { }
    public void setUnitIncrement(int m)    { }
    public void setVisibleAmount(int v)    { bar.setVisibleAmount(v); }
}
```

Because all the complexity has been encapsulated inside ThreeWay, the class is very easy to use. The following applet code updates its textfield with the value of its ThreeWay component whenever the user clicks the Show button. The applet is shown in Figure 3.9. The source code is also included on the CD-ROM in the file javadevhdbk\ch03\ThreeWayTest.java.

FIGURE 3.9:

A simple applet that uses
the ThreeWay component

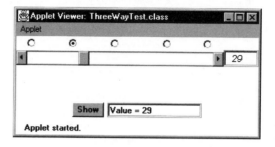

LIST 3.7   *ThreeWayTest.java*

```java
import  java.awt.*;
import  java.awt.event.*;
import  java.applet.Applet;


public class ThreeWayTest extends Applet implements ActionListener
{
    ThreeWay    threeway;
    Button      button;
    TextField   textfield;

    public void init()
    {
        setLayout(new BorderLayout());
        threeway = new ThreeWay(23, 0, 100);
        threeway.setFont(new Font("Helvetica", Font.ITALIC, 14));
        add(threeway, BorderLayout.NORTH);
        Panel panel = new Panel();
        button = new Button("Show");
        button.addActionListener(this);
        panel.add(button);
        textfield = new TextField("Value = 23", 15);
        panel.add(textfield);
        add(panel, BorderLayout.SOUTH);
    }
```

```
        public void actionPerformed(ActionEvent e)
        {
            textfield.setText("Value = " + threeway.getValue());
        }
    }
```

Subclassing a Standard Component: Validating Textfields

 Many programs require text validation. For example, the information typed into a textfield may need to be numeric, it may be required to fall within a certain range, or it may need to match a certain pattern. Because the standard AWT TextField class has no facilities for validation, you must create a custom component to incorporate this capability. For this example, we'll develop two alternatives: a simple IntTextField component for validating numeric input and a more sophisticated ValidatingTextField component that can check for specific input formats.

IntTextField's Look-and-Feel Issues

Obviously, a validating textfield should display its value in the same way that any textfield displays its value, and users should enter new values by typing. Our subclassing strategy is also obvious: A single component, TextField, requires enhancement. To begin, we will create a TextField subclass called IntTextField, which accepts only nonnegative integer input.

IntTextField's Design Issues

As with our previous examples, we will work through the list of design decisions to develop the validating textfield component.

Modifying the Component's Appearance

Programmatically modifying an IntTextField component's appearance is straightforward. Because IntTextField is a simple subclass, the setForeground(), setBackground(), and setFont() methods are inherited from TextField and will function as required without any additional effort.

Limiting the Value

The next issue is how to restrict values. For now, the class will insist on nonnegative integer values, and that will be the only restriction. When the user presses the Enter key, the input is checked to see if it represents a nonnegative integer; if it does not, the component is restored to its previous value.

Storing, Setting, and Retrieving Values

The new component will need to store its last valid value, so it will be able to restore itself if the user enters invalid input. The last valid value will be stored as an int, in an instance variable called intValue.

You may want to set the component's value from an int or from a string. To support setting from an int, the class has a setIntValue() method that takes an int argument and takes no action if the argument is negative. For setting from a string, the setText() method is overridden; again, the method has no effect if the argument is not valid. Both methods update the component's text as well as the intValue instance variable. These methods are listed here:

```
public void setText(String s)
{
    // Check for valid nonnegative int.
    int    newintval = 0;
    try
    {
        newintval = Integer.parseInt(s);
    }
    catch (NumberFormatException nfex)
    {
        return;
    }
    if (newintval < 0)
    {
        return;
    }

    // Valid input, update value and textfield.
    intValue = newintval;
    super.setText("" + newintval);
}
```

```
public void setIntValue(int newintval)
{
    if (newintval < 0)
    {
        return;
    }

    intValue = newintval;
    super.setText("" + newintval);
}
```

The value can be retrieved as a string by calling the inherited getText() method. However, that string most likely would be immediately converted to an int; therefore, an additional accessor called getIntValue() is provided:

```
public int getIntValue()
{
    return intValue;
}
```

Handling Events

Now consider the type of event that the IntTextField component should send. Programmers expect textfields to send Action events when the user presses Enter, so it is reasonable to expect the IntTextField component to do the same.

The new component will need to detect action events sent by itself and validate its contents. If the contents are valid, all Action listeners must be notified. If the contents are not valid, the value must be restored. This is a perfect opportunity to exploit the explicit event-enabling mechanism. The IntTextField class can enable Action events and only request notification of listeners if the input is valid. Recall that the way to request notification of listeners is simply to call the inherited version of the event-handler method.

The first step is to enable detection of Action events at construction time. Our class will provide two constructors. One that specifies just an initial int value and one that specifies both an initial int value and a width:

```
public IntTextField(int val)
{
    super((new Integer(val<0 ? 0 : val)).toString());
    intValue = val;
    enableEvents(AWTEvent.KEY_EVENT_MASK);
}
```

```
public IntTextField(int val, int width)
{
    super((new Integer(val<0 ? 0 : val)).toString(), width);
    intValue = val;
    enableEvents(AWTEvent.ACTION_EVENT_MASK);
}
```

Both constructors set the initial value to zero if the requested value is negative. It is difficult to check for this condition while still leaving the first line for the superclass constructor call, but the ternary operator comes to the rescue.

Now that explicit detection of Action events has been enabled, it is time to write a processActionEvent() method:

```
public void processActionEvent(ActionEvent e)
{
    int         newintval = 0;
    boolean     trouble = false;

    try
    {
        newintval = Integer.parseInt(getText());
        if (newintval < 0)
        {
            trouble = true;
        }
    }
    catch (NumberFormatException nfex)
    {
        trouble = true;
    }

    // Invalid char => undo.
    if (trouble)
    {
        setText("" + intValue);
    }

    // All is well.
    else
    {
        intValue = newintval;
        super.processActionEvent(e);
    }
}
```

Behaving under Stress

The issues of the component's behavior during multithreading and resizing are trivial for this example. The benefit of inheriting so much behavior from an industrial-strength superclass is that these matters have already been taken care of. No precautions need to be taken.

The IntTextField Component

The following is the complete listing for IntTextField (located on the CD-ROM in javadevhdbk\ch03\IntTextField.java and javadevhdbk\ch03\IntTextField.class).

LIST 3.8   *IntTextField.java*

```
import java.awt.*;
import java.awt.event.*;


public class IntTextField extends TextField
{
    private int      intValue;

    public IntTextField(int val)
    {
        super((new Integer(val<0 ? 0 : val)).toString());
        intValue = val;
        enableEvents(AWTEvent.KEY_EVENT_MASK);
    }


    public IntTextField(int val, int width)
    {
        super((new Integer(val<0 ? 0 : val)).toString(), width);
        intValue = val;
        enableEvents(AWTEvent.ACTION_EVENT_MASK);
    }


    public synchronized void setText(String s)
    {
        // Check for valid nonnegative int.
        int      newintval = 0;
```

```
    try
    {
        newintval = Integer.parseInt(s);
    }
    catch (NumberFormatException nfex)
    {
        return;
    }
    if (newintval < 0)
    {
        return;
    }

    // Valid input, update value and textfield.
    intValue = newintval;
    super.setText("" + newintval);
}


public synchronized void setIntValue(int newintval)
{
    if (newintval < 0)
    {
        return;
    }

    intValue = newintval;
    super.setText("" + newintval);
}


public int getIntValue()
{
    return intValue;
}


public void processActionEvent(ActionEvent e)
{
    int         newintval = 0;
    boolean     trouble = false;

    try
```

```
    {
        newintval = Integer.parseInt(getText());
        if (newintval < 0)
        {
            trouble = true;
        }
    }
    catch (NumberFormatException nfex)
    {
        trouble = true;
    }

    // Invalid char => undo.
    if (trouble)
    {
        setText("" + intValue);
    }

    // All is well.
    else
    {
        intValue = newintval;
        super.processActionEvent(e);
    }
    }
}
```

External Validation: The ValidatingTextField Component

The IntTextField subclass accepts only nonnegative integer input. Our next example is a variation that can check for other input formats. For the Validating-TextField component, validation is provided by an external object. An arbitrary validator is passed into the constructor and called upon to perform validation when the user presses the Enter key.

We begin by defining an interface called Validator, containing a single method:

```
public interface Validator
```

```
    {
        public boolean      validate(String s);
    }
```

The `ValidatingTextField` class is similar to the `IntTextField` class, with the following differences:

- The new class has a private instance variable, of type `Validator`, which is supplied via the constructor; when an `Action` event is detected, this object is consulted.

- No int value is maintained, since the class may not represent an int. Instead, the class has a string variable called `lastValidTextValue`, which is only used for restoring a previous value when invalid input is detected.

The source for the `ValidatingTextField` class listed in List 3.9 is also included on the CD-ROM in javadevhdbk\ch03\ValidatingTextField.java and javadevhdbk\ch03\ValidatingTextField.class.

LIST 3.9	*ValidatingTextField.java*

```
import  java.awt.*;
import  java.awt.event.*;


public class ValidatingTextField extends TextField
{
    private Validator    validator;
    private String       lastValidTextValue;


    public ValidatingTextField(String value,
                               int width,
                               Validator validator)
    {
        super(value, width);
        lastValidTextValue = value;
        this.validator = validator;
        if (!validator.validate(value))
        {
            lastValidTextValue = "";
```

```
            setText(lastValidTextValue);
        }
        enableEvents(AWTEvent.ACTION_EVENT_MASK);
    }


    public void processActionEvent(ActionEvent e)
    {
        String textValue = getText();
        if (!validator.validate(textValue))
        {
            // Invalid input.  Reset text, do not notify listeners.
            setText(lastValidTextValue);
            return;
        }

        // Valid input. Notify action listeners.
        lastValidTextValue = textValue;
        super.processActionEvent(e);
    }
```

Validating Textfields: Test Applet and Validator Classes

Figure 3.10 shows an applet that has three custom components. At the top is an instance of IntTextField. The other two components are instances of Validating-TextField. The middle textfield uses a validator that checks for a U.S. social security number format (as in 123-45-6789); the bottom textfield uses a validator that checks for a float value.

FIGURE 3.10:

Three subclasses of
TextField

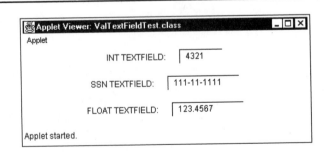

The code that produced Figure 3.10 is listed in List 3.10 along with the two validator classes. All source and bytecode files appear on the CD-ROM in the javadevhdbk\ ch03 directory.

LIST 3.10   *ValTextFieldTest.java*

```java
import  java.awt.*;
import  java.applet.Applet;


public class ValTextFieldTest extends Applet
{

    public void init()
    {
        setSize(420, 120);
        setLayout(new GridLayout(3, 1));

        Panel p = new Panel();
        p.add(new Label("INT TEXTFIELD:"));
        p.add(new IntTextField(4321, 6));
        add(p);

        p = new Panel();
        p.add(new Label("SSN TEXTFIELD:"));
        Validator val = new SSNValidator();
        p.add(new ValidatingTextField("111-11-1111", 12, val));
        add(p);

        p = new Panel();
        p.add(new Label("FLOAT TEXTFIELD:"));
        val = new FloatValidator();
        p.add(new ValidatingTextField("123.4567", 12, val));
        add(p);
    }
}
```

LIST 3.11   *SSNValidator.java*

```java
/*
 * A validator that checks if a string is a valid United States
 * social security number.  The format is three digits, a hyphen,
 * two digits, another hyphen, and four more digits, e.g. 123-45-6789.
 */

public class SSNValidator implements Validator
{
    public boolean validate(String s)
    {
        char      ch;

        if (s.length() != 11)                    // Check string length
            return false;

        for (int i=0; i<11; i++)
        {
            ch = s.charAt(i);
            if (i == 3  ||  i == 6)              // Hyphen expected
            {
                if (ch != '-')
                {
                    return(false);               // Not a hyphen
                }
            }
            else if (!Character.isDigit(ch))     // Digit expected
            {
                return(false);                   // Not a digit
            }
        }

        return true;                             // Valid
    }
}
```

LIST 3.12   *FloatValidator.java*

```java
/*
 * A validator that checks if a string is a valid float.
 */

public class FloatValidator implements Validator
{
    public boolean validate(String s)
    {
        try
        {
            Float.valueOf(s);
        }
        catch (NumberFormatException x)
        {
            return false;    // Invalid
        }

        return true;         // Valid
    }
}
```

Summary

This chapter covered the considerations and mechanics for creating custom components. For the sake of users, the component must have a reasonable and intuitive look and feel, and must behave well when resized by a layout manager. For the sake of programmers, the component must do a good job of communicating its value and posting events, and must behave well when subclassed.

We examined the design issues you should consider when deciding which approach to take for programming a custom component. We then developed examples of components using each approach. Using this framework, you can develop your own custom component classes that are robust and maintainable.

In the next chapter, we'll focus on layout managers, which manage the layout of components within containers.

CHAPTER
FOUR

Layout Managers

- Layout manager functions

- The five standard layout managers

- A spreadsheet without a layout manager

- A custom grid layout manager

- A custom interdependent layout manager

This chapter shows how to succeed with the standard set of layout managers, and how to create a custom one when the standard set is inadequate. We'll begin with an explanation of how layout managers work and why you need them. Then we'll describe each of the five layout managers in the AWT package and their main uses. Finally, we'll develop two custom layout managers: a grid-based manager that supports adding components at specific cells in a grid and an inter-dependent layout manager, which allows you to specify a component's position or size in relation to another component's position or size.

The Layout Manager Paradigm

Java's original platform-independence model forced a new philosophy of component layout. In 1995, nobody could predict how popular Java would become, and it seemed risky to attempt to introduce a new set of GUI components. The result was the AWT, which uses the peer mechanism to borrow the look and feel of the underlying window system. Thus, an instance of the java.awt.Button class looks like a Motif button when displayed on a Motif platform, like a Windows button when displayed on a Windows platform, and so on.

Unfortunately, different platforms have minute variations in fonts and moderate variations in component appearance. So, for example, a button with a particular label rendered in a particular font will vary in size from one platform to another. The same principle holds true for the other component types. The precise size of a component is not known until runtime, so dictating absolute component size and position at compile time may result in a GUI that looks fine on one platform but unbalanced or even corrupted on another.

Java's solution is the layout manager paradigm. The task of component layout is encapsulated into the LayoutManager interface. The paradigm discourages explicit sizing and positioning of components. Instead, a programmer associates a layout manager with each container, and the layout manager enforces a layout policy on the container's children. It is the layout manager that takes care of precise size and position issues.

This new paradigm can be frustrating for programmers who are accustomed to exercising complete layout control. In Java, successful GUI programming results from understanding the various policies that are implemented by the various layout managers and surrendering layout control to appropriate layout managers.

NOTE The JFC (Java Foundation Classes) components, which were introduced with release 2 of Java, have a platform-independent look and feel. For example, a JFC radio button will be the same size on all platforms (although there may be some minor font variations). With the new components, there is less need for layout managers. See Chapter 15 for information about the JFC components.

What a Layout Manager Does

A layout manager is a class that implements either the LayoutManager interface or the more modern LayoutManager2 interface. (All examples in this chapter use the simpler LayoutManager interface.) These interfaces provide a suite of methods that a container can call at appropriate times. It is important to note that the container initiates all layout activity. Even if you create your own layout manager class, you never need to worry about *when* to lay things out; you just need to be concerned with *how* to lay things out.

A layout manager's job is to enforce a layout policy on the components within a container. When a container adds a component to itself, it sets a flag, which marks the container as invalid. This means that the container is not up-to-date and must be laid out anew. When the container requires rendering—at initial display time or after resizing, for example—a call is made to the container's layout() method, which tells the layout manager to layoutContainer(). Within layoutContainer(), the layout manager calls setBounds() on the components, specifying whatever size and position best express the layout policy. Figure 4.1 shows the layout calling sequence of a container.

FIGURE 4.1:

Sample layout manager
calling sequence

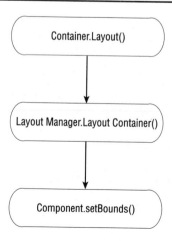

Container.Layout()

Layout Manager.Layout Container()

Component.setBounds()

Adding and Removing Components

Adding a component is done via the add() method of the Container class. This method is overloaded. The simplest form takes a component as its single parameter, as in add(okBtn). The container maintains an array, called component[], of child components that appear in the order in which they were added to the container. For order-dependent layout managers such as flow and grid, the manager itself does not keep its own list of components. Instead, the manager traverses the container's component[] array, positioning components as it encounters them.

Another form of add() that may be used with order-dependent layout managers is add(Component, int). The int specifies the component's place in the container's component[] array. Subsequent components in the array will be moved down.

More sophisticated layout managers, such as the border layout manager, use the add(Component, Object) version. In the case of the border layout manager, the object is really a string that specifies the component's position. Layout managers that require this form of add() generally ignore the container's component[] array. The component is indeed added to the container's array, but more important, the container calls the layout manager's addLayoutComponent(String, Component) method, passing in the string and the component. Typically, the layout manager maintains its own list of components, along with the associated strings.

Layout managers also support removing a component from a container. When a container receives a remove(Component) call, the container tells its layout manager to removeLayoutComponent(Component). Although the LayoutManager interface supports component removal, it is not usually good programming practice to take advantage of this functionality. It is much better to disable an extraneous control than to remove it.

The Case Against Removing Components

At first glance, the rationale for dynamically adding and removing components is sensible: When a component is not relevant to some mode or state of the program, why should the component occupy space on the screen? Isn't the best possible GUI one that configures itself moment by moment to present to the user only those controls that are needed? The answer is an emphatic no. The rationale makes sense in theory, but time after time, usability studies have found that what users really need in a GUI is stability. Accordingly, modern

Continued on next page

toolkits allow components to be disabled. A good GUI should deal with an irrelevant control not by removing it, but by graying it out.

When the GUI must be rearranged, it should be rearranged on a large scale, with nothing subtle about it. The user should know, in no uncertain terms, that something is different. Two situations come to mind where a dynamic GUI might be appropriate:

- A panel may need to display completely different contents. For example, a stock-trading applet might present one screen for buying shares, one for selling, and one for reviewing a customer's portfolio. In this case, the appropriate solution is to use the JFC tabbed-pane component, with one tab for each of the three modes. At any moment, the main panel displays one of the three major screens: the buying screen, the selling screen, or the portfolio screen. Clicking on a tab displays the appropriate screen. The tabs themselves are always available, and the three screens look so different that it is plain to the user which mode the applet is in.

- An applet or application may need to add or remove a toolbar. Toolbars are supported by the `java.awt.swing.JToolBar` class. A toolbar is like a panel that spans the entire width or height of its window. Generally, no component smaller than a toolbar should be dynamically added or removed from a GUI. When a toolbar is added, the program's working area is correspondingly reduced because the pixels for the toolbar come from the work area.

Laying Out the Container

When the container is laid out, the layout manager executes its `layoutContainer()` method, traversing either its own list of components or the container's, and calling `setBounds()` on each component. The layout manager must take into account the available space, its particular layout policy, and if possible, each component's preferred size. An additional consideration is the container's insets—a set of four integers that define how close any component may come to each of the container's four edges of the container. Many layout managers support gaps that specify the distance between adjacent components.

There is no guarantee that all of a container's components will be displayed. If the programmer provides contradictory instructions to the layout manager, some components may be omitted. This would happen, for example, if multiple components were added to any of a border layout manager's five regions.

The container, like any other component, may be called on to report its preferred size or its minimum size via the getPreferredSize() and getMinimumSize() methods, both of which return an instance of Dimension. Often, these values should be derived from the preferred or minimum sizes of the child components. Layout managers compute preferred and minimum size with the preferredLayoutSize(Container) and minimumLayoutSize(Container) methods.

The CD-ROM contains an applet called LoadLayoutLab to help you understand when a container lays out its components. The applet pops up a frame, because a frame can always be resized manually under any browser. In the middle of the frame is a panel composed of four subpanels. These subpanels appear to be managed, respectively, by a flow, a grid, a border, and a card layout manager, and they contain a variety of buttons. Actually, the layout managers and the buttons are subclasses that record activity in the applet's large text area. The layout managers report when they receive calls to addLayoutComponent(), layoutContainer(), preferredLayoutSize(), and minimumSize(). The buttons report when they receive getPreferredSize(), getMinimumSize(), and setBounds(). Because this makes for a cluttered text area, you can disable reporting via the checkboxes at the top of the frame. To learn more about one of the layout managers, first disable reporting from the others, then clear the text area and resize the frame.

The Standard Suite of Layout Managers

There are five layout managers in the AWT package: flow, grid, border, grid bag, and card. Keep in mind that it is rare to see a fully developed applet or frame that is controlled by a single layout manager. Generally, the applet or frame is subdivided into panels, each of which is controlled by its own layout manager. These smaller panels can contain other panels, and so on.

One of the key facts to know about any layout manager is whether it honors or ignores a component's preferred size. Some component classes should never be laid out in such a way that they can grow without limits. Usually a button, for example, only needs to be large enough to accommodate its label string; anything larger is a waste of pixels. Thus, a panel that contains buttons is an unlikely candidate for a grid layout manager, because every button would receive an equal share of the panel's available space. Similarly, sometimes it is desirable for a textfield to be as wide as possible, so using a border layout manager and putting the textfield at North or South is reasonable. However, if the textfield were added at East or West, its height would be unbounded; the upper portion of the textfield would be a blank waste.

In the following sections, we will examine each of the standard layout managers and discuss not only what they do, but also how to use them appropriately.

The Flow Layout Manager

The flow layout manager (class `java.awt.FlowLayout`) is the default for panels and applets. This layout manager arranges its components in horizontal rows. The preferred size of each child component is honored. The height of each row is determined by the height of the tallest component in that row. Within a row, the vertical centers of all components are aligned (not the tops or bottoms). The distance between components in a row is governed by the *horizontal gap*, which is an instance variable in the layout manager that defaults to 5 pixels but may be set in the manager's constructor. The components in a row default in such a way that they clump together in the middle of the row, but the manager can be constructed so that the components clump together to the right or the left.

Arranging Components

Components are added to the top row of the container until that row is full. Subsequent components are added to the second row, then the third, and so on. The distance between rows is governed by the vertical gap, which defaults to 5 pixels and may be set in the constructor.

The following are the constructors for `FlowLayout`:

`FlowLayout()`   Align components in the center of each row. Horizontal and vertical gaps are both 5 pixels.

`FlowLayout(int align)`   Align components at the left, in the center, or at the right of each row, according to whether `align` is `FlowLayout.LEFT`, `FlowLayout.CENTER`, or `FlowLayout.RIGHT`. Horizontal and vertical gaps are both 5 pixels.

`FlowLayout(int align, int hgap, int vgap)`   Align as above. Initialize horizontal and vertical gaps from `hgap` and `vgap`.

The minimum size of a container using a flow layout manager is found by computing the minimum width and height of every row, as follows:

- The container's minimum width is the largest minimum width of a row.

- The container's minimum height is the sum of the minimum heights of each row, plus extra pixels for gaps and insets.

- The minimum width for any individual row is the sum of the minimum widths of the row's components, plus extra pixels for gaps and insets.

- The minimum height for a row is the minimum height of that row's tallest component.

Preferred size is computed in a similar manner.

Using the Flow Layout Manager

The components managed by a flow layout manager are almost always noncontainer components—buttons, textfields, and so on, but not panels. Usually, there are not very many components. A single row of components looks fine on any platform, but a second row will often clash with the first. It is difficult to control where the row will break, and it is undesirable to have one or two components all by themselves in the bottom row when the upper rows are full.

More than two rows—and possibly more than one—is an indication that more organization is necessary. For example, the panel could be managed by a grid layout manager with one column. (The grid layout manager is discussed in the next section.) Each row would then contain a panel, managed by a flow layout manager. Rows would still contain neatly spaced and centered components, but you would have more control over which components went where.

You can implement a vertical column of components by setting hgap to an extremely large value such as 10,000. Because no container can possibly be this wide, no two components will ever share a row (because there would have to be 10,000 pixels between them).

Often, an applet or frame uses a border layout manager, populating only two regions. (The border layout manager is discussed in a subsequent section.) At North is a panel that contains all the program's controls, and at Center is everything else. The panel at North is laid out with a flow layout manager. This is one of the most common uses of the flow layout manager. For a program with only a few controls, this simple solution looks fine. Even if there are many components in the control panel, this design is helpful during the early stages of development.

During early program development, the concern is to make the program respond correctly when a button is clicked or a scrollbar is slid, without regard to where the button or scrollbar is situated. Frequent testing of these components will most likely suggest the need for additional components that you could not have anticipated during the early theoretical design phase. There is not much point in designing the perfect layout until you have decided on all the components. Meanwhile, tossing everything into a panel managed by a flow layout manager is perfectly acceptable.

The Grid Layout Manager

The grid layout manager (class java.awt.GridLayout) divides its container into a rectangular grid of equal-sized cells. Components occupy cells, filling them row by row from left to right in their order of appearance in the container's internal list. It is possible for some of the cells in the bottom row or rows to be empty.

Arranging Components

The constructor for GridLayout suggests a number of rows and a number of columns. Horizontal and vertical gaps, similar to those used by FlowLayout, may be specified optionally; they default to zero.

The following are the constructors for GridLayout:

GridLayout()   Place a single row, with one column per component.

GridLayout(int nrows, int ncols)   Place the specified number of rows and columns.

GridLayout(int nrows, int ncols, int hgap, int vgap)   Place the specified number of rows and columns, and the specified horizontal and vertical gaps.

Before it lays out its components, a grid layout manager determines how many rows and columns of cells to implement. These rows and columns may differ from the values passed into the constructor, especially if the container has only a few components.

The row and column count determine the height of every component as a function of the container's height, its top and bottom insets, nrows, and vgap. The number of columns is just enough to ensure that there is a cell for every component. Layout is rarely affected by ncols, which is used for computing minimum and preferred size. To illustrate how the grid layout manager lays out components,

Figure 4.2 shows a 4×4 grid with four buttons, and Figure 4.3 shows a 4×4 grid with twenty-three buttons.

FIGURE 4.2:

A 4×4 grid with four buttons

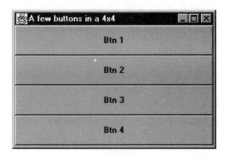

FIGURE 4.3:

A 4×4 grid with twenty-three buttons

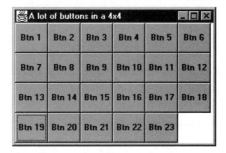

If the nrows parameter passed into the constructor is zero, then there will be exactly ncols columns. If the ncols parameter passed into the constructor is zero, then there will be exactly nrows rows.

Because the grid layout manager fills cells from left to right and top to bottom, there is no explicit way to skip a cell or to place a component in a particular cell. One way to give the illusion of skipping a cell is to insert an empty panel:

```
add(new Panel());
```

Of course, this solution is wasteful. It would be nice to be able to specify precisely where in the grid a component should go, so that unused space would not present a problem. The grid layout manager does not support this functionality. Later in this chapter, in the "A Custom Specific Grid Layout Manager" section, we will develop a custom layout manager that supports adding components at specific cells.

The minimum width of a grid-managed container is `ncols` times the widest child component minimum width, plus extra pixels for gaps and insets. The minimum height is computed similarly, as are the preferred width and the preferred height.

Using the Grid Layout Manager

Because the grid layout manager exerts full control over the size of its children, there are certain component classes that typically should not be managed by a grid. Buttons, checkboxes, and choices usually should be no larger than their minimum size; they should only appear in a grid-managed container if the container's own size is well controlled. If this can be ensured, it would be reasonable to manage related components this way. For example, radio buttons would look good in a grid if the grid were just the right size. Textfields and horizontal scrollbars might benefit from unlimited width, but not from unlimited height. (As explained in Chapter 3, unlimited height for a horizontal scrollbar can present a serious problem on Motif platforms.) Panels, canvases, and text areas do not present a problem.

It is common to see grids with just a single row or just a single column. For example, painting programs typically put their toolbars along the left or right edge. You could implement this type of toolbar by using a grid with one row and one column.

The Border Layout Manager

The border layout manager divides its container into, at most, five cells. Unlike the grid layout manager, the border layout manager does not arrange these cells in rows and columns.

Arranging Components

Components are added using the add(`Component, Object`) version of add(), where the object is a string specifying the name of the cell. The string must be one of the following:

"North"   The component is placed at the top of the container. Its height is its preferred height. Its width is the entire width of the container.

"South"   Like North, but the component is placed at the bottom of the container.

"East"   The component is placed at the right edge of the container. Its width is its preferred width. Vertically it extends up to the bottom of the North component if one is present, or all the way to the top of the panel if there is no North component. Horizontally it extends to the top of the South component if one is present, or all the way to the bottom of the panel if there is no South component.

"West"   Like East, but the component is placed at the left edge of the container.

"Center"   All the remaining space after North, South, East, and West have been considered. This is the default location if no second argument is specified.

The BorderLayout class has five defined constants that equal these string values:

```
BorderLayout.NORTH
BorderLayout.SOUTH
BorderLayout.EAST
BorderLayout.WEST
BorderLayout.CENTER
```

Using the constants requires more typing than using the literal values, but the constants result in more maintainable code. This is because if you misspell a constant, the compiler will let you know. If you misspell a literal, you are on your own to find the bug.

The constructor for border layout manager has two forms:

BorderLayout()   Creates a border layout manager with 5-pixel horizontal and vertical gaps.

BorderLayout(int hgap, int vgap)   Creates a border layout manager with the specified horizontal and vertical gaps.

The minimum width of a panel laid out with a border layout manager is the sum of the minimum widths of the West, Center, and East cells (or whichever of these are occupied), plus horizontal gaps and insets. The minimum height is the sum of the minimum heights of the North, Center, and South cells (or whichever of these are occupied), plus vertical gaps and insets. Preferred size is calculated similarly.

Using the Border Layout Manager

The border layout manager differentiates between components whose width or height is fixed and those that should expand or contract as the container expands or contracts. The typical case is a program with a control panel above a work area. The control panel, which is usually laid out with a flow layout manager, occupies the North cell, while the work area, usually a subclass of Panel or Canvas, occupies Center. This arrangement could easily be modified to add a status bar at South, implemented as a read-only textfield.

This example points out that panels that use the border layout manager rarely populate all five cells. The whole idea of border layout is that the work area in the center is able to grow in two dimensions, while the four regions around the edges are constrained to grow in only one dimension.

The Grid Bag Layout Manager

Of all the standard layout managers, grid bag offers the most control. It is also by far the most complicated.

Arranging Components

The grid bag layout manager consists of three conceptual layers: the container is divided into a grid, elements of the grid combine to form rectangular cells, and components occupy all or part of a cell. Figures 4.4, 4.5, and 4.6 illustrate each of these layers.

FIGURE 4.4:

Grid bag layout manager: the grid

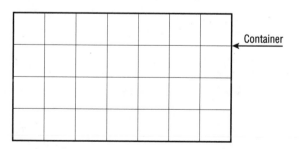

FIGURE 4.5:

Grid bag layout manager: cells within the grid

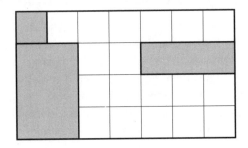

FIGURE 4.6:

Grid bag layout manager: components within the cells

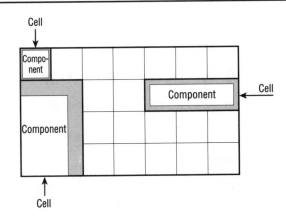

The constructor does not explicitly state the number of grid rows and columns. The layout manager infers the intended number of grid rows and columns from the per-component layout information supplied by the programmer; the cell sizes are inferred from the component sizes.

The GridBagLayout class uses GridBagConstraints as a helper class because describing a component requires more information than can reasonably be expressed in a string. When a component is added, an instance of GridBag-Constraints must have its instance variables set to the values that describe the component. Then the component is added to its container, with the GridBagConstraints passed as a second argument:

```
theContainer.add(okButton, myGridBagConstraints);
```

The layout manager stores a clone of the constraints, so the original may be reused. This is useful if the constraints for one component are almost the same as those for another.

GridBagConstraints specifies three pieces of information:

- The size and location within the container of the component's cell—width and height may span multiple rows and columns

- The size and location within the cell of the component

- What happens to the cell when the container is resized

Cell size and location are specified in the gridx, gridy, gridwidth, and grid-height instance variables of GridBagConstraints.

The fill instance variable determines whether the component's width and height will take their preferred values or completely fill the cell. The fill instance variable can take one of four values, which are defined as final ints in GridBag-Constraints and are described in Table 4.1.

TABLE 4.1   Values for Fill in GridBagConstraints

Fill	Width	Height
None (default)	Preferred	Preferred
Horizontal	Cell width	Preferred
Vertical	Preferred	Cell height
Both	Cell width	Cell height

If a component does not occupy its entire cell, its position within the cell must be specified. There are nine possibilities, represented by final ints in class Grid-BagConstraints. The default is CENTER, which places the component in the center of the cell. Four other options place it in the cell's corners: NORTHWEST, NORTHEAST, SOUTHEAST, and SOUTHWEST. Four more options place it in the center of the cell's edges: NORTH, EAST, SOUTH, and WEST.

These values are sufficient to dictate components' initial sizes and positions. GridBagLayout allows program control of where extra pixels are allocated when extra space becomes available (when the container resizes, for example).

The weightx and weighty instance variables of GridBagConstraints specify what proportion of extra space will be allocated to a cell. These values are not percentages, nor are they proportional to any particular scale. When there are new pixels to be allocated to a row, the total `weightx` for all the cells in that row is computed; the number of pixels allocated to a cell is in proportion to the contribution its `weightx` made to the total. Vertical allocation is based on a similar calculation with `weighty`. This imprecision makes for very easy use. Typically, some cells should not grow at all in a particular direction, while others should share equally in any extra pixels that come along. In this case, the cells that do not grow should have `weightx` or `weighty` set to zero.

The weight feature is useful for the same reason that the border layout manager is useful: When the container resizes, some components should resize, some should resize in just one direction, and some should remain as they are. Note that if different components have different weights, resizing will result in rows and columns of unequal widths and heights. In fact, since weight affects the entire row and column, inconsistent specifications of weight can mess up a layout.

The grid bag layout manager's computations of minimum and preferred size are similar to the grid layout manager's. Minimum or preferred size is summed across all rows and all columns. This is the theory. In practice, grid bag is like the other higher-level layout managers—in most situations, some features are used and some are not.

Using the Grid Bag Layout Manager

The grid bag layout manager may seem daunting at first, but once you understand how it works, it is easy to use. The trick is to achieve an intuitive understanding, and this can only come with use.

One way to rise up the learning curve is, of course, to write dozens of pieces of trial code. The CD-ROM that comes with this book offers an alternative. The `GridBagLab` applet presents six identical color-coded panels, each of which can be enabled or disabled, as shown in Figure 4.7. The panels contain controls for specifying values of a `GridBagConstraints`. When you click the Show button, the applet displays a frame that contains one button for each enabled panel. The panel is laid out using a grid bag, and the constraints of each button are set according to the corresponding panel. Clicking any button in the panel dismisses that panel. Spending 15 minutes experimenting with `GridBagLab` should help you understand how the grid bag layout manager works.

FIGURE 4.7:

The GridBagLab applet

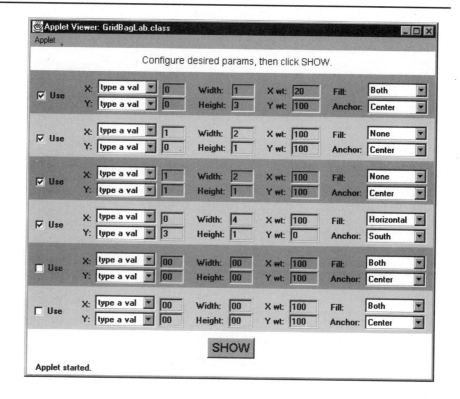

Table 4.2 shows sample values for four components. When you enter these values into the textfields in the GridBagLab applet, you get the layout shown in Figure 4.8. Figure 4.9 shows the same frame after horizontal resizing.

TABLE 4.2: Sample Values for Four GridBagLab Components

XY	Width	Height	X Weight	Y Weight	Fill	Anchor
0 0	1	3	20	100	Both	N/A
1 0	2	1	100	100	None	Center
1 1	2	1	100	100	None	Center
0 3	4	1	100	0	Horizontal	South

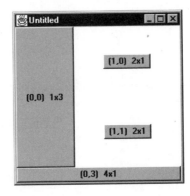

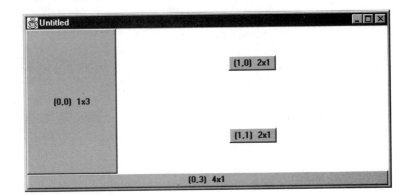

The Card Layout Manager

So far, we have looked at layout managers that position their components in 2-D space. The card layout manager positions components in time. This means that if a container uses a card layout manager, then exactly one of the container's components is visible at any moment. The result is similar to tabbed dialog boxes that are often used for setting options on Windows platforms (with the notable omission of the tabs; tabbed panels are provided in the JFC components, described in Chapter 15). Various methods are provided to tell the layout manager to display a different component.

Arranging Components

CardLayout has two constructors:

CardLayout()   The default. Both gaps are zero.

CardLayout(int hgap, int vgap)   Horizontal and vertical gaps are specified. Unlike other layout managers, which manage more than one component at a time, gaps here specify distance from the container's edges, like the container's gaps.

The following methods change the displayed component. Note that they are methods in the CardLayout class, and they all require the associated container to be passed in as a parameter:

next(Container)   Display the container's next child component in the container's list, using the order in which they were added.

previous(Container)   Display the container's previous child component in the container's list, using the order in which they were added.

first(Container)   Display the container's first child component in the container's list, using the order in which they were added.

last(Container)   Display the container's last child component in the container's list, using the order in which they were added.

show(Container, String)   Display the component specified by String. The component must have been added using add(Component, Object); the Object parameter is a unique string that identifies the component.

Each child component (or *card*) is resized to fill the container, less gaps and insets. The minimum width is the largest minimum width of any child. The minimum height is the largest minimum height of any child. The preferred width is the largest preferred width of any child. The preferred height is the largest preferred height of any child. (These might be different children.)

Using the Card Layout Manager

The card layout manager is useful whenever the purpose of a region of the screen changes. A text editor application, for example, might use a border layout manager, allocating the North region of its frame for tool panels and the Center region for its work area. A menu item would switch from Editing mode to Print Preview mode. The Center region would be occupied by a panel using a card layout manager, that controlled the Editing and Print Preview panels.

The card layout manager supports a dynamically changing user interface, and GUIs should be modified with extreme caution. Every card represents a mode of the program. A card change should happen only when the program really changes to a new major state. Each card should look sufficiently different from all the other cards so that the user cannot mistake which mode is currently in effect.

Property sheets and wizards are also excellent examples of the appropriate use of the card layout manager.

No Layout Manager

There is certainly no danger in calling `setLayout(null)` on a container. The `Component` class always checks to see if it has a null layout manager before calling on the layout manager to do anything. This strategy will not cause a null pointer exception, but there is little to be said in its favor.

The advantage of not using a layout manager is that calling `setSize()` and `setBounds()` on components actually works. On the other hand, the programmer is responsible for positioning the components, not only at initialization but whenever the container resizes. This requires overriding the container's `setBounds()` method, as shown below:

```
public void setBounds(int x, int y, int w, int h)
{
        super. setBounds(x, y, w, h);
        // Compute size/position for each child component
        component1. setBounds(x1, y1, w1, h1);
        component2. setBounds(x2, y2, w2, h2);
                . . .
}
```

TIP   `setSize(w, h)` just calls `setBounds(x, y, w, h)` using the component's current `x` and `y`. It is always sufficient to override `setBounds()` and leave `setSize()` alone.

For a very simple layout, using a null layout manager is easy, but as the GUI's complexity increases, the chore of laying out the components becomes increasingly burdensome. The `setBounds()` method must implement a layout policy. It is generally easier to implement a custom layout manager, because when you implement the `LayoutManager` interface, all you need to worry about is correctly writing five methods. All the subtleties of deciding when to lay out the container are taken care of. (Following this section, the remainder of this chapter deals with custom layout managers.)

That being said, when is it appropriate to set layout to null? The advantage comes when the container contains so few components that, in essence, there is no layout policy to encapsulate in a layout manager. This is rare. One example might be a spreadsheet, where clicking on a cell brings up a panel for viewing or editing the cell's formula. The spreadsheet can be implemented as a subclass of Applet. The subclass' constructor or init() calls setLayout(null). The paint() method renders the spreadsheet data. A mouse click in a cell reformats the formula panel, positions it, and adds it to the spreadsheet panel.

The code for a simplified version of this spreadsheet follows. Cells just display their coordinates, and the formula panel also shows the coordinates. The layout policy can be stated as follows: The formula panel, if it appears, has a constant width and height; if possible it should be centered over the cell it describes, but it should always be at least 5 pixels from any edge of the spreadsheet.

For the sake of simplicity, this example deliberately uses hardcoded cell width and height. The source code and the applet itself are on the CD-ROM in java-devhdbk\ch04\NoLayoutSpreadsheet.java.

LIST 4.1   *NoLayoutSpreadsheet.java*

```java
import    java.awt.*;
import    java.awt.event.*;
import    java.applet.Applet;


public class NoLayoutSpreadsheet extends Applet
                            implements ActionListener,
                                       MouseListener
{
    static final int    CELL_WIDTH_PIX      = 80;
    static final int    CELL_HEIGHT_PIX     = 60;
    static final int    N_ROWS              = 5;
    static final int    N_COLS              = 5;
    static final int    FORMULA_WIDTH       = 165;
    static final int    FORMULA_HEIGHT      = 80;
```

```
Panel              formulaPanel;
TextField          formulaTF;
Button             formulaOKBtn;


public void init()
{
    setBackground(Color.white);
    setLayout(null);

    formulaPanel = new Panel();
    formulaPanel.setBackground(Color.lightGray);
    formulaPanel.setLayout(new BorderLayout());
    formulaTF = new TextField(10);
    formulaTF.setEditable(false);
    formulaTF.setFont(new Font("Monospaced" , Font.PLAIN, 40));
    formulaPanel.add(formulaTF, BorderLayout.CENTER);
    Panel p = new Panel();
    formulaOKBtn = new Button("OK");
    formulaOKBtn.addActionListener(this);
    p.add(formulaOKBtn);
    formulaPanel.add(p, BorderLayout.SOUTH);

    addMouseListener(this);
}


public void paint(Graphics g)
{
    int     i, j, x, y;

    g.setColor(Color.blue);
    for (j=0; j<=N_ROWS; j++)
    {
        y = j * CELL_HEIGHT_PIX;
        g.drawLine(0, y, getSize().width, y);
    }
    for (i=0; i<=N_COLS; i++)
    {
        x = i * CELL_WIDTH_PIX;
        g.drawLine(x, 0, x, getSize().height);
    }
```

```java
        g.setColor(Color.black);
        for (j=0; j<N_ROWS; j++)
        {
            for (i=0; i<N_COLS; i++)
            {
                x = i * CELL_WIDTH_PIX;
                y = j * CELL_HEIGHT_PIX;
                String s = "(" + i + "," + j + ")";
                g.drawString(s, x+18, y+36);
            }
        }
    }


    public void mouseReleased(MouseEvent e)
    {
        int cellX = e.getX() / CELL_WIDTH_PIX;
        int cellY = e.getY() / CELL_HEIGHT_PIX;
        formulaTF.setText("(" + cellX + "," + cellY + ")");

        int panelX = cellX*CELL_WIDTH_PIX    +
                     CELL_WIDTH_PIX/2         -
                     FORMULA_WIDTH/2;
        panelX = Math.max(panelX, 5);
        panelX = Math.min(panelX,
                        getSize().width - FORMULA_WIDTH - 5);
        int panelY = cellY*CELL_HEIGHT_PIX    +
                     CELL_HEIGHT_PIX/2         -
                     FORMULA_HEIGHT/2;
        panelY = Math.max(panelY, 5);
        panelY = Math.min(panelY,
                        getSize().height - FORMULA_HEIGHT - 5);
        formulaPanel.setBounds(panelX, panelY,
                        FORMULA_WIDTH, FORMULA_HEIGHT);
        add(formulaPanel);
        validate();
        repaint();
    }


    public void actionPerformed(ActionEvent e)
    {
        remove(formulaPanel);
    }
```

```
        // Superfluous interface methods.
        public void mouseClicked(MouseEvent e)      {  }
        public void mouseEntered(MouseEvent e)      {  }
        public void mouseExited(MouseEvent e)       {  }
        public void mousePressed(MouseEvent e)      {  }
}
```

Note that when we add the formula panel in `mouseReleased()`, we need to call `validate()`. The `add()` call invalidates—it marks the applet as requiring fresh layout and rendering, but the layout and rendering are not invoked. This is not the case with the `remove()` call in `actionPerformed()`. When a component is removed, `validate()` is usually called automatically.

Note also that it is possible to add the formula panel when it has not yet been removed if the user clicks on a new cell while the formula panel is displayed. The `add()` method supports this; it checks to see if the component is already contained in the parent, and if so it removes before adding.

Figure 4.10 shows the spreadsheet with the formula panel displayed.

FIGURE 4.10:

A spreadsheet with no layout manager

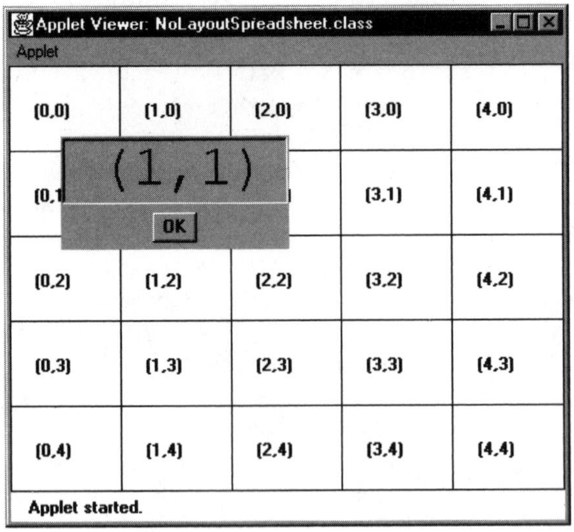

Custom Layout Managers

In order to create a new layout manager class, you need to understand the LayoutManager interface. After we examine the makeup of that interface, we'll develop two examples of custom layout managers. The first example is like GridLayout, but clients specify where in the grid a component is to go. The second is an interdependent layout manager in the spirit of Motif's Form widget, where component positions can be specified relative to other components.

The first example is moderately small. The second is quite long; in fact, it is the longest code example in this book. The code sizes themselves are part of the information. It is hoped that after having read this chapter, you will have two good points of reference for estimating how long it will take to develop a custom layout manager.

The LayoutManager Interface

LayoutManager is not a class but an interface. In other words, the various classes share no methods or instance variables. All they have in common are five method names.

A class that declares that it implements LayoutManager promises only to provide methods whose names and argument lists match the five methods named in the LayoutManager interface:

```
public void addLayoutComponent(String, Component)
public void removeLayoutComponent(Component)
public Dimension minimumLayoutSize(Container)
public Dimension preferredLayoutSize(Container)
public void layoutContainer(Container)
```

The code can do anything it pleases. Because interface methods are called blindly, it is especially important to know what behavior the caller expects. The following sections detail the behavior expected of the methods of the LayoutManager interface.

The addLayoutComponent() Method

The addLayoutComponent() method is called when a component is added to a container by means of the add(String, Component) method or the add(Component,

Object) method. The container keeps track of its components but not of the constraint strings or objects passed in with them, so it is the layout manager's job to associate components with constraints, typically by storing components in a hashtable that is keyed by the constraints.

The add() and add(int) methods of Container do not call addLayoutComponent(); if the layout manager cares about components added in this fashion, it must find out about them by calling the container's getComponent(), getComponent(int), or getComponents() method. It is acceptable for a layout manager that uses constraints to ignore components unless it hears about them via addLayoutComponent().

The removeLayoutComponent() Method

The only job of removeLayoutComponent() is to remove the component from any storage maintained by the layout manager (such as the hashtable suggested above). It is not necessary to rearrange the remaining components; when the time comes to do that, the container will call layoutContainer() explicitly.

The miminumLayoutComponent() Method

The minimumLayoutSize() method should return a value based on a geometrical aggregate of the minimum sizes of the child components. In practice, it is rarely called, and even more rarely does it affect anything. Therefore, if computation based on the children's minimum sizes is out of the question, it is reasonable to return some hardcoded value. The minimum size is used for reporting the container's own minimum size, rather than for laying out components within the container.

There is no guarantee that layout managers will honor a component's minimum size. Layout managers frequently report their preferred layout size as their minimum layout size. Frequently, this is implemented by calling the preferredLayoutSize() method.

The preferredLayoutSize() Method

Like the minimumLayoutSize() method, the preferredLayoutSize() method should return a value based on a geometrical consideration of the container's children.

This method also is used for computing the container's own preferred size, not for laying out its components. However, unlike minimumLayoutSize(), preferred-LayoutSize() is quite likely to be called. This means that it is more important to return a reasonable value, unless clients can be warned against adding the container to a container that uses, for instance, a flow or border layout manager.

WARNING   It is tempting to have minimumLayoutSize() and preferredLayoutSize() return the container's minimum or preferred size. This seems the courteous thing to do, as if the layout manager is saying to the container, "Oh, I don't much care, what size would *you* prefer?" This approach fails, because the layout manager's minimumLayoutSize() and preferredLayoutSize methods ordinarily are called by the container's getMinimumSize() and getPreferredSize(), and the result is a back-and-forth call loop that eventually blows its stack. The safe way to defer to the container's size is to return the size of the container.

A Custom Specific Grid Layout Manager

The standard grid layout manager insists on populating grid cells in the order in which components appear in the container's internal storage. Here, we will develop a custom manager class called SpecificGridLayout, which supports adding components at specific cells. The number of cell rows and columns is specified to the constructor, and that many rows and columns will always be present.

Clients add components with the add(component, String) version of add(). The string format is *x*,*y*, in which *x* and *y* are the cell coordinates where the component is to go. The upper-left cell is denoted by the string "0,0".

The only methods in SpecificGridLayout are a pair of constructors (one specifying just grid size and one specifying grid size and gaps) and the five methods of the LayoutManager interface.

We will go through the entire source file, method by method—comments and explanations are interspersed with the SpecificGridLayout.java listing, which follows. The complete source is on the CD-ROM in javadevhdbk\ch04\SpecificGrid-Layout.java.

LIST 4.2   *SpecificGridLayout.java*

```java
import  java.awt.*;
import  java.util.*;

public class SpecificGridLayout implements LayoutManager
{
    int         nrows;
    int         ncols;
    int         hgap;
    int         vgap;
    Hashtable   hash;


    public SpecificGridLayout(int nrows, int ncols)
    {
        this(nrows, ncols, 0, 0);
    }


    public SpecificGridLayout(int nrows, int ncols, int hgap, int vgap)
    {
        this.nrows = nrows;
        this.ncols = ncols;
        this.hgap = hgap;
        this.vgap = vgap;
        hash = new Hashtable();
    }
```

The constructors just initialize the instance variables and construct a new hashtable. The horizontal and vertical gap sizes default to 0.

```java
    public void addLayoutComponent(String position,
                                    Component component)
    {
        if (!(hash.containsKey(position)))
            hash.put(position, component);
    }
```

When a component is added, it is inserted into the hashtable; the hash key is the position string. If the position string is a duplicate, the new component is not inserted in the hashtable and will not be seen.

```
public void removeLayoutComponent(Component component)
{
    Enumeration keys = hash.keys();
    while (keys.hasMoreElements())
    {
        String key = (String)(keys.nextElement());
        if (hash.get(key) == component)
        {
            hash.remove(key);
            return;
        }
    }
}
```

When a component is to be removed, it is simply removed from the hashtable. Most likely, the removeLayoutComponent() call comes from the container's remove() method, which will later mark the container as invalid and call the layout manager's layout-Container() method.

```
public Dimension minimumLayoutSize(Container container)
{
    return xxxSize(container, SIZE_MIN);
}

public Dimension preferredLayoutSize(Container container)
{
    return xxxSize(container, SIZE_PREF);
}

private Dimension xxxSize(Container container, int type)
{
    Dimension    dim = null;
    int          maxWidth = 0;
    int          maxHeight = 0;

    Enumeration components = hash.elements();
```

```
while (components.hasMoreElements())
{
    Component comp = (Component)(components.nextElement());
    switch (type)
    {
        case SIZE_MIN:
            dim = comp.getMinimumSize();
            break;
        case SIZE_PREF:
            dim = comp.getPreferredSize();
            break;
    }
    maxWidth = Math.max(maxWidth, dim.width);
    maxHeight = Math.max(maxHeight, dim.height);
}

Insets insets = container.getInsets();
int width  = insets.left                    +
                maxWidth * ncols            +
                hgap * (ncols-1)            +
                insets.right;
int height = insets.top                     +
                maxHeight * nrows           +
                vgap * (ncols-1)            +
                container.getInsets().top;

    return new Dimension(width, height);
}
```

The minimumLayoutSize() and preferredLayoutSize() algorithms call, respectively, getMinimumSize() and getPreferredLayoutSize() on every component in the hashtable, determining the largest of the widths and heights. The minimum width for the container is the sum of the left and right container insets, plus one maximum component width for every column in the layout, plus one horizontal gap for every gap between columns. The minimum height for the container is computed similarly: It is the sum of the top and bottom container insets, plus one maximum component height for every row in the layout, plus one vertical gap for every gap between rows. The preferred size is computed according to the same recipe, but preferred component sizes are used instead of minimum sizes.

```java
public void layoutContainer(Container container)
{
    // Compute cell width and height.
    Insets insets = container.insets();
    int availableWidth =
            container.size().width - insets.left - insets.right;
    int compWidth = (availableWidth - hgap*(ncols-1)) / ncols;
    int availableHeight =
            container.size().height - insets.top - insets.bottom;
    int compHeight = (availableHeight - vgap*(nrows-1)) / nrows;

    // Position components.
    Enumeration keys = hash.keys();
    while (keys.hasMoreElements())
    {
        String key = (String)(keys.nextElement());
        StringTokenizer st = new StringTokenizer(key, ",");
        int cellx = Integer.parseInt((String)(st.nextToken()).trim());
        int x = insets.left + compWidth*cellx + hgap*(cellx);
        int celly = Integer.parseInt((String)(st.nextToken()).trim());
        int y = insets.top + compHeight*celly + vgap*(celly);
        Component comp = (Component)(hash.get(key));
        comp.reshape(x, y, compWidth, compHeight);
    }
}
```

To lay out its components, the layout manager just computes the size of each cell. Then it iterates through every component in the hashtable, computing x and y and then sizing/positioning the component. Most of the code accounts for insets and gaps. If the layout manager did not support insets and gaps, this method would be reduced to just a few lines.

Figure 4.11 shows an applet laid out using the specific grid layout manager, with five rows and five columns. This applet is on the CD-ROM in `javadevhdbk\ch04\SpecificGridTest.java`.

FIGURE 4.11:

The SpecificGridTest applet

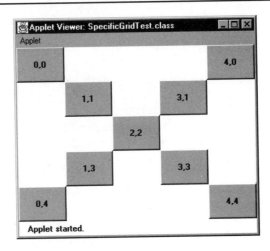

A Custom Interdependent Layout Manager

One very desirable bit of functionality that is not supported by any of the standard layout managers is the ability to specify some attribute of a component's size or position with respect to some other component's size or position. For example, you cannot specify that the top edge of the Cancel button is to be 15 pixels below the bottom edge of the OK button; the OK button's width is to be 75 percent of the Cancel button's width, and the two buttons' centers are to be vertically aligned.

Consider a panel with scrollbars at the right and the bottom edges, and the remainder occupied by a canvas depicting some kind of image. You can almost achieve this with a border layout manager, but not quite. With a border layout manager, one scrollbar goes at South and one at East; the canvas goes at Center. The problem is that the bottom scrollbar is too wide. It should not be wider than the canvas. Figure 4.12 illustrates the problem. If you could set the bottom scrollbar's width to be the width of the canvas, then the panel would appear as in Figure 4.13.

For the final example in this chapter, we will develop an *interdependent* layout manager—one that supports specifying component position or size as functions of another component's position or size. The layout policy will be similar to that of the Motif Form widget, and our new class will be called FormLayout. The applet shown in Figure 4.13 was laid out using this custom class. The source for the applet is quite simple and is listed in the "Using FormLayout" section later in this chapter. The source for the layout manager, on the other hand, is not at all simple.

FIGURE 4.12:

Imperfect bottom scrollbar

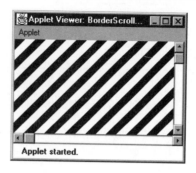

FIGURE 4.13:

Bottom scrollbar is
just right.

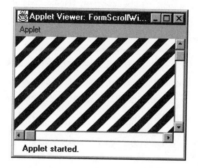

This is a lengthy example. The length itself conveys important information: this is about what it takes to create a layout manager that supports component interdependence.

Three major pieces must be designed before we can develop the FormLayout class:

- The layout policy, which is a statement of the functionality that FormLayout is to support.

- A mechanism for specifying component position and size, which is a way for clients to express programmatically the desired size and position of components.

- A dependency checker, which decides in which order the components' attributes (size and position) will be computed.

Each of these, and then the code for the layout manager itself, will be developed in turn.

NOTE   The entire listing for the layout manager is on the CD-ROM. Because it is just over 1000 lines long, some of the tedious parts have been abbreviated here (as noted in the text).

The Layout Policy

The form layout manager's layout policy is designed to be as simple as possible while still being of practical use.

The form layout manager takes the view that there are four attributes that describe a component's horizontal position and size: the position of the left edge, the position of the center, the position of the right edge, and the width. If any two of these are provided by the client program, the layout manager will be able to determine the other two.

Similarly, there are four attributes that describe a component's vertical position and size: the position of the top edge, the position of the center, the position of the bottom edge, and the height. Again, if any two of these are provided by the client program, the layout manager will be able to determine the other two.

Therefore, the layout policy is that for each component, the client program must specify two out of the four horizontal attributes and two out of the four vertical attributes.

Because every component has a preferred width, the form layout manager optionally permits clients to specify only one horizontal attribute instead of two, provided that attribute is not the width. In this case, the width will be taken to be the component's preferred width. Similarly, it is permitted to specify only one vertical attribute instead of two, provided that attribute is not the height. In this case, the height will be taken to be the component's preferred height.

The layout policy supports three ways for clients to specify these attributes:

- In absolute pixels: "The right-hand edge of this scrollbar is at pixel coordinate 365."

- In decimal fractions of the container's width or height: "The horizontal center of this button is at 0.25 times the entire width of the container."

- In terms of an attribute of another component: "The bottom edge of this checkbox is aligned with the bottom edge of that label."

Note that the decimal fraction form supports attaching a component to an edge of the container. For example, to attach a component to the top of the container, the client would specify that the top of the component is at 0.0 times the container's height. To attach to the bottom of the container, the client would specify that the bottom of the component is at 1.0 times the container's height.

The layout policy supports one further refinement: Any attribute, having been specified as above, may optionally be given a modification (or *delta*), specified in absolute pixels. Thus, a client could tell the layout manager that the left edge of the Cancel button is to be the right edge of the OK button, plus 15 pixels.

The intention of this layout policy is to permit programmers to describe layout relationships in a natural way. How well this is achieved can be gauged by looking at the layout shown in Figure 4.14.

This layout consists of a canvas, a scrollbar, and a button. If you had to describe this layout to somebody over the telephone using only words, you might say the following:

"There is an OK button in the lower-right corner. It is as large as it needs to be (given its huge font) and no larger. Above the OK button is a vertical scrollbar. It extends all the way up to the top. It is as wide as the OK button. The remainder of the container is occupied by a canvas."

FIGURE 4.14:

A simple layout

And here is how a client program would describe the layout to a form layout manager:

- The OK button's right edge is at 1.0 times the container's width. The OK button's width is its preferred width. Its bottom edge is at 1.0 times the container's height. Its height is its preferred height.

- The scrollbar's left edge is the same as the OK button's left edge. Its width is the same as the OK button's width. Its top edge is at the top of the container. Its bottom edge is 5 pixels less than the OK button's top edge.

- The canvas' left edge is at the container's left edge. Its right edge is the same as the scrollbar's left edge. The canvas's top is at the top of the container. Its bottom is at the bottom of the container.

In comparing these two verbal descriptions of the layout, it is clear that the first version (the informal description) is not very different from the second version (the formal description). This suggests that the layout policy will be useful because it supports the way people naturally think and talk about layouts.

Note that even this simple layout description requires 12 sentences, because for each of three components, two horizontal attributes and two vertical attributes must be specified. In practice, only 10 specifications are required for this example, because the OK button's width and height are to be its preferred width and height, and these are the assumed defaults if no width or height is explicitly requested.

Even so, 10 specifications for only three components are quite a few. This is unavoidable with interdependent layouts; keeping track of all these specifications will be a major portion of the development task.

Our next step will be to formalize the way client programs will describe layout attributes to the form layout manager.

Position and Size Specification

We need a way for computers to make statements to describe the layout, similar to those in the previous section. Client programs will pass the string into a container's add(Component, String) method; the container will pass the string along into the form layout manager's addLayoutComponent(String, Component) method.

Next, observe that many attributes will be specified in terms of attributes of other components. The required specification format will need to refer to other components. We will require that every component be given a unique name.

At this point, at the top level, specifying a component's layout requires three pieces of information: the component's name, its horizontal information, and its vertical information. The general form of a specification string will therefore be:

```
"component_name/horizontal_information/vertical_information"
```

Now we need to decide what goes between the slashes.

Horizontal specification involves specifying one or two of a component's horizontal attributes (left edge, center, right edge, or width) in one of the three supported formats (absolute pixels, decimal fraction, or relative to another component). The `horizontal_information` part of the formula will be expressed in one of the following formats:

X=*value*   The left edge

C=*value*   The horizontal center

R=*value*   The right edge

X=*value*;C=*value*   The left edge and the horizontal center

X=*value*;R=*value*   The left edge and the right edge

X=*value*;W=*value*   The left edge and the width

C=*value*;R=*value*   The horizontal center and the right edge

C=*value*;W=*value*   The horizontal center and the width

R=*value*;W=*value*   The right edge and the width

These are all the possible combinations (recall that we do not support specifying width only, because this does not provide enough information).

The *value* portion of the formula must support absolute pixel, decimal fraction, and component-relative formats. The supported formats are:

A*int*   The value is an absolute pixel position or size given by *int*.

F*fraction*   The value is a fraction of the container's width. The value of *fraction* is 0, 1, or any fractional number between 0 and 1.

X*other_component*   The value is the X (left edge) of *other_component*.

R*other_component*   The value is the R (right edge) of *other_component*.

C*other_component*   The value is the C (horizontal center) of *other_component*.

W*other_component*   The value is the W (width) of *other_component*.

Because the *Xs*, *Rs*, and so on are capitalized, this format encourages, but does not require, programmers to use lowercase for component names. The result is a quite readable formula.

Any attribute specification may optionally be followed by *+delta* or *–delta*. The following are examples of valid horizontal specifications:

X=A50   The left edge of this component is at 50. The width will be the component's preferred width.

X=Rokbtn+10;R=F1   The left edge of this component is 10 pixels to the right of *okbtn*'s right edge. The right edge of this component is the right edge of the container.

C=A.5   The horizontal center of this component is at half the container's width (thus the component is horizontally centered within its container). Width is the preferred width.

Vertical attributes are specified in a similar manner. The *vertical_information* portion of the overall formula must be in one of the following formats:

Y=*value*   The top edge

C=*value*   The vertical center

B=*value*   The bottom edge

Y=*value*;C=*value*   The top edge and the vertical center

Y=*value*;H=*value*   The top edge and the height

C=*value*;B=*value*   The vertical center and the bottom edge

C=*value*;H=*value*   The vertical center and the height

B=*value*;H=*value*   The bottom edge and the height

This completes the formula specification. As an example of the use of the formula, consider the layout pictured in Figure 4.14 (shown earlier, with the button, the vertical scrollbar, and the canvas). First, the formal verbal description of the layout stated that:

- The OK button's right edge is at 1.0 times the container's width. The OK button's width is its preferred width. Its bottom edge is at 1.0 times the container's height. Its height is its preferred height.

Assuming that the components are given the names okbtn, sbar, and can this specification becomes:

```
"okbtn/R=F1/B=F1"
```

The scrollbar was described as:

- The scrollbar's left edge is the same as the OK button's left edge. Its width is the same as the OK button's width. Its top edge is at the top of the container. Its bottom edge is 5 pixels less than the OK button's top edge.

This specification becomes:

```
"sbar/X=Xokbtn;W=Wokbtn/Y=A0;B=Yokbtn-5"
```

The canvas was described as:

- The canvas' left edge is at the container's left edge. Its right edge is the same as the scrollbar's left edge. The canvas's top is at the top of the container. Its bottom is at the bottom of the container.

This is specified as follows:

```
"can/X=A0;R=Xsbar/Y=A0;B=F1"
```

The following code fragment shows how these strings might be used to lay out the components (assuming successful development of the rest of the layout manager code!).

```
public class Snippet extends Applet
{
    Button          okButton;
    Scrollbar       sbar;
    Canvas          canvas;


    public void init()
    {
        okButton = new Button("OK");
        scrollbar = new Scrollbar(Scrollbar.VERTICAL);
        canvas = new Canvas();

        setLayout(new FormLayout());
        add(okButton, "okbtn/R=F1/B=F1");
```

```
        add(scrollbar, "sbar/X=Xokbtn;W=Wokbtn/Y=A0;B=Yokbtn-5");
        add(canvas, "can/X=A0;R=Xsbar/Y=A0;B=F1");
    }

                . . .

}
```

Now that we have defined a formula for specifying layout information, we need a way to keep track of all that information.

The Dependency Checker

The dependency checker makes sense out of a hodgepodge of interdependent layout information. Suppose a client program has specified that A goes to the right of B, and B goes to the right of C, and C is attached to the left-hand wall of the container. Now something has to figure out that C's layout must be computed first. Only then can B's position be computed, and only after that can A's position be computed.

For example, the layout described in the previous section specified that the bottom of the scrollbar should be 5 pixels above the top of the button. Therefore, the button's size and position must be known (at least, its *vertical* size and position must be known) before the layout manager can attempt to lay out the scrollbar.

There are two separate tasks. Clearly, the layout manager must compute layout attributes whose values depend on other attributes. In our example, the layout manager knows that the height of the scrollbar depends on the position of the button according to some mathematical formula. The layout manager must be able to apply the formula and derive the height of the scrollbar. Given any dependent attribute and the values on which that attribute depends, the layout manager must be able to compute the attribute's value.

The second task is to figure out which attributes depend on which other attributes. This information must be converted into an ordering of attributes, so that by the time the layout manager attempts to compute an attribute's value, all inputs to the appropriate formula have already been computed.

Another task related to dependencies is *validity checking*. If a Cancel button says that it goes to the right of an OK button, while the OK button goes to the left of the Cancel button, something had better notice and reject this circular dependency or the code will end up in an infinite loop. After all components have been added, something must determine whether or not there is enough information to resolve all dependencies.

At this point it becomes clear that dependency management is a separate task from component layout; it is a task that merits its own class. The class is called DependencyChecker.

The DependencyChecker class knows nothing about layout geometry. It only knows how to maintain a set of dependencies of things on other things. Within the dependency checker, the things being tracked are represented as strings.

In the course of building up the dependency structure, the programmer can tell the dependency checker two kinds of information:

- A depends on B (B must be known before A can be computed).

- Z is known at the outset (there is nothing that Z depends on).

Given two attributes A and B, with A depending on B, A is the *master* and B is the *puppet*. With this terminology, the four methods of the DependencyChecker class can be defined as follows:

void add(String puppet, String master) throws InvalidDependency-
Exception   Adds a single dependency relationship. Informs the dependency checker that attribute puppet depends on attribute master. Throws an exception if adding this dependency results in a self-contradictory dependency hierarchy.

void addKnown(String attribute) throws InvalidDependencyException
Informs the dependency checker that attribute is known; that is, it does not depend on anything. Throws an exception if adding this dependency results in a self-contradictory dependency hierarchy.

void validate() throws InvalidDependencyException   Instructs the dependency checker to check whether its set of dependencies can be completely resolved. Throws an exception if invalid; successful return without an exception indicates validity.

Vector sort() throws InvalidDependencyException   Instructs the dependency checker to determine an order for evaluating its attributes. Returns a vector of strings, which are the attribute names that were passed in via the add() and addKnown() calls. The order of appearance in the vector is such that if an attribute depends on other attributes (that is, if the attribute is puppet to one or more masters), then all the master attributes (and by recursion *their* masters, and so on) appear in the vector before their puppet appears. Thus attributes may be evaluated in their order of appearance in the vector.

When the dependency checker is used to support the form layout manager, the entities whose dependencies are managed are not components, but rather the layout attributes of components. For example, recall that the following code was used to add a canvas:

```
add("can/X=A0;R=Xsbar/Y=A0;B=F1", canvas);
```

The layout manager will need to parse the string. In the course of doing so, it will conclude that the R of can depends on the X of sbar. The form layout manager represents an attribute of a component by concatenating the attribute with the component's name, using a colon as a delimiter. The R of can would be represented as "R:can" and the X of sbar would be represented as "X:sbar". The layout manager will eventually make the following call to the dependency checker:

```
theDependencyChecker.add("R:can", "X:sbar");
```

The canvas's X value is specified as an absolute pixel location. It has no dependencies; it is known *a priori*. The layout manager will represent this to the dependency checker by calling:

```
theDependencyChecker.addKnown("X:can");
```

NOTE　The DependencyChecker class manages dependency relationships among strings. It has no knowledge of the meaning of those strings. The dependency checker's client is responsible for calling **sort()** and evaluating the sorted list as it sees fit. In our example, the client is the dependency checker, and its job is to compute layout values. However, the DependencyChecker class can be used to manage *any* set of dependency relationships. For example, you could use it to create a make facility for C or C++, where the client specifies which source modules depend on which other source modules. The client would call **sort()** and use the resulting list to dictate order of compilation.

The job of the dependency checker is to represent and analyze relationships among attributes of objects. Implementation is straightforward once it is understood that the way relationships should be represented is backwards from the way client programs wish to specify them. For example, a client would like to say, "His X depends on her Y," while the dependency checker would represent this as "Her Y controls his X." The dependency checker is not concerned with the actual value or meaning of either of these attributes, but only with the dependency relationships between them.

The DepNode Class   The DependencyChecker class is built around a set of *depnodes*. DepNode is a class that has a vector of strings. Each depnode instance represents a single attribute, and each string in that depnode's vector represents some other attribute that depends on the depnode. Thus, the fact that "A controls B" (in other words, "B depends on A") is represented by an entry in the vector of the depnode for "A"; this entry is the string "B."

NOTE

It is tempting to implement the **DepNode** class as a subclass of **Vector**. This would let us add or retrieve dependencies by calling the inherited **addElement()** and **elementAt() methods**. This would be poor object-oriented design, however. A depnode is not a kind of vector; it is a class that has a vector, and, indeed, that vector comprises most of DepNode's data, but there is no escaping the fact that a depnode is not a vector. The proper relationship is "has a," and not "is a." The **DepNode** class should aggregate **Vector**, not extend it.

The DepNode class listing is shown below (and is also included on the CD-ROM in javadevhdbk\ch04\DepNode.java). In addition to the vector (called puppets), there is an instance variable called name, which is the name that was passed into the dependency checker via the add() or addKnown() methods. The boolean instance variable marked is used for validity checking. The int instance variable refCount is used for validity checking and sorting.

LIST 4.3   *DepNode.java*

```
import     java.util.Hashtable;
import     java.util.Vector;
import     java.util.Enumeration;


/*
 *   A class containing a vector of strings, one for every node that
 *   depends on this node.
 */

class DepNode
{
    String       name;
    Vector       puppets;
```

```java
    boolean     marked;
    int         refCount;

DepNode(String name)
{
    this.name = name;
    puppets = new Vector(1, 1);
}


// Returns true if this depnode controls the specified puppet.
boolean controlsPuppet(String puppet)
{
    for (int i=0; i<puppets.size(); i++)
    {
        if (puppet.equals(puppets.elementAt(i)))
        {
            return true;
        }
    }

    return false;
}


int size()
{
    return puppets.size();
}


String puppetAt(int i)
{
    return (String)(puppets.elementAt(i));
}


void addPuppet(String s)
{
    puppets.addElement(s);
}
}
```

The Hashtable of Depnodes   The DependencyChecker class is built around a hashtable of depnodes. The keys are strings that represent attributes; the elements themselves are the depnodes that describe the puppets of those attributes. When a client calls add(String puppet, String master), the dependency checker will check the hashtable to see if there is a depnode representing puppet and a depnode representing master. If one or both of these depnodes do not already exist, they will be created and added to the hashtable.

After ensuring that both the puppet and the master are represented, the dependency checker adds an entry for the puppet in the master's depnode. The result is that client programs tell the dependency checker that "this thing depends on that thing"; the dependency checker stores the fact that "that thing controls this thing."

The dependency checker must also represent known attributes. This is done by creating a depnode at construction time, which is called *the known node* (in the source, its handle is theKnownNode). Every string that is added via the addKnown() call is registered as a puppet of this node.

Dependency Validation and Sorting   The three major tasks of the Dependency-Checker class are maintaining the dependency list, determining whether or not the dependencies are valid, and creating a sorted list of dependencies. Representation of dependencies has already been examined; the following discussion shows how the dependencies are validated and sorted.

In order for a set of dependencies to be valid, two conditions must hold: It must be possible to derive every attribute's value, and the web of masters and puppets must not contain any loops.

To determine whether every value can be computed, the dependency checker counts root depnodes. These are depnodes that are not puppets of any other depnodes. There should be only a single root depnode: the known node. Any other structure is invalid. Finding root depnodes is easy: The dependency checker traverses the depnodes, incrementing a puppet's reference count once for every master that controls it. (This reference count will be useful later when it comes time to sort.) A root depnode is one whose reference count is zero—that is, a depnode not controlled by any other depnode.

If there is only one root depnode, and that one is the known node, then it is time to check for loops. The algorithm starts at the known node and recursively traces every possible downward path, keeping track of path length. Any path longer than the total number of nodes must designate a loop.

The DependencyChecker class uses exceptions in the validation process. If an invalid configuration is detected, an InvalidDependencyException is thrown. Several layers of methods declare that they throw InvalidDependencyException. This makes the code much more readable, hence maintainable, than if its "train of thought" had to be constantly sidetracked in order to account for possible errors.

In order to sort its depnodes, the dependency checker once again recurses from the known node. The algorithm relies on the reference count in each depnode; this count is now valid, having been set in the validation process described above. A depnode's reference count is the number of masters on which it has a dependency. The sorting algorithm construes a slightly different meaning for the reference count. From now on, the reference count will represent the number of masters that have not yet been added to the sorted list.

The sorted list is implemented as a vector. A depnode is added to the list when the algorithm has determined that its dependencies have been resolved. When a depnode is added, all of its puppets get their reference counts decremented, meaning that each puppet has one fewer unresolved dependency. If a puppet's reference count reaches zero, all its dependencies have been resolved and it too can be added to the sorted list.

Clearly this is a recursive process. The algorithm starts at the known node. Because all puppets of the known node have zero dependencies, they can immediately be added to the sorted list, their reference counts can be zeroed, and their puppets can be recursively visited.

This recursive procedure continues until there are no more puppets (of puppets of puppets, and so on) to check. The validation requirement that there must not be any loops ensures that the procedure will terminate. And the validation requirement that every depnode should ultimately descend from the known node, which is where the recursion began, ensures that the procedure will visit every depnode.

At this point, you may be thinking that this discussion has little to do with layout management. It only seems so. Any layout manager that supports positioning components relative to other components cannot escape dependency management. The DependencyChecker and DepNode classes encapsulate efficient, minimal, maintainable algorithms.

The source code for DependencyChecker appears below. It is found on the CD-ROM in javadevhdbk\ch04\DependencyChecker.java.

TIP

The dependency checker presented here can be reused for any dependent layout manager. You are welcome to use and modify it for your own application development.

LIST 4.4   **_DependencyChecker.java_**

```
import      java.util.Hashtable;
import      java.util.Vector;
import      java.util.Enumeration;


public class DependencyChecker
{
      private Hashtable              nodes;
      private DepNode                theKnownNode;
      private int                    maxPathLength;
      private boolean                valid = false;
      private boolean                sorted = false;
      private Vector                 sortedNodes;

      private static final String    KNOWN      = "9";


      /*
       *      Constructs a hashtable with a single node for
       *      representing known values.
       */

      public DependencyChecker()
      {
          nodes = new Hashtable();
          theKnownNode = getNode("9");
      }


      /*
       *      If a node with the specified key exists in the
       *      hashtable, return it.  Otherwise construct one, put
       *      it in the hashtable, and return it.
       */

      private DepNode getNode(String key)
```

```
{
      DepNode n = (DepNode)(nodes.get(key));
      if (n == null)
      {
            n = new DepNode(key);
            nodes.put(key, n);
      }
      return n;
}


/*
 *      Adds an attribute whose value is known.  This is
 *      represented by a dependency for that attribute on the
 *      "KNOWN" node.
 */

public void addKnown(String puppetName)
      throws InvalidDependencyException
{
  add(puppetName, KNOWN);
}


/*
 *      Adds a dependency for a named component.  Throws if the
 *      dependency already exists.  This involves adding a
 *      String element to the master node's.  This String is the
 *      key in the hashtable of the puppet node.
 */

public void add(String puppetName, String masterName)
          throws InvalidDependencyException
{
      DepNode            masterNode;

      valid = false;
      sorted = false;

      getNode(puppetName);                  // Ensure an entry
      if (masterName.equals(KNOWN))
      {
            masterNode = theKnownNode;
```

```
        }
        else
        {
            masterNode = getNode(masterName);
        }
        if (masterNode.controlsPuppet(puppetName))
        {
            // Duplicate dependency.
            throw new InvalidDependencyException(puppetName,
                                    "Duplicate dependency");
        }
        else
        {
            masterNode.addAttribute(puppetName);
        }
    }


    /*
     *      Resets the "marked" flag and the reference count for
     *      each node, prior to validation and sorting.
     */

    private void clearAll()
    {
        DepNode             node;
        Enumeration             enum;

        enum = nodes.elements();
        while (enum.hasMoreElements())
        {
            node = (DepNode)(enum.nextElement());
            node.marked = false;
            node.refCount = 0;
        }
    }


    /*
     * Returns a vector containing all the root nodes, i.e., those
     * on which no other node depends.  Caller should make sure
     * all reference counts are zero before calling.
     */
```

```java
private Vector getRootNodes() throws InvalidDependencyException
{
        String          masterName;
        String          puppetName;
        DepNode         masterNode;
        DepNode         puppetNode;
        DepNode         rootNode;
        Enumeration     enum;
        int             i;

        // Count references to each node.
        enum = nodes.elements();
        while (enum.hasMoreElements())
        {
                masterNode = (DepNode)(enum.nextElement());
                masterName = masterNode.name;
                for (i=0; i<masterNode.size(); i++)
                {
                        puppetName = masterNode.attributeAt(i);
                        if (puppetName.equals(masterName))
                        {
                                // A loop!
                                throw new
                                    InvalidDependencyException(masterName,
                                                        "Self dependency");
                        }
                        puppetNode = (DepNode)(nodes.get(puppetName));
                        puppetNode.refCount++;
                }
        }

        // Return array of nodes with zero reference count.
        Vector vec = new Vector();
        enum = nodes.elements();
        while (enum.hasMoreElements())
        {
            rootNode = (DepNode)(enum.nextElement());
            if (rootNode.refCount == 0)
            {
                vec.addElement(rootNode);
            }
        }
```

```
        return vec;
    }



    /*
     * Recursively follows all paths from node, checking for length
     * violation.  The longest legal path is maxPathLength, which
     * is the total number of nodes.  If a path is longer than
     * that, at least one node must have been visited at least
     * twice, indicating a loop.
     */

    private void checkNodeForLoops(DepNode node, int depth)
        throws InvalidDependencyException
    {
        String              puppetString = null;
        DepNode             puppetNode = null;

        if (++depth > maxPathLength)
        {
            throw new InvalidDependencyException(node.name,
                                                "Loop");
        }

        for (int i=0; i<node.size(); i++)
        {
            puppetString = node.attributeAt(i);
            puppetNode = (DepNode)(nodes.get(puppetString));
            checkNodeForLoops(puppetNode, depth);
        }
    }


    /*
     *      Validates the set of dependencies by verifying that
     *      there are no loops and every dependent node can be
     *      resolved.  Return without an exception means the
     *      structure is valid.
     */

    public void validate() throws InvalidDependencyException
    {
        Vector          roots;
```

```
        valid = false;

        //
        //      Identify root nodes.  For every node to be
        //      resolvable, there must be exactly one root,
        //      namely, the "known" node.
        //
        clearAll();
        roots = getRootNodes();
        if (roots.size() != 1 || roots.elementAt(0) !=
                                    theKnownNode)
        {
                throw new InvalidDependencyException("???",
                                "Unresolved dependencies");
        }

        //
        //      Everything descends from the known.  Make sure
        //      there are no loops.
        //
        maxPathLength = nodes.size();
        checkNodeForLoops(theKnownNode, 0);
        valid = true;
    }


/*
 * Returns a vector of names, in dependency order.
 * Dependencies may be resolved in order of appearance in the
 * vector.
 *
 * Assumes reference counts are valid.  Recurses through
 * resolved nodes, decrementing child reference counts.  When a
 * child's reference count reaches zero, that child is
 * resolved; it is put in the vector and recursed upon.
 *
 * Throws InvalidDependencyException if structure was not
 * valid.
 */

public Vector sort() throws InvalidDependencyException
{
     if (sorted)
          return sortedNodes;
```

```
        if (!valid)
            validate();

        sortedNodes = new Vector();
        sortRecurse(sortedNodes, theKnownNode);
        sorted = true;
        return sortedNodes;
    }


/*
 *  Recursively sorts dependencies on a given node, adding
 *  resolved attributes to a vector.  Assumes the given node
 *  has been resolved.
 */

private void sortRecurse(Vector vec, DepNode masterNode)
{
    String          puppetName;
    DepNode         puppetNode;
    int             nNodes;

    nNodes = masterNode.size();
    for (int i=0; i<nNodes; i++)
    {
        puppetName = masterNode.attributeAt(i);
        puppetNode = (DepNode)(nodes.get(puppetName));
        if (-puppetNode.refCount == 0)
        {
            vec.addElement(puppetNode.name);
            sortRecurse(vec, puppetNode);
        }
    }
}
}
```

Inside FormLayout

With dependency management encapsulated in its own class, it is now time to look at the implementation of the FormLayout class.

The first thing to realize is that it takes a lot of information to represent a component. Information must be stored for each of the eight attributes of every component (horizontal attributes X, R, W, and C; vertical attributes Y, B, H, and C). For each attribute, it will be necessary to represent the corresponding substring of the descriptor string, the attribute's dependencies, the formula for deriving the attribute's value, and eventually, the value itself.

Consider the ongoing example of a scrollbar whose descriptor string (as passed into `Container.add()`) is:

```
"sbar/X=Xokbtn;W=Wokbtn/Y=A0;B=Yokbtn-5"
```

Consider what is required just to represent the coordinate of this scrollbar's bottom edge. The substring of the descriptor is `"Yokbtn-5."` There is a dependency on the Y value of okbtn. The formula is the Y value of okbtn minus five. The value must be stored in an int somewhere.

There is enough going on here that there should be a helper class. It is called `ComponentSpec`, and it encapsulates whatever information and behavior are required to represent a single component. The best way to design this class is to determine what `FormLayout` requires of it, so we begin by considering `FormLayout`.

The addLayoutComponent() Method   `FormLayout` has an instance of `DependencyChecker` and maintains a hashtable of its component specifications, keyed by descriptor string. The `addLayoutComponent()` method adds the new entry. At some point, every descriptor string will need to be parsed, and dependencies must be deduced from the string and reported to the dependency checker. `addLayoutComponent()` is an appropriate place to do this.

Because a descriptor refers to a single component, it is reasonable to construct a `ComponentSpec` for the component at this time and defer to that class the parsing of the descriptor and the management of dependencies. The layout manager just divides the descriptor string into the name portion (before the first slash) and the remainder, and constructs a component specification. The constructor for the component specification is passed the two pieces of the descriptor string, as well as references to the component, the dependency checker, and the layout manager itself. In the code fragment below, specs is the hashtable of component specifications.

```
/*
 *     The descriptor provides 3 fields, separated by slashes.   The
 *     1st field is a name for the component.  The other fields are
 *     descriptors for horizontal and vertical attributes of the
 *     component.
```

```
*/

public void addLayoutComponent(String descriptor,
                               Component component)
{
    ComponentSpec      cspec;
    StringTokenizer    st;
    String             name;
    String             subdesc;

    int slashIndex = descriptor.indexOf("/");
    name = descriptor.substring(0, slashIndex).trim();
    subdesc = descriptor.substring(slashIndex+1).trim();
    cspec = new ComponentSpec(name, component,
                                 subdesc, checker, this);
    specs.put(name, cspec);
}
```

The layoutContainer() Method   At layout time, the layout manager must determine the values of each component's attributes in the proper order. There is no sense trying to compute the *y* coordinate of a button if that value depends on the height of some scrollbar whose height is not yet known. The dependency checker's job is to tell the layout manager in what order to compute values.

Recall that the strings in the vector returned by the dependency checker's sort() method are in the format *attribute:componentname*. For example, the X coordinate of a component called zipcodetextfield would be represented by the string X:zipcodetextfield. The code below, which is form layout's layoutContainer() method, traverses the vector of sorted attributes. It splits each attribute into a parameter name (the part before the colon, called paramName), and a component name (the part after the colon, called componentName).

At this point, componentName can be used as an index into the form layout manager's hashtable. The hashtable contains specifications for the components. Recall that the functionality of the ComponentSpec class has not yet been defined; we are still in the process of figuring out what it needs to do. We now realize that we would like a component specification to be able to compute the value of an attribute; the layout manager will only require a component specification to do so once all the attribute's dependencies have been resolved.

So the first loop in layoutContainer() traverses the sorted list of attributes, telling the component that owns the attribute to compute the attribute's value. Once this is done, every component spec will know the x, y, width, and height (as well as the r, b, horizontal center, and vertical center) of every component. The second loop in layoutContainer() traverses the component specifications in the hashtable, instructing each component specification to reshape its corresponding component.

The code for the layoutContainer() method is shown below.

```java
public void layoutContainer(Container parent)
{
    Vector              sorted = null;
    String              nextAttrib;
    String              componentName;
    String              paramName;
    ComponentSpec       cspec;

    this.parent = parent;

    //
    //  Have the dependency checker provide a Vector of sorted
    //  attributes.  All value may safely be computed in the
    //  provided order.
    //
    try
    {
        sorted = checker.sort();
    }
    catch (InvalidDependencyException ex)
    {
        return;
    }

    //
    //      Compute all values.  The elements of sorted are
    //      strings which specify component attributes.
    //
    for (int i=0; i<sorted.size(); i++)
    {
        nextAttrib = (String)(sorted.elementAt(i));
        StringTokenizer st = new StringTokenizer(nextAttrib, ":");
        paramName = st.nextToken();
        componentName = st.nextToken();
        cspec = (ComponentSpec)(specs.get(componentName));
        cspec.computeAttributeValue(paramName);
    }
```

```
//
//        Reshape all components.
//
Enumeration enum = specs.elements();
while (enum.hasMoreElements())
{
    cspec = (ComponentSpec)(enum.nextElement());
    cspec.reshape();
}
}
```

Other Required Methods   The addLayoutComponent() and layoutContainer() methods are the important ones. The other three methods required by the Layout-Manager interface are trivial. removeLayoutComponent() does nothing; component removal is not supported, as it is likely to result in an incomplete set of dependencies. minimumLayoutSize() method and preferredLayoutSize() return hardcoded values. This suggests that a panel that uses this layout manager should not be added to a container whose own layout manager will query the panel's preferred size. This restriction is mild. A panel that uses form layout is unlikely to appear in a flow layout, for example, or anywhere except Center of a border layout.

The FormLayout Class   The complete code for FormLayout is listed below, and appears on the CD-ROM in javadevhdbk\ch04\FormLayout.java.

LIST 4.5	*FormLayout.java*

```
import     java.awt.*;
import     java.util.*;


public class FormLayout implements LayoutManager
{
    private Hashtable              specs;
    private DependencyChecker      checker;
    private Container              parent;


    public FormLayout()
    {
        specs = new Hashtable();
        checker = new DependencyChecker();
    }
```

```
ComponentSpec getComponentSpec(String name)
{
    return (ComponentSpec)(specs.get(name));
}


int parentWidth()
{
    return parent.getSize().width;
}


int parentHeight()
{
    return parent.getSize().width;
}


/*
 *    The descriptor provides 3 fields, separated by slashes.  The
 *    1st field is a name for the component.  The other fields are
 *    descriptors for horizontal and vertical attributes of the
 *    component.
 */

public void addLayoutComponent(String descriptor,
                               Component component)
{
    ComponentSpec     cspec;
    StringTokenizer   st;
    String            name;
    String            subdesc;

    int slashIndex = descriptor.indexOf("/");
    name = descriptor.substring(0, slashIndex).trim();
    subdesc = descriptor.substring(slashIndex+1).trim();
    cspec = new ComponentSpec(name, component,
                              subdesc, checker, this);
    specs.put(name, cspec);
}


public void layoutContainer(Container parent)
```

```
{
    Vector              sorted = null;
    String              nextAttrib;
    String              componentName;
    String              paramName;
    ComponentSpec       cspec;

    this.parent = parent;

    //
    //  Have the dependency checker provide a vector of sorted
    //  attributes.  All values may safely be computed in the
    //  provided order.
    //
    try
    {
        sorted = checker.sort();
    }
    catch (InvalidDependencyException ex)
    {
        return;
    }

    //
    //    Compute all values.  The elements of sorted are strings
    //    which specify component attributes.
    //
    for (int i=0; i<sorted.size(); i++)
    {
        nextAttrib = (String)(sorted.elementAt(i));
        StringTokenizer st = new StringTokenizer(nextAttrib, ":");
        paramName = st.nextToken();
        componentName = st.nextToken();
        cspec = (ComponentSpec)(specs.get(componentName));
        cspec.computeAttributeValue(paramName);
    }

    //
    //    Reshape all components.
    //
    Enumeration enum = specs.elements();
    while (enum.hasMoreElements())
```

```
          {
              cspec = (ComponentSpec)(enum.nextElement());
              cspec.setBounds();
          }
      }


  public void removeLayoutComponent(Component c)       { }


  public Dimension preferredLayoutSize(Container parent)
  {
      return parent.getSize();
  }


  public Dimension minimumLayoutSize(Container parent)
  {
      return(new Dimension(100, 100));
  }
}
```

The ComponentSpec Class

The FormLayout class constructs an instance of ComponentSpec for each component. The instances are stored in a hashtable and keyed by name. The class must be able to parse a descriptor string, report its dependencies to the dependency checker, and eventually compute the values of its attributes.

NOTE   The source for ComponentSpec is on the CD-ROM in javadevhdbk\ch04\ ComponentSpec.java. Because it is nearly 600 lines long, we will not present the entire listing here. This section shows just the top-level design of the class and explains how the ComponentSpec class works.

Every component has eight attributes: four for horizontal information and four for vertical. FormLayout has three eight-element arrays—called descriptors[], deltas[], and values[]—for storing attribute descriptors (substrings of the original descriptor string), deltas (the optional plus-or-minus value), and eventual values. At construction time, the descriptors and deltas are parsed out of the full descriptor string. The values are not computed until the layout manager executes `layoutContainer()`.

For easy array indexing, eight final static ints are defined, with names that correspond to the eight attribute names:

```
private final static int    PARAM_X     = 0;
private final static int    PARAM_HC    = 1;
private final static int    PARAM_R     = 2;
private final static int    PARAM_W     = 3;
private final static int    PARAM_Y     = 4;
private final static int    PARAM_VC    = 5;
private final static int    PARAM_B     = 6;
private final static int    PARAM_H     = 7;
```

Here and elsewhere, horizontal center (HC) begins to be distinguished from vertical center (VC). Until now, we have used C to denote both, as a convenience to programmers, and figured out from context which one was intended. From now on, they must be distinct.

The `ComponentSpec` class also has int instance variables for the horizontal and vertical "formulas." The formula represents which attributes were specified in the descriptor string. The X formula might be x coordinate only, for example, or x and width. Final static ints are also defined for the nine horizontal formulas and the nine vertical ones:

```
// Values for hFormula.
final static int H_FORMULA_X    = 0;  // x is specified
final static int H_FORMULA_C    = 1;  // center
final static int H_FORMULA_R    = 2;  // right
final static int H_FORMULA_XR   = 3;  // x, right
final static int H_FORMULA_XW   = 4;  // x, width
final static int H_FORMULA_RW   = 5;  // right, width
final static int H_FORMULA_CW   = 6;  // center, width
final static int H_FORMULA_XC   = 7;  // x, center
final static int H_FORMULA_RC   = 8;  // right, width

// Values for vFormula.
final static int V_FORMULA_Y    = 0;  // y is specified
final static int V_FORMULA_C    = 1;  // center specified
final static int V_FORMULA_B    = 2;  // bottom specified
final static int V_FORMULA_YB   = 3;  // y, bottom
final static int V_FORMULA_YH   = 4;  // y, height
final static int V_FORMULA_BH   = 5;  // bottom, height
```

```
final static int V_FORMULA_CH   = 6;  // center, height
final static int V_FORMULA_YC   = 7;  // top, center
final static int V_FORMULA_BC   = 8;  // bottom, center
```

The constructor for ComponentSpec is passed the component's descriptor string; it calls a method called parseDescriptor(), which initializes the descriptors[] and deltas[] arrays.

As an example, consider an OK button whose X is 50, whose right edge is 10 pixels in from the container's right edge, whose top is aligned with the top of a Cancel button, and whose height is one-quarter the height of the container. The descriptor for this button would be:

```
okbtn/X=A50;R=F1-10/Y=Ycancelbtn;H=F.25
```

The formulas would then be H_FORMULA_XR and V_FORMULA_YH. After parsing, the descriptors[] and deltas[] arrays contain the attributes shown in Table 4.3.

TABLE 4.3:   Attributes in the descriptors and deltas Arrays after Parsing

Attribute	descriptors[Attribute]	deltas[Attribute]
PARAM_X	A50	0
PARAM_HC		0

Continued on next page

TABLE 4.3 CONTINUED: Attributes in the descriptors and deltas Arrays after Parsing

Attribute	descriptors[Attribute]	deltas[Attribute]
PARAM_R	F1	-10
PARAM_W		0
PARAM_Y	Ycancelbtn	0
PARAM_VC .		0
PARAM_B		0
PARAM_H	F25	0

The constructor next calls the method registerDependencies(), which provides information to the dependency checker. This method and its subordinates must consider every possible formula case-by-case, and this is what makes the class so lengthy. For each formula, those parameters that are not provided must still be derived, because values for other components might depend on them. Given any two horizontal attributes, the other two can always be derived (if you know width and R, you can compute X and center). The same holds true for vertical attributes. The programmer must tell the dependency checker that those attributes that are not supplied by the formula string depend on those that are supplied. In the example, HC and W both have dependencies on X and R, while both VC and B depend on Y and H. The calls to add these attributes to the dependency checker might look like this:

```
checker.add("HC:okbtn", "X:okbtn");
checker.add("W:okbtn", "R:okbtn");
checker.add("HC:okbtn", "X:okbtn");
checker.add("W:okbtn", "R:okbtn");
checker.add("VC:okbtn", "Y:okbtn");
checker.add("B:okbtn", "H:okbtn");
checker.add("VC:okbtn", "Y:okbtn");
checker.add("B:okbtn", "H:okbtn");
```

Three of the attributes (X, R, and H) have their values explicitly stated by the descriptor. These are known values, so they will be passed to the dependency checker using the addKnown() method:

```
checker.addKnown("X:okbtn");
checker.addKnown("R:okbtn");
checker.addKnown("H:okbtn");
```

The last attribute to consider is Y, which depends on the Y of some other component. This relationship is communicated to the dependency checker as follows:

```
checker.add("Y:okbtn", "Y:cancelbtn");
```

Eventually, all dependencies for all components are reported to the dependency checker. Later, when the layout manager executes layoutContainer(), each component specification receives a number of calls to computeAttributeValue(String attributeName). This method inspects the formula for the desired attribute. If the formula begins with "A...", the value can be determined from the rest of the formula. If the formula begins with "F...", the value can be determined from the rest of the formula and the parent container's size. For all other formats, the value is the value of some other attribute of (possibly) some other component. Because the other component's name is known, its own component specification can be retrieved from the hashtable and the value can be looked up in the values[] array. The dependency checker guarantees that what is found in values[] is valid. After the value is computed, the delta is added to it.

Once `computeAttributeValue()` has been called in the proper order for every attribute of every component, all values are known and the components can be reshaped.

Length of the Layout Manager Design

This example should give you a clear idea of the effort involved in creating an interdependent layout manager. Any interdependent layout manager will require a dependency checker. The one developed here (`DependencyChecker.java`) is approximately 350 lines long.

An interdependent layout manager will also need a helper class to encapsulate a component's positional information as well as any parsing that may be required. The helper class should be responsible for registering dependencies with the dependency checker. In this example, the `ComponentSpec` helper class is around 600 lines long. The size comes from the large number of input formats supported by the layout policy, and not from any inherent complexity of interdependent layout managers.

The layout manager is so well supported by the dependency checker and the component specification that the manager is just over 100 lines long.

A Test Applet for FormLayout

With so much effort put into developing the form layout manager, there is every right to expect the client code to be simple. This is, in fact, the case. The code that generates a window with its scrollbars aligned correctly (see Figure 4.13 earlier in this chapter) is shown below, and is also on the CD-ROM in `javadevhdbk\ch04\FormScrollWin.java`.

LIST 4.6   *FormScroll Win.java*

```java
import java.awt.*;
import java.applet.Applet;


public class FormScrollWin extends Applet
{
    public void init()
    {
        Scrollbar       hbar, vbar;
        StripeCanvas    canvas;
```

```
        setLayout(new FormLayout());
        hbar = new Scrollbar(Scrollbar.HORIZONTAL);
        vbar = new Scrollbar(Scrollbar.VERTICAL);
        canvas = new StripeCanvas();
        add(canvas, "view/X=A0;R=Xvert/Y=A0;B=Yhoriz");
        add(hbar, "horiz/X=A0;R=Rview/B=F1");
        add(vbar, "vert/R=F1/Y=A0;B=Bview");      }
}


class StripeCanvas extends Canvas
{
    public void paint(Graphics g)
    {
        for (int i=0; i<size().width+size().height; i++)
            if ((i/15) % 2 == 0)
                g.drawLine(i, 0, 0, i);
    }
}
```

An Applet for Adding Descriptor Strings

The only difficult thing about using the form layout manager is entering the correct descriptor string for each component. One way to get it right is trial-and-error recompilation.

An easier way is to use the FormLab applet on the CD-ROM. This applet presents four color-coded panels in which to type descriptor strings, as shown in Figure 4.15. Each panel is activated by a checkbox. When you click the Show button, the applet displays a frame laid out using a form layout manager. The frame contains one button for each activated panel. Clicking any of these buttons dismisses the frame.

FormLab has several predefined sets of descriptor strings that can be selected via a choice button at the top of the applet. When you select a set, its descriptor strings are copied into the panels. You can also modify the layouts by editing the strings. Figure 4.16 shows one of the FormLab applet's predefined options, called Tapering in the choice button.

FIGURE 4.15:

The FormLab applet

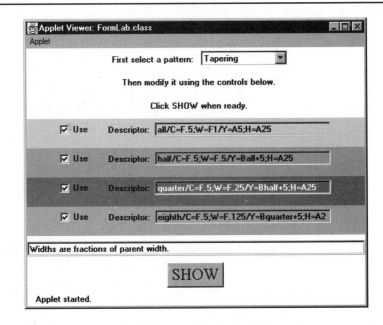

FIGURE 4.16:

The FormLab applet's
Tapering choice

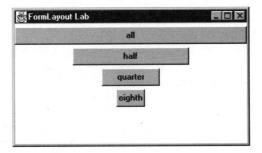

The four buttons in the panel shown in Figure 4.16 were added to their container using the following descriptor strings:

```
all/C=F.5;W=F1/Y=A5;H=A25
half/C=F.5;W=F.5/Y=Ball+5;H=A25
quarter/C=F.5;W=F.25/Y=Bhalf+5;H=A25
eighth/C=F.5;W=F.125/Y=Bquarter+5;H=A25
```

Summary

Java layout managers encapsulate component sizing and positioning. Programmers operate one step removed from precise layout by specifying layout policies rather than widths, heights, and positions. The standard suite of layout managers does a decent job of providing desired functionality. Effective use of the standard layout managers requires an understanding of each manager's algorithm. It is especially important to know when a manager honors a component's preferred size, and when the manager dictates size.

When the standard layout managers are inadequate, it is necessary to create a custom layout manager. This requires implementing the LayoutManager interface, which is not especially difficult. The alternative is to use no layout manager at all. Usually, this is more complicated than it seems, and may be more complicated than creating a custom layout manager class.

Ordinary layout managers may be arbitrarily simple or complicated. Interdependent layout managers, which support positioning components with respect to other components, are moderately complicated. A major portion of the work of developing an interdependent layout manager involves maintaining dependencies. The dependency checker presented here can be reused for any dependent layout manager.

The use of layout managers is one way that Java provides platform independence. The next chapter deals with other portability issues.

CHAPTER

FIVE

5

Portability Issues

- Data and character representation

- Timing of programs

- Availability of Java packages and classes

- File system navigation

- Fonts, colors, and GUI layout

- Property specifications

- Network class loading mechanism

- Security issues

This chapter discusses the design and implementation considerations that relate to writing genuinely platform-independent Java code. Platform independence presents some challenges that cannot be handled by a language and library set alone.

The entire Java system—both the design of the language and the libraries—is intended to provide the greatest possible inherent portability. This requires compilers that demand the exact same language for each platform. The detailed semantics of both the language and the libraries must be the same on all platforms. The compiler's binary code output must be independent of the platform. This demands the use of the runtime interpretation that is provided by the Java Virtual Machine (JVM). Even these rules, which are imposed at the language level, do not solve all portability problems.

Despite Java's design, the programmer must still take some care to avoid writing a program that is not portable. Many problems are easy to avoid, but some of the potential pitfalls when writing a portable program are less obvious. The issues that are discussed in this chapter cover a variety of topics.

The underlying platform can affect the format of data on network connections and in files. Variations in the speed of the CPU and in the thread-scheduling scheme of the host operating system can cause an incorrectly designed program to fail. Required support classes must be available at runtime. Although Java can load classes from either the local file system or the network, these classes must still be accessible. Also, Java has some rules that define the expected directory layout for classes.

The user interface presented by the AWT adopts the look and feel of the host platform and uses the resources of that platform for fonts and colors. This leads to presentation variations between platforms, and optimal behavior might require adjustment or configuration on each platform. This is often best achieved if the program allows the user a means of configuring preferences.

Applets run subordinate to security restrictions imposed by the browser. These restrictions are designed to maintain the security and integrity of the host but vary between browsers.

Data Representation

Java requires that data items always appear to have the same representation regardless of the platform or the compiler. An int, for example, must always behave as if it were a 32-bit 2's complement value. In fact, the specification does not require that this is actually how it is *stored*, but only how it *behaves* and *appears*. These aspects of the language are tightly defined and, in the absence of implementation error, do not cause difficulty when changing platforms.

Character Representation

The representation of characters is defined to appear to be a 16-bit unsigned quantity using the Unicode character set. However, most of the platforms on which Java runs do not support the full Unicode character set. This makes it difficult for the Java runtime system to do so. Because of these difficulties, a quite properly written program might still fail at the I/O level if it uses non-ASCII characters from the Unicode set.

Java supports those characters in the Unicode set that have direct equivalents on the current host system. For example, a machine running with a French Canadian keyboard and screen configuration is able to support accented characters. In Java, those characters will be handled correctly; they will be translated between the local machine representation and Unicode as they pass in and out of the program.

TIP

As additional support, the Java distribution includes the `native2ascii` tool. This command-line tool converts between local character sets and the ASCII-only file format expected by the remainder of the Java tools. The output of this program retains the special characters by translating them into, or from, Unicode escape sequences—the `\uxxxx` literal format. This allows you to edit your Java source programs and support files on a local text editor—using the characters available on your machine—and convert the result to a format suitable for Java. Additionally, `Reader` and `Writer` classes in the `java.io` package perform I/O that includes these conversions in a running program.

Data Outside the Java Program

When data leaves the confines of the Java program—for example, it's saved in a file or sent over a network—more difficulties can arise. Different systems often have their own ways of coding network or disk information, and these methods are often incompatible. Java can handle these problems in two ways:

- Any external data produced or received by Java programs, whether on a network or a disk, will have a format that is independent of the platform.

- Where data is being shared with a non-Java system, such as the conventional platform that is supporting the Java environment, Java allows the necessary control of individual bits and bytes to convert between the formats, provided that the definition is available for that other format.

A common problem that arises when data is shared between platforms is the representation of "end of line." This is done with the line-feed character on Unix, with a line-feed followed by a carriage-return in MS DOS, and with a carriage-return on Macintosh. The Java libraries hide these problems, but can only do so in Java programs. Files written from Java will still require conversion if taken to a non-Java program on another platform.

> **NOTE**   Inside a Java program, the ordering of bytes within longer numeric types is effectively invisible; in the absence of pointer manipulation, you can only break down an int, say, by using the shift operators (>>, >>>, and <<) or the bitwise AND (&) and OR (|) operators. When data is moved out of the Java program, however, it is often important to know that the byte ordering used by Java is high byte first, regardless of the conventions of the host platform.

Program Timing

For many programs, the time taken for execution is a matter of user convenience rather than correctness of operation. If the process takes a long time, the delay might be irritating, but the answer is usually still right, even when it is late.

However, this is not always the case. In the particular category of a program referred to as *real time*, the time taken for execution is as much a part of the correct operation as any other measure. An everyday example may be found in video player software (that is, MPEG or AVI players, not the kind that sit under television sets). In this case, the video player software is operating correctly only if the frames are updated at the proper rate and in proper synchronization with the sound output.

Unfortunately, even perfect software cannot make a CPU work any faster than the hardware dictates, so it is always possible that a program that executes perfectly well on one machine might fail on another machine that is operating at a different speed. There are two modes of failure related to timing.

In the obvious case, the slower processor is unable to complete a calculation in time, and the whole program fails in consequence. This problem can be addressed only in software by improving the algorithm or its implementation. If such improvements are insufficient, then more powerful hardware is required.

The other failure mode relates to the interactions between multiple threads. A loose description of a thread is that it is a mechanism that allows a single program to appear to be doing more than one thing at once. Some machines have multiple CPUs, and these can really do more than one thing at a time. In other systems with only a single CPU, the effect is only an illusion and results are achieved in the same way as by an office worker: by doing a little of one job, then a little of another, and so forth. The term *concurrent* is used to describe multiple threads that are "on the go" simultaneously but are not necessarily actually being worked on by physically separate CPUs. Where different CPUs are actually working on threads at the same time, the threads are said to be running *in parallel*.

In an office, workers who have more than one task in progress might keep working on one job for as long as they can usefully make progress on it, ignoring all other scheduled tasks until something prevents further progress or a higher-priority task requires immediate attention. For example, a worker might need to stop a task to help a colleague or answer the phone. If no more progress can be made on the current task, the workers move on to a different job. This style of working, when applied to threading, approximately describes the idea of a *preemptive* scheduling system. Other workers might take the view that they want to be able to demonstrate steady progress on all tasks. To do so, they might do half an hour on one job, and then move on to another task even if they could continue with the present one. This style of work, applied to a threading system, describes the idea of a *time-sharing* scheduling system. These and other threading concepts are described in detail in Chapter 7.

In a threaded system, a number of programming difficulties can arise specifically from the nature of threads. Suppose that a program has two threads that are operating concurrently. They might or might not be time-sharing—the Java environment does not specify one behavior rather than the other. If the program is written on a computationally slow machine, it could easily be that a thread involving a great deal of computation might take longer than another thread that is waiting for disk I/O. If the program depends for its correctness on the disk having completed its task before the computation completes, this might work correctly on the slow machine. If you run the same code on a machine with a comparable disk system but a faster processor, then the computation thread could complete sooner and thereby cause the whole program to fail.

A timing dependency of this type actually constitutes incorrect design or implementation of the program; however, the example of two uncoordinated threads shows again that a portable language and library set are not enough.

Java leaves one aspect of the threading model undefined. Given two or more threads of the same priority, all with useful work to perform, some systems might time-share the CPU between these threads. Other systems allow the current thread to run continuously for as long as it usefully can, changing to a different thread only if a higher priority one becomes runnable or this one cannot proceed. The time-sharing system is often considered to be easier to understand, but it is usually less efficient than the second approach. Whatever the relative merits of these approaches in any particular program, code must be correctly designed if it is to work properly on all possible systems.

Package and Class Availability

Java comes with a clearly defined set of core packages, offering a wide base of standard support. Any program, whether it is an application or an applet, can generally depend on the availability of the classes in these core packages. Only if a service is inapplicable to a particular platform might such a service be unavailable. For example, it is acceptable for sound support, or even the AWT itself, to be absent from a system that has no supporting hardware. More advanced or unusual programs might require additional support classes, and you must take care to ensure that these are available on the target machine.

It is safe and entirely reasonable to use core classes for general development. If, however, you use third-party classes, you must decide if these classes become required support for this product or if the program can operate in a reduced way without them. If it is possible, practical, and legal, you could supply these support packages with the product. If legal restrictions exist, it might be best to develop alternative classes.

Network speed constraints might make it undesirable to download large volumes of support classes. Furthermore, because of the time taken to set up an individual HTTP connection, transferring large numbers of classes individually will be time-consuming even if the classes are small. For this reason, all related class files should be packaged in an archive so they are transferred over the network in a single connection. The standard archive since JDK release 1.1 is the JAR format. Before release 1.1, there was no standard mechanism, and proprietary extensions were offered by both Netscape and Microsoft.

When a class is part of a developer's local support package—in other words, the class is directly accessible from the file system of the developer's machine but is not part of the JDK distribution itself—that class must be distributed with any program that uses it. It is very easy to fall into the habit of thinking that class loading happens by magic in Java, and that this will be the case over any TCP/IP network, too. Packages, and classes in packages, can be distributed along with an applet over the network. For this to happen, however, the package must be correctly installed on the server. This requires a little more thought than simply copying an applet into the classes directory beneath the invoking HTML page.

Locating Classes and Packages

When a browser loads an applet over the web, that browser has a notion of the codebase from which it was obtained. This is the return value from the applet method getCodeBase(). It is the base URL from which the main Applet class was loaded. If the applet asks for additional classes, the browser should search the local system—that is, the system that is running the browser—for them first using the CLASSPATH or other equivalent mechanism; if this fails, the browser should try to load them from the web server that supplied the applet.

Classes in the unnamed package are taken from the same directory as the codebase. For classes that are members of a package, the codebase is extended by the package name. Hence, the class must be located properly on the server. For example, suppose an applet is called `Complex`. It is loaded from a web page at the URL `http://www.unknown.org/examples/mathematical.html`. If the `<APPLET>` tag that invokes it is `<APPLET CODE=Complex.class WIDTH=100 HEIGHT=100>`, then the codebase value is `http://www.unknown.org/examples/`, and the file `Complex.class` must be placed in the same directory as the file `mathematical.html`. The diagram in Figure 5.1 shows this.

FIGURE 5.1:

Class location for an applet with the default codebase

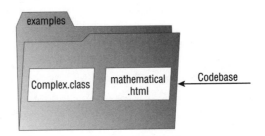

On the other hand, an `<APPLET>` tag `<APPLET CODE=Complex.class CODEBASE=classes WIDTH=100 HEIGHT=100>` would result in a codebase of `http://www.unknown.org/examples/classes/`. The file `Complex.class` should be placed in this subdirectory, beneath the directory containing the HTML file, as shown in Figure 5.2.

NOTE   The Applet Viewer does not reject an `<APPLET>` tag if the `.class` part is missing. Omitting it would make the detail of the `<APPLET>` tag more consistent with the command-line tools, but might result in problems with some other browsers.

If the `Complex` class requires a support class `unknown.utils.fft`—that is, the class is called `fft` and is a member of the package `unknown.utils`—then the class file `fft.class` must be placed in the appropriate directory. In either of these cases, the directory will be called `utils` and must be located in a directory called `unknown`. This in turn must be located in the same directory as the applet. Figures 5.3 and 5.4 show this modification to each of the earlier examples.

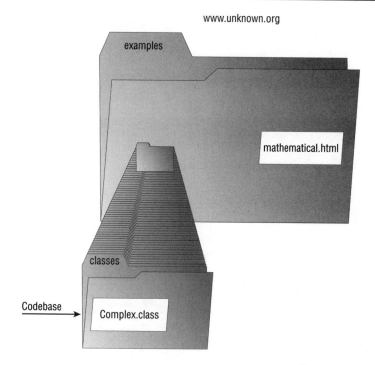

This concept can be extended to applets themselves. Although it is usual for applets to belong to the default or unnamed package, this is not actually required. If an applet is called unknown.math.Bessel, then it can still be loaded from a web server, but a slightly different setup is required. To load this class properly, the <APPLET> tag must reflect the proper codebase. The codebase is the directory for classes that belong to the unnamed package. Therefore, the following HTML is required: <APPLET CODE=unknown.math.Bessel.class WIDTH=100 HEIGHT=100>. In this case, the file Bessel.class must be located in a subdirectory called math, in a subdirectory called unknown, in the directory containing the HTML file. This is shown in Figure 5.5.

NOTE   Notice that the CODE=*xxx* part of the <APPLET> tag should really be considered as a class specification rather than a file specification. It is unfortunate, therefore, that the specification describes this as the filename and requires the .class file extension to be present. It is similarly somewhat misleading that the CODEBASE directive is so named, rather than being CLASSBASE or CLASSPATH, either of which would be more consistent with the operation of the command-line tools.

FIGURE 5.3:

Location of support class that is a package member with the default codebase

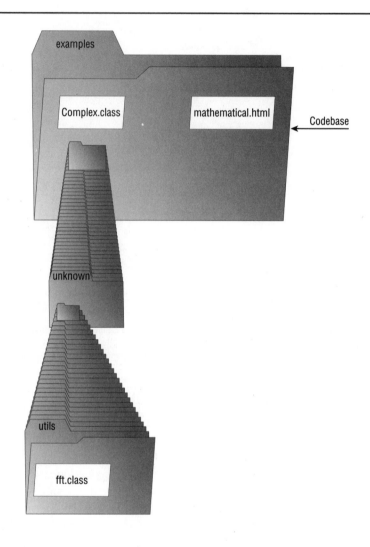

FIGURE 5.4:

Location of support class that is a package member with CODEBASE=classes

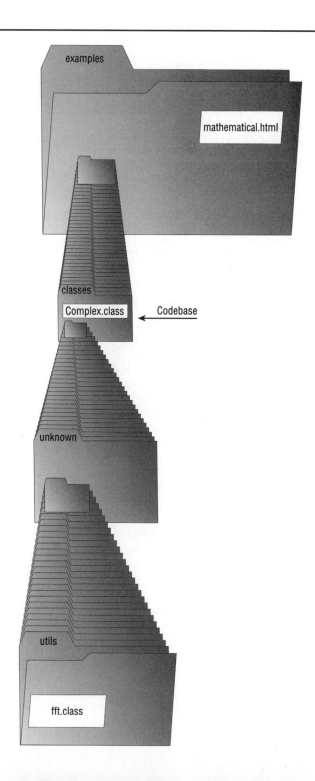

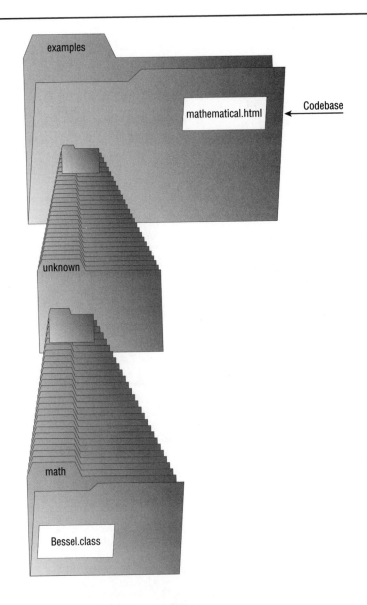

FIGURE 5.5:

Class location for an applet that is a package member with the default codebase

In this last example, it is both correct and workable for the <APPLET> tag to include a CODEBASE=*xxx* specification. In such a case, the directory structure must still reflect the package naming, but the directory containing the directory unknown must be that specified by the codebase directive.

Naming Packages

When classes are to be distributed widely over the Internet, there is great potential for difficulties arising from naming. If an applet tries to load a support class called `MyButton`, the intention of the programmer is probably that a class defining a customized UI component should be loaded from the same site as the applet. If, however, a class with this name exists on the local class path, then security rules demand that the local class should be loaded in preference. Because it is unlikely that the two classes will perform exactly comparable functions, with compatible public APIs, the result will almost certainly be the failure of the applet.

Avoiding this difficulty requires a little organization in the allocation of names. Ideally, all publicly distributed classes should belong to a package that uniquely belongs to the author of that class. For Internet-connected organizations, this need can be addressed by reversing the domain name and using the result as the first part of the package name. Hence, `MyButton` created at `unknown.org` would be `org.unknown.MyButton`. This convention is suggested by the Java documentation.

However, some problems remain with this suggested convention. First, if the unknown organization is large, several programmers might create classes called `MyButton`. Now there is a potential for local conflict and for problems when installing these on their web server. Therefore, in large organizations, the domain-package name should be extended with additional naming levels. Appropriate possibilities include the department name or an employee number. For example, the button might be placed in `org.unknown.research.MyButton` or `org.unknown.1234.MyButton`. (Of course, if two classes are so similarly named, they should be checked for duplication of effort.)

Laying Out Web Server Directories

Web servers that carry many applets requiring support packages might require many directories. For example, if applets are maintained for the support of ten different pages in different directories, and each applet requires three directories in a chain to properly represent package names, this results in a total of thirty specially created directories. The problem is compounded if many supporting classes by different programmers are used. Figure 5.6 illustrates this problem.

FIGURE 5.6:

Cumbersome directory
structure and duplication of
classes resulting from
individual class directories

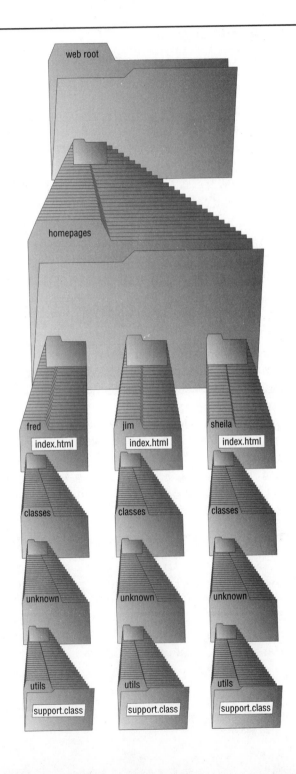

Under these conditions, it might be better to put all Java code in one specific directory tree and use an absolute codebase in the <APPLET> tags in the HTML files, as in this example:

```
<APPLET CODE=org.unknown.research.MyButton.class CODEBASE=/Java
WIDTH=100 HEIGHT=100>
```

Imagine another applet written by someone in the accounts department, called HerButton, shares the use of other supporting classes with MyButton. The second applet could be loaded from the tag:

```
<APPLET CODE=org.unknown.accounts.HerButton CODEBASE=/Java WIDTH=100
HEIGHT=100>
```

Under this layout, far fewer directories are needed, packages are shared, and at most, one copy of each class file is required. Figure 5.7 shows the effect of this modified approach applied to the same example that was used in Figure 5.6. Although this approach has many advantages, there is no clear link between the HTML pages and the applets that they invoke.

NOTE   In JDK 1.0.2, a path to an audio file, in the `getAudioClip()` and related methods, could not have a path that traverses up a directory tree beyond the codebase. There was no good reason for this, and the constraint was removed in JDK 1.1. However, if your applets are reasonably likely to be run in JDK 1.0.2 browsers, you might need to consider this restriction.

Using JAR Files

You can use JAR files to supply classes to browsers if you prefer. This can make the web server directory layouts considerably tidier, which will simplify maintenance and reduce mistakes.

Another potential advantage of using JAR files to deliver applets is the startup time of the applet. It is generally accepted that HTTP transfers are relatively time-consuming to set up. If an applet needs a dozen classes before it can get started and become visible to the user, then 12 separate HTTP transactions must be completed. If you use a JAR file containing those classes instead, then only one transaction is required. Usually, this will complete sooner, resulting in a shorter time to applet display.

FIGURE 5.7:

Simplified directory
structure with shared class
directories

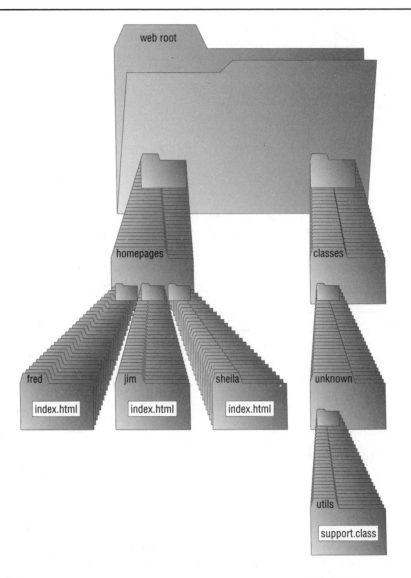

However, keep in mind that if you use a JAR archive, the entire JAR must be transferred to the browser before any class can be instantiated. Using individual classes, only those that are actually required for the applet to run are loaded. This means that the applet may be visible after, say, only three classes have been loaded. Similarly, if you have an applet that has many classes but can run without using all of them (for example, if your applet has a spell checker, the user might never run that facility), then forcing the browser to load the whole JAR could actually slow down the startup time. On the other hand, JARs may be compressed further, reducing the download time.

In general, it is usually a good idea to use JAR files to supply applets and supporting classes, but you should not always use a single JAR to contain the entire package. Instead, you should consider splitting the classes across a number of separate JARs if there are many classes.

NOTE   In JDK 1.1, all JARS listed in an ARCHIVE tag were loaded by the browser before the applet started. In Java 2, you can use the Java Extensions Framework to arrange for some JARs to be loaded only when required. The Java Extensions Framework is discussed shortly.

Storing Classes in JARs

So far, we have discussed storing classes in JAR files, without being specific about how this can be done. Well, it's very simple really. If you take a number of class files that make up one applet and collect them together in a JAR file, then you can modify your HTML page so that it specifies use of this JAR as the source of classes by using the ARCHIVE= modifier in your <APPLET> tag. Suppose your main applet class is called MyApplet and you have placed it and its supporting classes into an archive called MyAppletStuff.jar. You would use an <APPLET> tag like this:

```
<APPLET CODE=MyApplet ARCHIVE=MyAppletStuff.jar WIDTH=100 HEIGHT=100>
```

You can specify multiple archives using a comma-separated list. In this case, each of them will be loaded immediately.

Your applet class does not need to be located inside the JAR file. However, if you specify archives at all, they are preloaded, so there is nothing to be gained by keeping the main applet class out of the JAR.

Using the Java Extensions Framework

Since the release of Java 2, another mechanism for handling multiple JAR archives has been made available. This mechanism, called the Java Extensions Framework, is equally valid for both applets and applications, and admits the possibility of delaying the loading of supporting JAR files.

If you create a JAR archive that contains your applet and the immediate supporting classes, and place other support classes that might not be required at all in another JAR file, then you can refer to the second JAR file from the first by using an entry in the manifest file. For example, to refer to a JAR called `extras.jar` that is stored in the same directory on your web server as the main JAR that supplied the applet, add to the manifest an entry of this form:

```
Class-Path: extras.jar
```

The `Class-Path` manifest entry may list multiple JAR archives, and those archives can be relative to the referring JAR if desired. However, it is not possible to refer to an archive that is not on the same server as the original JAR because absolute URLs are not permitted (this is a current security-based restriction, which might be modified in future releases).

Handling Class Locations and Namespaces

In addition to segmenting and organizing your classes, the package mechanism is intended to provide part of the security mechanism that restricts untrusted code, such as applets. Each downloaded class is placed in a *namespace*, which reflects both the origin of the class file and the fully qualified package to which it belongs.

From the point of view of access control, default access to a class member is usually described as meaning that the member is accessible to other classes in the same package. In fact, this actually means the same namespace—two classes named `my.stuff.ClassA` and `my.stuff.ClassB` would not have access to each other's default access members if they were loaded from different web servers.

In JDK 1.1 and earlier, this mechanism was not clearly defined nor fully implemented, although the consequences of the bug were limited to allowing one applet to interfere with another applet, not with your system. With the release of Java 2, this has been rectified. Now each distinct remote codebase, not just each web server, has its own namespace. You might even find that separate JAR archives are given separate namespaces, depending on the browser's implementation.

WARNING   It is important to keep the namespace mechanism in mind; otherwise, you might find that splitting your applet across different codebases or putting it into multiple JAR files might keep it from running. This would happen only if you make use of default access to members of other classes. If you stick with a more pure object-oriented model, where members are either public (for selected methods) or private (for everything else), then this will not cause problems.

File System Semantics

On the whole, applets are not able to access file systems of the host that runs them. For portable applications, however, the variety of different path name conventions is an issue.

Browsing a Directory System

Many of the problems associated with path names are resolved by the java.io .File class. This class provides mechanisms that, in principle, allow browsing directory hierarchies without any need to know the local conventions. The following example shows how a directory system can be browsed in a largely platform-independent way. The source for this example is located on the CD-ROM in the directory \javadevhdbk\ch05\Directory.java.

LIST 5.1	*Directory.java*

```java
import java.io.*;
import java.util.*;

public class Directory {
  private File currentDir;

  public Directory() {
    // create any file in current directory
    currentDir = new File("x");
    // get the full path
    currentDir = new File(currentDir.getAbsolutePath());
    // and lose the fake filename.
    currentDir = new File(currentDir.getParent());
  }

  public Directory(String start) throws IOException {
    currentDir = new File(start);
    if (!currentDir.isDirectory()) {
      throw new IOException("Not a directory");
    }
    // this might not be absolute, make it so...
    currentDir = new File(currentDir.getAbsolutePath());
  }
```

```java
public File current() {
  return currentDir;
}

public static File at(File start, String move) throws IOException {
  if (File.separator.length() != 1) {
    throw new RuntimeException("Fatal: Unexpected platform." +
      " Multiple character separators not supported");
  }

  StringTokenizer tok = new StringTokenizer(move, File.separator);
  String nextDir = null;

  // absolute path ignores starting point
  if (File.separator.indexOf(move.charAt(0)) != -1) {
    start = new File(move);
  }
  else {
    // otherwise, work down the move string one element at at time
    while (tok.hasMoreTokens()) {
      nextDir = tok.nextToken();
      // dot is current directory, so no change
      if (nextDir.equals(".")) {
        continue;
      }
      // dot dot is parent, so move up
      else if (nextDir.equals("..")) {
        start = parentOf(start);
      }
      // anything else tries to move down
      else {
        start = new File(start, nextDir);
        // but the result must exist...
        if (!start.exists()) {
          throw new IOException("No such file or directory " +
            start);
        }
        // and be a directory
        if (!start.isDirectory()) {
          throw new IOException("Not a directory " + start);
        }
      }
    }
```

```java
      } // end of 'while more path tokens'
    }
    return start;
  }

  public static File parentOf(File child) throws IOException {
    File rv;
    try {
      rv = new File(child.getParent());
    }
    catch(NullPointerException e) {
      throw new IOException("Already at the top of the tree");
    }
    return rv;
  }

  public File parentDir() throws IOException {
    return parentOf(currentDir);
  }

  public void up() throws IOException {
    currentDir = parentDir();
  }

  public void cd(String dest) throws IOException {
    currentDir = at(currentDir, dest);
  }

  public String [] dir() {
    return currentDir.list();
  }

  public String [] dir(String target) throws IOException {
    return at(currentDir, target).list();
  }

  public static void main(String args[]) {
    boolean finished = false;
    String cmdline = null;
    String command = null;
    String argument = null;
    StringTokenizer tok = null;
```

```java
BufferedReader in = new BufferedReader(
                      new InputStreamReader(System.in));
Directory that;

if (args.length == 0) {
  that = new Directory();
}
else {
  try {
    that = new Directory(args[0]);
  }
  catch (IOException e) {
    System.out.println("Can't start at " + args[0] + "\n" + e);
    that = new Directory();
  }
}

while (!finished) {
  System.out.print(that.current() + "> ");
  System.out.flush();
  try {
    cmdline = in.readLine();
  }
  catch (IOException e) {
    finished = true;
    break;
  }
  tok = new StringTokenizer(cmdline, " \t");
  command = argument = null;
  if (tok.hasMoreTokens()) {
    command = tok.nextToken();
  }
  if (tok.hasMoreTokens()) {
    argument = tok.nextToken();
  }
  if (command == null) {
    continue;
  }
  if (command.equalsIgnoreCase("exit")) {
    finished = true;
  }
  if (command.equalsIgnoreCase("cd")) {
```

```
      if (argument == null) {
        System.out.println("Current directory is " + that.current());
      }
      else {
        try {
          that.cd(argument);
        }
        catch (IOException e) {
          System.err.println("Failed to change directory. " + e);
        }
      }
    }
    if (command.equalsIgnoreCase("up")) {
      try {
        that.up();
      }
      catch (IOException e) {
        System.err.println("Failed to change up directory. " + e);
      }
    }
    if (command.equalsIgnoreCase("dir")) {
      String [] files = null;
      if (argument == null) {
        files = that.dir();
      }
      else {
        try {
          files = that.dir(argument);
        }
        catch (IOException e) {
          System.out.println("Failed to list directory. " + e);
        }
      }
      if (files != null) {
        for (int i = 0; i < files.length; i++) {
          System.out.println(files[i]);
        }
      }
    }
    if (command.equalsIgnoreCase("help")) {
      System.out.println("cd [<directory>]\n" +
        "      Select the specified directory" +
```

```
                  " or print currently selected directory");
          System.out.println("dir [<directory>]\n" +
              "     List contents of the specified directory" +
              " or the current directory");
          System.out.println("exit\n" +
              "     Quit the program");
          System.out.println("help\n" +
              "     Ouputs this message");
          System.out.println("up\n" +
              "     Select the parent of the current directory");
        }
      }
    }
  }
```

Running the Directory Program

If you run the program without specifying a path name, the browser starts in the current directory; otherwise, it will start it in the specified directory.

When the program starts, it will issue a prompt that indicates the current directory. At the prompt, the following commands are accepted:

cd   Echo current directory.

cd *<path>*   Select new current directory, relative or absolute.

up   Move up one directory.

dir   List contents of current directory.

dir *<path>*   List contents of relative or absolute directory.

exit   Exit the program.

help   List these commands with brief explanations.

The commands cd and dir are similar to their MS-DOS equivalents. By itself, cd is equivalent to the Unix command pwd; with a command-line argument, cd is equivalent to its Unix counterpart of the same name. In Unix, ls performs broadly the same function as dir.

The command up is a shorthand for cd .. and selects the parent of the current directory. The commands exit and help quit the program and provide a brief description of each command, respectively.

On MS-DOS-type systems, the starting path can be specified as a different device, but the program does not operate properly if the root directory of a device is specified. So, the command java Directory C:\somedir works as expected, but the command java Directory C:\ fails to work properly and becomes confused. In the latter, the program works properly after the issue of an up command, which resets the current directory to C: without a trailing backslash (\). Unfortunately, the command java Directory C: fails because it treats C: as a directory name that it expects to find in the current directory of the default device. The easiest way to start the program in the root directory of a device is to use the command java Directory C:\., which, because it takes the first form, does work correctly.

Another weakness with this program is that it is not possible to change devices. If it is started on C:, then that is where it will stay.

WARNING   The parsing of user input splits text on space or tab characters; hence, the program will not operate correctly on directories that have spaces in them. This, however, is a limitation of the main() method itself and not of the File or Directory classes.

Using Methods for File System Navigation

There are two distinct bodies of code in the Directory class. The main() method represents a test harness and trivial application, while the class as a whole encapsulates some ideas about directories.

The main() method reads commands from the standard input and parses them for the small command set that it recognizes. The main() method then invokes the appropriate methods on the instance that of the Directory class, displaying any appropriate results.

The rest of the class represents a single directory and provides a number of methods that allow you to move up and down the file system and to list the contents of directories.

The at() and parentOf() Methods

The body of the class provides two static methods that supplement the facilities of the java.io.File class. These are called at() and parentOf(). Each takes a File instance as an argument and returns another File instance as the result. The at() method also takes a String. The returned File from at() describes the directory that results from changing the path of the first argument according to the path given as the second String. The parentOf() method simply returns a File that describes the parent directory of the File object supplied. In both cases, erroneous arguments, such as asking for the parent of a root directory or trying to move down through a nonexistent path, result in an IOException being thrown.

The parsing of path names by the at() method handles absolute references and the relative references dot (.) and dot dot (..). To operate successfully, the at() method depends on running on a platform that follows the basic Unix and MS DOS convention that a fully qualified filename consists of a list of directory names followed by the actual filename, and that the elements of the list are separated by a single, unique character. This character is a forward slash (/) in Unix and a backward one (\) in MS DOS. If the Directory class were used on a VAX/VMS system, which uses a more complex description, it would fail.

NOTE   The VAX/VMS file system uses a five-part mechanism for specifying a full path to a file. The outline looks like this: <Node>::<Device>:[<directory.parts>] <filename.ext>;<ver>. The <Node> part specifies a node on a DECNet network at which the file is stored. <Device> specifies the name of the device containing the file. The device names are multicharacter. The directory parts describe a hierarchical directory system, and elements of the directory are separated with periods. The whole directory specification is enclosed in square brackets. The filename and extension follow, with a version number after a semicolon. As with most file systems, most parts of these specifications, except the filename itself, are optional.

The separator used by the host file system is available from the system properties table. For convenience, this information is also available from the File class. Two members, called separator and separatorChar, are declared as public static final variables. The separator variable is a String object that, in principle, might contain multiple characters, although on Windows and Unix platforms it contains only one. The separatorChar variable is of type char and is the first character from the separator variable.

One aspect of the at() method warrants particular mention. The File class parses the relative directories dot (.) and dot dot (. .) only partly correctly. For instance, if a File object f refers to a directory x\y\z, and then a new File object f1 is constructed as f1 = new File(f, " .. "), the result will be that f1 refers to the directory x\y as expected.

Although this construction works, it unfortunately appears to be a feature of the underlying operating systems, rather than being behavior built into the File class itself. If the getAbsolutePath() method is applied to f1, it does not return the string x\y, but instead x\y\z\. ., which is rather ugly and might cause comparisons that attempt to determine if two paths are related in some way to fail.

NOTE

One of the security bugs in the alpha releases of the HotJava browser is related to directory specification. HotJava intended that the user be able to specify that files and directories in certain paths could be accessible to untrusted applets. Unfortunately, a file could be specified as, for example, . .\. .\autoexec.bat, and therefore any permitted path could be used to gain access to any part of the disk.

In the Directory class example, the at() method parses the individual parts of the path modifier and handles the dot (.) and dot dot (. .) as special cases. The result is a path that is tidied up and avoids messy dot and dot dot sequences being left in the path.

Other Features of the Directory Class

Based on the two utility routines and the preexisting facilities of the File class, a number of features are built into the Directory class. Two constructors are provided. The first constructor has no arguments, which extracts the current directory as the default. The second constructor allows the specification of a particular starting path and will throw an IOException if this argument does not describe a real path.

In addition to the constructors, the current() method reports the current directory. The cd() method allows changing of the current directory. Two methods called dir() allow the contents of either the current or a specified directory to be listed as an array of Strings.

Enhancing the Directory Program

The major weakness of the `Directory.java` code is that it does not properly handle device names such as `C:` in paths. This is tiresome on platforms like Windows that use this form. This problem could be fixed, although the resulting code would be rather fudged and would have to make platform-dependent assumptions about how to distinguish between a directory and a device name. Testing for a colon in the second position is appropriate for DOS/Windows platforms, VMS, and others; however, although this approach is quite general, it is not portable.

The `Directory` class has been written to provide a reasonable basis for reuse, although the `main()` method should probably be cut out if this is to be pursued. Many applications will require some ability to navigate the file system, and this class can be of assistance where the basic methods of the `File` class are lacking. Creating a GUI for the `Directory` class would provide a file-management tool.

TIP   This book's appendix, Frequently Asked Questions, gives an example of using the `java.lang.reflection` package to determine if a newly loaded class has a `main()` method and shows how to invoke this method if it exists. It would be a simple exercise to extend the `Directory.java` example to add this behavior. The `java.lang.reflection` package is not available in releases before JDK 1.1.

The example of the `Directory` class has shown that, to a large extent, the standard Java packages allow programs to access the host file system without specific knowledge of its platform. However, some difficulties need to be handled, and some aspects, most notably device names, still present significant barriers to a genuinely platform-independent solution.

Visual Aspects

The visual appearance of a GUI-based program is partly controlled by the programmer, but it is also partly controlled by the host windowing system. Programs are expected to have a look and feel that is comparable with others running in the same environment. In general, each platform that supports Java has a distinct look and feel of its own; Microsoft Windows, Macintosh, and X Windows all have different visual styles.

Java runtime systems using AWT adopt the look and feel of the host system. This is important as otherwise users might reject Java programs because of the "culture shock" that results from a strange-looking program. With the new components in the Swing set, a program can still adopt the local look and feel or it can use the "Metal" look and feel, which was designed to be largely familiar and hence avoid the culture shock effect. This conformity to the host system has an impact on the programmer. The three aspects of visual appearance that warrant discussion are fonts, colors, and layout.

Working with Fonts

Different platforms support different fonts. Even different installations of the same platform might have different fonts installed. GUIs might require a range of fonts and styles (although this is the exception rather than the rule). It is important that you write a program that is able to determine which fonts are available and is able to use them in an appropriate way without the final result being surprising or inappropriate.

You can write a program that extracts a full list of supported font names from the running system, and these fonts can, in principle, be used at any point size and style. Java supports the font styles plain, bold, italic, and bold italic.

In addition to polling the running system, a program can be written so the end user is allowed to configure the fonts used for various parts of the GUI.

Obtaining the Available Font List

You can obtain the list of available fonts from the running system via the Toolkit object. The Toolkit represents the underlying platform-specific windowing system, such as Microsoft Windows or X Windows. Every instance of a java.awt.Component has a reference to the Toolkit that currently implements it. There is also a static Toolkit method called getDefaultToolkit() that returns a reference to the default Toolkit.

Under certain conditions, it is possible that the default Toolkit might not be used by a particular Component. This can occur if the Component is not displayed on the local screen or if there are multiple local screens, which frequently occurs in X Windows environments. The getToolkit() method, called before the Component is actually displayed, will return the default Toolkit.

Obtaining a reference to the Toolkit from a Component is easy once that Component has been displayed, but not before that moment. This is awkward because, ideally, the program should be able to determine any information that might impact the displayed appearance before the display occurs. If this determination cannot happen, then when the program is first displayed, it is likely to flicker because it must be redrawn in the light of new information.

In fact, it is possible to extract the required data from the Component when it is just about to be displayed. The actual displayable part of a Component, known as the *peer*, is created by the method addNotify(). Building the peer is called *realizing* the Component. The addNotify() method may be overridden by a subclass of Component and the original method called at the start of the code. After the return of the parental addNotify() method, the return value from the getToolkit() method will be valid, and so will the response to any other queries that are made of it. This technique works for other facilities of Component, such as createImage(), which are unavailable before the realization of the Component.

As mentioned earlier, in principle, fonts can be constructed in four styles and any point size. However, the Java system might allow itself a little leeway with this; it is possible for a font to be provided that is not precisely the size requested. Typically, the tolerance allowed is six points, although this may vary among implementations. Also, a font that is reported by the getFontList() method might not actually be available in all the styles.

WARNING   Once a font has been created, the class has methods that return the font name, size, and attributes. It is not usually relevant, but is slightly unfortunate, that the values reflect the constructor arguments, not the actual results. Even obtaining a reference to the FontPeer object will not help, because this is different even for two consecutive calls to the getPeer() method of the same Font object. Hence, it is not possible to use these facilities to determine if two fonts are visibly distinguishable. The FontMetrics class, described later, can provide some assistance with this problem.

The following example provides a basic font-examination tool that generates a list of the font names available on your machine in a Java program. You can select a font and style and immediately see the appearance of that font with a sample of text in the window. This example is located on the CD-ROM in the directory javadevhdbk\ch05\Fontsel.java. The bytecode is located in the file Fontsel.class.

LIST 5.2	**Fontsel.java**

```java
import java.awt.*;
import java.awt.event.*;

public class Fontsel extends Frame
                      implements ActionListener,
                                 ItemListener,
                                 WindowListener {
  Label sample;
  Choice fontNames;
  TextField fontSize;
  int actualFontSize;
  Checkbox italic;
  Checkbox bold;

  public static void main(String args[]) {
    Fontsel that = new Fontsel();
    that.setVisible(true);
  }

  public Fontsel() {
    super("Font Selection");
    fontNames = new Choice();
    fontSize = new TextField("10", 5);
    actualFontSize = 10;
    Panel topPanel = new Panel();
    topPanel.setLayout(new BorderLayout());
    topPanel.add(fontSize, BorderLayout.WEST);
    topPanel.add(fontNames, BorderLayout.CENTER);
    add(topPanel, BorderLayout.NORTH);

    italic = new Checkbox("Italic");
    bold = new Checkbox("Bold");
    Panel leftPanel = new Panel();
    leftPanel.setLayout(new GridLayout(2, 1));
    leftPanel.add(italic);
    leftPanel.add(bold);
    add(leftPanel, BorderLayout.WEST);
```

```
      Panel centerPanel = new Panel();
      centerPanel.setLayout(new GridLayout(1, 1));
      sample = new Label("");
      centerPanel.add(sample);
      add("Center", centerPanel);
      pack();

      italic.addItemListener(this);
      bold.addItemListener(this);
      fontNames.addItemListener(this);

      fontSize.addActionListener(this);

      addWindowListener(this);
    }

  public void addNotify() {
    super.addNotify();
    Toolkit myToolkit = getToolkit();
    String [] fonts = myToolkit.getFontList();
    for (int i = 0; i < fonts.length; i++) {
      fontNames.addItem(fonts[i]);
    }
    showSample();
  }

  public void itemStateChanged(ItemEvent ev) {
    actionPerformed(null);
  }

  public void actionPerformed(ActionEvent e) {
    int guess = 0;
    try {
      guess = Integer.parseInt(fontSize.getText());
    }
    catch (NumberFormatException ex) {
      fontSize.setText("" + actualFontSize);
    }
    if ((guess >= 2) && (guess <= 144)) {
      actualFontSize = guess;
    }
```

```java
        showSample();
    }


    public void windowClosing(WindowEvent ev) {
        System.exit(0);
    }

    public void windowClosed(WindowEvent ev) {
    }

    public void windowDeiconified(WindowEvent ev) {
    }

    public void windowIconified(WindowEvent ev) {
    }

    public void windowOpened(WindowEvent ev) {
    }

    public void windowActivated(WindowEvent ev) {
    }

    public void windowDeactivated(WindowEvent ev) {
    }

    private void showSample() {
      int style = 0;
      if (italic.getState()) {
        style |= Font.ITALIC;
      }
      if (bold.getState()) {
        style |= Font.BOLD;
      }
      Font f = new Font(fontNames.getSelectedItem(),
                      style, actualFontSize);
      sample.setText(f.toString());
      sample.setFont(f);
    }
}
```

Running the Fontsel Program   When you run the program, it will start up and launch a new window, as shown in Figure 5.8. Across the top of the window is a textfield in which a font size (from 2 to 144 points) may be typed and a choice box that contains the names of all fonts known to Java. Along the left side of the window are two checkboxes, one labeled Italic and the other labeled Bold. An example of the chosen font is shown in the remainder of the window. Entering a new font size, checking or unchecking the checkboxes, or choosing a new font from the choices will update the sample text in the lower-right corner of the window.

FIGURE 5.8:

The Fontsel program

Building the Display and Getting the Font List   The program starts by creating the GUI layout. A list of fonts is extracted and installed in the Choice. The currently selected font is indicated in the Label area and is updated in both font and text whenever the user changes the values specified by the user interface. The important details of this program relate to the extraction of the font list and the use of the addNotify() method, although the majority of the code relates to building the display.

In the addNotify() method, just after the invocation of super.addNotify(), the getToolkit() method will return a correct reference to the underlying toolkit. The components are not displayed until after the return of the addNotify() method to its caller. From this Toolkit reference, the getFontList() method returns an array of strings representing the names of the available fonts.

As soon as the list of font names has been obtained, it is used to set up the Choice from which the font may be displayed.

Whenever an item or action event callback is received from any of the control AWT elements, the program reacts by constructing the required Font and setting the Label display to use that Font. The text of the Label is then set to the text that results from invoking the toString() method on the Font.

The `Fontsel` class is intended to demonstrate principles. It might be a useful utility for determining the available fonts on a platform, but because the bulk of the code provides a GUI for the program and only a line or two is actually of general utility, it is unlikely that this class will be reused.

One aspect is worth noting as a design pattern for use elsewhere; `addNotify()` is used obtain proper connection to the underlying `Toolkit` object before a component is actually visible. This connection is required for a number of facilities—including creating instances of the `Image` class, which is used, among other things, for double buffering.

Finding Out about the Font

When a `Font` object has been created and installed in a particular `Component` for use, it is possible to determine information about the dimensions of characters in the `Font`. This information is used by components to determine their own preferred sizes and is useful when coding new components.

To obtain the size information, an instance of the `FontMetrics` class is used. This instance is extracted from the component that uses the font by calling the method `getFontMetrics()`. Using the `FontMetrics` object, a number of methods are available. All the characteristic dimensions of the font are accessible, including the line height and advance width (the space to move forward to get to the position of the next character) of any single character. One particularly useful method is `getStringWidth()`, which takes a `String` argument and returns the total length of that `String` in units of pixels.

If two `Fonts` are visibly different, especially if they are of different point sizes, then it is likely that some detail of the associated `FontMetric` object will differ. This allows the possibility of determining if two `Fonts` are actually different from the user's point of view. This can be helpful because the `Font` object methods that return the name, size, and attributes do not report the attributes used on the display; rather, they report the arguments with which the `Font` was constructed.

Adding Fonts

You can add new fonts to the runtime system of the JDK. This might be useful either to give more control over the appearance of an application or to support a character set that is not normally provided. As a programmer, you should avoid depending on special fonts, but adding new fonts might allow you to get a program running well even if it was written to use special fonts.

Adding an Alias   At the simplest level, you can define an alias for a name. This allows a program that requests a special font by name to be redirected to one of the existing fonts (normally, if you request an unknown font, you will get sans serif). Adding an alias is simple. Using an editor of your choice, load the file `font.properties` from the `lib` subdirectory under your JDK installation. Then add a line like this, which defines the alias typewriter for monospaced:

```
alias.typewriter=monospaced
```

Adding an alias in this way does not add a new font as such. Instead, it allows you to use a different name for one that already exists. In other words, aliases allow a program to run adequately even if it has been hardcoded to look for a particular name that doesn't exist on your system.

Adding a Font Name   To add a font name properly, so that a new font is actually available, you must make a different kind of entry. Unfortunately, the details of the entry you need to make depend on the host platform somewhat. In a Windows system, to add a font called Traditional, based on a physical font called Bookman Old Style, you should add two entries like this:

```
traditional.0=Bookman Old Style,ANSI_CHARSET
exclusion.traditional.0=0100-ffff
```

The digit 0 after `traditional` indicates that this is the first entry that should be consulted when looking for a real font to use to satisfy the request for Traditional. The `ANSI_CHARSET` part indicates the range and indices of these characters against the range of Unicode. The `exclusion` statement indicates that the font only has characters for the Unicode index range 0 to 100 hex, and is only specified for the dot-zero, or entries ending in `.0`.

Providing an Index Translation   The ANSI character set includes characters in the same index positions in the font as for Unicode. For example, character 65 in the font is the letter A and Unicode character 65 is also A. Not all fonts have characters in the same index position as Unicode; for these, an index translation is required. To indicate that a font needs index conversion, Windows installations use entries of this form:

```
squiggle.1=Symbol,SYMBOL_CHARSET,NEED_CONVERTED
fontcharset.squiggle.1=sun.awt.windows.CharToByteWingDings
```

The digit 1 after `squiggle` indicates that this is the second choice (after the entry for `squiggle.0` elsewhere in the `font.properties` file) of font to fulfill requests for characters for the Squiggle font.

The tag SYMBOL_CHARSET refers to the CHARSET entry of the font in the Win32 API. There are a number of possibilities in addition to ANSI_CHARSET and SYMBOL_ CHARSET, such as GB2312_CHARSET (which indicates Chinese).

The NEED_CONVERTED part indicates that the font indices are not Unicode indices. Because of this tag, the fontcharset entry is required to indicate the fully qualified name of a class that provides the index translation. This class also provides a way to determine if the font can satisfy a request for a particular Unicode character, which is used to determine if the conversion should try the next lower priority entry in the font.properties file. That is, if the fontcharset converter for traditional.0 indicates that the character isn't available in this font, then the entry traditional.1 will be tried next.

Adding Fonts on a Unix Platform   On a Unix platform, the approach is slightly different. The entry that declares the font to use does not need a *xxx_* CHARSET entry, and the need for conversion is assumed—that is, a fontcharset entry specifying a converter class is always expected. A further complication is that the fonts used on a Unix system are different from the TrueType fonts used under Windows and are generally not scalable, nor are they suitable for italicizing or boldfacing. Because of this, different fonts need to be used to provide bold, italic, and bold/italic styles, and a mechanism is required to allow the required font size to be found on the host system.

To provide for different font attributes (bold, italic, and so forth), Unix systems use additional entries of this form:

```
traditional.0=<fontname>
traditional.italic.0=<fontname>
traditional.bold.0=<fontname>
traditional.bolditalic.0=<fontname>
```

This way, a different base font can be specified for each style.

We now have a mechanism for specifying the physical font for a given font name and style, but not for different sizes. Well, here the underlying X Windows system comes to the rescue. Fonts in X Windows generally have long names that are constructed from the properties of the font in question. One of these properties is the size in tenths of points. So, all we have to do is to specify whereabouts in the name this size field is located, and Java's font system does the rest. So a typical entry from the Unix version of font properties might be:

```
serif.plain.0=-linotype-times-medium-r-normal-*-%d-*-*-p-*-iso8859-1
```

Notice the use of "%d" in this line. When the font is actually loaded, this will be replaced with the required font size in tenths of points. For example, new Font("serif", Font.PLAIN, 24) would look for a font with the actual name:

```
serif.plain.0=-linotype-times-medium-r-normal-*-240-*-*-p-*-iso8859-1
```

Notice that 240 (10 times the requested point size) is substituted for the "%d".

Handling Font Properties and Locale

So far in this discussion of fonts, we have referred only to a file called font .properties. In fact, it might be that this is not the only file containing font information that your system consults.

If you have a locale set, then the Java runtime will look for a font properties file that reflects that locale name. For example, if you are running with the locale set to Japanese, then the file font.properties.ja will be read instead of the plain font.properties file. This feature allows you to run Java programs in the language of your choice, while keeping the font-loading time to a minimum by not loading fonts that are not needed for your particular locale.

Working with Colors

When defining a color in a Java program, a 24 + 8-bit true color representation is used in the API. The low-order 24 bits represent three separate 8-bit values. These indicate the intensity of red, green, and blue in the color. Red is the most significant byte, blue is the least significant, and green is in between. The extra 8 bits represent an opacity. The opacity is called the *alpha* value and occupies the most significant byte of the full 32-bit integer. An alpha value of 255 indicates that the color is fully opaque; 0 indicates a fully transparent color. Opacity does not affect a color on the display—it is used for mixing images together.

Java programs might be called on to run on platforms with widely differing color capabilities. Monochrome systems still exist, especially in laptops, and certainly not all systems have full 24-bit color facilities. Internally, Java translates the color definition into the best available representation. In some cases, the result might not bear much relationship to the original color definition.

It is possible to determine some information about the color system, such as the physical color resolution and the actual colors that are available. Based on this information, a program can choose an appropriate behavior when displaying colors. For example, if insufficient color resolution is available for displaying a photograph, a program might use dithering rather than precise color specifications.

Dithering is a technique that uses groups of nearby pixels and color mixing to give the appearance of more colors than are really available. Although this increases the effective color resolution, the effective pixel resolution is reduced.

Determining the Color Model

The java.awt.Component class has a method getColorModel(). This returns a subclass of java.awt.image.ColorModel.

The two most common color models used by the JDK are DirectColorModel and IndexColorModel. DirectColorModel represents a system that has a fixed, evenly distributed number of predefined colors. A range of intensities is available in red, green, and blue, and the three colors can be controlled effectively individually. For example, this model suits 16-bit color or 24-bit true color. The representation of the ranges of each color is done using a number of bits out of a larger value. An 8-bit-per-pixel range is typically treated as 3 bits each of red and green and 2 bits of blue. The range of each color is therefore 0 to 7 for red and green, and 0 to 3 for blue. Figure 5.9 shows a typical mapping between red, green, and blue ranges for a DirectColorModel with 8 bits per pixel.

FIGURE 5.9:

A typical DirectColorModel using 8 bits per pixel

The human eye is least sensitive to contrast in blue and most sensitive in green. This is why blue is chosen to have the lower resolution when allocating the short number of bits.

The IndexColorModel is used for systems that have a palette. This is typical of many X Windows systems and 256-color VGA adapters on IBM PC-type systems. In displays of this type, a limited number of different colors can be displayed simultaneously; however, each of those colors can be selected from a very large number of colors, allowing smooth graduation of color over a limited range. Figure 5.10 shows an example of a color palette that might be represented by an IndexColorModel.

FIGURE 5.10:

An example of an
IndexColorModel palette
mechanism

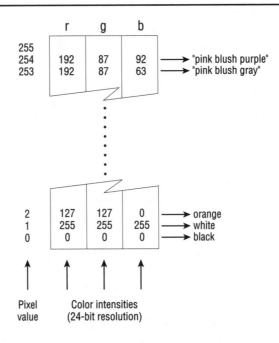

To determine the nature of the color system on the host running a Java program, first obtain the ColorModel from a displayed component. The instanceof operator determines which of the two available color models has been returned. The getPixelSize() method of the ColorModel class returns the number of bits used for each pixel. Assuming all the bits are used, the number of available colors is determined as two raised to the power of the number of bits per pixel.

The following example launches a new window and reports the ColorModel and color range, in terms of bits per pixel, in that window. This program may be run either as an application or an applet (using the Applet Viewer or a browser that supports Java 1.1 or later, launch the ColMod.html file). The source for this example is located on the CD-ROM in the directory javadevhdbk\ch05\ColMod.java. The corresponding bytecode is in the file javadevhdbk\ch05\ColMod.class.

LIST 5.3   **ColMod.java**

```java
import java.awt.*;
import java.awt.event.*;
import java.awt.image.*;
import java.applet.*;

public class ColMod extends Applet {
  Label model;
  Label bitsPerPixel;

  public static void main(String args[]) {
    Frame f = new Frame("ColorModel information");
    f.addWindowListener(
      new WindowAdapter() {
        public void windowClosing(WindowEvent ev) {
          System.exit(0);
        }
      }
    );
    ColMod that = new ColMod();
    f.add("Center", that);
    f.pack();
    f.setVisible(true);
  }

  public ColMod() {
    setLayout(new GridLayout(2, 1));
    model = new Label();
    add(model);
    bitsPerPixel = new Label();
    add(bitsPerPixel);
  }

  public void addNotify() {
    super.addNotify();
    ColorModel m = getColorModel();
    model.setText("ColorModel is " + m.getClass().getName());
    bitsPerPixel.setText(m.getPixelSize() + " Bits per pixel");
  }
}
```

The bulk of this program creates a basic GUI for displaying the information about the local color system. Three points of interest are the use of getColor-Model(), applied to the main Frame object; the getPixelSize() method, applied to the resulting ColorModel object; and the use of the instanceof operator to determine which particular ColorModel was reported.

NOTE   The ColMod class serves to demonstrate the use of the getColorModel() and getPixelSize() methods but, the example is not intended to support reuse.

Matching the Desktop

When running, a Java program should usually use display colors that match those of the current host platform. In general, AWT components will handle this directly. However, you might want to handle Desktop matching in your code, especially if you create your own custom components.

A number of constants are defined in the Color class to specify the colors in the Desktop of the host system. These constants are not defined in the source code of, and compiled into, an implementation, but are determined and configured in the running system when the java.awt.Toolkit class is loaded. There is no guarantee that they will be revised if the user selects a new color scheme during the execution of a Java program.

You can determine the settings of the colors by reading static final variables in the java.awt.SystemColor class. The variable names are listed in Table 5.1. Note that not every color scheme model uses all of these symbolic colors. Unused symbolic colors will be set to reasonable values.

TABLE 5.1: SystemColor Class Variables

Variable Name	Contents
activeCaption	Caption background color (the caption is the window's title bar area)
activeCaptionBorder	Caption border color
activeCaptionText	Caption text color
control	Control (noncontainer component) background color
controlDkShadow	Control dark shadow color

Continued on next page

TABLE 5.1 CONTINUED: SystemColor Class Variables

Variable Name	Contents
desktop	Desktop's background color
controlHighlight	Control regular highlighting color
controlLtHighlight	Control light highlighting color
controlShadow	Control shadow color
controlText	Control text color
inactiveCaption	Inactive caption background color
inactiveCaptionBorder	Inactive caption border color
inactiveCaptionText	Inactive caption text color
info	Spot-help background color
infoText	Spot-help text color
menu	Menu background color
menuText	Menu text color
scrollbar	Scrollbar background color
textHighlight	Background text highlighting color
textHighlightText	Foreground text highlight color
textInactiveText	Text color for disabled controls
textText	Text color in text components
window	Window background color
windowBorder	Window border color
windowText	Text color inside window

Consider a custom component that has a background and some text. Without using these color specifications, the paint() method might look like this:

```
public void paint(Graphics g)
{
    g.setColor(Color.black);
```

```
        g.drawString(labelstring, x, y);
        // Other rendering code …
    }
```

With Desktop colors, this code might be rewritten as follows:

```
    public void paint(Graphics g)
    {
        g.setColor(SystemColor.controlText);
        g.drawString(labelstring, x, y);
        // Other rendering code …
    }
```

WARNING   The equals() method does not work with system colors. To compare two system colors sc1 and sc2, do *not* use if (sc1.equals(sc2)). Instead, convert the colors to RGB values: if (sc1.getRGB() == sc2.getRGB()).

Working with the GUI Layout

The physical layout of a program's GUI depends to some degree on the sizes of the components that make it up. For this reason, it is important to resist any temptation to position components at absolute x,y coordinates. As explained in detail in Chapter 4, Java provides the layout manager mechanism to allow layouts to be described in logical terms so the platform can implement the correct absolute positioning required to achieve the desired effect.

Each component is able to express a preference for a particular size in terms of width and height, and is also able to state what minimum size is required for proper operation. If a LayoutManager object wishes to, it can inquire for these dimensions and use them in deciding how to lay out the display.

Different systems might use different fonts when running the same program. This typically changes the sizes of text strings and consequently the space required for labels and similar components. In such cases, an absolute layout would be spoiled. Fonts are not the only variations between platforms that might ruin an absolute layout. For example, there are different adornments around different components. On older versions of Windows NT, a TextField object has a single-pixel wide box around it; on Windows 95 and newer, the same component is enclosed in a 3-D box. Even when using the Metal look and feel with the Java

Swing set, which gives the same appearance for all platforms, the fonts, screen size, and resolution will vary between one system and the next (the Java Foundation Class components in the `java.awt.swing` package are covered in Chapter 15).

For conditions that require a customized layout, it is usually better if you code a special `LayoutManager` class rather than use ad hoc code to perform the layout externally. This provides two benefits:

- The detail of layout-management calculation does not clutter other parts of the code, which improves the readability and hence maintainability of the work.

- You can readily reuse the resulting `LayoutManager` class in other situations. Reuse of code results in retesting, which in turn results in better quality software.

Chapter 4 describes how to write layout managers and includes examples of custom layout managers.

> **NOTE**   It is important to realize that a layout manager might coerce the width, height, or both of each component it lays out. The `FlowLayout` class controls neither, while the `GridLayout` class controls both. The `BorderLayout` class controls the height of the East and West components, the width of the North and South components, and both dimensions of the Center component. In situations where *either* dimension of component is controlled by the layout manager, the use of `setSize()` or `setBounds()` methods will be ineffective because it will be overridden by the layout manager.

Local and User Configuration

Many of the platforms that support Java provide environment variables. These are ways for the user to define certain attributes of environment or preference—such as username, temporary file directory, or the color of a button—so a program can obtain this information at runtime and behave in a fashion to suit the local user. Not all systems provide this facility, however, and there are no standard conventions for the naming of these attributes. Furthermore, some information that is programmed into environment variables might be sensitive, so applets should not have access to it. Environment variables are commonly used to maintain username, home directory, and perhaps the names of local servers. None of this should be accessible to an applet.

WARNING   Even information that is apparently quite innocuous can be sensitive or dangerous in the hands of someone trying to break into your systems. The type of operating system you are running, for example, would tell the attacker what type of attacks should be tried. Even something as simple as your username and machine name can be used to send unwanted e-mail. For this reason, applets should be denied access to any information that is either not essential to operation or cannot be proven genuinely harmless.

Because environment variables are not platform independent, the Java system provides an alternative mechanism. This alternative is called properties.

Accessing Properties

Some properties are provided by the system itself, and others can be read by applications from both files and the command line. Some browsers support properties, some of which are usually read from a file. If the browser does support properties, they are generally available to applets in that browser. In such circumstances, each applet request to read a property is checked by the security manager, and some accesses are denied for security reasons.

Although the full list of defined properties depends on the individual browser and version of Java, there is a basic set of standard system properties that are defined in any environment. Table 5.2 shows the names of these properties and indicates if the property value is accessible from an applet.

TABLE 5.2: Standard System Properties

Property Name	Normally Accessible from Applet?
About the Java distribution	
java.class.version	Yes
java.vendor	Yes
java.vendor.url	Yes

Continued on next page

TABLE 5.2 CONTINUED: Standard System Properties

Property Name	Normally Accessible from Applet?
About the Java distribution	
java.version	Yes
java.specification.name	No
java.specification.vendor	No
java.specification.version	No
java.vendor.url.bug	No
About the Java installation	
java.class.path	No
java.home	No
java.library.path	No
awt.toolkit	No
java.awt.graphicsenv	No
java.tmpdir	No
java.awt.fonts	No
About the individual user	
user.dir	No
user.home	No
user.name	No
user.language	No
user.region	No
user.timezone	No
About the host I/O system	
file.separator	Yes

Continued on next page

TABLE 5.2 CONTINUED: Standard System Properties

Property Name	Normally Accessible from Applet?
About the host I/O system	
line.separator	Yes
path.separator	Yes
file.encoding	No
file.encoding.pkg	No
About the host operating system	
os.arch	Yes
os.name	Yes
os.version	Yes
About the Virtual Machine	
java-vm.name	No
java-vm.specification.vendor	No
java-vm.specification.version	No
java-vm.version	No
java-vm.specification.name	No
java-vm.vendor	No

These properties are actually defined or determined inside the Java runtime. Additional properties are often read from files. The Applet Viewer, for example, reads the contents of a file called hotjava.properties to find configuration information for itself. Although many, if not most, of these additional properties are accessible to an applet, they are generally specific to an individual browser, and hence you cannot safely program using them.

The Java interpreter allows *per session* properties to be defined using the -D command line option. A command line including the text -Dname=value provides for a property called `name` to have a value of `value`. The same format, without the `-D` part, is used in property files.

Note that in Java 2, the accessibility of properties from untrusted code, such as applets, is governed by the `java.policy` file and is user configurable. This is described in Chapter 18, which covers security.

The `java.lang` package provides a number of standard methods for obtaining property values of certain types, such as `String`, `int`, and `boolean`, inside programs. These methods are generally encapsulated in the wrapper classes in the `java.lang` package. Hence, the class `java.lang.Boolean` has a method called `getBoolean(String)`. This method returns a value of `true` if there is an entry in the property table that has the name specified by the string argument and the value part is set to `true`. Accessing string properties is done via the `getProperty()` method of the `System` class; since all properties are initially defined as `String` objects, this property type does not need any conversion.

Properties can be used to control the operation of both applets and applications. Applications are able to load their own property tables from specific files; in general, applets cannot read from files. Because of this, applets usually must use the property table offered by the browser. In some browsers, this can be extended by the user. Unfortunately, the current implementations of many popular browsers do not allow properties to be set in a file, reducing the utility of the mechanism in the short term.

Although applets generally cannot add their own properties to the system table and cannot read files either, properties can be read from any `InputStream` object. So, if appropriate, an applet could read properties from a network connection.

The following example demonstrates some of the fundamentals of using properties. The source for this example is located on the CD-ROM in the directory `javadevhdbk\ch05\PropView.java`. The corresponding bytecode file, `PropView.class`, is in the same directory.

LIST 5.4   *PropView.java*

```
import java.io.*;
import java.util.*;

public class PropView {
  public static void main(String args[]) {
    Properties properties = System.getProperties();
```

```
System.out.println("The system property table is:");
properties.list(System.out);

System.out.println("\nIndividual properties can be obtained" +
  "\nThe value of os.name is " + System.getProperty("os.name"));

if (args.length > 0) {
  FileInputStream in = null;
  boolean success = true;

  try {
    in = new FileInputStream(args[0]);
    properties.load(in);
    success = true;
  }
  catch (IOException ex) { /* do nothing, success remains false */
  }

  if (success) {
    System.out.println("\nThe property table can be extended by " +
      "applications from an InputStream");
    System.out.println("\nNew system property table is:");
    System.getProperties().list(System.out);
    System.out.println("\nValue of local.animal.defined is " +
      Boolean.getBoolean("local.animal.defined"));
    System.out.println("\nValue of local.animal.legcount is " +
      Integer.getInteger("local.animal.legcount"));
  }
  else {
    System.err.println("Unable to open the file " + args[0] +
      " for reading");
  }
}
  }
 }
}
```

To run the program, change to its directory and issue the command:

java PropView local.prop

The argument `local.prop` refers to a text file that defines a number of additional `Properties`. This argument is also located in the `javadevhdbk/ch05` directory. To experiment with alternative property sets, you can create your own file and provide the name of it in place of `local.prop`.

When the program starts, it prints the defined system properties to the standard output. It then outputs the value of the single property *os.name*, which is used to describe the name of the operating system. Finally, if an argument has been supplied, it is treated as a filename. That file is appended to the system properties and the aggregated table is listed.

Extracting the System Properties

The static `getProperties()` method in the `System` class extracts the table of all system properties. This is an instance of the class `java.util.Properties`. Next, the `list()` method is used on this returned object to write the entire table to the standard output.

The static `getProperty()` method of the `System` class is then used, demonstrating a more realistic mode of operation for normal programs. This method extracts from the table a specific system property by name, returning the value as a string.

Extending the Property Table

If an argument has been provided, this is used as the name of a file. That file is then opened for reading. The contents of the file are then appended to the system table, using the `load()` method of the `Properties` class.

If the supplied example file called `local.prop`, which is located in the same directory as the bytecode of this example, has been specified on the command line, then the resulting extended property table has two specific entries: `local.animal` and `local.animal.legcount`. The presence of the command-line argument causes the program to look for these properties using the methods built into the classes `Boolean` and `Integer` and then output the values that it finds.

TIP   Property-access methods are also available for several other types, such as `Font` and `Color`. The values returned by these methods have been converted from the original string into an object of the appropriate class. More details of these mechanisms are discussed later in this chapter.

Using Properties Effectively

You will find that properties are a versatile tool for creating a configurable program so a system administrator, or perhaps a user, can obtain optimal behavior on a specific platform. However, to make the best use of properties, a little advance planning is beneficial.

Each aspect of your program that might be affected by the platform on which it is run should be considered—fonts, colors, dimensions, label text, default directories, and more. For each aspect, a default value should be chosen along with a property name that is used to allow configuration. The program should be coded so if the property is undefined, the default is used. In some cases, this requires checking the return value of a `getXxx()` method. A return of `null` indicates that the property was not defined or the definition could not be interpreted properly. In other cases, a special `getXxx()` method takes a second argument that defines a default value to be returned if the property is not defined.

Careful use of properties for the messages used in a program can give easy and flexible support for programs that must run in a variety of languages. For example, the error messages issued by the standard Java compiler are defined in a property file that is read when the compiler starts up. This is easiest to achieve by using the `PropertyResourceBundle` class, which reads a text file of *name=value* assignments.

Creating a Property Specification Scheme

In the X Windows system, a powerful mechanism called *resources* provides parallel facilities to properties. In that system, a hierarchical naming scheme is used. For example, a resource can be defined as:

```
*.font: TimesRoman
```

This would cause X programs to use the Times Roman font by default. A specific program can be made to override this by another definition. For example, the following would cause the program called myProgram to ignore the default and use Helvetica instead:

```
myProgram.font: Helvetica
```

The X resources mechanism is powerful and complex, but the basic principles can be reused in Java via the properties mechanism. Using the example of fonts, you could write a suite of programs to check a series of property names when defining which font to use for warning labels. For example, consider this list:

```
font.mySuite.thisProgram.labels
font.mySuite.any.labels
font.mySuite.thisProgram.any
font.mySuite.any.any
```

The first element of these definitions is a property type. The second part defines the suite or group of related programs. The third element specifies a particular program. The elements beyond this point describe the particular aspect or category of aspects that will be controlled by the definition.

For example, if a program called thisProgram in the suite called mySuite wishes to know what Font to use for a general Label, it checks each of the properties listed in turn. As soon as a defined property is found, that property value is used to select the font. If some labels have special functions, such as issuing warnings, then the list could be extended by the addition of even more specific items at the start of the list, for example:

```
font.mySuite.thisProgram.labels.warning
```

The scheme is extensible as far as you require it to be. To define the fonts used for text entry, such as TextField or TextArea, you can use resources of the form font.mySuite.thisProgram.textEntry. You can handle menu items and any other group of fonts, and of course, the scheme is not restricted to Font specifications.

A sample implementation of this concept follows. The source for this example is on the CD-ROM in the directory javadevhdbk\ch05\Suite.java. The corresponding bytecode is in the file Suite.class in the same directory.

LIST 5.5   *Suite.java*

```
import java.util.*;
import java.io.*;

public class Suite {
  private String suite;
  private String progname;
  private static final boolean TRACE = true;
```

```
public Suite(String suite, String progname) {
  this.suite = suite;
  this.progname = progname;
}

public String findBest(String type, String [] matchList) {
  String [] base = new String[3];
  String s, p = null;
  int listElements = matchList.length;

  base[0] = type + "." + suite + "." + progname;
  base[1] = type + "." + suite + ".any";
  base[2] = type + ".any.any";

  outer:
  for (int b = 0; b < base.length; b++) {
    for (int l = listElements; l >= 0; l-) {
      s = base[b];
      for (int e = 0; e < l; e++) {
        s += "." + matchList[e];
      }
      if (TRACE) {
        System.out.println("checking " + s);
      }
      if ((p = System.getProperty(s)) != null) {
        break outer;
      }
    }
  }
  return p;
}

public static void main(String args[]) {
  Properties p = System.getProperties();
  try {
    p.load(new FileInputStream("Suite.prop"));
  }
  catch (IOException e) {
    System.err.println("Failed to open property file Suite.prop");
    System.exit(1);
  }
```

```
  if (args.length < 3) {
    System.err.println(
      "Usage: java Suite <suitename> <progname> <propertytype>" +
      " [<specifier>...]");
    System.exit(2);
  }

  Suite that = new Suite(args[0], args[1]);
  String type = args[2];
  String [] s = new String[args.length - 3];
  System.arraycopy(args, 3, s, 0, args.length - 3);

  System.out.println(that.findBest(type, s));
  }
}
```

Running the Suite Program

Run the program with each of the following command lines:

java Suite mySuite myProg font label

java Suite mySuite myProg font

java Suite mySuite yourProg font label

The output shows the property names that the program looks for and the final decision of the best-fit property found.

Finding the Best-Fit Property

The program appends the contents of a file Suite.prop to the system property table. A sample file of the name Suite.prop is on the CD-ROM in the same directory as the bytecode of this example. It contains:

```
font.mySuite.myProg=desperate
font.mySuite.myProg.label=labelStuff
font.mySuite.myProg.label.warning=danger
font.mySuite.any=lastDitch
```

The program then takes the first two arguments of the command line and treats them as the name of the suite and the name of this program, respectively. These values are used to create an object of the Suite class. The main() method, which serves as a test harness, then takes the third argument and an array built from the remaining arguments and asks the Suite object for the best-fit property from the system property table.

The program performs the search for the best fit by constructing test strings using the details of program and suite name, property type, and the specific details. If the "perfect fit" property is not found, the search proceeds by dropping items from the specific details list and checking for another property. If no match is found by the time the specific details have all been dropped, then the search proceeds again, substituting *any* in place of the program name. If this fails, then *any* is substituted in place of the suite name. Failure at this stage is considered to be complete failure of the match and returns null.

To support investigation of the behavior of this example, and to aid under-standing the hierarchical definition of these property names, the program prints out each property name as it is sought in the list.

Enhancing the Program

Suite.java can be used easily in any general program or suite of applications. Removing the main() method would improve the space efficiency of the class file, but is otherwise unnecessary. For real use, you should change the constant definition TRACE to false and recompile the program. It is not necessary to remove the code block that begins with:

```
if (TRACE) {
```

This is because the compiler optimization removes this block from the bytecode output altogether if TRACE is a constant of the value false.

For general use, construct the Suite object using an appropriate suite and pro-gram name and ensure that a property file that defines the property values is appended to the system properties at startup.

TIP   Although access to local files is generally prohibited to applets, the load() method in the **Properties** class expects an **InputStream** instance as its argu-ment. It is therefore perfectly possible to read properties from a URL if this is useful in a particular case. Using the method **getResourceAsStream()** in the **Class-Loader** class, reading properties from a URL is directly supported in a way that does not require an applet to be aware of its own origin. This method is discussed in the next section.

Locating Properties and Other Resources

The foregoing discussions have considered ways of using properties and of maximizing the convenience they offer to the user. However, we have not talked about where these properties are located.

As part of their design, some browsers—particularly the Applet Viewer and HotJava—read specific files for additional resources. It is generally not convenient for the user, system administrator, or software distributor to need to edit this file as part of software installation. Furthermore, because not all browsers use resources from a file, resources defined in any particular file are not available in all browsers. Finally, because these are browser-configuration files, it would be inappropriate to use the same files in the context of an application.

A mechanism introduced at JDK 1.1 allows general resources to be located by association with packages. The mechanism closely parallels that used for locating classes within packages; in fact, the mechanism is implemented by the class loaders. The mechanism is referred to as *resource location*.

NOTE

A *resource* in Java is often a file containing property definitions, but could be any other form of support file as needed in a particular program; for example, an image or sound file.

Recall that the `Properties` class provides a `load()` method that takes an `InputStream` object as its argument. The primary facility provided by the resource mechanism is to return an `InputStream` object suitable for use in this `load()` method. This is done by the `getResourceAsStream()` method in the `Object` class. The argument to the `getResourceAsStream()` method is a `String` object. This string, in the simplest case, is a filename. The `getResourceAsStream()` method attempts to load the specified file from the same location where the class file for the requesting object was loaded. In the case of a local class, loaded from the `CLASSPATH`, the file will be sought on each element of the `CLASSPATH`, too. If a class—for example, an `Applet` class—was loaded from a URL, the resource file will be loaded from the same base URL, if it exists.

In the "Package and Class Availability" section earlier in this chapter, we described the mechanism that uses package information as a relative directory path when loading classes. A similar approach is taken with the resource mechanism. If a resource is specified using the forward slash (/) character as part of its makeup, then the information up to the last of these will be taken as path information, and the search for the resource will be modified accordingly. (Regardless of the host platform, the forward slash (/) should always be used—in the implementation, any necessary translation is handled transparently.)

The resource mechanism allows a convenient way to provide configuration information on a per-class basis. Because an application must be started from a main() method in a specific class, this supports application configuration as well.

It is simple to support user-specific resources if required, and it can be achieved in several ways. For example, the username can be made part of the relative path of the resource name or can be the actual resource filename.

WARNING It might seem convenient to use a dot (.) as a part of the CLASSPATH, allowing the resource file to be loaded from the user's current directory. This approach is probably not to be encouraged because it might result in classes being loaded from the user's directories, too. This would allow the possibility of system attack, either directly by the user seeking to modify the working of the program or by an outsider who managed to breach the user's individual security and place a class file into that user's file space.

In addition to supporting property files via the getResourceAsStream() method, the resource mechanism allows arbitrary files to be located in the same way. You also can use the getResourceAsName() method, which describes the full path (perhaps including URL protocol information) of the resource location. You can then use any appropriate method to handle the resource directly. This is perhaps particularly appropriate when handling images and sounds.

TIP The resource-loading mechanism is built into the class loaders; thus, resources may be loaded from JAR files without any additional effort on your part whatsoever. This applies regardless of whether you load your code as an applet from a browser using the archive modifier or as an applet or application using the Java Extensions Framework mechanism. In fact, all provided class loaders, including the URLClassLoader (discussed in Chapter 10) provide this support. You will still find that resources can be loaded transparently from JAR archives, even if you explicitly use class loaders in your code.

Specifying Color Properties

Colors can be specified using property values, and a static method in the Color class is able to interpret the values directly. The method name is getColor(). It takes a string argument that should match the property name. For the mechanism to function correctly, the value of the property should be specified as a 24-bit integral value. This value is interpreted as 3 bytes. The highest order byte represents red, the middle byte represents green, and the low-order byte represents blue. In each case, the color is on a scale of 0 to 255. The property mechanism for reading integer values allows the use of decimal, hexadecimal, or octal if desired. These formats are represented using the same conventions as source code constants.

TIP

In addition to reading and interpreting the system properties directly, the Color class provides the decode() method. This is a static method that interprets its argument, which is a String object, as a number representing the 24-bit color value. This method can therefore be used to create Color objects conveniently from this form of representation. This method was introduced with the release of JDK 1.1.

 The following example simply displays a small window and sets the color of that window to a value specified by a property. The source of this example is on the CD-ROM in the directory javadevhdbk\ch05\ColorProp.java. The corresponding bytecode is in the same directory in the file ColorProp.class.

LIST 5.6	*ColorProp.java*

```
import java.awt.*;

public class ColorProp extends Frame {
  public static void main(String args[]) {
    ColorProp that = new ColorProp();
    that.setSize(100, 100);
    that.setVisible(true);
  }

  public ColorProp() {
    setBackground(Color.getColor("ColorProp.background"));
  }
}
```

Try running the program with the following command lines in turn:

java -DColorProp.background=0xff0000 ColorProp

java -DColorProp.background=0x00ff00 ColorProp

java -DColorProp.background=0x0000ff ColorProp

NOTE   Remember that an application can read properties from a file, and that is the normal place for properties to be defined. However, the command-line form used here is useful for experimentation because it avoids the need to edit a file before each test run. Instead, you simply change the argument list and run the program again.

This program is very simple, and for the purposes of the example, only one line is of interest:

```
setBackground(Color.getColor("ColorProp.background"));
```

Within this line, the `Color.getColor()` method is the one that does the interesting work. It attempts to load a property named `ColorProp.background` from the system properties table. If successful, it attempts to treat it as a number and create a new instance of the `Color` class from that number.

The remainder of the program provides a window and sets the background color of that window using the `Color` object returned by the `Color.getColor()` method.

Specifying Font Properties

The `Font` class is able to read and interpret properties to define fonts. The static method `getFont()` searches the system properties for a property with the string name that matches the string provided as an argument to the call. If the property name is found, then the value associated with it is interpreted as a font name. Font names contain three parts that define the font's name, style, and point size (specifying style and size is optional).

To specify only the font name, accepting the default of plain style and 12-point size, you include only the name of the font in the property value. If you want to specify either style or size, then the property value should be laid out as three parts, each separated by a dash (-). The font name should be first, followed by the style, and then the size. For example, Times Roman 36-point italic is specified with the property value:

```
TimesRoman-italic-36
```

Notice that there are no spaces in this value; the name TimesRoman is also a single string with no spaces.

To leave either the size or the style unspecified, include both hyphens but do not include a value for whichever aspect is to take the default. Hence, a default style 24-point Helvetica is indicated as:

```
Helvetica-24
```

This has the same effect as an explicit request for the plain style, which can be made as:

```
Helvetic-plain-24
```

Bold/italic style is indicated by the string bolditalic. For example, the following indicates a default size Courier typeface with both bold and italic attributes:

```
Courier-bolditalic-
```

TIP

In addition to reading and interpreting the system properties directly, the **Font** class provides the **decode()** method. This is a static method that takes a **String** object as its argument. It interprets the string and returns a new **Font** object constructed according to the rules just described. The **decode()** method was introduced with the release of JDK 1.1.

The following example reads a property to determine a font. The source and bytecode for this example are on the CD-ROM in the files FontProp.java and FontProp.class in the directory javadevhdbk/ch05.

LIST 5.7 *FontProp.java*

```java
import java.awt.*;

public class FontProp extends Frame {
  public static void main(String args[]) {
    FontProp that = new FontProp();
    that.pack();
    that.setVisible(true);
  }
```

```
public FontProp() {
  Font myFont = Font.getFont("FontProp.font");
  setLayout(new FlowLayout());
  setFont(myFont);
  add(new Label(myFont.toString()));
  }
}
```

Try running the program with the following command lines in turn:

java -DFontProp.font=TimesRoman-bold-26 FontProp

java -DFontProp.font=TimesRoman-bolditalic-16 FontProp

java -DFontProp.font=Courier—20 FontProp

Like `ColorProp.java`, this is a very simple program with one method of interest to this discussion. In this case, that method is called in this line:

```
Font myFont = Font.getFont("FontProp.font");
```

This line attempts to load a property called `FontProp.font` from the system properties table. Provided this is successful, the method treats the resulting value as a font name and creates a new `Font` object based on that value. The rest of the program serves only to present a label using this font.

An X Windows Security Weakness

A security weakness exists in font allocation on most X Windows platforms. Attempts to create fonts are not restricted by standard security managers. This opens a potentially nasty denial of service attack in X Windows environments.

If a request is made to create a font with a huge point size, the server will take a long time—perhaps several minutes—to create the necessary data structures. Unfortunately, most X servers, specifically X11-R5 and older, are single-threaded. This means that while the font is being prepared, no other display, keyboard, or mouse activity will be possible. The underlying Unix system will still be running, however, so you might be able to recover from the problem by logging into the machine from another host and issuing a `kill` command.

In addition to hanging the display, the resulting font will take up large amounts of server memory. This might cripple the X server even after the font has been allocated.

Localizing Programs

With the release of JDK 1.1, Java provided significantly more support for localization of programs. Using the idea of a *locale*, the local system administrator or user can specify a preference for the language and other styles, such as currency and data/time format, that the program should use for presenting output.

Several classes were added or enhanced to provide this functionality. The cornerstone of these facilities is the Locale class. The Locale class is used to represent a particular set of presentational preferences. There are up to three parts to a locale: the country, the language, and a variant.

Country and language are represented both with a readable string and with a code. The country codes are defined in ISO-3166; the language codes are defined in ISO-639. Variants describe other specific localizations. Typically, the platform can be represented as POSIX, WIN, or MAC for Posix, Microsoft Windows, or Macintosh, respectively.

A Locale object that reflects the preference of the user can be obtained using the static method Locale.getDefault(). Once a Locale object has been obtained, a number of methods can be used to extract the country, language, and variant from it. The methods getDisplayCountry(), getDisplayLanguage(), and getDisplayVariant() return full strings that are suitable for presentation to the user. Similarly, getDisplayName() represents all the locale information in a single string.

Inside programs, short form representations are often more useful. These may be obtained using the methods getISO3Country(), getISO3Language(), getCountry(), getLanguage(), and getVariant(). The ISO3 versions return the three-character codes specified by the ISO standards; the getCountry() and getLanguage() methods return the two-character strings that are normally used.

You can use the locale information to allow localization of properties. If properties are read from a file, then all that is needed is to build the filename to reflect the locale features. In practice, two modifications are made:

- Several files should be created, using the different aspects of the locale as a hierarchical representation. Hence, if the full locale was made up from country Great Britain, language English, variant Windows, then the files from which to load properties might be prefs, prefs_en, prefs_en_GB, and prefs_en_GB_WIN.

- Since JDK 1.1, the class loader allows you to obtain a stream from a file located in the same place that the class loader obtains classes. This modification allows applets to obtain properties (and other data) from their web servers in a platform- and location-independent way.

The following example demonstrates these principles. The source and bytecode files are located on the CD-ROM in the directory javadevhdbk\ch05.

LIST 5.8   *LocProp.java*

```java
import java.applet.*;
import java.awt.*;
import java.io.*;
import java.util.*;


public class LocProp extends Applet {
  TextArea ta = new TextArea(24, 60);
  Properties props = new Properties();

  Locale loc = Locale.getDefault();
  String extras[] = { "Resources",
                      "_" + loc.getLanguage(),
                      "_" + loc.getCountry(),
                      "_" + loc.getVariant() };

  public LocProp() {
    setLayout(new BorderLayout());
    add("Center", ta);
  }

  public void init() {

    ClassLoader c = getClass().getClassLoader();
    String base = "";

    InputStream resStream = null;

    try {
      for (int i = 0; i < extras.length; i++) {
        base += extras[i];
        System.out.print("Looking for " + base);
```

```
        if (c != null) {
          resStream = c.getResourceAsStream(base);
        }
        else {
          resStream = ClassLoader.getSystemResourceAsStream(base);
        }
        if (resStream != null) {
          System.out.print(" - found");
          props.load(resStream);
        }
        System.out.println();
      }
      ta.setText("");
      Enumeration pe = props.propertyNames();
      while (pe.hasMoreElements()) {
        String key = (String)(pe.nextElement());
        ta.append(key + " = ");
        ta.append(props.getProperty(key) + "\n");
      }
    }
    catch (IOException e) {
      System.err.println("Unexpected exception ");
      e.printStackTrace(System.err);
    }
  }

  public static void main(String args[]) throws Throwable {
    Frame f = new Frame("Localized Properties");
    Applet a = new LocProp();
    f.add("Center", a);
    f.pack();
    f.show();
    a.init();
  }
}
```

You can run this program either as an applet or an application. To run the program as an applet, use your browser or the Applet Viewer to load the HTML file LocProp.html, which is located in the same directory as the class file.

When you run the program, it indicates the names of four files that it tries to load. These filenames are built from the base name Resources, and each is successively extended with the language, country, and variant information of the current locale. Four resource files—Resources, Resources_en_US, Resources_en_GB, and Resources_fr—are provided in the same directory as this program. After the four resource files have been loaded, the resulting properties will be listed in a text area.

> **NOTE** If your locale is not US, British English, or French, then you should copy the locale resource files, along with the file **LocProp.class**, onto your hard disk and create a modified resource file that has a name that reflects your locale. Choose one of the filenames that the program reports it is looking for.

Using the ClassLoader Object

The LocProp.java program demonstrates the use of the ClassLoader object to obtain a stream from a location that depends on the origin of the class that makes the request. If the program is run as an application, the resource stream will originate from a file located in a directory somewhere on the CLASSPATH. If the program is run as an applet, the resource will originate from a file at the same base URL as the applet class file itself.

To load a resource in this way, the code must locate the class loader that is to be used. This is done by first using the getClass() method on the current object (which is the applet), and then using the getClassLoader() method on the Class object that was returned. The getClass() method is a member of the Object class; the getClassLoader() method is a member of the Class class.

If a class was loaded from the local system, then it is loaded by the *primordial* class loader—that is, the class loader that is built into the base Java distribution. Calling the getClassLoader() method on such a class returns null. Under these conditions, it is necessary to use the static method ClassLoader.getSystem-ResourceAsStream(). For classes loaded from remote systems, however, a non-null ClassLoader reference is returned by the getClassLoader() method, and that reference can be used to invoke the getResourceAsStream() method.

Internationalizing Programs

Along with the ability to load locally appropriate resources by using elements of the current locale as part of the filename, a generalized mechanism is built into Java (since JDK 1.1) for internationalization of programs. This internationalization mechanism depends on the locale element names in the same way as localization does (as demonstrated in the LocProp.java example).

Instead of simply defining properties, however, the internationalization mechanism defines whole subclasses and allows arbitrary objects to be written in a variety of locale-dependent ways. At runtime, the correct variant to load is determined according to the locale. This mechanism is embodied in the java.util.Resource-Bundle class. As with the LocProp.java example, the resources are loaded via the class loader, and are therefore obtained from the same location as the class that requests them.

The class PropertyResourceBundle allows you to create a resource bundle for key/value pairs that are Strings. The constructor for PropertyResourceBundle takes an InputStream as its argument and reads strings of the form *"key=value"* from that stream. In this way, you can create the same effect as the LocProp.java example by simply subclassing PropertyResourceBundle for each locale and in each subclass, specifying an appropriate FileInputStream in the constructor, like this:

```
public class MyProperties_en_GB extends PropertyResourceBundle {
  public MyProperties_en_GB() {
    try {
      super(new FileInputStream("myProps_en_GB");
    }
    catch (IOException e) {
      throw new RuntimeException("File Not Found");
    }
  }
}
```

Network Class Loading

Java is very flexible about the sources from which bytecode can be obtained. Because it is so easy to use a browser and see code being loaded from a web server or from the browser's own local machine, as required, it is easy to believe that Java has some "magic" and that classes are loaded automatically without any setup or intervention being needed. In reality, the user has this impression because the web site administrators and developers, of both Java and the individual programs, have done their jobs properly.

If you are to distribute your programs successfully, whether they are applets or applications, you will need an understanding of the mechanisms that Java uses to locate a class that it must load. This section discusses those mechanisms and the configuration options that are available to the developer and web site administrator when installing Java applets for distribution.

Deferring Class Loading

To construct an instance of a class, invoke a static method, or access a static variable, the definition for that class must first be loaded into the JVM. A class must also be loaded if it is a superclass of some other class that is also being used.

If an applet refers to several other classes but uses them only in special conditions, this means that usually these classes are not required at all. It would therefore be a waste of network bandwidth to insist on loading all of the classes every time the applet is loaded. The loading would also delay the startup of the applet.

For these reasons, class loading is deferred until the last possible moment. This is not restricted to applets, but applies to any Java class. So, if an applet has instance variables of types HerClass and HisClass, then the class files for these will not be loaded until they are actually required.

It is possible to demonstrate this effect. At the instant a class is loaded, before any constructor or static method can be called or any static variable accessed, the class undergoes static initialization. This process initializes all the static variables and also invokes any static initializer code blocks. Consider this class skeleton:

```
public class StaticStuff {
  static int x = 7;
  public StaticStuff() {
    // constructor code
  }
  static {
    // this is a static initializer block
    x += 3;
  }
}
```

When the class is loaded, *all* the static initialization is done in sequence, both variable and code blocks. Here, the value of x is first set to 7 and then the body of the static initializer is executed. This increases the value of x by 3, resulting in a value of 10. Multiple static initializer blocks are allowed in a class (although this looks odd and it is difficult to conceive a reason for wanting to do this).

The static initializer can be used to determine the instant that a class is loaded. The following example demonstrates that classes are only loaded when actually required. The source for this example is located on the CD-ROM in the directory javadevhdbk/ch05/C1.java. The corresponding bytecode is located in the same directory in the files C1.class and C2.class.

LIST 5.9   *C1.java*

```java
public class C1 {
  C2 that;

  public static void main(String args[]) {
    C2 other;
    System.out.println("I'm started. Pausing for effect....");
    try {
      Thread.sleep(3000);
    }
    catch (InterruptedException e) {
    }
    System.out.println("About to create a C2.");
    other = new C2();
    System.out.println("C2 created, bye.");
  }
}

class C2 {
  static {
    System.out.println("I'm C2 being loaded");
  }
}
```

The output of the program is:

```
I'm started. Pausing for effect....
About to create a C2.
I'm C2 being loaded
C2 created, bye.
```

This output shows that the static initializer block of the class C2 is not executed until immediately before the call is made to the constructor for that class. This demonstrates the loading of the class has been deferred until the class was actually needed.

Forcing Class Loading

It is possible to force loading of a class even in the absence of an immediately visible requirement for it. This might be done deliberately to enhance running response of a program at the expense of startup time. If the user has a dial-on-demand network connection with a standard modem, this approach might be particularly appropriate. Under such conditions, if the network remains idle for a period, the modem drops the phone line. The connection is reestablished automatically when needed. This reestablishment takes a significant amount of time and, if done regularly, also makes for very inefficient use of modem time.

You can achieve *forced loading* using a static method in the class java.lang .Class called forName(). This method takes a string argument that defines the fully qualified class name, which is the class name with the package name included. The following code fragment demonstrates this approach.

LIST 5.10   **ForceLoad.java**

```java
public class ForceLoad {
  ForceLoaded that;

  public static void main(String args[]) {
    ForceLoaded other;
    System.out.println("I'm started. Pausing for effect....");
    try {
      Thread.sleep(3000);
    }
    catch (InterruptedException e) {
    }
    System.out.println("About to create a ForceLoaded.");
    other = new ForceLoaded();
    System.out.println("ForceLoaded created, bye.");
  }

  static {
    try {
      Class.forName("ForceLoaded");
    }
```

```
        catch (ClassNotFoundException e) {
          // let it show up later
        }
      }
    }

    class ForceLoaded {
      static {
        System.out.println("I'm ForceLoaded being loaded");
      }
    }
```

This example is deliberately almost identical to the previous example, C1.java. ForceLoad.java. It is located on the CD-ROM in the same directory and may be run in the same way as C1.java. However, you will notice one main difference: the ForceLoaded class, which parallels the C2 class in the previous example, is actually loaded before any of the mainstream processing occurs.

Security Effects

Java provides a framework for security that allows a user to run an unknown applet with reasonable confidence that the applet will be prevented from performing any malicious actions, such as modifying files or stealing private data. From a programmer's point of view, such prevention can have an impact. For instance, many services that an applet developer might like to use, such as opening a temporary file, will be prohibited. Furthermore, the precise set of operations that are prohibited can vary to an extent between platforms and even between different browsers or different users on the same platform.

Java 2 introduced a configuration mechanism that allows each user to reconfigure his or her own security policy, so some hosts might be much more generous than normal, while others might reject even quite innocuous requests. Because of these considerations, it is important for a developer to understand the background to security and the ways in which the conventional applet restrictions in particular affect the programmer's freedom. This section discusses these points.

Java security is normally discussed in the context of applets. This is because applets, running in browsers, are governed by prewritten security code. However, it is important to be aware that the security mechanism that browsers apply to applets is a general one, and it is possible to design and implement specific security policies on applications. Also, modified security policies can be imposed on existing browsers, although sometimes it might require a specialist's knowledge of the innards of the particular browser—or persistent guesswork.

In general, security must cover two areas:

- During and after execution of the applet, the machine facilities, CPU, memory, and so forth should remain under the control of, and available to, the legitimate user. "Foreign" code should not be able to usurp that control or make runaway use of the system.

- Data stored on the machine and any network companions must be protected against modification, damage, or unauthorized access.

Protecting Against Denial of Service Attacks

Java, in its current versions, does not actively attempt to ensure that facilities remain under the user's control. Attacks in this category are termed *denial of service*. Competent operating systems allocate all resources to user processes on a "fair shares" basis and, as such, no single process should be able to make runaway use of the system. In practice, this assumption is possibly a shade optimistic.

It can be very irritating to have a browser's performance reduced by a greedy applet. At the worst, such an attack might necessitate exiting and restarting the browser. Java's fundamental assumption is that the denial of service attacks are irritating but not debilitating. Currently, most browsers arrange that the thread that runs an applet's init() method is in a thread group, which limits the maximum priority. However, this alone is not sufficient to protect against a denial of service attack. Future versions of Java are likely to tighten up protection in this situation.

Protecting Data

Protection of data is, by contrast, something that Java considers absolutely paramount. Several convenient facilities are strictly prohibited to applets on these grounds.

Data protection can be considered in two categories: protection against unauthorized reading and protection against unauthorized modification. Java browsers go to great lengths to prevent applets from obtaining information that they might be able to misuse. Several properties are unavailable to applets because even knowledge as apparently innocuous as the user's login name on the host machine could be misused. At the low-damage end of the scale, the login name could be used to direct unwanted marketing information via e-mail; at the serious end, it provides an attacker with a target username, which is a valuable first step towards a complete break-in.

It is in the nature of the World Wide Web and other Internet services that it is generally possible for an applet to transmit information to any host that is waiting to receive it. Because it is impossible to prevent an applet from talking to any cooperating remote server, it is therefore vital to restrict the information that it can obtain. You should not, therefore, write applets in such a way that they need to access anything on local file systems, HTML pages, or any other source that might be considered sensitive. To attempt to do so will almost certainly result in an applet that fails to run in a properly platform-independent way.

NOTE   In the controlled environment of an intranet, it might be acceptable to allow applets access to files in certain controlled directories. Some browsers, most notably the Applet Viewer, are able to support this facility. However, access should not be permitted if the browser has any ability to load applets from untrusted hosts.

Protection against unauthorized changes to data is enforced with no less rigor. Again, therefore, applets should be coded in such a way that they do not need to be able to access any local data. For example, any attempt to use the class `File-OutputStream` will normally be rejected.

Summary

This chapter has discussed a wide variety of topics, all loosely related by their impact on the portability of Java program code. Different platforms run with different native data formats, different file system layouts, different CPU speeds, and different thread-scheduling algorithms. Windowing systems affect the layout, appearance, colors, and size of visible elements of a GUI program. Individuals might want the opportunity to configure a running Java program to their own preferences. Classes must be accessible for loading at runtime, and applets are restricted by the security manager. All these aspects require consideration when a program is being developed if the result is to run smoothly and inconspicuously on all Java platforms.

PART II

Advanced Topics

CHAPTER

SIX

6

Images

- What an image really is

- Image observers

- Java's `MemoryImageSource` class

- Color models and images

- Image producers, consumers, and filters

- `java.awt.image.BufferedImage` class

Images have a big job to do. It takes a lot to make an image, especially if the source is some file out on the network. The bits that represent the image must be loaded from the network and stored locally. From the users' perspective, all of this processing should have a minimal impact on their computer's performance. From the programmers' perspective, the process of moving pixel information from the network to the windowing system should be encapsulated in the various support classes, so that to the greatest extent possible, the whole arrangement is hidden.

In practice, the whole arrangement is indeed hidden, but it's like a slightly fat bear hiding behind a slightly thin tree—there are places where bits of the bear stick out into view, alarming the casual passerby. Many image-related methods require a mysterious extra parameter of type `ImageObserver`. The `getImage()` method seems to return immediately, even when loading a large image from a slow network. Sometimes you can create an off-screen image, and sometimes you cannot.

There are two important things to learn from this chapter. The first is the way that the image infrastructure works. Equally important is an understanding of which parts of that infrastructure can be usefully modified and which are best left alone.

The Image Infrastructure

The `Image` class is abstract. You never construct one (that would be impossible because the class is abstract). Instead, you have two options: You can call the `createImage()` method or you can create an instance of the `java.awt.image` `.BufferedImage` class.

Most of this chapter concerns images that are created with `createImage()`. The `BufferedImage` class was introduced as part of the JDK release 1.2. This class is easy to use, but it does not offer the functionality that is available when you call `createImage()`. The `BufferedImage` class is discussed at the end of this chapter.

Image Creation and Retrieval

The `createImage()` method is part of the `Component` class. Usually, the component's `createImage()` method just tells its peer to `createImage()`. The peer is a platform-specific bundle of calls to native methods. Thus, the object returned by `createImage()` is a platform-specific subclass of `Image`. Not surprisingly, its methods are primarily calls to native methods.

For example, consider what happens in a `createImage()` call in the `init()` of an applet running on a Solaris/Motif platform. The applet's peer is a subclass of `MComponentPeer` in the `sun.awt.motif` package. The `MComponentPeer` class has its own `createImage()` method that constructs and returns an instance of `X11Image`, which is a concrete subclass of the abstract `Image` class. After much intricate processing, the `X11Image` constructor causes native calls into the Solaris/Motif version of the Java library; a pixel map is created in the X server, and the `X11Image` communicates with this map.

NOTE   The handling of the `Image` class is a perfect example of polymorphism. As programmers, we believe that we are using an instance of class **Image**. In fact, we are using whatever subclass of **Image** is appropriate to our platform; the chore of deciding which subclass to use is taken care of for us. The entire mechanism is so well encapsulated that we never even need to know about it. Many successful Java programs have been written by people who were not aware that **Image** is abstract.

Using `createImage()`, you can create a fresh image. You also can load an image from a remote file, via the `getImage()` method of the `Component` class. Here, Java goes to great lengths to optimize performance. The simplest strategy would be for `getImage()` to make a connection to the machine that owns the remote graphics file, load the file, parse it, and construct and return an image. This strategy would be adequate in a perfect world, but in the real world, it could likely introduce extreme delays, for two reasons:

- The connection to the remote machine might be slow. The applet would waste cycles idling while waiting for network response.

- The user might never bring the applet into a state where the image was needed. The time spent in loading the image would have been wasted.

To avoid these problems, Java enforces the following policies with respect to remote image files:

- All remote images are loaded by asynchronous threads.

- These threads do not begin to load until the corresponding image is used, or *observed*.

The mechanisms that enforce these policies are almost completely hidden from programmers. Programmatically, the biggest clue that something is going on is that certain methods require an extra parameter of type ImageObserver. Behaviorally, the biggest clue that Java is doing something complicated is when an applet flashes the first time it paints a large image.

Readers who are unfamiliar with image flashing are invited to run the Flasher applet. The first time the program runs in any browser session, the image does not appear all at once on the screen; rather, it grows in vertical chunks, with a repaint flash between chunks. The textfield at the top of the applet indicates that the applet is receiving an extraordinary number of repaint() calls. The code for the applet is quite simple and appears below and on the CD-ROM in javadevhdbk\ch06\ Flasher.java. The bytecode is on the CD-ROM in javadevhdbk\ch06\Flasher .class. At the end of the listing is a method that would eliminate the flashing if it were not commented out. The reasons for the flashing and the fix are explained in the next section.

LIST 6.1   *Flasher.java*

```java
import    java.awt.*;
import    java.awt.image.*;
import    java.applet.Applet;


public class Flasher extends Applet
{
    Image        im;
    TextField    tf;
    int          nRepaints;
    int          nPaints;

    public void init()
    {
        setLayout(new BorderLayout());
        tf = new TextField();
        add(tf, BorderLayout.NORTH);

        // Load image from server of applet.
        im = getImage(getDocumentBase(), "Hammock.jpg");
    }
```

```
// This is the version of repaint() called by imageUpdate().
public void repaint(long tm, int x, int y, int w, int h)
{
    nRepaints++;
    super.repaint(tm, x, y, w, h);
}

public void paint(Graphics g)
{
    nPaints++;
    tf.setText(nRepaints + " repaints, " + nPaints + " paints, " +
                "width = " + im.getWidth(this) +
                ", height = " + im.getHeight(this));
    g.drawImage(im, 0, 0, this);
}

/**** Un-comment this method to eliminate flashing *********
***** without using a MediaTracker. ************************
public boolean imageUpdate(Image img, int flags,
                            int x, int y, int width, int height)
{
    if ((flags & ImageObserver.ALLBITS) != 0)
        repaint();
    return true;
}
************************************************************/
}
```

Image Observers

The image-observer mechanism is an example of the Observer design pattern. The idea is to permit an object to be "observed" by an arbitrary number of other objects. When the object being observed experiences a change that the observers should know about, the observed object makes a method call to all the observers. The object being observed has the discretion to decide when the observers should be notified.

NOTE   For programmers who wish to apply the Observer/Observed paradigm to their own designs, Java offers the interfaces Observer and Observable in the util package. Images do not actually use these interfaces.

In Java's paradigm, the color values for an image are delivered by an object that implements the `ImageProducer` interface, which is covered in detail later in this chapter. For a remote image, the image producer is a thread that communicates via TCP/IP with the server that contains the image file.

Recall Java's policy that the producer thread will run asynchronously (in the background), not beginning its work until the image is observed. For this reason, `getImage()` returns immediately. The value returned is a reference to an instance of `Image` with width and height both set to -1. Eventually, the width and height will be set to the correct values.

Several methods can make the system decide that the image has been observed. The most common is `Graphics.drawImage()`, which renders the image onto the screen. This method requires an extra parameter of type `ImageObserver`, which is an interface, not a class. The `Component` class implements the interface. The easiest way to call `Graphics.drawImage()` is to pass as the image observer a reference to the component in which the image is being rendered.

The call to `drawImage()` causes the image's producer to start producing. Periodically, the producer delivers new information to the image and then makes a call to the `imageUpdate()` method of the image's observer. The meaning of the call is, "The image has changed, and here's how, and you might want to do something about it." The API for `imageUpdate()` is:

```
public boolean imageUpdate(Image im, int flags,
                           int x, int y, int width, int height)
```

The `flags` parameter describes the new information being reported by the current `imageUpdate()` call. The x, y, width, and height parameters specify the bounding box of the image data delivered so far. However, the four bounding box parameters cannot be depended on to be valid unless they are referred to by one of the flags. The `flags` values are described in Table 6.1.

TABLE 6.1: The flags Values for imageUpdate()

Value	Meaning
ImageObserver.WIDTH	The image's width has been updated and may be read from the `width` parameter or from the image's `getWidth()` method.
ImageObserver.HEIGHT	The image's height has been updated and may be read from the `height` parameter or from the image's `getHeight()` method.

Continued on next page

TABLE 6.1 CONTINUED: The flags Values for imageUpdate()

Value	Meaning
`ImageObserver.PROPERTIES`	The image's properties have been updated and may be read from the image's `getProperties()` method.
`ImageObserver.SOMEBITS`	More pixels have been delivered for an image.
`ImageObserver.FRAMEBITS`	A complete frame of a multiple-frame image has been delivered.
`ImageObserver.ALLBITS`	The image is complete.
`ImageObserver.ERROR`	An error has occurred in production.
`ImageObserver.ABORT`	Production has been abnormally terminated.

For example, the `width` parameter should not be used unless the `WIDTH` bit of the `flags` values is set. Even when set, the value of `width` is just the current width. In most cases, images are produced row by row so that `width` attains its ultimate value early in the process, but this cannot be guaranteed. Generally, `height` does not get set to its ultimate value until production is all but finished.

The `imageUpdate()` method of `Component` just calls `repaint()` so that the more complete image is rendered. This could easily result in several hundred calls to `repaint()`, which does little harm since most of those calls do nothing. Recall that `repaint()` just requests a call to `update()` in the near future. Most of the calls occur after some other call has already made the request but before the update thread has run, so nothing happens. The hundreds of calls to `repaint()` result in only a few calls to `update()` and `paint()`. Those few calls, however, will produce a visible flashing of the image as `update()` clears the screen and `paint()` draws the incomplete image. You saw how the flashing occurs in the `Flasher` applet presented in the previous section. `Flasher` demonstrates the flashing phenomenon, the number of calls to `paint()` and `repaint()`, and the image's size.

One way to eliminate the flashing is to override `imageUpdate()` so that it only repaints when the complete image is available. The code below does the trick (this is the code that is commented out in `Flasher`):

```
public boolean imageUpdate(Image img, int flags,
                           int x, int y, int width, int height)
{
    if ((flags & ImageObserver.ALLBITS) != 0)
```

```
        repaint();
    return true;
}
```

This fix certainly works, but if there are multiple images, the code gets a bit more complicated (it would be desirable to repaint only once, when all the images are complete). Moreover, if this is happening in an applet or frame of any complexity, layout considerations may call for subdivision into panels. In this case, some of the logic from imageUpdate() must be moved into the subpanel's own imageUpdate() method. Overriding imageUpdate() is generally not the best strategy for waiting for an image. A much better way is to use the java.awt.MediaTracker class, which is the subject of the next section.

The Media Tracker

It often happens that an applet or application cannot do anything useful until certain images are fully loaded. A prime example is an applet that just presents an animation. If the animation is begun before all the frames are available, somewhere there will be a delay or blank frame. As things stand, this situation is a deadlock. The image is not to be displayed until it is loaded, but the system will not even start to load the image until it tries to display the image.

The MediaTracker class solves the problem by providing a sly, unseen observer for each image so the pixel-loading thread can be kicked off on demand. This mechanism is hidden from the programmer, who simply registers images with the tracker.

The constructor for MediaTracker is:

```
MediaTracker(Component target)
```

The target parameter can be any component, but for ease of reading, it should be something simple, such as the applet.

After an image is created via getImage(), it can be registered with a tracker with the addImage() method:

```
tracker.addImage(image, n);
```

Here, image is the image to be tracked. The second parameter is an ID or category. The tracker can be asked to load all of its images or just those images with a certain ID. The methods are described below:

> void waitForAll() throws InterruptedException   Waits until all registered images are loaded.

void waitForID(int id) throws InterruptedException   Waits until all images with the specified ID are loaded.

Both methods block the current thread until the images are loaded. The Media-Tracker supports various other forms of waiting and offers several forms of checking; it also supports unregistering an image. These facilities are straightforward and are adequately documented in the class API.

NOTE

When a method such as waitForAll() blocks, its thread gives up the CPU and does not become eligible for running until the condition on which it blocked is satisfied (or, more rarely, until the call is interrupted). At that point, the thread does not necessarily run; it must contend with other runnable threads. See Chapter 7 for more information about threads.

Typically, a program that provides several different animations will use one ID for each animation. All frames (that is, images) for the first animation will use ID = 0, all frames for the second animation will use ID = 1, and so on.

The code to use a media tracker to load an image might look like this (the exception handler has been omitted for simplicity but should be present in any complete program):

```
public void init()
{
    MediaTracker tracker = new MediaTracker(this);
    im = getImage(getDocumentBase(), "images/xyz.gif");
    tracker.addImage(im, 0);
    try
    {
        tracker.waitForID(0);
    }
    catch (InterruptedException excep) { }
}
```

Images and Applications

For an applet, the obvious place to create or load an image is in the applet's init() method. Applications do not have an init() method, but they do have frames, and frames have constructors. As a general rule, tasks that an applet would perform in init() should be done in the constructor of an application's main frame.

This approach does not work with image initialization. Both getImage() and createImage() rely on the image-supporting resources of the underlying windowing system. In an applet, this is no problem; by the time init() is called, the applet has been installed within the browser and its connection with the windowing system has been established. This is not the case with a frame in an application.

In Java, all components—including applets and frames—are just ones and zeros somewhere in memory. They remain no more than abstract representations until they are "realized," which happens when a call is made to the component's addNotify() method. At this point, the underlying windowing system is called on (through native methods in the component's peer) to create its own local-style equivalent of the component. It is as if a component that has been realized casts a shadow onto the screen. A component's addNotify() method is most commonly called by the system when its container is realized.

The createImage() method only works if it is executed by a realized component. In an applet, by the time init() is called, the applet has been realized—its addNotify() method has been called, and it has been added into its browser. The applet is already "casting a shadow" onto the screen.

An application's frame is not realized until its show() method is executed. This method, inherited from the Window superclass, calls addNotify(). Before this happens, the frame's createImage() method will return null.

In general, images should be created as soon as possible after addNotify(). The best way to do this is to override addNotify(), calling the superclass version and then initializing the images. Because there is no guarantee that addNotify() will be called only once, it is a good idea to have a boolean instance variable to ensure that initialization happens only once. The code below implements this strategy:

```
public void addNotify()
{
    super.addNotify();
    if (!imagesInitialized)
    {
        image = createImage(100, 100);
        imagesInitialized = true;
    }
}
```

The Memory Image Source

So far, this chapter has been concerned with loading images from external files. Another source for images is memory. A program can build an int or byte array to represent pixel values and use Java's MemoryImageSource class to construct an instance of Image.

MemoryImageSource has a variety of options for representing colors. Only the simplest option will be discussed in this section; other ways to specify what Java calls "the color model" will be discussed in the next section.

The input to MemoryImageSource in its most simple form is an array of ints. Each int consists of 8 bits (position 0 to 7) to represent blue, 8 bits (8 to 15) to represent green, and 8 bits (16 to 23) to represent red. The most significant 8 bits (24 to 31) are the color's alpha or opacity.

> **NOTE** True opacity can be represented only on very expensive hardware. Affordable systems render inaccessible transparency combinations the same way that they render other inaccessible colors—by dithering.

Life would be easy if the array were two-dimensional. Unfortunately, it is one-dimensional, with pixel values laid out as might be expected. For an image with n columns, the first n ints represent the first scan line, the second n ints represent the second scan line, and so on.

After the array is formatted, a memory image source can be constructed from the entire array or from a portion of it. The MemoryImageSource constructor needs to be passed the size of the desired image, the int array, an offset into the array, and the width of the hypothetical image represented by the int array. This last parameter is required in case the desired image is to be a subset of the hypothetical full image.

The constructor for MemoryImageSource is called as follows:

```
MemoryImageSource(int width, int height, int[] pixels,
                  int arrayOffset, int scanwidth)
```

Figure 6.1 shows how the int array becomes an image. Bear in mind that no instance of Image is actually created until the MemoryImageSource is told to create one.

FIGURE 6.1:

How an int array becomes an image

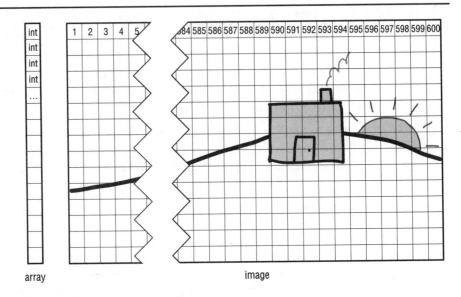

array

image

The Airbrush applet on the CD-ROM uses a MemoryImageSource to build nine airbrush images. Each image has pixels of a single color (red, green, and so on) but with an alpha that drops off with distance from the center of the image. The greater the distance from the center, the thinner the paint. The code that populates the nine arrays is as follows:

```
int sources[][] = new int[9][BRUSH_AREA];
for (j=0; j<BRUSH_SIZE; j++)
{
    for (i=0; i<BRUSH_SIZE; i++)
    {
        alpha = getAlpha(i, j);
        alpha <<= 24;
        sources[RED][index]     = 0x00ff0000 + alpha;
        sources[GREEN][index]   = 0x0000ff00 + alpha;
        sources[BLUE][index]    = 0x000000ff + alpha;
        sources[YELLOW][index]  = 0x00ffff00 + alpha;
        sources[MAGENTA][index] = 0x00ff00ff + alpha;
        sources[CYAN][index]    = 0x0000ffff + alpha;
        sources[BLACK][index]   = 0x00000000 + alpha;
        sources[GRAY][index]    = 0x00b8b8b8 + alpha;
        sources[WHITE][index]   = 0x00ffffff + alpha;
        index++;
    }
}
```

The getAlpha() method returns an alpha in the low 8 bits of an int. The alpha drops off in proportion to the sixth power of the distance from the center, because that seems to produce the most airbrush-like effect. The code is shown below:

```
int getAlpha(int x, int y)
{
    double deltaX = (double)(x - BRUSH_SIZE/2);
    double deltaY = (double)(y - BRUSH_SIZE/2);
    double distance = Math.sqrt(deltaX*deltaX +
                        deltaY*deltaY);
    double fracDistance = distance / (BRUSH_SIZE/2);
    if (fracDistance > 1.0)
        fracDistance = 1.0;
    fracDistance = 1.0 - fracDistance;
    fracDistance = Math.pow(fracDistance, 6);
    return (int)(255 * fracDistance);
}
```

Figure 6.2 shows a picture created with Airbrush. Of course, this is a monochrome screenshot, and readers are encouraged to create their own on-screen multicolor masterpieces.

FIGURE 6.2:

Airbrush special effects

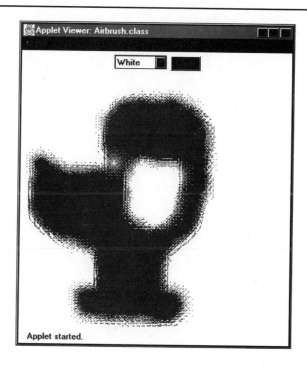

The `MemoryImageSource` class has methods that support multiple-frame images. The `setAnimate()` method tells the memory image source that it is to be the source of a multiple-frame image. The `newPixels()` method supplies the memory image source with the next frame's pixels.

Color Models

An image is a collection of zeros and ones. A rendered image is an arrangement of colors. Some sort of convention is required to translate between binary numbers and screen colors. In Java, that convention is encapsulated in color models. We discussed Java's color models in Chapter 5, in the context of portability and running Java programs on platforms with different color capabilities. Here, we'll go into more detail about the models and their relationship to images.

Recall that Java represents a color as 32 bits. By default, there are 8 bits for alpha, 8 for red, 8 for green, and 8 for blue. These values fit conveniently into an int, as shown in Figure 6.3.

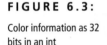

FIGURE 6.3:

Color information as 32 bits in an int

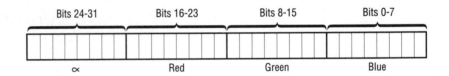

What Figure 6.3 really shows is Java's default color model; in other words, this is the convention by which Java maps bits to colors (and transparencies). When an int is passed to the constructor for a `Color`, it is expected to be in the format shown in the figure. When an array of ints is passed to the constructor for a `MemoryImageSource`, all the ints are likewise expected to be in this format.

A program is free to create other color models. The class `ColorModel` (in package `java.awt.image`) has several subclasses, including `DirectColorModel` and `Index-ColorModel`. These two subclasses are discussed in the following sections.

Direct Color Models

`DirectColorModel` supports a custom partition of the 32-bit int into bit positions and numbers of bits to represent alpha, red, green, and blue. With a direct color model, the program specifies which and how many bits of an int represent which of the four attributes (alpha, red, green, and blue). The bits of an attribute must be contiguous and may not overlap the bits of any other attribute.

There are two constructors for class `DirectColorModel`. Both expect an int to specify the width in bits of the model (32 for modern color models, but older systems might only use 8) and one int each for red, green, and blue. Optionally, a fifth int may be supplied to specify alpha. The API for the constructors is as follows:

```
DirectColorModel(int nbits, int redmask, int greenmask,
                 int bluemask)
DirectColorModel(int nbits, int redmask, int greenmask,
                 int bluemask, int alphamask)
```

The masks are just ints with bits set to mark where in the int the corresponding color will be found. For example, a color model that uses 1 bit to represent red, 3 bits for green, and 20 bits for blue would be constructed as follows:

```
model = new DirectColorModel(32, 0x800000, 0x700000, 0x0fffff);
```

 The applet DCModelLab, found on the CD-ROM in `javadevhdbk\ch06\`
`DCModelLab.java` and `DCModelLab.class`, makes it easy to see how an int will be translated into a color via the standard color model and also via a custom direct color model specified by the user. Figure 6.4 shows the program's window. You can run the program and enter the values shown in the figure. The pixel value is `0xff000f`. With the standard model, this means red = 255, green = 0, and blue = 15. This is very close to plain red, and the rectangle on the lower left, representing `0xff000f` as interpreted through the standard color model, is indeed red (unfortunately, you can't see this in the black-and-white figure).

With the custom color model, red is represented by 20 bits, or 5 hex digits. Green and blue get only 2 bits each. The red value is `ff000` out of a possible `fffff`, which amounts to 99.6 percent. Green and blue are both 3 out of a possible 3. Because all three colors are full intensity, or very nearly so, the result is white.

FIGURE 6.4:

FIGURE 6.4:

The DCModelLab program

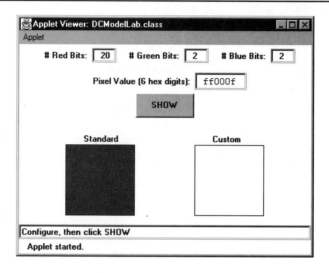

TIP

If you are developing your own custom direct color models, you can use the DCModelLab program to speed the process.

Indexed Color Models

IndexColorModel supports a lookup table of red, green, and blue values. Colors are represented by bytes, which are used to index into the table. The true color values are ints in the table, which are interpreted according to the default color model.

There are actually three lookup tables—one for each primary color (optionally, a fourth may be used for alpha). Each table entry contains 8 bits that specify color intensity. For example, if byte 3 is to represent cyan, element 3 in the red table should be 0, and in both the green and blue tables, it should be 255. When a byte color is to be rendered, a lookup is made into the tables, and the values retrieved are used to build up a 32-bit color value as it would be represented by the default color model.

For images that use relatively few colors, indexed color models provide a convenient mapping mechanism. This mechanism is especially useful when the image to be constructed represents digital information. For example, a weather satellite might generate two-dimensional arrays of ints that represent air pressure. A mapping satellite might generate maps in the form of ints representing altitude. The best way to portray this information visually is to correlate each int value in the map with a color.

Indexed color models are also useful for rendering fractals, for elementary ray tracing, and for other geometrical applications where a pixel's position is mapped to a bounded int, usually by a time-consuming algorithm in the domain of pure mathematics.

The constructor for the IndexColorModel class is heavily overloaded. The simplest form is:

```
IndexColorModel(int nbits, int ncolors,
                byte reds[], byte greens[], byte blues[])
```

Here nbits is the number of bits used in the index; small models need not use all 8 bits of the byte. The ncolors parameter is the number of colors in the model, which is the size of the lookup table. The next three parameters are byte arrays that give the red, green, and blue levels; the size of all three arrays should be ncolors.

The main benefit of an indexed color model is the encapsulation of the lookup process. A beneficial side effect is that it takes only 8 bits, rather than 32 bits, to represent a pixel. This is a 75 percent savings, which can mount up impressively if a program uses several large images. Yet another benefit is enhanced image-filtering performance, which is discussed later in this chapter.

 The SquareMIS applet shows how to use an indexed color model and a memory image source to draw a white box on a blue background. The applet is listed below and is on the CD-ROM in javadevhdbk\ch06\SquareMIS.java and SquareMIS.class.

LIST 6.2   *SquareMIS.java*

```
import  java.awt.*;
import  java.awt.image.*;
import  java.applet.Applet;
```

```
public class SquareMIS extends Applet
{
    Image    image;


    public void init()
    {
        ColorModel            model;
        MemoryImageSource     mis;

        // Build the color model.
        //                  color #0    color #1
        //                  white       blue
        byte reds[]   = {(byte)0xff, (byte)0x00};
        byte greens[] = {(byte)0xff, (byte)0x00};
        byte blues[]  = {(byte)0xff, (byte)0xff};
        model = new IndexColorModel(2, 2, reds, greens, blues);

        // Build array of bytes.
        int width = getSize().width;
        int height = getSize().height;
        byte pix[] = new byte[width*height];
        int n = 0;
        for (int j=0; j<height; j++)
        {
            for (int i=0; i<width; i++)
            {
                if (i > width/4   &&  i < width*3/4    &&
                    j > height/4  &&  j < height*3/4)
                {
                    pix[n] = 0;
                }
                else
                {
                    pix[n] = 1;
                }
                n++;
            }
        }

        // Build a memory image source and have it build an
        // image.
```

```
        mis = new MemoryImageSource(width, height,
                                    model, pix, 0, width);
        image = createImage(mis);
    }



    public void paint(Graphics g)
    {
        g.drawImage(image, 0, 0, this);
    }
}
```

Producers, Consumers, and Filters

Both the hidden objects that turn a remote GIF (Graphics Interchange Format) file into pixel values and the quite visible memory image source are examples of *image producers*. They implement the ImageProducer interface, which is found in the java.awt.image package. Image producers have the job of delivering pixel values to image consumers. In addition to ImageProducer, there is also an Image-Consumer interface in the java.awt.image package, and the creation of an image is the result of a dialogue between producer and consumer.

Java also supports a filter paradigm: between production and consumption there may be any number of filters. Figure 6.5 shows a metaphor for this process.

Image Producers and Image Consumers

Programmers are more concerned with creating image producers than with creating image consumers. However, there are many situations where creating a producer is not the best strategy, as you will see shortly.

The producer/consumer dialogue is initiated by the consumer, which tells the producer to start producing. The producer's appropriate response is to report the size of the image if possible and then to begin computing pixel values (or to begin marshaling them from a file on a remote server). From time to time, the producer delivers fresh pixels to the consumer and tells the consumer when that task is done. Figure 6.6 illustrates the sequence of calls.

FIGURE 6.5:

Production, consumption,
and filtering

The producer

Falling hot water

Falling charcoal-filtered hot water

Falling coffee...

The consumer

FIGURE 6.6:

The producer/consumer dialogue

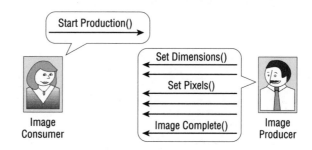

NOTE   Figure 6.6 is an oversimplification. Both interfaces are more extensive than shown.
ImageProducer has methods that permit more than one consumer to register
with the producer. **ImageConsumer** has methods that permit the producer to supply more information about the image and the production process.

The ImageProducer Interface

The API for ImageProducer is as follows:

> void addConsumer(ImageConsumer ic)   Registers the consumer with the
> producer.

> boolean isConsumer(ImageConsumer ic)   Tells whether the consumer is
> currently registered with the producer.

> void removeConsumer(ImageConsumer ic)   Unregisters the consumer with
> the producer.

> void startProduction(ImageConsumer ic)   Registers the consumer and
> directs the producer to begin computing pixel values.

> void requestTopDownLeftRightResend(ImageConsumer ic)   Requests the
> producer to resend the pixel data. This is called in the unlikely event that
> the producer generates pixels in random order. Presumably, it has previ-
> ously generated the image and cached the pixels so now it can very
> quickly resend everything, row by row. A producer that sends pixels row
> by row anyway may safely ignore this call.

An image producer is expected to maintain a list of its consumers and report
generated information to every consumer.

The ImageConsumer Interface

Image information is reported to image consumers via the calls of the Image-Consumer interface, as follows:

void setDimensions(int width, int height)   Tells the consumer the size of the image.

void setColorModel(ColorModel cm)   Tells the consumer which color model will be primarily used when pixels are sent. setPixels(), which is called arbitrarily many times, is free to use a different color model each call; setColorModel() tells the consumer which model will be most commonly used in case the consumer can use this information to improve performance.

void setHints(int hints)   Tells the consumer how the pixels will be generated in case the consumer can use this information to improve performance. The value of the hints parameter is an OR (|) of the following constants of ImageConsumer:

RANDOMPIXELORDER   Pixel values will be delivered in random order.

TOPDOWNLEFTRIGHT   Pixel values will be delivered row by row, and pixel by pixel within each row.

COMPLETESCANLINES   Every call to setPixels() will deliver complete scan lines.

SINGLEPASS   Every pixel value will be delivered exactly once (though there might still be multiple calls to setPixels()).

SINGLEFRAME   The image consists of one frame, not multiple frames.

void setProperties(Hashtable properties)   Defines a set of properties for the image. Properties are string values associated with string names. The properties parameter is a hashtable of the values keyed by property name. Clients may query properties by calling the getProperty() method of class Image.

void setPixels(int x, int y, int width, int height, ColorModel model, int pixels[], int offset, int scansize)   Delivers more pixels to the consumer. The pixels represent the rectangular area of the image defined by x, y, width, and height. The model parameter is the color model of this set of pixels only and is free to change from call to call. The pixels[] and offset parameters provide an array of pixel values and a starting place within that array. If the color model is indexed, only the low-order byte of each int in pixels[] is used. The scansize parameter is the number of pixels in a scan line (row).

void setPixels(int x, int y, int width, int height, ColorModel model, byte pixels[], int offset, int scansize)   Same as above, but pixels[] is an array of bytes rather than ints. The color model is generally an indexed color model, though this method is sometimes seen with direct color model GIF image files.

void imageComplete(int status)   Informs the consumer that a frame has been completely delivered or that some problem has occurred. Note that for multiple-frame images, there could be more frames to deliver, so the method name is misleading in this case. The status parameter is one of the following:

STATICIMAGEDONE   Production is complete.

SINGLEFRAMEDONE   One frame of a multiple-frame image is complete, but there are more frames to follow.

IMAGEERROR   The producer encountered an error.

IMAGEABORTED   Production has terminated prematurely.

A Producer That Uses a Memory Image Source

The applet ProdConLab uses a memory image source to draw a black circle. The MemoryImageSource class implements the ImageProducer interface, and the programmer overrides some of its methods so they will report when called. The applet actually creates a subclass of MemoryImageSource called LoudMIS, which writes a message to the applet's text area when one of the methods of the Image-Producer interface is called. Results will vary from platform to platform. Figure 6.7 shows the applet running on a Windows 95 machine. The calls to addConsumer(), removeConsumer(), and startProduction() are easily seen. The program is shown below and is on the CD-ROM in javadevhdbk\ch06\Prod-ConLab.java and ProdConLab.class.

FIGURE 6.7:

The ProdConLab program

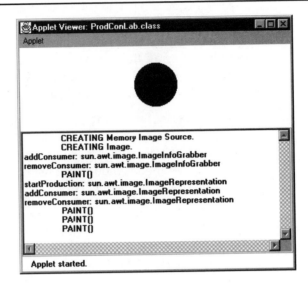

| LIST 6.3 | *ProdConLab.java* |

```
import        java.awt.*;
import        java.awt.image.*;
import        java.applet.Applet;


public class ProdConLab extends Applet
{
    Image        image;
    TextArea     ta;


    public void init()
    {
        LoudMIS        mis;

        // Add a text area for reporting.
        setLayout(new BorderLayout());
        ta = new TextArea(12, 12);
        add(ta, BorderLayout.SOUTH);

        // Build array to represent 100x100 pixels.
```

```java
        int blackInt = Color.black.getRGB();
        int whiteInt = Color.white.getRGB();
        int pix[] = new int[100*100];
        int n = 0;
        for (int i=0; i<100; i++)
        {
            for (int j=0; j<100; j++)
            {
                // Formula for a circle
                int r2 = (i-50)*(i-50) + (j-50)*(j-50);
                if (r2 < 1000)
                    pix[n] = blackInt;
                else
                    pix[n] = whiteInt;
                n++;
            }
        }

        // Build a memory image src, and use it to
        // build an image.
        report("        CREATING Memory Image Source.");
        mis = new LoudMIS(this, 100, 100, pix);
        report("        CREATING Image.");
        image = createImage(mis);
    }


    public void paint(Graphics g)
    {
        report("        PAINT()");
        g.drawImage(image, getSize().width/2 - 50, 5, this);
    }


    public void report(String s)
    {
        ta.append(s + "\n");
    }
}


class LoudMIS extends MemoryImageSource
```

```
{
    private ProdConLab        applet;


    LoudMIS(ProdConLab applet, int w, int h, int[] pix)
    {
        super(w, h, pix, 0, w);
        this.applet = applet;
    }


    public void addConsumer(ImageConsumer ic)
    {
        applet.report("addConsumer: " + ic.getClass().getName());
        super.addConsumer(ic);
    }


    public boolean isConsumer(ImageConsumer ic)
    {
        applet.report("isConsumer: " + ic.getClass().getName());
        return super.isConsumer(ic);
    }


    public void removeConsumer(ImageConsumer ic)
    {
        applet.report("removeConsumer: " + ic.getClass().getName());
        super.removeConsumer(ic);
    }


    public void startProduction(ImageConsumer ic)
    {
        applet.report("startProduction: " + ic.getClass().getName());
        super.startProduction(ic);
    }


    public void requestTopDownLeftRightResend(ImageConsumer ic)
    {
        applet.report("requestTopDownLeftRightResend: "
```

```
                               + ic.getClass().getName());
            requestTopDownLeftRightResend(ic);
    }
}
```

The next section will examine what it takes to create a custom image producer.

A Custom Producer

The SquareProducer applet uses a custom image producer to draw a white box on a blue background. The algorithm and results are identical to those of the memory image source example, SquareMIS, shown earlier in the section "Indexed Color Models." After the listing, we will compare the costs and benefits of using a custom image producer to those of using an indexed color model with a memory image source. The program is listed below and is on the CD-ROM in javadev-hdbk\ch06\SquareProducer.java and SquareProducer.class.

LIST 6.4	*SquareProducer.java*

```
import     java.awt.image.*;
import     java.awt.Color;
import     java.util.Vector;
import     java.util.Enumeration;


public class SquareProducer implements ImageProducer
{
    private ColorModel      model;
    private int             width, height;
    private byte[]          pix;
    private Vector          consumers;


    public SquareProducer(int width, int height, ColorModel model)
    {
        this.width = width;
        this.height = height;
        this.model = model;
        consumers = new Vector();
        pix = new byte[width];
    }
```

```
public void addConsumer(ImageConsumer ic)
{
    if (!isConsumer(ic))
    {
        consumers.addElement(ic);
    }
}


public boolean isConsumer(ImageConsumer ic)
{
    return consumers.contains(ic);
}


public void removeConsumer(ImageConsumer ic)
{
    consumers.removeElement(ic);
}


public void startProduction(ImageConsumer ic)
{
    ImageConsumer      consumer;
    Enumeration        enum;

    // Add input consumer.
    addConsumer(ic);

    // Set dimensions and hints for all consumers.
    enum = consumers.elements();
    while (enum.hasMoreElements())
    {
        consumer = (ImageConsumer)(enum.nextElement());
        consumer.setDimensions(width, height);
        consumer.setHints(ImageConsumer.TOPDOWNLEFTRIGHT   |
                          ImageConsumer.COMPLETESCANLINES  |
                          ImageConsumer.SINGLEPASS         |
                          ImageConsumer.SINGLEFRAME);
    }
```

```
// Compute pixel values. Set pixels for all consumers.
for (int j=0; j<height; j++)
{
    for (int i=0; i<width; i++)
    {
        if (i > width/4   &&   i < width*3/4    &&
            j > height/4   &&   j < height*3/4)
        {
            pix[i] = 0;
        }
        else
        {
            pix[i] = 1;
        }
    }
    enum = consumers.elements();
    while (enum.hasMoreElements())
    {
        consumer = (ImageConsumer)(enum.nextElement());
        consumer.setPixels(0, j, width, 1,
                           model, pix, 0, width);
    }
}

// Send image complete to all consumers.
enum = consumers.elements();
while (enum.hasMoreElements())
{
    consumer = (ImageConsumer)(enum.nextElement());
    consumer.imageComplete(ImageConsumer.STATICIMAGEDONE);
}

ic.imageComplete(ImageConsumer.STATICIMAGEDONE);
}


public void requestTopDownLeftRightResend(ImageConsumer ic)
{
    return;
}
}
```

The applet SquareProdTest uses the image producer listed above to create an image. The source for SquareProdTest is shown below and is on the CD-ROM in javadevhdbk\ch06\SquareProdTest.java and SquareProdTest.class.

LIST 6.5   *SquareProdTest.java*

```java
import     java.awt.*;
import     java.awt.image.*;
import     java.applet.Applet;


public class SquareProdTest extends Applet
{
    private Image    image;


    public void init()
    {
        ImageProducer    producer;
        ColorModel       model;
        byte reds[]   = { (byte)0xff, (byte)0x00 };
        byte greens[] = { (byte)0xff, (byte)0x40 };
        byte blues[]  = { (byte)0xff, (byte)0xff };
        model = new IndexColorModel(8, 2, reds, greens, blues);
        producer = new SquareProducer(size().width, size().height,
                                          model);
        image = createImage(producer);
    }


    public void paint(Graphics g)
    {
        g.drawImage(image, 0, 0, this);
    }
}
```

In comparing the SquareProducer listing to the version that uses a memory image source, you can see that there is very little benefit to be derived from using this image producer. The memory image source implementation must set pixel values in an array, and that is all it has to do. The custom image producer must not only generate pixel values, but it also needs to keep track of its consumers and correctly participate in the dialogue with those consumers. The MemoryImage-Source class merely needs to implement ImageProducer. Creating a custom producer requires reimplementing a lot of functionality instead of reusing what has already been provided.

These facts argue for using a MemoryImageSource unless there are compelling reasons not to. One possible reason is that with a custom producer, the producer does not need to allocate one int or byte for every pixel in the image. The custom producer example shows that it is easy to allocate just a small array that contains the current scan line. This could be an issue in programs with large images. With a 500×500-pixel image and a direct color model, a custom image producer implementation requires a modest 500 ints, or 2000 bytes. A memory image source implementation requires 250,000 ints, or 1MB. This is not the total memory requirement, of course (the image itself must be stored somewhere), but just the requirement at the production end of the pipeline.

Image Filters

Generally, image consumers are invisible to the programmer. Even when a custom image producer is created, the programmer is unaware of the details of the consumers with which the producer has its dialogue. Most implementation details, such as the true class of the consumers or when and how they are constructed, are hidden.

NOTE Figure 6.7, the screenshot of ProdConLab shown earlier in the chapter, shows that on the Windows 95 platform where ProdConLab ran, two consumer classes were involved: ImageInfoGrabber and ImageRepresentation. Neither of these classes is part of the visible portion of the JDK.

One type of image consumer is accessible to the programmer. The ImageFilter class is intended to consume image data, filter it in some way, and pass it on to a producer.

This process is made possible by an auxiliary class called FilteredImageSource. The constructor for FilteredImageSource takes as inputs a reference to an image producer and a reference to an image filter. Because `FilteredImageSource` implements the `ImageProducer` interface, a filtered image can be created, as in the following example:

```
SquareProducer prod = new SquareProducer(250, 250, colorModel);
ExampleImageFilter filter = new ExampleImageFilter();
FilteredImageSource filtSrc = new FilteredImageSource(prod, filter);
Image image = createImage(filtSrc);
```

Any number of filters may be chained together to create a highly filtered image. For example, the following code could be used to run an image through a color-to-grayscale filter and then through a contrast-enhancing filter:

```
Image originalImage = getImage(getDocumentBase(), "something.gif");
ImageProducer origProducer = originalImage.getSource();
FilteredImageSource grayProducer =
      new FilteredImageSource(origProducer, grayFilter);
FilteredImageSource contrastSource =
      new FilteredImageSource(grayProducer, contrastFilter);
Image finalImage = createImage(contrastSource);
```

Although this could be done with one filter that performs both functions, creating separate filter classes results in code that is much cleaner and more likely to be reusable.

Filter Subclasses

The `ImageFilter` class takes care of all image consumer behavior and all interactions with the `FilteredImageSource` class. It stands to reason that programmers should subclass `ImageFilter` rather than reinvent it, and in fact, the `java.awt` `.image` package provides four subclasses for handling major categories of filtering situations.

One subclass is called `CropImageFilter`. The constructor is passed `x`, `y`, `width`, and `height`. The filter extracts the subset of the image specified by these parameters.

Another subclass is `RGBImageFilter`. This is an abstract class whose abstract method `filterRGB(int x, int y, int rgb)` must be overridden by subclasses. The `x` and `y` parameters are the coordinates of the pixel being filtered, and `rgb` is the pixel value to be translated. Note that `rgb` is expressed with respect to the default color model (alpha:red:green:blue). The method should return an int representing the new translated pixel value. Commonly, `RGBImageFilter` is subclassed to produce a contextless filter. A contextless filter is one whose rgb translation algorithm does not depend on the position of the pixel being translated or on the values of any other pixels.

If an RGBImageFilter filter truly does not care about a pixel's surroundings (but only the pixel's color), the subclass of RGBImageFilter can make an important optimization. If the subclass sets the boolean instance variable canFilterIndex-ColorModel to true, then image producers that use an indexed color model do not need to translate every pixel. Instead, only the values in the color model's lookup table need to be translated. This is a significant performance bonus, especially if the translation algorithm is compute-intensive.

Two more filter classes are ReplicateScaleFilter and AverageScaleFilter. The ReplicateScaleFilter class is a simple size-scaling filter. Its constructor is passed two ints, which dictate the width and height of the filtered image. The Average-ScaleFilter class is a subclass of ReplicateScaleFilter that uses a more sophisticated smoothing algorithm than its superclass.

The Pixel Grabber

Another issue related to filters is what to do if a filtering algorithm is heavily dependent on a pixel's surrounding pixels as well as on the pixel itself. This is the case in edge-detection and convolution algorithms.

One strategy for handling this situation is to subclass ImageFilter so it consumes the entire source image, caching pixel values in an array. When the image is completely cached, the translation algorithm can be applied. The subclass will need code to cache pixels, code to apply the filtering algorithm, and code to participate in the dialogue with the FilteredImageSource. These are three distinct tasks.

It would be greatly preferable if the filter only had to filter, leaving the other tasks to more appropriate classes. What would be useful would be a way to convert an image producer to an array of pixel values—a kind of memory image source in reverse. The array could be processed and then a memory image source could be used to convert it to an image. This strategy bypasses the producer/filter/consumer model because the model is not appropriate to the task at hand.

As it turns out, there is a class that converts images to arrays of ints. The class is PixelGrabber in the java.awt.image package. There are two constructors for Pixel-Grabber; one takes an image and the other takes an image producer. The version that takes an image producer is more useful for filtering situations. The API for the constructors is as follows:

```
PixelGrabber(ImageProducer producer, int x, int y,
             int w, int h, int pixels[], int offset,
             int scansize)
PixelGrabber(Image image, int x, int y, int w, int h,
             int pixels[], int offset, int scansize)
```

In both cases, a subset of the image, as defined by x, y, w, and h, is "grabbed" into the entries of array pixels[], starting at offset. The array must be allocated and must be large enough. The scansize parameter gives the width of the original image.

Once the pixel grabber has been constructed, it can be told to grab pixels into its array of ints. The method is grabPixels(), and in its simplest form it takes no arguments. After calling grabPixels(), it is good practice to check for errors by calling the pixel grabber's getStatus() method.

Given the ease of use of the PixelGrabber class, the cleanest way to apply a contextual filter to the output of an image producer is as shown below:

```
int pixels[] = new int[width*height];
MyImageProducer producer = new MyImageProducer(width, height);
PixelGrabber grabber = new PixelGrabber(producer, 0, 0,
                                        width, height,
                                        pixels, 0, width);
CustomFilter myFilter = new CustomFilter();
myFilter.filterThis(pixels);
MemoryImageSource mis = new MemoryImageSource(width, height,
                                              pixels, 0, width);
```

Three Sample Filters

Because PixelGrabber is so easy to use, the appropriate time to use the filtering mechanism is when the filtering algorithm involves cropping the image or translating pixel values irrespective of the neighboring pixels. In these cases, the CropImageFilter and RGBImageFilter classes make life even easier than Pixel-Grabber does.

The applet FilterLab provides three filters: one cropping filter and two different custom filters. One of the custom filters converts white to green, and the other converts to grayscale. The user may activate any of these filters (or all or none of them) and view the result by clicking the Filter button. The original image is shown on the left, and the filtered image appears on the right. (Combining the white-to-green filter with the grayscale filter may produce a visually counter-intuitive result.)

The cropping filter is the easiest to create because no subclassing is required. The CropImageFilter class constructor takes the position, width, and height of the cropped region, so all that is required is to construct the filter:

```
cropFilter = new CropImageFilter(50, 20, 120, 140);
```

The other two filters require subclassing RGBImageFilter so that a new filterRGB() method can be provided. The constructors for these subclasses set canFilterIndexColorModel to true, so images that use indexed color models may be filtered quickly. This setting can be modified via the checkbox labeled Fast Filter. Even with these fairly small images, a performance decrease should be visible on most platforms if both the white-to-green and the grayscale filters are enabled.

NOTE   The FilterLab applet uses a GIF file for its original image. The GIF image used by the applet is indexed, so there is a visible performance difference between using and not using the Fast Filter checkbox to control the value of canFilterIndex-ColorModel. The JPEG format is not indexed, so if FilterLab used a JPEG file for its original image, setting canFilterIndexColorModel would not improve performance.

The white-to-green filter checks for pixel values whose red, green, and blue levels are all at least 75 percent (0xC0). Pixels that pass this test are converted to green (0xff00ff00: alpha and green full on, red and blue off). The algorithm is implemented in the filterRGB() method, as shown here.

```
public int filterRGB(int x, int y, int rgb)
{
    int red   = (rgb & 0x00ff0000) >> 16;
    int green = (rgb & 0x0000ff00) >> 8;
    int blue  = (rgb & 0x000000ff);

    if (blue >= 0xc0  &&  green >= 0xc0  &&  red >= 0xc0)
    {
        return 0xff00ff00;
    }
```

```
        else
        {
            return rgb;
        }
    }
```

The grayscale filter computes the average of the red, green, and blue intensities and returns a pixel value whose red, green, and blue levels are set to this average. Its filterRGB() method is shown below.

```
public int filterRGB(int x, int y, int rgb)
{
    int red   = (rgb & 0x00ff0000) >> 16;
    int green = (rgb & 0x0000ff00) >> 8;
    int blue  = (rgb & 0x000000ff);

    int mean = (red+green+blue) / 3;
    return 0xff000000 | mean<<16 | mean<<8 | mean;
}
```

The applet has a method called filter(), listed below, which applies filters to the original image's producer. The desired filters are requested via boolean inputs. Note how each producer in turn is used to create the next producer.

```
private void filter(boolean crop, boolean red, boolean gray)
{
    w2gFilter.setFast(fastCbox.getState());
    grayFilter.setFast(fastCbox.getState());

    ImageProducer producer = originalImage.getSource();

    if (crop)
        producer = new FilteredImageSource(producer, cropFilter);
    if (red)
        producer = new FilteredImageSource(producer, w2gFilter);
    if (gray)
        producer = new FilteredImageSource(producer, grayFilter);

    filteredImage = createImage(producer);
}
```

The complete listing for FilterLab, which can be found on the CD-ROM in javadevhdbk\ch06\FilterLab.java and FilterLab.class, follows.

LIST 6.6   *FilterLab.java*

```java
import    java.awt.*;
import    java.awt.event.*;
import    java.awt.image.*;
import    java.applet.Applet;


public class FilterLab extends Applet implements ActionListener
{
    private Image              originalImage, filteredImage;
    private Button             btn;
    private Checkbox           cropCbox, w2gCbox, grayCbox;
    private Checkbox           fastCbox;
    private CropImageFilter    cropFilter;
    private WhiteToGreenFilter w2gFilter;
    private GrayFilter         grayFilter;


    public void init()
    {
        // Get original image.
        originalImage = getImage(getDocumentBase(), "emily.gif");
        MediaTracker tracker = new MediaTracker(this);
        tracker.addImage(originalImage, 0);
        try
        {
            tracker.waitForAll();
        } catch (Exception e) { }
        filteredImage = originalImage;

        // Create filters.
        cropFilter = new CropImageFilter(50, 20, 120, 140);
        w2gFilter = new WhiteToGreenFilter();
        grayFilter = new GrayFilter();

        // Create GUI.
        fastCbox = new Checkbox("Fast Filters");
        fastCbox.setState(true);
        add(fastCbox);
        btn = new Button("FILTER");
```

```
        btn.addActionListener(this);
        add(btn);
        cropCbox = new Checkbox("Crop");
        w2gCbox = new Checkbox("White to Green");
        grayCbox = new Checkbox("Grayscale");
        add(cropCbox);
        add(w2gCbox);
        add(grayCbox);
    }


    public void actionPerformed(ActionEvent ev)
    {
        // Create new filteredImage based on checkbox selections.
        filter(cropCbox.getState(),
               w2gCbox.getState(),
               grayCbox.getState());
        repaint();
    }


    // Filters the original image using user-selected filters.
    private void filter(boolean crop, boolean red, boolean gray)
    {
        w2gFilter.setFast(fastCbox.getState());
        grayFilter.setFast(fastCbox.getState());

        ImageProducer producer = originalImage.getSource();

        if (crop)
            producer = new FilteredImageSource(producer, cropFilter);
        if (red)
            producer = new FilteredImageSource(producer, w2gFilter);
        if (gray)
            producer = new FilteredImageSource(producer, grayFilter);

        filteredImage = createImage(producer);
    }


    public void paint(Graphics g)
```

```
        {
            g.drawImage(originalImage, 10, 50, this);
            g.drawImage(filteredImage, 271, 50, this);

        }


    }



/*
 *  A filter class which translates moderately white pixels to green.
 */

class WhiteToGreenFilter extends RGBImageFilter
{
    public WhiteToGreenFilter()
    {
        canFilterIndexColorModel = true;
    }


    public void setFast(boolean fast)
    {
        canFilterIndexColorModel = fast;
    }


    public int filterRGB(int x, int y, int rgb)
    {
        int red   = (rgb & 0x00ff0000) >> 16;
        int green = (rgb & 0x0000ff00) >> 8;
        int blue  = (rgb & 0x000000ff);

        if (blue >= 0xc0  &&  green >= 0xc0  &&  red >= 0xc0)
        {
            return 0xff00ff00;
        }
        else
```

```
            {
                return rgb;
            }
        }
    }


    /*
     * A filter that translates to gray.  Each of the red, green, and
     * blue levels becomes the mean intensity.
     */

    class GrayFilter extends RGBImageFilter
    {
        int    nCalls;


        public GrayFilter()
        {
            canFilterIndexColorModel = true;
        }


        public void setFast(boolean fast)
        {
            canFilterIndexColorModel = fast;
        }


        public int filterRGB(int x, int y, int rgb)
        {
            int red   = (rgb & 0x00ff0000) >> 16;
            int green = (rgb & 0x0000ff00) >> 8;
            int blue  = (rgb & 0x000000ff);

            int mean = (red+green+blue) / 3;
            return 0xff000000 | mean<<16 | mean<<8 | mean;
        }
    }
```

Buffered Images

Revision 1.2 of the JDK includes the `java.awt.image.BufferedImage` class. This class is a nonabstract extension of the `java.awt.Image` abstract superclass. When you want to use a buffered image, you call a constructor rather than a factory method such as `createImage()`.

Most of the constructors for this class are complicated. The simplest constructor has the following signature:

```
public BufferedImage(int width, int height, int type)
```

Here, `width` and `height` are the pixel width and height of the image; `type` is one of the following two constants:

`BufferedImage.TYPE_BYTE_BINARY`   Specifies a monochrome image.

`BufferedImage.TYPE_BYTE_INDEXED`   Specifies a color image.

For the most common color image applications, you can create a byte-indexed buffered image, get a `Graphics` context, and then draw using the methods of the `Graphics` class. For example, the following code creates a 75×75 image and fills it with a blue line on a white background:

```
Image im = new BufferedImage(75, 75, BufferedImage.TYPE_BYTE_INDEXED);
Graphics g = im.getGraphics();
g.setColor(Color.white):
g.fillRect(0, 0, 75, 75);
g.setColor(Color.blue);
g.drawLine(5, 50, 70, 70);
```

Summary

Java goes to great lengths to ensure that image manipulation is efficient, platform independent, and well encapsulated. The casual programmer can generally write robust code without knowing anything about producers, consumers, color models, or behind-the-scenes threads.

Beginner image programmers only need to know two tricks: Use `this` wherever an image observer is required, and use a media tracker to coordinate image loading. Eventually, curiosity or need leads to further investigation, and the whole complicated infrastructure is revealed. Images are produced, filtered, consumed, and observed. Abstract classes abound, hiding the true type of platform-specific classes.

Programmers who wish to work on the level of the image infrastructure are encouraged to make the most of existing functionality. This chapter has shown an example (the white and blue squares) where creating a custom `ImageProducer` has no advantage over the much simpler approach of using a `MemoryImageSource`. This case is by no means universal, but it is common. This chapter has also made a case for considering a `PixelGrabber` design as an alternative to developing a custom `ImageFilter`.

The image infrastructure is for the most part, a model of good object-oriented design. The structure is far more complicated than image support on other platform-specific systems, but everything is there for a reason. The designers have made intelligent subclassing and partitioning decisions throughout. The complication ensures platform independence and good performance. It is likely that this part of Java will scale easily to new platforms for a long time to come.

The next chapter covers threading and how threads operate in Java programs.

CHAPTER

SEVEN

7

Threads

- How to create threads

- Thread scheduling

- Methods for controlling threads

- Thread group control and security

- Thread communications

- Deadlock causes and prevention

- The AWT thread

- Complex thread interaction

Traditional programming environments are generally single-threaded. Java, however, is multithreaded. Although multithreading is a powerful and elegant programming tool, it is not easy to use correctly and has a number of traps that even experienced programmers can fall into.

This chapter introduces the ideas of multithreading, describes the tools that Java provides that allow you to create and control threads, and discusses some of the essential programming techniques you will need to make effective use of threads in your programs.

Threading Concepts

To better understand threading, think of the CPU as an office worker, performing a task according to instructions. Think of that single task as the program for one thread of execution. In a single-threaded environment, each program is written and executed on the basis that at any one time, that program is concerned with only one sequence of processing. In our analogy, this is like an office worker who has been allocated a single task to be performed from start to finish without interruption or distraction.

In a real office, it is unlikely that a worker will have only one task at a time. Much more commonly, a worker will work on several tasks at once. The boss gives the tasks to the worker and expects that that worker will do a bit of one task, then a bit of another, and so forth. If progress becomes impossible on one task, perhaps because the worker is waiting for information from another department, the worker will put the task aside and make progress on some other task in the meantime. Generally, the boss expects that the worker will make progress on each job at some point throughout the day.

Multithreaded programming environments are much like this typical office. The CPU is given several tasks, or *threads*, at the same time. Like the office worker, a computer CPU is not actually able to do more than one thing at a time. Instead, time is divided between the various threads so that each one is moved forward a bit at a time. If no progress can be made on one particular thread—for example, if the thread requires keyboard input that has not been typed yet—then work is done on some other thread instead. Typically, the CPU switches between threads fast enough to give a human observer the appearance that all the threads are being performed simultaneously. This is not necessarily the case, however, as we will discuss later in this chapter.

There are three key aspects of any processing environment, whether single or multithreaded:

- The CPU, which actually does the computational activities
- The program code that is being executed
- The data on which the program operates

In a multithreaded programming environment, each thread has code to provide the behavior of the thread, and has data for that code to operate on. It is possible to have more than one thread working on the same code and data. It is equally possible to have different threads, each with unique code and data. In fact, the code and data parts are largely independent of each other and can be made available to a thread as needed. Hence, it is quite common to have several threads all working with the same code but different data. These ideas can be considered in our office worker analogy. An accountant can be asked to do the books for a single department or for several departments. In any case, the task of *do the books* is the same essential program code, but for each department the data is different. The accountant could also be asked to do the books for the whole company. In this case, there would be several tasks, but some of the data is shared because the company books require figures from each department.

Multithreaded programming environments use a convenient model to hide the fact that the CPU must switch between jobs. The model allows, in broad principle, the pretense that an unlimited number of CPUs are available. To set up another job, the programmer must ask for another "virtual CPU" and instruct it to start executing a particular piece of code, using a particular data set. Figure 7.1 compares a single CPU with a multiple virtual CPU computer. Each virtual CPU has one piece of code and one set of associated data.

In some systems, there really are multiple physical CPUs, in much the same way that an office commonly has multiple workers. Using the model of virtual CPUs, multiple threads can be written so that they are either executed a bit at a time by a single CPU or genuinely in parallel by multiple physical CPUs, depending on what is actually available at runtime.

FIGURE 7.1:

Comparing single and multithreaded programming environments

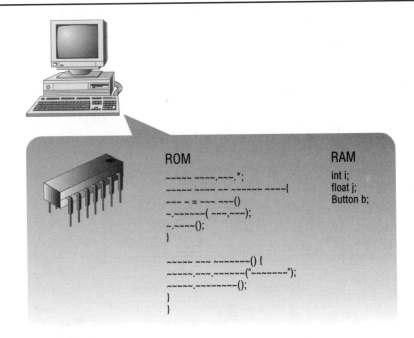

ROM
```
~~~~~ ~~~~.~~~.*;
~~~~~ ~~~~ ~~ ~~~~~~ ~~~~{
~~~ ~ = ~~~ ~~~()
~.~~~~~~( ~~~,~~~);
~.~~~~();
}

~~~~~ ~~~ ~~~~~~~() {
~~~~~.~~~.~~~~~~("~~~~~~~");
~~~~~.~~~~~~~~();
}
}
```

RAM
```
int i;
float j;
Button b;
```

Single computer, single thread

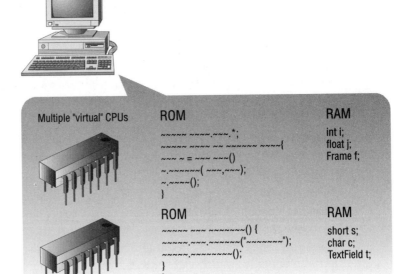

Multiple "virtual" CPUs

ROM
```
~~~~~ ~~~~.~~~.*;
~~~~~ ~~~~ ~~ ~~~~~~ ~~~~{
~~~ ~ = ~~~ ~~~()
~.~~~~~~( ~~~,~~~);
~.~~~~();
}
```

RAM
```
int i;
float j;
Frame f;
```

ROM
```
~~~~~ ~~~ ~~~~~~~() {
~~~~~.~~~.~~~~~~("~~~~~~~");
~~~~~.~~~~~~~~();
}
}
```

RAM
```
short s;
char c;
TextField t;
```

Single computer, multiple thread

Thread Creation

Creating threads in Java is not difficult. Again, the three things that are required are the code to be executed, the data for that code to operate on, and the virtual CPU that is to execute the code. In Java, the virtual CPU is encapsulated in an instance of the Thread class.

Rules for Creating Threads

When a Thread object is created, it must be provided with code to execute and data for that code to work on. Java's object-oriented model requires that program code can be written only as member methods of classes. Data can exist only as automatic (or local) variables inside methods or as class or instance members. These rules require that the code and data we provide for a thread must be in the form of a class instance.

When a thread starts to execute, it does so in a specific method called public void run(). This method is the starting point for a thread execution by definition, in much the same way that applications start at main() and applets start at init(). The data items that the thread operates on are the members of the object that were passed to the thread.

Any class can be used to provide the starting point for the execution of a new thread, and the class can be a subclass of any other single class, if the programmer requires it. The particular requirement is that the class must be declared to implement the interface Runnable, and in consequence of this declaration, it must have a nonabstract method called public void run(). Because of this interface, a class that provides the code for a thread is often simply referred to as a Runnable.

The following example demonstrates the steps for thread creation. You can find the code on the CD-ROM in javadevhdbk\ch07\SimpleRunnable.java and Simple-Runnable.class.

LIST 7.1   *SimpleRunnable.java*

```java
public class SimpleRunnable implements Runnable {
  private String message;

  public static void main(String args[]) {
    SimpleRunnable r1 = new SimpleRunnable("Hello");
```

```
      Thread t1 = new Thread(r1);
      t1.start();
    }

    public SimpleRunnable(String message) {
      this.message = message;
    }

    public void run() {
      for (;;) {
        System.out.println(message);
      }
    }
  }
```

First, the main() method constructs an instance of the SimpleRunnable class. Notice that the instance has its own data—in this case, a single string, which is initialized to "Hello." Because the instance, r1, is passed to the Thread class constructor, this is the data with which the thread will work when it runs. The code that will be executed will be the instance method run().

Creating a thread by creating an instance of the Thread class, and specifying the code and data using an instance of a Runnable class, allows the creation of multiple threads based on the same Runnable instance. In this case, they all will work with the same code and the same data. This could be achieved by simply issuing more lines like this:

```
Thread t2 = new Thread(r1);
Thread t3 = new Thread(r1);
```

This type of behavior is both legitimate and, in some cases, valuable.

WARNING When more than one thread is operating on the same data, some potentially undesirable interactions can occur. The "Interaction between Threads" section later in this chapter expands on these important issues.

The start() method, which is invoked on the threads after they are created, causes them to become runnable. Before this point, the run() method will not be executed. This and other basic thread-control methods are discussed in the "Essential Control of Threads" section later in this chapter.

Thread Names

Every thread in Java has a name. Java provides different Thread class constructors that allow a particular name to be specified. If you use a constructor without one of these specific names, Java automatically provides a unique, if unimaginative, name. Although it is possible, and sometimes useful, to determine the name of a thread in a running program, this facility is most useful in debugging.

To name the thread in the example, a different constructor can be invoked, like this:

```
Thread t1 = new Thread(r1, "First Thread");
```

Given an instance of the Thread class, the name can be extracted as a string using the getName() method. For example, this line would print the name of the Thread object referred to by the variable r1:

```
System.out.println(r1.getName()); // Outputs "First Thread"
```

Code and Data Sharing

In Java, it is possible to create threads that share program code but have different data to work on. Consider the code below to be a variation of the earlier example. You can find this code on the CD-ROM in javadevhdbk\ch07\SimpleRunnable2 .java and SimpleRunnable2.class.

LIST 7.2   *SimpleRunnable2.java*

```
public class SimpleRunnable2 implements Runnable {
  private String message;

  public static void main(String args[]) {
    SimpleRunnable2 r1 = new SimpleRunnable2("Hello");
    SimpleRunnable2 r2 = new SimpleRunnable2("Goodbye");
    Thread t1 = new Thread(r1);
    Thread t2 = new Thread(r2);
    t1.start();
    t2.start();
  }

  public SimpleRunnable2(String message) {
    this.message = message;
  }
```

```
public void run() {
  for (;;) {
    System.out.println(message);
  }
}
}
```

In this case, two different instances of the SimpleRunnable2 class—r1 and r2—are created having different, independent data. The code that each thread executes is the same run() method as before.

To run different code, different Runnable classes are usually provided.

```
public class OtherRunnable implements Runnable {
  // Constructor, methods, and data items
  public void run() {
    // Code to do something useful
  }
}
```

Given this class, it is possible to construct a thread by the following calls:

```
OtherRunnable r3 = new OtherRunnable();
Thread t3 = new Thread(r3);
```

In this case, a new thread is created. This new thread shares neither code nor data with the earlier threads created using SimpleRunnable2 objects.

Sharing Data with Different Code

The data that is used by a thread is the instance data of its Runnable object. This data can be primitive types or references to other objects. Therefore, sharing data between threads can be achieved simply by placing a reference to a shared object into each Runnable object. The following sample code demonstrates this idea:

```
public class TheData {
  int x;
  float f;
  // Other member data and methods
}

public class FirstRunnable implements Runnable {
```

```
    TheData sharedData;

    public FirstRunnable(TheData toUse) {
      sharedData = toUse;
    }

    public void run() {
      // Do things with 'sharedData'
    }
  }

  public class SecondRunnable implements Runnable {
    TheData sharedData;

    public SecondRunnable(TheData toUse) {
      sharedData = toUse;
    }

    public void run() {
      // Do things with 'sharedData'
    }
  }

    // Launch from some other method,
    // perhaps main() in another class...
    TheData data = new TheData();
    // Set up contents of 'data'
    FirstRunnable f = new FirstRunnable(data);
    SecondRunnable s = new SecondRunnable(data);
    Thread t1 = new Thread(f);
    Thread t2 = new Thread(s);
    // Start the threads...
```

Notice that the instance data of the Thread t1 is provided by the instance f of the class FirstRunnable. The code for this Thread is the run() method of that class. The instance data for Thread t2 is provided by the SecondRunnable s. Similarly, the code to execute is the run() method of the class SecondRunnable. In both cases, the instance data has a reference to the single object of class TheData, which was created during the first stage of setting up these threads. In this way, the two threads share common data even though they are using different code from a different class.

NOTE   The relationship between the virtual CPU, code, and data is summarized as follows. A Thread encapsulates the virtual CPU. The virtual CPU starts executing code in the run() method of the *class* of Runnable provided to the Thread constructor, while the data used is provided by the *instance* of that Runnable.

Using Different Code in the Same Runnable

It is also possible to share data between threads that are executing different code by making the run() method of a single Runnable class provide multiple different execution paths. Consider this sample:

```
public class TwoPath implements Runnable {
  static Thread t1;
  static Thread t2;

  public static void main(String args[]) {
    TwoPath r = new TwoPath();
    t1 = new Thread(r);
    t2 = new Thread(r);
    t1.start();
    t2.start();
  }

  public void run() {
    if (Thread.currentThread() == t1) {
      // Behavior one
    }
    else {
      // Behavior two
    }
  }
}
```

Here, the single run() method provides two different execution paths. The selection is made on the basis of which of two threads is executing it. References to each of the threads are made available to both instances of the Runnable TwoPath via the static variables. The current Thread is determined using the static method Thread.currentThread(), and this value is compared with the stored reference to t1 to determine the appropriate behavior. You can take a similar approach using a string comparison on the name returned from the Thread object getName() method.

Because this approach embeds multiple types of behavior in a single class, we do not generally recommend it. In most circumstances, it is unlikely to represent good object-oriented design.

Essential Control of Threads

You can control the execution of a thread in a variety of ways. So far, we have discussed the start() method briefly. The following sections discuss the start() method in more detail and introduce some other methods that provide the fundamental techniques for thread control.

Starting a Thread

To start the thread, all you need to provide is an instruction of this form:

```
t1.start();
```

The start() method causes the virtual CPU represented by the Thread object to begin executing. Before calling this method, it is as if the program and data memory associated with the CPU have been loaded but the CPU itself has not been switched on. After the start() method is invoked on the Thread instance, the new thread is able to start executing the run() method of the Runnable.

WARNING   It is important to have a clear understanding of the distinction between start() and run(). The start() method is a member of the Thread class and controls the virtual CPU. The run() method is a member of the Runnable object and provides the code that the thread actually executes. Calling the run() method directly is entirely legal in Java, but does not result in a new thread executing the code; rather it constitutes a simple method call like any other. Also, be sure to differentiate between the start() method of a Thread object and the start() method of an applet.

Stopping a Thread

After a thread stops, it is considered to be *dead*. A thread stops executing permanently if its run() method completes. Although there is a stop() method that kills a thread forcibly, this is deprecated since Java 2 and should be avoided. The stop() method is deprecated because it can cause a thread to die in an untidy state that might threaten the integrity of the whole program. If you need to have a thread die, code it in such a way that you can trigger it to complete its run() method at a time to suit you. For example, you can use the interrupt() method to break a thread out of waiting conditions, such as reading input, that might prevent a thread from noticing your request to stop. An example of using interrupt() in this way is provided in the "More Thread Control" section later in this chapter.

Once dead, the thread cannot execute any further code, even if the start() method is called again. The Thread object might be subject to garbage collection if no references to it remain.

WARNING Using resources of the underlying system—for example, non-lightweight AWT components such as Frames and, in particular, Threads—as disposable items is generally weak design and not necessary. The garbage collector can recognize when the system is running out of memory and attempt to rectify the situation, but it does not recognize shortages of other system resources. Such shortages can cause an otherwise correct program to fail.

Pausing Thread Execution

It is possible to temporarily pause a thread in a number of ways. There is a static method called sleep() that requests that the currently executing thread stop executing for *at least* a certain period. The time period is specified as the argument to the method.

There are two forms of the sleep() method, allowing specification of either a number of milliseconds or, using two arguments, a number of milliseconds and a number of nanoseconds. The second form might allow a more precise specification of the duration of sleep requested, but you should realize that the sleep time represents the *minimum* time for which the thread will be idle. The "Introduction to Thread Scheduling" section later in this chapter explains why the thread might be idle for much longer than was requested and how you can control this effect when the time is critical.

The sleep() method is declared as able to throw an InterruptedException. Because of this, and the compiler's rigid insistence on proper handling of exceptions, sleep() is usually coded inside a try{} block. Alternatively, the enclosing method can be declared to throw the exception. The InterruptedException is thrown if the thread receives an interrupt() method call while in the sleeping state.

The methods suspend() and resume() are deprecated since Java 2. These methods allowed you to put a thread on indefinite hold, and subsequently restart it under the control of another thread. However, subtle difficulties could arise from using these methods. You can get equivalent control more safely using the methods wait() and notify(), which are discussed later in this chapter.

An Example of Thread Creation

The ThreadTest.java program provides an example of the topics we've covered so far. To ensure clarity of the salient points, ThreadTest.java does not do anything either startling or useful in its threads. Three separate threads are created; two of these share an instance of a Runnable and hence have the same code and data to work on. The third has an instance of a different Runnable and, in addition, has a reference to the Runnable used by the other two threads. Each thread executes independently although data is shared, and this fact is demonstrated by the output.

The source for the following example can be found on the CD-ROM in java-devhdbk\ch07\ThreadTest.java. The corresponding bytecode files, ThreadTest .class and FirstRunnable.class, are in the same directory.

When you run ThreadTest.java, it begins issuing messages at random intervals. The program does not stop until it is killed manually, so be ready to do this by pressing Ctrl+C or by entering the appropriate kill command for your platform.

| **LIST 7.3** | **ThreadTest.java** |

```java
class FirstRunnable implements Runnable {
  public int value = 0;

  public void run() {
    for (;;) {
      try {
        Thread.sleep((int)(Math.random() * 2000));
      }
      catch (InterruptedException e) {
        // Ignore and carry on
      }
      value ++;
```

```
        System.out.println("Thread " +
          Thread.currentThread().getName() +
            " value is now " + value);
    }
  }
}

class ThreadTest implements Runnable {
  public FirstRunnable otherData;

  public void run() {
    for (;;) {
      try {
        Thread.sleep((int)(Math.random() * 2000));
      }
      catch (InterruptedException e) {
        // Ignore and carry on
      }
      System.out.println("Thread " +
          Thread.currentThread().getName() +
        " value in otherData is currently " +
          otherData.value);

    }
  }

  public ThreadTest(FirstRunnable other) {
    otherData = other;
  }

  public static void main(String args[]) {
    FirstRunnable r1 = new FirstRunnable();
    ThreadTest r2 = new ThreadTest(r1);
    Thread t1 = new Thread(r1, "FirstRunnable, first Thread");
    Thread t2 = new Thread(r1, "FirstRunnable, second Thread");
    Thread t3 = new Thread(r2, "ThreadTest, third Thread");
    t1.start();
    t2.start();
    t3.start();
  }
}
```

Creating the Runnables and Threads

The startup of ThreadTest.java, handled by the main() method of the ThreadTest class, creates an instance of the class FirstRunnable. The single data item in this class, called value, is initialized to zero. Actually this explicit initialization is redundant, but it seems to be good style to explicitly perform any initialization on which a program depends. Next, an instance of the ThreadTest class is created.

After the main() method of the ThreadTest class creates the three runnables, the three threads are constructed. Each of these is given a separate name that allows the various lines of output to be attributed to its originating thread. Two threads are created using the single Runnable r1, and the third is created using r2.

Running the Threads

When the threads have been started, each enters an infinite loop. The body of the loop pauses for a random period. This is achieved by using the Math .random() method to generate a random number in the range 0 to 2000 and using the sleep() method to cause the thread to remain idle for at least that many milliseconds. The net result is that the thread remains idle for a random time, somewhere between zero and two seconds. As noted earlier, the sleep() method can throw an InterruptedException, so this requires the try{} construction. In this program, there is no possibility that this exception will arise, so it can be ignored.

Each time the threads t1 and t2, executing the run() method in the First-Runnable class, awaken from sleep, they increment the contents of value and issue a message announcing the name of the current thread and stating the new incremented contents of value. The output indicates that both threads are sharing the same data.

When t3, executing the run() method in the ThreadTest class, awakens from sleep, it prints its name and the contents of value. This thread does not change the variable value, however. This demonstrates that despite running different code, the thread t3 is able to access the same data as the other runnables.

WARNING   Sharing data in this way is generally very risky. Consider the ThreadTest.java program as a demonstration of the principles of threading, not as an example of ways to share data. There is a small, but finite, chance that you might notice occasional strange behavior, such as the output value incrementing by two counts. The mechanisms of these problems are potentially platform-dependent. We will discuss controlled ways to share data between threads later in the chapter, in the section "Interaction between Threads."

Two Ways to Create a Class for Threading

Up to this point, we have discussed only one way to create a thread. That method requires a Runnable object to be created, and the Thread object is constructed to use that runnable. However, there is an alternative mechanism.

The Thread class implements the Runnable interface itself; that is, it actually defines a public void run() method. In the Thread class itself, this method is empty, but if another class is a subclass of Thread, then it has the opportunity to override the empty definition with a new one. When this is done, creating an instance of the class inherently creates a new Thread. All that is needed to start that thread executing is to invoke the start() method.

If an object is an instance of some subclass of the Thread class, then in the methods of that object, the this pointer is actually a reference to the currently executing Thread object. Because of this reference, Thread instance methods such as get-Name()may be executed directly, without requiring an explicit Thread reference.

Despite the ability to execute Thread instance methods directly in the context of a Runnable, in general it is probably not a good idea to use this approach. Because Java permits only single inheritance, if a class extends Thread, it cannot be a subclass of anything else. Other facilities, such as those of the Applet class, are available only through subclassing. Therefore, it is unwise to waste this ability when it is not necessary.

There is another reason why extending Thread might be considered a poor approach, although the reasoning is rather academic and has no pressing practical significance. In the object-oriented paradigm, subclassing is the mechanism by which a modified version of a predefined "something" is produced. In this way, for example, the object-oriented approach allows modeling of entries in a pet show so that a Dog class can be specialized, by subclassing, to produce a Terrier class. Note that a terrier is a dog, but a particular type of dog.

Consider now the original description of the Thread class as encapsulating the virtual CPU. The CPU is a separate entity from the code and data on which it operates; hence, the proper reason for subclassing a Thread is to produce a CPU with new behavior, not to modify the code that it executes. Of course, some designs might actually call for a modified version of the Thread class, such as a thread with special processing or scheduling characteristics. Under such conditions, it would be not only correct but also necessary to subclass Thread.

When Not to Create a Thread

It is easy to get carried away and treat threads as disposable items. However, creating a new **Thread** object each time a job or service must be performed and letting the thread stop when that service is completed is wasteful. The better approach is to create a single **Thread** object to perform the particular job or service. If the service is needed multiple times, then the same thread should be reused.

In general, constructing instances of classes is a matter of allocating memory space and invoking a constructor to initialize the object. Although the same is broadly true of a **Thread** object, there is an additional aspect for you to consider. Most implementations of Java use the underlying operating system to provide threads. The operating system mechanisms used with threads can involve quite significant overhead. Therefore, setting up a single thread to do a job repeatedly saves CPU time and improves overall efficiency. Usually, it also results in a tidier and more elegant solution.

To have a single thread operate in a loop, handling requests as they become available, requires a communication mechanism. Somehow, the thread must be told that there is work for it to do. Communication between threads is discussed later in this chapter.

An Introduction to Thread Scheduling

The discussion at the beginning of this chapter suggested that the effect of virtual CPUs is achieved by doing a part of a job and then moving on to do part of another job. The scheme by which decisions are made about which thread is actually executing at any one instant on a physical CPU is called the *thread scheduling model*. In Java, this model is platform-dependent, but you still need some understanding of the various possibilities in order to program with threads effectively.

The following sections discuss the two main types of scheduling models: the preemptive scheduler and the time-sharing (or time-slicing) scheduler. Strictly speaking, time-slicing is a superset of preemptive scheduling, but from a programmer's viewpoint, there are a number of significant differences.

Preemptive Scheduling

In a preemptive scheduling model, each thread is either runnable or not. Threads that are in the *runnable* (ready to run) state are either running or waiting to run. A thread is not runnable if it needs some condition to be satisfied or some resource—such as input from the user—before it can proceed. The *not ready* state is usually referred to as *blocked*. The physical CPU will execute one of the runnable threads.

Choosing Threads for Execution

Each thread has an associated priority that describes how important the thread is relative to the others. With a preemptive scheduler, whenever a CPU is available, runnable threads are checked according to priority, and the highest priority runnable thread is chosen for execution. If more than one thread of the same priority tie for this privilege, then usually the one that has been waiting the longest is chosen.

The next question is, "When does a thread get taken off a CPU to allow others a chance to run?" In a purely preemptive scheduling model, the thread is descheduled under only two conditions:

- If a higher-priority thread becomes runnable. For example, suppose that a thread was blocked and waiting for user input, and that input has now arrived. In such a case, we say that the higher-priority thread *preempts* the lower-priority one—hence the name of the scheduler.

- If the original thread is actually unable to continue. This condition might occur if the thread requires an I/O operation or executes the sleep() method.

Threads in this model can be very selfish and this, at least at first sight, appears to make the pure preemptive scheduling model a difficult one to program.

Programming for a Preemptive Scheduler

When threads are working on a common task, the preemptive scheduling model is actually very elegant and easy to use.

To illustrate our point, we'll use a restaurant analogy. One thread represents a customer, another represents a waiter, and a third represents a chef. Because of the nature of their respective tasks, the chef and waiter threads cannot do anything until the customer thread orders. When the customer thread begins, it prepares some data and then needs to communicate its request to the waiter. At that instant, the waiter thread, which has been blocked, waiting for input from the customer, is ready to run. The customer thread then blocks, waiting for the waiter to bring food. Then the waiter thread actually can start to run because the customer is no longer using the CPU. The same kind of interaction occurs between the waiter and the chef.

When this type of dependency exists between threads, the preemptive scheduler is highly efficient. Each thread typically gets the CPU quite soon after it is able to use it, but the overhead of switching between different threads is kept to an absolute minimum.

The following incomplete sample puts this idea into outline Java code for the customer/waiter part of the relationship. Observe how there are specific points at which the control is transferred between the threads, but do not concern yourself with how the communication occurs. We'll talk about the communication techniques later in the chapter, in the "Communication between Threads" section.

```java
class Customer implements Runnable {
  public void run() {
    chooseFromMenu();        // Uses CPU to think
    waiter.orderMeal();      // Passes information to waiter,
                             // making waiter able to run
    waiter.waitForMeal();    // Blocked until waiter returns,
                             // CPU not used here
    eatMeal();               // Once food arrives, we can use
                             // the CPU to process chewing,
                             // swallowing, and enjoying food
  }
}

class Waiter implements Runnable {
  public void run() {
    while (restaurantIsOpen()) {
      waitForCustomerToOrder(); // No CPU time used until
                                // an order is placed
      chef.takeOrder();         // Pass the order to the chef
                                // Now the chef needs the CPU
                                // to be able to do the cooking
      chef.waitForOrder();      // Blocks, releasing CPU (which
                                // the chef will use) until food
```

```
                                        // is ready
            takeOrderToCustomer();      // Now the customer can use CPU
                                        // and will get it when we loop
                                        // round to wait for next order

        }
      }
    }
```

NOTE

The programming task becomes harder, and the scheduler less efficient, when threads being coded do not exhibit this type of interdependence. Entirely independent tasks must be given otherwise arbitrary blocking calls, such as the `sleep()` or the `yield()` method, as discussed in the "More Thread Control" section later in this chapter.

Time-Sharing Scheduling

Although purely preemptive scheduling is elegant and expressive for controlling threads that are working on related aspects of some greater task, there are many situations where threads are working on tasks that do not have such clear-cut interactions. Therefore, many operating systems provide a means of sharing time between unrelated jobs without those jobs having to give up time voluntarily. This sharing is generally referred to as a *time-sharing* or *time-slicing scheduler*, and it is strictly a superset of the preemptive system.

In general, it is easy to construct a time-sharing mechanism on the basis of a pure preemptive scheduling model. All that is required is a high-priority task that deschedules running jobs at intervals.

The time-sharing model has two potential drawbacks:

- For interrelated threads, it is generally less efficient than pure preemptive scheduling.

- The currently executing thread can change without warning or particular reason. Where threads share data, this can give rise to disastrous data corruption.

These difficulties are discussed in detail later in this chapter.

Java's Platform-Dependence

Our discussion so far has left one important question unanswered: Just what is the thread scheduling model used in Java—preemptive or time-sharing? Unfortunately, the Java specification does not require any particular model. Rather, it is expected that the underlying scheduling system of the host platform will be used. This is a concession to the difficulty of implementing a thread-control scheme outside an operating system. In general, the degree of interaction between the operating system and the thread scheduler is too great to allow for an efficient implementation if the two aspects are separated.

So, just what is guaranteed by Java? Very little actually, but enough that platform-independent programs can be written, although the result might be rather inefficient. Note, however, that it is very easy to write programs that are platform-*dependent* if you make incorrect assumptions about threading models, so a clear understanding of these aspects is important. The following points can be made:

- All Java implementations provide threads.

- The scheduling mechanism is *not* specified.

- Synchronization and communication *are* possible in a platform-independent manner but require techniques that are discussed in the "Communication between Threads" section later in this chapter.

- Java allows control of thread priorities, but the meaning of *priority* is not specified, is platform-dependent, and might not have the effect you expect.

The usual implication of a priority is that if a task of a particular priority is ready to run, then it will definitely be given the CPU in preference to any task of lower priority. However, this is *not* required of Java implementations. Implementations are at liberty to use the priority value as an indication of the relative amount of time that each thread should receive (sometimes called a *nice* value) or even to ignore the priority specification altogether. In Solaris, for example, "green threads" implement purely preemptive priorities to give exclusive rights to higher-priority threads, while "native threads" provide time-sharing among threads of the same priority. Windows 95 threads, however, allow lower-priority threads to execute, but with a smaller share of CPU time.

The result of this lack of specification is that the programmer must work much harder to produce a reliable, portable application. You must not depend on time-sharing because this might not be provided. You must not rely on runnable high-priority threads preventing lower-priority ones from running, because this also might not be the case. The only definite way to control which of your threads executes at any given time is to use advanced thread communication and synchronization facilities. These facilities are discussed later in this chapter in the "Communication between Threads" section.

More Thread Control

Java provides several mechanisms for controlling the execution of threads. The following sections discuss the uses of various methods and describe user and daemon threads.

Thread Methods

We'll begin our discussion of the methods for controlling thread execution with more details about the sleep() method, which was introduced earlier in this chapter. Then we will cover the interrupt() and join() methods.

Using the sleep() Method

The sleep() method can be used to make a thread cooperate with other threads and allow them a chance to execute. It is most appropriate, however, when a thread must perform an action at regular intervals. To achieve this kind of regular scheduling, a main loop in the thread's run() method should contain a fixed-length sleep() call. This call will ensure that the remainder of the body of the loop is executed at regular intervals.

This approach does not result in precise timing. There are two main reasons for the inaccuracies. The most obvious failing is that the scheduler might well leave the thread in the runnable state for a significant period of time before actually running it again. If the underlying implementation provides meaningful priorities, this effect can be reduced by raising the priority of the thread using the setPriority() method. If you cannot raise the thread's priority because of other considerations, you may need to make some compromises, such as accepting lower timing accuracy.

This approach also fails to take into account the time it takes for the body of the loop itself to execute. If this situation is not corrected, the timing of the thread will tend to *creep*, because each time the main loop runs, the timing error will be added, compounding the previous errors. To address this, a high-priority thread should be created that performs only a single action in the loop body. This action is to "trigger" the work required. The work must then be performed in another thread. In this way, the incremental error can be limited. Note, however, that this technique is effective only if priorities are meaningful on the host platform and it is not possible to eliminate these timing errors using software alone.

Further improvement can be made to the timing of this loop by marking the absolute start time of the loop and then calculating the target wakeup time each time around. This eliminates incremental creep errors, leaving only variations in individual times for the loop. The following incomplete sample code demonstrates the idea.

```
public static final int INCREMENT = 50;
public void run () {
  int targettime = (int)System.currentTimeMillis();
  for (;;) {
    // Loop body
    targettime += INCREMENT;
    int sleeptime = targettime - (int)System.currentTimeMillis();
    while (sleeptime >0) {
      try {
        Thread.sleep(sleeptime);
      }
      catch (InterruptedException e) {
        // Ignore
      }
      sleeptime = targettime - (int)System.currentTimeMillis();
    }
  }
}
```

Using the yield() Method

If you use the sleep() method to write multiple cooperating threads, then it is possible that CPU time might be wasted. This can occur if all the threads are sleeping for cooperation, despite some of them having useful work to perform. Under these conditions, the CPU does not do any work, even though there is work to be done.

For this reason, cooperating processes should not *all* use the sleep() method. If you can choose one that is able to use all the CPU time made available when others are sleeping, but is itself not time critical, then it might be possible to run it without sleeping but at a lower priority. Unfortunately, because you cannot rely on priorities being effective on every platform, this approach is not reliably portable.

In many cases, it is more appropriate to use the yield() method to enforce cooperation between threads. This method will cause a thread to be descheduled in favor of some other runnable thread. If no other thread is currently runnable, then this thread continues immediately. Clearly, this mechanism has the advantage over the use of sleep() because it ensures the CPU is never idle when work can be done.

Using the interrupt() Method

There are many conditions that cause a thread to stop executing temporarily, such as executing the sleep() method or performing some I/O operation. You might need to make a thread abandon whatever it is waiting for and continue down some alternative path. For example, you might decide that an input operation should timeout if is incomplete after 20 seconds. You can achieve this using an external thread and the interrupt() method.

Where a thread is blocked in some method, such as sleep(), invoking the interrupt() method causes the blocking method to abort and throw an InterruptedException. You can then catch this exception to process the timeout. You can use this same approach to be able to stop a thread entirely. The following code fragment shows how this can be done:

```
public class ThreadStopper implements Runnable {
  private Thread myThread;
  private boolean stopNow = false;

  public void run() {
    while (!stopNow) { // Keep going until asked to stop
      try {
        // Lots of work, including sleep() and other blocking methods
      }
      catch (InterruptedException ex) {
        break;
      }
```

```
      }
    }

  public void stopPlease() {
    stopNow = true;
    myThread.interrupt();
  }
}
```

Using the join() Method

The join() instance method causes the current thread to stop executing until the thread for which the method is invoked stops. This provides a useful way to wait for the completion of one thread before proceeding in the current one. The following incomplete sample shows how this is achieved:

```
Thread t1 = new Thread(someRunnable);
Thread t2 = new Thread(otherRunnable);
t1.start();
t2.start();
System.out.println("Threads now running");
t1.join();
t2.join();
System.out.println("Threads have now finished");
```

This is a rudimentary form of communication between threads. More control is available using other methods, which are described in the "Interaction between Threads" section later in this chapter.

Daemon and User Threads

Threads in the Java system can be marked as either user or daemon threads. A newly created thread inherits this characteristic from the thread that invoked its constructor. The significance of the distinction between the two is that the JVM exits, stopping the entire program, when zero user threads are alive. Hence, creating a user thread prevents the program from exiting until that thread has completed. In contrast, marking the thread as a daemon thread allows the JVM to consider it as being a service provider, without value in the absence of user threads acting as clients of the service.

Daemon threads are commonly used for housekeeping tasks and services that support a program but are not themselves an active part of that program. In the Java system itself, the garbage collector and finalizer are daemon threads. Similarly, the threads that are used to load images for the getImage() method are daemon threads. Generally, any thread providing a service that is useful only if some other thread exists to use the service is a good contender to be a daemon thread.

To create a daemon thread, invoke the setDaemon() method on the newly created Thread object, with the argument true, before the thread is started.

WARNING   There was a bug in JDK 1.0.2 for 32-bit Windows platforms that prevented the proper exit of a program that has multiple threads. The workaround is to use the join() method in main() to wait for the completion of one of the threads, and you will often see such code in examples. The bug was fixed in the 1.1 release of the JDK.

Thread Groups

Every Thread object created in Java is a member of a ThreadGroup object. The relationship between a thread and a thread group is very similar to the relationship between a file and a directory. A thread group can contain many instances of both Thread and ThreadGroup objects in a hierarchical layout.

The thread group mechanism creates an association between related threads. By default, a newly created Thread object belongs to the same group as the Thread object that constructs it. Several Thread class constructors allow the specification of an explicit ThreadGroup object, overriding this default. The following sections discuss the uses of the thread group mechanism.

Thread Group Control

Putting threads into thread groups allows the threads to be associated, and controlled together, via the ThreadGroup interrupt() method. The security manager can prevent threads in one group from controlling threads in another group.

Group control is useful when a number of threads are operating on related work. An applet, for example, could create a new thread group for multiple threads working on a complex simulation. This allows the entire simulation to be interrupted if the user visits a different page.

Thread Group Security

Another benefit of using thread groups is that the security system can use the mechanism to decide if one thread should be permitted to operate on another. For example, it would be undesirable for an applet to be able to suspend() or stop() any thread that controls the browser.

When you execute thread methods, any installed SecurityManager object is checked to see if the method is permitted. This mechanism is intended to check if the Thread object issuing the call is a member of the same group or a parent group. If the Thread object is not such a member, it would be appropriate to reject the attempt and throw a SecurityException.

NOTE   Although restricting the ability of one thread to manipulate another thread based on the thread group mechanism appears to be a good way to protect browsers from malicious applets that try to deny browser service, the restriction is not implemented in many browsers.

Interaction between Threads

As we've noted earlier, difficulties can arise when multiple threads share data. As an example of what can go wrong, consider the following example, called Crunch. This program is intended to increment the value of x in two concurrent threads; however, it fails to achieve this. The program creates two threads, and these share the data of the Crunch object. When you look at the code, you may think that each thread will increment the value of x and output the thread's name and the result of incrementing x, but this is not the case.

The source code for this example is on the CD-ROM in the directory java-devhdbk\ch07\Crunch.java. The bytecode is in the corresponding .class file in the same directory.

LIST 7.4   *Crunch.java*

```java
public class Crunch implements Runnable {
  public int x;

  public static void main(String args[]) {
    Crunch r1 = new Crunch();
    Thread t1 = new Thread(r1);
    Thread t2 = new Thread(r1);
    t1.start();
    t2.start();
  }

  public void run() {
    int hold;
    for (;;) {
      hold = x + 1;
      try {
        Thread.sleep(1000);
      }
      catch (InterruptedException e) {
      }
      x = hold;
      System.out.println(Thread.currentThread().getName() +
        " value is now " + x);
    }
  }
}
```

When you run the program, it begins issuing messages similar to this (after half a dozen or so messages have been issued, you can exit the program):

```
Thread-1 value is now 1
Thread-2 value is now 1
Thread-1 value is now 2
Thread-2 value is now 2
Thread-1 value is now 3
Thread-2 value is now 3
Thread-1 value is now 4
Thread-2 value is now 4
```

Each thread runs by picking up the value of x, adding one to it, and storing the result in a holding variable called hold. The thread then sleeps for one second. After this, the stored value is replaced in the variable x and written to the standard output.

It is clear in Crunch.java that the second thread will pick up the same value of x as the first, and hence the value in each of the two variables called hold will be the same. This happens because of the long delay between picking up the value of x and the moment at which the newly calculated value is written back into x.

Although this example is greatly exaggerated, it demonstrates the essential nature of the problem. Consider a modified run() method:

```
public void run() {
    for (;;) {
        x++;
        System.out.println(Thread.currentThread().getName() +
            "value is now " + x);
    }
}
```

In this case, it might appear that the difficulty cannot arise, but this isn't so. It is true that the problem arises much less often, because the time when the value of x is vulnerable is greatly reduced, but the statement x++ is actually shorthand for several machine operations. These operations usually take the following general form:

- Load the value from the address of x into a register.
- Increment the register.
- Store the register value at the address of x.

Because these three operations of this read/modify/write cycle are quite distinct and take a finite time to complete, it is possible that the scheduler might change the current thread in the middle of the sequence. In such conditions, the error still arises.

Controlling Multiple Access

The fundamental cause of the difficulty just described is that during manipulation, a data item or group of items might pass through a *delicate* state. This can be a state in which the value is temporarily duplicated in a working variable, a calculation is partially completed, or items in a related data set have been partially changed so the set as a whole is inconsistent. If the current thread happens to stop running while the data is in this delicate state, and some other thread begins instead and also tries to access the data in this delicate state, then a problem arises.

One common feature of all mechanisms that handle these difficulties is that they prevent any other thread from accessing data items while they are in the delicate state. The region of code that has data in a delicate condition like this is known as a *critical section*.

Another common feature of all such mechanisms is that the programmer is responsible for determining the existence of these critical sections and for specifying when the data must be protected.

Applying the Object Lock

Java's protection mechanism hinges on a feature of the Object class called a *lock*. Perhaps somewhat perversely, the object lock may best be described if it is likened to a key. The key fits a particular door that is this grammatical construction:

```
synchronized(obj) {  // Enter through the door,
                     // taking the key with you
                     // Do delicate work
}                    // Leave through the door,
                     // leaving the key on the outside
```

For a thread's execution to proceed inside this block, it must hold the key belonging to obj. Normally, the key is held by the obj itself and is available for the asking. However, when a thread holds the key, it is removed from obj. The key behaves like a physical key in that it is only in one place at a time—it is moved rather than copied.

Now suppose that while it is inside the synchronized block, the currently executing thread is descheduled and another thread starts to run. If the second thread tries to pass through the door, the key will be missing and the thread cannot pass. At this point, this thread is descheduled and waits for the key to be returned to obj.

If one thread is holding the key inside the synchronized block in the context of one particular object, no other thread can enter that region in the context of the same object until the key is replaced. This happens when the thread that holds the key passes the closing curly brace at the end of the block. When the key is replaced, it is possible for the thread that tried to enter earlier to pick it up and proceed.

It is vital to realize that the lock is associated with an instance of a class, not with the code itself. It is entirely possible for two different threads to be executing the code of a single synchronized block, provided that they are doing so in the context of different instances.

This protection has been coded in the example Crunch2.java. The source and bytecode files for this example are on the CD-ROM in javadevhdbk\ch07. The only functional change that has been made is to the body of the run() method. Crunch2.java looks like this:

```
for (;;) {
      synchronized(this) {
        hold = x + 1;
        try {
          Thread.sleep(1000);
        }
        catch (InterruptedException e) {
        }
        x = hold;
        System.out.println(Thread.currentThread().getName() +
          "value is now " + x);
      }
}
```

Given this modification, the output now looks something like this:

```
Thread-1 value is now 1
Thread-2 value is now 2
Thread-2 value is now 3
Thread-1 value is now 4
Thread-1 value is now 5
Thread-2 value is now 6
```

Notice that this version increments x successfully each time that a thread executes the body of the main loop. However, the scheduling has changed unexpectedly, and as a result, the execution order has changed. The scheduling issues will be addressed later in the chapter in the "Communication between Threads" section.

The behavior of the object lock and the synchronized() instruction can be summarized as follows:

- Every object has a lock. This lock is normally attached to the object itself.

- To execute a statement synchronized(obj), a thread must be able to claim the lock belonging to the object obj. Claiming the lock effectively removes it from the object.

- If the lock is not attached to obj when a thread begins executing the synchronized(obj) instruction, the thread is made to stop running until the lock is returned to the object.

- A thread returns the lock to the object when it leaves the block that originally caused it to take the lock.

Notice that an object lock by itself does not prevent data from being corrupted; it only provides a mechanism that allows you to protect critical sections against concurrent execution.

Fully Protecting Data Access

To fully protect a data item, you must use additional mechanisms. Consider the following partial example:

```
public class Crunch3 {
  public int x;
}


    // Threads A and B share an instance of Crunch3 called obj
    // Thread A executes this:
    synchronized(obj) {
      int hold = x + 1;
      x = hold;
    }

    // Thread B executes this:
    int hold2 = x + 1;
    x = hold2;
```

Suppose that Thread A is executing and is just about to store hold into x. If Thread B is run, preempting Thread A, then despite the fact that Thread A holds the lock for obj, the data is still corrupted. This is because Thread B had not been programmed to require the lock for obj before starting the delicate operation.

Remember that the synchronized() instruction does not protect data; it only provides a mechanism that allows the programmer to limit to one the number of threads concurrently executing a critical section. To protect the data, you must treat all potentially delicate accesses as critical and guarded by using synchronized() calls.

To protect all accesses to a data item using the synchronized() mechanism, three conditions must be imposed:

- The data items to be protected must be private members of an object.

- The object that is used for synchronization is this.

- You need to ensure that any accesses made to these data items must be performed inside a synchronized(this) block.

The data must be private because if not, methods in other classes can be written to access the data directly. These methods in other classes might not be in a synchronized block, which would leave the data unprotected.

Different objects can require their own critical sections. Just because a thread is doing something to data on one particular instance of a class does not mean that another thread should not operate on data in a different instance of the same class. This means that the lock that should be used is the one associated with the object that contains the data being manipulated.

Because the data must be private, it can be accessed only by methods inside its own class. Therefore, the lock that should be used is the one belonging to the object this.

Finally, having prevented any stray code in other classes from making indelicate access to the data, you must ensure that all accesses in this class are properly protected. You should examine every method in the class to determine whether it has any critical sections. All such sections must then be protected with a synchronized block.

You may be familiar with a popular mechanism for handling critical sections called a *monitor*. It is important to appreciate that a Java class as a whole is not a monitor in the conventional sense unless *all* its nonprivate methods use `synchronized` to protect all data accesses and all its data items are marked as `private`.

Using Synchronized Methods

Because `synchronized` is used most commonly on the `this` object, a convenient shorthand is provided in the language. For example, consider a method of this form:

```
void method() {
  synchronized(this) {
    // Lots of work
  }
}
```

This can be shortened, without changing the meaning, to this form:

```
synchronized void method() {
  // Lots of work
}
```

In the `synchronized` method, the entire method is treated as a critical section. This treatment might result in protecting a larger region of code than is strictly necessary. Although this is often not of consequence, it may reduce the efficiency of the scheduler.

Using Nested Synchronization

Sometimes the design of a piece of software might make it desirable to call a method that synchronizes on an object from a method that is already synchronized on that object. In some types of multithreading systems, this can cause a fatal condition called *deadlock*, in which the thread waits forever for itself to release the lock it already holds (deadlock is discussed in more detail shortly). However, Java's synchronization mechanism does not have any difficulty with this scenario.

The rules for the behavior of the synchronized() call specify that to proceed past the point of the call, the thread must hold the lock. If the thread already holds the lock, then it proceeds without any difficulty. When a thread exits a synchronized block, it returns the lock to the object if, and only if, it first obtained the lock at the entry to this particular block. Because of these rules, Java's synchronization elegantly avoids the self-deadlock problems that can be tricky to avoid in other systems.

The object-oriented nature of Java makes this feature very valuable. Consider a method in a derived class that is marked as synchronized. This method might need to call the method that it overrides, using the construction super .method(). If the superclass method is also synchronized, this would cause deadlock if the mechanism was not as just described.

Synchronizing on Other Objects

Java allows the use of object references other than this in the synchronized call. Using other object references might not be a sound way to create critical sections because it might be impossible to control those references. However, there are conditions where it is appropriate to synchronize on an object other than this.

The simplest way that it can be appropriate and safe to synchronize on an object other than this is with private member variables or method local variables that you know refer to objects that are *never* passed outside the this object. Under such conditions, you are effectively synchronizing on a subset of this. It must, however, be emphasized that it is absolutely crucial to be sure that there are no references to the same object that are accessible outside the this object.

Another situation where it might be appropriate to issue the synchronized() call on an object other than this is when you want to allow a thread to be idle until it is needed. This is accomplished by using the wait() and notify() methods, as discussed in the "Communication between Threads" section later in this chapter.

Synchronizing on Static Members

In addition to the ability to synchronize on an object other than this, Java allows synchronization on classes. To support this, in addition to the lock associated with every object, there is also a lock associated with each class. In a static method, there is no this object, and consequently it would not be meaningful to say that the method obtains the lock of the object `this`. In fact, a static synchronized method obtains the lock associated with the class instead.

In a static method, the only data that can normally be accessed is the static members of the class. Provided these members are marked as private, static synchronized methods form critical sections and can provide some protection for those data items. There is a problem, however. Although a static method cannot access instance data items (unless an instance is passed to the method as an argument), the converse is not true; that is, an instance method is fully able to access static data.

If an instance method is marked as synchronized, the lock that is obtained is the *instance* lock of the object `this`. This lock is not the same as the *class* lock, and hence concurrent access to the static data items remains possible. Because of this, if static data items require controlled access, instance methods must not access static data items directly; rather, they must do so by calling static synchronized methods to perform the access for them.

The data items in an object instance can be protected over part of a method by using the construction `synchronized(this)`. However, Java does not allow the use of a class name in the `synchronized()` statement. Instead, inside an instance method, it is possible to access the class lock by issuing the call `synchronized(this.get-Class())`. This call works because the class lock is actually the instance lock of the class's defining instance of `java.lang.Class`. Unfortunately, the `getClass()` call is an *instance* method of the `Object` class and therefore cannot be invoked inside a static method. Because of this limitation, static methods must be either entirely synchronized or not at all.

Deadlock Considerations

We mentioned deadlock in the previous section. Here, we will describe the causes of deadlock and some broad strategies for avoiding it.

Causes of Deadlock

To prevent concurrent access to data items, those data items must be marked `private` and accessed only via synchronized regions of instance methods in the class itself. To proceed into the critical section, a thread must obtain the lock associated with the object.

Suppose that a thread requires exclusive access to the data of not one, but two distinct objects. To do so, it must obtain two distinct locks—one from each object. So far, there are no difficulties with this description. Now suppose that another thread also requires exclusive access to the same two objects. It cannot proceed until it has both locks.

Because both locks are required, a fatal deadlock condition can occur if the programming is not done with care. Imagine that the first thread has obtained the lock for object A and is about to try to get the lock for object B. Meanwhile, the second thread has obtained the lock for object B and is now trying to obtain the lock for object A. Neither thread can proceed because the other holds the lock that it needs. Because neither can proceed, neither can leave the synchronized block that it has already entered. This means that neither can relinquish the lock it now holds.

This particular type of deadlock, where two threads have each grabbed something the other requires to proceed and cannot release it until able to proceed, is called *starvation* (or sometimes *deadly embrace*) and is a classic textbook case of deadlock.

Other types of deadlock can occur, but all have one feature in common. They all reflect a design error that permits a thread to get into a situation in which it cannot proceed without some change in circumstances, and that change will never occur.

Designs for Avoiding Deadlock

You can avoid deadlock by careful design. Whenever a thread might block because of some prevailing condition, such as the need for a lock flag, there must be no possibility that the stagnation of the thread might itself prevent that condition from changing.

If multiple resources are to be obtained, such as the locks for two distinct objects, you must create a rule defining the order in which the resources will be obtained. If the locks for objects A and B are always obtained in alphabetical order, then there can be no possibility of the starvation condition just described.

Because of the nature of the synchronization mechanism and the danger of deadlock conditions, it is unwise to issue synchronized() calls on objects that might already be involved in synchronization in unknown ways. In other words, if the source is not available for a class, its superclasses, and classes that use the same instance of the class that you are using, do not synchronize on that class. The reason is that if the object is already being used in synchronization, it is not possible to determine if the ordering rules have been adhered to. Additionally, if the class is being used for thread communication, it is possible to break its behavior. For example, it is unsafe to synchronize on an applet because the AWT already does this as part of the painting mechanism.

Threading in the AWT

Java makes use of threading to support several features of the runtime system. Garbage collection and object finalization are both performed by low-priority daemon threads that are created when the JVM starts up. An additional thread is used to handle features of the AWT.

The AWT Thread

The AWT thread handles events and painting. It runs in a loop that waits until an event occurs in the underlying windowing system. Waiting for events blocks a thread, so it is convenient that this is not done in the primary thread of the program. The use of this secondary thread allows the main program design to ignore the problems of *polling* for input. Rather than requiring that the program look for the input, the input comes to the program.

The AWT thread spends most of the time idle—it's blocked, waiting until there is work for it to do. It wakes up when an event occurs. This event happens in response to user input, such as key presses or mouse movements. It also happens when an area of the AWT display has been obscured by another window and is exposed.

When you want an AWT component redrawn, use the repaint() method. This method simulates the exposure of the entire region of the component to be redrawn. The simulated exposure causes the AWT thread to wake in the same way as a real exposure would, and hence the component's paint() method is called.

To allow the AWT thread to be woken up by the main thread via `repaint()` requires a mechanism for the two threads to communicate. This communication is the subject of the "Communication between Threads" section later in this chapter.

AWT Thread Cautions

In an application, there is only one thread handling the AWT behavior, even in a browser that might have many applets displayed simultaneously. Because the AWT thread executes the event-handling methods, it is important not to tie the AWT thread up with long processing. The same caveat applies inside the `update()` and `paint()` methods.

Suppose that an application wishes to perform some processing that takes a significant duration, and this work is to be done in response to clicking the mouse. A good example might be a fractal generator program that allows the user to zoom in on a particular region by clicking the mouse. Consider the flow diagram shown in Figure 7.2.

FIGURE 7.2:

Flow of control handling a calculation during event handling

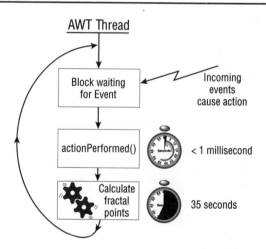

Normally, the time taken for the AWT thread to service the event, via `action-Performed()` or a similar method, would seem very short to the user. This would mean that the AWT thread had returned to the block point and would be ready for the next event fast enough for human eyes to perceive the reaction to the next event as instantaneous.

Now suppose that the calculation of the fractal points takes 35 seconds, as shown in Figure 7.2. This means that the AWT thread is tied up doing this processing for this amount of time; any events that occur during this time will not be serviced until later. The events are not lost, but they cannot be handled until the earlier one completes. One particularly unfortunate consequence of this situation is that if a user clicks a button labeled Abort, it will not be possible for that command to take effect until after the earlier behavior completes.

There is a demonstration of this problem on the CD-ROM. The file can be found in the directory javadevhdbk\ch07\SlowService.java. This code creates a deliberately time-consuming handler for the action of a button. While the `actionPerformed()` method is busy, the example is unable to react effectively to any other events. For example, resizing the frame of the application or attempting to close it down is not acted on until the button press has been serviced completely. (Because the example is very simple, it is neither listed nor described in detail here.)

The program launches a frame containing a button and a label. Try resizing the frame first, and notice that the button and label are redrawn promptly. Next, click the button with the mouse. The program generates numbers on the standard output and takes a significant amount of time to complete the operation. The exact amount of time depends, of course, on the platform. While the output is still counting, try to resize the frame. Notice that the components are not redrawn until after the count is completed. You will notice the same delay if you try to close down the program from the window's control menu while the count is in progress.

To avoid these difficulties, it is important to avoid using the AWT thread for performing protracted processing. Previous sections have described mechanisms that allow one thread to share information with another. For example, your program could pass the coordinates of a mouse-click to a thread that will calculate the zoomed image. What is needed to complete the picture is a mechanism that permits one thread to trigger another to start running so it performs the calculations when needed. Figure 7.3 shows the flow that must be arranged to implement this design elegantly.

The AWT thread is used only to determine that the recalculation should be made and to collect the parameters for that calculation. The work is then done by a separate thread that is dedicated to performing this calculation. In this way, all the remaining features of the user interface remain active, and it is possible to react to an Abort button, for example.

FIGURE 7.3:

Using a separate thread to handle protracted calculation outside of AWT event handling

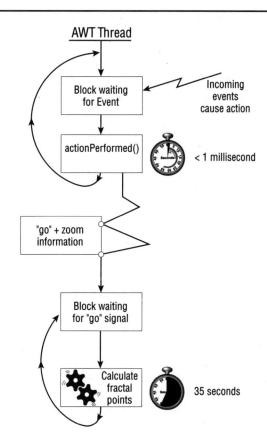

Communication between Threads

A common technique for programming thread communications is by using the `PipedInputStream` and `PipedOuputStream` classes, and we will cover that method first. However, although pipes are easy and convenient to use, they do not suit all situations in which threads need to communicate. In fact, pipe input and output streams are not the most fundamental forms of thread communication in Java. In the following sections, we will cover Java's wait/notify mechanism as well as some other thread-communication techniques.

Pipes for Communications

The simplest way to arrange communication between threads is by using the classes `PipedInputStream` and `PipedOutputStream`. Consider the following example, named `Pipe.java`. This program creates two threads, which communicate over a `PipedInputStream`/`PipedOutputStream` pair. The sender thread issues five bytes, chosen at random, at random intervals of less than one second. The receiver thread collects these bytes and prints them when they arrive. The source code for this example is on the CD-ROM in the directory `javadevhdbk\ch07\Pipe.java`; the three corresponding bytecode files are in the same directory.

LIST 7.5   *Pipe.java*

```java
import java.io.*;

public class Pipe {
  public static void main(String args[]) throws Exception {
    PipedInputStream in = new PipedInputStream();
    PipedOutputStream out = new PipedOutputStream(in);

    Sender s = new Sender(out);
    Receiver r = new Receiver(in);
    Thread t1 = new Thread(s);
    Thread t2 = new Thread(r);
    t1.start();
    t2.start();
  }
}

class Sender implements Runnable {
  OutputStream out;

  public Sender(OutputStream out) {
    this.out = out;
  }

  public void run() {
    byte value;

    try {
      for (int i = 0; i < 5; i++) {
```

```
            value = (byte)(Math.random() * 256);
            System.out.print("About to send " + value + ".. ");
            out.write(value);
            System.out.println("..sent..");
            Thread.sleep((long)(Math.random() * 1000));
          }
          out.close();
        }
      catch (Exception e) {
        e.printStackTrace();
      }
    }
  }
}

class Receiver implements Runnable {
  InputStream in;

  public Receiver(InputStream in) {
    this.in = in;
  }

  public void run() {
    int value;

    try {
      while ((value = in.read()) != -1) {
        System.out.println("received " + (byte)value);
      }
      System.out.println("Pipe closed");
    }
    catch (Exception e) {
      e.printStackTrace();
    }
  }
}
```

The combination of PipedInputStream and PipedOutputStream acts as a conveyer
belt for bytes between the two threads. Bytes written into the PipedOutputStream
will arrive at the PipedInputStream in the same order in which they were sent,
with none missing. The nature of these streams is that the receiver thread is made

nonrunnable while it is waiting for characters and is made runnable again when characters are available.

A typical output from the program looks like this:

```
About to send -8.. ..sent..
received -8
About to send -87.. ..sent..
About to send 24.. ..sent..
received -87
received 24
About to send -52.. ..sent..
About to send 92.. ..sent..
received -52
received 92
Pipe closed
```

Notice that all the bytes that were sent were received in the correct order, and the receiver thread is able to correctly determine when the sender has closed the connection. However, the receiver does not wake up the instant that the sender places the output byte into the stream. In some cases, several characters have been written before the receiver gets a chance to run.

NOTE The `Pipe` program output shown here was obtained on a Windows 95 system, where priorities are not viewed strictly according to the preemptive scheduling model, but rather are taken as indications of relative proportion of CPU time. On that platform, raising the priority of the receiver does not significantly change the output seen. Other platforms, such as Solaris, do implement preemptive scheduling style priorities, and the receiver does indeed pick up the bytes immediately if its priority is raised. This example is typical of the type of scheduling differences that occur between different platforms and the kind of effects these differences can have on how a program runs.

Flag Variables

The general approach for all communication between threads is that one thread prepares an item of data, another thread is informed, and then that other thread picks up and uses that item.

Suppose that the data item is a simple integer. As a first suggestion, an int member variable could be defined in the Runnable class of the sender thread, and the Runnable class of the receiving thread could be written so it could read that value. Clearly, this is not sufficient by itself, because the receiver cannot be informed when the variable contains a value that is valid. Some value is always present in the variable, hence the reader cannot distinguish between a proper value it should read and any other value, such as an old one, that happens to be in the variable.

This problem can be overcome by the use of a flag variable of some sort, typically a boolean value. The sender sets this to true just after it deposits a value in the variable. This solution has another improvement over the first suggestion— the receiver must set the flag back to false when it has read the value. This provides a means for the sender to know that the value has been read, and hence to know that it is safe to write the next value into the variable.

Consider the following example, which implements this idea. The file can be found on the CD-ROM in the directory javadevhdbk\ch07\FlagComm.java. The three corresponding class files are located in the same directory.

LIST 7.6   *FlagComm.java*

```java
public class FlagComm {
  public static void main(String args[]) {
    FlagSend s = new FlagSend();
    FlagRec r = new FlagRec(s);
    Thread st = new Thread(s);
    Thread rt = new Thread(r);
    rt.setDaemon(true);             // The receiver doesn't die
    st.start();
    rt.start();
    try {
      while (s.isValid) {           // Give receiver a chance to
        Thread.sleep(100);          // read the final value
      }
    }
    catch (InterruptedException e) {
      e.printStackTrace();
    }
  }
}
```

```
class FlagSend implements Runnable {
  volatile int theValue;
  volatile boolean isValid;

  public void run() {
    for (int i = 0; i < 5; i++) {
      while (isValid) {
        Thread.yield();
      }
      theValue = (int)(Math.random() * 256);
      System.out.println("sending " + theValue);
      isValid = true;
    }
  }
}

class FlagRec implements Runnable {
  FlagSend theSender;

  public FlagRec(FlagSend sender) {
    theSender = sender;
  }

  public void run() {
    while (true) {
      while (!theSender.isValid) {
        Thread.yield();
      }
      System.out.println("received " + theSender.theValue);
      theSender.isValid = false;
    }
  }
}
```

When you run the program, it generates output similar to this:

```
sending 177
received 177
sending 236
received 236
sending 181
```

```
received 181
sending 53
received 53
sending 140
received 140
```

Sending Values

The main() method in the FlagComm class creates an instance of each of the classes FlagRec and FlagSend. These instances are used to create two threads that are run. The sender and receiver threads then communicate using the principles just outlined.

The two shared variables are theValue and isValid, both in the FlagSend class. When the instance of FlagSend is constructed, these are initialized to zero and false, respectively. When the sender wishes to transmit a value, it loops waiting until the value of isValid is false. Because this is the starting condition, the value is written immediately. Once the value has been written, the flag isValid is set to true. The sender then loops round to send the next value. Because isValid is true, it will wait in the loop until this variable is changed by the receiving thread.

When the receiver thread starts, isValid is initially false. This causes it to loop until the sender thread changes this to true. As just described, this happens after the variable theValue has been set to a proper value. At this point, the loop test returns false, and the loop exits. Hence, the receiver thread reads theValue and writes it to the output. After reading this value, the receiver thread sets isValid back to false, which informs the sender thread that it is able to place the next value in theValue.

Testing the isValid Value

Notice how the value of isValid is crucial to the correct operation of this program design. It acts as a gate, allowing the sender to write a value without destroying a previous value that has not been used, and it ensures that the receiver is able to read a value without the risk of picking up an old value.

The drawback with this approach is that it is inefficient. Consider a situation in which these two threads communicate rarely—perhaps if the sender thread takes a significant time to prepare the data or the receiver takes time to handle the value sent. Under these conditions, one or the other thread would be looping round, testing the value of isValid many times until it finally changed.

Note that in this program, the declarations of theValue and isValid are marked with the modifier volatile. If this marking were not done, the Java compiler would be at liberty to consider the value of these variables as being under the sole control of this thread. Hence, the compiler could optimize the loop so it does not read the value each time round, but instead remembers the value in a register. This would prevent it from noticing the change. The keyword volatile tells the compiler not to make such assumptions, informing it that the value might be affected unexpectedly from outside the scope of its execution flow analysis.

Java's Wait/Notify Mechanism

Java provides mechanisms that allow a thread, such as the sender and receivers in FlagComm.java, to be blocked and wake up at the moment that conditions would allow them to usefully proceed. This mechanism is built around two methods of the Object class: wait() and notify().

Every object in Java has the ability to keep track of a pool of blocked threads attached to it. A thread joins this pool by issuing the wait() call on the object whose pool it wishes to join. At some later time, another thread can issue the notify() call. If only the one thread were waiting in the pool, and the notify() method were invoked on the same object as the one on which wait() was called, then the first thread would leave the waiting pool.

 For reasons that will be discussed later, wait() and notify() must only be issued inside a synchronized block. The WaitComm program demonstrates the use of wait() and notify (). The basic algorithm of this example is the same as that used in FlagComm.java. The differences are in the handling of the wait phase that each thread has when it is unable to proceed. The source code for this example is on the CD-ROM in the directory javadevhdbk\ch07\WaitComm.java. The corresponding bytecode files are in the same directory.

LIST 7.7   *WaitComm.java*

```java
public class WaitComm {
  public static void main(String args[]) {
    WFlagSend s = new WFlagSend();
    WFlagRec r = new WFlagRec(s);
    Thread st = new Thread(s);
    Thread rt = new Thread(r);
    rt.setDaemon(true);              // The receiver doesn't die
    st.start();
```

```
      rt.start();
      try {
        st.join();                  // Wait for sender to exit
        while (s.isValid) {         // Give receiver a chance to
          Thread.sleep(100);        // read the final value
        }
      }
      catch (InterruptedException e) {
        e.printStackTrace();
      }
    }
  }
}

class WFlagSend implements Runnable {
  volatile int theValue;
  boolean isValid;

  public void run() {
    for (int i = 0; i < 5; i++) {
      synchronized(this) {
        while (isValid) {
          try {
            this.wait();
          }
          catch (InterruptedException e) {
            e.printStackTrace();
          }
        }
      }
      theValue = (int)(Math.random() * 256);
      System.out.println("sending " + theValue);
      synchronized(this) {
        isValid = true;
        this.notify();
      }
    }
  }
}

class WFlagRec implements Runnable {
  WFlagSend theSender;
```

```java
      public WFlagRec(WFlagSend sender) {
        theSender = sender;
      }

      public void run() {
        while (true) {
          synchronized(theSender) {
            while (!theSender.isValid) {
              try {
                theSender.wait();
              }
              catch (InterruptedException e) {
                e.printStackTrace();
              }
            }
          }
          System.out.println("received " + theSender.theValue);
          synchronized(theSender) {
            theSender.isValid = false;
            theSender.notify();
          }
        }
      }
    }
```

NOTE
The variable `isValid` is not marked as `volatile` in `WaitComm.java`. This is because all accesses are protected by `synchronized` blocks. These blocks prevent the value from being accessed or modified by one thread when the other needs to access to it. Furthermore, the specification of a `synchronized` block guarantees to write back into main memory any values that have been copied by the thread for optimization.

Checking the Test Condition

In the case of both the sender and receiver, the threads use the following approach to check the test condition before proceeding. One half of the approach is:

• Enter a `synchronized` block. This is synchronized on the object that supplies both the flag value and the wait pool.

- Test the flag value.

- If the flag value is such that the thread can properly continue immediately, then do so. Exit the synchronized block on the way out.

- If the flag value says that the thread cannot proceed, then it calls the wait() method on the synchronized object. This causes it to become blocked and temporarily release the lock.

The other half of the approach, used by the other thread, is:

- Enter a synchronized block, which is also synchronized on the same object that was used by the other thread; that is, the object that provides the flag value.

- Set the flag to the value that allows the other thread to proceed.

- Call the notify() method on the synchronized object. If the other thread was idle in the wait() method, this call causes it to stop waiting, which is appropriate because the flag value now has the state required to allow it to proceed.

When either of the threads in WaitComm.java is woken up by a notify() call, it loops around to check if the state of the flag variable is set to the value required for it to proceed. This is not strictly necessary because, provided the program has been written correctly, the thread leaves the wait() method only when the variable has the correct value.

> **WARNING** As the try{}/catch() blocks that surround the wait() method call suggest, it is possible for wait() to exit under conditions other than receipt of a notify(). This can happen if the thread receives an interrupt() call. It is therefore common to see a loop of this form that tests the flag condition and calls the wait() method inside the loop. Although this is not necessary if the program is correctly written, the use of imported classes from unknown or untrusted sources, such as Internet servers, makes this an unverifiable assumption. Hence, we recommend using a loop as a matter of general course.

Synchronizing wait() and notify()

The Java language requires that the wait() and notify() methods be called only by a thread that holds the lock for the object on which the methods are invoked.

In other words, the thread must be synchronized on that object, because the data that controls the coordination of the threads must usually be protected from the kind of problems that were described earlier in the chapter, in the "Interaction between Threads" section. As an example of the type of problem that can arise, consider the following scenario.

Multiple threads are operating independently but sharing a particular counter value that represents a number of items currently available for use (it does not matter what the items are). A thread that wishes to use one of these items must first check if one is available. If there is, then it must reduce the count and proceed to use that item. After it has finished with the item, it increases the count to reflect this. The wait() and notify() methods are used to allow a thread that releases one of the items to wake up another thread that might be currently waiting. Consider this code fragment, which describes an attempt to address part of this design:

```
int countOfItems = 3;

void useItem() {
  while (countOfItems < 1)
    wait();
  countOfItems -;

  //Do the work
  countOfItems++;
  notify();
}
```

The design intention is that a thread that needs to use an item enters this method and loops, testing the value of countOfItems. If the value is found to be zero, the thread enters the wait() method. When another thread relinquishes one of these items, it increases the count and issues the notify() method. At this point, the first thread retests the value of countOfItems and determines that it is now greater than zero. So far, all is well, but consider what happens if another thread happens to start running and immediately performs the same test: It also will decide that at least one of the shared items is available and will proceed to the section that does the work. Therefore, clearly this implementation does not succeed in coordinating the threads properly.

The solution for this problem, as described in the earlier discussion, is to place the entire read/modify/write cycle of the access inside a synchronized block.

Releasing the Lock in wait()

Closer consideration of the use of synchronized blocks around wait() and notify() calls raises an interesting problem. As we've discussed previously, to enter a synchronized block, a thread must be able to obtain the lock for the object in question. This appears to mean that when one thread blocks inside the wait() call, no other thread can possibly enter the synchronized block to issue the notify() call. Clearly, because the example works, there must be some special exception being made here.

When a thread issues a wait() call, it actually releases the lock that it holds. This is done deliberately to avoid the kind of deadlock just described. Because the lock is released, the other thread is able to enter its synchronized block and issue the notify() call. At this point, it might be expected that the newly notified thread might become runnable, but this is *not* the case. To enforce the semantics of the synchronized block, the thread actually waits to reclaim the lock for the object. Only when the lock is reclaimed does the thread again become runnable.

This means that the significance of the synchronized block is slightly different from the earlier description. It is not actually true to say that the thread holds the lock flag for as long as it is inside the synchronized block, but more precisely, it is guaranteed to perform no processing unless it has the lock. Hence, the synchronized block is still an effective way to protect data from multiple concurrent accesses.

WARNING   With the sole exception of wait(), you should generally avoid using methods that might block a thread inside a synchronized block. If other methods such as sleep() are used, the lock is retained during the blocked time, and other threads are locked out of any synchronized blocks. Sometimes, this kind of lockout is precisely what you require, but be sure of this before you code such a construction. An example of just this type of behavior is shown in the last example in this chapter, ReadWrite.java.

Timing wait() and notify()

There is a crucial feature of the wait()/notify() pair that we have not yet discussed: If no thread is waiting in an object's wait pool at the instant that a notify() is issued, then the notify() does nothing and is lost. In other words, the next thread to issue the wait() call does, in fact, wait until a further notify() is issued. It does not return from wait() immediately on the basis of the earlier notify().

This is another reason that wait() and notify() are not usually used in isolation, but rather in conjunction with a flag variable of some sort. To keep track of the number of notify() calls made, you could use an integer counter.

Handling Timeout Conditions

Sometimes, it is necessary for a thread to wait for some condition that might not occur or might not occur soon enough. In these cases, it is desirable to be able to cause the wait to be abandoned after a certain period of time. This is generally called a *timeout period*.

Java provides two modified versions of the wait() method, which accept arguments indicating a maximum period to wait. After that period, the wait is timed out and abandoned. One of these methods accepts a single long value that is taken to be a number of milliseconds. The other takes a long indicating milliseconds and an int indicating additional nanoseconds.

If a wait() method times out, there is no indication in the calling thread that the wait() ended in a timeout rather than by receipt of a notify(). Use of a flag variable will allow this situation to be recognized.

WARNING   In principle, the second version of the wait() method allows quite precise control over the maximum wait period. In practice, as is the case with the sleep() methods that have similar argument choices, the thread will not start running immediately when the wait() period expires, but some time later when the scheduler sees fit. Therefore, the higher-resolution version is meaningful only if the target platform and thread-scheduling mechanism are known and care is taken, based on that platform knowledge, to ensure that the thread will start executing immediately if the wait() times out.

Although Java provides the ability to limit the wait() method with a timeout, the same is not true of the synchronized() call. In general, the lock for any object should not be held for a protracted period of time. Instead, the synchronized() mechanism should be used only to protect data items against the damage caused by concurrent access. The actual communication should be done using variables that are protected in this way. Adopting this approach, combined with the use of wait() and notify(), to advise threads of when conditions have changed should mean that it is never necessary to hold the lock for long.

Another useful approach that can minimize the need to hold locks is to perform I/O or similar operations using temporary space created exclusively for a single call. In this approach, a synchronized block is used only while the data block is copied to or from that exclusive space.

Ordering Exit from wait()

As we stated earlier, a thread will awaken from the wait() method if it is the only thread waiting on the object notified. If more than one thread is waiting and a single notify() is issued, then only one of the waiting threads will be removed from the wait pool and will start waiting to reclaim the object lock before becoming runnable.

In many systems that implement a wait/notify mechanism, the thread that wakes up is the one that has been waiting longest. In other words, threads are placed in a *first in, first out*, or *FIFO*, queue. However, Java does not provide this guarantee. All that is required by the language specification is that when notify() is called on an object, if there are threads currently idle in the wait() method, one of them will be removed. Nothing is specified about which one. This lack of specification is deliberate to allow Java to be implemented reasonably efficiently on any underlying threading mechanism. Your programs must ensure that if multiple threads are waiting on the same object, they are all equally appropriate choices to be woken by a notify() call.

Waking Up Multiple Threads

In most cases, communication between threads is a point-to-point affair. One thread needs some kind of input from some other single thread. However, occasionally it might be that multiple threads are waiting for a condition and some other thread needs to restart them all. This is possible using the method notifyAll().

As with the single notify() method, be aware that the threads released by notifyAll() do not become immediately runnable. Because wait() can be issued only in a synchronized block, none of the threads that leave the wait state can become runnable until it regains the object lock. This can happen to only one thread at a time.

Controlling Wakeup Order

If a design calls for threads to be released in a particular order, then additional efforts must be made to ensure this. To control wakeup order, you must keep track of all the threads that are waiting and the order in which they should be woken. Typically, the desired wakeup order will be the same order in which the threads started to wait. When one is to be notified, that thread's identity is placed in another variable and the notifyAll() method is invoked. Each waiting thread is then able to continue execution, subject to reclaiming the lock. When each one does actually start, it checks its own identity against that noted in the variable. If the identities do not match, the thread reenters the wait() call.

A drawback of this approach is that all waiting threads must restart and make their own decisions about which should continue. This is wasteful of both CPU and elapsed time. A better approach would be to direct the notify() call at the single thread that should be woken. This can be done if each thread issues its wait() call on a different object. You can put the objects on which the threads are waiting into a Vector object or other appropriate container that maintains the sequence order of the objects it contains.

The following example implements this idea to guarantee that threads are woken in the same order in which they waited. The source code is on the CD-ROM in the directory javadevhdbk\ch07\Wake.java. The corresponding class files are in the same directory.

LIST 7.8	*Wake.java*

```java
import java.util.*;

public class Wake {
  private Vector stopped = new Vector();

  public void stopOne() {
    Object myLock = new Object();
    synchronized(myLock) {
      stopped.addElement(myLock);
      try {
        myLock.wait();
      }
      catch (InterruptedException e) {
      }
```

```
      }
    }

  public void wakeOne() {
    Object theLock = null;
    synchronized(stopped) {
      if (stopped.size() != 0) {
        theLock = stopped.firstElement();
        stopped.removeElementAt(0);
      }
    }
    if (theLock != null) {
      synchronized(theLock) {
        theLock.notify();
      }
    }
  }

  public static void main(String args[]) {
    Wake queue = new Wake();
    Runnable r = new RunThis(queue);
    Thread t;
    for (int i = 0; i < 10; i++) {
      t = new Thread(r);
      t.start();
    }

    for (int i = 0; i < 11; i++) {
      try {
        Thread.sleep((long)(Math.random() * 1000));
      }
      catch (InterruptedException e) {
      }
      System.out.println("About to wake one thread");
      queue.wakeOne();
    }
  }
}

class RunThis implements Runnable {
  Wake w;
```

```
public RunThis(Wake w) {
  this.w = w;
}

public void run() {
  System.out.println("Thread starting, name is " +
    Thread.currentThread().getName());
  w.stopOne();
  System.out.println("Thread woken up, name is " +
    Thread.currentThread().getName());
  }
}
```

Queuing Threads

The Wake.main() method creates an instance of the Wake class, which implements the queue mechanism for threads described in the previous section. The main() method then creates an instance of the RunThis class, which will be used to create 10 threads. The RunThis object is given a reference to the Wake object so that each of the threads can attach to the queue that the Wake class implements.

TIP   In your own programs, you can use the Wake class for circumstances that require threads to be woken in a strictly FIFO fashion. If a particular program required it, you could add priority handling to allow some threads to jump part of the queue. To do this, you would need to create a specific class, rather than using the Object class, so the priority of each thread could be marked in the queue.

When the threads are started, they issue a message announcing their name, and then they attach themselves to the Wake object's queue using the stopOne() method. The main() method proceeds by issuing wakeOne() method calls at intervals. Each of these calls will restart one thread from the queue. When the threads restart, they issue another message announcing their name.

The important parts of the Wake.java example are the stopOne() and wakeOne() methods.

The stopOne() Method   The stopOne() method starts by creating an Object instance that will be used for the wait() method call. The reference to this object is retained in the variable myLock. The thread must be synchronized() on myLock to allow it to call myLock.wait().

To enforce the order of thread waking, the objects on which the threads wait are placed at the end of a vector. After the object has been appended to the queue, the thread issues the wait() method call. At this point, the thread ceases executing until after a notify() method call has been invoked on the myLock object.

The wakeOne() Method   The wakeOne() method must first determine if there are any objects in the vector. If one is present, it removes that one from position zero, which constitutes the front of the queue.

TIP

Although Java classes, including Vector, are thread-safe in themselves, the potential problems that can arise if the size(), firstElement(), and remove-ElementAt() methods are not used in a synchronized block demonstrate the importance of using classes correctly in a threaded program. In this particular case, it would be useful to have a single additional method in the Vector class that removes and returns the first element of the Vector instance and returns null if the vector is empty. A parallel method, called pop(), is actually provided in the Stack class.

The size(), firstElement(), and removeElementAt() methods are invoked in a block that is synchronized on the stopped object, which forms the queue. This is done to prevent other threads from modifying the stopped vector contents in the middle of this block. The three methods form a critical section of code operating on the vector.

Once an object has been removed from the front of the queue, the wakeOne() method synchronizes on that object and then issues the notify() method.

WARNING

Most versions of Java actually implement the wait pool as a FIFO queue, so it may be an acceptable pragmatic solution simply to assume that this behavior will prevail if you use wait() calls on a single object. However, this cannot be relied on, and bugs arising from this assumption proving false might be very difficult to track down.

Semaphores for Thread Communications

Academic textbooks that discuss multithreaded programming usually introduce a variety of communication and synchronization mechanisms. Although most of these mechanisms have some particular advantages, these advantages are generally related to the readability of the resulting solution in a particular circumstance. In general, the methods are interchangeable, and any one mechanism can be written in terms of any other.

One of the mechanisms that is commonly described is the *semaphore*. A semaphore is usually implemented as a numeric value. Before entering a critical section of code, the programmer issues a down() call. This effectively says, "If the value of the semaphore counter is greater than zero, decrement it and carry on." At the exit from the critical section, you issue an up() call. The up() call says, "Increment the value of the semaphore counter." If the value of the semaphore is already zero when a down() call is issued, the thread is blocked until an up() call is issued by some other thread. In this way, if the semaphore is initialized to a value of one and you are careful to always properly pair the calls to down() and up(), critical sections of code can be protected. Many programming languages and operating systems use the semaphore mechanism as a main way to protect critical sections, similar to how Java's synchronized mechanism is used.

NOTE   A semaphore gets its name from the flag that was used on railroad tracks to ensure that trains did not collide on a section of track. Before the days of electronic communication, in places where a single track was used by trains in both directions, the signalman would have a flag, or semaphore. No train was allowed on the track unless the driver held that flag. When the train passed off the track, the driver returned the flag to the signalman, allowing other trains to use the track. Presumably, the signalman had to walk the length of the track if two trains wanted to go in the same direction, one after the other.

Semaphores that change between the only two values, often one and zero, are called *binary semaphores*. These are typically used to guard critical sections of code.

It is also quite common to work with semaphores that are not restricted to the values one and zero but count from zero up to arbitrarily high numbers. Such a nonbinary semaphore is usually written so the counter is kept nonnegative. Operations are provided that can add an amount to the value and subtract an amount from the value. If an attempt to reduce the value of the counter would produce a negative result, then the counter is left unchanged and the thread waits. Whenever the counter value is increased, waiting threads might be restarted if the count increases to the amount required to permit the decrement operation to proceed. (The partial example discussed earlier in this chapter, in the "Synchronizing wait() and notify()" section, demonstrates a basic nonbinary semaphore.)

The nonbinary semaphore is often used to allocate restricted resources. For example, if three tape devices are available on a computer system, a semaphore could be created and initialized to the value 3. If a thread requires use of a tape drive, it must reduce the count in the semaphore by 1. This action either "allocates" a tape drive for the exclusive use of that thread or blocks the thread until one can be allocated. After the thread has finished with the tape drive, it increases the semaphore value by 1 to indicate that another tape drive is now available. Notice that this scheme also works if one thread requires multiple tape drives. It can attempt to decrement the semaphore counter by, say, 2. When the thread returns from the decrement call, it knows that two tapes are available. Of course, this example does not consider how the tape drives themselves are allocated; it considers only the availability of the devices.

NOTE   The increment and decrement operations are sometimes referred to in academic papers as *V* and *P*. These names are derived from the initials of the Dutch words used for them by their inventor, and as such are not easy to remember. It is more mnemonic to call them *up* and *down*.

 Semaphores can be implemented quite easily in Java. The following code does just that. The source code for this example is on the CD-ROM in the directory javadevhdbk\ch07\Semaphore.java. The two bytecode files, Semaphore.class and SemTest.class, are located in the same directory.

The SemTest class creates two threads; each generates a random number between 1 and 5. One thread attempts to issue a down() operation on a semaphore by the amount of its random number. The other thread sleeps for a while and then increases the semaphore value by its random number using the up() method. Each thread runs in an infinite loop. After a dozen or so lines of output have been generated, stop the program with the appropriate key sequence for your platform.

LIST 7.9   *Semaphore.java*

```
public class Semaphore {
  int value;

  public Semaphore() {
    this(1); // Default value of 1
  }
```

```java
public Semaphore(int initial) {
  value = initial;
}

public void down() {
  down(1);
}

public synchronized void down(int count) {
  while (value < count) {
    try {
      System.out.println("down() has to wait()");
      wait();
    }
    catch (InterruptedException e) {
      // Ignore it, we test the condition again
    }
  }
  value -= count;
}

public void up() {
  up(1);
}

public synchronized void up(int count) {
  value += count;
  notify();
}
}

class SemTest implements Runnable {
  static Thread pThread;
  static Thread cThread;
  Semaphore theSemaphore;

  public static void main(String args[]) {
    Semaphore theSemaphore = new Semaphore();
    SemTest producer = new SemTest(theSemaphore);
```

```
    SemTest consumer = new SemTest(theSemaphore);

    pThread = new Thread(producer);
    cThread = new Thread(consumer);
    pThread.start();
    cThread.start();
  }

  public SemTest(Semaphore s) {
    theSemaphore = s;
  }

  public void run()
    if (Thread.currentThread() == pThread) {
      produce();
    }
    else {
      consume();
    }
  }

  private void produce() {
    int count;

    while (true) {
      try {
        Thread.sleep((long)(Math.random() * 1000));
      }
      catch (InterruptedException e) {
        // Ignore
      }
      count = (int)(Math.random() * 4) + 1;
      System.out.println(
        "producer increasing semaphore by " +
        count);
      theSemaphore.up(count);
    }
  }
```

```
private void consume() {
    int count;

    while (true) {
        count = (int)(Math.random() * 4) + 1;
        theSemaphore.down(count);
        System.out.println(
            "consumer decremented semaphore by " +
            count);
    }
}
}
```

The keys to Semaphore.java are in the methods down(int) and up(int) in the Semaphore class. Both of these are synchronized methods for two reasons:

- These methods perform read/modify/write sequences on the count value. Because this value is shared between multiple threads, it is necessary to handle this modification as a critical section.

- The communication methods wait() and notify() are issued in the down() and up() methods, and the wait() and notify() methods may be invoked on an object only when the thread holds the lock for that object.

The down() method starts with a loop. The loop body is executed until the count value is large enough to allow the decrement operation to proceed without resulting in a negative value. The body of the loop effectively contains only a wait() call.

The up() method, under the protection of a synchronized block, increases the value of the count and then issues a notify() call. This notify() will awaken at most one thread blocked in a wait() call. The affected thread, if any, will be blocked inside the down() method. Therefore, that thread loops around to test if the count value is great enough to allow the decrement it wishes to perform. If this is the case, then the decrement proceeds and the thread returns from the down() method. If the decrement cannot proceed, then the thread goes back into the wait() method, where it remains until another notify() is issued; then the test is repeated.

Thread-Safe Design

This section describes the main considerations that must be given when producing library code that is required to be thread-safe. Remember that all the Java library code is thread-safe, and programmers are entitled to expect published Java packages to be thread-safe (unless a specific warning is included in the documentation—swing is in this category).

The main issues relate to protecting data against the effects of uncontrolled changes. Several earlier examples have demonstrated the nature of the divisible read/modify/write cycle and described the problems this can cause. Consideration of this concept forms the hub of thread-safe design.

Many data representations require more than one primitive variable. For example, consider the idea of a calendar date. To represent this, several forms are possible, but a likely possibility is to use three integer values: one for the day of month, one for the month of the year, and the third for the year itself. What happens when a date is incremented? First, the day field is incremented. If this results in a value that is greater than the number of days in the indicated month, then the month is incremented and the day is reset to one. Similarly, the month and year are modified if the month is increased beyond December. If two threads simultaneously attempt to modify a date that is represented in this way, it is easy to see that severe difficulties could arise. The algorithm described here can be represented like this:

```
day++
if (day > days_in_month(month, year)) {
   day = 1;
   month++;
   // Handle end of year…
}
```

Now suppose that one thread has just incremented the day and is preempted by another thread. That second thread enters this method and increments the day again. If this results in a day past the last day of the month, this thread will enter the body of the condition. Suppose that the original thread now begins running again. It tests the value of day and finds it to be greater than the number of days in the month. It proceeds by entering the body of the conditional, too. After this scenario, the day will end up set to one, apparently having been incremented once instead of twice, but the month has been incremented twice instead of once.

Here is a summary of how problems can arise when two threads attempt to increment a date in the absence of proper protection:

Thread 1	Thread 2	Values
		day = 31, month = 1
day++		day = 32
	day++	day = 33
if (day > ...) {		true, enter body
	if (day > ...) {	true, enter body
day = 1;		day = 1
	day = 1;	day = 1
month++;		month = 2
	month++;	month = 3

Many kinds of data structures exhibit a self-consistency; that is, one part of the data might need to be changed if other parts are changed. Where such a situation exists, the data must be protected using critical sections to ensure that once a thread starts to change a value set, the change proceeds to completion without any other threads breaking in on the incomplete process.

Updating Long and Double Data Items

Most of the primitive data items in Java are *atomic*, that is, they are effectively single indivisible items rather than aggregates of several parts, and it is not possible for such data items to be only partially updated when a thread is descheduled. An `int`, for example, is a single, indivisible value. It is read into the JVM from memory as a single instruction without any possibility of the thread that performs the read being preempted partway through the operation. The same is true for writing such a value from the JVM back into memory.

Continued on next page

However, this is not the case for items of `long` or `double` type. These values occupy 64 bits, and the Java specification allows the possibility that they could be read or written in two *separate* 32-bit operations. Furthermore, the specification allows the possibility that the thread performing the operation could be preempted between the two operations. Hence, if a `long` or `double` value is to be used in a package, it must be treated the same as a compound data structure and be protected with `synchronized` blocks if it is to be properly and reliably thread-safe.

Advanced Thread Interaction: Multiple Reader, Single Writer Locks

All the essential details required for successful thread control and communication have now been introduced. All other thread control and communication methods can be constructed on the basis of the basic `synchronized` block and the `wait()`/ `notify()` method pair provided by Java. This section will describe one final example of more complex thread interaction.

A standard textbook example of more complex thread control is the problem of allowing multiple threads to have concurrent access to a database record for reading, but restricting threads wishing to write. It is generally safe for any number of threads to perform concurrent read operations on a single record, provided that no threads are writing to that record. In the absence of writers, because no data is changing, there is no possibility of reading anything in an inconsistent state.

For any thread to write to a record, that thread must be the only one accessing the record for either a read or write operation. If any other thread attempts to read during the write operation, it might read some parts of the new record and some parts of the old record. If another thread attempts to write at the same time, the record might be committed to the disk with partial information from one thread and partial information from the other. The example presented here demonstrates one of the common solutions to this problem. The source code for this example is on the CD-ROM in the directory javadevhdbk\ch07\ReadWrite .java. This file contains two class definitions; the second class is called `TestReadWrite` and is a basic test and demonstration harness for the `ReadWrite` class. The corresponding bytecode files, `ReadWrite.class` and `TestReadWrite.class`, are in the same directory.

When you run `TestReadWrite`, `ReadWrite.java` creates five threads that each loop continuously. The body of the loop chooses at random either to perform a read or a write operation. The probability of reading is greater than that of writing. To perform the read, the thread calls the `enterRead()` method of the `ReadWrite` object. When the `enterRead()` method returns, the thread sleeps for 100 milliseconds to simulate performing the read operation. After sleeping, the thread calls `leaveRead()`. If the thread chooses to perform a write operation, a similar sequence is used, but the methods `enterWrite()` and `leaveWrite()` are called instead.

LIST 7.10	*ReadWrite.java*

```java
public class ReadWrite {
  Semaphore db = new Semaphore();
  int readers = 0;

  public synchronized void enterRead() {
    readers++;
    if (readers == 1) {
      db.down();
    }
  }

  public synchronized void leaveRead() {
    readers-;
    if (readers == 0) {
      db.up();
    }
  }

  public void enterWrite() {
    db.down();
  }

  public void leaveWrite() {
    db.up();
  }
}

class TestReadWrite implements Runnable {
  public static final int IDLE = 0;
```

```java
public static final int READING = 1;
public static final int WRITING = 2;

private static int nextIdx = 0;
private int stateIdx;
private static int [] states = {IDLE, IDLE, IDLE, IDLE, IDLE, IDLE};
private ReadWrite controller;


public static void main(String args[]) {
  ReadWrite that = new ReadWrite();

  Thread t1 = new Thread(new TestReadWrite(that));
  Thread t2 = new Thread(new TestReadWrite(that));
  Thread t3 = new Thread(new TestReadWrite(that));
  Thread t4 = new Thread(new TestReadWrite(that));
  Thread t5 = new Thread(new TestReadWrite(that));
  t1.start();
  t2.start();
  t3.start();
  t4.start();
  t5.start();
}

public TestReadWrite(ReadWrite c) {
  controller = c;
  stateIdx = nextIdx++;
}

public void run() {
  String name = Thread.currentThread().getName();
  while (true) {
    if (Math.random() > 0.1) {
      controller.enterRead();
      states[stateIdx] = READING;
      showStates();
      try {
        Thread.sleep(100);
      }
      catch (InterruptedException e) {
      }
      states[stateIdx] = IDLE;
```

```
        controller.leaveRead();
        showStates();
      }
      else {
        controller.enterWrite();
        states[stateIdx] = WRITING;
        showStates();
        try {
          Thread.sleep(100);
        }
        catch (InterruptedException e) {
        }
        states[stateIdx] = IDLE;
        controller.leaveWrite();
        showStates();
      }
    }
  }

  private void showStates() {
    for (int i = 0; i < nextIdx; i++) {
      System.out.print(states[i] == IDLE ? " " :
                      (states[i] == READING ? "R" : "W"));
    }
    System.out.println();
  }
}
```

The Behavior of the ReadWrite Class Methods

The main focus of this discussion is the behavior of the four methods in the Read-Write class. An instance of the Semaphore class, developed earlier in this chapter, indicates if the database is in use. When the semaphore value is 1, the database is idle. In this condition, an attempt to claim read or write access will immediately succeed, reducing the semaphore value to 0. After this has happened, further attempts to reduce the value of the semaphore block in a wait() method call until after the value has been restored.

Using the enterRead() and leaveRead() Methods

The methods enterRead() and leaveRead() are both synchronized. This ensures that the value of the variable readers can be modified and tested in an atomic fashion. The Semaphore object operations that are triggered by the value of this variable are included in the synchronized region to ensure that the condition that caused the operations is not changed before the operation takes place.

When a thread executes the enterRead() method, it first increments the value of the counter variable readers. If the value becomes 1, indicating that no other threads are currently reading, then it proceeds by executing the down() method on the database semaphore. If no other threads are currently writing, the down() method returns immediately; otherwise, it blocks. If the thread does block in the down() method, then other threads executing the enterRead() method will block on entry because the method is synchronized and the other thread still holds the lock. On the other hand, if other threads execute the enterRead() method when the first did not block, they will not block, either. They do not block at the entry to the synchronized method because the first thread did not stay in this method; because the value of readers is already nonzero, they do not execute the down() operation on the semaphore.

When a thread executes the leaveRead() method, provided that it is calling it in the correct sequence, no thread can be blocked in the semaphore down() operation. Hence, this thread must be able to enter the synchronized region without significant delay. When it does so, it reduces the value of readers. If this value becomes 0, then the semaphore up() operation is issued, which will potentially unblock a thread currently waiting to write.

Using the enterWrite() and leaveWrite() Methods

Threads entering the enterWrite() method simply perform a down() operation on the semaphore. If no threads are currently either reading or writing, then the down() operation will proceed immediately. If any other kind of access is in progress, then the semaphore value will already be 0 and the down() operation will block.

Threads entering the leaveWrite() method simply perform an up() operation on the semaphore. If a thread is waiting either to read or to write, the up() operation will potentially unblock it.

Reuse of the ReadWrite Class

In your own programs, you can use the ReadWrite class wherever a multiple read, single write lock is required. However, you should understand one crucial aspect of its design. As with the Semaphore class, it is imperative that the program that uses the ReadWrite class should be correctly designed to pair up calls to the enter and leave methods correctly.

If a leave method is called by a thread that has not called the corresponding enter method, the lock will be broken and improper access might be granted to some other thread. Similarly, if a thread fails to call the corresponding leave method after calling an enter method, then the lock becomes sealed permanently against some types of access. Specifically, failing to call leaveRead() will prevent any further write operations; failing to call leaveWrite() will lock out all access. Wherever possible, these calls should be wrapped directly around the database-access methods themselves to produce a new compound method. In this way, the danger of incorrect coding can be reduced to a minimum.

Summary

This chapter has described the threading mechanism in Java. Some of the ideas are specific to the implementation of Java threads, but most of the ideas relate to threading in any language. Specific discussions have covered creation and control of Java threads and the significance of the AWT event-handler thread. Ideas that relate to threading in any environment include the scheduling of threads on platforms that have fewer physical CPUs than threads and the problems of interaction between threads. A substantial discussion, with a number of examples, covered the control of this type of interaction as well as the communication between threads.

In the next chapter, we will cover programming techniques for animation, which put to use the threading concepts presented in this chapter.

CHAPTER

EIGHT

8

Animation

- In-place animation techniques

- Rubber banding techniques

- Ticker-tape animation techniques

- Sprite animation techniques

Animation is the display of graphics that change over time. The Java core API provides limited support for animation. There are no explicit animation classes, although the upcoming Animation and JavaMedia APIs will eventually provide sophisticated support. However, with a solid understanding of images (discussed in Chapter 6) and threads (discussed in Chapter 7), you can implement a number of animation techniques. This chapter investigates four of these techniques: in-place animation, rubber-band animation, ticker-tape animation, and sprite animation.

In-Place Animation

With in-place animation, changing visuals are displayed in a dedicated region of the screen. The individual frames of the animation are generally loaded from external files or generated by software before the animation begins. Either way, the frames are typically stored in an array of images. The job of the animation software is to draw the appropriate image onto the screen at the appropriate time.

In-place animation is, for the most part, straightforward. What requires care is ensuring that the GUI of an animating applet or application continues to be sensitive to user input while the animation is running. This is done with a thread.

In its most common form, in-place animation uses an array of images to store the frames of an animation and an int instance variable to indicate the index in the array of the next frame to be displayed. The animation thread executes an infinite loop in which it sleeps, bumps the index, and calls `repaint()`.

In-Place Animation Pitfalls

A simple applet that implements in-place animation is listed below. It is assumed that the `initImages()` method somehow initializes the `images[]` array. Code like this is a good first step, but a few important details are overlooked; as it stands, this code is not robust (and therefore does not appear on the CD-ROM).

```java
import      java.awt.*;
import      java.applet.Applet;


public class Bogus extends Applet implements Runnable
{
    Image       images[];
    int         index;
    Thread      animator;


    public void init()
    {
        images = initImages();
        index = 0;
        animator = new Thread(this);
        animator.start();
    }


    public void run()
    {
        while (true)
        {
            try
            {
                Thread.sleep(100);
            }
            catch (InterruptedException ex) { }
            repaint();
            index = ++index % images.length;
        }
    }


    public void paint(Graphics g)
    {
        g.drawImage(images[index], 0, 0, this);
    }

    // ...
}
```

This design is simple and probably familiar. The animation thread spends most of its time asleep. Every now and then it wakes up, calls repaint(), and bumps the image index. The call to repaint() schedules a call to update(), which calls paint(); all of this happens in a thread separate from the animator thread, which is asleep while the screen refresh is going on.

> **NOTE**
>
> The example in this section uses an array of images built from scratch in the init() method. Animations that load their images from files should use a media tracker to ensure that all images are fully loaded. See Chapter 6 for a discussion of how and why a media tracker is used.

There are several problems with this code:

- When the user browses away from the page containing the applet (either by surfing to a different page or by iconifying the browser), the animator thread continues to run, wasting CPU cycles in support of an animation that cannot be seen. There needs to be code to pause and resume the animation at the appropriate times.

- It is an oversimplification to assume that the animation really should run throughout the lifetime of the applet. The applet itself may want to pause and resume the animation.

- Because update() clears the screen prior to calling paint(), there will be a noticeable flicker.

- The worst part of the design is that there is a potential problem with the integrity of the index instance variable. This variable is written by the animator thread (in run()) and read by the update thread (in paint()). On a platform with preemptive thread scheduling, the run() method might be preempted at any moment, including the moment between incrementing index and computing the modulo.

In the next section, a robust example that deals with each of these issues will be developed.

An In-Place Animation Example

As an example of in-place animation, we will develop an applet called AnimInPlace, which displays a multicolored series of concentric cycloids. The shapes will be familiar to anybody who has played with a Spirograph. The animation begins with just the outermost cycloid. The second frame adds a second cycloid, the third frame adds a third, and so on. Figure 8.1 shows the first frame; Figure 8.2 shows the fourth frame. (The cycloid-generating algorithm is irrelevant to the topic at hand; its code appears on the CD-ROM but is not listed here.)

FIGURE 8.1:

The first frame of the AnimInPlace applet

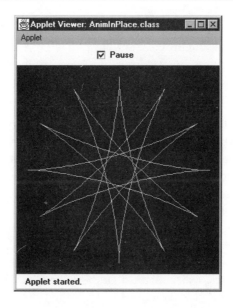

FIGURE 8.2:

The fourth frame of the AnimInPlace applet

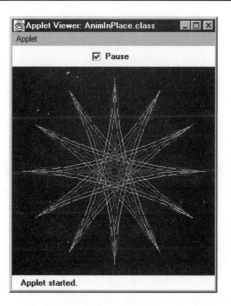

The Pause checkbox is initially not checked. The user may click here at any time to pause the animation; clicking again resumes the animation.

This applet was designed by addressing the four areas where the example of the previous section falls short, as explained in the following sections.

Browser-Initiated Pausing

First, the browser should pause (and resume) the animation when the user browses away from (and returns to) the page containing the applet. The stop() and start() methods of the Applet class are specifically designed to support this functionality.

In theory, the intention of stop() is to provide hooks for suspending CPU activity that does not contribute to the currently visible page. In practice, stop() is most often used for suspending animations and sound clips. The browser should call stop() when the user iconifies or browses to a new page; Netscape Navigator products comply with this, but some versions of Applet Viewer do not. Similarly, the browser should call start() when it is de-iconified or when the user revisits an applet's page. Again, Netscape Navigator products comply and some versions of Applet Viewer do not. The browser automatically makes one extra call to start() at the beginning of execution, shortly after init() terminates, which means that the start() code cannot assume that a corresponding stop() has previously been called. (However, it *is* safe for the stop() code to assume that a corresponding start() has been called previously.)

In the example, stop() should simply suspend the animation thread and start() should resume it. Prior to release 2 of the JDK, this would have been easy: stop() could have called animator.suspend(), and start() could have called animator.resume(). Unfortunately, as of release 2, the suspend() and resume() methods of the Thread class are deprecated, so a more sophisticated technique is required.

The class is given a new boolean instance variable called suspendRequest, which can be set by any code that wishes to pause the animator thread and can be cleared by any code that wishes the animator thread to continue execution. The thread's run() method will need to check this flag each time it executes its loop. If the flag is set, the thread executes wait(), so that it cannot continue until the animator's notify() is executed by some other thread.

The resulting stop() and start() methods look like this:

```
public void stop()
{
    suspendRequest = true;
}

public void start()
{
    synchronized(this)
    {
        suspendRequest = false;
        notify();
    }
}
```

The thread's run() loop must be modified as follows:

```
public void run()
{
    while (true)
    {
        if (suspendRequest)
        {
            synchronized(this)
            {
                try
                {
                    wait();
                }
                catch (InterruptedException x) { }
            }
        }
        try
        {
            Thread.sleep(100);
        }
        catch (InterruptedException e) { }
        index = ++index % images.length;
        repaint();
    }
}
```

User-Initiated Pausing

The applet should support pausing under user control. The Pause checkbox is called pauseBox, and it is the applet's only component. The itemStateChanged() method should pause or restart the animator thread, depending on the state of the checkbox. Pausing and restarting are done exactly as they were in the stop() and start() methods:

```
public void itemStateChanged(ItemEvent ev)
{
    if (pauseBox.getState() == true)
        suspendRequest = true;
    else
    {
        synchronized(this)
        {
            suspendRequest = false;
            notify();
        }
    }
}
```

This causes a problem for the start() method. If the user pauses animation by clicking in the checkbox, browses to a different page, and then browses back again, start() will resume the animator thread even though the animation should still be paused. This means that start() must be refined:

```
public void start()
{
    if (pauseBox.getState() == false)        // if not paused ...
    {
        synchronized(this)
        {
            suspendRequest = false;
            notify();
        }
    }
}
```

Avoiding Screen Flicker

The next issue is screen flicker. When the animator thread decides that a new image should be shown, it calls repaint(), which schedules update(), which clears the applet to its background color and then calls paint(). For a brief time (after update() clears but before paint() draws the next animation frame), the applet just shows a blank rectangle. The user will perceive this as a sporadic flash of color. This color flashing will be more noticeable the more the applet's background color differs from the predominant color of the animation frames.

The solution is to override update(). This method is inherited from the Component class and by default it does the following:

```
public void update(Graphics g)
{
    g.setColor(getBackground());
    g.fillRect(0, 0, width, height);
    g.setColor(getForeground());
    paint(g);
}
```

To eliminate the flash, update() needs to be rewritten so that it just calls paint():

```
public void update(Graphics g)
{
    paint(g);
}
```

Maintaining Data Integrity

The last issue is data integrity. The images of the animation are stored in an array called images[], which is indexed by index. This index is modified in the run() method's infinite loop. The inadequate implementation of the run() loop ends with the following line:

```
index = ++index % images.length;
```

The problem is that this line could be interrupted by the update thread. Consider what happens if the interrupt occurs after index is incremented but before the modulo operation. There are 24 frames in the animation, so index might be anything from 0 through 23, inclusive. An interrupt when index is any value through 22 is no problem. The trouble occurs when index is 23 and its value is incremented to 24. If the interrupt occurs before the modulo operation takes it back down to 0, then paint() will find itself accessing images[24], which throws an array index out-of-bounds exception.

It is instructive to use javap, the Java disassembler, to verify that the code that modifies index really is nonatomic. One nice feature of javap is that for simple examples, it is possible to get valuable information from the disassembled code without actually knowing anything about the JVM's architecture. Begin by building a class that contains a single method that consists of just the line of code to be disassembled:

```
class Atomic
{
    int     index;

    void bump()
    {
        index = ++index % 24;
    }
}
```

Compiling this and then executing javap -c Atomic produces the following output (on the Solaris JDK; other compilers may produce different results):

```
Method void bump()
   0 aload_0
   1 aload_0
   2 dup
   3 getfield #3 <Field Atomic.index I>
   6 iconst_1
   7 iadd
   8 dup_x1
   9 putfield #3 <Field Atomic.index I>
  12 bipush 24
  14 irem
  15 putfield #3 <Field Atomic.index I>
  18 return
```

Line 3 loads the value of index into a virtual register in the JVM. Line 7 adds 1. Line 9 writes the incremented value from the register back into index. Line 14 does the modulo computation (*irem* stands for *integer remainder*), and line 15 stores the final result in index. Clearly, a problem interrupt could happen anywhere between lines 9 and 15.

In the vocabulary of assembly-language programming, an *atomic* operation is one that cannot be interrupted; interrupt requests are not serviced until the atomic operation has completed. In Java, one common interrupt source is thread preemption. Since bumping index is not atomic, there is the possibility of being preempted by the update thread in the middle of incrementing and modulo'ing index.

There are two ways to resolve this data integrity problem: by making sure that index is incremented in an atomic fashion or by synchronizing critical parts of the code to prevent interrupts.

It is not difficult to increment index atomically. The following code will work:

```
int temp = index;
temp = ++temp % images.length;
index = temp;
```

The JVM specification states that 32-bit writes (such as index=temp) are atomic (64-bit writes are not, so it is fortunate that array indexes are ints and not longs). This code certainly does the job, but it is a maintenance risk. If the bumping algorithm changes, the person who modifies the code needs to know that the new code should be atomic and must know enough about the JVM to make it so. In the long run, it is much safer to synchronize the critical sections of the code.

The synchronization solution requires us to look at the code that modifies index (the run() method). The current version of run() is:

```
public void run()
{
    while (true)
    {
        . . .                   // Check for suspend request
        try
        {
            Thread.sleep(100);
        }
        catch (InterruptedException e) { }
        index = ++index % images.length;
        repaint();
    }
}
```

Synchronizing this method would be a disaster—since the method is an infinite loop, no other thread would ever get a chance to execute. From the standpoint of maintainability, the most robust solution is to create a new synchronized method just for incrementing index; this method can be called from run(). Anybody who needs to modify the bumping algorithm knows exactly where to go, and no amount of modification of the new synchronized method can break the synchronization.

The new code is as follows:

```java
public void run()
{
    while (true)
    {
        . . .                    // Check for suspend request
        try
        {
            Thread.sleep(100);
        }
        catch (InterruptedException e) { }
        bumpIndex();
        repaint();
    }
}


private synchronized void bumpIndex()
{
    index = ++index % images.length;
}
```

The AnimInPlace Applet

The four issues of browser-initiated pausing, user-initiated pausing, screen flicker, and index data integrity have now been addressed. The nearly complete listing follows. The omitted method, which is not relevant to the topic of animation, returns the array of images. The full code, including the class that renders Spirograph-style cycloids in an image, is on the CD-ROM in javadevhdbk\ch08.

LIST 8.1   *AnimInPlace.java*

```java
import java.awt.*;
import java.awt.event.*;
import java.applet.Applet;



public class AnimInPlace extends Applet
                    implements Runnable, ItemListener
{
    int             index;
    Image           images[];
    Thread          animator;
    Checkbox        pauseBox;
    boolean         suspendRequest;

    static final int    IMAGE_SIZE = 300;


    public void init()
    {
        pauseBox = new Checkbox("Pause");
        pauseBox.addItemListener(this);
        add(pauseBox);

        index = 0;

        images = initImages(IMAGE_SIZE);

        animator = new Thread(this);
        animator.start();
    }


    private Image[] initImages(int imageSize)
    {
        int         i;
```

```
Color        colors[] =
             {
                 Color.yellow, Color.red, Color.magenta,
                 Color.cyan, Color.blue, Color.green,
                 Color.yellow, Color.red, Color.magenta,
                 Color.cyan, Color.blue, Color.green,
                 Color.yellow
             };


    int nFrames = 2 * (colors.length-1);
    Image frames[] = new Image[nFrames];
    for (i=0; i<colors.length; i++)
    {
        frames[i] = createImage(imageSize, imageSize);
        Graphics g = frames[i].getGraphics();
        g.setColor(Color.black);
        g.fillRect(0, 0, imageSize, imageSize);
        if (i > 0)
            g.drawImage(frames[i-1], 0, 0, this);
        CycloidMaker maker = new CycloidMaker(imageSize, g);
        maker.draw1Curve(7, 12, i, colors[i]);
    }
    for (i=colors.length; i<nFrames; i++)
    {
        frames[i] = frames[nFrames-i];
    }

    return frames;
}


public void stop()
{
    suspendRequest = true;
}


public void start()
{
    if (pauseBox.getState() == false)        // if not paused ...
    {
        synchronized(this)
```

```
        {
            suspendRequest = false;
            notify();
        }
    }
}


public void itemStateChanged(ItemEvent ev)
{
    if (pauseBox.getState() == true)
        suspendRequest = true;
    else
    {
        synchronized(this)
        {
            suspendRequest = false;
            notify();
        }
    }
}


public synchronized void paint(Graphics g)
{
    g.drawImage(images[index], 0, 30, this);
}


public void update(Graphics g)
{
    paint(g);
}


public void run()
{
    while (true)
    {
        if (suspendRequest)
        {
            synchronized(this)
```

```
                {
                    try
                    {
                        wait();
                    }
                    catch (InterruptedException x) { }
                }
            }
            try
            {
                Thread.sleep(100);
            }
            catch (InterruptedException e) { }
            bumpIndex();
            repaint();
        }
    }


    private synchronized void bumpIndex()
    {
        index = ++index % images.length;
    }
}
```

Rubber-Band Techniques

Rubber-band lines are user-drawn outlines of regions of the screen. They are often seen in drawing programs to support user selection of a particular visible object or objects.

Usually, a rubber-band operation begins when the user presses a mouse button and continues while the mouse is dragged. Through the duration of the operation, a rectangle appears on the screen, tracking the movement of the mouse. One corner of the rectangle is defined by the point where the mouse button went down. The opposite corner is defined by the position of the mouse pointer. Since this corner changes as the mouse moves, the user sees a rectangle that stretches and retracts in response to mouse movement, as if it were made of rubber.

Drawing the rectangle presents no difficulty—drawing rectangles is easy in Java. The trick is to undraw the rectangle when it is time to draw a new one. The pixels that the old rectangle overwrote must be restored. In Java there are two alternative techniques, which will be presented in the next two sections.

Rubber Banding with Repainting

The simplest strategy for implementing rubber banding is to use a call to repaint(). Here are the essential points of this strategy:

- When the mouse button goes down, record x and y coordinates in instance variables. This is the "anchor" corner of the rubber-band box.

- When the mouse is dragged or its button goes up, record the new x and y coordinates in instance variables. This is the "tracking" corner of the rubber-band box. Call repaint() so that the screen reflects the proper position of the box.

- In paint(), first redraw the entire background; this erases the previous rubber-band box no matter where it might have been. Draw the new box as indicated by the instance variables for the anchor and tracking corners.

The major benefit of this approach is its simplicity. Implementation is straightforward and easy to refine. The only drawback is a certain lack of efficiency. In order to erase the previous box, the entire drawing area (applet, frame, canvas, or panel) is redrawn. Typically, this involves rendering tens or hundreds of thousands of pixels, all for the sake of erasing a few hundred. Generally, this is not a significant problem; since the program is waiting for the user to tell it what to do next, this is not a time when cycles are precious.

The frequent calls to repaint() during mouse drags can result in flicker if the region being painted is of any appreciable size. It is advisable to eliminate the flicker by overriding update(), as was done in the previous example, so that it calls paint() without clearing.

The RubberBandRepaint Applet

The example below uses this technique to support drawing rubber-band boxes on an image. The applet is called RubberBandRepaint, and the source is found on the CD-ROM in c:\javadevhdbk\ch08\RubberBandRepaint.java. The background is an image that is loaded from an external file.

LIST 8.2	*RubberBandRepaint.java*

```java
import java.awt.*;
import java.awt.event.*;
import java.applet.Applet;


public class RubberBandRepaint extends Applet
            implements MouseListener, MouseMotionListener
{

    Image         image;
    int           xDown, yDown;
    int           xOpposite, yOpposite;


    public void init()
    {
        // Load the image.
        MediaTracker tracker = new MediaTracker(this);
        image = getImage(getDocumentBase(), "Emily.gif");
        tracker.addImage(image, 0);
        try
        {
            tracker.waitForAll();
        }
        catch (InterruptedException ex) { }

        // Handle our own mouse input.
        addMouseListener(this);
        addMouseMotionListener(this);
    }


    public void update(Graphics g)
    {
        paint(g);
    }


    public void paint(Graphics g)
```

```java
    {
        g.drawImage(image, 0, 0, this);

        int x = Math.min(xDown, xOpposite);
        int y = Math.min(yDown, yOpposite);
        int w = Math.abs(xDown-xOpposite);
        int h = Math.abs(yDown-yOpposite);
        g.drawRect(x, y, w, h);
    }


    public void mousePressed(MouseEvent e)
    {
        xDown = xOpposite = e.getX();
        yDown = yOpposite = e.getY();
        repaint();
    }


    public void mouseDragged(MouseEvent e)
    {
        xOpposite = e.getX();
        yOpposite = e.getY();
        repaint();
    }


    public void mouseReleased(MouseEvent e)
    {
        xOpposite = e.getX();
        yOpposite = e.getY();
        repaint();
    }


    // Superfluous listener interface methods.
    public void mouseClicked(MouseEvent e)      { }
    public void mouseEntered(MouseEvent e)      { }
    public void mouseExited(MouseEvent e)       { }
    public void mouseMoved(MouseEvent e)        { }
}
```

One strength of this program is that it follows a very robust design strategy. The event handlers do not directly draw onto the screen. Instead, they record state information in instance variables and then call `repaint()`.

Centralized Drawing versus Direct Drawing

The alternative to this design pattern is to have the event handlers draw directly to the screen. Instead of calling `repaint()`, a handler such as `mouseDragged()` would call `getGraphics()` to get a `Graphics` object and would use that `Graphics` object to undraw the old box and draw the new one. It is worthwhile to compare these two approaches.

Centralizing all screen-drawing operations, as is done in the `RubberBandRepaint` code example, results in code that is much more maintainable. Consider a program that is 100,000 lines long with a `paint()` method that is 1000 lines long. If the screen could be drawn from anywhere in the program, then fixing a screen-related bug or adding a screen-related feature could entail consideration of all 100,000 lines. If, on the other hand, the program follows the guideline of only drawing in `paint()`, only 1000 lines need to be considered.

The centralized painting approach has a second maintenance benefit. Since the screen's appearance is completely determined by state instance variables, the program has accurate knowledge of the screen's state at every moment. If event handlers modify the screen directly, without the intermediate step of recording all state changes, there is no software record of the screen's appearance. With centralized painting, you cannot avoid the discipline of storing all screen state information in instance variables.

There is a third advantage to centralized painting. A frame in an application may receive a `paint()` call at any moment in order to repair damage caused by exposure. When an applet is damaged, some browsers repair via a backing store, but others (notably the Applet Viewer) do not. If a rubber-band box is drawn directly in the `mouseDragged()` method and the frame or applet is subsequently hidden and exposed, then a call to `paint()` would not draw the rubber-band box. It is uncommon for a frame or browser to be covered and exposed while the user is dragging the mouse, but it is possible. For example, many calendar managers spontaneously pop up a dialog box to remind the user of a coming appointment; later the program removes the dialog box. At the moment of removal, whatever was underneath the dialog box is damaged.

NOTE   In the vocabulary of windowing systems, when two windows overlap and the topmost window is moved to expose new portions of the lower window, the lower window is said to be *damaged*. The pixels that formerly belonged to the topmost window must be redrawn because they now belong to the lower window. This redrawing is known as *repairing*. Some programs (Netscape Navigator browsers, for example) maintain a copy in memory of their window's appearance; this copy is called a *backing store*. Such programs can repair damage very quickly simply by copying pixel values from the backing store. Programs that do not use a backing store must repeat the computations that generated the original pixels.

Rubber Banding with XOR

XOR drawing is a technique for drawing graphics in such a way that they may be easily undrawn.

With ordinary drawing (Java calls it *paint mode drawing*), graphic shapes are rendered by setting pixel values without regard to the previous pixel colors. The new pixel value is simply the current color set in the instance of Graphics. With XOR drawing, the new pixel value is (mostly) computed by XORing the current color with the previous color.

To select XOR drawing, call the setXORMode() method of the current instance of Graphics. Subsequent drawing operations will happen in XOR mode until the graphics object executes the setPaintMode() method.

The setXORMode() method takes an instance of Color as an argument, which becomes the XOR color of the graphics object. At this point, the result of calling a drawing method (such as drawLine() or drawRect()) on the graphics object is a function of the current color, the XOR color, and the colors of the pixels being overwritten. The formula for the new pixel value is:

new pixel = old pixel ^ current color ^ XOR color

This formula produces several surprising effects:

- Drawing twice in this mode returns any pixel to its original value.
- Drawing over a pixel that is the current color results in the XOR color.

- Drawing over a pixel that is the XOR color results in the current color.

- Drawing over a pixel that is any other color results in some other unpredictable color.

The important point is that drawing twice is the same as not drawing at all. Thus if graphics object gc is in XOR mode, a box can be drawn by calling gc.drawRect(x, y, w, h), and then undrawn with the very same call.

XOR Mode Trade-Offs

Although using XOR mode provides fast erasure, there are some trade-offs in the potential for color imprecision and programming overhead.

Shapes erased in XOR mode must be erased precisely; any imprecision will show up on the screen. Since colors in XOR mode are determined in part by the color being overwritten, drawing a box over a digitized photograph or any other color-rich background results in a multicolored box, which can be distracting or difficult to see.

The unpredictability of the resulting color can be a problem. Colors cannot really be XORed, after all. The binary numbers that *represent* colors are XORed. These numbers could be true 24-bit red/green/blue values, or they could be indexes into color tables. In the latter case, the resulting color is some new arbitrary color table index. There is no guarantee that the resulting color will even be distinct from the previous color.

The programming overhead results from the additional state variables and the extra logic required in paint(). The paint() method must perform all drawing, so it needs to know what kind of box is currently displayed (none, plain, or XOR) and what kind of box to draw next. An XOR box can be erased cheaply by redrawing; a plain box must be erased by redrawing the background.

The RubberBandXOR Applet

The applet listed here, RubberBandXOR, illustrates drawing a rubber-band box using XOR mode. The box is rendered in XOR mode while the mouse is being dragged and as a solid paint-mode rectangle after the mouse button goes up. The left-hand portion of the applet shows the same digitized image as was used in the RubberBandRepaint example; concentric colored squares appear on the right side of the applet. The applet shows that an XOR box drawn over a color-rich photo is much busier than one drawn over large solid regions.

The code also illustrates the programming overhead required to support this style of rubber-band box. The three constants BOX_NONE, BOX_PLAIN, and BOX_XOR are used to indicate the box state. The box state variables are lastBoxState and nextBoxState. When a new box is painted, the value in nextBoxState is copied into lastBoxState, so that the next pass will know the prior state.

The applet source is on the CD-ROM in c:\javadevhdbk\ch08\RubberBandXOR.java.

LIST 8.3   *RubberBandXOR.java*

```java
import java.awt.*;
import java.awt.event.*;
import java.applet.Applet;


public class RubberBandXOR extends Applet
            implements MouseListener, MouseMotionListener
{
    Image       backgroundImage;
    int         xDown, yDown;              // Where mouse went down
    int         xOpposite, yOpposite;      // Where mouse dragged to
    int         boxX, boxY, boxW, boxH;
    boolean     dragging;
    int         state;
    static final int BOX_NONE   = 0;
    static final int BOX_PLAIN  = 1;
    static final int BOX_1ST_RB = 2;
    static final int BOX_RB     = 3;

    public void init()
    {
        Color colors[] = {Color.red, Color.blue, Color.green,
                          Color.yellow, Color.magenta, Color.cyan};

        // Build the background image.
        MediaTracker tracker = new MediaTracker(this);
        Image emily = getImage(getDocumentBase(), "Emily.gif");
        tracker.addImage(emily, 0);
```

```
        try
        {
            tracker.waitForAll();
        }
        catch (InterruptedException ex) { }
        backgroundImage = createImage(500, 250);
        Graphics g = backgroundImage.getGraphics();
        g.drawImage(emily, 0, 0, this);
        int x = 270;
        int y = 0;
        int wh = 210;
        for (int i=0; i<colors.length; i++)
        {
            g.setColor(colors[i]);
            g.fillRect(x, y, wh, wh);
            x += 20;
            y += 20;
            wh -= 40;
        }

        // Handle our own mouse input.
        addMouseListener(this);
        addMouseMotionListener(this);
    }


    public void update(Graphics g)
    {
        paint(g);
    }


    public void paint(Graphics g)
    {
        // Plain box or no box. Better refresh background.
        if (state == BOX_NONE  ||  state == BOX_PLAIN)
        {
            g.drawImage(backgroundImage, 0, 0, this);
            if (state == BOX_PLAIN)
            {
                g.setColor(Color.black);
                g.drawRect(boxX, boxY, boxW, boxH);
```

```
        }
        return;
    }

    // 1st or subsequent drag box. Keep background.
    g.setColor(Color.yellow);
    g.setXORMode(Color.blue);
    if (state == BOX_RB)       // Subsequent => erase previous box
    {
        g.drawRect(boxX, boxY, boxW, boxH);
    }
    state = BOX_RB;            // In case state was BOX_1ST_RB

    // Draw new box.
    boxX = Math.min(xDown, xOpposite);
    boxY = Math.min(yDown, yOpposite);
    boxW = Math.abs(xDown-xOpposite);
    boxH = Math.abs(yDown-yOpposite);
    g.drawRect(boxX, boxY, boxW, boxH);
}


public void mousePressed(MouseEvent e)
{
    xDown = e.getX();
    yDown = e.getY();
    dragging = false;
    state = BOX_NONE;
    repaint();
}


public void mouseDragged(MouseEvent e)
{
    xOpposite = e.getX();
    yOpposite = e.getY();
    if (state == BOX_NONE)
        state = BOX_1ST_RB;
    repaint();
}
```

```
public void mouseReleased(MouseEvent e)
{
    xOpposite = e.getX();
    yOpposite = e.getY();
    dragging = false;
    state = BOX_PLAIN;
    repaint();
}


// Superfluous listener interface methods.
public void mouseClicked(MouseEvent e)      { }
public void mouseEntered(MouseEvent e)      { }
public void mouseExited(MouseEvent e)       { }
public void mouseMoved(MouseEvent e)        { }
}
```

Ticker-Tape Animation

Ticker-tape animation is a technique for scrolling text horizontally from right to left. The result is similar to the illuminated news flash billboard in Times Square or the live stock market displays found in trendy eating and drinking establishments around the world.

This kind of animation is useful in any program that has access to real-time textual information. Stock market transactions are a perfect example. Here, we will demonstrate how to implement ticker-tape animation in Java without considering the source of the information. The result will be a ticker-tape component class that can be told to display arbitrary strings.

Ticker-Tape Requirements and API

The new ticker-tape class will be called Ticker. It should have the following characteristics:

- Messages should scroll completely. At first, only the leftmost portion of a message's first character should appear. The message should scroll smoothly across the component and disappear off the left edge. The last part to be seen should be the rightmost portion of the last character.

- The component should queue up messages. There should be a reasonable minimum spacing between the end of one message and the beginning of the next.

- The component should be efficient. Clearly, there will be a thread to manage scrolling as long as there are messages to display. When there are no messages, this thread should not consume any resources.

- Client programs should be able to set the font.

- The component should compute its preferred height based on its font size. Tickers often appear in border layouts at North or South, where an accurate preferred height is essential.

With these requirements in mind, a simple API can be specified:

`public Ticker()`   Constructs a ticker that uses the default font (28-point Times Roman plain).

`public Ticker(Font font)`   Constructs a ticker that uses the specified font.

`public void addMessage(String message)`   Tells the ticker to display the message.

Ticker-Tape Class Design

The first design consideration for the `Ticker` class is the handling of the animation thread. This thread's `run()` method should execute an infinite loop. The loop should first see if there are any messages to display; if there are not, the thread should be suspended. If there are messages to display, the thread should sleep for a while, then bump some counter that dictates the horizontal position of the message (called `messageInsetRight`), and lastly call `repaint()`. The `addMessage()` method will need to resume the animation thread if it has been suspended due to lack of messages.

Using a Semaphore for Thread Control

As was the case with the in-place animation example, life would have been easier if the `suspend()` and `resume()` methods of the `Thread` class were not deprecated. In the `AnimInPlace` example, thread control is implemented with `wait()` and notify() calls within the AnimInPlace class. Here, we will take a slightly different approach; we will use a separate object as a semaphore.

The semaphore class is very simple:

```
public class Semaphore
{
    //
    // Should be called by the thread that wishes to suspend.
    //
    public synchronized void suspend()
    {
        try
        {
            wait();
        }
        catch (InterruptedException x) { }
    }


    //
    // Should be called by a different thread, to revive the
    // suspended thread.
    //
    public synchronized void resume()
    {
        notify();
    }
}
```

Our Ticker class will construct an instance of this semaphore and use the semaphore's suspend() and resume() methods for thread traffic control.

Storing Messages

The next issue to consider is how to store the messages. At first glance, it seems natural to store them in a vector using the addElement() method. When a message scrolls off the display, it can be removed from the beginning of the vector with a call to removeElementAt(0). This is in fact what is done, but it will be necessary to maintain additional data.

If addMessage() is called while the ticker component is idle, it is enough simply to begin displaying the new message. However, if the ticker is already displaying something, the code may need to wait for a while before displaying the new message. One of the requirements of the class is that there should be a minimum spacing between messages. We need a way to determine if and how long a new message should wait.

One solution to this problem would be to maintain a record of the position of every message on the screen. Given the position and the width of the message (width is determined by using the FontMetrics class), it is possible to find the right-hand edge. If this is too close to the right-hand edge of the component, the new message must be delayed. This approach can be made to work, but it is cumbersome because the position of each message changes with each pass through the animator thread's loop.

Rather than keeping track of each message's position in space, this implementation records the time at which each message started (or will start) to scroll. (After all, Einstein assures us that there is no real difference between space and time.) The class has two vectors. One, called messages, contains strings. The other, called times, contains times. The unit of time is one iteration through the animation thread's infinite loop. The loop increments a variable of type long, called now; when a new message arrives, the addMessage() method constructs an instance of Long (the wrapper class, not the primitive) based on the current value of now, and adds it to the times vector.

This provides enough information to write the run() method used by the animator thread. The semaphore described earlier will be referenced by a variable called sema.

```
public void run()
{
    while (true)
    {
        while (messages.size() == 0)
            sema.suspend();    // addMessage() will call resume()
        try
        {
            Thread.sleep(TICK_PERIOD);
        }
        catch (InterruptedException ex) { }
         now++;                         // Bump clock time
        messageInsetRight++;    // Bump leftmost message position
        repaint();
    }
}
```

It is now possible to write the addMessage() method. The difficulty here is deciding what value to add to the times vector if there are other messages being displayed. Consider the last message in the messages vector. The time when it began scrolling is recorded in the last element in the times vector; ever since then, it has been scrolling to the left at a rate of one pixel per clock tick. The soonest that displaying of the new message can begin is the last time recorded in the vector, plus the width in pixels of the last message, plus the minimum spacing between messages. This total is called earliestLegal in the code. If earliestLegal is more than the current time (called now in the code), then earliestLegal is stored in the times vector; the new message will be delayed. If earliestLegal is less than the current time, then the message may be displayed immediately, with now stored in the vector.

The addMessage() method looks like this:

```
public void addMessage(String msg)
{
    int size = messages.size();
    if (size == 0)
    {
        // No other messages, start display now.
        times.addElement(new Long(now));
    }
    else
    {
        // Other messages are displayed. May need to delay.
        long lastTime = getTime(size-1);
        String lastMsg = (String)(messages.elementAt(size-1));
        int lastWidth = metrics.stringWidth(lastMsg);
        long earliestLegal = lastTime + (long)(lastWidth+SPACING);
        long scrollStartTime = Math.max(now, earliestLegal);
        times.addElement(new Long(scrollStartTime));
    }
    messages.addElement(msg);
    sema.resume();    // Does no harm if thread is not waiting
}
```

Painting Messages

The last difficult piece of code is the paint() method. It has two jobs. First, it must check the messages at the beginning of the messages vector. If any of them have scrolled completely off the screen, they need to be removed from the vector, and their scroll-start times must be removed from the times vector. The paint() method maintains an instance variable called messageInsetRight, which is the distance from the start of the first message to the component's right-hand edge. If any scrolled-off messages have been deleted, messageInsetRight must be decremented to reflect the position of the new leftmost message.

Next, paint() needs to render messages. The vertical position of every message is controlled by the instance variable messageInsetY, which is computed in the constructor based on the metrics of the font. The horizontal position of the first message is controlled by messageInsetY. The horizontal position of any subsequent messages is controlled by that message's entry in the times vector.

The paint() method looks like this:

```
public void paint(Graphics g)
{
    int             spacing;
    int             canvasWidth;
    int             msgWidth;
    long            lastTime;
    long            nextTime;
    int             deltaTime;

    // Bail if no messages to display.
    if (messages.size() == 0)
    {
        messageInsetRight = 0;
        return;
    }


    //
    //  Delete any messages that have scrolled off.

    canvasWidth = size().width;
    while (messages.size() > 0)
    {
        String msg = (String)(messages.elementAt(0));
        msgWidth = metrics.stringWidth(msg);
        if (canvasWidth - messageInsetRight + msgWidth >= 0)
        {
```

```
            // 1st message in vector is still on screen.
            break;
        }
        // 1st message in vector has scrolled off.
        if (messages.size() >= 2)
        {
            // More messages => adjust messageInsetRight.
            lastTime = getTime(0);
            nextTime = getTime(1);
            deltaTime = (int)(nextTime - lastTime);
            if (msgWidth + SPACING  >  deltaTime)
                messageInsetRight -= msgWidth + SPACING;
             else
                messageInsetRight -= deltaTime;
        }
        // Remove 1st message in vector.
        messages.removeElementAt(0);
        times.removeElementAt(0);
    }

    if (messages.size() == 0)
    {
        messageInsetRight = 0;
        return;
    }

//
// Draw messages.
//
g.setFont(font);
int x = canvasWidth - messageInsetRight;
int y = size().height - messageInsetY;
for (int i=0; i<messages.size(); i++)
{
    String msg = (String)(messages.elementAt(i));
    msgWidth = metrics.stringWidth(msg);
    g.drawString(msg, x, y);          // Draw 1 message
    if (i < messages.size()-1)
    {
        // Determine x of next message
        lastTime = getTime(i);
```

```
            nextTime = getTime(i+1);
            deltaTime = (int)(nextTime - lastTime);
            if (msgWidth + SPACING  >  deltaTime)
                x += msgWidth + SPACING;
            else
                x += deltaTime;
        }

        if (x > canvasWidth)  // Remaining messages are beyond
            return;           // right edge
    }
}
```

The Ticker Class

The complete listing for the Ticker class follows. The code can be found on the CD-ROM in c:\javadevhdbk\ch08\Ticker.java.

LIST 8.4	**_Ticker.java_**

```
import  java.awt.*;
import  java.util.Vector;


public class Ticker extends Canvas implements Runnable
{
    private Font               font;
    private FontMetrics        metrics;
    private Vector             messages, times;
    private int                messageInsetRight;
    private int                messageInsetY;
    private long               now;
    private Semaphore          sema;

    static final int    TICK_PERIOD = 50;    // msecs
    static final int    SPACING = 50;        // pixels


    public Ticker()
    {
        this(new Font("TimesRoman", Font.PLAIN, 28));
    }
```

```java
public Ticker(Font font)
{
    messages = new Vector();
    times = new Vector();

    this.font = font;
    metrics = Toolkit.getDefaultToolkit().getFontMetrics(font);

    messageInsetRight = 0;
    messageInsetY = metrics.getMaxDescent() + 2;

     sema = new Semaphore();
    Thread animatorThread = new Thread(this);
    animatorThread.start();
}


public Dimension getPreferredSize()
{
    int h = metrics.getMaxAscent() + metrics.getMaxDescent() + 4;
    return new Dimension(100, h);
}


public void run()
{
    while (true)
    {
        while (messages.size() == 0)
            sema.suspend();     // addMessage() will call resume()
        try
        {
            Thread.sleep(TICK_PERIOD);
        }
        catch (InterruptedException ex) { }
        now++;                      // Bump clock time
        messageInsetRight++;    // Bump leftmost message position
        repaint();
    }
}
```

```java
public void addMessage(String msg)
{
    int size = messages.size();
    if (size == 0)
    {
        // No other messages, start display now.
        times.addElement(new Long(now));
    }
    else
    {
        // Other messages are displayed. May need to delay.
        long lastTime = getTime(size-1);
        String lastMsg = (String)(messages.elementAt(size-1));
        int lastWidth = metrics.stringWidth(lastMsg);
        long earliestLegal = lastTime + (long)(lastWidth+SPACING);
        long scrollStartTime = Math.max(now, earliestLegal);
        times.addElement(new Long(scrollStartTime));
    }
    messages.addElement(msg);
    sema.resume();    // Does no harm if thread is not waiting
}


private long getTime(int i)
{
    return ((Long)(times.elementAt(i))).longValue();
}


public void paint(Graphics g)
{
    int          spacing;
    int          canvasWidth;
    int          msgWidth;
    long         lastTime;
    long         nextTime;
    nit          deltaTime;

    // Bail if no messages to display.
    if (messages.size() == 0)
    {
        messageInsetRight = 0;
        return;
    }
```

```
//
//  Delete any messages that have scrolled off.
//
canvasWidth = getSize().width;
while (messages.size() > 0)
{
    String msg = (String)(messages.elementAt(0));
    msgWidth = metrics.stringWidth(msg);
    if (canvasWidth - messageInsetRight + msgWidth >= 0)
    {
        // 1st message in vector is still on screen.
        break;
    }
    // 1st message in vector has scrolled off.
    if (messages.size() >= 2)
    {
        // More messages => adjust messageInsetRight.
        lastTime = getTime(0);
        nextTime = getTime(1);
        deltaTime = (int)(nextTime - lastTime);
        if (msgWidth + SPACING  >  deltaTime)
            messageInsetRight -= msgWidth + SPACING;
        else
            messageInsetRight -= deltaTime;
    }
    // Remove 1st message in vector.
    messages.removeElementAt(0);
    times.removeElementAt(0);
}

if (messages.size() == 0)
{
    messageInsetRight = 0;
    return;
}

//
//  Draw messages.
//
g.setFont(font);
int x = canvasWidth - messageInsetRight;
int y = getSize().height - messageInsetY;
```

```
        for (int i=0; i<messages.size(); i++)
        {
            String msg = (String)(messages.elementAt(i));
            msgWidth = metrics.stringWidth(msg);
            g.drawString(msg, x, y);          // Draw 1 message
            if (i < messages.size()-1)
            {
                // Determine x of next message
                lastTime = getTime(i);
                nextTime = getTime(i+1);
                deltaTime = (int)(nextTime - lastTime);
                if (msgWidth + SPACING  >  deltaTime)
                    x += msgWidth + SPACING;
                else
                    x += deltaTime;
            }

    if (x > canvasWidth)  // Remaining messages are beyond
        return;           // right edge
      }
   }
}
```

The Ticker Demo Applet

The `TickerDemo` applet illustrates the use of the `Ticker` class. You type a message into the textfield and then click the Add Message button (or press Enter) to display the message as a ticker-tape animation in the bottom part of the applet. Figure 8.3 shows the `TickerDemo` applet as it begins to show a message, and Figure 8.4 shows the applet as it finishes showing the same message.

FIGURE 8.3:

The TickerDemo applet beginning a message

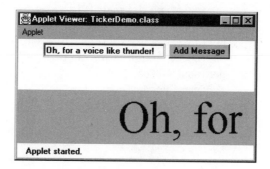

FIGURE 8.4:

The TickerDemo applet
finishing a message

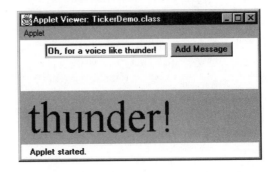

The code for `TickerDemo` is listed below and is also included on the CD-ROM in `c:\javadevhdbk\ch08\TickerDemo.java`.

LIST 8.5 *TickerDemo.java*

```java
import java.awt.*;
import java.awt.event.*;
import java.applet.Applet;


public class TickerDemo extends Applet implements ActionListener
{
    TextField      tf;
    Button         button;
    Ticker         ticker;

    public void init()
    {
        setLayout(new BorderLayout());
        Panel pan = new Panel();
        tf = new TextField(20);
        tf.addActionListener(this);
        pan.add(tf);
        button = new Button("Add Message");
        button.addActionListener(this);
        pan.add(button);
        add(pan, BorderLayout.NORTH);
        ticker = new Ticker(new Font("TimesRoman", Font.PLAIN, 64));
        ticker.setBackground(Color.lightGray);
        add(ticker, BorderLayout.SOUTH);
    }
```

```
    public void actionPerformed(ActionEvent e)
    {
        ticker.addMessage(tf.getText());
    }
}
```

Sprite Animation

Sprites are shapes that move across the screen, often tracking the mouse. Rollover help messages are sprites, and so are drag icons in drag-and-drop systems.

Sprite Implementation Issues

The general problem of sprite animation is how to repair a piece of the display after the sprite has moved past that piece. With sprite animation, elimination of flashing becomes a dominating concern.

The top-level design of a rollover sprite program is easy. The `mouseMove()` method should be overridden; the new version should determine which rollover region (if any) the mouse cursor is in. The old sprite should be erased, and the new one should then be displayed at the cursor position.

In practice, this approach is unsatisfactory. Appearance is fine when the mouse is stationary; but when the mouse moves, the entire screen, including the sprite, flashes severely. There are three techniques for dealing with this problem:

- Override `update()`.
- Adjust the clip region of the graphics object.
- Buffer the clip region off-screen.

These techniques may be used separately or in combination.

Overriding the update() Method

We have already seen how overriding `update()` eliminates flashing in a rubber-band animation, as demonstrated in the `RubberBandRepaint` applet. The technique is to modify `update()` so that it no longer clears before calling `paint()`.

Adjusting the Clip Region

Adjusting the clip region involves calling the `clipRect()` method of the `Graphics` class. The four inputs to this method are the x, y, width, and height of the clipping region. Subsequent graphics operations will take effect only if they fall within the clipping region. As the sprite moves, the only portion of the screen that needs to be refreshed is the union of the old position and the new position. (Fortunately, Java's `Rectangle` class has a `union()` method.) The clip region can be adjusted so that it is the smallest rectangle that contains both the old and the new sprite positions, as illustrated in Figure 8.5.

FIGURE 8.5:

Adjusting the clip region for old and new sprite positions

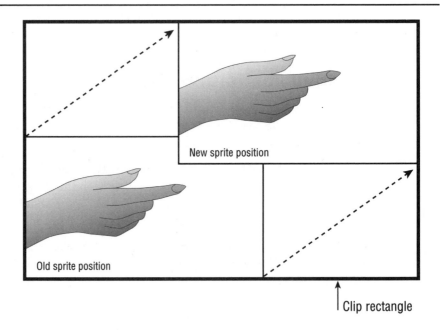

New sprite position

Old sprite position

Clip rectangle

Adjusting the clip region requires a simple three-step algorithm, which sets the clip region, draws the background image, and draws the sprite at its new position. Clip regions are usually considerably smaller than the entire screen, so relatively very few pixels are modified when the sprite moves. This reduces flashing dramatically but not completely. Every time the sprite moves, the portion of the screen at the new sprite position is first set to the background (in the example, this will be the bar chart). Then the sprite is rendered over the background. The background may be momentarily visible, which causes a small flash that can be eliminated with the buffering technique.

Buffering the Clip Region

The buffering technique is used in conjunction with clipping. An off-screen image is first cleared to the background. Next, the sprite is drawn to the off-screen image. Then the off-screen image is drawn to the screen. Since the screen is only drawn once, there is no flash. Figure 8.6 illustrates the use of the off-screen buffer.

FIGURE 8.6:

Using an off-screen buffer for old and new sprite positions

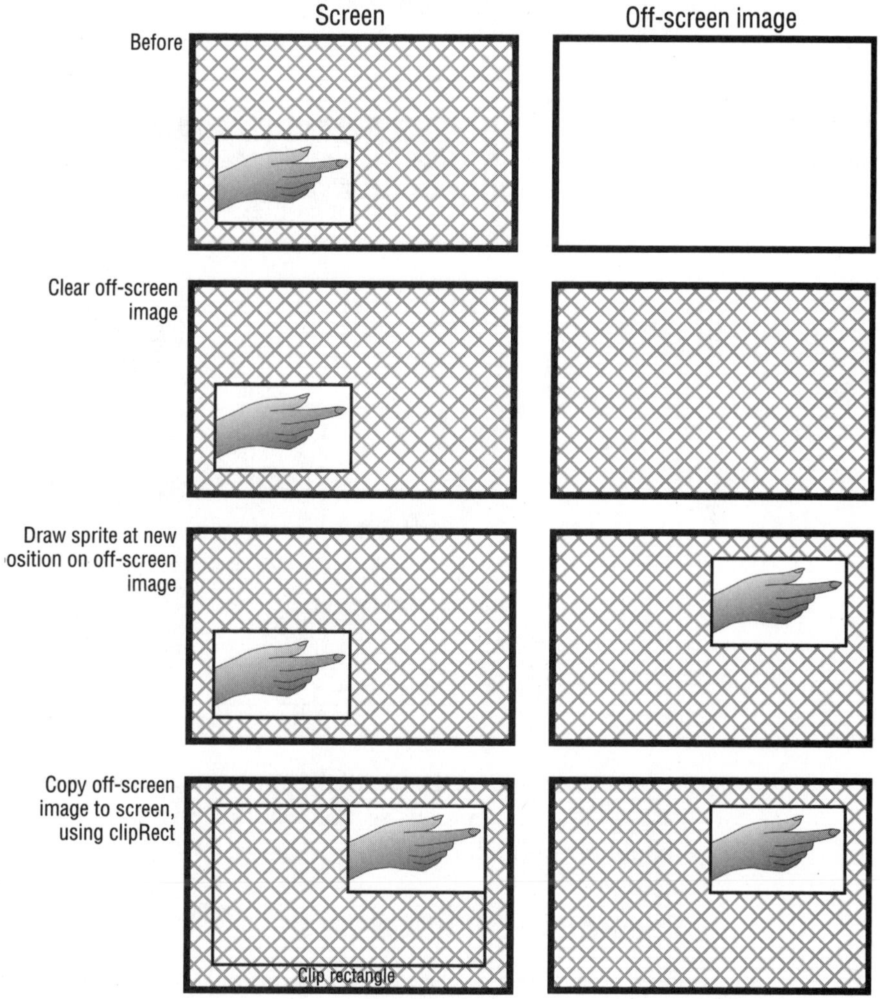

A Sprite Animation Example

As an example of sprite animation, we will develop a bar chart with rollover details. When the cursor "rolls over" one of the bars, a window pops up to give detailed information about the bar. This window appears at the mouse cursor position and tracks the cursor as it moves. This example is implemented using two classes. The first, RolloverRegion, is a helper class that represents a single bar of the bar chart. The second class, called Rollover, is an applet that constructs a number of rollover regions and manages the sprite animation. Figure 8.7 shows the Rollover applet.

FIGURE 8.7:

The Rollover applet

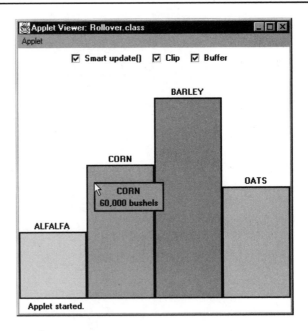

The checkboxes at the top of the applet enable or disable the three techniques discussed in the previous section. For the most satisfactory results, all three boxes should be checked.

The RolloverRegion Class

The RolloverRegion class represents a single bar of a bar chart. It has a number of instance variables that must be set by the client applet; these include color and position information. There are also two string instance variables: shortLabel appears on the screen just above the bar and both shortLabel and longLabel appear in the pop-up image.

The RolloverRegion class has two methods:

public void buildPopupImage(Applet applet)   Builds the off-screen image that will be displayed when the bar is rolled over.

public void paint(Graphics g)   Paints the bar on the screen using the specified graphics object.

The pop-up image displays the short label above the long label, as shown below:

Most of the code of the buildPopupImage() method is concerned with computing the size of the image and centering the text. A reference to the pop-up image is stored in the instance variable popupImage so that the client applet can access it.

The paint() method is not concerned with the pop-up sprite; it simply paints the vertical bar with a centered label.

The code for the RolloverRegion class is listed below. It is implemented as an inner class of the Rollover class, which appears on the CD-ROM in c:\javadevhdbk\ch08.

LIST 8.6   *RolloverRegion.java*

```
class RolloverRegion
{
        Rectangle       bounds;
        String          shortLabel;
        String          longLabel;
        Color           color;
        Font            font;
        Image           popupImage;
        int             popupWidth;
        int             popupHeight;

        public void buildPopupImage(Applet applet)
```

```
    {
        FontMetrics      fm;
        Graphics         g;
        int              fontHeight;

        // Create image. Size is a little bigger than long label.
        fm = Toolkit.getDefaultToolkit().getFontMetrics(font);
        popupWidth = fm.stringWidth(longLabel) + 2*8;
        fontHeight = fm.getHeight();
        popupHeight = (fontHeight + 8) * 2;
        popupImage = applet.createImage(popupWidth, popupHeight);

        // Fill with solid color, bordered in black.
        g = popupImage.getGraphics();
        g.setColor(Color.black);
        g.fillRect(0, 0, popupWidth, popupHeight);
        g.setColor(color);
        g.fillRect(2, 2, popupWidth-4, popupHeight-4);

        // Draw short and long label, centered.
        g.setColor(Color.black);
        int x = (popupWidth - fm.stringWidth(shortLabel)) / 2;
        g.drawString(shortLabel, x, 4+fontHeight);
        g.drawString(longLabel, 8, 8+2*fontHeight);
    }

    public void paint(Graphics g)
    {
        // Draw colored rectangle with a 2-pixel black border.
        g.fillRect(bounds.x, bounds.y, bounds.width, bounds.height);
        g.setColor(color);
        g.fillRect(bounds.x + 2, bounds.y + 2,
                bounds.width - 4, bounds.height - 4);

        // Draw short label above colored rectangle and centered.
        FontMetrics fm = g.getFontMetrics();
        int stringWidth = fm.stringWidth(shortLabel);
        int x = bounds.x + (bounds.width-stringWidth)/2;
        g.setColor(Color.black);
        g.drawString(shortLabel, x, bounds.y-4);

    }
}
```

The Rollover Applet Class

The code for the Rollover class is about 200 lines long, but, for the most part, it is straightforward. First, let's take a look at the paint() method:

```
public void paint(Graphics g)
{
    int       regionNum;
    Image     popup;

    // Determine which region, if any, was rolled over.
    for (regionNum=0; regionNum<nRegions; regionNum++)
    {
        if (regions[regionNum].bounds.inside(mouseX, mouseY))
        {
            break;
        }
    }
    if (regionNum == nRegions)        // Not in any region
    {                                 // => Just redraw all
        lastPopupRect.x = -1;
        g.drawImage(backgroundImage, 0, 0, this);
        return;
    }
    popup = regions[regionNum].popupImage;
```

The mouseMove() method records the new mouse position in instance variables mouseX and mouseY, and then calls repaint(). The paint() method begins by traversing the regions[] array, which contains references to all the rollover regions. If the cursor is not inside one of the regions, paint() draws the background image (to erase any defunct sprite that might still be on the screen) and returns. If the cursor is inside one of the regions, the index of the region is stored in regionNum, and a reference to the sprite image is stored in popup.

The next part of paint() sets the clip region if the user has requested this feature:

```
// Clip g if requested.
if (clipCbox.getState())
{
    currentPopupRect.x = mouseX;
    currentPopupRect.y = mouseY;
    currentPopupRect.width = regions[regionNum].popupWidth;
    currentPopupRect.height = regions[regionNum].popupHeight;
    if (lastPopupRect.x == -1)
```

```
        {
            // No previous sprite position; clip to current bounds.
            g.clipRect(currentPopupRect.x,
                    currentPopupRect.y,
                    currentPopupRect.width,
                    currentPopupRect.height);
        }
        else
        {
            // Clip to union of current and prev sprite positions.
            Rectangle clip = currentPopupRect.union(lastPopupRect);
            g.clipRect(clip.x, clip.y, clip.width, clip.height);
        }
    }
```

The code that sets the clip region uses the two instance variables currentPopup-
Rect and lastPopupRect to store the past and present location of the pop-up
sprite. (At the end of the paint() method, lastPopupRect will be set to current-
PopupRect.) There are two possible cases. If there was no previous sprite (indicated by lastPopupRect = -1), the clip region is set to the bounds of the new
sprite. If there was a previous sprite, the clip region is set to the union of the old
and new bounds.

Next, the sprite is drawn to the screen. Depending on the user's choice, this can
happen directly or via the off-screen image called buffer. The graphics object for
buffer is called bufferG.

```
    // Draw directly to screen.
    if (bufferCbox.getState() == false)
    {
        g.drawImage(backgroundImage, 0, 0, this);
        // Might see a flash right here.
        g.drawImage(popup, mouseX, mouseY, this);
    }

    // Draw to screen via buffer.
    else
    {
        bufferG.drawImage(backgroundImage, 0, 0, this);
        bufferG.drawImage(popup, mouseX, mouseY, this);
        g.drawImage(buffer, 0, 0, this);
    }
```

If buffering is not requested, the checkbox state is `false`. The code erases the old sprite by drawing the background image and then draws the new sprite. Note that the graphics object g may or may not have had its clip region adjusted.

If buffering has been requested, the code draws the background and the sprite to `buffer`. Then `buffer` is drawn to the screen. Again, the graphics object g may or may not have had its clip region adjusted.

Last, `paint()` sets the old pop-up rectangle from the current pop-up rectangle:

```
lastPopupRect.x = currentPopupRect.x;
lastPopupRect.y = currentPopupRect.y;
lastPopupRect.width = currentPopupRect.width;
lastPopupRect.height = currentPopupRect.height;
}
```

The complete listing for the `Rollover` class appears below. It is also on the CD-ROM in c:\javadevhdbk\ch08\Rollover.java.

LIST 8.7   *Rollover.java*

```java
import  java.awt.*;
import  java.awt.event.*;
import  java.applet.Applet;


public class Rollover extends Applet
                    implements MouseMotionListener,
                            MouseListener
{
    private RolloverRegion  regions[];
    private Rectangle       lastPopupRect, currentPopupRect;
    private boolean         firstPaint;
    private Image           backgroundImage, buffer;
    private Graphics        bufferG;
    private int             nRegions;
    private int             mouseX, mouseY;
    private Checkbox        smartUpdateCbox, clipCbox, bufferCbox;


    String          shortLabels[] =
                        {
                            "ALFALFA",
```

```
                              "CORN",
                              "BARLEY",
                              "OATS"
                    };
String              longLabels[] =
                    {
                         "30,000 bushels",
                         "60,000 bushels",
                         "90,000 bushels",
                         "50,000 bushels"
                    };
int                 values[] =
                    {
                         30, 60, 90, 50
                    };
Color               colors[] =
                    {
                         Color.yellow, Color.lightGray,
                         Color.cyan, Color.blue
                    };


class RolloverRegion
{
    Rectangle       bounds;
    String          shortLabel;
    String          longLabel;
    Color           color;
    Font            font;
    Image           popupImage;
    int             popupWidth;
    int             popupHeight;

    public void buildPopupImage(Applet applet)
    {
        FontMetrics     fm;
        Graphics        g;
        int             fontHeight;

        // Create image. Size is a little bigger than long label.
        fm = Toolkit.getDefaultToolkit().getFontMetrics(font);
        popupWidth = fm.stringWidth(longLabel) + 2*8;
```

```
            fontHeight = fm.getHeight();
            popupHeight = (fontHeight + 8) * 2;
            popupImage = applet.createImage(popupWidth, popupHeight);

            // Fill with solid color, bordered in black.
            g = popupImage.getGraphics();
            g.setColor(Color.black);
            g.fillRect(0, 0, popupWidth, popupHeight);
            g.setColor(color);
            g.fillRect(2, 2, popupWidth-4, popupHeight-4);

            // Draw short and long label, centered.
            g.setColor(Color.black);
            int x = (popupWidth - fm.stringWidth(shortLabel)) / 2;
            g.drawString(shortLabel, x, 4+fontHeight);
            g.drawString(longLabel, 8, 8+2*fontHeight);
        }

        public void paint(Graphics g)
        {
            // Draw colored rectangle with a 2-pixel black border.
            g.fillRect(bounds.x, bounds.y, bounds.width, bounds.height);
            g.setColor(color);
            g.fillRect(bounds.x + 2, bounds.y + 2,
                        bounds.width - 4, bounds.height - 4);

            // Draw short label above colored rectangle and centered.
            FontMetrics fm = g.getFontMetrics();
            int stringWidth = fm.stringWidth(shortLabel);
            int x = bounds.x + (bounds.width-stringWidth)/2;
            g.setColor(Color.black);
            g.drawString(shortLabel, x, bounds.y-4);
        }
    }

    public void init()
    {
        int         i;
        int         regionWidth;
        double      valuePerPixel;
        Graphics    backgroundG;
```

```
mouseX = mouseY = -1;
lastPopupRect = new Rectangle(-1, -1, -1, -1);
currentPopupRect = new Rectangle(-1, -1, -1, -1);
firstPaint = true;

// Catch our own mouse events.
addMouseListener(this);
addMouseMotionListener(this);

// Create background and buffer images.
backgroundImage = createImage(getSize().width,
                              getSize().height);
backgroundG = backgroundImage.getGraphics();
buffer = createImage(getSize().width,
                     getSize().height);
bufferG = buffer.getGraphics();

// Build GUI.
smartUpdateCbox = new Checkbox("Smart update()");
add(smartUpdateCbox);
clipCbox = new Checkbox("Clip");
add(clipCbox);
bufferCbox = new Checkbox("Buffer");
add(bufferCbox);

// Create and init regions.
nRegions = shortLabels.length;
regions = new RolloverRegion[nRegions];
int maxValue = 0;
for (i=0; i<nRegions; i++)
{
    regions[i] = new RolloverRegion();
    regions[i].shortLabel = shortLabels[i];
    regions[i].longLabel = longLabels[i];
    regions[i].color = colors[i];
    regions[i].font = getFont();
    regions[i].buildPopupImage(this);
    if (values[i] > maxValue)
        maxValue = values[i];
}

// Determine drawing scale.  Tell each region where it is.
regionWidth = getSize().width / nRegions;
```

```
        valuePerPixel = maxValue / (getSize().height * 0.8);
        for (i=0; i<nRegions; i++)
        {
            int height = (int) ((double)values[i] / valuePerPixel);
            regions[i].bounds = new Rectangle(i * regionWidth,
                                              getSize().height - height,
                                              regionWidth,
                                              height);
        }

        // Draw each region into the background image.
        for (i=0; i<nRegions; i++)
        {
            regions[i].paint(backgroundG);
        }
    }


    public void mouseMoved(MouseEvent e)
    {
        mouseX = e.getX();
        mouseY = e.getY();
        repaint();
    }


    public void mouseExited(MouseEvent e)
    {
        mouseX = mouseY = -1;
        repaint();
    }


    public void update(Graphics g)
    {
        if (smartUpdateCbox.getState())
            paint(g);
        else
            super.update(g);
    }


    public void paint(Graphics g)
```

```
{
    int     regionNum;
    Image   popup;

    // Determine which region, if any, was rolled over.
    for (regionNum=0; regionNum<nRegions; regionNum++)
    {
        if (regions[regionNum].bounds.contains(mouseX, mouseY))
        {
            break;
        }
    }
    if (firstPaint || regionNum == nRegions) // Not in a region
    {                                         // => Redraw all
        lastPopupRect.x = -1;
        g.drawImage(backgroundImage, 0, 0, this);
        firstPaint = false;
        return;
    }
    popup = regions[regionNum].popupImage;

    // Clip g if requested.
    if (clipCbox.getState())
    {
        currentPopupRect.x = mouseX;
        currentPopupRect.y = mouseY;
        currentPopupRect.width = regions[regionNum].popupWidth;
        currentPopupRect.height = regions[regionNum].popupHeight;
        if (lastPopupRect.x == -1)
        {
            // No previous sprite position, clip to current bounds.
            g.clipRect(currentPopupRect.x,
                    currentPopupRect.y,
                    currentPopupRect.width,
                    currentPopupRect.height);
        }
        else
        {
            // Clip to union of current and prev. sprite positions.
            Rectangle clip = currentPopupRect.union(lastPopupRect);
            g.clipRect(clip.x, clip.y, clip.width, clip.height);
        }
    }
}
```

```
        // Draw directly to screen.
        if (bufferCbox.getState() == false)
        {
            g.drawImage(backgroundImage, 0, 0, this);
            // Might see a flash right here.
            g.drawImage(popup, mouseX, mouseY, this);
        }

        // Draw to screen via buffer.
        else
        {
            bufferG.drawImage(backgroundImage, 0, 0, this);
            bufferG.drawImage(popup, mouseX, mouseY, this);
            g.drawImage(buffer, 0, 0, this);
        }

        lastPopupRect.x = currentPopupRect.x;
        lastPopupRect.y = currentPopupRect.y;
        lastPopupRect.width = currentPopupRect.width;
        lastPopupRect.height = currentPopupRect.height;
    }


    // Superfluous listener interface methods.
    public void mouseClicked(MouseEvent e)      { }
    public void mouseEntered(MouseEvent e)      { }
    public void mousePressed(MouseEvent e)      { }
    public void mouseReleased(MouseEvent e)     { }
    public void mouseDragged(MouseEvent e)      { }
}
```

Summary

Java's animation support is limited. However, by using any of the four techniques discussed in this chapter—in-place animation, rubber-band animation, ticker-tape animation, and sprite animation—you can achieve some sophisticated effects. In the future, you will be able to create really dazzling special effects with the upcoming support of the Animation API.

In the next chapter, we will explore Java's file input/output support and how the various stream classes work.

File I/O and Streams

- The input and output stream abstract classes

- The reader and writer abstract classes

- Low-level stream classes

- High-level stream classes

- Nonstream classes

Java's file input/output (I/O) support classes reside in the java.io package. Most of these classes support a stream-based model of reading and writing files. There are low-level stream classes for communicating with disk files and high-level classes for organizing the information that moves through the low-level streams. The high-level streams are also useful for organizing information sent to or received from the network.

This chapter investigates all the low-level and high-level stream classes, as well as the few classes that communicate with disk files without using the streams mechanism. Here, we will describe what the file I/O and stream classes and methods do. The next chapter demonstrates various techniques for using streams in network reading and writing applications.

An Overview of Streams

A *stream* can be thought of as a conduit for data, somewhat like a straw or a siphon, with a *source* at one end and a *consumer* at the other end. For example, a Java program can read bytes from a disk file with the FileInputStream class, as shown in Figure 9.1. In the figure, the Java program makes a read call to the FileInputStream, which reads bytes from the disk and delivers them to the caller. In Figure 9.2, a program writes to a file with the FileOutputStream class.

FIGURE 9.1:

A simple input stream

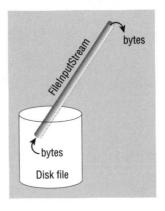

bytes

bytes

Disk file

FIGURE 9.2:

A simple output stream

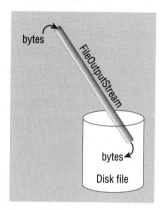

In practice, this mechanism is not particularly useful. Files usually contain highly structured information. The bytes are to be construed as numbers, text, source code, and so on. The java.io package provides a number of high-level input streams that read bytes from a low-level stream and return more sophisticated data. For example, the DataInputStream class consumes bytes and produces Java primitive types and strings, as illustrated in Figure 9.3. The technique of attaching a sophisticated stream to a lower-level one, as shown in the figure, is called *chaining*.

FIGURE 9.3:

Two levels of input streams

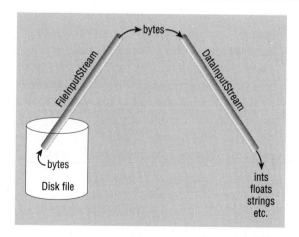

Similarly, writing bytes to a file is cumbersome. Usually, a program needs to write structured information to a file. The DataOutputStream class has methods for writing primitive data types and strings. The data-output stream converts its source data to bytes, which are passed to the stream's output. In Figure 9.4, the data-output stream's output is chained to a file-output stream; the result is that when a program writes primitives to the data-output stream, the corresponding bytes are written to the disk. The bytes are written in a platform-independent order; thus a file written by a big-endian machine can be read on a little-endian machine.

FIGURE 9.4:

Two levels of output streams

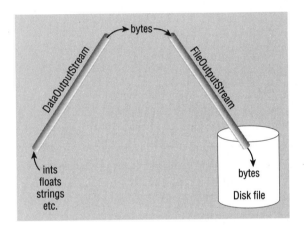

Traditionally, Java's low-level streams have operated on bytes. Release 1.1 of the JDK introduced character-based streams. These stream classes look very similar to their byte-based counterparts, but they permit programmers to operate on a level independent of any character-encoding scheme because all translations between characters and bytes are hidden by the class methods. This makes it easier to develop programs that are simple to internationalize. Moreover, character streams have been optimized for reading and writing multiple characters at a time. For these reasons, for character-based I/O, it is generally preferable to use character streams rather than byte streams whenever possible.

The Abstract Superclasses

Java's byte-oriented input and output streams are derived from the InputStream and OutputStream abstract classes. The character-oriented classes are derived from Reader and Writer.

The InputStream Class

Most of the InputStream class methods interact with system resources and have the potential for encountering platform-specific system problems and throwing an IOException. The following are the methods of InputStream:

int read() throws IOException   Reads one byte from the data source. Returns the byte in the low-order 8 bits of the return value. If no more data is available, returns -1. If data is not available at the moment of the call, the calling thread is blocked (see Chapter 7 for more information about blocking).

int read(byte[] dest) throws IOException   Reads bytes from the data source into the dest array. Returns when the array is full or when the data source has no more data. The return value is the number of bytes read. Note that you can convert an array of bytes to a string by calling the String(byte) constructor.

int read(byte[] dest, int offset, int length) throws IOException Just like read(byte[] dest) above, but only attempts to read length bytes into the portion of the byte array beginning at offset. Returns -1 at the end of the input.

void close() throws IOException   Releases system resources associated with the data source. For example, on a Unix platform, a file-input stream consumes one file descriptor. The close() call releases this file descriptor, and the stream then becomes permanently unavailable for reading.

int available() throws IOException   Returns the number of bytes that may be read immediately without blocking. This call is not reliable on all systems; some implementations of Java are known to return 0.

`long skip(long nbytes) throws IOException`   Attempts to skip over and discard `nbytes` bytes from the data source. It skips fewer bytes if no more data is available. It returns the number of bytes skipped.

`boolean markSupported()`   Returns `true` if the mark/reset mechanism is supported; otherwise, returns `false`. (See the `mark()` method description below.)

`void mark(int readlimit)`   Sets a mark in the input stream. If in the future, a `reset()` call is made and `markSupported()` is `true`, subsequent reads from the input stream will repeat all bytes read since the mark call. If more than `readlimit` bytes are read before the next `reset()` call, the mark is lost.

`void reset() throws IOException`   Repositions the stream so that subsequent reads repeat the values read since the last `mark()` call. Throws `IO-Exception` if the file has not been marked.

The OutputStream Class

As with input streams, most of the `OutputStream` class methods interact with system resources and inform the caller of platform-specific system problems by throwing an `IOException`. The following are the methods of `OutputStream`:

`void write(int b) throws IOException`   Writes the byte that appears in the low-order 8 bits of the argument, discarding the higher 24 bits.

`void write(byte b[]) throws IOException`   Writes an array of bytes. Note that a string can be converted to a char array by calling the `getBytes()` method, but any information in the high-order byte of each Unicode character will be lost.

`void write(byte b[],int offset, int length) throws IOException`   Writes the subset of the byte array beginning at `offset` and is `length` bytes long.

`void flush() throws IOException`   Writes any bytes that the stream has buffered.

`void close() throws IOException`   Releases system resources associated with the data source. The stream becomes permanently unavailable for writing. An output stream should be flushed before it is closed.

The Reader Class

The character-oriented abstract classes `Reader` and `Writer` both define two constructors in addition to their various methods. The following are the constructors for `Reader`:

`Reader()`   Constructs an instance of the class.

`Reader(Object lock)`   Constructs an instance of the class. Critical sections of class methods will synchronize on `lock`.

The following are the methods of the `Reader` class. Only two of these methods—`read(char[], int, int)` and `close()`—are abstract and must be supplied by concrete subclasses. All of the other methods are implemented.

`int read() throws IOException`   Reads one character from the data source into the low-order 16 bits of the return value. If the data source has no more data, returns the int -1. If data is not available at the moment of the call, the calling thread is blocked (see Chapter 7 for more information about threads and blocking).

`int read(char[] dest) throws IOException`   Reads characters from the data source into the `dest` array. Returns when the array is full or when the data source has no more data. The return value is the number of characters read, or -1 if there is no more data.

`int read(char[] dest, int offset, int length) throws IOException`   Just like `read(char[] dest)` (above), but attempts to read `length` characters into the portion of the character array beginning at `offset`. Returns -1 when there is no more data.

`void close() throws IOException`   Releases system resources associated with the data source. For example, on a Unix platform, a file-input stream consumes one file descriptor. The `close()` call releases this file descriptor, and the stream then becomes permanently unavailable for reading.

`long skip(long nchars) throws IOException`   Attempts to skip over and discard `nchars` bytes from the data source. It skips fewer bytes if no more data is available. It returns the number of bytes skipped.

`boolean markSupported()`   Returns `true` if the mark/reset mechanism is supported; otherwise, returns `false`. (See the `mark()` method description below.)

`void mark(int readlimit)`   Sets a mark in the input stream. If in the future, a `reset()` call is made and `markSupported()` returns `true`, subsequent reads from the input stream will repeat all characters read since the mark call. If more than `readlimit` characters are read before the next `reset()` call, the mark is lost.

`void reset() throws IOException`   Repositions the stream so that subsequent reads repeat the values read since the last `mark()` call.

`void ready()throws IOException`   Returns `true` if the stream has data immediately available, so that a `read()` call will not block. Returns `false` if block prevention cannot be assured.

The Writer Class

Like `Reader`, the `Writer` class has an overloaded constructor that offers the option of synchronizing on any arbitrary object. `Writer` has two constructors:

`Writer()`   Constructs an instance of the class.

`Writer(Object lock)`   Constructs an instance of the class. Critical sections of class methods will synchronize on `lock`.

`Writer` has the following methods:

`void write(int c) throws IOException`   Writes the character that appears in the low-order 16 bits of the argument.

`void write(char[] c) throws IOException`   Writes an array of characters.

`void write(char[] c, int offset, int length) throws IOException` Writes a subset of an array of characters.

`void write(String s) throws IOException`   Writes a string.

`void write(byte[] b,int offset, int length) throws IOException`   Writes a subset of a string.

`void flush() throws IOException`   Writes any characters that the stream has buffered.

`void close() throws IOException`   Releases system resources associated with the data source. The stream becomes permanently unavailable for writing. Writers should be flushed before they are closed.

The Low-Level Stream Classes

The java.io package provides four low-level stream classes for file access. These classes are FileInputStream for byte input, FileOutputStream for byte output, FileReader for character input, and FileWriter for character output.

The FileInputStream Class

The FileInputStream class is a byte-based input stream that reads from a file. In addition to the inherited methods described in the previous sections, this class has three constructors. All three constructors require arguments to specify the file to be opened:

FileInputStream(String path) throws FileNotFoundException   Attempts to open a stream to the file described by path. Throws an exception if the file does not exist.

FileInputStream(File file) throws FileNotFoundException   Attempts to open a stream to the file described by file. Throws an exception if the file described by file does not exist.

FileInputStream(FileDescriptor fd)   Opens a stream to the file described by fd.

> **NOTE**   On Windows machines, a file path can use either forward or backward slashes as separators.

The FileOutputStream Class

The FileOutputStream class is an output stream that writes to a file. This class has four constructors:

FileOutputStream(String path) throws IOException   Attempts to open a stream to the file described by path. The file is created if it does not already exist.

FileOutputStream(String path, boolean append) throws IOException   Attempts to open a stream to the file described by path. If append is true, the file will be opened in append mode; this means that if the file already exists, data will be written to the end of the file rather than replacing the file's existing contents. The file is created if it does not already exist.

`FileOutputStream(File file) throws IOException`   Attempts to open a stream to the file described by `file`. The file is created if it does not already exist.

`FileOutputStream(FileDescriptor fd)`   Opens a stream to the file described by fd.

NOTE   In an applet, permission to access files is granted or denied by the browser's security manager. If permission is denied, all the `FileOutputStream` class constructors throw a `SecurityException`. Because `SecurityException` is a type of runtime exception, it does not need to be caught.

The FileReader Class

The `FileReader` class is a character-based stream for reading from a file. It is a subclass of the `Reader` and `InputStreamReader` classes (discussed later, in the "The InputStreamReader and OutputStreamWriter Classes" section) and adds no methods of its own except for the following three constructors:

`FileReader(String path) throws FileNotFoundException`   Attempts to open a stream to the file described by path.

`FileReader(File file) throws FileNotFoundException`   Attempts to open a stream to the file described by `file`.

`FileReader(FileDescriptor fd)`   Opens a stream to the file described by fd.

The FileWriter Class

The `FileWriter` class is a character-based stream for writing to a file. It is a subclass of the `Writer` and `OutputStreamWriter` classes (discussed later, in the "The

InputStreamReader and OutputStreamWriter Classes" section) and adds no methods of its own except for the following four constructors:

`FileWriter(String path) throws IOException`   Attempts to open a stream to the file described by path.

`FileWriter(String path, boolean append) throws IOException`   Attempts to open a stream to the file described by path. If append is `true`, the file will be opened in append mode; this means that if the file already exists, data will be written to the end of the file rather than replacing the file's existing contents.

`FileWriter(File file) throws IOException`   Attempts to open a stream to the file described by `file`.

`FileWriter(FileDescriptor fd)`   Opens a stream to the file described by fd.

Other Low-Level Stream Classes

In addition to `FileInputStream`, the `java.io` package contains several other low-level input stream classes: `ByteArrayInputStream` and `PipedInputStream` for byte input; and `CharArrayReader`, `PipedReader`, and `StringReader` for character input. These classes read from sources other than a disk file. Otherwise, they are similar to `FileInputStream` and `StringReader`—they inherit from the `InputStream` or `Reader` class, and they read bytes or characters from a data source. A program may use the data directly, or it may chain a high-level input stream for more sophisticated processing.

There are also several low-level output classes in addition to `FileOutputStream`: `ByteArrayOutputStream` and `PipedOutputStream` for byte output; and `CharArrayWriter`, `PipedWriter`, and `StringWriter` for character output. These classes write to destinations that are not files. Otherwise, they are similar to `FileOutputStream` and `Writer`—they inherit from the `OutputStream` or `Writer` class, and they write bytes or characters. A program may write data to any of these classes, or it may chain a higher-level output stream to facilitate writing of more structured information.

The following sections examine these classes in more detail.

Stream Classes That Connect to Arrays

The `ByteArrayInputStream` class takes its input from a byte array or from a piece of a byte array. There are two constructors:

`ByteArrayInputStream(byte[] buf)`   Constructs an input stream that reads bytes from array buf.

`ByteArrayInputStream(byte[] buf, int offset, int length)` Constructs an input stream that reads bytes from a subset of array buf. The subset begins at offset and is length bytes long.

The `ByteArrayOutputStream` class writes to a byte array. The array grows automatically as needed. There are two constructors:

`ByteArrayOutputStream()`   Creates a new instance.

`ByteArrayOutputStream(int size)`   Creates a new instance with an initial destination array of the specified size. If the number of bytes written to the stream exceeds size, the destination array will grow automatically.

There are three methods for converting a byte array output stream into more accessible data:

`String toString()`   Returns a String consisting of all the bytes written to the stream so far.

`String toString(String encoding) throws UnsupportedEncodingException` Returns a String consisting of all the bytes written to the stream so far. The string is created using the specified encoding.

`byte[] toByteArray()`   Returns an array containing all bytes written to the stream so far. This array is a copy of the stream's contents, so it may be modified without corrupting the original data.

These two classes have character-based analogues that extend the Reader and Writer abstract superclasses. The `CharArrayReader` class reads characters from a character array; the `CharArrayWriter` class writes characters to a character array. Except for constructors, neither class introduces any new methods beyond those inherited from their respective superclasses.

The following are the constructors for `CharArrayReader`:

`CharArrayReader(char[] chars)`   Creates a character array reader from array `chars[]`.

`CharArrayReader(char[] chars, int start, int length)`   Creates a character array reader from a subset of array `chars[]`.

The following are the constructors for `CharArrayWriter`:

`CharArrayWriter()`   Creates a character array writer.

`CharArrayWriter(int length)`   Creates a character array writer whose internal array has the initial size of `length`.

Stream Classes That Connect to Strings

The `StringReader` and `StringWriter` classes communicate with Java strings and string buffers. The `StringReader` class reads characters from a string. The `StringWriter` class writes characters to a string buffer (*not* a string!).

The `StringReader` class has the following constructor:

`StringReader(String s)`   Constructs an input stream that reads characters from the specified string.

The `StringWriter` class accumulates its characters in a string buffer. It has two constructors.

`StringWriter()`   Constructs a string writer with a default-sized internal buffer.

`StringWriter(int size)`   Constructs a string writer with an internal string buffer whose initial size is specified by `size`.

NOTE   Release 1.1 of the JDK included a `StringBufferInputStream` class. This class is deprecated as of release 2.

Stream Classes That Connect to Each Other

The `java.io` package contains four *piped* classes that operate in pairs and in tandem. A piped input stream reads bytes that are written to a corresponding piped output stream; a piped reader reads characters that are written to a corresponding piped writer. The most common use for these classes is for interthread communications: One thread writes to a piped writer or output stream, while another thread reads the same data from a piped reader input stream. For character-based communication, it is generally preferable to use a reader/writer pair because those classes are optimized for block transfers. (See Chapter 7 for details on the use of these classes in the context of threads.) Each of these classes has two constructors.

The `PipedInputStream` class has the following constructors:

`PipedInputStream()`   Constructs a piped input stream with no data source. The stream is useless until it is associated with a piped output stream. This is accomplished by calling the `connect(PipedOutputStream)` method.

`PipedInputStream(PipedOutputStream source)`   Constructs a piped input stream whose data source is the bytes written to the `source` output stream.

The `PipedOutputStream` class has these two constructors:

`PipedOutputStream()`   Constructs a piped output stream with no data receiver. The stream is useless until it is associated with a piped input stream. This is accomplished by calling the `connect(PipedInputStream)` method.

`PipedOutputStream(PipedInputStream receiver)`   Constructs a piped output stream whose data is written into the `receiver` piped input stream.

The following are the constructors for `PipedReader`:

`PipedReader()`   Constructs a piped reader with no data source. The stream is useless until it is associated with a piped writer. This is accomplished by calling the `connect(PipedWriter)` method.

`PipedReader(PipedWriter source)`   Constructs a piped reader whose data source is the characters written to the `source` writer.

The following are the constructors for `PipedWriter`:

`PipedWriter()`   Constructs a piped writer with no data receiver. The stream is useless until it is associated with a piped reader. This is accomplished by calling the `connect(PipedReader)` method.

`PipedWriter(PipedReader receiver)`   Constructs a piped writer whose data is written into the `receiver` reader.

A stream of any type can be associated with a stream of the opposite type by calling the `connect()` method.

There are two ways to create a paired set of piped streams. The first way is to start with a piped input stream:

```
PipedInputStream instream = new PipedInputStream();
PipedOutputStream outstream = new PipedOutputStream(instream);
instream.connect(outstream);
```

The alternative way is to start with a piped output stream:

```
PipedOutputStream outstream = new PipedOutputStream();
PipedInputStream instream = new PipedInputStream(outstream);
outstream.connect(instream);
```

The same principle applies to creating a piped reader/writer pair. One way is to start with a reader:

```
PipedReader reader = new PipedReader();
PipedWriter writer = new PipedWriter(reader);
instream.connect(writer);
```

The alternative is to start with a piped writer:

```
PipedWriter writer = new PipedWriter();
PipedReader reader = new PipedReader(writer);
outstream.connect(instream);
```

The High-Level Stream Classes

High-level input streams take their input from other input streams. High-level output streams direct their output to other output streams.

Each of these classes is constructed by passing as an argument to the constructor an instance of another stream type. The new stream is chained onto the argument stream; a high-level input stream will read bytes from the argument stream, and a high-level output stream will write bytes to the argument stream. The argument stream may itself be a high-level stream.

The following sections discuss each of the high-level input and output stream classes.

The Buffered Classes

The BufferedInputStream class maintains an internal array of characters in which it buffers the data it reads from its source. The default size of the buffer is 2048 bytes. The first time one of the read() methods is called on the buffered input stream, it fills its buffer from its own data source. Subsequent reads on the buffered input stream return bytes from the buffer until the buffer is empty. At this point, the buffered input stream again fills its buffer from the data source.

A buffered input stream is beneficial in situations where reading a large number of consecutive bytes from a data source is not significantly more costly than reading a single byte. For example, when reading from a disk file, a large amount of time is spent in positioning the disk drive's read head and in waiting for the disk to spin into position under the read head. This time expenditure must be made no matter how many consecutive bytes are to be read. In this case, it would be advantageous to read an entire block of disk data (512 or 1048 bytes on most systems) and buffer the undesired bytes in case they are needed in the future.

There are two constructors for the BufferedInputStream class. One version creates a buffer with a default size of 2048 bytes; the other version lets the caller specify the buffer size:

BufferedInputStream(InputStream source)   Creates a buffered input stream with a 2048-byte buffer. The input stream uses source as its data source.

BufferedInputStream(InputStream source, int bufsize)   Creates a buffered input stream with a buffer of bufsize bytes. The input stream uses source as its data source.

The BufferedReader class is the character-based analogue of the buffered input stream. Because of the benefit conferred by the buffer, this class is the preferred tool for reading lines of input. Not surprisingly, there are two constructors:

BufferedReader(Reader source)   Creates a buffered reader with an 8192-character buffer. The reader uses source as its data source.

`BufferedReader(Reader source int bufsize)`   Creates a buffered reader with a buffer of `bufsize` characters. The reader uses `source` as its data source.

The `BufferedOutputStream` class also maintains a buffer of bytes. Data written to a buffered output stream is accumulated in the buffer until the buffer is full. Then the bytes are written in a single operation to whatever output stream is chained to the buffered output stream.

Like `BufferedInputStream`, the `BufferedOutputStream` class has two constructors. One version creates a buffer with a default size of 512 bytes; the other version lets the caller specify the buffer size:

`BufferedOutputStream(OutputStream dest)`   Creates a buffered output stream with a 512-byte buffer. The stream writes its data to `dest`.

`BufferedOutputStream(OutputStream dest, int bufsize)`   Creates a buffered output stream with a buffer of `bufsize` bytes. The stream writes its data to `dest`.

The `BufferedWriter` class is analogous:

`BufferedWriter(Writer dest)`   Creates a buffered writer with a 512-byte buffer. The writer writes its data to `dest`.

`BufferedWriter(Writer dest, int bufsize)`   Creates a buffered writer with a buffer of `bufsize` characters. The stream writes its data to `dest`.

NOTE   The largest network packet size is 64KB. If a buffered writer is to be used for network output, there is no benefit to creating it with a buffer larger than 64KB.

The DataInputStream and DataOutputStream Classes

The `DataInputStream` class reads bytes from another stream and interprets them as Java primitives, char arrays, and strings. There is no corresponding character-oriented reader class, because it makes no sense to write primitives in character form. The constructor expects to be passed an input stream:

`DataInputStream(InputStream source)`   Creates a data-input stream that takes its data from stream `source`.

In addition to the usual inherited `read` methods, data-input streams support the following methods:

`boolean readBoolean() throws IOException`   Reads a boolean value.

`byte readByte() throws IOException`   Reads a signed 2's-complement byte.

`int readUnsignedByte() throws IOException`   Reads an unsigned byte, returned as an int.

`short readShort() throws IOException`   Reads a signed 2's-complement short. The first byte read is interpreted as the high-order byte of the short value.

`int readUnsignedShort() throws IOException`   Reads an unsigned short. The first byte read is interpreted as the high-order byte of the short value.

`char readChar() throws IOException`   Reads a 2-byte Unicode char. The first byte read is interpreted as the high-order byte of the char.

`int readInt() throws IOException`   Reads a signed 2's-complement 4-byte Java int. The first byte read is interpreted as the high-order byte of the int.

`long readLong() throws IOException`   Reads a signed 2's-complement 8-byte Java long. The first byte read is interpreted as the high-order byte of the long.

`float readFloat() throws IOException`   Reads a 4-byte representation of a Java float.

`double readDouble() throws IOException`   Reads an 8-byte representation of a Java double.

`String readUTF() throws IOException`   Reads a series of bytes and interprets them as a Java modified Universal Text Format (UTF-8) string.

NOTE   UTF is an emerging international standard that uses one, two, or three bytes to represent each character. There are no string-termination issues because a UTF string includes length information.

`static String readUTF(DataInput din) throws IOException` A static method. Reads a UTF string from the specified input stream.

`void readFully(byte[] dest) throws IOException` Attempts to fill byte array `dest` with bytes from the data source. The executing thread blocks if enough bytes are not available, and it throws an `EOFException` if the data source is depleted before `dest` is filled.

`void readFully(byte[] dest, int offset, int length) throws IOException` Like `readFully()` (above), but only attempts to fill a subset of `dest`. The subset begins at index `offset` and is `length` bytes long.

`void skipBytes(int offset nbytes) throws IOException` Like `readFully()` (above), but discards bytes rather than storing them in an array. The executing thread blocks if not enough bytes are available.

The `DataOutputStream` class supports the writing of Java's primitive data types to an output stream. Strings and byte arrays may also be written. There is no analogous character-oriented writer class. Both `DataOutputStream` and `DataInputStream` communicate in a platform-independent way. The constructor expects to be passed an output stream:

`DataOutputStream(OutputStream dest)` Creates a data-output stream that writes its data to `dest`.

The data written to a data-output stream is broken up into its constituent bytes, which are written to whatever output stream is chained to the data-output stream. In addition to the various byte-writing methods inherited from its `DataOutput` superclass, the `DataOutputStream` class supports the following methods for writing:

`void writeBoolean(boolean b) throws IOException` Writes a boolean value. A value of `true` is represented by `(byte)0`; a value of `false` is represented by `(byte)1`.

`void writeByte(int i) throws IOException` Writes the low-order byte of `i`.

`void writeShort(int i) throws IOException` Writes the two low-order bytes of `i`. Of the 2 bytes written, the higher-order byte is written first (bits 8 to 15), followed by the lower-order byte (bits 0 to 7).

void writeInt(int i) throws IOException   Writes all 4 bytes of i, starting with the highest-order byte (bits 24 to 31).

void writeLong(long theLong) throws IOException   Writes all 4 bytes of theLong, starting with the highest-order byte (bits 56 to 63).

void writeFloat(float f) throws IOException   Writes the 4-byte representation of f.

void writeDouble(double d) throws IOException   Writes the 8-byte representation of d.

void writeBytes(String s) throws IOException   Writes s as a series of bytes. Only the low-order byte of each 2-byte Unicode character is written.

void writeChars(String s) throws IOException   Writes s as a series of Unicode characters. Starting with the high-order byte, 2 bytes are written for each Unicode character.

void writeUTF(String s) throws IOException   Writes s as a UTF string.

The LineNumberReader Class

The LineNumberReader class maintains an internal count of the number of lines it has read. A line is considered to be any number of bytes, terminated by a return character ('\r'), a newline character ('\n'), or a return followed by a newline. This class is a subclass of BufferedReader.

The constructors expect to be passed a reader:

LineNumberReader(Reader source)   Creates a line-number reader that takes its data from source.

LineNumberReader(Reader source, int size)   Creates a line-number reader that takes its data from source. The internal buffer size is given by size.

This class introduces the following methods:

int getLineNumber()   Returns the current line number.

void setLineNumber(int newvalue)   Sets the current line number to newvalue.

`public String readLine() throws IOException`   Returns the next line of input.

NOTE

Release 1.0 of the JDK provided a `LineNumberInputStream` class. This class is deprecated in releases 1.1 and Java 2.

The PrintStream and PrintWriter Classes

The `PrintStream` and `PrintWriter` classes have methods that support printing text. This support consists of data-type conversion and automatic flushing.

The `PrintStream` class has two constructors:

`PrintStream(OutputStream dest)`   Constructs a print stream and chains its output to `dest`. Automatic flushing is not supported.

`PrintStream(OutputStream dest, boolean autoflush)`   Constructs a print stream and chains its output to `dest`. The value of `autoflush` determines whether automatic flushing is supported; if this value it `true`, the print stream will be flushed whenever a newline character is written.

The `PrintStream` class has numerous methods for converting and writing different data types. For each data type, there is a `print()` method, which writes the data as a string, and a `println()` method, which writes the data as a string and appends a newline character. The supported methods are listed in Table 9.1.

TABLE 9.1: PrintStream Methods for Data Types

Method	Description
`void print(char c)`	Prints a character
`void println(char c)`	Prints a character followed by a newline character
`void print(int i)`	Prints an int
`void println(int i)`	Prints an int followed by a newline character
`void print(long ln)`	Prints a long

Continued on next page

TABLE 9.1 CONTINUED: PrintStream Methods for Data Types

Method	Description
void println(long ln)	Prints a long followed by a newline character.
void print(float f)	Prints a float.
void println(float f)	Prints a float followed by a newline character.
void print(double d)	Prints a double.
void println(double d)	Prints a double followed by a newline character.
void print(boolean b)	Prints a boolean. If the boolean value is **true**, prints the string **true**, otherwise prints the string **false.**
void println(boolean b)	Prints a boolean followed by a newline character.
void print(char[] c)	Prints a character array.
void println(char[] c)	Prints a character array followed by a newline character.
void print(String s)	Prints a string.
void println(String s)	Prints a string followed by a newline character.
void print(Object ob)	Prints an object. The string that is printed is the result of calling **ob.toString()**.
void println(Object ob)	Prints a character followed by a newline character.
void println()	Prints a newline character.

WARNING   Print streams should be used only in programs based on pre-1.1 versions of the JDK. Since 1.1, the entire class has been periodically deprecated and rehabilitated. Print writers are the preferred choice. The one exception is the phenomenally useful System.out, which is a PrintStream.

The PrintWriter class has two constructors:

PrintWriter(Writer dest)   Constructs a print writer and chains its output to dest. Automatic flushing is not supported.

PrintWriter(Writer dest, boolean autoflush)   Constructs a print writer and chains its output to dest. The value of autoflush determines whether automatic flushing is supported; if this value is `true`, the print stream will be flushed whenever a newline character is written.

The names of the writing methods for this class precisely match those of the `PrintStream` class (see Table 9.1). The only functional difference is that a print writer writes characters rather than bytes.

There is nothing inherent in `PrintStream` or `PrintWriter` that requires that the output be a printing device. A print writer might, for example, be chained to a string writer (which writes to a string buffer, not to a string!); when output to the print writer is completed, the string buffer can be converted to a string and written to a text-area component.

The Pushback Classes

The `PushbackInputStream` and `PushbackReader` classes permits data to be *unread* or *pushed back* into the data source. The classes maintain internal stacks for pushed-back bytes and chars. Read operations pop data from the stack until the stack is empty—only then is the data source accessed again.

NOTE   In pre-1.1 versions of the JDK, only one byte at a time could be pushed back; as of release 1.1, constructors are provided for specifying the size of the internal pushback buffer.

The following are the constructors for `PushbackInputStream`:

`PushbackInputStream(InputStream source)`   Creates a pushback input stream connected to `source`. The stream's buffer accommodates a single byte.

`PushbackInputStream(InputStream source, int bufsize)`   Creates a pushback input stream connected to `source`. The stream's buffer accommodates `bufsize` bytes. This constructor is not supported in pre-1.1 releases of the JDK.

The following are the constructors for `PushbackReader`:

`PushbackReader(Reader source)`   Creates a pushback reader connected to `source`. The stream's buffer accommodates a single byte.

`PushbackReader(Reader source, int bufsize)`   Creates a reader stream connected to source. The stream's buffer accommodates bufsize bytes.

For pushback input streams, the following methods support pushing back:

`void unread(int ch) throws IOException`   Stores the low-order byte of ch in an internal buffer. The next read operation from the stream will return ch as a byte.

`void unread(byte bytes[]) throws IOException`   Undoes the reading of all the bytes in array bytes[]. Not supported in pre-1.1 releases of the JDK.

`void unread(byte bytes[], int start, int length) throws IOException` Unreads a subset of array bytes[]. Not supported in pre-1.1 releases of the JDK.

The pushback readers have the following methods:

`void unread(int ch) throws IOException`   Pushes back the low-order two bytes of ch.

`void unread(char chars[]) throws IOException`   Undoes the reading of all the characters in array chars[].

`void unread(char bytes[], int start, int length) throws IOException` Undoes the reading of a subset of array chars[].

All the pushback methods for both classes throw an IOException if the internal pushback buffer does not have space to accommodate the operation. This can happen if the operation pushes more data than the capacity of the buffer or if there have not been enough reads since the last pushback to create sufficient buffer space.

Finding Fields within Nondelimited Input

The pushback input classes are useful for finding fields within nondelimited input. Consider the problem of finding a field within delimited input. Suppose that an input stream consists of various nonnumeric data, followed by a single slash character (/), followed by a number. Now suppose that the stream is currently somewhere in the nonnumeric data, and it is necessary to skip to the numeric field. Because the input is delimited (the fields are separated), this is easy to do, as shown in the following code fragment. This code fragment assumes that the input stream is called inreader.

```
// Assume inreader is somewhere in nonnumeric field.
int intchar;
while ((intchar=inreader.read()) != -1)
{
    if (intchar == '/')
        break;
}
// Now inreader is positioned at 1st char after '/'
```

Unfortunately, not all input is delimited. If the input data does not have a slash between its two fields, it is tempting to do something like the following:

```
int intchar;
while ((intchar=inreader.read()) != -1)
{
    if (Character.isDigit((char)intchar))
        break;
}
```

This code fails because, by the time the loop is exited, the first character of the numeric field has been read and the input stream is positioned at the second character. The code must undo the reading of the first numeric character. Reading is undone by chaining a pushback input stream onto inreader.

```
int intchar;
PushbackInputStream pbis = new PushbackInputStream(inreader);
while ((intchar=pbis.read()) != -1)
{
    if (Character.isDigit((char)intchar))
    {
        pbis.unread(intchar);
        break;
    }
}
```

The ability to push a single byte back into the data source does not seem impressive, but it permits the easy parsing of structured, nondelimited input.

The SequenceInputStream Class

The `SequenceInputStream` class is a mechanism for combining two or more input streams. There is no corresponding character-based reader class. A sequence input stream reads from its first input stream until that stream is exhausted; it then reads from its second input stream, continuing until the last input stream is emptied. Only then does a read of the sequence input stream return -1.

This class has two constructors:

`SequenceInputStream(InputStream s1, InputStream s2)` Creates a sequence input stream out of s1 and s2.

`SequenceInputStream(Enumeration enum)` Creates a sequence input stream out of the list of input streams given by enum.

The second constructor requires an enumeration—that is, an object that implements the `Enumeration` interface. The easiest way to build an enumeration is to add all the input streams to a vector and then have the vector return an enumeration of its elements. Thus, the following code constructs a sequence input stream out of input streams s1, s2, s3, s4, and s5:

```
Vector vec = new Vector();
vec.addElement(s1);
vec.addElement(s2);
vec.addElement(s3);
vec.addElement(s4);
vec.addElement(s5);
SequenceInputStream sis = new SequenceInputStream(vec.elements());
```

The InputStreamReader and OutputStreamWriter Classes

The `InputStreamReader` class, when chained onto any subclass of `InputStream`, reads bytes from the input stream and converts them to characters. The `OutputStreamWriter` class, when chained onto any subclass of `OutputStream`, converts characters written to it into bytes and writes the bytes to the output stream. The conversion is illustrated in Figure 9.5.

Both classes need to know how to convert between 16-bit characters and 8-bit bytes. Conversion mappings are represented by string names. Either of these classes may be constructed with an optional string argument to specify a mapping other than the default.

FIGURE 9.5:

Converting with Input-StreamReader and Output-StreamWriter

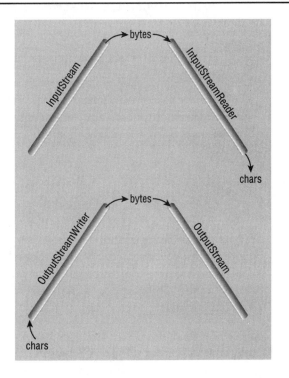

If you have downloaded the Java 2 documentation, you can find a list of encodings in **docs/tooldocs/win32/native2ascii.html**.

The following are the constructors for InputStreamReader:

InputStreamReader(InputStream source)   Constructs an input stream reader whose data source is source. Note that the recommended way to read standard input is to use this constructor to create an InputStream-Reader that reads from System.in.

InputStreamReader(InputStream source, String encodingName)   Constructs an input stream reader whose data source is source. Bytes will be converted to chars using the encoding specified by encodingName.

The constructors for `OutputStreamWriter` offer the same combinations of options:

`OutputStreamWriter(OutputStream out)`   Constructs an output stream writer connected to out.

`OutputStreamWriter(OutputStream out, String encodingName)`   Constructs an output stream writer connected to out. Bytes will be converted to chars using the encoding specified by `encodingName`.

The Non-Stream Classes

The `java.io` package contains several classes that are not streams. These include `File`, `FileDescriptor`, `RandomAccessFile`, and `StreamTokenizer`. `File` and `FileDescriptor` are straightforward and are adequately described in Sun's API documentation. The next two sections discuss the `RandomAccessFile` and `StreamTokenizer` classes.

The RandomAccessFile Class

The `RandomAccessFile` class supports reading and writing of a file, as well as file-pointer positioning. Because it does not treat the file as an ordered sequence of pure input or pure output, it operates outside the streams model.

There are two constructors for `RandomAccessFile`:

`RandomAccessFile(String path, String mode)`   Creates a random-access file connected to the file path. Access permission is described by the string permissions, which must be either `"r"` for read-only mode or `"rw"` for read-write mode.

`RandomAccessFile(File file, String permissions)`   Same as above, but the file path is taken from an instance of the `File` class.

Random-access files support a wide variety of methods for reading and writing various data types. These methods have the same names as the methods for the `DataInputStream` and `DataOutputStream` classes, which are listed earlier in this chapter.

Unix programmers who are accustomed to the standard I/O library are used to being able to position a file pointer relative to the start of the file, the end of the file, or the current file-pointer position. The `RandomAccessFile` class offers only a single `seek()` method, which positions with respect to the start of the file. In order to achieve the other two modes of seeking, it is necessary to retrieve the file length or the current position and do an explicit subtraction.

The following methods support positioning:

`void seek(long newPosition)`   Sets the file's pointer to `newPosition`.

`long length()`   Returns the current length of the file in bytes.

`long getFilePointer()`   Returns the current location of the file pointer.

The StreamTokenizer Class

The `StreamTokenizer` class is a parser, useful for analyzing input whose format is similar to Java, C, or C++ source code.

The first step in using a stream tokenizer is, of course, to construct one:

`StreamTokenizer(Reader reader)`   Constructs a stream tokenizer that takes its input from `reader`.

The next step is to parse the input reader `reader`. Parsing is typically done in a `while` loop, calling the tokenizer's `nextToken()` method until the end of the input is reached. The `nextToken()` method returns an int that describes the type of the next token. There are four possible return values for `nextToken()`:

`StreamTokenizer.TT_NUMBER`   Indicates that the token just read was a number. The number's value may be read from the tokenizer's `nval` instance variable, which is of type double.

`StreamTokenizer.TT_WORD`   Indicates that the token just read was a nonnumerical word (an identifier, for example). The word may be read from the tokenizer's `sval` instance variable, which is of type String.

`StreamTokenizer.TT_EOL`   Indicates that the token just read was an end-of-line character.

`StreamTokenizer.TT_EOF`   Indicates that the end of the input stream has been reached.

A stream tokenizer can be customized to recognize caller-specified characters, such as whitespace, comment delimiters, string delimiters, and other format-specific values. The customization methods are listed in Table 9.2.

TABLE 9.2: StreamTokenizer Customization Methods

Method	Description
void commentChar(int comment)	Specifies that comment is to denote the first character of a single-line comment.
void quoteChar(int quote)	Specifies that quote is to delimit the beginning and end of string constants.
void whitespaceChars(int low, int high)	Specifies that all input characters in the range low through high (inclusive) are to be interpreted as whitespace.
void wordChars(int low, int high)	Specifies that all input characters in the range low through high (inclusive) are to be interpreted as word characters.
void ordinaryChar(int ord)	Specifies that ord is an ordinary character and is not a quote delimiter, comment-line delimiter, whitespace character, word character, or number character. This "turns off" any special significance previously assigned using the calls listed above.
void ordinaryChars(int low, int high)	Specifies that all input characters in the range low through high (inclusive) are to be interpreted as ordinary characters.
void eolIsSignificant(boolean flag)	If flag is true, specifies that the parser will recognize end-of-line characters as tokens. If flag is false, end-of-line characters will not be recognized.
void parseNumbers(boolean flag)	If flag is true, specifies that the parser will recognize numbers as tokens. If flag is false, numbers will not be recognized.
void slashStarComments(boolean flag)	If flag is true, specifies that the parser will recognize C-style comments and skip over the comment body. If flag is false, C-style comments will not be recognized. C-style comments begin with a slash character followed by an asterisk character (/*) and end with an asterisk followed by a slash (*/); they may span multiple lines.

Continued on next page

TABLE 9.2 CONTINUED: StreamTokenizer Customization Methods

Method	Description
void slashSlashComments(boolean flag)	If **flag** is **true**, specifies that the parser will recognize C++-style comments. If **flag** is **false**, C++-style comments will not be recognized. C++-style comments begin with two slash characters (//) and end at the end of the current line.
void resetSyntax()	Resets the significance of all characters to be ordinary.

NOTE Notice that the values for the **StreamTokenizer** customization methods listed in Table 9.2, such as **comment**, **quote**, **low**, and **high** are ints, not bytes or chars. However, the values should certainly represent characters.

With the methods listed in Table 9.2, the StreamTokenizer class can be configured as a flexible and moderately powerful parser for an input stream whose format resembles Java, C, or C++ source code. Parsing of more general formats would require a powerful lexical analyzer and compiler generator, similar to the lex and yacc tools found in Unix.

Summary

The java.io package offers a variety of low-level input and output streams that read or write files, byte arrays, and strings. There are also a number of high-level streams that process or filter data. Streams can be chained together into arbitrarily long sequences.

One common use of streams is for disk file input and output. However, chains of streams can be a powerful solution for any programming problem involving the processing of structured sequential data. A prime example of this situation is network communication. The next chapter shows some examples of how to use streams for network reading and writing.

CHAPTER

TEN

10

Java Networking

■ TCP/IP networking

■ A TCP server and client

■ An SMTP mail client

■ URL retrieval and content handling

■ CGI connections

■ A mini-Applet Viewer

■ Methods for getting connection information

■ UDP services

Java networking uses TCP/IP—the same network system used by the Internet. TCP/IP defines protocols for providing services, such as file transfer and remote login, as well as protocols for the underlying communication system.

This chapter begins by discussing some of the fundamental issues that relate to the TCP/IP communication system. An understanding of the nature of the network, along with its strengths and limitations, is crucial when producing programmed systems to run over it.

The rest of the chapter will look at techniques for programming network systems with Java. The topics that will be covered include client and server programming, handling URLs (Uniform Resource Locators), and CGI (Common Gateway Interface) mechanisms. We will develop a mini-Applet Viewer application to demonstrate the use of Java class loaders. We will also explore the networking facilities provided by the java.net package for getting network address information. Another important topic we will address is security considerations for network programming. Finally, the chapter will describe the use of UDP (User Datagram Protocol), along with examples of both broadcasting and multicasting.

Fundamentals of TCP/IP Networking

The primary function of TCP/IP is to provide a point-to-point communication mechanism. One process on one machine communicates with another process on another machine. This communication appears as two streams of data: One stream carries data from one process to the other, and the other carries data in the other direction. Each process can read the data that has been written by the other. Under normal conditions, the data received is the same and in the same order as when it was sent.

TCP/IP Addressing

To support a point-to-point communication system, each node requires a unique address, which is analogous to a telephone number. In the current version of TCP/IP, the address takes the form of a 32-bit binary number. Conventionally, because humans do not cope well with long binary numbers, these addresses are represented as four decimal numbers, each in the range 0 to 255. Even with this improvement, humans still have difficulty remembering addresses. For this reason, mechanisms have been developed to allow more natural names to be used.

A name service provides a means of translating between names, which are easy for users to understand, and 32-bit binary numbers, which the machine can understand. Figure 10.1 shows a comparison of addresses in 32-bit binary format, dotted decimal format, and name service names.

FIGURE 10.1:

A comparison of addressing formats used in TCP/IP

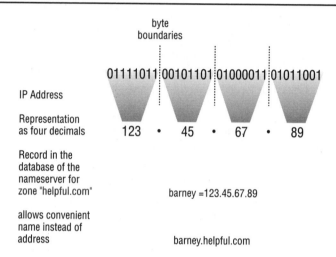

byte
boundaries

01111011 00101101 01000011 01011001

IP Address

Representation
as four decimals   123 • 45 • 67 • 89

Record in the
database of the
nameserver for
zone "helpful.com"   barney =123.45.67.89

allows convenient
name instead of
address   barney.helpful.com

A variety of naming schemes are available and in regular use on private TCP/IP networks, but only one system is accepted for use on the Internet as a whole. That system is called the Domain Name System (DNS). DNS allows machines to be addressed using textual names instead of numbers. To allow network administrators a degree of autonomy with machine names, a hierarchical approach is used for these names.

A DNS name is made up of a number of parts, separated by periods. In the same way that a street address has the city at the end and the individual house number at the beginning, a DNS name has a broad specification at the right, with more detail added with each element to the left. Hence, an address like www.javasoft.com indicates that the machine is called www, that name is known in the context of a zone called javasoft, and the name javasoft is known in the context of a larger zone called com.

In addition to the machine addresses provided by the Internet Protocol (IP) part of the network system, TCP/IP has a mechanism for identifying individual processes on a machine, analogous to an office block. The building has a telephone number, but each room inside is also identified by an extension number. When a call arrives at the building, it must be connected to the correct room for handling—payment requests go to accounts payable, orders to sales, and so forth. In the TCP/IP system, the extension numbers are called *ports*, and they are represented by a 16-bit binary number.

NOTE   A TCP/IP connection is identified by four numbers: the source machine address, the destination machine address, the source port, and the destination port. Usually, only the server port is important for deciding which service is being used, and ports at the client end are allocated according to what is available. Because both port numbers are considered when identifying a connection, the server port can be reused—even from the same client machine—without confusion.

To communicate with the correct part of a particular computer, the sending machine must know both the machine address and the port number to which the message should be sent. The organization of port numbers is rather more rigid than that of telephone extensions. Most public services use port numbers defined in *Request for Comment* standards (RFCs). A list of these is found in most Unix systems in a file called /etc/services or on Windows systems in \WINDOWS\SERVICES. The full set of RFC documents can be obtained from a number of sites, including ftp://nic.ddn.mil/rfc. Relevant RFCs are included on the CD-ROM, in the javadevhdbk\rfcs directory.

Recent Internet systems, such as Gopher and the World Wide Web, use URLs to specify individual services. A URL is able to define a port number, protocol, machine, and specific file. Because of this expressiveness, URL-based services are able to use nonstandard port numbers. In most other cases, however, a service will be associated with one particular port. For example, SMTP, the Internet mail service, is found on port number 25, and the Telnet server is found at port 23.

TCP/IP Internals

The TCP/IP system is actually made up of a number of logical layers. Each layer communicates with both its neighbor layers. In this way, clearly defined responsibilities can be allocated to different parts of the system.

The First Layer

The lowest layer handles physical transmission and reception of data from the network cable itself. This is not actually part of the TCP/IP system as such, but is usually provided by another protocol. This layer is sent a block of bytes—conventionally called a *datagram*—by the layer above it. Then it sends the datagram to the network, or it receives data from the network and passes the data to the layer above it.

The first layer service is not expected to know if transmitted data successfully reached the intended destination or what the destination was intended to be. When receiving data, this layer is not required to know if this machine is the intended recipient, nor if the data has been received correctly.

NOTE   Many implementations of the first layer, such as Ethernet, actually do know if the data is correct and intended for this machine. Although TCP/IP does not require it, it is common for implementations to be optimized to take advantage of these benefits when they are available.

The IP Layer

The next layer is the IP layer. IP knows that it has a physical transport layer available for carrying datagrams. IP takes the data it is to send and adds special control information, called a *header*, to it. The headers describe, among other things, the address of the destination machine. In this way, when the IP layer at the receiving machine is passed a datagram by its physical transport layer, it is able to look at the header and decide whether it is the intended recipient. As with the physical transport layer, datagrams are passed down from above to be transmitted (along with the destination address), and received datagrams are passed up when the address has been verified. (IP provides other important services, including network system configuration and control over routing, but these are not available to Java programmers, so they are not directly relevant to this discussion.)

The TCP and UDP Layers

Above the IP layer are a number of other layers at the same level. Two parts of the system occupying this level are interesting here. These are the Transmission Control Protocol (TCP) and the User Datagram Protocol (UDP, often referred to descriptively as the Unreliable Datagram Protocol). In later sections, you will find descriptions of ways to use Java to handle both of these services.

TCP and UDP are intended for programs to use when communicating with each other, and they provide one facility in common: port numbers. In the same way that the IP layer builds a header and attaches it to the front of the data to be transmitted to identify the target machine, TCP and UDP build headers of their own to identify the target port number. When a datagram is passed up to one of these layers by the IP layer, the header is examined so that the target port number can be identified and the data passed to the correct process.

During transmission, each layer of these protocols takes data and control information from the layer above and creates a sort of envelope to wrap the data in. The combined data and control block is passed down to the layer below, where the whole block is regarded simply as data. At the receiving end, each layer in turn "unwraps" the parcel of data, extracting the control information from it. This control information is used, for example, by the receiving IP layer to distinguish UDP and TCP datagrams. The separated data and control information are then passed up to the layer above. Figure 10.2 illustrates this idea.

FIGURE 10.2:

Data blocks are wrapped in envelopes by each successive layer of TCP/IP transmission.

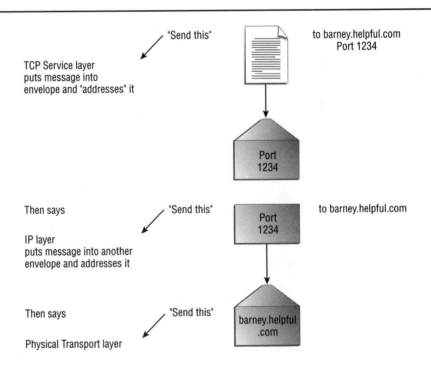

TCP and UDP have important differences. UDP is called the User Datagram Protocol precisely because it takes the IP layer, which provides a datagram protocol, and provides a programming interface that makes it suitable for use in general programming. The user referred to in the name is the user process that makes use of the network system.

UDP has a facility for determining whether the received data has been corrupted, but it is not used often. Even if the data is read incorrectly, UDP does not implement any kind of acknowledgment mechanism, so this layer cannot inform the sender of the failure.

Significantly more facilities are provided by TCP. When a TCP data block, usually called a *segment*, is transmitted, the sender labels it with a *sequence number* and a *checksum*. The sequence number is a label to uniquely identify this segment and its position in the ordered flow of segments. The checksum allows the receiver to determine whether the segment has been received correctly. The data sent is stored along with the time of sending and the sequence number. If the segment is received correctly by the intended recipient and the recipient was ready to receive it, then the recipient sends an acknowledgment. This is a message that says, in effect, "I got your message; it was correct, and it had this label on it." When the sender sees this message, it can discard its copy of the segment data. If the sender does not receive the acknowledgment in a reasonable time, then it retransmits the segment.

If too many failures occur, the TCP system abandons the attempt on the assumption that there is a physical problem with the network. The program using the TCP system, and in turn the human user, can be informed that a failure has occurred.

Clearly, TCP is the easier system to use from a programming point of view, because the channels it creates can be treated as reliable. This means that, unless something catastrophic happens, the bytes that are read and written are known by both the sender and the receiver to have been received correctly, in the same order, by the intended process on the intended machine. The sender knows that it will be informed if successful transmission is not possible or cannot be verified. Using UDP, all these issues remain for the programmer to resolve.

NOTE   It is easy enough to conceive of how a datagram might get damaged or lost entirely—all that is needed for that to happen is a power surge on a transmission line or a computer failure somewhere along the route. It is perhaps less clear why two datagrams might arrive out of order. In a TCP/IP network, it is common to have multiple possible routes between two systems. Each datagram that is transmitted follows a route chosen for it by the network system as a whole, and two successive datagrams might follow different routes. If the first datagram follows a route that takes longer to complete (either because it is physically further or, more commonly, because it uses slower links), then the first datagram might arrive after the second.

Despite the added complexity incumbent in its use, UDP is not without appropriate application. It is a simpler protocol, involving less CPU time and less network overhead in terms of additional "management" data. Therefore, on networks that are reasonably reliable, such as most modern LANs, UDP is faster. Also, UDP is necessary for broadcast and multicast systems. When using UDP, the programmer must either provide verification and recovery mechanisms or accept the possibility of lost data. If the verification and recovery mechanisms are not carefully designed to match the reliability of the network, the performance of the UDP system will drop. This reduction of performance can be dramatic.

What Java Does Not Provide

There are some facilities offered by traditional TCP/IP programming libraries that are not supported by Java: raw sockets, out-of-band data, socket half-close, and direct access to the full facilities of DNS.

Raw sockets allow the programmer to develop new protocol sets, parallel to TCP or UDP. They are also used to implement services that use the Internet Control Message Protocol (ICMP) protocol, such as the `ping` utility.

Out-of-band data allows sending "urgent" messages so that the receiver will be notified of their arrival. The receiver would then be able to read the urgent data before reading the other data that arrived first. Some standard Internet services use urgent messages, but it is the exception rather than the rule.

Socket half-close is a little-used facility that allows one end of a connection to close down its transmission while the other end is still sending data in the other direction. In Java, closing either of the streams will close the underlying socket.

The core Java networking classes also do not provide the full facilities of name services. *Name services* typically provide information about machine names and addresses, service names and port numbers, and the routing of e-mail. Some systems provide even more. However, the core Java facilities provide access to only hostname and address information.

Network Programming Basics

The following sections introduce the basics of creating network connections using Java. We will develop a simple TCP client and server to demonstrate the techniques covered here.

A Simple TCP Client

The daytime service is a traditional TCP service available on Unix systems. If you have a system that does not provide this service, there is a simulation of the service on the CD-ROM accompanying this book. The daytime protocol is defined in RFC 867; a copy of this document can be found in the file `javadevhdbk\rfcs\rfc867.txt` on the CD-ROM accompanying this book.

The Daytime server accepts connections on its designated port and sends to the client a single line of text representing the current date and time. The code for a simple client that connects to this service follows. The algorithm of this client is very simple. A socket is created and connected to a named host using the command-line argument provided. When the connection is established, an input stream reads characters from the network. One line of input is read and copied to the standard output. You can find the source code for this example in the directory `javadevhdbk\ch10\DayClient1.java`. The bytecode is in the file `javadevhdbk\ch10\DayClient1.class`.

LIST 10.1   *DayClient1.java*

```java
import java.net.*;
import java.io.*;

public class DayClient1 {
  public static final int DAYTIME_PORT = 13;
  String host;
  Socket s;

  public static void main(String args[]) throws IOException {
    DayClient1 that = new DayClient1(args[0]);
    that.go();
  }
```

```
public DayClient1(String host) {
  this.host = host;
}

public void go() throws IOException {
  s = new Socket(host, DAYTIME_PORT);
  BufferedReader i = new BufferedReader(
    new InputStreamReader(s.getInputStream()));
  System.out.println(i.readLine());
  i.close();
  s.close();
}
}
```

Running the TCP Client

It is not necessary to determine whether your system currently provides a day-time service. Most Unix systems do; most other systems do not. Simply attempt to run the Java version of the server. If there is a server already running, the Java version will be unable to use the socket and will fail; otherwise, it will start correctly.

Attempt to start the Java server by issuing the command:

java DayServer1

Note that the DayServer.class file is located on the CD-ROM along with the DayClient1.class file. If no other server is already using port 13, the server will start and run until killed.

In a different window, run the example by issuing the command:

java DayClient1 localhost

Be careful to supply a hostname; this example does not check for it.

TIP   There are two ways to refer to the local machine without needing to know its proper name. Traditionally, the name localhost is reserved for this purpose. Also, a special address is reserved for a machine to refer to itself: This address is 127.0.0.1.

If no hostname is given, an `ArrayIndexOutOfBoundsException` will be thrown. (Checks for this error have been omitted to avoid distracting you from the point of the code.) Provided your system networking is installed correctly, the program will run, connect to the server, and read and output the current date and time. The client will exit after this process is completed.

If your machine is connected to a network, try giving the names of other machines. Some might be running the daytime service, especially if they are Unix-based. On the Internet, some publicly accessible systems run the service, including www.sgi.com (at the time of this writing).

NOTE
The Java networking packages insist that hosts must be known by name; otherwise, an `IOException` indicating "Unknown host" will be thrown. It is possible to use numeric addresses in string form, but they must match some entry in the name table used by the network. If a numeric address is not listed in the network's name database, it will be rejected.

Providing Machine and Port Information

The `Socket` constructor arguments describe the machine on which the server is located and the port number on which the service is provided. The conventional port number for the daytime service is 13, and a constant declaration is made for this in the `DayClient1` class. The name of the server host machine is taken from the first command-line argument of the program itself. Typically, for this example, use `localhost` to refer to the current machine.

The `Socket` constructor documentation states that it might throw an `IOException`. This occurs if the hostname provided is not known or if the machine to which it refers is not offering any service on the specified port. This example concentrates on the working of sockets, rather than the failure modes, so the `main()` method is declared to ignore the problem and to throw the exception up to the interpreter. In the event of a problem, the whole program will simply dump an error report and a stack trace, and then stop.

When the `go()` method is executed, it waits until the connection is established and then returns the new `Socket` object. At this point, the socket is ready to use. Anyone who has programmed with the traditional sockets libraries (for example, in C) will know that this is a much simpler mechanism.

Connecting to the Streams

After the socket is connected, two streams are obtained from it: One is an Output-Stream object and the other is an InputStream object. Both streams are connected to the server via the network. Bytes written to the output stream are sent across the network for the server to read. Similarly, bytes transmitted by the server are readable from the client's input stream. This particular program only reads data from the server; no data is output.

Two methods are provided by the Socket class to allow connection to the streams: getInputStream() and getOutputStream(). Rather than use the basic stream interfaces, you would usually plug an additional layer of filtering into them. In this example, this filtering layer is a combination of a BufferedReader and InputStreamReader object. The constructor for this InputStreamReader object takes the feeder InputStream object as an argument and connects to it automatically. Similarly, the constructor for the BufferedReader object takes the Input-StreamReader object as an argument.

The final operation of this example, prior to closing the connection, is to read the output of the server, using the in.readLine() method of the BufferedReader class. This method collects one line of characters from the stream, and the resulting String object is printed on the standard output channel using the System.out.println() method.

Java streams are generally closed from the top of the stream. This example is no exception. The BufferedReader object is closed, which closes the underlying input stream in the socket. It is important to be aware that closing either the input stream or output stream of a Socket object closes that socket entirely. Explicitly closing both the streams and the socket is a matter of convention and clarity.

Enhancing the TCP Client

You can use the TCP client example to connect to a number of services similar to the daytime service. Changing the code so it uses a second command-line argument to define the port number for the connection will allow this code to connect to any service that outputs a single line of text.

To read multiple lines, you can place the readLine() method call inside a loop. This requires an additional modification to recognize the end of the communication. In this case, the end-of-file condition is indicated by the readLine() method returning a null value. Other variations of read() methods return -1.

These modifications have been made, and you can find the resulting code on the CD-ROM, in javadevhdbk\ch10\GeneralClient.java.

> **NOTE**
>
> In JDK versions up to 1.0.2, there was a bug in the Socket class implementation under Windows platforms. The bug affected socket closing, so when a socket was closed at one end of the connection, the other end—which should have read an end-of-file indication—remained unaware of the closing until an IOException occurred during a read(). Many protocols include a specific high-level command indicating that the connection is to be closed. This behavior is useful because it conveniently sidesteps this particular problem.

A Simple TCP Server

It is important to be able to offer services as well as connect to them. To this end, a ServerSocket object is used. This section examines the code for a basic server that achieves the same effect as the daytime service. This code is basically the same server that was used in the preceding section for systems without the daytime service. In this version, the port number is different to allow the server to coexist with the standard daytime service on machines that provide it. To operate with this modified server, the client must also use this different port number.

> **NOTE**
>
> Port numbers up to 1024 are reserved for system services. In the case of Unix systems, a program cannot generally use these ports unless it is run by the superuser root. Ports in the range 6000 to 6999 are used for X Windows. A number of services, such as NFS, use ports in the range 2000 to 2999. For these reasons, port numbers cannot be chosen entirely arbitrarily. Nonstandard servers should generally use ports higher than 5000, but the essential point is that you must avoid port numbers used by any other services running on the same server, and for clarity, avoid ports already in use on the local network.

For this server, the ServerSocket object is created and associated with the chosen port, number 13013. When the socket has been created, the program enters an infinite loop. The body of this loop accepts a single connection, extracts the output stream from the resulting Socket object, and writes the message onto it in ASCII via a buffered writer and an output stream writer. The output message is followed by a newline and closure of both the stream and socket, as an indication to the client that the message is completed. You'll find the source code for this example in javadevhdbk\ch10\DayServer2.java. The corresponding bytecode is in the file javadevhdbk\ch10\DayServer2.class.

LIST 10.2	***DayServer2.java***

```java
import java.io.*;
import java.net.*;
import java.util.*;

public class DayServer2 {
  private ServerSocket ss;
  public static final int DAYTIME_PORT = 13013;

  public static void main(String args[]) throws IOException {
    DayServer2 d = new DayServer2();
    d.go();
  }

  public void go() throws IOException {
    Socket s = null;
    ss = new ServerSocket(DAYTIME_PORT, 5);
    for (;;) {
      s = ss.accept();
      BufferedWriter out = new BufferedWriter(
        new OutputStreamWriter(s.getOutputStream(),"8859_1"));
      out.write("Java Daytime server: " +
        (new Date()).toString() + "\n");
      out.close();
      s.close();
    }
  }
}
```

Running the TCP Server

To run the program, change to the directory javadevhdbk\ch10 and issue the command:

java DayServer2

The server will start and run until it is stopped.

In a different window, run the client DayClient2 by typing the command:

java DayClient2 localhost

Provided your system networking is correctly set up, the client will run, connect to the server, and print the time and date message that the server transmits.

Accepting Connections

The first argument to the constructor of the ServerSocket class is the port number on which connections will be accepted. The second is for a value called *queue depth* or *backlog*. The significance of the second argument is discussed later.

After the ServerSocket object has been created, it is able to accept connections from clients. A connection is established by issuing the accept() method call. This method blocks the current thread until a client has made a connection. When the connection has been established, accept() returns a new Socket object. From this object, in the same way as with the client code, InputStream and Output-Stream objects may be obtained. The handling of these streams is identical to that in the TCP client described in the previous section.

Enhancing the TCP Server

This trivial server can be easily modified to provide for a variety of simple circumstances. As with the simple client example, reading the port to use from the command line improves the code's versatility.

More general utility may be achieved by modifying the server to read the data to be transmitted from the command line, a file, or perhaps even a separate program.

TIP   Under Unix systems the standard utility inetd provides for all these options from a standard facility. The inetd utility can be very useful for debugging.

In javadevhdbk\ch10\GeneralServer.java, you can find the source and bytecode for a modification that implements the port number control and reads the message to be sent from a file. (That file is also named on the command line.) Be aware that the trivial client example DayClient1.java, which expects a single line, will not work properly with the GeneralServer.java example if the file specified contains more than a single line. The `GeneralClient.java` example, however, handles multiple lines correctly.

In the examples discussed so far, only the server has transmitted any data and only the client has read data. If you understand the basics of creating client and server sockets, extracting the streams, and passing data from server to client, programming bidirectional communications is easy. Implementing bidirectional communications in Java is simply a matter of extracting the output stream for the client and the input stream for the server. However, there are some issues you need to consider when designing programs that connect clients and servers. The next section discusses the key issues.

Client-Server Communication Considerations

The basic construction of a network connection between client and server using Java is quite simple—much simpler than with most other programming interfaces. However, once the connection is established, the ensuing communication must be handled and controlled. In designing your programs, you need to consider server types, queue depth, and protocol issues.

Server Types

Some servers, including the examples discussed in the previous sections, accept a single connection, handle it to completion, and then shut down that connection. Only then can a new connection be made. Servers of this type are often called *sequential* or *iterative*. Many servers can handle more than one connection simultaneously. Servers that can handle multiple connections are generally described as *parallel* or *concurrent*.

A server that keeps itself busy throughout its connection with a client gains nothing from handling multiple connections simultaneously, which would necessarily result in each of the connections taking longer to complete. On the other hand, a server idle for periods while the connection is established could be used to serve another client.

But, in your choice of server type, you must consider what specifically is meant by the server being idle. At least three components are involved: the CPU, the disk, and the network interface. A fully laden network interface might appear to constitute a busy server, but while the interface is busy, the CPU or disk might be available to prepare more data for another connection. In general, on a modern operating system that schedules the use of its devices, a parallel server will offer some improvement in overall throughput compared with a sequential one.

The sequential server does offer some advantages, but they are in simplicity of design and coding rather than overall throughput. A parallel server requires a threaded implementation, so its design is more complicated, especially if the data used to support the server must be protected from multiple overlapping accesses. If a situation requires a rapid solution, then pragmatism might suggest a sequential server.

We will develop an example of a parallel server after discussing the other server design considerations.

The Queue Depth

New connections can only be established if the server program is waiting in the accept() call. When this is not the case, however, clients are not refused connection immediately, nor are they left to time out. Rather, the underlying TCP/IP system will hold a number of new clients in a queue. The size of this queue is determined by the second argument to the ServerSocket class constructor, which is called the queue depth or backlog.

NOTE   The queue depth parameter has been incorrectly documented throughout the JDK sources where it is described as a timeout. This error was propagated into the API documentation until later versions of JDK 1.0.2. Server sockets, in the underlying TCP/IP system do *not* generally have a timeout period. Although many servers will apply a timeout to a connected socket if it remains inactive for a long time, the ServerSocket itself, once created and configured, continues to listen for incoming connections until the controlling program shuts it down. There is, however, a timeout facility available with the accept() method. Using the setSoTimeout() method, it is possible to configure the socket so that an accept() that does not receive a connection in a reasonable time will be abandoned. The Java 1.1 and 2 documentation correctly reflects all these issues.

If the queue depth is set to five, the server socket can have at most five connections waiting to be accepted. Current or past connections are not part of this count. If more clients attempt to connect after five are in the queue, the new connections are ignored. If the queue remains full while the client socket retries, the client socket times out and fails. In a Java client program, this causes the Socket object constructor to fail. The period before a client socket timeout occurs is typically around three to five minutes, although this depends on the platform. A Java Socket that fails to make a connection throws an IOException with the message "Connection timed out."

Although the usual maximum queue depth is five, individual implementations may vary, and some systems, especially Unix-based ones, allow the limit to be reconfigured. However, arbitrarily increasing the figure will not necessarily improve a server's throughput. As with any performance tuning, you must first carefully analyze the actual bottleneck and determine if the proposed changes will help or simply move the bottleneck elsewhere.

Configuring a server socket with enough queue depth to ensure that new clients are never made to wait will generally allow faster service, because the `accept()` call will not have to wait. On the other hand, if clients are made to retry because the TCP/IP queue is full, the retries happen at comparatively long intervals, which will result in a greater average waiting time in the `accept()` method.

In a parallel server design, there is less chance that the queue will be needed, because more connections will be handled directly. However, in a sequential server design, it becomes more important to avoid forcing the clients to retry, because they are less likely to be able to connect to the server on their first attempt.

Protocol Issues

If a client and server are to communicate, they must have a prior agreement on how to do so. This agreement is known as a *protocol*. In some cases, a protocol can be trivially simple. The daytime example is one such protocol. In that service, the client and server agree that the client will connect on port 13 and listen for one line of output. In most cases, such a degree of simplicity is unacceptable.

A common requirement in a client/server relationship is some form of command/response mechanism: The client connects and asks a question, and the server then determines the proper response and transmits it. Two major decisions must be made in this regard: the data format for the communication and the nature of the relationship between request and response.

Stop-and-Wait and Asynchronous Protocols   In order to maintain control of the interaction between client and server, the design must define when each is permitted to send requests or responses and when each should be listening for replies. In a common design pattern, known as *stop-and-wait* or *lockstep*, one end sends a message that the other end must fully process before replying. While the message is being processed, neither end sends anything. Following the response, nothing is transmitted until more is heard from the original station. Such protocols are rather like "walkie-talkie" radio systems and are simple to implement and easy to debug. Probably for these reasons, they are also very common.

Another possibility exists, however, which might be appropriate in some circumstances. Where both client and server are multithreaded, it might be possible for either or both to perform useful actions during times when a stop-and-wait protocol would restrict them from sending network traffic. If those other activities happen to require network support, then the overall use of bandwidth, and possibly the use of CPU resources at one or both ends, could be improved if the stop-and-wait rule were waived.

If a protocol of this type, called *asynchronous*, is to be implemented, a mechanism must be devised to allow a response to be associated with the message, and perhaps the thread, that requested it. A number of mechanisms can be employed. If requests are small, responses can reasonably carry copies of the original requests. In circumstances where the requests are large, a *serial number* mechanism might be more appropriate. Clearly, one feature of asynchronous protocols is inevitable: They are more complex to design than the traditional stop-and-wait approach. They can also prove substantially harder to debug in "live" conditions.

There is a limitation in the Java networking libraries that might encourage the design of asynchronous services. Standard TCP/IP sockets allow the transmission of *out-of-band* (OOB) or urgent data. Messages of this type can *jump the queue* of data waiting to be handled at the receiving end. The java.net package does not, however, provide access to these facilities. In traditional stop-and-wait protocols, the out-of-band data mechanism can be used to provide an "emergency stop" facility. Because OOB transmission is not available, an asynchronous protocol with appropriate handling at each end can provide an alternative way to achieve this functionality. This kind of facility can be useful, for example, if a long database request is being handled and the user decides to cancel the request while waiting.

Data Formats

The data that is sent over the network may be carried in a number of different formats. Binary and ASCII have been used for many systems in many languages. Java actually raises two more possibilities: Unicode and Universal Transfer Format (UTF), which are not normally considered in other systems. The advantages and disadvantages of each of these formats are explained in the following sections.

ASCII Format   Many of the familiar TCP/IP services use ASCII-based data formats for their communications, which has a number of advantages. Perhaps the most persuasive is that debugging the system becomes much easier. Given an ASCII-based TCP protocol, it is possible to test the server manually using the standard Telnet client. For example, even without a client, the Daytime server can be tested (on a Unix system and some Windows systems) simply by issuing the following command:

$ telnet localhost 13

This would output date and time information directly to the screen. (Later in the chapter, in the "Investigation of the SMTP Protocol" section, we'll discuss using the Telnet technique to examine a working network server.)

Although the daytime service is sufficiently simple to hide the need for debugging, it is easy to see that in a more typical and complex server, an ASCII-based format can offer great advantages. Commands can be typed at the keyboard, and the responses are displayed directly on the console. It is then easy to verify whether the server is working correctly.

In many operating systems, particularly Unix-based ones, it is possible to construct a server using standard operating system services, with only a simple shell script and a one-line configuration entry in a text file. For example, a server that records the messages sent to it by clients and transmits the contents of a file to a connecting client. (This may be achieved in Unix by using the inetd facility.)

Another advantage of ASCII is that it is platform independent. This aspect forms the foundation for many of the services that built the Internet.

The disadvantage of ASCII as the basic encoding mechanism for a network connection is that it is rather inefficient in bandwidth terms.

As with the sequential server design, where a rapid solution is required, ASCII may be your best choice.

Unicode Format   Because Java uses Unicode for encoding all characters and strings internally, Unicode is clearly a possible choice for network communication. Its disadvantages are that it does not offer the ease of debugging that ASCII does, and it is not necessarily readily supported in systems that are not written using Java. Unicode is a 16-bit representation, which gives it the range it requires but also means that it needs twice the bandwidth of an equivalent ASCII transmission. However, it might be a good choice if a variety of languages are to be handled using the service.

UTF Format   The Java libraries offer a third possible variation on the theme of text-based communication. Java supports a variation of UTF that can represent all the characters in the Unicode set. The representation uses a variable number of bytes for each character. Seven-bit ASCII is represented unchanged. Eight-bit characters and many of the Unicode set are represented using two bytes, while those characters remaining are represented using three bytes. This means that UTF is able to represent non-ASCII characters as comprehensively as Unicode, but, where the bulk of characters are seven-bit ASCII, UTF does not require additional bandwidth. Also, because of its equivalence with seven-bit ASCII, UTF can make some use of Telnet as a debugging tool for viewing a server's output.

An additional feature of UTF is that it represents record boundaries using a length prefix field rather than by using normal characters. In ASCII systems, it is common to use a carriage return or similar character to indicate record boundaries, but this makes it inconvenient to use the delimiter character itself as data for communication. With UTF, however, each message can contain any character, including carriage return, linefeed, null, and so forth. Unfortunately, however, you can't transmit these record-oriented strings from Telnet.

Binary Format   Where nontext data is being communicated, the most compact form of data transmission, excluding compression, normally results from direct use of binary. Of course, compressed data is binary anyway. This efficiency, especially in conjunction with compression, can make binary the most appropriate choice when large amounts of data are involved. Even for applications that are not handling large data volume, many small transmissions build up to a large bandwidth demand. Hence, it is prudent to consider the bandwidth efficiency of any design.

In most designs, one of the major disadvantages of using binary communication over a network link is the difficulties that can arise if dissimilar platforms are involved. Different systems commonly have different data formats in terms of byte order and size and representation of primitive types. Java provides an environment in which data formats are consistent between platforms, both in running programs and flowing over streams. Using the various stream, reader, writer, character-to-byte, and byte-to-character conversion classes, two Java programs can be connected over a network and may communicate in binary without concern about data-type mismatches resulting from different platforms.

NOTE   The Java standards do not actually require data representations in memory to be the same between platforms. They only require that the appearance and external representation of data items are the same. For example, it is permitted to use 128-bit values to represent int items, provided that the extra resolution is hidden, so overflow and all side effects of representation behave as if 32-bit two's complement were used.

A Parallel Server

In a single-threaded server, the behavior is to accept a connection and handle it to completion before looping round to another accept() call. The essence of the parallel server is that several threads are available for handling connections simultaneously.

One common way to approach the parallel server is to create a new thread each time that accept() returns a new connection. Code of the following form would achieve this:

```
for (;;) {
  s = ss.accept();
  handler = new ConnectionHandler(s);
  handlerThread = new Thread(handler);
  handlerThread.start();
}
```

In this hypothetical example, the ConnectionHandler class implements the Runnable interface so that it can be used to construct threads. The run() method services the connection. The connected Socket object is passed into the ConnectionHandler instance via its constructor.

This approach, in its simple form, has a major drawback: Some Java garbage collectors do not reclaim the space allocated to any object of the Thread class. Furthermore, because the Thread is never considered collectable, data to which the Thread has access cannot be collected either. If the approach shown above is implemented, the JVM steadily runs out of memory during operation. (See Chapter 7 for more details about this problem.)

Another weakness of the design shown is that it has no mechanism for limiting the number of simultaneous connections. Although the parallel server is likely to produce a higher overall throughput by keeping the CPU, network interface, and disk busy, too many connections will degrade performance. This can happen because of the overhead of switching contexts and because slow servers might cause their clients to retry their requests. Sending a retry to a server already responding slowly only exacerbates the problem by further increasing its load.

To produce a workable solution that does not suffer from the apparent problems of this model, a modified approach must be taken. A fixed number of threads must be launched, each with access to the same ServerSocket object. Each of these threads can then run independently, each calling the accept() method when it is able to handle another connection.

The parallel server example presented here constructs a ServerSocket object connected to the same port as was used by the DayServer2.java example. The three threads share this ServerSocket object. The behavior of the threads is very similar to that of the DayServer2.java example. In a loop, a connection is picked up via the accept() call. From the Socket object that this returns, the OutputStream object is extracted, and the date and time message is transmitted to the client. The source for this example is located on the CD-ROM in the directory javadevhdbk\ch10\ MultiServe.java. The bytecode is in the file javadevhdbk\ch10\MultiServe.class.

LIST 10.3	*MultiServe.java*

```java
import java.net.*;
import java.io.*;
import java.util.*;

public class MultiServe implements Runnable {
  private ServerSocket ss;

  public static void main(String args[]) throws Exception {
    MultiServe m = new MultiServe();
    m.go();
  }

  public void go() throws Exception {
    ss = new ServerSocket(DayClient2.DAYTIME_PORT, 5);
    Thread t1 = new Thread(this, "1");
    Thread t2 = new Thread(this, "2");
    Thread t3 = new Thread(this, "3");
    t1.start();
```

```
      t2.start();
      t3.start();
  }

  public void run() {
    Socket s = null;
    BufferedWriter out = null;
    String myname = Thread.currentThread().getName();

    for (;;) {
      try {
        System.out.println("thread " + myname +
          " about to accept..");
        s = ss.accept();
        System.out.println("thread " + myname +
          " accepted a connection");
        out = new BufferedWriter(
                new OutputStreamWriter(s.getOutputStream()));
        out.write(myname + " " + new Date());
        Thread.sleep(10000);
        out.write("\n");
        out.close();
      }
      catch (Exception e) {
        e.printStackTrace();
      }
    }
  }
}
```

Running the Parallel Server

The server provides a multithreaded version of the DayServer2.java example, and hence should be run alongside the DayClient2.java example. A number of "logging" messages have been added to the output of the server to allow its behavior to be monitored.

When the server is running, select a different window and run the DayClient2 program. Ideally, you should use several windows and run the client program nearly simultaneously from each window.

Messages are issued as each thread goes into the accept() statement and again when that statement returns, at which point the thread will be about to send the message to the client. Each successive running of the client will show that the request is served by the next thread in rotation.

NOTE

Actually, any available thread might be used to pick up the next request. Java does not guarantee any particular one, but a "round-robin" use of threads is common. See Chapter 7 for more details about threads.

Defining the MultiServer Class

A single object of the MultiServe class is created. In this object is a member variable of type ServerSocket, which is bound to the port chosen for this service.

The MultiServe class implements the Runnable interface, which allows it to be used as the basis for construction of the three threads. Because the threads are all built from the same Runnable instance, they share the same instance variables; specifically, they share the same ServerSocket object. Inside the run() method, each thread has its own local variables for Socket s, BufferedWriter out, and String myname.

Threads and Server Design

It might seem wasteful to create multiple threads before the server's load warrants it. Once created, however, a thread should not be destroyed if there is any chance that it might be needed again. Furthermore, there is a significant CPU overhead to creating a new thread (some operating systems are very poor in this area), and it is generally advantageous to do all this activity only once, at program startup.

Creating a predetermined number of threads in this way is quite common practice in server design. If necessary, the number of threads can be controlled with a command-line argument or a property, allowing tuning for each installation.

If you really need a variable number of threads, you can use the **setSoTimeout()** method to cause **accept()** calls to time out if they do not receive connections in a reasonable time. This approach would allow you to determine a suitable moment for reducing the number of threads.

Handling the Threads

The body of the run() method determines the behavior of the thread. In this case, this is a loop virtually identical to the one at the heart of the single-threaded Day-Server2.java example. A number of logging messages have been added. Each thread prints a message just before it enters the accept() method and immediately on its return from that method.

NOTE   This daytime service provided by MultiServe.java does not benefit particularly from a threaded server implementation because the time taken to handle the service is very small. For this reason, a deliberate delay has been introduced into the output. After the main date and time information is sent, the thread is sent to sleep for 10 seconds before it is able to complete the transmission by sending a newline. This delay gives you enough time to type the client command in separate windows. Quick typing should prove that the server actually can handle a new connection before the old one has been completed.

This approach solves the difficulties of the simple TCP server discussed earlier in the chapter. Multiple simultaneous connections are supported but are limited by the number of threads constructed. Furthermore, because each of the threads is reused rather than being wasted after handling a single connection, the problems of memory leakage are avoided.

Sharing one ServerSocket object directly is possible because the implementation of the accept() method protects the underlying system from multiple simultaneous access. The Java packages are generally described as *thread-safe*. In the current JDK, the accept() method calls a "sister" accept() method in the socket implementation class (usually PlainSocketImpl). That method is marked as synchronized, which prevents multiple threads from entering the body of the method simultaneously.

As you can see, the design of this parallel server is not complex. In your own server designs, you really only need to use single-threaded servers for the most basic situations or in circumstances where the data set supporting the server must be protected from concurrent accesses.

Enhancing the Parallel Server

You can adapt the overall design of this server to provide a multithreaded server for any application. A real application should not have the sleep() call, which is included in the example only to demonstrate how the threaded server behaves under load. The number of threads should be controlled via a command-line argument, perhaps with some default built in, to allow balancing resource usage against anticipated load.

Remember that as the number of threads increases, the server's throughput increases to a point and then falls off again. The only reliable guide for the optimum number of threads in any application on any particular platform is to experiment with different amounts. Such experiments should be carried out under live conditions or the results might be invalid.

Preexisting Protocols

Many preexisting network services are commonly available on TCP/IP networks. Here, we will consider the implications of writing Java code to interface with them.

In general, Java programs for connecting to, or providing, predefined network services are simpler than the equivalent programs written using other languages and libraries. Provided a proper definition of the protocol is available, all that remains is to design and implement code to handle it.

Many of the "core" TCP/IP services use ASCII-based protocols and a stop-and-wait approach to command and response. These features tend to simplify the job of debugging network code regardless of the language or libraries used.

As an example, we will develop a basic Java client for the Internet mail service SMTP (Simple Mail Transport Protocol), which is the standard protocol used for transporting e-mail over TCP/IP networks. (Other protocols, such as Post Office Protocol, or POP, are also used for e-mail, especially for communication with single-user machines.) The SMTP protocol is a good example of an ASCII-based stop-and-wait protocol. At each stage, only one machine is listening while the other is allowed to transmit. When the transmission is complete, the other machine is expected to send.

Before examining the example, you might find it useful to take a few minutes to investigate the operation of SMTP.

NOTE This investigation and the code that is presented are intended to demonstrate the typical nature of Internet services. Although the code works and can be reused, a suite of mail services is available in the Java Mail package. For most purposes, the services in this package are more suitable.

Investigation of the SMTP Protocol

If you are familiar with the SMTP protocol, you can safely skip this section and go directly to the description of a simple SMTP client. If not, and you can get access to an SMTP server and a Telnet client, you can gain some insight into the workings of the protocol by connecting to a mail server using Telnet.

SMTP uses a variety of simple commands, and most servers will actually offer a level of interactive help. This feature makes "manual" operation of the mail service quite easy.

Connect your Telnet client to the SMTP server using port 25. This will typically mean using one of the following two commands:

telnet *<serverhost>* **25**

or

telnet *<serverhost>* **smtp**

Substitute the name of the machine running your SMTP server in place of *<serverhost>*. If the server is running on the machine you are working at, you can use the name localhost. Note that 25 is the standard port number of the SMTP protocol as defined by RFC 821.

NOTE   The SMTP protocol, like Telnet, is defined in RFC documents. Copies of RFCs 821 and 822, the core description of SMTP, are located on the CD-ROM in the files javadevhdbk\rfcs\rfc821.txt and javadevhdbk\rfcs\rfc822.txt. Also, see Chapter 14 for more information about the Telnet protocol.

After the Telnet client connects, you will see the SMTP server sign on. Connecting to a system called freddy.helpful.org might result in the following output:

```
220 freddy.helpful.org Sendmail SMI-8.6/SMI-SVR4 ready at Wed, 21 Aug
1996 23:56:33 -0100
```

If you then enter either the **help** or **?** command, you should see a list of the commands that the server accepts (although some servers, especially non-Unix or enhanced-security versions, might not issue help messages). The output might be similar to this:

```
214-Commands:
214- HELO  MAIL  RCPT  DATA  RSET
```

```
214- NOOP  QUIT  HELP  VRFY  EXPN
214-For more info use "HELP <topic>".
```

Notice that all the responses from the server start with a three-digit code. These codes describe the status—successful or otherwise—of the command to which the server is responding. Codes starting with a 2 indicate successful completion; codes starting with a 3 indicate success so far of a command that is not yet completed. Other codes indicate difficulties. The full specification is given in the RFCs.

To send a mail message, a sign-on is first required. The client must introduce itself by using the command HELO. If your local machine is called talkative, your sign-on would be:

```
HELO talkative
```

Note that some security-conscious servers might take the trouble to check the address you gave against your real address, but in general, they will sign the message as being from whatever address the client machine claims.

In response to the client sign-on, the server will respond. This response generally takes a very friendly format:

```
Hello, talkative, pleased to meet you…
```

After sign-on, to send a mail message, the SMTP server must be provided with three pieces of data: the name of the sender, the name of the recipient, and the body of the message. Each of these items is supplied with a particular command.

A new message is introduced by the command MAIL FROM: sendername. Again, the server will believe whatever you tell it. This means that you can reasonably expect to be able send mail that shows a name completely different from the real sender's. Mail from cupid@olympus.com or president@whitehouse.gov does not necessarily mean that mysterious or powerful forces are trying to tell you something.

The recipient of the message is specified using the RCPT TO: recipient. In this case, if the specified recipient is local to the server, the server will attempt to verify that the destination is correct and will issue an error message if it is not.

Finally, the text of the message is sent. The command DATA is used to introduce the message text. The message should be sent as lines of text. To indicate that the text has been completed, a single period character (.) should be entered as the only character on a line.

NOTE   The definition of SMTP suggests that lines in mail messages should not exceed "about 1000 characters." This is because long lines might overflow buffers in some implementations. Special error codes should be returned in such conditions, but it is easier to keep lines short than to handle the errors.

A transcript of a typical (though trivial and fictional) SMTP session is shown below.

```
$ telnet freddy.helpful.org 25
Trying 1.2.3.4...
Connected to freddy.helpful.org.
Escape character is '^]'.
220 freddy.helpful.org Sendmail V7 ready at
    Wed, 21 Aug 1996 23:56:33 -0100
helo topsecret.whitehouse.gov
250 freddy.helpful.org Hello topsecret.whitehouse.gov,
    pleased to meet you
help
214-Commands:
214- HELO  MAIL  RCPT  DATA  RSET
214- NOOP  QUIT  HELP  VRFY  EXPN
214-For more info use "HELP <topic>".
214-smtp
214-For local information contact postmaster at this site.
214 End of HELP info
mail from: president@whitehouse.gov
250 president@whitehouse.gov... Sender ok
rcpt to: simon
250 simon... Recipient ok
data
354 Enter mail, end with "." on a line by itself
Your country needs you! Please report for official
duty tomorrow 5:15am sharp in the oval office.

BC

.
250 ACSE759 Message accepted for delivery
quit
221 freddy.helpful.org closing connection
Connection closed by foreign host.
$
```

A Simple SMTP Mail Client

The SMTP mail client presented here provides for only sending, not receiving, mail. A server would be required to receive mail.

In the SMTP mail client example, the main() method of the SMTP class is really a test harness. It collects the address information of the sender and recipient and then the body of the message. Given these, a new object of the SMTP class is constructed. The method send() is then invoked on that object, which goes through the basic SMTP protocol to deliver the message.

The source of the SMTP mail client follows. The source code for this example is located on the CD-ROM in the directory javadevhdbk\ch10\SMTP.java. The corresponding bytecode is in the file javadevhdbk\ch10\SMTP.class.

LIST 10.4   *SMTP.java*

```
import java.net.*;
import java.io.*;

public class SMTP {
  private String message;
  private String localMachine;
  private String senderName;
  private String recipient;
  private boolean valid_and_unsent = false;

  private BufferedReader in;
  private BufferedWriter out;

  // class constants
  public static final int SMTP_PORT = 25;
  private static final boolean logging = true;

  public SMTP() {
  }

  public SMTP(String sender) {
    int indexOfAtSign = sender.indexOf('@');
    if (indexOfAtSign < 0) {
      throw new RuntimeException("Malformed sender address." +
        " Need full user@host format");
    }
```

```java
    this.senderName = sender.substring(0, indexOfAtSign);
    this.localMachine = sender.substring(indexOfAtSign + 1);
}

public SMTP(String sender, String recipient, String message) {
  this(sender);
  setMessage(recipient, message);
}

public void setMessage(String recipient, String message) {
  this.recipient = recipient;
  this.message = message;
  valid_and_unsent = true;
}

public void send() throws IOException {
  if (!valid_and_unsent) {
    throw new RuntimeException("Attempt to send incomplete message,"
                               + " or send message twice");
  }

  // if this message is legitimate, continue to extract
  // the remote machine name
  int indexOfAtSign = recipient.indexOf('@');
  if (indexOfAtSign < 0) {
    throw new RuntimeException("Malformed recipient address." +
      " Need full user@host format");
  }
  String destinationMachine = recipient.substring(indexOfAtSign + 1);

  // attempt to make the connection, this might throw an exception
  Socket s = new Socket(destinationMachine, SMTP_PORT);
  in = new BufferedReader(
        new InputStreamReader(s.getInputStream(),"8859_1"));
  out = new BufferedWriter(
        new OutputStreamWriter(s.getOutputStream(),"8859_1"));
  String response;

  // discard signon message, introduce ourselves, and discard reply
  response = hear();
  say("HELO " + localMachine + "\n");
  response = hear();
```

```
      say("MAIL FROM: " + senderName + "\n");
      response = hear();
      say("RCPT TO: " + recipient + "\n");
      response = hear();
      say("DATA\n");
      response = hear();
      say(message + "\n.\n");
      response = hear();
      say("QUIT\n");

      // now close down the connection..
      s.close();
    }

    private void say(String toSay) throws IOException {
      out.write(toSay);
      out.flush();
      if (logging) {
        System.out.println(toSay);
      }
    }

    private String hear() throws IOException {
      String inString = in.readLine();
      if ("23".indexOf(inString.charAt(0)) < 0) {
        throw new IOException("SMTP problem: " + inString);
      }
      if (logging) {
        System.out.println(inString);
      }
      return inString;
    }

    public static void main(String args[]) throws Exception {
      BufferedReader in = new BufferedReader(
                                new InputStreamReader(System.in));
      System.out.print("Your address: ");
      System.out.flush();
      String sender = in.readLine();
      System.out.print("Recipient address: ");
      System.out.flush();
      String recipient = in.readLine();
      String message = "";
```

```
String part;
System.out.println("Message, end with '.' by itself:");
for (;;) {
  part = in.readLine();
  if ((part == null) || part.equals(".")) {
    break;
  }
  message += part + "\n";
}
SMTP mailer = new SMTP(sender, recipient, message);
mailer.send();
  }
}
```

Running the SMTP Client

To run this program, you will require network access to an SMTP server and knowledge of at least one valid mail account that is accessible to that server. Ideally, the account should be your own, so that you can see the results of the mail you send.

When the program starts, it prompts for the sender's username and that of the recipient. These should be given in the form *user@machine*. Be sure to give the SMTP server name, not the mail domain if these are different. Next, the program prompts for the body of the message. Enter text a line at a time (keep in mind that there are no editing facilities beyond those of the Delete key). When you have finished the message, type a single period on a line by itself.

When all the input has been given, the program will connect to the SMTP server on the recipient's machine and send the message. The whole protocol transaction will be copied to the standard output so you can see it progress.

NOTE   Normally, mail is not sent to a specific machine but to a mail domain. Hence, in the mail address simon@helpful.org it is unlikely that helpful.org is an actual machine; instead, the DNS name service translates it into a number of machines that act as mailboxes for that domain.

Remaining in Lockstep

In the SMTP protocol, the client and server remain in *lockstep*; that is, when the connection is established, the server is expected to transmit first and the client and server then proceed by taking turns. After that phase has been completed and the receiver has actually read the contents of the buffers, the "right to transmit" changes to the other party. In this approach, unexpected data is not possible, which simplifies the protocol because a main control loop can simply operate by receiving an input, generating the required output, and so forth.

If all is well, the SMTP responses are simply courtesy acknowledgments. However, there are two reasons that the client must read the text of the server's response. First, server implementations sometimes refuse to proceed if their responses have not been read.

The other reason, which is perhaps more important for a practical mail client, is that the responses carry a numeric status code at the beginning of the line. Numbers starting with a 2 indicate a successful completion, and numbers beginning with a 3 indicate a successful intermediate response, implying "OK so far, go ahead and finish off." Other values indicate some kind of difficulty; for example, if the mail recipient is described as a local user of the server but is not known by the server, the response will be error code 550. This client simply checks that a 2 or 3 starts the response line and throws an exception on everything else. (More details of the error status codes are provided in the RFCs on the CD-ROM, in the directory `javadevhdbk\rfcs`.)

Collecting the Message and Addresses

The work of the client is to collect the message data and addresses for recipient and sender. In a production program, the sender's name would be taken from a parameter file, and a menu entry would be offered to allow modification of this file. Non-Java systems might use an environment variable, but environment variables are not useful in Java because they are not platform independent and hence are not supported. In this example, for simplicity, the sender's name is also typed in.

TIP   Java provides a facility called properties that would be entirely suitable as a means of defining the sender's name. Properties are described in detail in Chapter 5.

The SMTP class requires the specification of sender and recipient addresses in *user@hostname* format, and the destination machine address is extracted from that form. The message can be provided as part of the constructor if preferred. When both addresses and a message have been supplied, the send() method can be invoked to handle the protocol transfer.

Before making the connection, the recipient address must be split into a machine name and a username. The machine name is then used to connect the client to the server, and the protocol messages are generated in the proper sequence by the body of the send() method.

To perform the transfer, two private methods are used: say() and hear(). These handle the logging of the transactions. The hear() method checks the SMTP return status to determine if any problems have arisen and throws an IOException when trouble occurs. To aid in determining the problem, the response that contained the error status is attached, in String form, to the exception that is thrown.

NOTE   The InputStreamReader and OutputStreamWriter objects in the SMTP.java example are created using an explicit converter to handle the translation between Unicode and byte-character encodings to ensure that the encoding of characters used in the network transactions is fixed. Normally, creating an InputStream-Reader uses the local default conversion; naturally, this is platform dependent. To avoid this platform dependency, the SMTP.java example makes explicit requests to convert between Unicode and ISO 8859-1 encoding. A list of the string names of converters that are supported in Java is provided in the documentation of the native2ascii utility.

To provide a useful, self-contained demonstration, the SMTP class also contains a main() method. If the program is invoked directly, it will prompt for user and destination addresses and a message body. When these have been entered, an instance of the SMTP class is constructed, and the message is sent.

The SMTP class includes a constant declaration called *logging*. This is set to true in the source, so the class will echo the protocol exchanges to System.out. The Java compiler optimizes conditional blocks of code if it sees a constant expression in the condition. Hence, this construction can be used to give conditional compilation, very similarly to the use of #ifdef or #if defined() in a C or C++ preprocessor.

Using Java Mail Facilities

This example is intended to demonstrate how sockets may be used in Java, rather than for reuse. Comprehensive mail facilities are provided in Java Mail. In particular, Java Mail provides POP in addition to SMTP.

In general, the mail domain name part of an e-mail address is not necessarily a machine name. DNS provides mail exchanger (MX) records, which map a single domain name onto several different physical machines. There is no provision for MX record lookup in the java.net package, but these facilities are embedded in Java Mail and can be accessed directly using the Java Naming and Directory Interfaces (JNDI).

An applet can connect only to its originating host, so MX lookup is not useful for applets. A suitably configured SMTP server on the host that originates the applet should be used to handle mail forwarding instead.

URL Operations

The URL is a crucial part of the World Wide Web, facilitating navigation for both human and machine alike. The java.net package includes two key classes specifically for working with URLs. The classes are called URL and URLConnection.

The most fundamental network facility provided by the URL class is the ability to read, as stream, the data to which that URL refers. An instance of the URL class can be created using a text string that represents the URL; for example:

```
URL theUrl = new URL("http://www.sun.com/");
```

This constructor throws an IOException if the URL text is malformed, or if the protocol part, http in this case, is not known to the system. Because of the validity checks imposed by the compiler, an IOException must be handled via a try {}/ catch(){} block, or the calling method must be declared to pass the exception on.

Once the URL is constructed, the openStream() method provides a simple mechanism for reading the data that the URL describes. This allows the input to be handled by any of the standard InputStream class facilities, including the chaining of other types of input streams or readers, such as the DataInputStream or Input-StreamReader classes. Other mechanisms permit writing to the server for services such as CGI POST.

Java 2 introduces a new protocol called `jar:` that allows data to be read from a JAR archive. For example, the URL `jar:http://accounts.myco.com/records/accounts.jar!/jan/data.dat` describes a file called **data.dat**, which is located in a subdirectory called **jan** in a JAR archive called **accounts.jar**, where the JAR archive is itself located on a web server at the URL `http://accounts.myco.com/records/accounts.jar`.

A URL Retrieval Example

Our next example uses the `openStream()` method to load a file over HTTP. This could be a class file, image, or any other data offered on a web server. The contents of the URL will be saved to a disk file so that they are available locally. This would allow you, for example, to take an applet from a remote site and place it onto your own server without needing to obtain the source for it.

Java code loaded from the local system will be treated as trusted and will bypass all the normal security restrictions. Any other type of executable will also present a risk, just as if an unknown program is loaded from an FTP site.

For each command-line argument, the `main()` method invokes the `getURL()` method. This method constructs a `URL` from the string supplied by the user and opens the connection to it. When the connection is opened, the data is read into a buffer and then saved to disk.

The source code for this example is located on the CD-ROM in the directory java-devhdbk\ch10\GetURL.java. The corresponding bytecode is in the file javadev-hdbk\ch10\GetURL.class.

LIST 10.5   *GetURL.java*

```
import java.io.*;
import java.net.*;


public class GetURL {
  public static void main(String args[]) {
    if (args.length < 1) {
      System.err.println("Usage: java GetURL <URL>...");
```

```
      System.exit(1);
    }
    else {
      for (int i = 0; i < args.length; i++) {
        getURL(args[i]);
      }
    }
}

private static void getURL(String urlname) {
  URL url = null;
  InputStream urlstream = null;
  byte [] returned;
  try {
    url = new URL(urlname);
  }
  catch (Exception e) {
    System.err.println("URL " + urlname + " failed, reason is:");
    System.err.println(e.toString());
    return;
  }

  try {
    urlstream = url.openStream();
  }
  catch (Exception e) {
    System.err.println("URL " + urlname + " failed open,
                        reason is:");
    System.err.println(e.toString());
    return;
  }

  returned = getURLFile(urlstream);

  String filename = (url.getFile()).replace('/', File.separatorChar);
  File f1 = new File(filename);
  filename = f1.getName();
  FileOutputStream f = null;
  try {
    f = new FileOutputStream(filename);

    f.write(returned);
    f.close();
```

```
    }
  catch (Exception e) {
    System.err.println("Error handling output file: " + filename);
    return;
  }
}

private static byte [] getURLFile(InputStream s) {
  byte [] buffer = new byte [0];
  byte [] chunk = new byte [4096];
  int count;

  try {
    while ((count = s.read(chunk)) >= 0) {
      byte [] t = new byte [buffer.length + count];
      System.arraycopy(buffer, 0, t, 0, buffer.length);
      System.arraycopy(chunk, 0, t, buffer.length,count);
      buffer = t;
    }
  }
  catch (Exception e) {
    System.err.println("Error during reading:" + e);
  }

  return buffer;
  }
}
```

Running the GetURL Program

You do not need to have a network connection to run this program; you can use a
file:// URL instead. The contents of the URL are not important in themselves,
but they should be something recognizable. When the contents are copied to the
local disk, you should be able to determine that they have arrived correctly. To
run the example, issue the command:

java GetURL *<chosen-URL>*

The program will start, connect to the URL using the specified protocol, fetch
the data, and write the data to the disk. The output is placed in a file with the
same name as the filename part of the original URL.

Transferring the Data

Provided the URL constructor is successful, the result is used to execute the method openStream(). This method returns an instance of the InputStream class from which the data may be read directly. In this example, the resulting stream is passed to the private method getURLFile(), which collects data in a buffer. Data is read in chunks of up to 4KB, and each chunk is coalesced with the data that has already been loaded to produce a single larger array. This is done with the two calls to System.arraycopy(), which move both the old and new data into the newly allocated buffer:

```
System.arraycopy(buffer, 0, t, 0, buffer.length);
System.arraycopy(chunk, 0, t, buffer.length, count);
```

One aspect that might warrant a moment of attention if the technique is unfamiliar is the use of System.arraycopy() and the two buffers in the getURLFile() method. The smaller buffer is used to read sizable chunks of data at a time. Each time the read() method returns, a new buffer is created that is large enough for all the data so far loaded. The holding buffer is copied to this new buffer, and then the newly read data is copied in. Finally, the new buffer becomes the holding buffer.

When loading is completed, the resulting array of bytes is returned by getURL-File() to its caller, which then saves the bytes to the disk file.

TIP

Some servers, for some protocols, can tell the client how much data is to be sent. This information is available in Java if a two-stage process is used to read the URL. First, use the openConnection() method of the URL class. This returns an instance of a URLConnection. On the URLConnection object, use the get-ContentLength() method. To obtain the data from the URLConnection, a method called getInputStream() is provided. Using the URLConnection allows other additional information, such as content type, to be queried.

The constructor of the URL object might fail if the URL is badly formed. A badly formed URL is reported if some essential part of the URL, such as the ://, is missing or if the protocol specified—FTP, for example—is not known to the running Java system. If the specified URL is invalid at the server, or the server is not providing a requested service, the openStream() call will fail.

The openStream() method is very easy to use and should not present difficulties for incorporation into other programs. The bulk of this particular piece of sample code is dedicated to the file and buffer handling. As such, this example might be useful for copying data from Internet servers directly to a disk file, but it is unlikely to form the basis for direct extension into a larger utility.

NOTE   This example does not use readers or byte-to-character conversion because the data is pure binary bytes. Conversion to Unicode text would be inappropriate and would damage the data.

In the next sections, we'll introduce some other techniques that allow more control over the handling of URLs.

A URL Content Handling Example

When an HTTP server transmits the data for a URL, it first sends some header information. This information might, but does not always, include the amount of data that is to be sent, a validity time for the data (a kind of electronic sell-by date intended to allow the server a chance to reduce the time for which the client caches the information), and a content type. The content type is expressed as a MIME type string and can be used to allow a program, such as a browser, to handle the data appropriately and automatically.

MIME type strings are a hierarchical description of a particular content. The hierarchy is described rather like a directory structure. An HTML document has a MIME type string of text/html. Similarly, plain, unformatted text has a type string of text/plain. Another hierarchy is used for images, so image/gif describes an image file in .gif format, while image/xpm describes an image in X Windows pixmap form.

Content type should ideally be reported by the HTTP server as one of the header fields, but in some cases, especially those where a non-http:// URL is used, this information isn't available. Unfortunately, in many cases, a server will report a MIME type of content/unknown, which implies that it does not know what the content type of the document is. Under these conditions, the client is left to guess based on the filename and the actual contents of the data stream. Java's content handling has some hard-coded guesses built in for this purpose.

Content handling in Java is achieved via the URL class method called getContent(). When invoked, this method first makes the connection to the server, then fetches the header information to find the MIME content type. If the MIME specification is missing or unknown, then ad-hoc techniques are used to make a guess. Based on this content type, getContent() then looks for an appropriate subclass of Content-Handler. This ContentHandler object is invoked to load the actual data and create a Java object that represents it. In this way, if a URL refers to an image stored in a .jpeg file, the content type would be image/jpeg. Provided a content handler is available for this, it constructs an object of some subclass of java.awt.ImageProducer and returns this object to its caller.

The following example demonstrates loading content from a URL using the getContent() method. When an image is fetched in this way, the getContent() method returns an object that is a subclass of ImageProducer. Given such an object, it is a simple matter to create an Image, as is required for display in AWT, using the createImage() method in the Toolkit class. The Toolkit object may be obtained by using getDefaultToolkit(), which is a static method in the Toolkit class, or directly from any visible AWT Component using the getToolkit() method.

The source code for this example is located on the CD-ROM in the directory javadevhdbk\ch10\GetImage.java. The corresponding bytecode is in the directory javadevhdbk\ch10\GetImage.class.

LIST 10.6   *GetImage.java*

```java
import java.awt.*;
import java.awt.image.*;
import java.net.*;

class myCanvas extends Canvas {
  Image i;

  public myCanvas(Image i) {
    this.i = i;
  }

  public void paint(Graphics g) {
    g.drawImage(i, 0, 0, this);
  }
}
```

```
public class GetImage {
  String name;
  Frame f;
  Image i;
  myCanvas c;
  MediaTracker m;
  Toolkit t = Toolkit.getDefaultToolkit();

  public static void main(String args[]) {
    if (args.length != 1) {
      System.out.println("Usage: java GetImage <image-URL>");
      System.exit(1);
    }
    GetImage that = new GetImage(args[0]);
    that.go();
  }

  public GetImage(String name) {
    this.name = name;
  }

  public void go() {
    Object o = null;
    f = new Frame("Image from " + name);
    URL source = null;
    URLConnection con = null;

    try {
      source = new URL(name);
      o = source.getContent();
    }
    catch (Exception e) {
      System.out.println("Problem with URL " + source);
      e.printStackTrace(System.out);
      System.exit(2);
    }

    if (o instanceof ImageProducer) {
      i = t.createImage((ImageProducer)o);
    }
    else {
```

```
        System.out.println("URL " + source +
                            " didn't give me an ImageProducer");
        System.out.println("but a " + o.getClass().getName() +
                            "instead");
        System.exit(3);
    }

    c = new myCanvas(i);
    m = new MediaTracker(c);
    m.addImage(i, 0);
    try {
      m.waitForAll();
    }
    catch (Exception e) { /* do nothing */ }

    f.add("Center", c);
    c.setSize(i.getWidth(c), i.getHeight(c));
    f.pack();
    f.setVisible(true);
  }
}
```

Running the GetImage Program

As with the GetURL program, you do not need to have a network connection to run the GetImage program; you can use a file:// URL if necessary. The contents of the file should be an image in a format that Java understands. The standard release can handle GIF, JPEG, and XBM formats. To run the example, issue the command:

java GetImage *<image-URL>*

The program will start, connect to the URL using the specified protocol, load the image, and display that image in a window.

This example exploits the built-in handling of image file types. The command line should have a single argument that is taken to be a URL. The program connects to the URL and loads the image. An auxiliary class provides a means of displaying the resulting Image object so it can recover from being obscured by other windows.

Performing Automatic Content Handling

The GetURL example used the URL method openStream() to access the data from a URL. In the GetImage example, the data is handled automatically, based on its type. For this example to work, the type must be an image in a supported format.

The automatic content handling is performed via the URL method getContent(), which establishes the protocol connection and determines the content type. When the content type is determined, it is used to select a ContentHandler object. The job of a content handler is to load the data and interpret it. The return value of the content handler should be some object that represents the content of the URL. In the case of an image file, the return from the content handler is an instance of the class ImageProducer. From this, an Image object can be created, which in turn can be displayed.

In this example, the content handler's return type is checked at runtime. The instanceof method is applied to determine if an ImageProducer has indeed been returned. If some other type is found, this program issues an error message, reporting the actual class of the object found.

> **NOTE**
>
> Although Java—and more specifically the HotJava browser—comes equipped with some content handlers, there are many content types in use, and new types are added regularly. For this reason, the Java system allows you to add new content handlers. Chapter 13 discusses writing and installing content handlers. Most notable is the omission of audio content handling from the core Java API. The audio handlers are part of the **sun.audio** classes, used by HotJava and the Applet Viewer.

As with the previous example, this code serves mainly to demonstrate the use of a particular method, in this case, getContent(). As a result, the body of the code is not of real use as the basis of extension. In some conditions, the support class myCanvas might be useful, if a static image is to be displayed and the immediately enclosing part of the GUI is not directly suited to the task of refreshing the image.

CGI Connections

In addition to handling conventional noninteractive content types, the URL class can be used to handle CGI connections. CGI (Common Gateway Interface) is a well-established mechanism for generating customized output for a web page. The request carries user-originated data with it, and the web server runs a program to interpret the data and produce a new, dynamically created HTML page in response.

CGI requests are made using URLs, but there are two forms:

- A GET request simply encodes the request into the URL itself. This form can be handled directly using little more than a URL and the openStream() method. The GET method, although simple, has some technical difficulties. For example, the security of the web server can be compromised by a request that has a very long argument list.

- In the POST mechanism, the URL is used to initiate the connection, but then two streams are used. One is an output stream that transmits the parameters to the web server. The other is the traditional input stream used to read the results of the request.

Both of these forms of CGI are directly supported by Java, and both are simple to implement. The POST mechanism is generally preferred for new CGI programs. However, the GET mechanism introduces some ground that is common to both approaches and will be described first.

A CGI GET Example

In practical use, the data returned from the server is normally presented to the user in an applet. This example, for simplicity, dumps the output to the standard output channel.

The source is on the CD-ROM in the directory javadevhdbk\ch10\CGIGet.java. The corresponding bytecode is in the directory javadevhdbk\ch10\CGIGet.class. This program requires access to a live network and an HTTP server that offers some GET-type CGI facility.

LIST 10.7   *CGIGet.java*

```java
import java.net.*;
import java.io.*;

public class CGIGet {
  public static void main(String args[]) {
    if (args.length <= 1) {
      System.err.println("Usage: java CGIGet <baseURL>" +
      "<CGI argument>...");
      System.exit(1);
    }
```

```java
String fullURL = args[0];
String arguments = args[1];
for (int i = 2; i < args.length; i++) {
  arguments += " " + args[i];
}
arguments = URLEncoder.encode(arguments);
fullURL += "?" + arguments;
InputStream theData = null;

URL u = null;
URLConnection uc = null;
try {
  u = new URL(fullURL);
  uc = u.openConnection();
  theData = uc.getInputStream();
}
catch (Exception e) {
  System.err.println("Trouble with URL " + fullURL + " " + e);
  System.exit(1);
}

String contentType = uc.getContentType();
if (contentType.toLowerCase().startsWith("text")) {
  BufferedReader in = new BufferedReader(
                      new InputStreamReader(theData));
  String line;
  try {
    while ((line = in.readLine()) != null) {
      System.out.println(line);
    }
  }
  catch (IOException e) {
    System.err.println("Trouble with IO" + e);
    System.exit(2);
  }
}
else {
  System.out.println("This program only handles text responses");
  System.out.println("I got " + contentType);
}
}
}
```

To run the program, determine the URL of the CGI program you wish to execute and the parameters that it requires. Then issue the command:

java CGIGet *<baseURL> <otherParameters>*...

You must provide at least one parameter. When the connection is made, the response type is checked. If a text response is received from the server, then that response will be dumped to the standard output channel. If the response is not text of some sort, a message is issued reporting the difficulty and the reported MIME content type.

Each parameter that is supplied is joined using spaces, and the result is converted into the external form required for CGI. This is then joined to the base URL using the ? symbol. Given the resulting composite URL, a stream is opened to collect the server's response. As characters are read from this stream, they are copied to the standard output.

Two aspects of this code are new: the first is the conversion of the URL to the external form, the second is the determination of the content type.

Converting the URL to External Form   This conversion is handled by the method `encode()`, which is the only method of the `URLEncoder` class. The external form of a URL makes a simple translation designed to minimize the character set used by the transfer and thereby to prevent intermediate programs interpreting characters as special and altering them. Unix shells, for example, would coalesce multiple spaces and treat asterisks and other characters as wildcard specifications to be expanded.

The conversion process changes spaces to +. Other nonalphanumeric characters are translated to %*xx*, where *xx* represents the hexadecimal ASCII value of the character to be sent.

Determining the Content Type   The content type is determined simply by using the `getContentType()` method on the `URLConnection` object, which returns the MIME type string that the server reported in the headers sent as part of an HTTP response.

A CGI POST Example

As with the CGI GET example, the CGI POST example sends the data returned from the server to the standard output. Like the GET example, this program requires access to a live network and an HTTP server with a POST-type CGI facility. The source for this example is on the CD-ROM in the directory javadev-hdbk\ch10\CGIPost.java. The corresponding bytecode is located in the directory javadevhdbk\ch10\CGIPost.java.

LIST 10.8   *CGIPost.java*

```java
import java.net.*;
import java.io.*;

public class CGIPost {
  public static void main(String args[]) {
    if (args.length <= 1) {
      System.err.println("Usage: java GCIPost
        <baseURL> <GCI argument>...");
      System.exit(1);
    }

    String fullURL = args[0];

    URLConnection conn = null;
    OutputStream theControl = null;
    InputStream theData = null;

    URL u = null;
    try {
      u = new URL(fullURL);
      conn = u.openConnection();
      conn.setDoOutput(true);
      theControl = conn.getOutputStream();
    }
    catch (Exception e) {
      System.err.println("Trouble with URL " + fullURL + " " + e);
      System.exit(1);
    }

    try {
      BufferedWriter out = new BufferedWriter(
                         new OutputStreamWriter(theControl));
      String encoded = null;
      for (int i = 1; i < args.length; i++) {
        encoded = URLEncoder.encode(args[i]);
```

```
      out.write(encoded + "\n");
    }
    out.close();
    theData = conn.getInputStream();

    String contentType = conn.getContentType();
    if (contentType.toLowerCase().startsWith("text")) {
      BufferedReader in = new BufferedReader(
                          new InputStreamReader(theData));
      String line;
      while ((line = in.readLine()) != null) {
        System.out.println(line);
      }
    }
    else {
      System.out.println("This program only handles
        text responses");
      System.out.println("I got " + contentType);
    }
  }
  catch (IOException e) {
    System.err.println("Trouble with IO" + e);
    System.exit(2);
  }
}
}
```

To run the program, determine the URL of the CGI program you wish to execute and the parameters that it requires. Then issue the command:

java CGIPost *<baseURL> <otherParameters>...*

As with the GET program, you must supply at least one parameter. When the connection is made, the response of the server will be dumped to the standard output channel. For this reason, a POST CGI script that produces fairly plain HTML is preferable.

This program expects at least two arguments: the base URL and a list of CGI parameters. The URL object is created and used to establish an output stream. The parameters are encoded into the external form and sent to that stream. The response is then read from the input stream and copied to the standard output.

The crucial detail of this example is that the URL class is very particular about how it should be used when the URL it describes expects to receive input from the client. The OutputStream object must be enabled, using the setDoOutput(true) call and the OutputStream object obtained with the call to getOutputStream(). This must happen, in this order, before the InputStream object is obtained. If a URL has obtained its InputStream object and the OutputStream object has not previously been opened, the class assumes that this is a traditional input-only URL and will generate an exception if the OutputStream object is requested.

WARNING   Although the specifications require that setDoOutput(true) should be issued before getOutputStream(), early versions of JDK did not enforce this rule but instead allowed the OutputStream to be obtained anyway. This behavior was not matched on other platforms, such as Netscape Navigator, leading to platform-dependent behavior. Therefore, you should be careful to call setDoOutput(true) at the correct point.

A Network Class Loading Example—A Mini Applet Viewer

This section demonstrates the use of the URLClassLoader. Class loaders are used to take an array of bytes and create a new class in the running JVM. This is the approach by which Java-enabled browsers are able to run code that has been dynamically loaded from the network.

As a network class loading example, we will develop a rudimentary Applet Viewer-like program. The example loads classes from a URL. When the class has been defined, an instance is created, and the reference to it is assigned into a variable of type java.applet.Applet. From this variable, the init() and start() methods will be invoked, so the applet can be given a working environment.

Two classes are used to create this program. One is the main class, and the other provides an implementation of the AppletStub and AppletContext interfaces that are required by most applets.

The source code for this example is on the CD-ROM located in the directory javadevhdbk\ch10. The files are called MinAppletViewer.java and AppSupport .java. The class files with corresponding names are in the same directory.

The MinAppletviewer Class

MinAppletViewer.java is the "glue" class for this example. It takes the command-line arguments and parses them to produce the components of the supplied URL. These details are used to determine the origin of the Applet class that is to be loaded and the class name associated with it. The main() method uses this information to configure the other parts of the system.

Provided the class file is loaded correctly, this part creates the Applet instance and simulates its life cycle, providing a window environment and calling the init() and start() methods. The applet is not provided with a thread of its own.

LIST 10.9	*MinAppletviewer.java*

```java
import java.awt.*;
import java.awt.event.*;
import java.applet.*;
import java.io.*;
import java.net.*;
import java.util.*;

public class MinAppletviewer {
  public static void main(String args[]) {
    URL toload = null;
    String host = null;
    String protocol = null;
    int port = 80;
    String path = null;
    String file = null;

    Applet theApplet = null;
    AppSupport theAppSupport = new AppSupport();
    Frame f;
    Class theAppletClass = null;
    URLClassLoader loader = null;

    f = new Frame("Minimum Appletviewer: " + args[0]);
    try {
      toload = new URL(args[0]);
      host = toload.getHost();
```

```java
        port = toload.getPort();
        protocol = toload.getProtocol();
        path = toload.getFile();
        int join = path.lastIndexOf('/');
        file = path.substring(join + 1);
        path = path.substring(0, join + 1);

        theAppSupport.setCodeBase(
          new URL(protocol, host, port, path));
        theAppSupport.setDocumentBase(theAppSupport.getCodeBase());

        URL [] bases = { theAppSupport.getCodeBase() };
        loader = new URLClassLoader(bases);
        theAppletClass = loader.loadClass(file);
        theApplet = (Applet)(theAppletClass.newInstance());
      }
      catch (Exception e) {
        System.err.println("Problem creating class for " + args[0] +
          "\n Exception: " + e.toString());
        System.exit(1);
      }

      f.addWindowListener(
        new WindowAdapter() {
          public void windowClosing(WindowEvent ev) {
            System.exit(0);
          }
        }
      );

      f.add(theApplet, BorderLayout.CENTER);

      theApplet.setStub(theAppSupport);

      f.setSize(200, 200);
      f.setVisible(true);
      theApplet.init();
      theApplet.start();
    }
  }
```

The five aspects of the applet's environment whose configuration is controlled from this piece of code are as follows:

- Invoking the class loader to load the class file and create a new `Class` object
- Instantiating the `Applet` object
- Supplying an `AppletContext` object
- Providing a graphical environment
- Calling the life-cycle methods `init()` and `start()`

Invoking the Class Loader   The `ClassLoader` object needs to know the URL base from which to load classes. These details are determined by splitting up the supplied URL using the calls `getHost()`, `getPort()`, `getProtocol()`, and `getFile()` on the URL. The `ClassLoader` class expects just the path part of the file information in the constructor, as it is also used to load other classes from the same base URL. This typically happens if the applet requires other support classes.

When the class has been loaded, an instance of it is created by invoking the `newInstance()` method on the `Class` object.

NOTE   Notice that the java class called `java.lang.Class`—`Class` with a capital C—is a class that *describes* other classes. Given an instance of a `Class`, methods can be invoked to inquire about aspects of the described class, such as its name. The method `newInstance()` invokes the default—that is, zero arguments—constructor of the described class. The `Class` object returned by the `ClassLoader` describes the applet and so creates a new instance of that applet.

Instantiating the Applet Object   The return type of the `newInstance()` method is declared as `Object`. In this case, we expect that the new object is actually an applet. If the browser is to be able to handle the object successfully, it is required that this be the case.

WARNING   It is possible to test if the `Object` is an applet using the `instanceof` operator, but this possibility is omitted in this example. If the loaded class is not in fact of the `Applet` class, then a `ClassCastException` will be thrown when the reference is cast to `Applet`. A full program should check for, and handle gracefully, this exception.

The following line creates the instance, casts it to a reference of type `Applet`, and assigns the result to the variable `theApplet`:

```
theApplet = (Applet)(theAppletClass.newInstance());
```

This, therefore, is the line that might throw a `ClassCastException`.

Supplying an AppletContext Object   When running, an applet depends on browser features called `AppletContext` and `AppletStub` for a number of services. This `main()` method creates an instance of the supporting class `AppSupport`, which implements these two interfaces. The `Applet` instance method `setStub()` is used to inform the applet of these support services. To find its `AppletContext`, the applet invokes a method in the `AppletStub` called `getAppletContext()`. `AppletStub` and `AppletContext` are used to provide such features as the method `getDocumentBase()`.

Providing a Graphical Environment   Because the `Applet` class is sub-classed from `java.awt.Panel` and is essentially graphical in nature, the mini-Applet Viewer must provide a GUI environment. This environment is achieved by creating a `Frame` object and using the `add()` method to install the applet in the center region of that `Frame`. The applet is launched in this program without the aid of HTML, so an arbitrary width and height are chosen—in this case, 200 pixels square.

Calling init() and start()   After the applet has been loaded, instantiated, and given support and a GUI, the methods `init()` and `start()` are called in turn. This is possible via the reference `theApplet`, because the type of this reference is `java.applet.Applet`.

The AppSupport Class

As mentioned earlier, to provide environmental support, an applet requires an `AppletStub` and `AppletContext`. Both of these are interface definitions that may be implemented by the browser directly or by a special class. The `AppSupport` class provides both these facilities.

LIST 10.10   *AppSupport.java*

```java
import java.applet.*;
import java.awt.*;
import java.net.*;
import java.util.*;
import java.io.*;

public class AppSupport implements AppletStub, AppletContext {
  private URL codeBase;
  private URL documentBase;

  public AppSupport() {
    URL url = null;
    try {
        String urlpart = System.getProperty("user.dir");
        urlpart = urlpart.replace(File.separatorChar, '/');
        url = new URL("file://" + URLEncoder.encode(urlpart) + "/");
    }
    catch (Exception e) { /* do nothing. url will remain null */ }

    codeBase = documentBase = url;
  }

  public void appletResize(int w, int h) {
  }

  public AppletContext getAppletContext() {
    return (AppletContext)this;
  }

  public URL getDocumentBase() {
    return documentBase;
  }

  public void setDocumentBase(URL url) {
    documentBase = url;
  }
```

```java
    public URL getCodeBase() {
      return codeBase;
    }

    public void setCodeBase(URL url) {
      codeBase = url;
    }

    public String getParameter(String s) {
      return null;
    }

    public boolean isActive() {
      return true;
    }

// AppletContext parts

    public Applet getApplet(String name) {
      return null;
    }

    public Enumeration getApplets() {
      return new Enumeration() {
        public boolean hasMoreElements() {
          return false;
        }

        public Object nextElement() {
          return null;
        }
      };
    }

    public AudioClip getAudioClip(URL url) {
      return Applet.newAudioClip(url);
    }

    public Image getImage(URL url) {
      return Toolkit.getDefaultToolkit().getImage(url);
    }
```

```
    public void showDocument(URL url) {
    }

    public void showDocument(URL url, String target) {
    }

    public void showStatus(String status) {
      System.err.println(status);
    }
}
```

Defining the AppleStub Methods The interface AppletStub defines the following six methods:

```
public void appletResize(int w, int h)
public AppletContext getAppletContext()
public URL getDocumentBase()
public URL getCodeBase()
public String getParameter(String s)
public boolean isActive()
```

These methods provide basic environmental support for the applet. The method appletResize() is called to advise the browser that the applet is trying to resize. The method isActive() may be used by an applet to determine its state. An active applet is somewhere between a start() and stop() call in terms of its life cycle. Both these methods are implemented with "dummy" code and hence are effectively nonfunctional for this class.

The method getParameter() is used by the applet to extract, by name, any arguments to the applet provided by the HTML document <PARAM> tags. Again, this example simply returns null from this method. A more advanced mini-Applet Viewer could be written to parse the command line to extract parameters.

The location of the invoking HTML page and the class file are available to an applet via the methods getDocumentBase() and getCodeBase(), respectively. The AppSupport class provides two routes for providing this information. The class constructor determines a default for code and document base derived from the current working directory. This is achieved by the following code:

```
String urlpart = System.getProperty("user.dir");
urlpart = urlpart.replace(File.separatorChar, '/');
url = new URL("file://" + URLEncoder.encode(urlpart) + "/");
```

The File class constructor invoked as new File("x") provides a reference to a file in the current directory; it does not matter that this file probably does not exist. When the getAbsolutePath() method is invoked on it, this returns a path specification as a String object, which includes the full path of the current working directory. This string is used to construct a new File object from which the directory part is extracted using the getParent() method. Because the getParent() method returns a string that might not use the forward slash character required for URLs, these are then translated using the replace() method. Finally, because the path might include colons or other characters that are not permitted in a URL, the encode() method is used to convert the string so it may be appended to the string constant file:// to produce a valid local URL describing the current directory.

In operation, the MinAppletviewer class does not make use of this facility. Rather, it determines the location of the class file from the supplied URL and uses the methods setCodeBase() and setDocumentBase() to configure these. Neither of these methods are part of the AppletStub interface definition.

The method getAppletContext() is used by the applet to retrieve a reference to the AppletContext, which provides additional utility methods. In this example, a single class implements both interfaces, so this method simply returns the reference this.

Defining the AppleContext Methods   The AppletContext interface defines the following seven methods:

```
public Applet getApplet(String  name)
public Enumeration getApplets()
public AudioClip getAudioClip(URL  url)
public Image getImage(URL  url)
public void showDocument(URL  url)
public void showDocument(URL  url, String  target)
public void showStatus(String  status)
```

The method getApplet() allows one applet to obtain a reference to another applet running in the same browser page, using a name associated with that applet in the HTML document. Because this example displays only a single applet at a time, this method returns null. Similarly, the method getApplets() is intended to return an Enumeration listing all the applets on this page, implemented here by returning a reference to this. Because this class implements the Enumeration interface, this approach is acceptable. When the Enumeration methods are called, they report that no elements are in the list.

The two `showDocument()` methods are intended to make the browser jump to a new HTML page. These are implemented as empty methods here. Similarly, the `showStatus()` method just causes the status message to be printed on the standard error stream.

The methods `getAudioClip()` and `getImage()` provide the applet with convenient methods of loading sounds and pictures.

Running the Mini Applet Viewer

Unlike the Applet Viewer supplied with the JDK distribution, this example does not require an HTML file. In fact, it cannot use one; instead, it takes a URL that describes the class to load directly. Also unlike the HTML <APPLET> tag, the URL for this example should not include the `.class` extension, because this extension is assumed. The absence of an HTML document also means that no dimensions or parameters can be specified.

To run the example, choose an applet that does not require additional parameters. The standard JDK demonstrations include a number of these, including one called `CardTest`, which demonstrates the `CardLayout` class, which is a layout manager (layout managers are discussed in Chapter 4). Invoke the example by issuing the command:

java MinAppletViewer <*url*>

For example, to run the `CardTest` demo from the CD-ROM mounted as drive D: in a DOS-like system, issue a command of this form:

java MinAppletViewer file:///D:/java/demo/CardTest/CardTest

Substitute the path to your Java installation. (Notice that the URL ends ... /Card-Test, not ... /CardTest.class.) The `CardTest` applet will start in a window of its own.

TIP

Although many methods in this class are not operational, the class can form the basis of a more comprehensive implementation. Passing parameters into the class from a parsed command line would be a simple but useful extension. Similarly, the `showStatus()` method could be implemented by adding a label in the South region of the browser window and arranging that the method updates the label text. If the `MinAppletviewer` class were modified suitably, it would be possible to implement the `showDocument()` option. Since this would require a parser for HTML, the HotJava Bean would be a good contender for such an implementation.

Connection Information

The networking facilities provided by the java.net package include a variety of informational methods. This section discusses those that allow conversion of network addresses between domain names and numeric IP addresses and those that obtain the addresses and port numbers from a connected socket.

The data that supports these methods is obtained from the underlying networking system. In an Internet environment, DNS is usually responsible for supplying this information. In local environments, the information might be obtained from text files or some other database system.

Network Address Conversion

The package java.net includes a class called InetAddress, which provides a number of facilities for manipulating addresses in the Internet domain. Two static methods provide conversion from textual domain name format into objects of the InetAddress class:

```
public static InetAddress getByName(String host)
   throws UnknownHostException
```

```
public static InetAddress[] getAllByName(String host)
   throws UnknownHostException
```

The first of these takes a DNS-type name, such as www.javasoft.com, and returns a single instance of the InetAddress class that represents a valid IP address of that name. Because it is possible for a name to translate to more than one IP address (to allow redundancy in important servers), the second method provides a means to obtain all the IP addresses associated with a name.

NOTE   When you use multiple IP addresses and attempt to connect to a single DNS name, such as nic.ddn.mil, you might connect to any one of a number of different machines. This allows load distribution. Because a client that fails to connect to one of the listed physical machines can try a different one after the timeout period, a greater service reliability is also achieved.

Where an InetAddress object already exists, such as is returned by either of the two methods above, the IP address may be retrieved in the form of an array of bytes (four with the current implementation of IP) so that the numerical form of the address can be manipulated directly. The following method provides this facility:

```
public byte[] getAddress()
```

Another instance method in the InetAddress class allows determination of the DNS name for an IP address:

```
public String getHostName()
```

The final method of interest here extracts an InetAddress object that refers to the local machine:

```
public static InetAddress getLocalHost()
```

Applets running subject to the security constraints of a browser usually find that the behavior of this method is modified so that the IP address is reported as 127.0.0.1 and the name is reported as localhost.

Connection Detail Determination

When a Socket is connected, three methods allow determination of the connection details. The following is probably the most useful of these methods:

```
public InetAddress getInetAddress()
```

This method reports the IP address of the remote end of the connection. In general, for a client socket, this address will already be known. However, where this Socket object has been extracted from a ServerSocket object, the address of the client is not known in advance, so this method can be used to obtain it. Using the method getHostName() in the InetAddress class, the hostname can be extracted.

A connected Socket has two port numbers associated with it. One port is associated with each end of a Socket. A method is available for finding each of these port numbers:

```
public int getPort()
public int getLocalPort()
```

In general, the port number of the client is not of interest. Only the port number at the server end is relevant to the service being offered. Because the server port number is the one that carries immediate significance and is also the one that is always known in any program, these methods are not likely to be of general use in TCP programs. They might, however, be useful in UDP systems, which are discussed later in this chapter.

Security Considerations

Java programs, whether applets in a browser or stand-alone applications, are able to load and run code from anywhere. This ability, combined with the fact that many networks now extend into the Internet, and thereby to untrusted machines, opens up serious security concerns. Because the network is the first point of attack, it must also be the first line of defense.

Java security measures operate by imposing restrictions on the abilities of running code. Code that tries to perform prohibited operations will fail, so it is important to understand the nature of these restrictions when writing portable programs.

As you've learned in previous chapters, security rules are imposed by a SecurityManager object. This is not part of the JVM, but must be installed by an application when it starts up. Until this is done, no restrictions are applied. The unrestricted mode is the usual domain of applications, although it does not have to be. If appropriate, each application can install its own security manager, and hence impose its own set of rules. Browsers should be expected to install a security manager, and the applets they run are therefore subject to its restrictions.

Despite this potential for flexibility, most browsers impose broadly the same security restrictions, and this is likely to remain true. This section will describe the significance of these constraints in relation to network programming.

Sockets and Server Sockets

Network services are often denied to requests that originate from "foreign" machines; these might be machines outside a firewall or perhaps any machine other than a specially chosen list of trusted machines. This security practice substantially reduces the chance that information will be accessed improperly.

If an applet opens a socket to another machine, that socket originates from the machine running the applet, not from the machine that provided the applet code. However, the behavior is provided by the applet writer. Unless something else prevents access, this would appear to give an applet the potential to access privileged network-based services that should be denied to the author of the applet. The most draconian approach to this problem, and that taken by early versions of the Netscape Navigator, is to prohibit all network access by any applet.

The current convention, adopted by the Applet Viewer and most web browsers, is to permit a client socket to be connected to the host from which the applet originated. This is considered safe from the browser host's point of view, because the only information available from services on that host is at the discretion, and under the control, of the supplier of the applet. The security of the machine supplying the applet is not the concern of the browser running the applet or of the local user.

> **NOTE**   Because of the requirement that an applet can only connect to the originating host, an applet should always expect to be denied the privilege of creating a server socket. It is in the nature of a server socket that it can accept a connection from anywhere, which would make it impossible to restrict the behavior of the applet.

Name and Address Access

Applets should, in general, be denied access to any information unless they have a legitimate need for it and it can be shown that this information is not considered private.

Because knowledge of IP addresses and hostnames can be useful to an attacker, the address access methods of the InetAddress class normally return modified information about the local host. Specifically, the address will be returned as 127.0.0.1 and the hostname either as localhost or as 127.0.0.1 in text form.

Covert Channels

Although the security restrictions applied to sockets and server sockets are soundly designed, a difficulty remains. Because of the nature of other Internet services, it is impossible to prevent a Java applet from communicating with any host programmed to cooperate with it. In other words, without regard to the host that originated it, the applet is able to covertly send any data to which it has access to any host on the Internet that is cooperating with the subterfuge. It is also able to receive data from any such host. Because of this difficulty, it is important to restrict the information that an applet can obtain in the first place.

There are a number of different mechanisms by which a covert channel can be obtained. For example, a low-bandwidth bidirectional channel can be established simply by using DNS. An applet is entitled to look up any hostname it needs; this is an essential service for the Internet to be useful. For an applet to communicate the message, "Hello, I am here" to its covert partner, the partner simply needs to run a modified domain name server, and the applet only needs to perform a name lookup on a host called `hello.i.am.here.spy.com`. Because the request for this name translation is passed to the name server for the domain `spy.com`, it is a trivial matter to extract the first part of the message from it. Further, a DNS lookup expects a response, in the form of one or more four-byte IP addresses. It is again simple for this response to be used to return information, which is then accessible in the applet.

The DNS mechanism for covert channels is slow but easy to understand and fairly easy to implement. More important, it is not the only available channel. It is therefore vital to address the security of information in terms of preventing an applet from gaining access in the first place. Fortunately, the other Java security mechanisms do achieve a high measure of success.

UDP Systems

For most network programs, TCP will be the service of choice. TCP offers reliable, ordered stream connection and relieves the programmer from most of the troublesome work involved in maintaining a connection. As explained earlier in the chapter, UDP does not send acknowledgments, so it cannot report the success or failure of a transmission, and it does not handle ordering of packets received.

It is important to appreciate the weaknesses of UDP. Data transmitted by UDP can be lost entirely or duplicated at the recipient. Multiple datagrams can be received in an order different from that in which they were sent. The two benefits of UDP are the reduced overhead that results from the greatly reduced complexity and, to an extent, the record-oriented nature of the system.

In some cases, UDP might be a more appropriate, or even necessary, choice. There are three main reasons why UDP might be chosen:

- For preexisting services that use UDP
- For maximum throughput on a fairly reliable network
- For services that require broadcast or multicast

Using UDP in Java is not difficult, although the problems of reliability and ordering must be addressed. The examples presented here do not attempt to handle these problems, because they do not have much impact on the functionality of the service provided. In fact, even if a large proportion of transmissions were to be lost, the resulting service would be usable, if intermittent.

A UDP-Based Daytime System

As an example, we will develop a service that uses UDP to send date and time information. The standard daytime service, described in earlier sections of this chapter, does have a UDP equivalent. In that service, the server waits passively for a message from a client and then responds with time information. In this example, the server transmits time information at one-second intervals regardless of whether the client is listening. This exemplifies the fundamental difference between TCP and UDP services—there is no concept of a "connection" in the UDP system, and hence transmission of data onto the network does not require any other host to be listening.

There are two classes that make up the UDP-based daytime system: the server and the client. When started, both client and server continue to run indefinitely. Each time the client notices a new message, it prints it to the standard output channel. If a message is lost, no difficulties arise, but the client's output will pause for more than one second and then jump when a packet is received.

The source code for these examples is located on the CD-ROM in the directory javadevhdbk\ch10. The files are called DayBcast.java and DayWatch.java, respectively. The corresponding class files are in the same directory.

The UDP Daytime Server

The server code has a very simple algorithm. The target address is determined from the command-line argument. An uncommitted DatagramSocket object is created and then the code loops, once per second, sending a text representation (in the platform's default encoding) of the current date and time over the network. Each transmission is accompanied by the message "Sending" on the standard output.

This code uses port 1313, which is the same port as was used for the unofficial TCP daytime service. Although TCP and UDP port numbers cover the same range, they are in a different namespace and do not interfere with each other. Because of this, it is possible to have a TCP and UDP server both running simultaneously, using the same port number.

LIST 10.11   *DayBcast.java*

```java
import java.net.*;
import java.util.*;

public class DayBcast {
  DatagramSocket ds;
  DatagramPacket dp;
  InetAddress addr;

  public static final int DAYTIME_PORT = 1313;

  public static void main(String args[]) throws Exception {
    DayBcast db = new DayBcast(args[0]);
    db.go();
  }

  public DayBcast(String target) throws Exception {
    addr = InetAddress.getByName(target);
    ds = new DatagramSocket();
  }

  public void go() throws Exception {
    byte [] buff;
    for (;;) {
      Thread.sleep(1000);
      System.out.println("Sending");
      String s = (new Date()).toString();
      buff = s.getBytes();
      dp = new DatagramPacket(buff, buff.length, addr, DAYTIME_PORT);
      ds.send(dp);
    }
  }
}
```

Initializing the Address and Socket   The first step is to construct an InetAddress object that describes the remote host to which the date and time information is to be sent. This is achieved with the method call InetAddress .getByName(target), which was described earlier in the chapter, in the "Network Address Conversion" section.

Once the address information has been obtained, the DatagramSocket object is created. The fact that the socket is created without a specific port number is the only indication that it is a server program. In UDP, it is necessary to specify the port number of the receiver. If this datagram socket were to be used for receiving data, it would need to be configured at a specific port. The absence of this configuration suggests that this datagram socket will be starting the communication, and hence is probably the server end.

Preparing the DatagramPacket Object   When a proper address and socket have been initialized, a DatagramPacket object must be prepared. The socket is then used to send that packet. The DatagramPacket object is constructed by the following line:

```
dp = new DatagramPacket(buff, buff.length, addr, DAYTIME_PORT);
```

The first two arguments provide the data to be transmitted (buff) and the length of that data (buff.length). The argument addr specifies the destination address of this packet. The final argument, DAYTIME_PORT, indicates the port number to which the packet is to be sent. Note that this information is provided in the DatagramPacket object rather than the socket.

After the DatagramPacket object has been prepared, the data is transmitted by the call to ds.send(dp).

The UDP Daytime Client

The client end for this example is no more complex than the server program. In fact, the algorithm of this client is even simpler than that of its server. A buffer is created to hold the received characters. A socket is created that is bound to a particular port, and a DatagramPacket object is created to collect the data. The code then enters an infinite loop that receives and then prints data to the standard output.

LIST 10.12   *DayWatch.java*

```java
import java.net.*;

public class DayWatch {
  private DatagramSocket ds;
  private DatagramPacket dp;

  public static void main(String args[]) throws Exception {
    DayWatch d = new DayWatch();
    d.go();
  }
```

```
public void go() throws Exception {
  byte [] buff = new byte[64];
  String s;
  ds = new DatagramSocket(DayBcast.DAYTIME_PORT);
  dp = new DatagramPacket(buff, buff.length);
  for (;;) {
    ds.receive(dp);
    s = new String(dp.getData());
    System.out.println("Time signal received from " +
      dp.getAddress() + "\n  Time is: " + s);
  }
}
}
```

Setting Up the DatagramSocket and DatagramPacket Objects   The client creates a DatagramSocket object, bound to the port number previously chosen. It also constructs a DatagramPacket object that will be used to hold the received data. To support this reception, the DatagramPacket object is provided with storage space for the received data—this is the array of 64 bytes, which should be more than enough for the date and time string that is expected. In general, a buffer size of 512 bytes is a sensible choice, because this is the largest UDP packet size that can be handled reliably by all TCP/IP networks.

WARNING   In principle, UDP datagrams can be up to 65,536 bytes in length. However, IP implementation standards only require a minimum packet size of 576 bytes. After allowing for the length of headers, this results in a conventional limit on UDP datagrams of 512 bytes. If a longer packet is sent, excess data might simply be truncated.

Calling the receive() Method   Once the socket and packet objects are set up, all that is required to receive data is to call the receive() method of the Datagram-Socket class, providing as an argument the DatagramPacket object that is to hold the returned data. The client must be in the receive() method when the server sends, for three reasons:

- There is no connection involved.

- There is no way for the sender to know if the receiver got the message.

- The protocol does not perform retries.

After the receive() method returns, the DatagramPacket object will contain the received data and will also have been updated with the address of the sending machine. This address can be extracted with the getAddress() method, which returns an InetAddress object. This object provides the methods described earlier for manipulating addresses. The toString() method of the InetAddress class conveniently returns a printable form of the address. If preferred, the getHostName() can be used.

NOTE

The method getHostName() will not provide a useful text string unless some form of naming service is functioning on your system. Systems without a real network should be expected to return the dotted form of the IP address. This behavior will be found on most systems that are non-Unix and are not connected to a real TCP/IP network.

Running the Daytime System

Using two separate windows, start both parts of the system. Start the server first, by issuing the command:

java DayBcast *<target machine>*

If you are running both client and server on the same machine, use the name localhost to describe the target machine.

When the server has started, it will print the message "Sending" on its output at one-second intervals. Some of these might well have been output before you start the client, because there is no "connection" with UDP, and so the sender has no way to know whether the packets were lost.

To start the client, issue the command:

java DayWatch

When the client starts, it should print a date and time message each time the server sends. If the server is killed, the client does not exit, but sits waiting for more packets. Indeed, the server can even be restarted, in which case, the client will continue to print output messages without noticing the failure or recovery.

UDP Broadcasting

Because UDP does not attempt to set up a connection between the two machines before transmitting data, it is possible to use it to create a broadcast server. The name of the server class in the previous example, `DayBcast.java`, was a strong indication of this potentially valuable feature of UDP.

Broadcasting can occur in a TCP/IP network on two levels:

- The data can be sent to all the machines connected to the same subnet as the sender, which is called a *subnet broadcast*. The term *subnet* describes a particular collection of local machines, determined by a network parameter called the *subnet mask*.

- The data can be sent to all machines on the same network. Broadcasts to an entire network are potentially expensive in terms of bandwidth; packets might propagate through many bridges and routers. Most bridges and routers provide configuration options to allow broadcast packets to be suppressed, and this option is commonly enabled.

The Broadcast Address

In a broadcast message, the destination of the data is not specified as a single machine with a unique address. Instead, a special address, called a *broadcast address*, is given.

The broadcast address is calculated from other configuration parameters of the local network. For a subnet broadcast, the required data is the local IP address and the subnet mask. If the IP address is I and the subnet mask is M, using bitwise binary logic, the subnet broadcast address A is calculated as follows:

$$A = I \text{ or } (\text{not } M)$$

To put this algebra into words, the local IP address is modified by forcing to 1 all the bits that correspond to a 0 in the subnet mask. For example, if the IP address of a machine is 146.188.4.192 and the subnet mask is 255.255.254.0, the subnet broadcast address is calculated as follows:

```
146.188.4.192 => 10010010 10111100.00000100.11000000
255.255.254.0 => 11111111.11111111.11111110.00000000
```

Forcing to 1 each bit of the IP address corresponding to a 0 in the subnet mask gives:

```
146.188.5.255 => 10010010 10111100.00000101.11111111
                                    ^ ^^^^^^^^
```

The caret symbol (^) indicates the bits that have been forced to 1.

A broadcast address for the whole logical network is calculated similarly, but instead of using the subnet mask, the default netmask is used for the network. The netmask can be determined from the first byte of the IP address. A first byte in the range 0 to 126 indicates a class A network, the range 128 to 191 indicates a class B network, and the range 192 to 223 indicates class C. For each of these network classes, the default netmask is listed below:

Class	Netmask
A	255.0.0.0
B	255.255.0.0
C	255.255.255.0

Using the classes DayBcast and DayWatch from the previous example, you can see how UDP broadcasting works. Set the transmit address used by the server to the local subnet broadcast address. Any machine on the local subnet can then run the DayWatch client successfully.

NOTE Although a broadcast UDP packet can be received by multiple machines, it usually can be received by only a single process on each machine. If two clients are started on the same port, one will receive each incoming packet and the other will not see the data.

Broadcasting Drawbacks

Broadcasting provides a valuable mechanism for communicating between multiple hosts simultaneously. There are, however, drawbacks in its use:

- The communication must take place between hosts on the local subnet or, at the widest, hosts on the same logical network.

- Every host that receives a broadcast must perform some processing before it is able to determine whether it wants the data or not. This wastes CPU resources on a potentially great number of machines.

- Where a network is divided by bridges or, for logical network broadcasts, routers, the packet must be propagated to every network segment, even if no hosts on that segment are interested. This can add significant network-bandwidth demand. In some cases, this forwarding might cause a broadcast packet to reach a network segment that constitutes a security risk.

UDP Multicasting

Multicasting is a mechanism that allows communication between multiple hosts but avoids most of the problems of broadcasting. Multicasting is achieved by using a special range of IP addresses. These addresses are not associated with particular machines; instead, groups of machines associate themselves with a particular address. This association is in addition to the normal IP address for each machine.

WARNING   Not all TCP/IP implementations support multicasting. While workstations running Unix will generally be able to handle the service, PC-based implementations might not.

For a group of machines to become associated with a particular multicast address, the routers that connect them must all be aware of the associations and the routes between the machines. When a machine becomes associated with a particular multicast address, the routers that connect it with the rest of the group are notified. These routers then ensure that when a message is sent to the group, it passes only to those parts of the network where it will be useful. This reduces the number of machines that need to waste CPU time examining and rejecting the message.

The directed nature of multicast packets addresses all of the difficulties listed for normal UDP broadcasts. The packets are not restricted by network topology, CPU time is not wasted rejecting data, and network bandwidth is not used on unnecessary network cable. To an extent, multicasting is also more secure than broadcasting, because the packets are not propagated on irrelevant cable and are not read into machines unnecessarily.

WARNING   As a general point, in the absence of encryption, many LAN technologies are hardly more secure than the cable they use. Because each user's machine is connected to that cable, only good faith or lack of technical knowledge will protect data from other users of the same network cable. Multicasting merely reduces the availability of the data.

Applications of Multicasting

Multicasting is generally suited to any application that requires a number of machines in a distributed group to receive the same data. For example, you might use multicasting for conferencing, group mail and news distribution, and network management.

A typical application of multicasting is RIP-2 (Route Information Protocol-2). This protocol propagates routing information among routers (hosts are sometimes interested too, but less often) to ensure that large, dynamic networks have the best possible knowledge of what routes are currently available for traffic. Clearly, it would be counterproductive to use extensive broadcasting, with its associated bandwidth demand, for a protocol that attempts to ensure the best network throughput for user applications.

Multicasting also has uses in less mundane applications, such as communication between systems in networked multiuser games and simulations. Some games communicate using ordinary broadcast techniques and have become notorious for overloading previously quiet office networks.

A Multicast Server and Client

Programming Java to use multicasting is not difficult in principle. Most of the techniques are the same as those used by UDP technology.

Consider the following pair of examples of a multicast server and companion client. The basic algorithms of both the server and client, along with much of the code, is taken from the DayBcast.java and DayWatch.java examples presented earlier. The essential differences are the use of the MulticastSocket class in place of the DatagramSocket class and the need to explicitly join the multicast group address.

The source code for this example is on the CD-ROM in the directory javadev-hdbk\ch10\MCastServ.java. The bytecode is in the file MCastServ.class in the same directory.

LIST 10.13   *MCastServ.java*

```java
import java.net.*;
import java.io.*;
import java.util.*;

public class MCastServ {
  MulticastSocket ms;
  DatagramPacket dp;
  InetAddress addr;

  public static final int MC_DAYTIME_PORT = 13013;

  public static void main(String args[]) throws Exception {
    MCastServ mcs = new MCastServ(args[0]);
    mcs.go();
  }

  public MCastServ(String target) throws Exception {
    addr = InetAddress.getByName(target);
    ms = new MulticastSocket();
    ms.joinGroup(addr);
  }

  public void go() throws Exception {
    byte [] buff = null;
    for (;;) {
      Thread.sleep(1000);
      System.out.println("Sending");
      String s = (new Date()).toString();
      buff = s.getBytes();
      dp = new DatagramPacket(buff, buff.length, addr,
                              MC_DAYTIME_PORT);
      ms.send(dp, (byte)1);
    }
  }
}
```

LIST 10.14   *MCastWatch.java*

```java
import java.net.*;
import java.io.*;

public class MCastWatch {
  private MulticastSocket ms;
  private DatagramPacket dp;

  public static void main(String args[]) throws Exception {
    MCastWatch d = new MCastWatch(args[0]);
    d.go();
  }

  public MCastWatch(String groupAddr) throws Exception {
    ms = new MulticastSocket(MCastServ.MC_DAYTIME_PORT);
    ms.joinGroup(InetAddress.getByName(groupAddr));
  }

  public void go() throws Exception {
    byte [] buff = new byte[64];
    String s;
    dp = new DatagramPacket(buff, buff.length);
    for (;;) {
      ms.receive(dp);
      s = new String(dp.getData());
      System.out.println("Time signal received from " +
        dp.getAddress() + "\n  Time is: " + s);
    }
  }
}
```

Defining the MulticastSocket Methods

The joinGroup() method of the MulticastSocket class associates the socket with the group IP address and instructs the underlying TCP/IP system to join the group. This must be done on the client as well as the server because, in the multicast scenario, the address is a meeting point rather than a definition of either of the two machines.

The send() method in the MulticastSocket class takes two arguments. The first is the DatagramPacket that is to be transmitted. This aspect is exactly parallel with the use of standard UDP. The second argument is called the *time to live*. This parameter is used to control the number of routers that the packet can be passed through before it is dropped, and as such is rather misnamed since it represents not a time, but a hop count. This precaution ensures that if a packet gets misdirected, perhaps because of the dynamic nature of the multicast group address, the packet does not go bouncing around between routers indefinitely.

In addition to the facilities shown here, there is another important method in the MulticastSocket class: the leaveGroup() method. After joining a group, a program should advise the underlying TCP/IP system that it is no longer interested in the packets. The TCP/IP system informs the routers that ensure packets reach the machine so no more unnecessary traffic is generated.

Running the Multicast Programs

To run the multicast programs, you need a multicast address, it is highly likely that 224.1.1.1 will be suitable. Also, if you are using a Java version older than 2, you need to ensure that a name is associated with a suitable multicast address. This requires access to—and understanding of—your system's configuration. Add a suitable name, such as mcast-test, and assign it the address you chose.

> **NOTE**
>
> As written the multicast example does not work on JDK 1.0.2. If you need it to work in that environment, you can edit both files to include the line import sun.net.*; at the top of each. Recompiling will produce new versions of the programs. Be aware, however, that the example might well fail depending on your platform, because multicast sockets were not fully supported by JDK 1.0.2.

Now run the server program by issuing the following command:

java MCastServ *multicast address name*

If all is well, if the multicast address name is successfully installed, and if multicasting is supported by your machine and your version of JDK, you should see the "Sending" message appear at one-second intervals. This suggests that the server is running.

Run the client by issuing the command

java MCastWatch *multicast address name*

Note that for this example the address must be provided for both client and server.

You should now see the date and time information being printed at one-second intervals.

In this chapter, we introduced a full spectrum of techniques in Java network programming. You have seen techniques for programming clients and servers using both TCP and UDP services. URL handling for standard content types and for both POST and GET CGI has been demonstrated. You have also seen how easy it is to use the URLClassLoader to load classes dynamically from any URL. If you have previous experience in these areas, you will probably agree that Java makes network programming much easier than it is in most other languages.

The next chapter describes how to use Java as a database front end, taking advantage of the Java Database Connectivity (JDBC) API.

CHAPTER

ELEVEN

11

Database Connectivity (JDBC)

- Database client/server methodology

- Java's JDBC API

- JDBC's drivers

- The JDBC-ODBC bridge

In the information age, the database is a tool used to collect and manipulate data. While the database system is well-suited to the storage and retrieval of data, human beings need some sort of front-end application in order to see and use the data stored.

In developing database front-end applications, programmers face the challenge of the heterogeneous nature of the computers in most companies. For example, you may find that the art and marketing departments have Macintosh systems, the engineers have high-end Unix workstations, and the sales department people are using PCs.

This chapter will look at Java as the way to solve the Tower of Babel of database front ends by providing a single and consistent application programming interface: the Java Database Connectivity (JDBC) API. First, we will briefly review database models, and then we will examine how to use the JDBC API to connect Java applications and applets to database servers.

RDBMS Models

In a relational database management system (RDBMS), data is stored as rows of distinct information in tables. A structured language (Structured Query Language, or SQL) is used to query (retrieve), store, and change the data. SQL is an ANSI standard, and all major commercial RDBMS vendors provide mechanisms for issuing SQL commands.

NOTE The evolution of relational data storage began in 1970 with the work of Dr. E. F. Codd. Codd's rules for relational modeling of data formed the basis for the development of systems to manage data. Today, RDBMSs are the result of Codd's vision.

Single-Tier Database Design

The early RDBMS applications were developed based on an integrated model of user interface code, application code, and database libraries. This single binary model ran only on a local machine, typically a mainframe. Figure 11.1 illustrates the monolithic single-tier database design.

FIGURE 11.1:

The monolithic single-tier database design

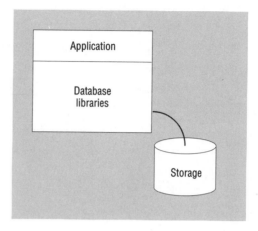

These applications were simple but inefficient, and they did not work over LANs. The model did not scale, and the application and user interface code were tightly coupled to the database libraries. Furthermore, the monolithic approach did not allow multiple instances of the application to communicate with *each other*, so there was often contention between instances of the application.

> **NOTE**   It is typical for the terms *RDBMS* and *DBMS* (Database Management System) to be used interchangeably because almost all major commercial databases are relational and support some form of SQL to allow the user to query the relations between data tables.

Two-Tier Database Design

Two-tier RDBMS models appeared with the advent of server technology. Communication-protocol development and extensive use of LANs and WANs allowed the database developer to create an application front end that typically accessed data through a connection (*socket*) to the back-end server. Figure 11.2 illustrates a two-tier database design, where the client software is connected to the database through a socket connection.

FIGURE 11.2:

The two-tier database design

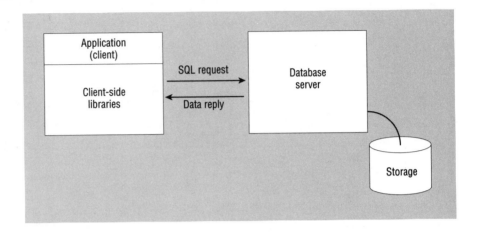

Client programs (applying a user interface) send SQL requests to the database server. The server returns the appropriate results, and the client is responsible for formatting the data. Clients still use a vendor-provided library of functions that manages the communication between client and server. Most of these libraries are written in the C language.

Despite the success of client/server architectures, two-tier database models suffer a number of limitations:

- They are limited by the vendor-provided library. Switching from one database vendor to another requires rewriting a significant amount of the client application's code.

- Version control is an issue. When the vendor updates the client-side libraries, the applications that use the database must be recompiled and redistributed.

- Vendor libraries deal with low-level data manipulation. Typically, the base library deals only with fetches and updates on single rows or columns of data. This can be enhanced on the server-side by creating a stored procedure, but the complexity of the system then increases.

- All of the intelligence associated with using and manipulating the data is implemented in the client application, creating large client-side runtimes. This drives the cost of each client seat up.

Multitier Database Design

In a multitier design, the client communicates with an intermediate server that provides a layer of abstraction from the RDBMS. Figure 11.3 illustrates a three-tier database design.

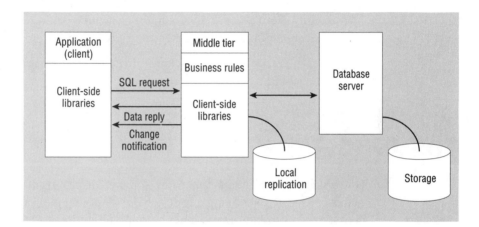

The intermediate layer is designed to handle multiple client requests and manage the connection to one or more database servers. The intermediate-tier design provides several advantages over the two-tier design. The middle tier has the following characteristics:

- It is multithreaded to manage multiple client connections simultaneously.

- This tier can accept connections from clients on a variety of vendor-neutral protocols (from HTTP to TCP/IP), then marshal the requests to the appropriate vendor-specific database servers and return the replies to the appropriate clients.

- Developers can program the middle tier with a set of "business rules" that manage the manipulation of the data. Business rules might include anything from restricting access to certain portions of data to making sure that data is properly formatted before being inserted or updated.

- The tier prevents the client from becoming too heavy by centralizing process-intensive tasks and abstracting data representation to a higher level.

- Having the tier in the middle isolates the client application from the database system and frees a company to switch database systems without needing to rework the business rules.

- The tier can asynchronously provide the client with the status of a current data table or row. For example, suppose that a client application had just completed a query of a particular table. If a subsequent action by another distinct client *changed* that data, the first client could receive notification from an intelligent middle-tier program.

- The tier can provide significant security benefits by handling the real database behind a gateway system.

The JDBC API

Java offers several benefits to the developer creating a front-end application for a database server. Just having a common development platform is a big advantage, because programmers are no longer required to write to the many platforms a large corporation may have. Also, a single Java program can satisfy the requirements of a large corporate customer.

In addition, there is a cost associated with the deployment and maintenance of the hardware and software of any system (client) the corporation owns. Microsoft Windows, Macintosh, and Unix desktop-centric clients (*fat clients*) can cost corporations between $10,000 and $15,000 per installation seat. Java technology makes it possible to use a smaller system footprint. These systems are based on a Java chip set and can run any and all Java programs from a built-in Java operating system. Java-based clients (*thin clients*) that operate with a minimum of hard resources and yet run the complete Java environment can cost less than $2,500 per seat. According to various studies, the savings for a corporation moving 10,000 fat client systems to thin clients could be as much as $100 million annually.

For the developer, Java-based database applications and applets represent a huge market opportunity. Most medium-sized to large organizations use databases for some portion of their business operations; many use databases for *every* aspect of their business, from human resources to front-line customer sales.

The JDBC API is designed to allow developers to create database front ends without needing to continually rewrite their code. Despite standards set by the

ANSI committee, each database system vendor has a unique way of connecting to its system.

Features of the JDBC API

The JDBC API was first introduced with release 1.1 of the JDK. JDBC provides application developers with a single API that is uniform and database independent. The API provides a standard to write to, as well as a standard that takes all of the various application designs into account.

The API's database independence is due to a set of Java interfaces that are implemented by a driver. The driver takes care of translating the standard JDBC calls into the specific calls required by the database it supports. The application is written once and moved to the various drivers. The application remains the same; the drivers change. Drivers may be used to develop the middle tier of a multitier database design, as illustrated in Figure 11.4.

FIGURE 11.4:

JDBC database designs

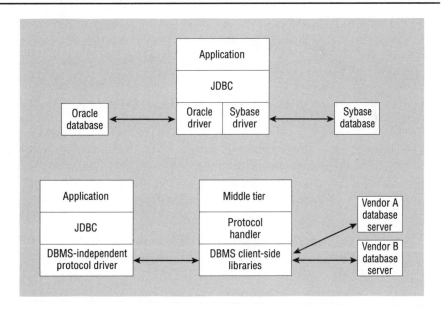

There is a subtle difference between the terms *middle-tier software* and *middleware*. Middle-tier software performs some kind of data processing. Middleware simply packages and transports data without doing any processing.

In addition to providing developers with a uniform and database-independent framework, JDBC also provides a means of allowing developers to retain the specific functionality that their database vendor offers. JDBC drivers must support ANSI SQL-2 Entry Level, but JDBC allows developers to pass query strings directly to the connected driver. These strings may or may not be ANSI SQL, or SQL at all. The use of these strings is up to the underlying driver. (Of course, using this feature limits your freedom to change database back ends.)

Every JDBC application (or applet) must have at least one JDBC driver, and each driver is specific to the type of DBMS used. A driver does not, however, need to be directly associated with a database.

JDBC is *not* a derivative of Microsoft's Open Database Connectivity (ODBC) specification. JDBC is written entirely in Java; ODBC is a C interface. However, both JDBC and ODBC are based on the X/Open SQL Command Level Interface (CLI). JavaSoft provides a JDBC–ODBC bridge that translates JDBC to ODBC. This implementation, done with native methods, is very small and efficient. (The JDBC-ODBC bridge is discussed later in the chapter.)

JDBC Interface Levels

There are two JDBC interface levels:

- The Application layer is where the developer uses the API to make calls to the database via SQL and retrieve the results.

- The Driver layer handles all communication with a specific driver implementation.

Figure 11.5 illustrates the Driver and Application layers.

Fortunately, the application developer only needs to use the standard API interfaces in order to guarantee JDBC compliance. The driver developer is responsible for developing code that interfaces to the database and supports the JDBC application level calls. However, it is important to understand the Driver layer and how some of the objects that are used at the Application layer are created by the driver.

There are four main interfaces that every driver layer must implement, and one class that bridges the Application and Driver layers. The four interfaces are `Driver`, `Connection`, `Statement`, and `ResultSet`. The `Driver` interface implementation is where the connection to the database is made. In most applications, the `Driver` is accessed through the `DriverManager` class—providing one more layer of abstraction for the developer.

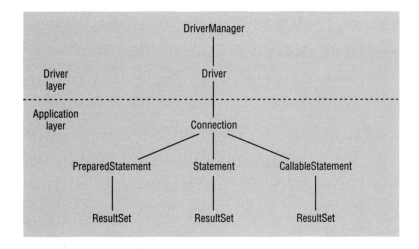

The Connection, Statement, and ResultSet interfaces are implemented by the driver vendor, but these interfaces specify the methods that the application developer can use. They allow the developer to create statements and retrieve results without having to think about where the objects are coming from or worry about what specific driver the application will use. The following sections discuss the Driver and Application layers in more detail.

The Driver Layer

Driver is an interface. Each vendor supplies a class that implements this interface. The other important class is the DriverManager class, which sits above the Driver and Application layers. The DriverManager class is responsible for loading and unloading drivers and making connections through drivers. The DriverManager class also provides features for logging and database login timeouts.

NOTE   Remember that the driver does not need to connect directly to a database and can support a new protocol for a multitier database design.

The Driver Interface   Every JDBC application must have at least one JDBC driver implementation. The Driver interface allows the DriverManager and JDBC Application layers to exist independently of the particular database used. A JDBC driver is an implementation of the Driver interface class.

Drivers use a string to locate and access databases. The syntax of this string is similar to a URL string and is referred to as a "URL." The purpose of a JDBC URL string is to separate the application developer from the driver developer. JavaSoft defines the following goals for driver URLs:

- The name of the driver-access URL should define the type of database being used.

- The user (application developer) should be free from any of the administration of creating the database connection. Therefore, any database connection information (host, port, database name, user access, and passwords) should be encoded in the URL.

- A network naming system may be used so that the user does not need to specifically encode the exact hostname and port number of the database.

The URL syntax used by the World Wide Web supports a standard syntax that satisfies these goals. JDBC URLs have the following syntax and structure:

```
jdbc:<subprotocol>:<subname>
```

where *<subprotocol>* defines the type of driver, and *<subname>* provides the network encoded name, as in:

```
jdbc:oracle:products
```

In this example, the database driver is an Oracle driver and the subname is a local database called `products`. This driver is designed to know how to use the subname when making the connection to the Oracle database.

A network naming service may also be specified as the subprotocol, rather than using a specific database driver name. In this case, the subprotocol would define the naming service:

```
jdbc: localnaming:human-resources
```

In this example, the subprotocol defines a local service that can resolve the subname `human-resources` to a database server. This approach can be very useful when the application developer wants to isolate the user from the actual location, name, database username, and database password. This URL specifies a driver named `localnaming`; this could be a Java program that contains a simple flat-file lookup, translates `human-resources` into `hrdatabase1.eng:888/personnel`, and knows to use the username `user` and password `matilda`. The details of the connection are kept hidden from the user.

Typically, the application developer will know specifically where the database is located and may not wish to use network indirection to locate the database. In this case, the URL may be expanded to include the location of the host and specific port and database information:

```
jdbc:msql://dbserver.eng:1112/bugreports
```

In this example, an `msql` database driver type is used to locate a server named `dbserver` in the `eng` domain and attempt to connect to a database server on port 1112 that contains a `bugreports` database, using the default username and password to connect.

Subprotocol names will eventually overlap, and there will need to be a registry of reserved names. For more information about registering a JDBC subprotocol name, consult the JDBC Specification.

The `Driver` interface specifies several methods. From a practical programming point of view, the two most important methods look like this:

`public Connection connect (String url, Properties info) throws SQLException`   Checks the subprotocol name of the URL string passed for a match with this driver. If there is a match, the driver should then attempt to make a connection to the database using the information passed in the remainder of the URL. A successful database connection will return an instance of the driver's implementation of a `Connection` interface. The `SQLException` should be thrown only if the driver recognizes the URL subprotocol but cannot make the database connection. A `null` is returned if the URL does not match a URL the driver expected. The username and password are included in an instance of the `Properties` container class.

`public boolean acceptsURL (String url) throws SQLException`   Explicitly "asks" the driver if the URL is valid. Note that, typically, the implementation of this method checks only the subprotocol specified in the URL, not whether the connection can be made.

Both of these methods throw `SQLException` if there is trouble with the remote database.

The `Driver connect()` method is the most important method, and is called by `DriverManager` to obtain a `Connection` object. The `Connection` object is the starting point of the JDBC Application layer (see Figure 11.5, shown earlier). The `Connection` object is used to create `Statement` objects that perform queries.

The `Driver connect()` method typically performs the following steps:

- Checks to see if the given URL string is valid.
- Opens a TCP connection to the host and port number specified.
- Attempts to access the named database table (if any).
- Returns an instance of a `Connection`.

NOTE   `Connection` is a Java interface, so the object returned is actually an instance of the vendor's implementation of the `Connection` interface.

The DriverManager Class   The `DriverManager` class is actually a utility class used to manage JDBC drivers. The class provides methods to obtain a connection through a driver, register and deregister drivers, set up logging, and set login timeouts for database access. The important `DriverManager` methods are listed below. Since they are static, they may be referenced through the interface. `SQL-Exception` is thrown if there is trouble with the remote database.

`public static synchronized Connection getConnection (String url, Properties info) throws SQLException`   Attempts to return a reference to an object implemented from the `Connection` interface. The method sweeps through a vector of stored `Driver` classes, passing the URL string and `Properties` object `info` to each in turn. The first `Driver` class that returns a `Connection` is used. `info` is a reference to a `Properties` container object of tag/value pairs, typically username/password. This method allows several attempts to make an authorized connection for each driver in the vector.

`public static synchronized Connection getConnection (String url) throws SQLException`   Calls `getConnection (url, info)` with an empty `Properties` object (`info`).

`public static synchronized Connection getConnection (String url, String user, String password) throws SQLException`   Creates a `Properties` object (`info`), stores the user and password strings into it, and then calls `getConnection (url, info)`.

`public static synchronized void registerDriver(java.sql.Driver driver) throws SQLException`   Stores the instance of the `Driver` interface implementation into a vector of drivers, along with an instance of `securityContext`, that identifies where the driver came from.

public static void setLogWriter(java.io.PrintWriter out)   Sets a private static java.io.PrintWriter reference to the PrintWriter object passed to the method.

The driver implementation can make use of two static object references that are stored through set*Type* methods and accessed by the driver through get*Type* methods: an integer that specifies login timeout and a PrintStream object used to log driver information.

Drivers are registered with the DriverManager class, either at initialization of the DriverManager class or when an instance of the driver is created.

When the DriverManager class is loaded, a section of static code (in the class) is run, and the class names of drivers listed in a Java property named jdbc.drivers are loaded. This property can be used to define a list of colon-separated driver class names, such as:

```
jdbc.drivers=imaginary.sql.Driver:oracle.sql.Driver:weblogic.sql.Driver
```

Each driver name is a class name (including the package declaration) that the DriverManager will attempt to load through the current CLASSPATH. The Driver-Manager uses the following call to locate, load, and link the named class:

```
Class.forName(driver);
```

If the jdbc.drivers property is empty (unspecified), then the application programmer must create an instance of a Driver class.

In both cases, the Driver class implementation must explicitly register itself with the DriverManager by calling:

```
DriverManager.registerDriver (this);
```

Here is a segment of code from the imaginary Driver (for the Mini-SQL database). The Driver registers itself whenever an instance of the imaginary driver is created:

```
...
public class iMsqlDriver implements java.sql.Driver
{
    static
    {
        try
```

```
          {
              new iMsqlDriver();
          }
          catch (SQLException e)
          {
              e.printStackTrace();
          }
      }
      /**
       * Constructs a new driver and registers it with
       * java.sql.DriverManager.registerDriver() as specified by the
       * JDBC protocol.
       */
      public iMsqlDriver() throws SQLException {
          java.sql.DriverManager.registerDriver(this);
      }
  }
  ...
```

The primary use of DriverManager is to get a Connection object reference through the getConnection() method:

```
Connection conn = null;
conn = DriverManager.getConnection
          ("jdbc:sybase://dbserver:8080/billing", dbuser, dbpasswd);
```

This method goes through the list of registered drivers and passes the URL string and parameters to each driver in turn through the driver's connect() method. If the driver supports the subprotocol and subname information, a Connection object reference is returned.

The DriverManager class is not required to create JDBC applications; it is possible to get a Connection object directly from the driver. For example, if a driver class name is XxxDriver, then the code below can be used to get a connection from the driver:

```
Connection conn;
conn = new XxxDriver().connect("jdbc:sybase://dbserver:8080/billing",
                               props);
```

However, this means of obtaining a connection is not as clean, and leaves the application developer dependent on the Driver implementation class to provide security checks. Also, the driver class is now hardcoded into the software, so the advantages of JDBC's vendor independence are lost.

The Application Layer

The Application layer encompasses three interfaces that are implemented at the Driver layer but are used by the application developer. In Java, the interface provides a means of using a general type to indicate a specific class. The interface defines methods that *must* be implemented by the specific classes. For the application developer, this means that the specific `Driver` class implementation is irrelevant; simply coding to the standard JDBC APIs will be sufficient. (Of course, this is assuming that the driver is JDBC-compliant, which means that the database is at least ANSI SQL-2 Entry Level.)

The three main interfaces are `Connection`, `Statement`, and `ResultSet`. A `Connection` object is obtained from the driver implementation through the `DriverManager.getConnection()` method call. Once a `Connection` object is returned, the application developer may create a `Statement` object to issue SQL against the database. If the SQL that was submitted was a `SELECT` query, then the result set is returned in a `ResultSet` object.

The Connection Interface   The `Connection` interface represents a session with the database connection provided by the `Driver`. Typical database connections include the ability to control changes made to the actual data stored through transactions. On creation, JDBC connections are in an *auto-commit* mode—there is no rollback possible. So after getting a `Connection` object from the driver, the developer should consider setting auto-commit to `false` with the `setAutoCommit (boolean b)` method. When auto-commit is disabled, the `Connection` will support both `Connection.commit()` and `Connection.rollback()` method calls. The level of support for transaction isolation depends on the underlying support for transactions in the database.

NOTE   A *transaction* is a set of operations that are completed in order. A *commit* action makes the operations store (or change) data in the database. A *rollback* action undoes the previous transaction before it has been committed.

A portion of the `Connection` interface definition follows. As usual, `SQLException` is thrown in case of trouble with the remote database.

> `Statement createStatement () throws SQLException`   The `Connection` object implementation will return an instance of an implementation of a `Statement` object. The `Statement` object is then used to issue queries.

`PreparedStatement prepareStatement (String sql) throws SQLException` The `Connection` object implementation will return an instance of a `Prepared-Statement` object that is configured with the `sql` string passed. The driver may then send the statement to the database, if the database (driver) handles precompiled statements. Otherwise, the driver may wait until the `PreparedStatement` is executed by an execute method.

`CallableStatement prepareCall (String sql) throws SQLException` The `Connection` object implementation will return an instance of a `Callable-Statement`. `CallableStatements` are optimized for handling stored procedures. The driver implementation may send the `sql` string immediately when `prepareCall()` is complete or may wait until an execute method occurs.

`void setAutoCommit (boolean autoCommit) throws SQLException` Sets a flag in the driver implementation that enables commit/rollback (`false`) or makes all transactions commit immediately (`true`).

`void commit () throws SQLException` Makes all changes made since the beginning of the current transaction (either since the opening of the `Connection` or since the last `commit()` or `rollback()`).

`void rollback() throws SQLException` Drops all changes made since the beginning of the current transaction.

The primary use of the `Connection` interface is to create a statement:

```
Connection conn;
Statement stmt;

conn = DriverManager.getConnection(url);
stmt = c.createStatement();
```

This statement may be used to send SQL statements that return a single result set in a `ResultSet` object reference. Statements that need to be called a number of times with slight variations may be executed more efficiently using a `Prepared-Statement`. The `Connection` interface is also used to create a `CallableStatement` whose purpose is to execute stored procedures.

Most of the time, the developer knows the database schema beforehand and creates the application based on the schema. However, JDBC provides an interface that may be used to dynamically determine the schema of a database. The `Connection` interface `getMetaData()` method will return a `DatabaseMetaData` object.

The instance of the class that implements the interface provides information about the database as a whole, including access information about tables and procedures, column names, data types, and so on. The implementation details of DatabaseMetaData are dependent on the database vendor's ability to return this type of information.

The Statement Interface   A *statement* is the vehicle for sending SQL queries to the database and retrieving a set of results. Statements can be SQL updates, inserts, deletes, or queries; statements may also create or drop tables. The Statement interface provides a number of methods designed to ease the job of writing queries to the database. The important Statement methods are listed below. As usual, SQLException is thrown if there is a problem with the remote database.

ResultSet executeQuery(String sql) throws SQLException   Executes a single SQL query and return the results in an object of type ResultSet.

int executeUpdate(String sql) throws SQLException   Executes a single SQL query that returns a count of rows affected rather than a set of results.

boolean execute(String sql) throws SQLException   A general way to execute SQL statements that may return multiple result sets and/or update counts. This method is also used to execute stored procedures that return out and inout parameters. The getResultSet(), getUpdateCount(), and getMoreResults() methods are used to retrieve the data returned. (This method is less likely to be used than executeUpdate() and executeQuery().)

NOTE   The in parameters are parameters that are passed into an operation. The out parameters are parameters passed by reference; they are expected to return a result of the reference type. The inout parameters are out parameters that contain an initial value that may change as a result of the operation. JDBC supports all three parameter types.

ResultSet getResultSet () throws SQLException   Returns the result of a statement execution as a ResultSet object. Note that if there are no results to be read or if the result is an update count, this method returns null. Also note that once read, the results are cleared.

int getUpdateCount() throws SQLException   Returns the status of an Update, an Insert, or a Delete query; a stored procedure; or a DDL statement. The value returned is the number of rows affected. A -1 is returned if there is no update count or if the data returned is a result set. Once read, the update count is cleared.

`boolean getMoreResults() throws SQLException`   Moves to the next result in a set of multiple results/update counts. This method returns `true` if the next result is a `ResultSet` object. This method will also close any previous `ResultSet` read.

Statement methods may or may not return a `ResultSet` object, depending on the `Statement` method used. The `executeUpdate()` method, for example, is used to execute SQL statements that do not expect a result (except a row-count status):

```
int rowCount;
rowCount = stmt.executeUpdate
    ("DELETE FROM Customer WHERE CustomerID = 'McG10233'");
```

SQL statements that return a single set of results can use the `executeQuery()` method. This method returns a single `ResultSet` object. The object represents the row information returned as a result of the query:

```
ResultSet results;
results = stmt.executeQuery("SELECT * FROM Stock");
```

SQL statements that execute stored procedures (or trigger a stored procedure) may return more than one set of results. The `execute()` method is a general-purpose method that can return either a single result set or multiple result sets. The method returns a boolean flag that is used to determine whether there are more result sets. Because a result set could contain either data or the count of an operation that returns a row count, the `getResultSet()`, `getMoreResults()`, and `getUpdate-Count()` methods are used. Here is an example:

```
// Assume SQLString returns multiple result sets
// returns true if a ResultSet is returned
int count;
ResultSet results;
if (stmt.execute (SQLstring))
{
    results = stmt.getResultSet();
    // false, an UpdateCount was returned
}
else
{
    count = stmt.getUpdateCount();
}
```

```
    // Process the first results here ....

    // Now loop until there are no more results or update counts
    do
    {
        // Is the next result a ResultSet?
        if (stmt.getMoreResults())
        {
            results = stmt.getResultSet();
        }
        else
        {
            count = stmt.getUpdateCount();
        }

        // Process next results (if any) here ....

    }
    while ((results != null) && (count != -1));
```

The PreparedStatement Interface   The PreparedStatement interface extends the Statement interface. When there is a SQL statement that requires repetition with minor variations, the PreparedStatement provides the mechanism for passing a pre-compiled SQL statement that uses parameters.

```
public interface PreparedStatement extends Statement
```

PreparedStatement parameters are used to pass data into a SQL statement, so they are considered in parameters and are filled in by using set*Type* methods:

```
// Assume priceList is an array of prices that needs
// to be reduced for a 10% off sale, and reducedItems
// is an array of item IDs
int reduction = 10;
PreparedStatement ps =
  conn.prepareStatment("UPDATE Catalog SET Price = ? WHERE ItemID = ?");
// Do the updates in a loop
for (int i = 0; i < reducedItems.length; i++)
{
    // Note that the setType methods set the value of the
    // parameters noted in the SQL statement with question
    // marks (?). They are indexed, starting from 1 to n.
    ps.setFloat(1, (priceList[i]*((float)(100-reduction)/100)));
```

```
    ps.setString(2, reducedItems[i]);
    if (ps.executeUpdate() == 0)
    {
        throw new ApplicationSpecificException ("No Item ID: " +
                                            reducedItems[i]);
    }
}
```

> **NOTE** The set*Type* methods fill the value of parameters (marked by question marks) in a PreparedStatement. These parameters are indexed from 1 to *n*.

Parameters hold their current values until either a new set*Type* method is called or the method clearParameters() is called for the PreparedStatement object. In addition to the execute methods inherited from Statement, Prepared-Statement declares the set*Type* methods listed in Table 11.1. Each method takes two arguments: a parameter index and the primitive or class type, as shown in Table 11.1.

TABLE 11.1: The set*Type* Methods

Method Signature	Java Type	SQL Type from the Database
void setBigDecimal (int index, BigDecimal x)	java.math. BigDecimal	NUMERIC
void setBoolean (int index, boolean b)	boolean	BIT
void setByte (int index, byte b)	byte	TINYINT
void setBytes (int index, byte x[])	byte array	VARBINARY or LONGVAR BINARY
void setDate (int index, Date d)	java.sql.Date	DATE
void setDouble (int index, double d)	double	DOUBLE
void setFloat (int index, float f)	float	FLOAT

Continued on next page

TABLE 11.1 CONTINUED: The set*Type* Methods

Method Signature	Java Type	SQL Type from the Database
`void setInt (int index, int i)`	`int`	INTEGER
`void setLong (int index, long l)`	`long`	BIGINT
`void setNull (int index, int sqlType)`	—	`java.sql.Types` lists SQL types by number, and **null** is integer 0 (zero)
`void setShort (int index, short x)`	`short`	SMALLINT
`void setString (int index, String s)`	`java.lang.String`	VARCHAR or LONGVAR CHAR
`void setTime (int index, Time t)`	`java.sql.Time`	TIME
`void setTimestamp (int index, Timestamp ts)`	`java.sql.Timestamp`	TIMESTAMP
`void setAsciiStream(int index, InputStream istr, int length)`	`InputStream`	LONGVARCHAR
`void setBinaryStream(int index, InputStream istr, int length)`	`InputStream`	LONGVARBINARY
`void setUnicodeStream(int index, InputStream istr, int length)`	`InputStream`	LONGVARCHAR

The CallableStatement Interface   The `CallableStatement` interface is used to execute SQL stored procedures. `CallableStatement` inherits from the `Prepared-Statement` interface, so all of the `execute` and set*Type* methods are available. The syntax of stored procedures varies among database vendors, so JDBC defines a standard way to call stored procedures in all RDBMSs.

```
public interface CallableStatement extends PreparedStatement
```

The JDBC uses an escape syntax that allows parameters to be passed as in parameters and out parameters. The syntax also allows a result to be returned. If this syntax is used, the parameter must be registered as an out parameter.

Here is an example of a `CallableStatement` with an out parameter:

```
CallableStatement cs = conn.prepareCall("{call getQuote(?, ?)}");
cs.setString (1, stockName);
// java.sql.Types defines SQL data types that are returned
// as out parameters
cs.registerOutParameter(2, Types.FLOAT);
cs.executeUpdate();
float quote = cs.getFloat(2);
```

`CallableStatement` defines a set of get*Type* methods that convert the SQL types returned from the database to Java types. These methods match the set*Type* methods declared by `PreparedStatement` and are listed in Table 11.2.

NOTE   The get*Type* methods access data in each column as the result of a query. Each column can be accessed by either its position in the row, numbered from 1 to *n* columns, or by its name, like `custID`.

TABLE 11.2:   The get*Type* Methods

Method Signature	Java Type	SQL Type from the Database
BigDecimal getBigDecimal (int index, int scale)	java.math. BigDecimal	NUMERIC
boolean getBoolean (int index)	boolean	BIT
byte getByte(int index)	byte	TINYINT
byte[] getBytes(int index)	byte array	BINARY or VARBINARY
Date getDate(int index)	java.sql.Date	DATE
double getDouble(int index)	double	DOUBLE
float getFloat(int index)	float	FLOAT
int getInt(int index)	int	INTEGER
long getLong(int index)	long	BIGINT

Continued on next page

TABLE 11.2 CONTINUED: The get*Type* Methods

Method Signature	Java Type	SQL Type from the Database
`short getShort(int index)`	`short`	SMALLINT
`String getString(int index)`	`string`	CHAR, VAR CHAR or LONGVAR CHAR
`Time getTime(int index)`	`java.sql.Time`	TIME
`Timestamp getTimestamp (int index)`	`java.sql.Timestamp`	TIMESTAMP

NOTE   It is the responsibility of the JDBC driver to convert the data passed from the database as SQL data types into Java values.

The ResultSet Interface   The `ResultSet` interface defines methods for accessing tables of data generated as the result of executing a `Statement`. `ResultSet` column values may be accessed in any order—they are indexed and may be selected by either the name or the number (from 1 to *n*) of the column. `ResultSet` maintains the position of the current row, starting with the first row of data returned. The `next()` method moves to the next row of data.

A partial look at the `ResultSet` interface follows. Vendors that implement this interface have the option of caching the results on the remote side, so there is the possibility of a communication problem. For this reason, the methods listed below throw `SQLException`.

> `boolean next() throws SQLException`   Positions the `ResultSet` to the next row. The `ResultSet` row position is initially just before the first row of the result set.

> `ResultSetMetaData getMetaData() throws SQLException`   Returns an object that contains a description of the current result set, including the number of columns, the type of each column, and properties of the results.

> `void close() throws SQLException`   Normally a `ResultSet` is closed when another SQL statement is executed, but it may be desirable to release the resources earlier.

As with the `CallableStatement` interface discussed earlier, the resulting data can be read through get*Type*() methods. Note, however, that values can be accessed either via column names or column numbers; callable statements can use only column numbers. Recall that column numbers begin at 1. Here is an example:

```
// Pass a query to the statement object
ResultSet rs =
    stmt.executeQuery("SELECT * FROM Stock WHERE quantity = 0");


// Get the results as their Java types
// Note that columns are indexed by an integer starting with 1,
// or by the name of column, as in "ItemID"
System.out.println("Stock replenishment list");
while (rs.next())
{
    System.out.println ("Item ID: " + rs.getString("ItemID"));
    System.out.println ("Next ship date: " + rs.getDate(2));
    System.out.println ("");
}
```

The ResultSetMetaData Interface   Besides being able to read data from a `ResultSet` object, JDBC provides an interface to allow the developer to determine what type of data was returned. The `ResultSetMetaData` interface is similar to the `DatabaseMetaData` interface in concept, but it is specific to the current `ResultSet`. As with `DatabaseMetaData`, it is unlikely that many developers will use this interface, because most applications are written with an understanding of the database schema and column names and values. However, `ResultSetMetaData` is useful in dynamically determining the `MetaData` of a `ResultSet` returned from a stored procedure.

NOTE   SQL LONGVARBINARY and LONGVARCHAR data types can be of arbitrary size. The `getBytes()` and `getString()` methods can read these types up to the limits imposed by the driver. The limits can be read through the `Statement.getMaxFieldSize()` method. For larger blocks of data, the JDBC allows developers to use input streams to return the data in chunks. (Streams must be read immediately following the query execution—they are automatically closed at the next get of a `ResultSet`.) You can also send large blocks of data by using `java.io.OutputStream` as a parameter. When a statement is executed, the JDBC driver makes repeated calls to read and transmit the data in the streams.

JDBC Applications versus Applets

You may be wondering whether a Java applet or application would work best for your database front-end development. Each has its advantages and disadvantages.

JDBC Applications

Because Java applications are developed as stand-alone executables, the user is expected to have access to the program executable (class file) and the Java interpreter locally. For an intranet-based database front end, this strategy offers the benefits of faster startup (class files are local) and local disk utilization. In addition, Java applications are trusted and are allowed greater flexibility with socket connections—making it possible for the client program to access multiple database systems on remote servers.

Java applications are becoming more prevalent as tools become available for GUI development and speed improvements are made possible through Just-In-Time (JIT) compilers/interpreters. Applications can also reduce or eliminate issues with browser security models and the differences in the browser's implementation of Java widgets.

JDBC Applets

The process of executing a JDBC applet includes downloading the necessary Java applet code (including JDBC drivers and application layer software), automatically checking security restrictions on the code, and running the applet.

As with other types of applets, JDBC applets have the benefits of being easy to modify, easy to use, and capable of including embedded help links. However, like other types of applets, JDBC applets also are severely constrained by the browser environment—they cannot access any local files, connect to arbitrary hosts, or load or run drivers that contain native methods (C language calls). Additionally, there is a considerable performance hit involved in loading applet code across an Internet (WAN) connection.

Some of these constraints may be lifted or reduced with the introduction of trusted applets and browsers that accept them. Trusted applets may be code-signed with a cryptographic key or may be stored in a trusted location. If the browser environment believes that the applet's source is trusted, then for security purposes, it may be treated like an application, although there may still be limits regarding the location of databases on a network that are not related to the Java security manager.

A typical use of JDBC applets might be for training within a large organization, where the data being delivered is not critical and access can be limited to a two-tier model. Another use may be the simple presentation of a limited amount of data to the Internet community, when the security of the data message is not paramount.

Another alternative is the use of a three-tier model. In this approach, the applet is loaded from a middleware tier that provides both the HTML page and HTTP server, and a multithreaded application (Java, C, or C++) that supports socket connections for multiple clients and, in turn, contacts remote database systems. Calls to the third tier can be managed by developing a custom (proprietary) protocol, by using Remote Method Invocation (RMI), or by using an Object Request Broker (ORB). RMI is discussed in Chapter 12, and ORB is covered in Chapter 13.

Security Considerations

The JDBC API follows the standard Java security model. In short, applications are considered trusted code, and applets are considered untrusted. In general, the job of writing a secure JDBC driver is left to the driver vendor.

The JVM employs its own well-documented security checks for untrusted applets, including the aforementioned restrictions. However, if JDBC driver vendors want to extend the model by adding features to their drivers—for example, allowing multiple applets to use the same TCP socket connection to talk to a database—then it becomes the responsibility of the vendors to check that each applet is allowed to use the connection.

In addition to maintaining the integrity of the Java security model, both the JDBC driver vendor and JDBC application developer need to keep in mind that the JDBC API defines a means of executing database calls and does not define a network security model. The data sent over the network to the database and the resulting table information (for example, to request customer credit card information) are exposed and can be read by any terminal that is capable of snooping the network.

A JDBC Database Example

As an example of the concepts presented in this chapter, we'll work with a hypothetical database that stores information related to a large catalog ordering system. This simple database includes a table called Customer, which has the following schema:

CustomerID	VARCHAR
LastName	VARCHAR
FirstName	VARCHAR
Phonenumber	VARCHAR
StreetAddress	VARCHAR
Zipcode	VARCHAR

Here is the definition of a simple `Customer` object with two primary methods, `insertNewCustomer()` and `getCustomer()`:

`public Customer(Connection conn)` The constructor for the class. The `Customer` constructor receives a `Connection` object, which it uses to create `Statement` references. In addition, the constructor creates a `PreparedStatement` and three `CallableStatements`.

`public String insertNewCustomer(String lname, String fname, String pnum, String addr, String zip) throws insertFailedException, SQLException` Creates a new customer record, including a new ID. The ID is created through a stored procedure that reads the current list of customer IDs and creates a new reference. The method returns the new ID created or throws an exception if the insert failed.

`public CustomerInfo getCustomer(String custID) throws selectException, SQLException` Returns an object that contains the data in the Customer table. An exception is thrown if the customer ID passed does not exist or is not properly formatted, or if the SQL statement fails.

`public static synchronized boolean validateZip(String zip) throws SQLException` A utility method to validate the zip code. A true value is returned if the zip code exists in the ZipCode table in the database.

public static synchronized boolean validateID(String id) throws SQLException   A utility method to validate a customer ID. If the ID exists, the method returns true.

The source for Customer.java follows. It is also included on the CD-ROM in javadevhdbk\ch11\Customer.java.

LIST 11.1   *Customer.java*

```java
// Customer record class
// This class is used to store and access customer data from the
// database
import java.sql.*;

public class Customer
{
    private Connection conn;
    private PreparedStatement insertNewCustomer;
    private CallableStatement getNewID;
    public static CallableStatement checkZip;
    public static CallableStatement checkID;

    // Customer constructor: store a local copy of the
    // Connection object create statements for use later
    public Customer (Connection c)
    {
        conn = c;

        try
        {
            insertNewCustomer = conn.prepareStatement
                ("INSERT INTO Customers VALUES (?, ?, ?, ?, ?, ?)");
                getNewID = conn.prepareCall("{call getNewID (?)}");
                checkID = conn.prepareCall("{call checkID (?,?)}");
                checkZip = conn.prepareCall("{call checkZip (?, ?)}");
        }
        catch (SQLException e)
        {
            System.out.println("Cannot create statements");
        }
    }
```

```java
// Method for creating a new customer record.
// The customerID is generated by a stored procedure
// call on the database
public String insertNewCustomer
    (String lname, String fname, String pnum,
     String addr, String zip)
        throws insertFailedException, SQLException
{
    String newID;

    // Get a new customer ID through the stored procedure
    if ((newID = getNewID ()) == null)
    {
        throw new insertFailedException("could not get new ID");
    }

    // Insert the new customer ID
    insertNewCustomer.setString (1, newID);
    insertNewCustomer.setString (2, lname);
    insertNewCustomer.setString (3, fname);
    insertNewCustomer.setString (4, pnum);
    insertNewCustomer.setString (5, addr);
    insertNewCustomer.setString (6, zip);

    // Execute the statement
    if (insertNewCustomer.executeUpdate() != 1)
    {
        throw new insertFailedException ("could not insert");
    }
    return (newID);
}

// Get a single customer record with this ID
// Note: this method maps the returned data onto a
// CustomerInfo container object
public CustomerInfo getCustomer(String custID)
    throws selectException, SQLException
{
    // Check the ID first
    if (!validateID (custID))
    {
```

```java
            throw new selectException("no customer with ID: " +
                                                    custID);
        }

        // Create the select statement
        Statement stmt = conn.createStatement();

        // Get the results
        ResultSet rs = stmt.executeQuery
            ("SELECT * FROM Customer WHERE CustID = " + custID);
        rs.next();

        // Create a CustomerInfo container object
        CustomerInfo info = new CustomerInfo();

        // Populate the CustomerInfo object
        // Columns are indexed starting with 1
        info.CustomerID = rs.getString(1);
        info.LastName = rs.getString(2);
        info.FirstName = rs.getString(3);
        info.PhoneNumber = rs.getString(4);
        info.StreetAddress = rs.getString(5);
        info.Zip = rs.getString(6);

        return (info);
    }

    // Method for validation of a customer's zip code
    // This method is public so that it can be called from
    // a user interface
    public static synchronized boolean validateZip(String zip)
        throws SQLException
    {
        // Make call to stored procedure to validate zip code
        checkZip.setString (1, zip);
        checkZip.registerOutParameter (2, Types.BIT);
        checkZip.executeUpdate();
        return (checkZip.getBoolean(2));
    }

    // Method for validating a customer ID
    // This method is public so that it can be called from
    // a user interface
```

```java
        public static synchronized boolean validateID(String id)
            throws SQLException
        {
            // Make call to stored procedure to validate
            // customer ID
            checkID.setString (1, id);
            checkID.registerOutParameter (2, Types.BIT);
            checkID.executeUpdate();
            return (checkID.getBoolean(2));
        }

        // Method for retrieving a new customer ID from the database
        private String getNewID() throws SQLException
        {
            // Make call to stored procedure to get
            // customer ID from DB
            getNewID.registerOutParameter(1, Types.VARCHAR);
            getNewID.executeUpdate();
            return getNewID.getString(1);
        }
}

// Exceptions

// insertFailedException is a general exception for
// SQL insert problems
class insertFailedException extends SQLException
{
    public insertFailedException(String reason)
    {
        super (reason);
    }
    public insertFailedException()
    {
        super();
    }
}

// selectException is a general exception for SQL select problems
class selectException extends SQLException
{
    public selectException(String reason)
```

```
        {
            super (reason);
        }

        public selectException()
        {
            super ();
        }
    }
```

The CustomerInfo class is a simple container object. Container classes make it easier to pass a complete customer record to and from any method that manipulates the Customer table in the database. Data can be stored in the container class and passed as a single object reference, rather than having to pass each element as a single reference.

The following code can be found in javadevhdbk\ch11\CustomerInfo.java.

LIST 11.2   *CustomerInfo.java*

```
// A container object for the Customer table
public class CustomerInfo
{
    String CustomerID;
    String LastName;
    String FirstName;
    String PhoneNumber;
    String StreetAddress;
    String Zip;
}
```

Finally, to test the simple Customer class, here is a simple Java application that illustrates loading a Sybase driver, then making a connection, and passing the Connection object returned to a new instance of a Customer object. The following code can be found on the CD-ROM in javadevhdbk\ch11\Example.java.

LIST 11.3   *Example.java*

```
// A simple Java application that illustrates the use of
// DriverManager,
```

```java
// Driver, Connection, Statement and ResultSet

import java.sql.*;


public class Example
{
    Connection sybaseConn;

    // main
    public static void main(String arg[])
    {
        // Look for the URL, username and password
        if (arg.length < 3)
        {
            System.out.println("Example use:");
            System.out.println
                ("java Example <url> <username> <password>");
                System.exit(1);
        }

        // Create an instance of the class
        Example ex = new Example();

        // Initialize the connection
        ex.initdb(arg[0], arg[1], arg[2]);

        // Test the connection—write a customer and
        // then read it back
        ex.testdb();
    }

    // method to initialize the database connection
    // The Connection object reference is kept globally
    public void initdb(String url, String user, String passwd)
    {
        // Try to open the database and get the connection
        try
        {
            // Note that this example assumes that
            // Java property "jdbc.drivers"
            // that is loading the appropriate driver(s) for
            // the URL passed in the getConnection call.
```

```
            // It is possible to explicitly create an
            // instance of a driver as well, for example:
            // new sybase.sql.Driver(); or
            // Class.forName("sybase.sql.Driver");

            // Create a connection
            sybaseConn = DriverManager.getConnection(url, user, passwd);

        }
        catch (SQLException e)
        {
            System.out.println("Database connection failed:");
            System.out.println(e.getMessage());
            System.exit(1);
        }
    }

    // Simple method to test the Customer class methods
    public void testdb()
    {
        String custID = null;

        // Create the instance of the Customer class
        Customer cust = new Customer (sybaseConn);

        try
        {
            // Now insert a new Customer
            custID = cust.insertNewCustomer
                    ("Jones", "Bill", "555-1234", "5 Main Street","01234");
        }
        catch (SQLException e)
        {
            System.out.println("Insert failed:");
            System.out.println(e.getMessage());
            System.exit(1);
        }

        try
        {
            // Read it back from the database
                CustomerInfo info = cust.getCustomer(custID);
        }
```

```
catch (SQLException e)
{
    System.out.println("Read failed:");
    System.out.println(e.getMessage());
    System.exit(1);
}
}
}
```

This example illustrates the use of the CallableStatements to issue stored procedure calls that validate the zip code and validate the customer ID, and the PreparedStatement to issue an Insert SQL statement with parameters that will change with each insert.

This example also illustrates code that will run with any JDBC driver that will support the stored procedures used in the Customer class. The driver class names are loaded from the jdbc.drivers property so code recompilation is not required.

JDBC Drivers

One of the real attractions of the JDBC API is the ability to develop applications knowing that all of the major database vendors are working in parallel to create drivers. A number of drivers are available both from database vendors and from third-party developers. In most cases, it is wise to shop around for the best features, cost, and support.

TIP
JDBC drivers are being released from so many vendors and at such a rapid rate that a definitive list is just not practical and would be obsolete by the time it was printed. For information on current driver vendors, their product names, and what databases they support, a good source is http://splash.javasoft.com/jdbc/jdbc.drivers.html.

Types of Drivers

Drivers come in a variety of flavors according to their construction and the type of database they are intended to support. JavaSoft categorizes database drivers four ways:

- A JDBC-ODBC bridge driver, shown in Figure 11.6, implemented with ODBC binary code, and in some cases, a client library as well. The bridge driver is made up of three parts: a set of C libraries that connects the JDBC to the ODBC driver manager, the ODBC driver manager, and the ODBC driver. (See the next section for more information about the JDBC-ODBC bridge.)

FIGURE 11.6:

JDBC-ODBC bridge driver

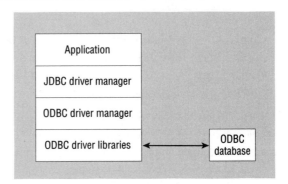

- A native library-to-Java implementation, as shown in Figure 11.7. This driver uses native C language library calls to translate JDBC to the native client library. The drivers use C language libraries that provide vendor-specific functionality and tie these libraries (through native method calls) to the JDBC. These drivers were the first available for Oracle, Sybase, Informix, DB2, and other client-library-based RDBMSs.

FIGURE 11.7:

Native library-to-Java driver

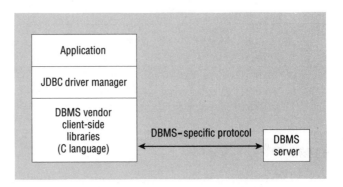

- A network-protocol Java driver, as shown in Figure 11.8. JDBC calls are translated by this driver into a DBMS-independent protocol and sent to a middle-tier server over a socket. The middle-tier code contacts a variety of databases on behalf of the client. This approach is becoming the most popular and is by far the most flexible. This approach also deals specifically with issues relating to network security, including passing data through firewalls.

FIGURE 11.8:

DBMS-independent
network protocol driver

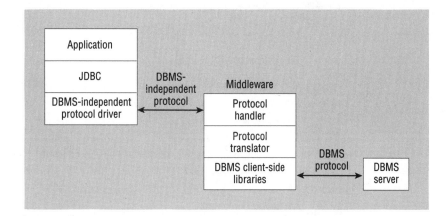

- A native-protocol Java driver, as shown in Figure 11.9. JDBC calls are converted directly to the network protocol used by the DBMS server. In this driver scenario, the database vendor supports a network socket, and the JDBC driver communicates over a socket connection directly to the database server. The client-side code can be written in Java. This solution is very practical for intranet use. However, because the network protocol is defined by the vendor and is typically proprietary, the driver usually comes only from the database vendor.

FIGURE 11.9:

DBMS-protocol all-Java
driver

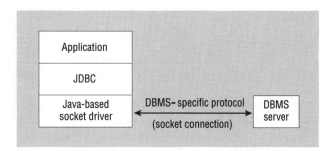

The JDBC-ODBC Bridge

The JDBC-ODBC bridge is a JDBC driver that provides translation of JDBC calls to ODBC operations. There are a number of DBMSs that support ODBC. When a company the size of Microsoft creates a standard for database access, there are sure to be vendors that follow, and in fact there are more than 50 different ODBC drivers available.

As mentioned earlier in this chapter, both JDBC and ODBC are based on the X/Open CLI, so the translation between JDBC and ODBC is relatively straightforward. ODBC is a client-side set of libraries and a driver that is specific to the client's operating system and, in some cases, machine architecture.

From the developer's perspective, using a JDBC-ODBC bridge driver is an easy choice—applications will still speak directly to the JDBC interface classes, so it is exactly the same as using any other JDBC driver. However, the implementation of a JDBC-ODBC bridge requires that the developer be aware of what is required to run the application. Because ODBC calls are made using binary C calls, the client must have a local copy of the ODBC driver, the ODBC driver manager, and the client-side libraries.

For these reasons, JavaSoft makes the recommendation that the JDBC-ODBC bridge not be used for web-based database access. For intranet access, the developer must distribute the Java program to the client machines as either a Java application or Java applet (which would run as a trusted source from the local client file system).

Summary

The interest in Java has created a number of new strategies for moving data between the database system and the front-end user. In this chapter, the JDBC API was presented as the primary technique for connecting Java applications to database systems. The JDBC solves the problem of connecting a single application to a multitude of database systems by isolating the interface that the developer uses and the driver that is used to connect to the database.

As alternative database connectivity strategies, both RMI (Remote Method Invocation) and CORBA (Common Object Request Broker Architecture) can be used to connect client applications to databases. RMI is the subject of Chapter 12, and CORBA is covered in Chapter 13.

CHAPTER

TWELVE

12

Persistence and Remote Method Invocation

- Object persistence and serialization

- RMI basics

- Callbacks in RMI

- Dynamic class loading in RMI

- Remote object activation

Java 2 includes support for object persistence and for making method calls on remote objects. This chapter explains these two concepts, discusses Java's support for them, and shows how they are related. The final section of the chapter covers the new features of Remote Method Invocation (RMI) that were introduced with JDK release 1.2.

Object Persistence

A Java object ordinarily lasts no longer than the program that created it. An object may cease to exist during runtime if it is reaped by the garbage collector. If it avoids that fate, it still goes away when the user terminates the browser (for an applet) or the object's runtime environment (for an application).

In this context, *persistence* is the ability of an object to record its state so that it can be reproduced in the future, perhaps in another environment. For example, a persistent object might store its state in a file. The file can be used to restore the object in a different runtime environment. It is not really the object itself that persists, but rather the information necessary to construct a replica of the object. When an object is *serialized*, all of the object's data, but not its methods or class definition, is written to a stream.

Serialization

An object records itself by writing out the values that describe its state. This process is known as *serialization* because the object is represented by an ordered series of bytes. Java provides classes that write objects to streams and restore objects from streams.

The main task of serialization is to write out the values of an object's instance variables. If a variable is a reference to another object, the referenced object must also be serialized. Serialization may involve serializing a complex tree structure that consists of the original object, the object's objects, the object's object's objects, and so on. An object's ownership hierarchy is known as its *graph*.

Not all classes are capable of being serialized. Only objects that implement the `Serializable` or `Externalizable` interfaces may successfully be serialized. Both interfaces are in the `java.io` package. A serializable object can be serialized by another object, which in practice is a type of output stream. An externalizable object must be capable of writing its own state, rather than letting the work be done by another object.

The Serializable Interface

The `Serializable` interface does not have any methods. When a class declares that it implements `Serializable`, it is declaring that it participates in the serialization protocol. When an object is serializable, and the object's state is written to a stream, the stream must contain enough information to restore the object. This must hold true even if the class being restored has been updated to a more recent (but compatible) version.

You can serialize any class as long as the class meets the following criteria:

- The class, or one of its superclasses, must implement the `java.io.Serializable` interface.

- The class can implement the `writeObject()` method to control data that is being saved and append new data to existing saved data.

- The class can implement the `readObject()` method to read the data that was written by the corresponding `writeObject()` method.

If a serializable class has variables that should not be serialized, those variables must be marked with the `transient` keyword. The serialization process will ignore any variables marked as `transient`. In general, references to AWT classes that rely on system peers should be marked as `transient`. Many things—like static data, open file handles, socket connections, and threads—will not be serializable, because they represent items that are very JVM-specific.

The Externalizable Interface

The `Externalizable` interface identifies objects that can be saved to a stream but are responsible for their own states. When an externalizable object is written to a stream, the stream is responsible for storing the name of the object's class; the object must write its own data. The `Externalizable` interface is defined as:

```
public interface Externalizable extends Serializable {

    public void writeExternal (ObjectOutput out)
        throws IOException;
```

```
public void readExternal (ObjectInput in)
     throws IOException, ClassNotFoundException;
}
```

An externalizable class must adhere to this interface by providing a write-External() method for storing its state during serialization and a readExternal() method for restoring its state during deserialization.

Object Output Streams

Objects that can serialize other objects implement the ObjectOutput interface from the java.io package. This interface is intended to be implemented by output stream classes. The interface's definition is:

```
public interface ObjectOutput extends DataOutput {
    public void writeObject(Object obj)
        throws IOException;
    public void write (int b) throws IOException;
    public void write(byte b[]) throws IOException;
    public void write(byte b[], int off, int len)
        throws IOException;
    public void flush() throws IOException;
    public void close() throws IOException;
}
```

The essential method of the interface is writeObject(Object obj), which writes obj to a stream. Static and transient data of obj are ignored; all other variables, including private ones, are written.

Exceptions can occur while accessing the object or its fields, or when attempting to write to the storage stream. If an exception occurs, the stream that the interface is built on will be left in an unknown and unusable state, and the external representation of the object will be corrupted.

The ObjectOutput interface extends the DataOutput interface. DataOutput methods support writing of primitive data types. For example, the writeDouble() method writes data of type double, and writeBoolean() writes data of type boolean. These primitive-type writing methods are used for writing out an object's primitive instance variables.

The primary class that implements the ObjectOutput interface is ObjectOutput-Stream. This class is similar to other output stream classes, which are discussed in Chapter 9.

Serializable objects are represented as streams of bytes, rather than as characters. Therefore, they are handled by streams rather than by character-oriented writers.

When an object is to be serialized to a file, the first step is to create an output stream that talks to the file:

```
FileOutputStream fos = new FileOutputStream("obj.file");
```

The next step is to create an object output stream and chain it to the file output stream:

```
ObjectOutput objout = new ObjectOutputStream(fos);
```

The object output stream automatically writes a header into the stream; the header contains a magic number and a version. This data is written automatically with the writeStreamHeader() method when the object output stream is created. Later in this chapter, we will demonstrate how an object input stream reads this header and verifies the object before returning its state.

After writing the header, the object output stream can write the bit representation of an object to the output stream using the writeObject() method. For example, the following code constructs an instance of the Point class and serializes it:

```
objout.writeObject(new Point(15, 20));
objout.flush();
```

This example shows that serializing an object to a stream is not very different from writing primitive data to a stream. The example writes objects to a file, but the output stream can just as easily be chained to a network connection stream.

Without calling the reset() method of java.io.ObjectOutputStream, you cannot use the same stream to write the same object reference twice.

Deserialization

The ObjectInputStream class reads serialized object data. By using the methods of this class, a program can restore a serialized object, along with the entire tree of objects referred to by the primary object, from the stream. Primitive data types may also be read from an object input stream.

Object Input Streams

There is only one class constructor in the ObjectInputStream class:

```
public ObjectInputStream(InputStream in) throws IOException,
StreamCorruptedException
```

The constructor calls the class's readStreamHeader() method to verify the header and the version that were written into the stream by the corresponding object output stream. If a problem is detected with the header or the version, a Stream-CorruptedException is thrown.

The primary method of the ObjectInputStream class is readObject(), which deserializes an object from the data source stream. The deserialized object is returned as an Object; the caller is responsible for casting it to the correct type.

The Known Objects Table

During deserialization, a list is maintained of objects that have been restored from the stream. This list is called the *known objects table*.

If the data being written is of a primitive type, it is simply treated as a sequence of bytes and restored from the input stream. If the data being restored is a string, it is read using the string's UTF encoding; the string will be added to the known objects table.

If the object being restored is an array, the type and length of the array are determined. Next, memory for the array is allocated, and each of the elements contained in the array is read using the appropriate read method. Once the array is reconstructed, it is added to the known objects table. If it is an array of objects (as opposed to primitives), then each object is deserialized and added to the known objects table.

When an object is restored, it is added to the known objects table. Then the objects to which the original object refers are restored recursively and added to the known objects table.

Object Validation

Once an object has been retrieved from a stream, it must be validated so it can become a full-fledged object and be used by the program that deserialized it. The validateObject() method is called when a complete graph of objects has been retrieved from a stream. If the primary object cannot be made valid, the validation process will stop, and an exception will be thrown.

Security for Serialized Objects

Serialization can involve storing an object's data on a disk file or transmitting the data across a network. In both cases, there is a potential security problem because the data is located outside the Java runtime environment—beyond the reach of Java's security mechanisms.

The `writeExternal()` method is public, so any object can make an externalizable or serializable object write itself to a stream. You should be careful when deciding whether or not `writeExternal()` should serialize sensitive private data. When an object is restored via an ordinary `readExternal()` call, its sensitive values are restored into private variables, and no harm is done. However, while the serialized data is outside the system, an attacker could access the data, decode its format, and obtain the sensitive values. A similar form of attack would involve modifying data values—for example, replacing a password or incrementing a bank balance. A less precise attack would simply corrupt the serialized data.

When an object is serialized, all the reachable objects of its ownership graph are potentially exposed. For example, a serialized object might have a reference to a reference to a reference to an instance of the `FileDescriptor` class. An attacker could reserialize the file descriptor and gain access to the file system of the machine where the serialized object originated.

The best protection for an object that has fields that should not be stored is to label those fields with the `transient` keyword. Transient fields, like static fields, are not serialized and therefore are not exposed.

If a class cannot be serialized in a manner that upholds the integrity of the system containing it, then it should avoid implementing the `Serializable` interface. Moreover, it should not be referred to by any class that will be serialized, unless its reference is marked `transient`.

Externalizable objects (that is, ones that take care of writing their own data) often use the technique of including invariant data among their instance variables. These invariants serve no useful purpose during normal operation of the class. They are inspected after deserialization; an unexpected value indicates that the external serialized representation has been corrupted.

Serialization Exceptions

There are six types of exceptions that can be thrown during serialization or deserialization of an object:

InvalidClassException   Typically thrown when the class type cannot be determined by the reserializing stream or when the class that is being returned cannot be represented on the system retrieving the object. This exception is also thrown if the deserialized class is not declared public or if it does not have a public default (no-argument) constructor.

NotSerializableException   Typically thrown by externalizable objects (which are responsible for their own reserialization) on detection of a corrupted input stream. The corruption is generally indicated by an unexpected invariant value or simply when you try to serialize a nonserializable object.

StreamCorruptedException   Thrown when a stored object's header or control data is invalid.

OptionalDataException   Thrown when a stream is supposed to contain an object, but it actually contains only primitive data.

ClassNotFoundException   Thrown when the class of the deserialized object cannot be found on the read-side of the stream.

IOException   Thrown when there is an error related to the stream that the object is being written to or read from.

Object Stream Processes

Writing an object to a stream is a simple process, similar to the process of writing any other kind of high-level structure. This process is explained in detail in Chapter 9. You must create a low-level output stream to provide access to the external medium (generally a file or network). Next, a high-level stream is chained to the low-level stream; for serialization, the high-level stream is an object output stream.

The following code fragment constructs an instance of Point and writes it to a file called Point.ser on the local file system (note that the .ser extension is the conventional extension for serialized objects):

```
Point p = new Point(13, 10);
FileOutputStream f = new FileOutputStream("Point.ser");
ObjectOutputStream s = new ObjectOutputStream (f);
```

```
try
{
    s.writeObject (p);
    s.flush ();
} catch (IOException e) { }
```

Restoring the object involves opening a file input stream on the file and chaining an object input stream to the file input stream. The Point object is read by calling readObject() from the object input stream; the return value is of type Object and must be cast by the caller. The following code fragment shows how this is done:

```
Point p = null;
FileInputStream f = new FileInputStream("Point.ser");
ObjectInputStream s = new ObjectInputStream (f);
try
{
    p = (Point)s.readObject ();
}
catch (IOException e) {}
```

In the next section, we will develop a simple example that saves and restores an object.

A Serialization Example

As an example of serialization, we will develop a simple painting program, call PersisTest, that can store its display list to a file. (A display list is a data structure that contains an abstract description of what should appear on the screen.) The program allows the user to draw rectangles with the mouse; pressing the mouse button defines one corner of a rectangle, and releasing the button defines the opposite corner. The display list is a vector that contains two instances of the Point class for each rectangle. Each point represents a corner of the rectangle.

The PersisTest application is a subclass of Frame. A panel across the top of the frame contains four control buttons. The frame's paint() method clears the screen to white and then traverses the display list vector, drawing one black rectangle for each pair of points in the vector.

The four control buttons support clearing, saving, restoring, and quitting. The handler for the Save button uses the writing technique discussed in the previous section to store the display list vector in a file. The filename must be specified in the command-line argument. The handler for the Restore button deserializes a vector, replacing the old display list with the new vector.

To test the application, invoke it with a filename as a command-line argument:

java PersisTest *filename*

Then use the mouse to draw some rectangles. Next, click on the Save button to write the display list to the file. Clear the screen or draw more rectangles. Finally, click the Restore button. The display will change back to the state it was in when the Save button was clicked. You can even terminate the application and restart it; it will still restore correctly from the external file.

This example could achieve the same result by opening a data output stream instead of an object output stream and writing four ints for each rectangle. The benefit of using serialization lies in the dramatic improvement in program maintainability. If you were to store and restore the display list by using data input and output streams, any change in the format of the display list would force a change in both the writing and the reading code. With serialization, the display list data format is irrelevant (although the data graph is still important—changing the data in the object would make restoring old data impossible).

 The source code for the example follows, and it is also included on the CD-ROM in the file javadevhkbk\ch12\serial\PersisTest.java.

LIST 12.1   *PersisTest.java*

```java
import java.awt.*;
import java.awt.event.*;
import java.io.*;
import java.util.Vector;


public class PersisTest extends Frame
implements MouseListener, ActionListener
{
    Vector      displayList;
    String      pathname;
    Button      clearBtn, saveBtn, restoreBtn, quitBtn;


    public static void main(String args[])
    {
        if (args.length == 0)
        {
            System.out.println("Usage: java PersisTest filename");
            System.exit(0);
```

```java
        }

        PersisTest that = new PersisTest(args[0]);
        that.show();
    }


    public PersisTest(String pathname)
    {
        this.pathname = pathname;
        displayList = new Vector();

        // Handle our own mouse clicks.
        addMouseListener(this);

        // Build the GUI. Make this object a listener for all actions.
        setLayout(new BorderLayout());
        Panel pan = new Panel();
        clearBtn = new Button("Clear");
        clearBtn.addActionListener(this);
        pan.add(clearBtn);
        saveBtn = new Button("Save");
        saveBtn.addActionListener(this);
        pan.add(saveBtn);
        restoreBtn = new Button("Restore");
        restoreBtn.addActionListener(this);
        pan.add(restoreBtn);
        quitBtn = new Button("Quit");
        quitBtn.addActionListener(this);
        pan.add(quitBtn);
        add("North", pan);
        setSize (350, 200);
    }


    public void paint(Graphics g)
    {
        // Clear to white.
        g.setColor(Color.white);
        g.fillRect(0, 0, getSize().width, getSize().height);

        // Traverse display list, drawing 1 rect for each 2 points
        // in the vector.
```

```java
        g.setColor(Color.black);
        int i = 0;
        while (i < displayList.size())
        {
            Point p0 = (Point)(displayList.elementAt(i++));
            Point p1 = (Point)(displayList.elementAt(i++));
            int x = Math.min(p0.x, p1.x);
            int y = Math.min(p0.y, p1.y);
            int w = Math.abs(p0.x - p1.x);
            int h = Math.abs(p0.y - p1.y);
            g.drawRect(x, y, w, h);
        }
    }


    public void mousePressed(MouseEvent e)
    {
        // Store x and y in display list vector.
        Point p = new Point(e.getX(), e.getY());
        displayList.addElement(p);
    }


    public void mouseReleased(MouseEvent e)
    {
        // Store x and y in display list vector, and request repaint.
        Point p = new Point(e.getX(), e.getY());
        displayList.addElement(p);
        repaint();
    }


    // Unused methods of MouseListener interface.
    public void mouseClicked(MouseEvent e) { }
    public void mouseEntered(MouseEvent e) { }
    public void mouseExited(MouseEvent e)  { }


    public void actionPerformed(ActionEvent e)
    {
        if (e.getSource() == clearBtn)
        {
            // Repaint with an empty display list.
            displayList = new Vector();
```

```
            repaint();
        }
        else if (e.getSource() == saveBtn)
        {
            // Write display list vector to an object output stream.
            try
            {
                FileOutputStream fos = new FileOutputStream(pathname);
                ObjectOutputStream oos = new ObjectOutputStream(fos);
                oos.writeObject(displayList);
                oos.flush();
                oos.close();
                fos.close();
            }
            catch (Exception ex)
            {
                System.out.println("Trouble writing display list vector");
            }
        }
        else if (e.getSource() == restoreBtn)
        {
            // Read a new display list vector from an object input stream.
            try
            {
                FileInputStream fis = new FileInputStream(pathname);
                ObjectInputStream ois = new ObjectInputStream(fis);
                displayList = (Vector)(ois.readObject());
                ois.close();
                fis.close();
                repaint();
            }
            catch (Exception ex)
            {
                System.out.println("Trouble reading display list vector");
            }
        }
        else if (e.getSource() == quitBtn)
        {
            setVisible(false);
            dispose();
            System.exit(0);
        }
    }
}
```

An Introduction to Remote Method Invocation

Java's Remote Method Invocation (RMI) feature enables a program in one JVM to make method calls on an object located in a different JVM, which could be running on a remote machine. The RMI feature gives Java programmers the ability to distribute computing across a networked environment. Object-oriented design requires that every task be executed by the object most appropriate to that task. RMI takes this concept one step further by allowing a task to be performed on the *machine* most appropriate to the task.

RMI defines a remote interface that can be used to create remote objects. A client can invoke the methods of a remote object with the same syntax that it uses to invoke methods on a local object. The RMI API provides classes and methods that handle all of the underlying communication and parameter referencing requirements of accessing remote methods. RMI also handles the serialization of objects that are passed as arguments to methods of remote objects.

The java.rmi and the java.rmi.server packages contain the interfaces and classes that define building blocks for creating server-side objects and client-side object stubs. A *stub* is a local representation of a remote object. The client makes calls to the stub, which automatically communicates with the server.

Object Persistence and RMI

When a Java program uses RMI, method parameters must be transmitted to the server and a return value must be sent back to the client. Primitive values can be simply sent byte by byte. However, passing objects, either as parameters or return values, requires a more sophisticated solution.

The remote object instance needs access to the entire graph of objects referenced by a parameter passed to its method. The remote method might construct and return a complicated object that holds references to other objects. If this is the case, the entire graph must be returned, so any object passed to or returned from a remote method must implement either the Serializable or the Externalizable interface.

NOTE   RMI is similar to the Remote Procedure Call (RPC) feature that Sun introduced in 1985. RPC also required a way to serialize parameter and return value data, although the situation was simpler because of the absence of objects. Sun developed a system called External Data Representation (XDR) to support data serialization. One significant difference between RPC and RMI is that RPC uses the fast but not very reliable UDP protocol; by default, RMI uses the slower but more reliable TCP/IP protocol. However, by implementing your own subclass of `java.rmi.server` `.RMISocketFactory`, you can choose to run RMI over other socket protocols.

The RMI Architecture

The RMI architecture consists of three layers: the stubs/skeleton layer, the remote reference layer, and the transport layer. The relationships among these layers are shown in Figure 12.1.

FIGURE 12.1:

An overview of the
RMI architecture

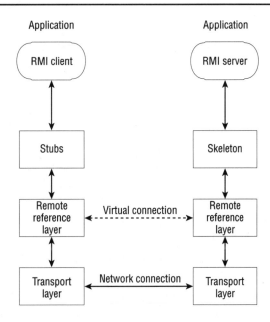

When a client invokes a remote method, the request starts at the top with the stub on the client side. The client references the stub as a proxy for the object on the remote machine; all the underlying functionality shown in Figure 12.1 is invisible to the client. The stub code is generated with the `rmic` compiler and uses the remote reference layer (RRL) to pass method invocation requests to the server object.

Stubs

The stub is the client-side proxy representing the remote object. Stubs define all of the interfaces that the remote object implementation supports. The stub is referenced like any other local object by a program running on the client machine. It is a local object on the client side; it also maintains a connection to the server-side object.

The RRL on the client side returns a *marshal stream* to the stub. The marshal stream is used by the RRL to communicate to the RRL on the server side. The stub serializes parameter data, passing the serialized data into the marshal stream.

After the remote method has been executed, the RRL passes any serialized return values back to the stub, which is responsible for deserializing.

The Skeleton

The skeleton is the server-side construct that interfaces with the server-side RRL. The skeleton receives method invocation requests from the client-side RRL. The server-side RRL must unmarshal any arguments that are sent to a remote method. The skeleton then makes a call to the actual object implementation on the server side. The skeleton is also responsible for receiving any return values from the remote object and marshaling them onto the marshal stream.

The RRL

The RRL is responsible for maintaining an independent reference protocol that is not specific to any stub or skeleton model. The RRL deals with the lower-level transport interface and is responsible for providing a stream to the stubs and skeleton layers.

The RRL uses a server-side and a client-side component to communicate via the transport layer. The client-side component contains information specific to the remote server. This information is passed to the server-side component and, therefore, is dependent only on the server-side RRL. The RRL on the server side is responsible for the reference semantics and deals with those semantics before delivering the RMI to the skeleton. The communication between client- and server-side components is handled by the transport layer.

The Transport Layer

The transport layer is responsible for creating and maintaining connections between the client and server. The transport layer consists of four abstractions:

- An *endpoint* is used to reference the address space that contains a JVM. An endpoint is a reference to a specific transport instance.

- A *channel* is the pathway between two address spaces. This channel is responsible for managing any connections from the client to the server and vice versa.

- A *connection* is an abstraction for transferring data (arguments and return values) between client and server.

- The *transport* abstraction is responsible for setting up a channel between a local address space and a remote endpoint. The transport abstraction is also responsible for accepting incoming connections to the address space containing the abstraction.

The transport layer sets up connections, manages existing connections, and handles remote objects residing in its address space.

When the transport layer receives a request from the client-side RRL, it establishes a socket connection to the server. Next, the transport layer passes the established connection to the client-side RRL and adds a reference to the remote object to an internal table. At this point, the client is connected to the server.

The transport layer monitors the "liveness" of the connection. If a significant amount of time passes with no activity on the connection, the transport layer is responsible for shutting down the connection. The timeout period is 10 minutes.

An RMI Example

Creating an application that is accessible to remote clients involves a number of steps:

1. Define interfaces for the remote classes.

2. Create and compile implementation classes for the remote classes.

3. Create stub and skeleton classes using the `rmic` command.

4. Create and compile a server application.

5. Start the `rmiregistry` and the server application.

6. Create and compile a client program to access the remote objects.

7. Test the client.

As an example of an RMI application, we will develop a simple credit card system. The server will support creating a new account, as well as performing transactions against an existing account. Because the intention of the example is to show you how to use RMI, there will not be a client-side user interface; the client will simply make a few hardcoded invocations.

The source code for this example, which is shown in the following sections, includes the following files:

- `CreditCard.java`

- `CreditManager.java`

- `CreditCardImpl.java`

- `CreditManagerImpl.java`

- `CardBank.java`

- `Shopper.java`

All of these files are also included on the CD-ROM in the directory javadevhdbk\ ch12\remote. (There are four trivial exception classes that appear on the CD-ROM but are not listed in the chapter; they extend `Exception` without adding new data or methods.)

Defining Interfaces for Remote Classes

The program will use two remote classes. The `CreditCardImpl` class will maintain the username, balance, available credit, and personal ID signature number for a single credit card account. The `CreditManagerImpl` class will maintain a list of `Account` objects and create new ones when necessary. The server-side application will construct a single instance of `CreditManagerImpl` and make it available to remote clients.

Each of these classes must be described by an interface: `CreditCard` and `CreditManager`. The client-side stubs will implement these interfaces. The stub classes will be created in a later step by the `rmic` utility. Note that `rmic` imposes several requirements: the interfaces must be public and extend the `Remote` interface; each method must throw `RemoteException`; and the stub and implementation code must reside in a package. The listings for `CreditCard` and `CreditManager` follow.

LIST 12.2   *CreditCard.java*

```java
package credit;

import credit.*;
import java.rmi.*;

public interface CreditCard extends java.rmi.Remote {

    /** This method returns a credit card's credit line. */
    public float getCreditLine() throws java.rmi.RemoteException;

    /** This method allows a card holder to pay all or some
        of a balance. Throws InvalidMoneyException if the
        money param is invalid. */
    public void payTowardsBalance(float money) throws
        java.rmi.RemoteException, InvalidMoneyException;

    /** This method allows the card holder to make purchases
        against the line of credit. Throws
        CreditLineExceededException
        if the purchase exceeds available credit. */
    public void makePurchase(float amount, int signature) throws
        java.rmi.RemoteException, InvalidSignatureException,
        CreditLineExceededException;

    /** This method sets the card's personal ID signature. */
    public void setSignature(int pin)throws java.rmi.RemoteException;
}
```

LIST 12.3   *CreditManager.java*

```java
package credit;

import credit.*;
import java.rmi.*;
import java.rmi.RemoteException;
```

```
public interface CreditManager extends java.rmi.Remote {

    /** This method finds an existing credit card for a given customer
        name. If the customer does not have an account, a new card will
        be "issued" with a random personal ID signature and a $5000
        starting credit line. */
    public CreditCard findCreditAccount(String Customer) throws
        DuplicateAccountException, java.rmi.RemoteException;


    /** This method creates a new credit account with a random
        personal ID signature and a $5000 starting credit line. */
    public CreditCard newCreditAccount(String newCustomer) throws
        java.rmi.RemoteException;
}
```

Creating and Compiling Implementation Classes

The implementation classes are server-side classes that implement the CreditCard and CreditManager interfaces.

The CreditCard interface is implemented by the CreditCardImpl class. This class must implement all of the methods in the CreditCard interface, and it must extend UnicastRemoteObject. To date, there is no support for multicast objects.

The interfaces and classes declare that they belong to the credit package. Each of the source files should be compiled with the -d <directoryname> option to specify a destination directory for the resulting .class files. Within the destination directory, the compiler will automatically create a subdirectory called credit (if one does not already exist), and then the class files will be created in the credit subdirectory. The destination directory supplied to the -d option should be in the class path. An easy way to compile the interfaces and classes is to create a "credit" directory; change directories to the credit directory, and compile the source, as follows:

```
cd credit
javac -d ..\. CreditCard.java
javac -d ..\. CreditCardImpl.java
javac -d ..\. CreditManager.java
javac -d ..\. CreditManagerImpl.java
```

The CreditManagerImpl class is responsible for creating and storing new accounts (as CreditImpl objects). This class uses a hashtable to store the account objects, keyed by owner name. The source code for the CreditCardImpl and CreditManagerImpl classes follows.

LIST 12.4   *CreditCardImpl.java*

```java
package credit;

import java.rmi.*;
import java.rmi.server.*;
import java.io.Serializable;

/** This class is the remote object that will referenced by the
    skeleton on the server side and the stub on the client side. */

public class CreditCardImpl
    extends UnicastRemoteObject
    implements CreditCard
  {
    private float currentBalance = 0;
    private float creditLine = 5000f;
    private int signature = 0;          // Like a PIN number
    private String accountName;         // Name of owner

    /** Class constructor generates an initial PIN.*/
    public CreditCardImpl(String customer) throws
    java.rmi.RemoteException, DuplicateAccountException {
        accountName = customer;
        signature = (int)(Math.random() * 10000);
    }

    /** Returns credit line. */
    public float getCreditLine() throws java.rmi.RemoteException {
        return creditLine;
    }

    /** Pays off some debt. */
    public void payTowardsBalance(float money) throws
    java.rmi.RemoteException, credit.InvalidMoneyException {
        if (money <= 0) {
            throw new InvalidMoneyException ();
```

```
        } else {
            currentBalance -= money;
        }
    }

    /** Changes signature. */
    public void setSignature(int pin) throws java.rmi.RemoteException {
        signature = pin;
    }

    /** Makes a purchase. Makes sure enough credit is available,
        then increments balance and decrements available credit. */
    public void makePurchase(float amount, int signature) throws
    java.rmi.RemoteException, credit.InvalidSignatureException,
    credit.CreditLineExceededException {
        if (signature != this.signature) {
            throw new InvalidSignatureException();
        }
        if (currentBalance+amount > creditLine) {
            throw new CreditLineExceededException();
        } else {
            currentBalance += amount;
            creditLine -= amount;
        }
    }
}
```

LIST 12.5　　　*CreditManagerImpl.java*

```
package credit;

import java.rmi.*;
import java.rmi.server.*;
import java.util.Hashtable;

public class CreditManagerImpl extends UnicastRemoteObject
implements CreditManager {
    private static transient Hashtable accounts = new Hashtable();

    /** This is the default class constructor that does nothing
        but implicitly calls super() which throws a RemoteException. */
    public CreditManagerImpl() throws RemoteException { }
```

```
/** Creates a new account. Puts the customer name and the customer's
    credit card in the hashtable. */
public CreditCard newCreditAccount(String customerName)
throws java.rmi.RemoteException {
    CreditCardImpl newCard = null;
    try {
        newCard = new CreditCardImpl(customerName);
    } catch (DuplicateAccountException e) {
        return null;
    }
    accounts.put(customerName, newCard);
    return newCard;
}

/** Searches the hashtable for an existing account. If no account
    for customer name, one is created and added to hashtable.
    Returns the account. */
public CreditCard findCreditAccount(String customer)
throws DuplicateAccountException, RemoteException {
    CreditCardImpl account = (CreditCardImpl)accounts.get(customer);
    if (account != null) {
        return account;
    }
    // Creates new account. Adds credit card to hashtable.
    account = new CreditCardImpl(customer);
    accounts.put(customer, account);
    return account;
}
}
```

Creating Stub and Skeleton Classes

Once the implementation classes are compiled, the next step is to create the stub and skeleton class files that are used to access the implementation classes. The stub classes are used by the client code to communicate with the server skeleton code.

The rmic command automatically creates stub and skeleton code from the interface and implementation class definitions. The syntax of the command is:

```
rmic [options] package.interfaceImpl ...
```

For our example, the following command creates the stubs and skeletons for the CreditCard and CreditManager remote classes:

```
rmic -d . credit.CreditCardImpl credit.CreditManagerImpl
```

Note that the command requires specification of the package in which the class files reside. This is why all the source modules for the implementation classes declare that they belong to the credit package.

The rmic command creates four class files in the credit package directory:

- CreditCardImpl_Skel.class

- CreditCardImpl_Stub.class

- CreditManagerImpl_Skel.class

- CreditManagerImpl_Stub.class

Creating and Compiling the Server Application

Now that the stubs and skeletons have been created, the next step is to create a server-side application that makes these classes available to clients for remote invocation.

The server-side application will be an application class called CardBank, whose main job is to construct an instance of CreditManager. Except for the line that calls the CreditManager constructor, all of the CardBank code involves making the Credit-Manager object available to remote clients. The details of this process are explained after the following code listing.

LIST 12.6   *CardBank.java*

```java
import java.util.*;
import java.rmi.*;
import java.rmi.RMISecurityManager;
import credit.*;

public class CardBank {

    public static void main (String args[]) {
        // Create and install a security manager.
        System.setSecurityManager(new RMISecurityManager());
```

```
    try {
        // Create an instance of our Credit Manager.
        System.out.println
            ("CreditManagerImpl: create a CreditManager");
        CreditManagerImpl cmi = new CreditManagerImpl();

        // Bind the object instance to the remote registry. Use the
        // static rebind() method to avoid conflicts.
        System.out.println("CreditManagerImpl: bind it to a name");
        Naming.rebind("cardManager", cmi);

        System.out.println("CreditManager is now ready");

    } catch (Exception e) {
        System.out.println("An error occured");
        e.printStackTrace();
        System.out.println(e.getMessage());
    }
  }
}
```

Applications, by default, run without security managers. In the main method of CardBank, the setSecurityManager() call installs an RMI security manager.

The server "publishes" an object instance by binding a specified name to the instance and registering that name with the RMI registry. There are two methods that allow an instance to be bound and registered:

```
public static void bind(String name, Remote obj) throws
AlreadyBoundException, MalformedUrlException, UnknownHostException,
RemoteException
```

```
public static void rebind(String name, Remote obj) throws
MalformedUrlException, UnknownHostException, RemoteException
```

Notice that both methods are static and ask for a name to reference the object, as well as the remote object instance that is bound to the name. In our example, the object name is cardManager. Any machine on the network can refer to this object by specifying the host machine and the object name.

The name argument required by both bind() and rebind() is a URL-like string. This string can be in this format:

protocol://*host*:*port*/*bindingName*

Here *protocol* is rmi, *host* is the name of the RMI server, *port* is the port number on which the server should listen for requests, and *bindingName* is the exact name that should be used by a client when requesting access to the object. If just a name is given in the string, then default values are used. The defaults are rmi for the protocol, localhost for the server name, and 1099 for the port number.

WARNING   An attempt to bind to any host other than the localhost will result in a SecurityException.

Both bind() and rebind() associate a name with an object. They differ in their behavior when the name being bound has already been bound to an object. In this case, bind() will throw AlreadyBoundException, and rebind() will discard the old binding and use the new one.

Starting the Registry and Server Application

The rmiregistry is an application that provides a simple naming lookup service. When the CardBank calls rebind(), it is the registry that maintains the binding. The registry can be run as an independent program or it can created by calling the java.rmi.registry.LocateRegistry.createRegistry method, and it must be running before the server-side application is invoked. The program resides in the jdk/bin directory.

The following two command lines invoke the registry and start up the card bank server:

```
start rmiregistry
java CardBank
```

The card bank application prints several status lines as it starts up the service. If there are no errors, you should see the following output:

```
CreditManagerImpl: create a CreditManager
CreditManagerImpl: bind it to a name
CreditManager is now ready
```

Once an object has been passed to the registry, a client may request that the registry provide a reference to the remote object. The next section shows how this is done.

Creating and Compiling the Client Program

The Shopper application needs to find a CreditManager object on the remote server. The program assumes that the server name has been passed in as the first command-line argument. This name is used to create a URL-like string of this format:

```
rmi://<hostname>/cardManager
```

The string is passed to the static lookup() method of the Naming class. The lookup() call communicates with the rmiregistry and returns a handle to the remote object that was constructed and registered. More accurately, what is returned is a handle to a stub that communicates with the remote object.

The return type from lookup() is Remote, which is the parent of all stub interfaces. When the return value is cast to type CreditManager, the methods of CreditManager can be invoked on it. The following sample code, titled Shopper.java, shows how this is done.

| LIST 12.7 | *Shopper.java* |

```java
import java.rmi.*;
import java.rmi.RMISecurityManager;
import credit.*;

public class Shopper {

    public static void main(String args[]) {

        CreditManager cm = null;
        CreditCard account = null;

        // Check the command line.
        if (args.length < 2) {
            System.err.println("Usage:");
            System.err.println("java Shopper <server> <account name>");
            System.exit (1);
        }

        // Create and install a security manager.
        System.setSecurityManager(new RMISecurityManager());

        // Obtain reference to card manager.
        try {
            String url = new String ("//" + args[0] + "/cardManager");
```

```java
            System.out.println ("Shopper: lookup cardManager, url = "
                                + url);
            cm = (CreditManager)Naming.lookup(url);
        } catch (Exception e) {
            System.out.println("Error in getting card manager" + e);
            System.exit (1);
        }


        // Get user's account.
        try {
            account = cm.findCreditAccount(args[1]);
            System.out.println ("Found account for " + args[1]);
        } catch (Exception e) {
            System.out.println("Error in getting account for " +
            args[1]);
            System.exit (1);
        }


        // Do some transactions.
        try {
            System.out.println("Available credit is: "
                               + account.getCreditLine());
            System.out.println("Changing pin number for account");
            account.setSignature(1234);
            System.out.println("Buying a new watch for $100");
            account.makePurchase(100.00f, 1234);
            System.out.println("Available credit is now: " +
                               account.getCreditLine());
            System.out.println("Buying a new pair of shoes for $160");
            account.makePurchase(160.00f, 1234);
            System.out.println("CardHolder: Paying off $136 of
            balance");
            account.payTowardsBalance(136.00f);
            System.out.println("Available credit is now: "+
                               account.getCreditLine());
        } catch (Exception e) {
            System.out.println("Transaction error for " + args[1]);
        }

        System.exit(0);
    }
}
```

The client expects two command-line arguments. The first argument specifies the server. (For testing on a single machine, specify localhost for the server name.) The second argument is a string that provides an account name. The client program asks the server-side credit manager object for a handle to the credit card object that represents this customer's account. (If the customer has no account yet, one will be created.) The initial random PIN number is modified to something a user will find easier to remember. The client program then makes several purchases and one payment, reporting the available credit after each transaction.

Testing the Client

The final step is to execute the client code. It can be run from any computer that has access to the server and to the supporting classes. Here is a sample session output on a Unix machine, with the remote service running on a host named sunbert (the first line is the invocation; the rest is output):

```
% java Shopper sunbert pogo
Shopper: lookup cardManager, url = //sunbert/cardManager
Found account for pogo
Available credit is: 5000.0
Changing pin number for account
Buying a new watch for $100
Available credit is now: 4900.0
Buying a new pair of shoes for $160
CardHolder: Paying off $136 of balance
Available credit is now: 4740.0
```

After the client program has finished running, the remote objects are still alive. The execution shown above created a new account for the customer. A second invocation of the client will work with that account; the available credit numbers in the listing below reflect the current state of the account:

```
% java Shopper sunbert pogo
Shopper: lookup cardManager, url = //sunbert/cardManager
Found account for pogo
Available credit is: 4740.0
Changing pin number for account
Buying a new watch for $100
Available credit is now: 4640.0
Buying a new pair of shoes for $160
CardHolder: Paying off $136 of balance
Available credit is now: 4480.0
```

Advanced RMI

So far, the examples shown in this chapter have just scratched the surface of what RMI has to offer. The RMI system released with JDK 1.1 demonstrated that it was poised to be a strong candidate for distributed Java systems; RMI in Java 2 proves that JavaSoft is not willing to let RMI be a flash in the pan.

Here are some of the new features in RMI, which we will explore in the following sections:

- The ability to perform callbacks

- Dynamic class loading

- Object activation, which allows a client to request a reference to a remote object that is not currently active in a JVM

TIP   The RMI in Java 2 also allows you to define and use a custom socket protocol. By subclassing the `RMISocketFactory` class, you can create your own network protocols, change the network protocol on a per-object basis, or make use of secure network protocols like SSL (Secure Socket Layer).

Callback Operations

The simple credit card system we developed in the previous section demonstrates a typical client/server application. The `CardBank` server creates an instance of a `CardManager` object and serves the instance of the object to the `Shopper` client using RMI. That example illustrates some of the underlying communications that RMI handles on the developer's behalf, like the creation and use of network sockets.

However, what that example does not show is that RMI is capable of providing two-way communications between objects. For an object's reference to be sent from one place to another, the object's class only needs to implement a `Remote` interface and be exported in order to receive remote method calls (by extending `UnicastRemoteObject`, an object is automatically exported).

Once these two requirements have been met, it is possible to send a remote object from a client to a server in such a way that the server is actually calling the remote methods of the client object. This is the nature of truly distributed applications: There is no distinction between "client" and "server"—each application provides or uses the services of another.

To demonstrate this concept with a practical example, we will extend the Credit application. In that example, the customer receives a credit line by simply passing his or her name to the CreditManager. In this example, the customer will fill out CreditApplication and send that application to the CreditManager. The Credit-Manager instance will use methods provided by a CreditApplication to fill in data that the customer can then validate for the final credit application.

In this example, the client creates a local instance of a CreditApplication object and passes a reference to that instance to the server through the CreditManager, obtained through the registry. The server executes methods on the Credit-Application reference using the same mechanism the client uses—the server holds a reference to a stub instance that forwards requests to the client's local object.

This example uses the code listed in the following sections, which is also included on the CD-ROM in the directory javadevhdbk\ch12\callback.

Creating the CreditApplication Object

The CreditApplication object is created in the same way as any other RMI remote object. The object's remote methods are defined in an interface class that extends java.rmi.Remote.

LIST 12.8   *CreditApplication.java*

```java
package credit;

import java.rmi.*;

public interface CreditApplication extends Remote {

    public String getCustName ()
    throws RemoteException;

    public void setCreditLine (float amount)
    throws RemoteException;

    public void setCreditCardNumber (String cardNumber)
    throws RemoteException;

}
```

Implementing CreditApplication

The `CreditApplicationImpl` object is an implementation of `CreditApplication` and provides bodies for each of the methods defined in the interface. In addition, `CreditApplicationImpl` defines the data that a credit application is expected to store. This class extends `UnicastRemoteObject` so that it is automatically exported upon creation, and it implements a remote interface, `CreditApplication`, so that it may be passed *by reference* to the server. For cases where a class cannot extend `UnicastRemoteObject`, the developer can explicitly export an object through the static method, `UnicastRemoteObject.exportObject`.

LIST 12.9   *CreditApplicationImpl.java*

```java
package credit;

import java.rmi.*;
import java.rmi.server.*;

public class CreditApplicationImpl extends UnicastRemoteObject
implements CreditApplication {

    private float creditLine;
    private float creditRate;
    private String creditCardNumber;
    private String custName;
    private String ssn;

    public CreditApplicationImpl (String name, String soc)
    throws RemoteException {
        custName = name;
        ssn = soc;
    }

    public String getCustName () {
        return custName;
    }

    public void setCreditLine (float amount) {
        creditLine = amount;
    }

    public float getCreditLine () {
        return creditLine;
    }
```

```
    public void setCreditCardNumber (String cardNumber) {
        creditCardNumber = new String (cardNumber);
    }

    public String getCreditCardNumber () {
        return creditCardNumber;
    }
}
```

Modifying CreditManager

The CreditManager interface is modified so that the CreditApplication object can be sent to the credit manager. If the customer's application is accepted, the customer will then be issued a valid CreditCard.

LIST 12.10   *CreditManager.java*

```
package credit;

import java.rmi.*;


public interface CreditManager extends java.rmi.Remote {

    /** This method finds an existing credit card for a
        given customer credit number. If the customer
        does not have an account, an InvalidAccountException
        is thrown. */
    public CreditCard findCreditAccount(String customer)
        throws InvalidAccountException, RemoteException;


    /** This method receives an CreditApplication object from
        the customer. On the customer's behalf the server will
        fill in the missing account number, initial credit line
        and rate. */
    public void applyForCard (CreditApplication app)
        throws DuplicateAccountException,
               AccountRejectedException, RemoteException;
}
```

Implementing CreditManager

The implementation of a CreditManager object is changed to reflect the new design. The CreditManagerImpl now uses a private method to create a credit account, which is called only if the customer's credit application is approved.

LIST 12.11   *CreditManagerImpl.java*

```java
package credit;

import java.rmi.*;
import java.rmi.server.*;
import java.util.Hashtable;

public class CreditManagerImpl extends UnicastRemoteObject
implements CreditManager {
    private static transient Hashtable accounts =
    new Hashtable();

    /** This is the default class constructor that does nothing
        but implicitly call super(). */
    public CreditManagerImpl() throws RemoteException { }

    /** Creates a new account. Puts the customer name and the
        customer's credit card in the hashtable. */
    private void newCreditAccount(String name, String cardNumber,
        float creditLine) throws DuplicateAccountException,
        RemoteException {
        CreditCardImpl newCard =
            new CreditCardImpl(name, cardNumber, creditLine);
        accounts.put(cardNumber, newCard);
    }

    /** Searches the hashtable for an existing account. If no
        account for customer name, an InvalidAccountException
        is thrown. */
    public CreditCard findCreditAccount(String cardNumber)
    throws InvalidAccountException, RemoteException {
        CreditCardImpl account =
            (CreditCardImpl)accounts.get(cardNumber);
        if (account != null) {
            return account;
        } else {
```

```
                      throw new InvalidAccountException ();
              }
      }

      /** The Account Manager will determine (based on the
          customer name and social security number) the credit line
          and credit rate. */

      public void applyForCard (CreditApplication app)
          throws DuplicateAccountException,
                  AccountRejectedException, RemoteException {

              // Here, some other process would determine the
              // customer's credit rating...
              // For now, we'll hardcode that number to 5000.
              app.setCreditLine (5000.0f);

              // Generate a credit card number the user can use.
              String cardNumber = app.getCustName() +
                  (int)(Math.random() * 10000);
              app.setCreditCardNumber (cardNumber);

              // Generate the customer credit card.
              newCreditAccount (app.getCustName(), cardNumber,
              5000.0f);
      }
  }
```

Modifying the Client

The client application is modified only slightly to include the step of applying for credit through a CreditApplication object.

LIST 12.12   *Customer.java*

```
import credit.*;
import java.rmi.*;

public class Customer {

    public static void main(String args[]) {
```

```
CreditManager cm = null;
CreditApplicationImpl cardApp = null;
CreditCard account = null;

// Check the command line.
if (args.length < 3) {
    System.err.println("Usage:");
    System.err.println("java Customer <server> <account
                        name> <social security number>");
    System.exit (1);
}

// Create and install a security manager.
System.setSecurityManager(new RMISecurityManager());

// Obtain reference to card manager.
try {
    String url = new String ("//" + args[0] +
    "/cardManager");
    System.out.println ("Shopper: lookup cardManager, url =
                        " + url);
    cm = (CreditManager)Naming.lookup(url);
} catch (Exception e) {
    System.out.println("Error in getting card manager" +
    e);
    System.exit(1);
}

// Apply for a credit card.

// Create an instance of a credit card application.

// Send the credit application to the Credit Manager.
try {
    cardApp = new CreditApplicationImpl(args[1],args[2]);
    cm.applyForCard (cardApp);
} catch (DuplicateAccountException e) {
    System.out.println ("Duplicate Exception applying for
                        credit");
    System.exit (1);
} catch (AccountRejectedException e) {
    System.out.println ("Reject Exception applying for credit");
    System.exit (1);
```

```java
} catch (RemoteException e) {
    System.out.println ("Remote Exception applying for
                        credit " + e);
    System.exit (1);
}


// The application was accepted, let's use the new card!
try {

    System.out.println ("New credit card number is: " +
    cardApp.getCreditCardNumber() + " with a credit line of: " +
    cardApp.getCreditLine());
    account =
    cm.findCreditAccount(cardApp.getCreditCardNumber());
    System.out.println ("Found account: " +
        cardApp.getCreditCardNumber());
} catch (Exception e) {
    System.out.println("Error in getting account for " +
    args[1]);
    System.exit(1);
}


// Do some transactions.
try {
    System.out.println("Available credit is: "
                        + account.getCreditLine());
    System.out.println("Changing pin number for account");
    account.setSignature(1234);
    System.out.println("Buying a new watch for $100");
    account.makePurchase(100.00f, 1234);
    System.out.println("Available credit is now: " +
                        account.getCreditLine());
    System.out.println("Buying a new pair of shoes for $160");
    account.makePurchase(160.00f, 1234);
    System.out.println("CardHolder: Paying off $136 of balance");
    account.payTowardsBalance(136.00f);
    System.out.println("Available credit is now: "+
                        account.getCreditLine());
} catch (Exception e) {
    System.out.println("Transaction error for " +
    args[1]);
```

```
        }

        System.exit(0);
    }
}
```

All that remains is to run `rmic` on the client-side `CreditApplicationImpl` class. The `rmic` utility creates a set of stub classes that the server will use as proxies to the implementation class.

Dynamic Class Loading

One of the primary features of RMI is that it has been designed from the ground up as a Java-to-Java distributed object system. RMI is distinct from other systems such as CORBA (discussed in the next chapter) in that it is possible to send a complete object from one remote address space to another. This feature makes it possible to not only pass data over the network, but also to pass behavior—complete class definitions can be passed using the magic of the `RMIClassLoader` and serialization. RMI makes it easy to send a full object graph by passing an object as the argument to a method call. The only requirement for passing an object is that the object be serializable.

How is this useful? Passing an object to another address space makes it possible to use the resources of that address space—CPU cycles, files, database access, and so on. If the type of computation required by the object is complex, sending it from a slower machine to a faster machine is worth the overhead of transferring the object over the network.

NOTE By default, the RMI system communicates between remote address spaces using a custom protocol (the Java Remote Method Protocol) over a standard TCP/IP protocol. In March 1998, at JavaOne, JavaSoft demonstrated an implementation of the Internet-Inter ORB Protocol (IIOP) for RMI. This feature should be available soon.

As an example of dynamic class loading, we will continue the bank paradigm of the previous examples and apply RMI to the process of obtaining a loan. Although this example is by no means computation-intensive and could be easily executed locally, the example demonstrates the mechanics of sending an object from one address space to another.

In the example, the client and server both share the definition of an abstract class called LoanType. The LoanType class defines the `calculatePayment()` method, which returns a LoanType object. On the client side, a subclass of LoanType defines what the `calculatePayment` method should do.

The client application requests a reference to a LoanOfficer class, then sends an instance of a LoanType object to the LoanOfficer.processLoan method. This method executes the `calculatePayment` method of the object passed and returns an instance of a LoanType object.

NOTE   The `LoanOfficer` doesn't know in advance what code it is going to run. It depends on which subtype of **LoanType** it receives.

Although this looks a little like the callback presented in the previous section, in this example, the server application must recreate (through class loading and serialization) an instance of the object passed as a LoanType object before executing the method. The server is working on a copy of the client's LoanType.

NOTE   Both the callback mechanism and the dynamic class loading mechanism are triggered by passing objects as arguments to remote methods. The key difference between passing a remote reference (which contains a stub instance) used in a callback versus the serialized instance of an object, is whether or not the object being passed implements the **java.rmi.Remote** interface. If an object implements a remote interface, its stub is serialized; otherwise, the object instance is serialized.

    The loan-processing example uses the code presented in the following sections, which is also included on the CD-ROM in the directory javadevhdbk\ch12\dynamic.

Defining the LoanType Class

The LoanType class is abstract (as opposed to the interfaces used so far) because many different types of loans could have similar data and methods, differing only in how the interest and monthly payment are calculated (for example, an adjustable rate mortgage or a balloon payment).

LIST 12.13   *LoanType.java*

```java
package bank.loan;
import java.io.Serializable;

public abstract class LoanType implements Serializable {

    private float monthlyPayment,interestRate;
    private int loanAmount, loanDuration;

    // This method is executed by the server on behalf of
    // the client.
    public abstract void calculatePayment();

    public LoanType(int amount, float rate, int term)
    {
        loanAmount=amount;
        interestRate=rate;
        loanDuration=term;
    }

    public void setMonthlyPayment(float payment)
    {
        monthlyPayment = payment;
    }

    public float getMonthlyPayment()
    {
        return monthlyPayment;
    }

    public int getLoanAmount()
    {
        return loanAmount;
    }

    public float getInterestRate()
    {
        return interestRate;
    }

    public int getLoanDuration()
```

```
    {
        return loanDuration;
    }

}
```

Defining the ConventionalLoan Class

The client defines an instance of a LoanType object by extending the abstract class and providing a method body for calculatePayment. This class, ConventionalLoan, calculates the monthly payment for conventional mortgages.

ConventionalLoan.java

```java
package bank.loan;

public class ConventionalLoan extends LoanType {

    public ConventionalLoan(int amount, float rate, int term)
    {
        super(amount, rate, term);
    }

    public void calculatePayment()
    {
        // convert the interest rate to decimal percentage
        float interestRate = getInterestRate()/100;

        // calculate the monthly interest rate
        float monthlyInterestRate = interestRate/12;

        // convert the duration of the loan from years in to
        // months
        int numberOfMonths = getLoanDuration() * 12;

        float pmt = (float)(getLoanAmount()*(monthlyInterestRate/
        (1 - Math.pow((1 + monthlyInterestRate), -numberOfMonths))));

        setMonthlyPayment(pmt);
    }

}
```

Creating the LoanOfficer Interface

The client requests a reference to a LoanOfficer instance from the server application. The LoanOfficer interface defines the processLoan method, which takes a single LoanType argument and returns a LoanType object, from which the client may extract the monthly payment amount.

LIST 12.15   *LoanOfficer.java*

```
package bank.loan;

import java.rmi.Remote;
import java.rmi.RemoteException;

public interface LoanOfficer extends Remote
{
    public LoanType processLoan(LoanType loan) throws RemoteException;
}
```

Implementing LoanOffice

The implementation of the LoanOfficer interface provides a method body for processLoan, which executes the calculatePayment method of the object passed.

LIST 12.16   *LoanOfficerImpl.java*

```
package bank.loan;

import java.rmi.Remote;
import java.rmi.RemoteException;
import java.rmi.server.UnicastRemoteObject;

public class LoanOfficerImpl extends UnicastRemoteObject
    implements LoanOfficer {

    public LoanOfficerImpl() throws RemoteException
    {
    }
```

```
    public LoanType processLoan(LoanType loan) throws RemoteException
    {
        loan.calculatePayment();
        return loan;
    }

}
```

Setting Up the Server

Finally, the server application creates an instance of a LoanOfficerImpl object and registers the implementation with the rmiregistry.

LIST 12.17   *Lender.java*

```
import java.rmi.Naming;
import java.rmi.RemoteException;
import java.rmi.RMISecurityManager;
import bank.loan.*;

public class Lender {

    public static void main (String args[]) {
        // Create and install a security manager.
        System.setSecurityManager(new RMISecurityManager());

        try {
            // Create an instance of our loan officer.
            System.out.println("Lender: create a LoanOfficer");
            LoanOfficerImpl loi = new LoanOfficerImpl();

            // Bind the object instance to the remote registry.
            // Use the static rebind() method to avoid conflicts.
            System.out.println("Lender: bind the LoanOfficer to a
                            name");
            Naming.rebind("loanOfficer", loi);

            System.out.println("The LoanOfficer is ready to process
                            requests");
```

```
        } catch (Exception e) {
            e.printStackTrace();
            System.out.println(e.getMessage());
        }
    }
}
```

Setting Up the Client

The client application creates an instance of ConventionalLoan, then obtains a remote reference to a LoanOfficer object and passes the instance of the ConventionalLoan to LoanOfficer through the processLoan method. First, the LoanOfficerImpl will look in its CLASSPATH for the class file. When the class is not found, it will use the URL supplied in the object's serialized form. This URL would have been set from the client's command line, via the java.rmi.server.codebase property. If the server cannot load the ConventionalLoan class from the client-supplied URL, it will fail with a ClassNotFoundException.

The client application takes four arguments: the hostname of the server, the amount of the loan, the annual percentage rate (as a float), and the number of years for the life of the loan.

LIST 12.18	***ConventionalLoanClient.java***

```
import java.rmi.Naming;
import java.rmi.RemoteException;
import java.rmi.RMISecurityManager;
import bank.loan.*;

public class ConventionalLoanClient {

    public static void main(String [] args) throws Exception {

        LoanOfficer officer;
        ConventionalLoan conv;

        // Check the command line.
        if (args.length < 4) {
            System.err.println("Usage:");
            System.err.println("java ConventionalLoanClient <server>
                                " +
```

```java
                          "<mortgage amount> <interest rate> " +
                              "<number of years>");
                System.exit (1);
        }
        int amount = Integer.parseInt(args[1]);
        float rate = (new Float(args[2])).floatValue();
        int length = Integer.parseInt(args[3]);

        // Create a new loan instance.
        conv = new ConventionalLoan(amount, rate, length);

            // Create and install a security manager.
            System.setSecurityManager(new RMISecurityManager());

            // Obtain reference to loan officer.
            try {
                String url = new String ("//" + args[0] + "/loanOfficer");
                System.out.println ("Conventional Client: lookup
                                        loanOfficer, " +
                    "url = " + url);
                officer = (LoanOfficer)Naming.lookup(url);
            } catch (Exception e) {
                System.err.println("Error in getting loan officer " + e);
            throw e;
                System.exit(1);
    }

        // Get the monthly payment.
            try {
            // Use the existing reference to get back
            // the changed instance information.
            conv = (ConventionalLoan)officer.processLoan(conv);
            System.out.println("Your monthly payment will be " +
                    conv.getMonthlyPayment());
        } catch (Exception e1) {
                System.err.println("Error in processing loan " + e1);
            throw e1;
            }

        }
    }
```

Running the Loan-Processing Application

So far, the examples illustrated in this chapter have made use of two (or three, if you count the rmiregistry) JVMs running on the same host with the same CLASS-PATH variable set. For this example, in order to illustrate that the classes are actually loaded over the network, the rmiregistry, server, and client will be isolated from each other through three steps:

- The server classes (including the stub classes created by rmic) will not be physically located in the same directory as the client application.

- The client class to be uploaded to the server (ConventionalLoan) will not be in the same directory as the server.

- The registry will be completely isolated from both the client and the server.

In order to load classes dynamically, the client and server applications must create and install an instance of an RMISecurityManager, because the RMIClass-Loader requires that a security manager be installed. Furthermore, the client and server must declare the URL path to the classes that they are "serving" in order for applications running in other JVMs to find these classes. The server will be "serving" the stub class for the LoanOfficerImpl, and the client will be "serving" the ConventionalLoan class definition.

To prove that the client's ConventionalLoan class and the server's stub classes are actually transferred between JVMs, do not set the CLASSPATH variable and start the rmiregistry in a directory isolated from the client and server.

WARNING   If the rmiregistry can find the class definitions locally, it will ignore the java.rmi.server.codebase property set from the command line. This is a problem because other JVMs will not be able to download the class definitions.

From the command line, enter:

C:\> **start rmiregistry**

Start the server application from the server directory—again, without setting the CLASSPATH variable. The server must let the registry and the client know where to load classes that are being made available by the server, so set the java.rmi.server.codebase property. From the command line, type:

C:\RMI\agent\server> **java
-Djava.rmi.server.codebase=file:/RMI/agent/server/ bank.loan.Lender**

NOTE   The `java.rmi.server.codebase` property requires forward slashes to separate the directory names (of the path), and there must be a trailing slash on the last directory.

The output from the server looks like this:

```
Lender: create a LoanOfficer
Lender: bind the LoanOfficer to a name
The LoanOfficer is ready to process requests
```

Start the client application from the client directory—again, do not set the CLASSPATH variable. The client must let the server know where the ConventionalLoan class is located, so the client application also sets its codebase property:

C:\RMI\agent\client> **java
-Djava.rmi.server.codebase=file:/RMI/agent/client/ bank.loan
.ConventionalLoanClient gus 250000 7.25 30**

This example shows a $250,000 mortgage at an annual percentage rate of 7¼ for 30 years, on a server named "gus."

Object Activation

In previous versions of RMI, in order to obtain a reference to a remote object, the server that generated the instance of the object had to be running (live) in a JVM. This simple mechanism is sufficient for most applications. However, for large systems that create a number of objects that are not used at the same time (or some objects that are not used at all), it is useful to have a mechanism to suspend those objects until they are needed.

The activation mechanism in Java 2 provides this facility. Activation allows a Java object to be bound (named by the registry) and then "activated" at some later date simply by referencing the object through the registry. One of the primary benefits to this approach is that the application that creates the instance of the remote object can terminate or exit normally before the object is ever used. The ability to activate remote objects on request allows RMI system designers much greater flexibility in designing smaller "servers." In order to make activation work, the RMI team created another daemon process, the Java RMI Activation System Daemon (`rmid`).

The process of finding an object reference is illustrated in Figure 12.2.

FIGURE 12.2:

Object activation in RMI

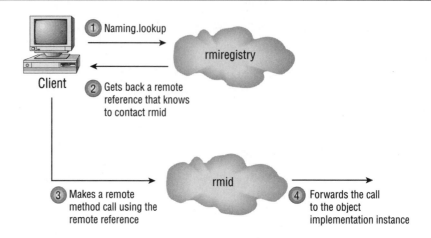

1. Naming.lookup

Client

2. Gets back a remote reference that knows to contact rmid

3. Makes a remote method call using the remote reference

4. Forwards the call to the object implementation instance

The rmid process must be run first, through the command line:

C:\> **start rmid**

By default, rmid will start on port number 1098 (rmiregistry is on port 1099), but you can specify an alternate port:

C:\> **start rmid -port 2001**

To demonstrate the object activation feature, we will extend the loan-processing example presented in the previous section by activating LoanOfficer to approve the mortgage loan application.

The client side of this example is just like any other RMI client class, since the client requests a remote reference and has no idea that the object is activatable or running as a standard UnicastRemoteObject. The "server" side however is very different, since the server must register the activatable object with the activation system before it terminates.

The extended loan-processing example uses the code presented in the following sections, which is also included on the CD-ROM in the directory javadevhdbk\ch12\activation.

NOTE Since the server is not run again when the object is activated, the term "server" does not really apply, and thus the RMI team came up with the term *setup*, which better defines what the activation application does before it exits.

Modifying LoanOfficer

To simplify the example and focus on the elements that make an object activatable, the `LoanOfficer` interface now defines a single method—`isApproved`—which takes a single argument—a `LoanApplication` object—and returns a boolean result.

LIST 12.19	*LoanOfficer.java*

```
package bank.loan;

import java.rmi.Remote;
import java.rmi.RemoteException;

public interface LoanOfficer extends Remote
{
    public boolean isApproved(LoanApplication app)
        throws RemoteException;
}
```

Implementing LoanOfficer and Extending Activatable

The `LoanOfficerImpl` class implements the `LoanOfficer` interface and extends the `Activatable` class instead of `UnicastRemoteObject`. Note that there is an additional constructor that could be defined for an `Activatable` class, but this one constructor is all that is necessary for this example.

Like the `UnicastRemoteObject` examples seen earlier, an `Activatable` class needs only to implement a remote interface and to be exported to accept incoming method requests. By extending `java.rmi.activation.Activatable`, the `LoanOfficerImpl` class is exported automatically upon construction, but any class (except those that extend `UnicastRemoteObject` or `Activatable`) may be exported by using the static method, `Activatable.exportObject`, as long as it directly or indirectly implements `java.rmi.Remote`.

LIST 12.20	*LoanOfficerImpl.java*

```
package bank.loan;

import java.rmi.activation.Activatable;
import java.rmi.activation.ActivationID;
import java.rmi.MarshalledObject;
```

```java
import java.rmi.Remote;
import java.rmi.RemoteException;

public class LoanOfficerImpl extends Activatable
    implements LoanOfficer {

    public LoanOfficerImpl(ActivationID id, MarshalledObject data)
        throws RemoteException {

        // Register the LoanOfficerImpl with the activation
        // daemon and "export" it on an anonymous port.
        super(id, 0);
    }

    public boolean isApproved(LoanApplication app)
        throws RemoteException
    {
        // Here, some other process would determine whether the
        // customer was approved for the loan.
        // For now, we'll let everyone be approved!
        return true;
    }

}
```

Creating the Activation Setup Class

The setup class, a rewritten Lender class, is a bit more complex than the server class for a UnicastRemoteObject; however, it is likely that this mechanism will be simplified in future releases.

The Lender creates an instance of a URL object that represents the location of the activatable class, LoanOfficerImpl. An ActivationGroupID is passed to the ActivationDesc object, which is registered with rmid. Each new JVM that is started by rmid will activate objects for only a single ActivationGroupID. If a JVM is already running that is associated with this class's ActivationGroupID, then this object will be created in that JVM rather than starting a new JVM. The ActivationGroupID gives greater control over which JVM the activated object runs in.

Next, the static method Activatable.register passes the ActivationDesc up to rmid. The activation group descriptor is all the information that rmid will need to create an instance of the Activatable class. The Activatable.register method returns a remote reference that is then used to register the `Activatable` class with the `rmiregistry`. The setup class, `Lender`, then explicitly exits with `System.exit`.

| **LIST 12.21** | ***Lender.java*** |

```
import java.net.URL;
import java.rmi.activation.Activatable;
import java.rmi.activation.ActivationDesc;
import java.rmi.activation.ActivationGroup;
import java.rmi.activation.ActivationGroupDesc;
import java.rmi.activation.ActivationGroupID;
import java.rmi.MarshalledObject;
import java.rmi.Naming;
import java.rmi.RemoteException;
import java.rmi.RMISecurityManager;
import java.security.CodeSource;
import java.security.PublicKey;
import java.util.Properties;
import bank.loan.*;

public class Lender {

    public static void main (String args[]) {
        if (args.length < 1) {
            System.out.println ("Usage: java bank.loan.Lender
                                 <absolute path to class files>");
            System.exit (0);
        }
        //  Create and install a security manager.
        System.setSecurityManager(new RMISecurityManager());

        try {
            // Create an instance of our loan officer.
            System.out.println("Lender: create a LoanOfficer");

            URL whereTheClassFileIs = new
                URL("file:"+args[0]+"/");

          // These are required for Java 2 Beta 3
            PublicKey [] mySecurity = null;
            CodeSource directions =
                new CodeSource(whereTheClassFileIs, mySecurity);
```

```
    Properties env =
    (Properties)System.getProperties().clone();
    ActivationGroupID groupID =
        ActivationGroup.getSystem().registerGroup(
        new ActivationGroupDesc(env));

// Marshaled object is typically used to tell the activated
// object where to find its persistent data.
// Right here it is unused, but required for the
// ActivationDesc
    MarshalledObject commandLineInfo = null;
    ActivationDesc ad =
        new ActivationDesc(groupID, "bank.loan.
                                LoanOfficerImpl",
            directions, commandLineInfo);

// Register the activatable class with rmid.
LoanOfficer lo = (LoanOfficer)Activatable.register(ad);
    System.out.println("Registered with rmid");

    // Bind the object instance to the remote registry. Use the
    // static rebind() method to avoid conflicts.
    System.out.println("Lender: bind the LoanOfficer to a
                            name");
    Naming.rebind("loanOfficer", lo);

    System.out.println("The LoanOfficer is ready to process
                            requests");

} catch (Exception e) {
    e.printStackTrace();
    System.out.println(e.getMessage());
}

// The work is done, now exit the program.
System.exit(0);
    }
}
```

On the client, the LoanApplication object is passed to the LoanOfficer object. The LoanApplication is a simple class that is constructed with the customer's social security number and the loan amount.

LIST 12.22   *LoanApplication.java*

```
package bank.loan;

public class LoanApplication implements java.io.Serializable {

    private String ssn;
    private int loanAmount;

    public LoanApplication(String loanInfo, int amount) {

    ssn = loanInfo;
    loanAmount = amount;
    }

    public String getApplicant() {
    return ssn;
    }

    public int getRequestedAmount() {
    return loanAmount;
    }
}
```

The client creates an instance of a LoanApplication and requests a LoanOfficer reference from the registry.

LIST 12.23   *LoanClient.java*

```
import java.rmi.Naming;
import java.rmi.RemoteException;
import java.rmi.RMISecurityManager;
import bank.loan.*;

public class LoanClient {

    public static void main(String [] args) throws Exception {

        LoanOfficer officer;
        LoanApplication app;

        // Check the command line.
```

```
    if (args.length < 3) {
        System.err.println("Usage:");
        System.err.println("java LoanClient <server> " +
                "<social security number> <mortgage amount>");
        System.exit (1);
    }
String applicant = args[1];
int loanAmount = Integer.parseInt(args[2]);

// Create the LoanApplication instance.
app = new LoanApplication(applicant, loanAmount);

    // Create and install a security manager.
    System.setSecurityManager(new RMISecurityManager());

    // Obtain reference to loan officer.
    try {
        String url = new String ("rmi://" + args[0] + "
                                /loanOfficer");
        System.out.println ("LoanClient: lookup loanOfficer, " +
            "url = " + url);
        officer = (LoanOfficer)Naming.lookup(url);
    } catch (Exception e) {
        System.err.println("Error in getting loan officer " + e);
        throw e;
    }

    // Get the loan approval.
    try {
        boolean approved = officer.isApproved(app);
        System.out.print("Your request for " + loanAmount +
                        " was ");
        if (!approved) {
            System.out.print("not ");
        }
        System.out.println("approved!");

    } catch (Exception e1) {
        System.err.println("Error in processing loan " + e1);
        throw e1;
```

```
            }

        System.exit(0);
    }
}
```

The registry looks up the `LoanOfficer` object that was registered by the setup application and returns to the client a remote reference that contacts `rmid` to create an instance of the class.

Summary

Java's persistent object support provides a very useful facility for storing and reconstituting objects. This feature is valuable in its own right; moreover, it plays an essential role in remote object invocation by providing a Java-standard protocol for reading and writing object data to and from I/O streams. While successful RMI programming involves a number of steps, the individual steps are not difficult. The examples presented in this chapter provide a template for your own development efforts.

While RMI is constantly compared to CORBA as a distributed object technology, it is important to bear in mind that RMI is capable of sending a full object data graph from one remote JVM to another. This is a feature that is not available in standard CORBA implementations. Furthermore, RMI systems are becoming more widely integrated as customers find that RMI is easier to develop and understand than CORBA. With the addition of activation and the future integration of the IIOP protocol, RMI is well positioned to continue as an inexpensive and powerful tool for creating object frameworks.

The next chapter discusses CORBA, IIOP, and Java IDL in detail.

Java IDL and CORBA Connectivity

- Heterogeneous environment problems

- An introduction to CORBA

- An introduction to IDL

- CORBA service development

- Mapping language from IDL to Java

- Legacy code wrapping

Java IDL, which was introduced with release 1.2 of the JDK, provides an implementation of the CORBA 2.0 (Common Object Request Broker Architecture) specification. CORBA is a distributed framework designed to support heterogeneous architectures. With CORBA, it is possible to connect two systems that differ not only in their hardware (CPU and memory), but also in their operating systems and programming languages.

This chapter begins with a discussion of the problem that CORBA was designed to solve. Then it covers the CORBA components and IDL, and examines how to develop CORBA services. After the examples, we'll go into some of the details of IDL-to Java language mapping. Finally, we'll describe how legacy code wrapping works.

The Compatibility Problem

CORBA was created to solve a common problem for most large companies. This problem is that there are different computer systems at work within the company. For example, the graphics department may have Macintoshes running MacOS, the engineering department may have Sun workstations running Solaris, and management may have PCs running either Windows 95 or NT. In addition to these systems, a large mainframe may run a proprietary operating system that is central to the operation of the company.

Traditionally, computer manufacturers have attempted to solve the compatibility problem of a heterogeneous environment by creating a line of products that reaches into all areas of a company's business. For example, a single vendor may offer a low-end system, a graphics system, and a high-end server system. This can sometimes solve the problem of compatibility, but it also is costly and leads to vendor dependence; the company must commit to spending more money on a single vendor's solution.

A Heterogeneous Environment Case Study

In order to understand why companies frequently have heterogeneous environments, let's consider the case of a fictional book publishing company, Sullivan Publishing.

Since the early 1900s, Sullivan Publishing has printed and bound books, all by hand. The initial "plant" was little more than a small warehouse with several bulky manual printing presses and a leather-cutting table for the book covers.

Over the next 70 years, the business grew, so Sullivan Publishing moved into larger quarters and bought automatic printing presses and binding machines. As the company grew, so did the quantity of data associated with book inventories and production and marketing costs. In order to remain competitive, the company needed an information system that would support its manufacturing and inventory goals.

The Mainframe's Role

During the 1970s and 1980s, the company purchased a large mainframe computer and hired a group of programmers to write and maintain programs to translate the publisher's business process into computer applications:

- Management used programs to produce reports that could be used to evaluate the information compiled by the computer and to make decisions based on that information.

- The production group used programs to track the costs of raw goods and to decide when to buy quality products from paper and ink dealers, so inventory did not sit idle on shelves for too long.

- The marketing group used programs to analyze readership trends and to ensure that specific target markets were not missed.

- The graphics department created programs that helped the designers standardize logos and product branding, and used other programs to produce the books' cover artwork.

It is important to note that the *purpose* of the mainframe computer was to provide the decision-makers in the company with tools to maintain and expand the business. The computer, the operating system, and the programming language(s) used to develop the programs were irrelevant to the real purpose of the system, which was to make more money for Sullivan Publishing.

The Evolution of the PC and the Network

As time went on, two events in the evolution of computer technology brought changes to Sullivan Publishing's computer system. The first event was the evolution of the PC as an inexpensive business computer. The PC made it possible for a single department within the company to make relatively small purchases (compared to the mainframe) of computer equipment that would have no impact on the mainframe environment. The local PC resources provided an attractive alternative to the terminals attached to the mainframe—more programs, better performance, local storage, and better games!

The second evolution was the network, which allowed companies to tie their different computer resources together and to share files and data. The network was technically capable of connecting disparate systems because the protocols for the network were designed as standards, independent of a computer's hardware or operating system. This is important because without the network, there is no concept of a distributed software architecture. Figure 13.1 illustrates Sullivan Publishing's network.

FIGURE 13.1:

The network of Sullivan Publishing company (our hypothetical example)

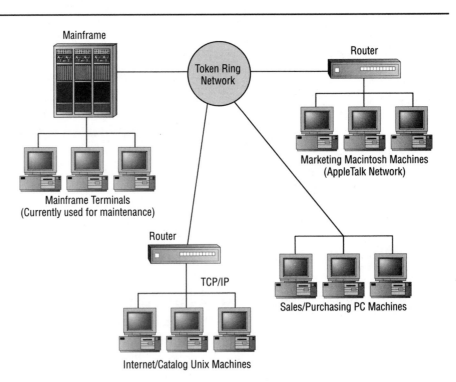

Unfortunately, the dream of sharing information between different systems proved difficult and expensive to implement. Programs could share data only if the data was properly formatted to the computing environment that used it. Computer companies were not interested in the data needs of a printing company, and they developed standards for data formats suited for their own hardware and operating systems. Thus, data and files from the mainframe word processor were incompatible with the word processing programs on the PCs.

Modern Challenges

So now we come to the challenges of the late 1990s. First, the company's managers would like all of their computers to seamlessly be able to share information. Second, they would like to offer an online buying service.

Sullivan Publishing has evaluated several alternative proposals from a variety of computer vendors. Each vendor promises to integrate the company's business onto a single platform that would make the computers work together as a system again. However, each vendor's proposal involves significant rewriting of the existing code base in addition to the purchase of new hardware.

Migration to the Network-Centric Model

The dilemma of the hypothetical publishing company is very common in many real companies, although perhaps not as severe. The short-term costs of a migration to a desktop-centric computing model are lower than the initial mainframe costs, but such a solution leads to incompatibilities between systems because they are heterogeneous in nature.

What companies with heterogeneous systems would really like to do is invest in a new software framework that allows them to leave the existing hardware intact and migrate existing software toward a network-centric model, where each computer system is part of the overall business system. Companies want to move applications and systems toward a central model that emphasizes a common look at the business application, regardless of the operating system and programming language the application requires.

Furthermore, companies would like to be able to use the current "legacy" code in its current state, until all of the code can be understood, documented, and rewritten for more modern hardware.

An Overview of CORBA

Several years ago, a group of engineers decided to form a consortium of their respective companies and design a reusable "system" that would enable multiple programming and operating system environments to work together. These engineers formed the Object Management Group (OMG). Working together, the OMG members have developed several hundred pages of specifications that define a framework of reusable components. The specification covers the architectural elements that are required to allow one hardware and software system to communicate with another. The OMG is now a consortium of more than 800 companies, and CORBA is the framework that is the result of their work.

A *framework* is a reusable collection of code that is almost "ready-to-use," which means that with some customization, it can be applied to specific implementations. The CORBA framework is designed to make communication between remote address spaces easier to implement. The primary goal of CORBA is to provide software developers with a means for developing systems that do not rely on a single operating system, programming language, or even hardware architecture.

CORBA by itself is not a product that you can buy from a store. The CORBA standard defines how companies can create implementations of the standard. You can purchase implementations from companies like Iona Technologies and Visigenic (now part of Borland).

A CORBA implementation is composed of several pieces, depending on the vendor's individual application of each standard. A typical CORBA vendor will supply the following components:

- An Object Request Broker (ORB) implementation

- An Interface Definition Language (IDL) compiler

- One or more implementations of Common Object Services (COS), also known as CORBAServices

- Common Frameworks, also known as CORBAFacilities

The Object Request Broker (ORB)

The primary mechanism for connecting objects in different address spaces is a function of the ORB. You can consider the ORB to be an object bus or object pathway. When two CORBA systems wish to communicate between different address spaces, the ORB takes care of making sure that regardless of the hardware, operating system, and software development language used, the remote object invocations will succeed. Figure 13.2 illustrates how an ORB connects objects between a client and a server.

FIGURE 13.2:

ORB communication

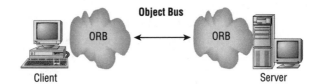

Typically, an ORB is implemented in one of two ways:

- As a "library" of objects that form an extension of the CORBA runtime

- As a daemon process

In either case, the ORB is responsible for establishing communications with the remote system, marshaling parameters to make remote calls, and managing concurrency of simultaneous requests from multiple clients.

Common Object Services (COS) and Common Frameworks

The ORB does not make up the entire CORBA implementation. Common Object Services such as the following are developed to assist the ORB:

- The Naming Service provides a way for CORBA clients to find objects on the network. An implementation server registers an object with a Naming Service using a hierarchical representation similar to a path used by a filename. Clients can request a reference to the object by name, using the Naming Service.

- The Event Service allows a client or server to send a message in the form of an event object to one or more receivers. Objects can request to listen to a specific event channel, and the Event Service will notify them of an event on that channel. The Event Service will store events before delivering them, so that clients and servers do not need to be connected.

- The Security Service provides a means to authenticate messages, authorize access to objects, and provide secure communications.

- The Transaction Service defines a means to control an action against a database or other subsystem. The Transaction Service allows clients and servers to commit or roll back a transaction, even when the transaction affects multiple databases.

Currently, there are a total of 15 services. Along with those listed above, the services are Persistent Object Service, Concurrency Control Service, Life Cycle Service, Relationship Service, Externalization Service, Query Service, Licensing Service, Property Service, Time Service, Object Trader Service, and Object Collections Service.

In addition to the Common Object Services, there are Common Frameworks. The Common Frameworks define application-level services, typically for vertical markets, such as Oil and Gas, Transportation, and Document Preparation. Currently, the majority of the specifications for these frameworks are in review, but few vendors have developed services that support portions of these specifications.

An Overview of IDL and IIOP

The ORB, Common Object Services, and Common Frameworks would be difficult for any one vendor to implement if there were not some standard way to define the interfaces that each of these elements requires. The definitions of the interfaces in CORBA are created through a set of language constructs that are specified by the Interface Definition Language (IDL).

Additionally, the CORBA 2.0 specification introduced the Internet Inter-ORB Protocol (IIOP) standard that specifies how ORBs communicate over networks.

IDL Definitions

IDL provides a programming-language neutral way to define how a service is implemented. The constructs that make up IDL are syntactically similar to C and C++ (and even Java), but they cannot be compiled into a binary program directly. Instead, IDL is intended to be an intermediary language that defines the interfaces that a client will use and a server will implement. IDL is best thought of as a "contract" between the system that makes use of an object and a system that implements an object.

A developer creating a CORBA system models a system using IDL to define the interface that the system will support. This model is an abstract representation of the actual system. For example, the following is a simple IDL file:

```
module Calculator {
        interface Functions {
                float square_root ( in float number );
                float power (in float base, in float exponent );
        };
};
```

This IDL file describes two function keys on a calculator: a square root function and a power function (a number raised to a power). The definition of these functions is abstract—there is no code describing the implementation of these functions, nor is there any definition of the language to be used to implement the functions.

This IDL specification is "compiled" using a tool that creates code for the specific operating system and programming language that the developer needs. Currently, CORBA vendors support C, C++, Java, SmallTalk, and Ada. Some companies have their own implementations of other languages such as COBOL. We'll cover the Java mapping of the most useful IDL constructs later in this chapter.

NOTE   IDL files are "compiled," but this is really a misnomer and illustrates the limited nature of computer terms. An IDL file is actually *translated* from the general constructs that make up IDL to specific programming language constructs (like C, C++ or Java). However, the files generated by the translation process are not complete; they require the implementation details, which the developer must fill in.

IIOP Communications

The IIOP is a TCP/IP implementation of the General Inter-ORB Protocol (GIOP). The GIOP specification defines how ORBs communicate, including how messages are sent, how byte ordering is done for integers and floating-point numbers, and how parameters are marshaled for remote object invocations.

NOTE   While not a CORBA component per se, IIOP compatibility is required of CORBA vendors who wish to advertise that they are 2.0-compliant. The IIOP specification has probably done more to further the cause of CORBA than any other specification. Without IIOP, CORBA vendors are free to implement their own ORB communication protocols, effectively creating a vendor lock—any additional service would need to be purchased from the single vendor.

With CORBA, it is possible to build a client application using one vendor's ORB and IDL compiler, build a server or object implementation with a second vendor's ORB and IDL compiler, and create a set of common services for both client and server with yet a third vendor's ORB and IDL compiler. The IIOP allows each of the three different vendors' products to communicate with each other using a standard set of protocol semantics. (And when you consider that all three of these ORBs could be using a different programming language and running on a different hardware and operating system platform, you get the idea that CORBA is pretty cool!)

A Working CORBA System

Now that we've introduced the CORBA components and specifications, let's see how each of these is used to develop a working CORBA system.

Java IDL is now part of the Java 2. The current release includes a 100% Pure Java ORB, a set of APIs, and a Naming Service (`tnameserv`) that follows the COS Naming Service specification. An IDL compiler (`idltojava`) is available separately. Java IDL is CORBA 2.0-compliant, so it also communicates with any other IIOP (version 1.0) ORB. The description here applies in particular to Java IDL, but the process will be similar in most other CORBA implementations.

The process of creating a CORBA system starts with the development of a design, or the outline of what functionality the system is to provide. From there, the design is translated into objects that provide the functionality required by the design. These objects are expressed in terms of IDL interfaces and collected into related modules. The IDL file(s) is then compiled to generate stub and skeleton code. Stubs represent the interfaces that client applications will use, and skeletons provide interfaces to object implementations that servers will provide.

Once the IDL file is compiled, object implementations are created from the files that are generated, and a server application is created to provide a means for publishing the object references by name through the Naming Service or through their Interoperable Object Reference (IOR). The client application requests a reference to an object through the Naming Service by name and is returned a reference to a generic CORBA object. This object reference is narrowed (like Java casting) to a reference that is actually the stub representation of the remote CORBA object.

The IDL File

CORBA objects are first described by their interface in an IDL file. A CORBA object is also known as a "service." CORBA services provide operations that may or may not return result(s).

NOTE   Actually, you could develop a CORBA application without using IDL. In fact, there are CORBA products that allow the developer to create Java and C++ code from a visual development tool, skipping over the creation of IDL files. However, an IDL file provides a road map for the development of a sound CORBA system, forcing the developer to think through the problem before generating any executable code. The IDL file also provides written documentation of the creation process and preserves the software design investment. An IDL file from 1998 will continue to provide insight into the design of a system long after CORBA is transformed into a new software paradigm.

There is no concept of data in an IDL definition, because IDL interface definitions of services are true object-oriented descriptions. The data is not shown because it is always private and accessed only by an operation, which is public.

For example, consider our sample IDL file:

```
module Calculator {
        interface Functions {
                float square_root ( in float number );
                float power ( in float base, in float exponent );
        };
};
```

Functions is a CORBA service (encapsulated in a package or library called Calculator) that describes two operations, square_root and power. An IDL compiler will generate language-specific files, depending on the purpose of the compiler. For example, the IDL compiler for Java IDL will generate Java files.

Stubs and Skeletons

The names of the files generated by the IDL compiler depend on the contents of the IDL file and the IDL compiler used. In our sample IDL file (shown in the previous section), a package directory Calculator is generated and a Java interface file named Functions.java is generated in the Calculator directory. Functions.java contains an interface declaration for the two operations.

Other generated files include stub and skeleton files. Stub files are used by client code to communicate with remote CORBA objects. Skeleton files are used by the ORB to make up-calls to server object implementations. Both stub and skeleton classes extend a common ORB class that allows these two objects to communicate. Both client and server applications utilize the Naming Service (tnameserv) to provide information about the remote object that is requested and served, respectively. Figure 13.3 illustrates how stubs and skeletons are used in a CORBA application.

FIGURE 13.3:

Using stubs and skeletons in a CORBA application

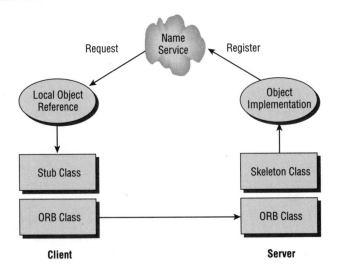

When the server is started, it creates or is passed an object that is to be referenced. This object implements the operations defined in the IDL file; in our example, it provides method bodies for the square_root and power methods. The Java class that provides the implementation of the operations defined in the IDL interface Functions also extends a generated class that defines skeleton methods. The server registers the reference to this object with the Naming Service.

The client requests a reference to a remote object through the Naming Service. The reference that is returned is passed to a stub object. The client then invokes methods through the stub reference as if the object were local to the client. The stub, in turn, passes requests to the skeleton reference obtained through the Naming Service.

CORBA Servers

The Naming Service provides a reference to a CORBA object provided by a server. There are two types of CORBA objects: transient and persistent. Transient objects have the same lifetime as the server that created them—as long as the server is running, the object is available. Persistent objects do not require a running server. If a request is made of an object that is not available because the server that created the object is not running, an ORB daemon will start the appropriate server to activate an object and return its reference. As of this writing, Java IDL provides only transient servers, but Java IDL clients can access persistent servers provided by other CORBA vendors.

Static versus Dynamic Skeletons

CORBA servers can refer to object implementations either statically or dynamically. In both cases, client requests are not sent directly to the object implementation, but instead pass through a skeleton. The skeleton provides methods for handling the order of arguments passed to the method invocation on the object it represents and provides methods for marshaling results to be passed back to the stub.

Static skeletons are generated directly from the IDL interface declarations. These are the easiest to create because the order of the arguments and their type is known in advance (at compile time). Dynamic skeletons are more flexible, allowing method invocations on an object to be handled dynamically at runtime. By default, the Java IDL compiler generates skeletons that use Java IDL's Dynamic Skeleton Interface (DSI). The use of the DSI skeletons is transparent; the client still makes calls to the operations declared in the IDL interface declarations.

Subclassed Skeleton Classes versus Ties

With Java IDL, you can connect the skeleton interfaces with the actual object implementation in two ways. One way is to inherit skeleton methods directly, by subclassing the skeleton class generated by the IDL compiler. This approach is straightforward—each IDL interface method has a direct correlation to a skeleton method.

However, for some applications, you may want to reserve the superclass slot for another class, particularly in instances when the classes that are being wrapped by the CORBA skeleton classes already exist. In this case, another class may be used in between the skeleton and the implementation that delegates the method calls to the appropriate implementation class. These delegation-based skeletons are referred to as *Ties*. Java IDL provides a mechanism for creating a Tie implementation by simply specifying the `-ftie` flag to the `idltojava` application on the command line.

CORBA Clients

A client application invokes methods on CORBA objects. In order to invoke a method on a CORBA object, the client must know what methods are available and what arguments each method takes. A client can be written with static or dynamic method invocations.

Static method invocations are the easiest to write because they are generated and type-checked at compile time. A static invocation uses the methods declared by the Java interfaces generated from IDL interface definitions.

Dynamic method invocations are more flexible. They allow the client to discover the object definitions at runtime. However, dynamic method invocations do not type-check arguments, so it is the responsibility of the client to make sure that arguments are valid. Dynamic invocation also requires that the server supports an Interface Repository. The Interface Repository is used to provide the client with method names, types, and argument lists. As of this writing, Java IDL does not provide an Interface Repository, although Java IDL clients can access the Interface Repository provided by another ORB. The method `org.omg.CORBA.Object` `.get_interface` will throw an exception if the server side is implemented in Java IDL, but it will return a valid reference if the server is another ORB.

The Object Adapter

Some CORBA implementations support the concept of an Object Adapter. The Object Adapter is responsible for creating server objects and returning the object reference (object ID). The Object Adapter is only used on the server side. CORBA specifies that at least one Basic Object Adapter (BOA) is supported. However, the current specification for the BOA is quite vague, so there are different semantics for the implementation of the BOA from vendor to vendor. These differences have made it difficult to port server-side code from one vendor's implementation to another.

The OMG recently released a new specification, deprecating the BOA and replacing it with the Portable Object Adapter (POA). This new specification carefully defines the requirements for a POA, making it possible to move server-side code from one vendor's implementation to another. The POA is described in the IDL and will be instantiated as a CORBA object. As of this writing, the POA is still in the specification phase and has not yet been implemented.

Java IDL currently supports only transient object servers, and therefore does not implement a BOA; instead, a simplified object adapter for transient objects is built into the Java ORB class.

A Simple CORBA Service

As described earlier, CORBA services are expressed in terms of IDL interfaces. The Naming Service is actually an IDL file that describes the interfaces required to provide this "service." To introduce how Java IDL is used, we'll develop a simple CORBA service.

There are ten basic steps to developing the CORBA service:

1. Create an IDL file that represents the interfaces desired.
2. Compile the IDL file using `idltojava`.
3. Compile the generated classes using `javac`.
4. Create an implementation class.
5. Create the implementation server.

6. Create the client application (or applet).

7. Compile the implementation, server, and client code.

8. Start the Naming Service application, `tnameserv`.

9. Start the server (which registers with the Naming Service).

10. Start the client.

WARNING   The most important of these steps is the first, but many developers spend too little time in design. One of the drawbacks to a flexible framework is that the design of the framework is what drives the implementation. Changes that are made to the implementation are not reflected in the IDL file automatically. Furthermore, tools for converting an implementation back to IDL are not provided by most CORBA vendors.

The steps and the code for the CORBA service example are described in the following sections. The full code is also on the CD-ROM in `javadevhdbk\ch13`.

Creating the IDL File

For our example, we'll use the same sample IDL file presented in earlier sections:

```
module Calculator {
        interface Functions {
                float square_root ( in float number );
                float power (in float base, in float exponent );
        };
};
```

In this IDL file, an IDL interface named `Functions` is enclosed in the naming scope of a module named `Calculator`. The IDL interface `Functions` describes a single service that contains two operations: square_root and power. The square_root operation takes a single floating-point argument, passed by value to the operation, and returns a single float result. The operation power takes two float arguments passed by value, and returns a single float result. The service `Functions` is enclosed in the `Calculator` naming scope. (We'll discuss the semantics of Java IDL in the "IDL to Java Language Mapping" section later in the chapter.)

Compiling the IDL File

For this example, assume that our sample IDL file is in a file named `calc.idl`. To compile the IDL file, use the `idltojava` compiler.

```
idltojava -fno-cpp calc.idl
```

The `-fno-cpp` option is used to turn off C/C++ preprocessing. This option is useful only if you plan to add preprocessing commands to your IDL files. Other options are described in the document `jidlCompiler.html`, which is shipped with the `idltojava` compiler.

The IDL compiler uses the constructs specified in the IDL file to generate specific Java files and directories. The `module` construct is used as a package specification, and the `interface` construct is used as a Java interface definition. In our sample IDL file, the package name is `Calculator`, and the Java interface file generated is named `Functions.java`. The Java IDL compiler generates the following files for this example:

`Calculator`	The directory/package created by the module declaration.
`Functions`	A Java interface that declares the operations and methods.
`_FunctionsImplBase`	A class that implements the `Functions` interface and provides a single class that the implementation class can extend.
`_FunctionsStub`	Another class that implements the `Functions` interface. This class is extended by the client class to access the methods declared in `Functions`.
`FunctionsHolder`	A utility class provided to allow client applications to pass a `Functions` object as a value to the server. It is not needed in this example.
`FunctionsHelper`	Another utility class that the client uses to classify object references received from the server as `Functions` objects.

Compiling the Generated Classes

The idltojava IDL compiler generates only Java source code, so the generated classes must be compiled. The nice thing about this step is that none of the generated classes will throw compilation exceptions! To compile the generated classes, use the following compiler command:

```
javac Calculator\*.java
```

Creating the Implementation Class

The next step is to provide a Java class that implements the Java interface generated by the IDL compiler. It is recommended that the physical location of the classes that you create remain separate from the generated classes. The generated classes are in the Calculator directory already, so the created classes can be created one directory level above them.

Java IDL provides a file that makes this step easy. The _FunctionsImplBase.java file is an abstract class file that extends org.omg.CORBA.DynamicImplementation and implements Functions.java . Extending this class provides the appropriate skeleton methods that are required to perform the up-calls from the ORB to the implementation methods.

The implementation class must provide method bodies for the interface methods described by the Functions interface (generated from the IDL file calc.idl).

LIST 13.1   *Functions.java*

```
/*
 * File: ./Calculator/Functions.java
 * From: calc.idl
 * Date: Wed Dec 31 13:44:56 1997
 *   By: C:\JDK1~1.2BE\BIN\IDLTOJ~1.EXE Java IDL 1.2 Nov 10 1997
 *   13:52:11
 */

package Calculator;
public interface Functions
    extends org.omg.CORBA.Object {
    float square_root(float number);
    float power(float base, float exponent);
}
```

NOTE   As of JDK 1.1, all methods defined in an interface are implicitly public.

Therefore, the implementation class must provide methods for the square_root and power methods. By convention, the implementation class adds an Impl suffix to the interface name. The implementation class created is shown below.

LIST 13.2   *FunctionsImpl.java*

```java
// Implementation file for the Functions interface

package Calculator;

// First, extend the Implementation Base class
public class FunctionsImpl extends _FunctionsImplBase {

        // A constructor is not required, but is recommended
        public FunctionsImpl () {
        }

        // Implement the two special methods
        public float square_root (float number) {
                return (float)Math.sqrt ((double)number);
        }

        public float power (float base, float exponent) {
                return (float)Math.pow ((double)base,
                (double)exponent);
        }
}
```

This simple implementation returns a square root using the sqrt() method and the pow() method of the java.lang.Math class. Note that these methods take double type arguments and return a double as a result, so the arguments and the results of the methods should be cast to a float.

Creating the Implementation Server

The next step is to create a server class that will register the implementation object with the ORB and Naming Service and provide the connection to the

implementation class. Like the implementation class, this Java class is not generated by the idltojava compiler.

LIST 13.3	***CalculatorServer.java***

```
// The Calculator Server class

import Calculator.*;

import org.omg.CosNaming.*;
import org.omg.CosNaming.NamingContextPackage.*;
import org.omg.CORBA.*;

public class CalculatorServer {

    public static void main(String args[])
    {
      try{
        // Create and initialize an instance of an ORB
        ORB orb = ORB.init(args, null);

        // Create implementation object and register with ORB
        FunctionsImpl fRef = new FunctionsImpl();
        orb.connect(fRef);

        // Get a handle to the name server
        org.omg.CORBA.Object objRef =
            orb.resolve_initial_references("NameService");
        NamingContext ncRef = NamingContextHelper.narrow(objRef);

          // Bind the Object Reference in Naming
          NameComponent nc = new NameComponent("Calc", "");
          NameComponent path[] = {nc};
        ncRef.rebind(path, fRef);

        // Wait for invocations from clients
            java.lang.Object sync = new java.lang.Object();
            synchronized (sync) {
                sync.wait();
            }

      } catch (Exception e) {
```

```
                     System.err.println("ERROR: " + e);
                     e.printStackTrace(System.out);
             }
        }
    }
```

The server code creates and initializes an ORB object, then creates a reference to the object implementation FunctionsImpl. The server must publish the object reference to the Naming Service in order for the object to be located. The name of the object reference is arbitrary and formed by creating a naming scope, similar to a filename and path. In our example, the FunctionsImpl reference is named "Calc" and is a top-level name. Finally, the server waits (indefinitely) for an object request (through the newly created ORB reference). This server is an example of a transient object server; the object reference and the ORB require that server application to remain running.

Creating the Client Application

The client application will locate a reference to the Functions object using the Naming Service. The object reference returned is a CORBA object reference that must be cast or narrowed to the appropriate reference type. The server published the name of the reference as "Calc", so this is the object reference that the client will request of the Naming Service.

LIST 13.4   *CalculatorClient.java*

```java
// Calculator Client

import Calculator.*;
import org.omg.CosNaming.*;
import org.omg.CORBA.*;

public class CalculatorClient
{
    public static void main(String args[])
    {
    try{
        // Create and initialize an instance of an ORB
        ORB orb = ORB.init(args, null);
```

```
// Get a handle to the name server
org.omg.CORBA.Object objRef =
    orb.resolve_initial_references("NameService");
NamingContext ncRef = NamingContextHelper.narrow(objRef);

// Look up the object bound to the name "Calc"
NameComponent nc = new NameComponent("Calc", "");
NameComponent path[] = {nc};

// Use the Helper class to "cast" the generic CORBA object
// reference to a Functions implementation. The object returned
// by the narrow method is actually a _FunctionsStub object
// that implements the methods in the Functions interface
Functions fRef = FunctionsHelper.narrow(ncRef.resolve(path));

// Use the reference to execute the interface methods
float sqrt = fRef.square_root (10f);
float pow = fRef.power (2f, 8f);

System.out.println ("The square root of 10 is: " + sqrt);
System.out.println ("2 to the 8th power is: " + pow);

} catch (Exception e) {
    System.out.println("ERROR : " + e) ;
    e.printStackTrace(System.out);
}
}
}
```

The client program also creates an instance of an ORB, then requests a reference to an object that matches the naming scope created through the NamingContext reference. The object reference that the Naming Service returns is a general CORBA reference and must be cast before the object methods can be called. In addition, the object reference will be represented by a stub, on which the client application will invoke methods. The helper class, generated by idltojava, makes this easy by providing a method called narrow(), which returns a reference to a FunctionsStub. With this reference, the square_root and power methods can be called.

Compiling the Implementation, Client, and Server Code

The newly created implementation, server, and client Java class files are compiled next with the following command line:

```
javac FunctionsImpl.java CalculatorServer.java CalculatorClient.java
```

Starting the Naming Service Application

The Naming Service application, `tnameserv`, is provided with Java 2. The Naming Service will listen on a port—number 900 by default—for name resolution and binding requests. You can change the default port number by specifying an argument to `tnameserv`. For example, here the default port number is changed to 1050:

```
tnameserv -ORBInitialPort 1050
```

The Naming Service application responds with something similar to the following output:

```
Initial Naming Context:
IOR:000000000000002849444c3a6f6d672e6f72672f436f734e616d696
e672f4e616d696e67436f6e746578743a312e3000000000010000000000
0000340001000000000000864656661756c740000040300000000001cafabc
afe0000000234ba207b00000000000000080000000000000000
TransientNameServer: setting port for initial object
references to: 1050
```

The output lists the Naming Service's Interoperable Object Reference (IOR) and the current port number that the Naming Service is listing on. The IOR string is another mechanism for locating a CORBA object reference. The IOR contains information about the location of the object, including the hostname and IP address, and what services the object provides. The IOR is most useful for passing an object reference between two ORB implementations without the need for a Naming Service to locate an object reference.

This works as follows: The server publishes a "stringified" object reference (the string representation of the CORBA object reference) by converting the object reference to a string. For example, the `CalculatorServer` class definition shown earlier includes:

```
try{

    // Create and initialize the ORB
    ORB orb = ORB.init(args, null);
```

```
        // Create implementation object and register it with the ORB
        FunctionsImpl fRef = new FunctionsImpl();
        orb.connect(fRef);
        System.out.println (orb.object_to_string (fRef));
    }
```

The server will then report the IOR for the FunctionsImpl object. The Calculator-Client is passed the entire string output as an argument on the command line, and it converts the IOR string to an object reference:

```
    try{
        // Create and initialize the ORB
        ORB orb = ORB.init(args, null);

        // Get a reference to an object from third argument
        // on the command line
        org.omg.CORBA.Object objRef = orb.string_to_object (args[2]);

        // Use the interface Functions to resolve the actual
        // object reference
        Functions fRef = FunctionsHelper.narrow(objRef);
    }
```

Starting the Server

Next, the server is started to register the implementation object with the Naming Service. The server must locate the Naming Service by using the same port number or by using the IOR that the Naming Service published on startup. In this example, the port number is used.

```
    java CalculatorServer -ORBInitialPort 1050
```

The server will run until it is killed.

Starting the Client

Now we can run the client application. The client must also be able to locate the Naming Service in order to contact the appropriate server for a reference to the implementation object:

```
    java CalculatorClient -ORBInitialPort 1050
```

The client application produces the following output, indicating that it was successful in locating the server, receiving a reference to the `FunctionsImpl` object, and executing a `square_root` and `power` operation:

```
The square root of 10 is: 3.1622777
2 to the 8th power is: 256.0
```

IDL-to-Java Language Mapping

Programming conventions for Java and IDL differ slightly. IDL conventions do not require capitalization for the names of modules, interfaces, or operations. In addition, IDL convention uses underscores instead of mixed case for long names. Some of the IDL conventions are the result of the OMG's adoption of a definition language that crosses several programming languages and the attempt to create a standard that satisfies the capabilities of all of these languages.

Here are some general guidelines to follow when developing IDL files:

- An IDL file is composed of several elements that together create a naming scope.

- IDL does not support the overloading and overriding of operations, although inheritance (single and multiple) is supported.

The following sections present an overview of the IDL-to-Java language mapping, focusing on the most commonly used constructs.

TIP

For the complete IDL-to-Java language mapping, refer to `http://www.omg.org/library/schedule/Technology_Adoption.htm`. Also, Chapters 5 through 8 of the Java mapping specification are provided as part of the Java IDL documentation (shipped with Java 2). These chapters are available through the file `/JDK1.2 document installation directory/docs/guide/idl/mapping/jidlMapping.html`.

IDL Constructs

As examples of how to use some common IDL constructs, we'll look at sample IDL files that might be used by Sullivan Publishing, the fictional book publishing company described at the beginning of this chapter.

IDL Modules

The IDL `module` construct is used to define the enclosing scope of a group of IDL interfaces. A `module` can contain one or more interfaces, and can nest other `module` constructs. Each `module` construct compiles to a Java package name. Here is an example of a nested `module` construct:

```
//IDL
module SullivanBooks {
    module BookStore {
        interface Account {
            ...
        };
    };
};
```

The Java code generated by `idltojava` would include the following package declaration:

```
// Java code
package SullivanBooks.BookStore;
...
```

IDL Interfaces

The IDL `interface` construct maps to a Java `interface` class. The `idltojava` compiler generates several Java files from a single IDL `interface` construct:

- A Java `interface` class with the same name as the interface identifier

- A generated implementation base class that contains the skeleton code required for the server-side application

- A stub class

- A helper class that is used to narrow the object reference returned from a Naming Service to the stub object required by the client

- A holder class that is used to contain a reference to the IDL type if the interface is passed as an argument in an operation

Given the IDL `module` definition shown in the previous section, the following files are generated (under the `SullivanBooks.BookStore` package directory) using `idltojava`:

> `Account.java`
>
> `AccountHolder.java`
>
> `_AccountStub.java`
>
> `AccountHelper.java`
>
> `_AccountImplBase.java`

IDL interfaces can contain attributes, exceptions, and operations.

IDL Attributes   An attribute defines a CORBA variable type that may be accessed by predefined methods. CORBA types can either be standard IDL types (listed in Table 13.1) or another IDL interface.

TABLE 13.1: IDL-to-Java Type Mappings

IDL	Java
`float`	`float`
`double`	`double`
`long, unsigned long`	`int`
`long long, unsigned long long`	`long`
`short, unsigned short`	`short`
`char, wchar`	`char`
`boolean`	`boolean`
`octet`	`byte`
`string, wstring`	`java.lang.String`
`enum, struct, union`	`class`

An attribute will generate an accessor and mutator method for the type declared. For example:

```
//IDL
attribute float price;
```

will generate the following Java methods:

```
// Generated Java methods
    float price();
    void price(float arg);
```

The attribute may also be declared read-only, in which case only an accessor method is declared. Note that the IDL compiler does not generate a price variable, just the methods to access the variable.

IDL Operations   IDL operations are compiled to Java methods. Each operation must declare a return type and may have zero or more arguments. Arguments to operations declare the call semantics of the argument. These may be in, out, or inout.

An in parameter is call-by-value and is mapped directly to the corresponding Java type (see Table 13.1). An out parameter uses call-by-reference semantics. Java does not use call-by-reference, so out parameters are mapped onto a Java Holder class. This class encapsulates a data variable that contains the parameter, and the value of the class reference is passed. Finally, the inout parameter semantics are call-by-value/result. This too is mapped onto a Java Holder class.

Operations That Raise Exceptions   Operations can declare that they raise an exception using the construct raises (exception). Exceptions in the raises clause must be declared before they can be used. Here is an example:

```
// IDL
// ... code above not shown
interface account {
    void orderBooks ( in BookList books, out string orderID )
        raises (StockException);
};
```

The above operation, orderBooks, declares an in parameter named books of type BookList and an out parameter that is a string, and raises an exception StockException.

An IDL File to Define Three Services

To continue the discussion of IDL constructs, let's look at a more complete example. Here is the IDL file that Sullivan Publishing will use for its online bookstore:

```
// Sample IDL
module BookStore {

    exception StockException {
        string reason;
    };

    exception AccountException {
        string reason;
        float creditLine;
    };

    struct Book {
        string title;
        string author;
        string isbn_number;
        float price;
    };

    typedef sequence <Book> BookList;

    interface BookOrder {
        readonly attribute BookList theOrder;
        void addBook (in Book theBook) raises (StockException);
        void removeBook (in Book theBook);
        void searchBook (in Book theBook, out Book result)
            raises (StockException);
    };

    interface BookOrderManager {
        BookOrder generateOrder ();
    };

    interface Account {
        readonly attribute string accountID;
        BookOrder getBookOrder ();
```

```
        void orderBooks ( in BookOrder order ) raises
            (AccountException);
        void checkStatus ( in BookOrder order, out string status );
    };

    struct PayType {
        string cardType;
        string cardNumber;
        string expirationDate;
    };

    interface AccountManager {
        Account getAccount ( in string name, in PayType payment );
    };
};
```

This IDL file defines four services:

- The AccountManager service will generate an Account for the customer and allow the customer to generate a book order.

- The Account service is used to generate a book order, order books, and check the status of a book order.

- The BookOrder service is used to add or remove books from an order.

- The BookOrderManager service generates a new order that the Account object uses to order books.

Customers will open an account, then generate a book order with one or more books they add to the order, then place the order.

If a book is not in stock, then a StockException is raised to let the customer know that the book is out of stock. An AccountException is raised if the credit card used to open the account is overdrawn or invalid at the time of ordering.

Object Factories

The factory concept is very important in the development of CORBA services. It is sometimes desirable to be able to create new objects on the fly at runtime. This capability is important when the number of objects to be created is not known in advance.

The IDL file shown in the previous section uses object factories. The number of accounts that Sullivan Publishing will have over the life of the company cannot be predetermined. It might be possible to create a number of objects in advance that can then be doled out, but how many is enough? Should you create 10 or 100?

Rather than describe each object as a discrete service that exists on the server, an object factory allows the server to create an instance of an `Account` object for each new customer request. The `AccountManager` service is responsible for receiving a request for a new account, and then creating a new `Account` object for that request. Subsequent requests will always return the same object reference given that the account name is the same. Granted, using a single string to create a unique object is probably not enough, but the idea is that some given set of parameters defines what object reference to return. Figure 13.4 illustrates this use of an object factory.

FIGURE 13.4:

Using an object factory

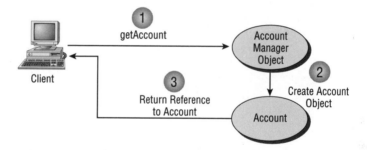

Likewise, each `Account` may have one or more `BookOrder` objects. Again, a factory is used to generate new `BookOrder` objects from the `BookOrderManager` object on request.

IDL Exceptions

IDL exceptions are passed as object references, as in Java, but they do not map directly onto the Java Exception API. IDL exceptions extend the `org.omg.CORBA` `.UserException` class. Exceptions may contain data that is accessed as public members of the named class and may be passed in the construction of the exception. For example, this `exception` construct:

```
// IDL
    exception StockException {
        string reason;
    };
```

is compiled into a Java class (`AccountException.java`):

```
/*
 * File: ./BookStore/AccountException.java
 * From: bookstore2.idl
 * Date: Tue Jan  6 14:13:36 1998
 *   By: idltojava Java IDL 1.2 Nov 12 1997 12:23:47
 */

package BookStore;
public final class AccountException
    extends org.omg.CORBA.UserException {
    //    instance variables
    public String reason;
    public float creditLine;
    //    constructors
    public AccountException() {
    super();
    }
    public AccountException(String __reason, float __creditLine) {
    super();
    reason = __reason;
    creditLine = __creditLine;
    }
}
```

IDL Structures

The IDL `struct` is a container class that may be used to pass a collection of data as a single object. An IDL `struct` maps to a Java class with public data members. For example, this `struct` construct:

```
// IDL
    struct Book {
        string title;
        string author;
        string isbn_number;
        float price;
    };
```

maps to a Java final class:

```
/*
 * File: ./BookStore/Book.java
 * From: bookstore2.idl
 * Date: Tue Jan  6 14:13:36 1998
 *   By: idltojava Java IDL 1.2 Nov 12 1997 12:23:47
 */

package BookStore;
public final class Book {
    //    instance variables
    public String title;
    public String author;
    public String isbn_number;
    public float price;
    //    constructors
    public Book() { }
    public Book(String __title, String __author,
                String __isbn_number, float __price) {
    title = __title;
    author = __author;
    isbn_number = __isbn_number;
    price = __price;
    }
}
```

IDL Type Definitions

IDL provides a construct for naming new IDL types from existing types. The typedef construct does not directly map to Java, so the IDL compiler will substitute and replace any instance of the typedef name for the actual type in the IDL before compiling it. The typedef construct makes it easier to write IDL files, particularly when sequences are required. Here are some examples of typedef constructs:

```
// IDL
typedef string CustomerName;
typedef long CustomerSalary;
typedef sequence <long> CustomerOrderID;
```

IDL Sequences

IDL sequences are single-dimension arrays that may be bounded or unbounded. A bounded sequence defines its maximum size in the declaration of the sequence. For example, in this sequence construct:

```
// IDL
typedef sequence <long, 10> openOrders;
```

A bounded sequence of ten IDL long numbers is defined as the type openOrders.

The bounds of a bounded sequence are checked as the argument is marshaled and sent. If the bounds of a bounded sequence are exceeded, a MARSHAL system exception is raised. Both bounded and unbounded sequences generate a Java helper and holder class for each sequence.

IDL Arrays

The IDL array construct is used to create a single-dimension bounded array of any IDL type. The array construct is mapped to Java the same way as the bounded sequence, but uses different semantics. Here is an example:

```
// IDL
const long length = 20;
typedef string custName[length];
```

IDL Enumerations

The IDL enum construct is used to represent an enumerated list, as in this example:

```
enum CityList {Boston, NewYork, Philadelphia, Baltimore};
```

The enum construct maps to a Java final class with the same name:

```
/*
 * File: ./BookStore/CityList.java
 * From: test.idl
 * Date: Tue Jan  6 16:32:56 1998
 *   By: idltojava Java IDL 1.2 Nov 12 1997 12:23:47
 */
package BookStore;
public final class CityList {
    public static final int _Boston = 0,
                    _NewYork = 1,
```

```
                              _Philadelphia = 2,
                              _Baltimore = 3;
            // code deleted
}
```

Legacy Applications and CORBA

A business application may include code that is not current or state-of-the-art, but works perfectly well. That code may have been written by engineers who left the company long ago. This type of code is referred to as "legacy" code. One of the drawbacks to legacy code is that it is often deployed on a legacy hardware system as well. The company needs to access this code on its existing hardware platform and be able to use it across its network.

One of CORBA's primary benefits is that it allows developers to wrap legacy code with a CORBA object approach. An IDL description of the legacy interfaces is used to produce a set of CORBA objects. These objects can then make calls into the legacy code and expose the legacy system to a network. Figure 13.5 illustrates this approach.

FIGURE 13.5:

Legacy COBOL code wrapping

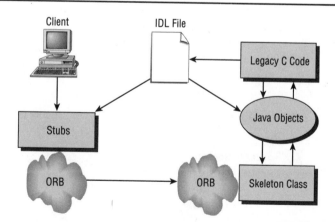

Wrapping legacy code does require some understanding of the way that the code works. The low-level implementation details are not important, but an understanding of the way that the code is called or interfaced with other code modules is necessary. The interfaces and access methods become the foundation of an IDL interface, which is then used to create a CORBA system.

As an example, suppose that Sullivan Publishing (our fictional book publishing company discussed at the beginning of this chapter), in one of its expansions, has purchased a book catalog service. Part of this purchase involved the acquisition of some C code used to search for book records in a database. The current book catalog service is a phone-only service. Sullivan Publishing would like to use the Internet to allow customers to order books, but still preserve the current code that exists for searching the book database. This is an excellent application for CORBA. The legacy C code can be used as is, but will be wrapped by an implementation that will expose the C code to the network.

In this example, Sullivan Publishing purchased inventory-tracking software that was designed to run on a Windows NT computer. The original code was not designed to run on a network, and the original source code is not available, so it is not practical to port the code directly to Java. However, the interface to the code is fairly straightforward—the C code is compiled into a library. For example, calls to the search routines are made as follows:

```
void search (Book *toFind, Book *result);
```

where the parameters are passed as a pointer to a struct:

```
struct Book {
    char title [100];
    char author [100];
    char isbn[25];
    float price;
};
```

The developer defined the C function call and the C struct in IDL as follows:

```
// IDL
    struct Book {
        string title;
        string author;
        string isbn_number;
        float price;
    };

    interface BookOrder {
        readonly attribute BookList theOrder;
        void addBook (in Book theBook) raises (StockException);
```

```
        void removeBook (in Book theBook);
        void searchBook (in Book theBook, out Book result)
            raises (StockException);
    };
```

Since Sullivan Publishing would like to preserve the legacy C code for the search routine, the BookOrder object must be implemented on the Windows NT computer. There are a couple ways to do this.

- Use a CORBA vendor that supports a C language mapping and a Windows NT ORB. Implement the BookOrder object in C, directly integrating the library call to the search function.

- Write the implementation class for BookOrder in Java on the Windows NT machine, and use a native method to call into the search function.

This is a book about Java, so we'll demonstrate the latter approach:

```
// Implementation file for the BookOrder interface

import BookStore.*;
import java.util.Vector;

// First, extend the Implementation Base class
public class BookOrderImpl extends _BookOrderImplBase {

    // Keep a vector of books to be ordered
    private Vector bookList;

    // Constructor
    public BookOrderImpl () {
        // Initialize the vector
        bookList = new Vector ();
    }

    // Implement the method to return the current list of books
    public Book[] theOrder() {
        Book [] bookOrder;
        // Turn the vector into an array
        bookOrder = new Book [bookList.size()];
        bookList.copyInto(bookOrder);
    }

        return bookOrder;
    }
```

```
public void removeBook(Book theBook) {
    // Remove an element from the bookList
    bookList.removeElement (theBook);
}

public void searchBook(Book theBook, BookHolder result)
    throws BookStore.StockException {
    // Call the native search function
    search (theBook, result);
    if (result == null) {
     throw new StockException ("No book found with ISBN number:
     " + theBook.isbn_number);
    }
}

    // The native method for search
    private native void search (Book theBook, BookHolder result);

    // Load the native method from the specified library
    static {
        System.loadLibrary ("orderlib");
    }
}
```

Note that the server application for the `AccountManager` object can reside on another machine, like a Sun workstation. The client application will request a reference to an `AccountManager`. Using this object reference, the client application will request an instance of an `Account` (by calling the `getAccount` method). With this object reference, the client can generate a new `BookOrder` object by calling the `getBookOrder` method. This method gets a reference to the `BookOrderManager` on the Windows NT machine and returns a `BookOrder` object. To the client application, this all happens through local stub invocations!

The Java Enterprise Server API/Enterprise Java Beans

Sun has announced that its flagship CORBA implementation, NEO, will no longer be supported after this year. This announcement came on the heels of Sun's announcement of the Java Enterprise Server API, also known as Enterprise Java Beans (EJB).

Continued on next page

The EJB specification outlines Sun's intent to continue to promote Java in the enterprise and to create a cohesive strategy for bringing industry leaders into the party. The Java Enterprise Server API describes a collection of services and methodologies that allow for tremendous flexibility in the development of enterprise-level applications.

Several companies have begun implementing the concepts outlined in the EJB specification, including BEA, GemStone, and Novera. For more information, see the following web pages:

- BEA Systems: `http://www.beasys.com`
- Novera: `http://www.novera.com`
- GemStone: `http://www.gemstone.com`

Summary

CORBA makes it possible to develop systems that are independent of a programming language and operating system. The introduction of Java to the programming world and the development of protocol standards have propelled CORBA into the current mainstream of computing.

CORBA provides an intermediary solution to the problem of rewriting code. CORBA makes it possible to preserve a company's current investment in COBOL, C, C++, and Ada applications while making the transition to Java in the long-term. CORBA's standards-based approach also frees decision-makers from making a single vendor choice. Systems that are developed using the CORBA framework and standards are easily adapted to other vendors' products with a minimum of code rewriting.

The future of distributed object programming will undoubtedly include CORBA. It is likely that in a few years, systems will be developed with visually driven tools, eliminating the need to develop IDL files altogether. Furthermore, it is becoming increasingly apparent that software vendors have embraced the standards set forth by the OMG, and the future will include more interoperability across both software and hardware domains.

CHAPTER
FOURTEEN

14

Content and Protocol Handlers

- Protocol and handler types

- Protocols and the URL

- Approaches to content and protocol handling

- Protocol handlers

- Content handlers

- Server-side handling

The Internet, mainly in the guise of the World Wide Web, allows data to be shifted around in a wide variety of formats. Despite appearances, the Internet has many more components besides HTTP and the World Wide Web. In fact, a wide variety of different protocols—such as FTP, Telnet, and Gopher—exist on the Internet and are quite well known. Java programs may be required to handle any or all of these protocols and data formats.

This chapter looks at the issues that are raised by these requirements and the mechanism that is built into the Java core packages for coping with the variety. The first sections discuss the background issues and consider how problems are handled in other related systems. Later sections describe the implementation and installation of Java content and protocol handlers.

Protocol and Content Types

The Internet contains information resources in a wide variety of formats. A corporate intranet also offers various formats, including all those that are normally found on the Internet. For example, it might be advantageous to publish figures using the native format of a spreadsheet application, which would also allow the work to be modified and might even result in smaller files when compared to, for example, PostScript files. Each of these different formats constitutes a different *content type*.

Two things are required to support multiple content types and to be able to view them in a web browser without user intervention:

- The browser must be able to recognize the content type in some way.

- The browser must be able to invoke code that handles the content correctly.

It has long been a tradition to use an extension, such as .txt or .cmd, in a filename to indicate the nature of the contents of a file. In a web environment, especially one with many dissimilar platforms, this mechanism is not sufficiently expressive nor widely standardized. Problems can arise when such mnemonic extensions are reused by different applications for incompatible files. This situation is handled on the web by making more detailed content type information available as part of the protocol. The nature of a data set is described using a string called the MIME content type.

MIME Description of Content Type

MIME, the Multipurpose Internet Mail Extensions system, was first invented, as the name suggests, to facilitate sending files representing images and sounds over Internet mail links. Strictly speaking, Internet e-mail is a 7-bit ASCII-only protocol; therefore, sending binary files directly is not possible. MIME, in the mail context, addresses two separate issues: how to represent 8-bit binary data using only 7-bit ASCII and how to describe the significance of the files that are being transmitted.

A number of general, or "top-level," categories are defined by MIME, including text, audio, image, and video. These categories are further subdivided to indicate the particular type of encoding used. So, for example, normal web pages are encoded using HTML, and the MIME type string representing that is text/html. Notice that the parts that make up the type are separated by a forward slash, in a fashion similar to that used to separate elements of a URL.

TIP   Like all Internet protocols, MIME is defined by Request For Comment documents (RFCs). In this case, the documents are RFC 1521 and 1522. These are on the CD-ROM in the directory javadevhdbk\rfcs.

Protocols and the URL

Identifying the protocol to be used for a data transfer is at least as important as identifying the contents of that transfer. In a URL, the protocol to be used is defined by the part of the URL immediately before the first colon. For example, a URL that starts with http: specifies the use of the HTTP protocol; a URL that starts with telnet: indicates that Telnet is the protocol to be used.

Each protocol has a default port number associated with it, but this can be overridden in the body of the URL by adding a number, prefixed with a full colon (:) between the end of the target machine name and the start of the path part of the URL. For example, if an HTTP connection is to be made using port 8080 rather than the default port of 80, to a machine www.fred.com, the URL would start like this:

```
http://www.fred.com:8080/
```

A number of well-known protocols exist, and the URL concept allows the possibility of adding new ones. Such additions might be particularly appropriate in a closed environment like a corporate intranet.

Nested Protocol Handlers

An interesting capability introduced with Java 2 is offered by the idea of a nested protocol handler. A *nested protocol handler* uses another protocol to do part of its work.

Specifically, Java 2 includes a new protocol called `jar:` that allows data to be read from a JAR archive. This protocol is nested in the sense that the location of the JAR archive itself is specified using another URL, and hence another protocol. For example, suppose that you want to specify a URL that describes a file called `data.dat`, which is located in a subdirectory called `jan` in a JAR archive called `accounts.jar`, and the JAR archive is itself located on a web server at the URL `http://accounts.myco.com/records/accounts.jar`. You would use the URL `jar:http://accounts.myco.com/records/accounts.jar!/jan/data.dat`.

To create a nested protocol handler; you simply parse the overall URL and separate the two parts. One part of the URL is used in handling the connection aspects, and the other part is used in handling the aspects that are specific to the new protocol. This approach has the potential to provide a convenient means for HTTP tunneling.

Extensibility in Java

Modern browsers must handle the wide variety of content types and protocols that exist on the Internet. Ideally, it should be possible to enhance a browser to cope with new standards that arise without needing to upgrade the whole browser. The same extensibility is required in Java.

> **NOTE** The software that handles a particular content type is referred to as a *content handler*. The software that handles a particular protocol is called a *protocol handler*.

One of the earliest techniques for extending a browser was to allow the configuration of an external "helper" program that could be used when an otherwise unsupported protocol or content type was encountered. This approach does not allow the resulting data to be displayed in the same browser window as the rest of the data being loaded, but it is easy to implement in a variety of systems. Its limitations are that the browser must be configured manually for each new content type or protocol and that the handling program must be obtained separately.

Another approach involves designing the browser to be extended by means of additional code modules provided after the original browser has been written. This extensibility eliminates the need to load and run external programs to work with additional protocols and content types. This code-module approach is the principle underlying the plug-ins used by the Netscape Navigator browser.

The JVM provides a mechanism for loading code into a running program. This dynamic-linking idea is fundamental to the design of Java and is ideally suited to the particular case of content or protocol handlers.

The key to creating a program that can be readily extended later lies in a carefully considered object-oriented design. Consider a drawing program that is being created to handle lines, circles, and rectangles. If it is coded so that these items are handled explicitly, then a later extension will require changes to the source, recompilation, and redistribution of the whole program. On the other hand, if the program deals instead with a more generalized object of a class called Drawable (as an example), then it can quite easily be extended to handle any other subclass of Drawable without needing recompilation.

For this to work in practice, two things must be done. First, the Drawable class must be designed carefully to ensure that it provides an interface flexible enough to allow any future ideas to be expressed, at least as far as possible within the broad context of drawing. Second, a mechanism must be provided for the program to determine which implementations of Drawable are available for use at runtime. These must be able to express their names and make themselves available via the user interface.

In the case of a drawing program, it is reasonable to arrange that all specific Drawable classes be placed in one particular directory. The program can then scan that directory to determine the names of the Drawable classes that are available to it.

Default Protocol and Content Handler Mechanisms

In the case of both content and protocol handlers, the mechanism by which the program determines the availability of the handler code is quite simple. If a particular handler is required, there is a convention that determines what the names of both the package and the class should be based on the name of the protocol or content type in question. Given this convention, it is a simple matter for the browser program to ask for the handler by name. If the attempt to load that driver fails, then the protocol or content type is unsupported.

NOTE   Java's framework for locating content and protocol handlers allows, in principle, for these handlers to be loaded from the same web server that supplies the data. However, in the current implementations of the Applet Viewer and HotJava, this ease of loading is not possible. Current browsers only support searching for either type of handler on the local machine CLASSPATH, which is a significant limitation.

As explained earlier, the protocol name is specified as the first part of the URL text string immediately before the :// separator. It is easy to extract this, and the mechanism for doing so is consistent regardless of the protocol. Furthermore, the URL class in the java.net package provides a built-in method for this purpose.

Because the protocol name is part of the URL, the primary responsibility for locating handler code for any particular protocol rests with the URL class. When the method openConnection() is called on a URL object, a protocol handler is located, if possible, and invoked. The protocol handler returns a URLConnection object over which the data can be transferred.

The URL class provides three routes for obtaining a protocol handler:

- Locate a class called Handler using the local CLASSPATH and a package name built using the protocol name and a predefined prefix.

- Locate a class called Handler using the local CLASSPATH and a package name built using the protocol name and a user-specified prefix.

- Invoke a *factory*. A factory takes a protocol name and attempts to return an instance of a ProtocolHandler. It can use any algorithm to achieve this, limited only by the programmer's imagination. (You will see later that the factory concept is also employed in content handling.)

Whatever the name of the protocol, the class that handles it is conventionally called Handler. To allow handlers for a variety of protocols to be installed, each Handler class is placed in a package that reflects the protocol name. For example, given the textual name of a protocol, finger, the Handler class is located in a sub-package called finger. This subpackage is located in a particular parent package that is called, by default, sun.net.www, so the full class name is sun.net.www .protocol.finger.Handler.

NOTE   The `finger` protocol, where available, allows you to find out information about users on other machines. Conventionally, `finger` would report the full name, last login time, and related personal information about either users currently logged in or about an individual specified by login name. The `finger` service is often disabled, because this kind of information is of potential use to malicious hackers.

It is possible to override this parent package name. If a property called `java.handler.protocol.pkgs` is defined, it is taken to be a list of package names. The elements of the list should be separated with the vertical bar character (|). For each element of this list, a tentative package name is created by appending the protocol name. If a class called `Handler` is found within the package and it is a protocol hander, then it will be used. If, for example, the property was defined to have the value `myhandlers`, then a `finger` protocol handler could be found first in the class `myhandlers.finger.Handler`, or, if that failed, in the default class `sun.net.www.protocol.finger.Handler`. (This mechanism, based on the property `java.handler.protocol.pkgs`, was added to the URL class in Java 1.1.)

Protocol Handlers and Class Loading

Java 2 includes a new class called `java.net.URLClassLoader`. This class loader has two significant benefits over the basic class loader that was defined in earlier JDK versions:

- It is a subclass of the `java.security.SecureClassLoader` class (also new with Java 2) that provides handling of code source and signatures to support the new protected domains security model.

- It can load the bytecode file from any supported URL.

The latter benefit effectively means that there is no longer any need for you to write a class loader yourself. Instead, you only need to create a new URL type, or more precisely, a new protocol handler. Such an approach can deal with simple problems, such as loading a file that is in an unusual place or stored in an unusual way. Furthermore, this approach allows you to handle more difficult problems, such as caching and version management, local copies of remote classes for use if the remote server is unavailable, or even dynamically created classes.

If you create a new protocol handler instead of writing a class loader, you work will be simpler, since you need only concern yourself with obtaining the bytecode data, not with installing a class. Perhaps more important, your work will also be less security sensitive—the worst mistakes you can make when writing a protocol handler would prevent the handler from working or perhaps corrupt the data. On the other hand, when you write a class loader, you can easily risk compromising your system's security entirely.

Factory Invocation

As described earlier, the default mechanisms in Java build a package name using the protocol name and search for a standard class in the resulting package. This describes the behavior of the Applet Viewer, too. A third option that exists in the URL class is to use a factory. However, the standard security manager prohibits its use by applets, so this option is available only to applications.

The interface URLStreamHandlerFactory defines a single method called create-URLStreamHandler(). This method takes a String argument, which names the protocol. The return from the method is an instance of a protocol handler (URL-StreamHandler class). The method can make whatever decisions are required to choose a protocol handler and can load it from anywhere it deems suitable.

To use a factory as a source of protocol handlers, an application must create an object that implements the URLStreamHandlerFactory interface. Once this object has been created, it can be installed in the system by invoking the static method of the URL class URL.setURLStreamHandlerFactory(). The URLStreamHandlerFactory class is passed to this method as its single argument. We'll present an example of creating and installing a URLStreamHandlerFactory in the "Server-Side Handlers" section later in this chapter.

NOTE   The setURLStreamHandlerFactory() method can be issued only once and cannot be called by untrusted code, such as an applet. Therefore, an application can have only a single factory, which must be able to locate all the protocol handlers that are not located according to the package name conventions.

If the factory fails to find an appropriate protocol handler, then the search proceeds with the mechanisms described earlier, involving packages defined by the property java.handler.protocol.pkgs and the default package sun.net.www.protocol.

The search process results in the selection of a single class that will support handling of the protocol. This will be a subclass of URLStreamHandler, because that is the defined return type of the createURLStreamHandler() method in the handler factory. This object itself is not expected to handle the protocol; rather, it acts as an intermediary and is called on to create other objects that actually handle the protocol. The method that is called to do this is openConnection(). The return type of this method is URLConnection. The actual returned object is a subclass of this method, written to handle the protocol.

URLConnection itself is an abstract class, and the method connect() must be overridden to make the connection. Doing so generally involves creating and connecting the socket that will actually handle the data transfer, and performing any required protocol transactions that might be needed to set up or configure the connection.

The methods getInputStream() and getOutputStream() of the URLConnection class can also be overridden, if appropriate. They allow the actual streams to be obtained by the program. Typically, these methods simply return the InputStream and OutputStream, respectively, from the socket that is handling the data transfers. In some cases, this behavior is modified. Protocols that provide only unidirectional communication will not want to provide access to one stream or the other. In this case, the parental method is left without being overridden, and an Unknown-ServiceException will be thrown if the method is called.

Unidirectional communication usually means reading from the server. In this case, the getOuputStream() method will be left unchanged. However, the get-InputStream() method will be overridden.

There are a series of methods for accessing information about the nature of the data to be transferred. These methods have a strong flavor of HTML about them, but they provide a useful mechanism for requesting general information about the connection. Standard HTTP header fields that can be queried are content-type, content-length, content-encoding, date, expires, and last-modified. These specific query methods use a general method that simply takes a string to indicate the name of the field to be returned. This method can be overridden to provide any information that might be required for a particular protocol. In the absence of an overriding method, the base method returns null for any field inquiry.

TIP   If you use the Netscape Navigator, you can see the HTTP headers that apply to a page by selecting the View ➤ Page Info menu item.

An Example of a Protocol Handler

Now we will develop a simple but complete protocol handler. The daytime protocol, which was discussed in Chapter 10, is used for this example. In Chapter 10, we developed a server for the daytime protocol, and that server will be used here to support the sample protocol handler.

Using the daytime protocol, a client connects to the server and reads one line of ASCII data. The protocol specifies that the service is normally provided on port 13, but to avoid conflict with the built-in daytime service of some operating systems, the one we develop here uses port 13013.

This example uses the default mechanism for locating a protocol handler, which is to use a package name that starts with sun.net.www.protocol followed by the protocol name. This protocol is called *daytime*, so the essential class must be called sun.net.www.protocol.daytime.Handler. This class must extend the URLStream-Handler class.

The job of the Handler class is to return a reference to a newly constructed subclass of URLConnection. This, by convention, should be located in the same package as the Handler class. This example will adopt that convention.

The name of the URLConnection subclass is not important, although it is conventional for the name to reflect the protocol that is handled and to end with the word *Connection*. Again, this example sticks with the conventions, and the class is called DaytimeConnection. (Since starting class names with a capital letter is the standard convention, we call this class DaytimeConnection with a capital *D*, even though the protocol is called *daytime* with a lowercase *d*.)

 The code for the Handler and DaytimeConnection classes follows, and it is on the CD-ROM in the javadevhdbk\ch14 directory. In that directory, you will also find the sun\net\www\protocol\daytime subdirectory, which contains two class files: Handler.class and DaytimeConnection.class. These correspond to the source files Handler.java and DaytimeConnection.java, which are located in the ch14 directory.

LIST 14.1   *Handler.java*

```
package sun.net.www.protocol.daytime;

import java.net.*;
import java.io.*;
```

```
public class Handler extends URLStreamHandler {
  public URLConnection openConnection(URL u) {
    return new DaytimeConnection(u);
  }
}
```

LIST 14.2   *DaytimeConnection.java*

```
package sun.net.www.protocol.daytime;

import java.net.*;
import java.io.*;

public class DaytimeConnection extends URLConnection {
  Socket s;

  protected DaytimeConnection(URL u) {
    super(u);
  }

  public void connect() throws IOException {
    int port;
    String host;

    if (connected) {
      return;
    }

    if ((port = url.getPort()) == -1) {
      port = 13;
    }

    if ((host = url.getHost()) == null) {
      host = "localhost";
    }

    s = new Socket(host, port);
    connected = true;
  }

  public InputStream getInputStream() throws IOException {
```

```
    if (!connected) {
      connect();
    }
    return s.getInputStream();
  }

  public String getHeaderField(String fieldName) {
    if ("content-type".equalsIgnoreCase(fieldName)) {
      return "text/plain";
    }
    else {
      return null;
    }
  }
}
```

Running the Protocol Handler

Because this code provides a protocol handler, you can only run it indirectly, which you can do from the Applet Viewer or an applet or application. Here, we will see how it works from the Applet Viewer. After we take a look at this example, we will develop a simple applet from which we will be able to run the protocol handler.

First, let's investigate the behavior of the Applet Viewer without a protocol handler for the daytime protocol. Make sure that you have *not* selected the directory for ch14 (so that the handler is unavailable). Then invoke the Applet Viewer like this:

appletviewer daytime://localhost:13013/

The Applet Viewer should show a message similar to this:

```
Bad URL: daytime://localhost:13013/ (unknown protocol: daytime)
```

Next, select the CD-ROM directory javadevhdbk\ch14 and invoke the Applet Viewer as before. This time, the URL is not rejected. You will see a message like this:

```
I/O exception while reading: 127.0.0.1
Is daytime: the correct URL?
```

This indicates that the URL was considered valid, which means that the protocol handler was located successfully. However, the connection failed because no server is available.

NOTE 127.0.0.1 is the address defined in the TCP/IP protocols for referring to the local machine, which is why the error report refers to that address, even though you asked to load the applet from `localhost` by name.

Now, using a different window, issue the following command (`DayServer` is an example developed in Chapter 10):

java DayServer

Then run the Applet Viewer again. This time you will see a new error message:

```
Warning: No Applets were started, make sure the input contains an
<applet> tag.
usage: appletviewer [-debug] [-J<javaflag>] [-encoding <character
encoding type>] url|file
```

This indicates that the URL was recognized as valid and that the connection to the server was opened. The problem is that the `DayServer` program returns a date and time string, not an HTML file. Therefore, the Applet Viewer is unable to proceed.

Understanding the Handler and DaytimeConnection Classes

The first class, `Handler`, is very simple. It serves only to satisfy the naming conventions required by the protocol-handling mechanisms. It accepts the `URL` object and returns a newly constructed instance of `DaytimeConnection`, based on the object.

The `DaytimeConnection` class has more work to do than `Handler`. First, using the facilities of its parent class `URLConnection`, it keeps a reference to the `URL` object that it is to work on. The `URLConnection` class has a protected variable called `url`, which is set up by the `URLConnection` constructor. That constructor is invoked by the `super(u)` call issued in the `DaytimeConnection` constructor.

The constructor for `DaytimeConnection` is marked as protected. It could be public but is not for security reasons. The protected constructor is accessible only to members of the same package and subclasses. In this case, that is the `sun.net.www`

.protocol.daytime package. By default, the security manager will not allow imported classes to reside in the sun.* package hierarchies, so the protected constructor prevents imported classes from constructing instances of the Daytime-Connection class. The constructor is still accessible to the Handler class, which is the only place that it should be constructed because Handler is part of the same package.

Making the Connection

The bulk of the work is done in the connect() method. Connection is performed only the first time it is asked for; subsequent attempts are quietly ignored. A boolean variable called connected is inherited from the URLConnection class and is used to keep track of connection attempts. Because many of the methods in the URLConnection class that have not been overridden make use of this variable, it must be used.

To perform the connection, the URL is parsed to determine whether a specific host and port number have been specified. These default to localhost and 13, respectively, in this protocol. Although there is no requirement to supply a default, it is normal to at least provide a default port. If you do not provide a default, then your code should throw a MalformedURLException in the absence of a specification. The documentation for the connect() method indicates that it should throw an IOException. In fact, MalformedURLException is a subclass of IOException.

Once the host and port have been determined, the Socket object that actually handles the data transfer is created. Notice that the Socket constructor might throw an exception, but this is simply passed up to the caller of this connect() method. Some protocols may have a mechanism for attempting to handle such difficulties—perhaps retrying the server or trying alternate servers—before failing completely.

Getting the Data from the URL

The connect() method does nothing with the connection aside from establishing it. The next job is to get the data from the URL so it can be handled locally. The getInputStream() method returns some subclass of InputStream that allows access to that data. In fact, two methods are defined in the URLConnection class—getInputStream() and getOutputStream()—because some protocols involve sending user data as distinct from protocol messages.

Separating the input and output methods allows for the possibility that a protocol might be read-only, write-only, or read-write. The definition of these methods in the URLConnection class simply throws an UnknownServiceException. Because of this, it is important to override both methods where a protocol requires both input and output.

In this example, the InputStream returned by the getInputStream() method is simply the one extracted from the Socket object. This implies that the data stream does not require any processing as part of the protocol. In many cases, the protocol is not so simple. To perform processing on the data stream, a subclass of Filter-InputStream must be created to handle the aspects of the protocol that are involved in the data transfer. The returned InputStream should then be an instance of that filter connected to the socket. For example, if a TelnetInputStream class had been created to handle the Telnet line protocols, the last line of the connect() method would look like this:

```
return new TelnetInputStream(s.getInputStream());
```

Because it is legitimate, and actually normal, to call the getInputStream() method on a URLConnection object before it has been connected, it is necessary to conditionally perform the connect() method at the start of the getInput-Stream() method.

This example also overrides the getHeaderField() method. This method relates mainly to the HTTP protocol, where it is used to extract certain standard bits of header information, such as the content type. Although the daytime protocol does not have such header information, it is valuable to pretend that the content-type field is supported because the content-handler mechanism, discussed later in this chapter, determines which content handler to use based on the content type. If no information is available, automatic content handling will not work. The type text/plain is a suitable default for any protocol that returns plain text. Other content types either should be recognized MIME types or should use the approach specified for "experimental" additions in the MIME RFC.

An Applet to Test the Protocol Handler

To actually make use of the daytime protocol handler, you need an applet or application that will invoke it. The following example is a simple applet that connects to a URL and presents the returned data to the user in a label. This example, located on the CD-ROM in the javadevhdbk\ch14 directory, runs as an applet. The supporting HTML file is called DayApplet.html and is in the same directory.

LIST 14.3   *DayApplet.java*

```java
import java.applet.*;
import java.awt.*;
import java.net.*;
import java.io.*;

public class DayApplet extends Applet {
  Label l;

  public void init() {
    String source = getParameter("source");
    if (source == null) {
      source = "daytime://localhost:13013/";
    }
    URL u = null;
    URLConnection c = null;

    try {
      u = new URL(source);
      c = u.openConnection();
    }
    catch (Exception e) {
      System.out.println("Problem creating URL: " + source);
      e.printStackTrace();
      return;
    }


    BufferedReader in = null;
    String value = null;
    try {
      in = new BufferedReader(
        new InputStreamReader(c.getInputStream(), "8859_1"));
      value = in.readLine();
    }
    catch (Exception e) {
      System.out.println("Problem establishing communication:");
      e.printStackTrace();
```

```
      return;
    }

    if (l == null) {
      l = new Label(value);
      add(l);
    }
    else {
      l.setText(value);
    }
  }
}
```

The DayApplet class reads a parameter called source if it is defined in the HTML file. If no such definition is found, which is the case in the supplied HTML, then a default is used instead. The resulting String is used to construct a URL object. To demonstrate the use of the protocol handler, this URL object should be based on the daytime protocol; hence, the default is daytime://localhost:13013/, which is intended to connect to the DayServer.java example (developed in Chapter 10).

Once the URL object has been constructed, which requires that the URL class be able to locate an appropriate protocol handler, the resulting URLConnection is connected, and the InputStream is extracted. Any errors that arise in this process cause exceptions that are caught and displayed.

Provided that the InputStream is successfully obtained, one line of data is read through a DataInputStream and is displayed in the label in the body of the applet.

You can run this applet in any Java-enabled browser, provided that the CLASS-PATH variable is set to include the ch14 directory and is available from the web pages of the CD-ROM. The daytime server program should be running on your local machine. To run the applet under the Applet Viewer, select the ch14 directory and issue this command:

appletviewer DayApplet.html

The applet displays a single text string with the output message of the daytime server.

In-Stream Protocols

The daytime protocol used in our protocol handler example requires only that a connection be made to a particular port and a single line of plain ASCII read from it. In many protocols, this is not sufficient. Some protocols, such as HTTP, require an initial configuration phase where the client expresses a particular need to the server. The server might return some preliminary status information, such as the size of the data to be transferred.

One requirement that is quite common is the handling of in-band protocol data, which appears, for example, in the Telnet protocol. The Telnet protocol allows the negotiation of certain facilities, such as whether characters typed at the keyboard should be automatically echoed by the terminal or by the remote computer. These options can be renegotiated and modified during the lifetime of the connection.

Protocols of this type are quite common and should be handled in subclasses of FilterInputStream. Bidirectional protocols require a matching pair of input and output filters. The next example demonstrates these ideas by implementing a minimal Telnet protocol handler. However, before we develop that example, let's take a look at the Telnet protocol from a programmer's viewpoint.

Telnet Protocol Programming Considerations

The Telnet protocol addresses a number of requirements. One requirement is for bidirectional communication, allowing both client and server to transmit information. This type of communication is simple in Java and requires only the extraction of both InputStream and OutputStream from the Socket.

Telnet also provides a control facility that allows the protocol to handle a variety of programmable options. For example, it allows the server to specify that characters should not be echoed to the screen when they are typed. Transmitting commands and data over the same connection requires a mechanism to distinguish between them. This idea, known as *escaping*, is a fundamental part of the control mechanism design.

NOTE   The Telnet protocol, like all core TCP/IP services, is defined in an RFC. The RFCs may be obtained from ftp://nic.ddn.mil/ftp. RFC854, which describes the core Telnet protocol, is on the CD-ROM in the file javadevhdbk\rfcs\ rfc854.txt.

Unlike many standard services in the TCP/IP suite, Telnet does not use ASCII for commands; it uses binary. A prefix (the byte value 255) is used to indicate that a command follows. Immediately following this byte value is a command of some form. If either system actually needs to send a real 255 value, then it is sent as two 255 bytes in sequence. This type of command escape mechanism is quite common in binary protocols.

Many of the commands defined in the Telnet protocol are used for *option negotiation*, which consists of requests for, or offers of, particular facilities. These messages pass both ways between server and client.

Requests for an option to be enabled are made using the DO message; an offer to use an option is made using the WILL message. Each of these is followed by further data indicating the particular facility to which the message relates. The possible responses to a DO message are either WILL or WONT; the responses to a WILL message are DO or DONT. This protocol is elegantly designed so that if one end offers a service that the other is simultaneously requesting, each end sees the other's request as a positive acknowledgment of its own message. Here are the possibilities:

Request received:	Means:	To say:	Send this:
DO *xxxx*	I would like you to use *xxxx* mode	I am willing and able to do *xxxx*.	WILL
		NO, sorry, I cannot or do not wish to do *xxxx*.	WONT *xxxx*
WILL *xxxx*	I am willing and able to use *xxxx* mode.	I would like you to use *xxxx* mode.	DO *xxxx*
		Please do not use *xxxx* mode.	DONT *xxxx*

Notice that the same format is used for an offer and a positive acknowledgment of a request, and vice versa. If a DONT or WONT is received, the facility *must* be disabled. This feature ensures that a common service set will always be found, even if this is the most basic communication with all features disabled.

Many facilities can be controlled using this option-negotiation scheme, and it is transparently extensible to allow future enhancements. Typical of the type of facility that can be controlled is the local echoing of typed characters to the screen. A server might ask for this to be turned off when passwords are entered. It is permissible for either end to say that it WONT do something that it has been asked to DO. Under these conditions, the end that issued the request is aware of the limitation and is expected to make the best of it.

A Simple Telnet Example

To demonstrate a more complete protocol-handling scheme than the one shown in the previous daytime protocol handler example, we will develop a simple Telnet client. All the aspects previously shown—a handler and connection class located in the sun.net.www.protocol.telnet package—are required for this client. Additionally, stream protocol handling is required.

This particular client reacts to any DO or WILL message by issuing a WONT or DONT reply without even examining what service is being requested. The important part of the example is that although the services are unimplemented, the protocol itself is implemented. Hence, the code serves as an example and as a starting point for enhancement. No matter what facilities are offered, the Telnet protocol specification requires that the connection must be able to operate in this fundamental mode. This minimal behavior is known as an NVT (Network Virtual Terminal).

 The minimal Telnet client is made up of several classes. First, we will discuss each class individually, and then we will describe the overall program. The source and bytecode files for this example are located on the CD-ROM in the directory javadevhdbk\ch14. You will recall that the protocol-handler mechanisms require that the handler be a class called Handler. Because Java requires public classes be declared in a file with a name that matches the class name, the source file is therefore always called Handler.java, regardless of the actual protocol. This subdirectory has been used to avoid a name conflict with the Handler.java source file used in the daytime protocol handler example.

Defining the TelnetDefs Class

The TelnetDefs class provides definitions of the standard commands used by the Telnet protocol. The meaning of these commands is described in the RFCs. Only five elements are actually used in this example: IAC (which stands for Interpret as Command), DO, DONT, WILL, and WONT (which were described in the previous section).

LIST 14.4	**TelnetDefs.java**

```java
package sun.net.www.protocol.telnet;

public class TelnetDefs {
  public static final int IAC   = 255;
  public static final int DONT  = 254;
  public static final int DO    = 253;
  public static final int WONT  = 252;
  public static final int WILL  = 251;
  public static final int SB    = 250;
  public static final int GA    = 249;
  public static final int EL    = 248;
  public static final int EC    = 247;
  public static final int AYT   = 246;
  public static final int AO    = 245;
  public static final int IP    = 244;
  public static final int BRK   = 243;
  public static final int DM    = 242;
  public static final int NOP   = 241;
  public static final int SE    = 240;
  public static final int EOR   = 239;
  public static final int ABORT = 238;
  public static final int SUSP  = 237;
  public static final int EOF   = 236;
}
```

Defining the TelnetOutputStream Class

The TelnetOutputStream class is a subclass of FilterOutputStream, modifying a flow of characters to suit the demands of the Telnet protocol. When a data byte in the flow is the same as IAC, it must be doubled to distinguish it from a real command introduction. The class provides two convenience methods, called sendCommand(), which allow the sending of one- or two-byte commands with the Telnet IAC flag in front of them.

The TelnetOutputStream class, like any FilterOutputStream, must be constructed with an OutputStream argument. It is used to write the combined data and command stream.

LIST 14.5	*TelnetOutputStream.java*

```
package sun.net.www.protocol.telnet;

import java.io.*;

public class TelnetOutputStream extends FilterOutputStream {

  public TelnetOutputStream(OutputStream out) {
    super(out);
  }

  public void sendCommand(int cmd)
    throws IOException{
    out.write(TelnetDefs.IAC);
    out.write(cmd);
  }

  public void sendCommand(int cmd, int arg)
    throws IOException {
    sendCommand(cmd);
    out.write(arg);
  }

  public void write(int b) throws IOException {
    // Data bytes of IAC need to be doubled
    if ((b & TelnetDefs.IAC) == TelnetDefs.IAC) {
      out.write(TelnetDefs.IAC);
    }
    out.write(b);
  }
}
```

Defining the TelnetInputStream Class

The TelnetInputStream class is a FilterInputStream, which reads a flow of characters and separates commands in the Telnet protocol from the data stream. IAC
control bytes are recognized, and WILL and DO commands that are found result in
a DONT or WONT reply. WONT or DONT messages that are received are not acknowl-
edged because the protocol definition requires ignoring instructions to set a mode
that is already current.

When this class is constructed, it is given a reference to an InputStream, which is used as the character source from the remote end of the connection. A Telnet-OutputStream object, connected to the outgoing channel of the network connection, should be provided. This object is used to send responses to the protocol commands.

When a WILL or DO command is recognized, the option byte is collected and a corresponding negative acknowledgment, DONT or WONT, is constructed and sent by the TelnetOutputStream object. If WONT or DONT commands are received, these do not require acknowledgment because the Telnet protocol does not permit refusal of them.

LIST 14.6   *TelnetInputStream.java*

```java
package sun.net.www.protocol.telnet;

import java.io.*;

public class TelnetInputStream extends FilterInputStream {
  protected TelnetOutputStream outChannel;

  public TelnetInputStream(InputStream source,
                           TelnetOutputStream out) {
    super(source);
    outChannel = out;
  }

  public int read() throws IOException {
    int b = in.read();
    // If we have a command introduction, go into
    // the processing body
    while (b == TelnetDefs.IAC)
    {
      // start by fetching the follow on byte
      b = in.read();
      // the byte after IAC is the command byte
      switch (b)
      {
        // another IAC implies that we have a data byte of 255
        case TelnetDefs.IAC:
          return b;
          // break; not reached..
```

```
        case TelnetDefs.WILL:
          b = in.read();
          outChannel.sendCommand(TelnetDefs.DONT, b);
          break;
        case TelnetDefs.WONT:
          b = in.read();
          break;
        case TelnetDefs.DO:
          b = in.read();
          outChannel.sendCommand(TelnetDefs.WONT, b);
          break;
        case TelnetDefs.DONT:
          b = in.read();
          break;
      }
      b = in.read();
    }
    return b;
  }
}
```

Defining the GlassTTY Class

The GlassTTY class provides a basic *glass teletype,* or crude terminal program. It takes keystrokes and transmits them to an OutputStream. Characters received from an InputStream are pasted onto the 80×24-character display. To support the basic NVT mode of Telnet, characters typed at the keyboard are echoed to the display as well as being sent to the output.

To support the two streams simultaneously, this class creates a separate Thread, which is used to read characters from the InputStream. Characters typed at the keyboard cause calls to the processKeyEvent() method and are processed and sent to the output channel from there.

The display is maintained very crudely. A two-dimensional array holds 24 rows of 80 characters. Whenever the display requires updating, this entire array is copied to the screen. The getMinimumSize() and getPreferredSize() methods use the Font-Metrics for the Fixedwidth font to provide size information so that a LayoutManager can properly display this window.

LIST 14.7   *GlassTTY.java*

```java
import java.awt.*;
import java.awt.event.*;
import java.io.*;

public class GlassTTY extends Canvas implements Runnable {
  private Font font;
  private FontMetrics metrics;

  private InputStream in;
  private OutputStream out;
  private Thread inHandler;

  private char [][] display = new char[24][80];
  private char[] blankLine = new char[display[0].length];
  private int x, y;

  public GlassTTY() {
    for (int i = 0; i < blankLine.length; i++) {
      blankLine[i] = ' ';
    }
    font = new Font("Monospaced", Font.PLAIN, 10);
    setFont(font);
    enableEvents(AWTEvent.KEY_EVENT_MASK);
  }

  public void connect(InputStream source, OutputStream dest) {
    in = source;
    out = dest;
    inHandler = new Thread(this, "input handler");
    inHandler.start();
  }

  public Dimension getPreferredSize() {
    return getMinimumSize();
  }

  public Dimension getMinimumSize() {
    int x = 0;
    int y = 0;
```

```java
      if (metrics != null) {
        x = display[0].length * metrics.charWidth(' ');
        y = display.length * metrics.getHeight();
      }
      return new Dimension(x, y);
  }

  public void addNotify() {
    super.addNotify();
    metrics = getToolkit().getFontMetrics(font);
    for (int y = 0; y < display.length; y++) {
      System.arraycopy(blankLine, 0, display[y], 0, blankLine.length);
    }
  }

  public void join() {
    boolean success = true;
    do {
      try {
        inHandler.join();
      }
      catch (InterruptedException e) {
        success = false;
      }
    } while (!success);
  }

  public void run() {
    int c = 0;

    for (;;) {
      try {
        c = in.read();
        if (c == -1) {
          break;
        }
      }
      catch (IOException e) {
        e.printStackTrace();
        System.exit(1);
      }
      switch(c) {
```

```
        case 0x08:
          doBS();
          break;
        case 0x0a:
          doCR();
        case 0x0d:
          doLF();
          break;
        default:
          newChar(c);
          break;
        }
        repaint();
      }
    }

    private synchronized void doBS() {
      if (x > 0) {
        x-;
      }
    }

    private synchronized void doLF() {
      if (y < display.length - 1) {
        y++;
      }
      else {
        for (int y = 0; y < display.length - 1; y++) {
          System.arraycopy(display[y+1], 0, display[y], 0,
                           display[y].length);
        }
        System.arraycopy(blankLine, 0, display[y], 0, blankLine.length);
      }
    }

    private synchronized void doCR() {
      x = 0;
    }

    private synchronized void newChar(int c) {
      display[y][x] = ((char)c);
      if (++x >= display[y].length) {
```

```java
        x = 0;
        doLF();
      }
    }

    public void paint(Graphics g) {
      for (int y = 0; y < display.length; y++) {
        g.drawChars(display[y], 0, display[y].length,
                    0, (y * metrics.getHeight()) +
                    metrics.getLeading() +
                    metrics.getAscent());
      }
      putCursor(g);
    }

    public void putCursor(Graphics g) {
      int x, y, w, h;
      Rectangle r = cursor();
      x = r.x;
      y = r.y;
      w = r.width;
      h = r.height;
      g.drawRect(x, y, w, h);
    }

    private Rectangle cursor() {
      return new Rectangle(x * metrics.charWidth(' '),
                    y * metrics.getHeight(),
                    metrics.charWidth(' ') - 1,
                    metrics.getHeight() - 1);

    }

    public void processKeyEvent(KeyEvent ev) {
      try {
        if (ev.getID() == KeyEvent.KEY_PRESSED) {
          switch (ev.getKeyCode()) {
          case KeyEvent.VK_ENTER:
            System.out.println("Got an ENTER");
            doLF();
            doCR();
            out.write('\n');
```

```
          repaint();
          break;
        case KeyEvent.VK_BACK_SPACE:
          System.out.println("Got BS");
          doBS();
          newChar(' ');
          doBS();
          out.write('\010');
          repaint();
          break;
      }
    }
    else if (ev.getID() == KeyEvent.KEY_TYPED) {
      char c = ev.getKeyChar();
      System.out.println("Got typed char " + c);
      if (!Character.isISOControl(c)) {
        System.out.println("char is not control");
        newChar(ev.getKeyChar());
        out.write(ev.getKeyChar());
        repaint();
      }
    }
  }
  catch (IOException e) {
    e.printStackTrace();
    System.exit(1);
  }
}

public void ec() {
  display[y][x] = (' ');
  repaint();
}

public void el() {
  System.arraycopy(blankLine, 0, display[y], 0, display[y].length);
}

public static void main(String args[]) throws Exception {
  PipedInputStream i = new PipedInputStream();
  PipedOutputStream o = new PipedOutputStream(i);
  Frame f = new Frame("GlassTTY test");
```

```
        GlassTTY that = new GlassTTY();
        f.add(that, BorderLayout.CENTER);
        f.pack();
        f.setVisible(true);
        that.connect(i, o);
    }
}
```

Defining the GlassTelnet Class

The GlassTelnet class provides the glue that holds the other classes in the example together in a workable program. It creates the network connection and the other objects.

The command-line argument, if any, should be a URL. The URL should use the telnet: protocol and may include an optional port number. A URL is created based on that argument or on the default telnet://localhost/ if no argument has been supplied. This requires that the Telnet protocol handler be found by the underlying system. Once the URL has been created, it is connected, and a GlassTTY is created based on the input and output streams of the resulting URLConnection.

After all the parts have been constructed, a Frame is built, and the GlassTTY object is added to it. The Frame is sized and shown. After that, the main thread waits for the GlassTTY object to kill its input thread. It is killed when the input stream to that object returns -1, indicating the end of the file.

LIST 14.8   *GlassTelnet.java*

```
import java.awt.*;
import java.net.*;
import java.io.*;

public class GlassTelnet
{
  public static void main(String args[]) throws Exception
  {
    URL u = new URL((args.length > 0) ?
                    args[0] : "telnet://localhost/");
```

```
        URLConnection c = u.openConnection();
        GlassTTY glass = new GlassTTY();
        glass.connect(c.getInputStream(), c.getOutputStream());

        Frame f = new Frame("GlassTelnet to " + args[0]);
        f.add(glass, BorderLayout.CENTER);
        f.pack();
        f.show();
        glass.join();
        System.out.println("Connection closed. Press <return> to exit");
        System.in.read();
        System.exit(0);
    }
}
```

Running the Telnet Program

To run the program, you must have a network service to connect to. Although the program will work adequately as a general client, the Telnet protocol parts will not be exercised at all unless the program connects to a Telnet server. If you have a network connection to a Unix machine, you can log in to that. If you have an Internet connection, there are a number of services that allow you to use a Telnet client. Some of these services require specific terminal emulation, which the Telnet client cannot offer. You should therefore select one that allows the use of a *glass TTY*.

TIP

A service called Hytelnet was set up some time ago to attempt to organize services that allow you use a Telnet client over the Internet. A web search for *Hytelnet* should yield an interesting server to connect to for the example.

When you have located a suitable server, start the Telnet client by issuing the command:

java GlassTelnet *<remoteURL>*

The program will run, set up the connection, and display the terminal window. The server will usually issue a login prompt first. From that point, the operation is governed by the remote server.

WARNING   Because of the absence of controls in this client, passwords entered using it will be echoed. It should not be used for any serious applications without being modified.

Enhancing the Telnet Example

Although this is quite a large example, it implements only the absolute minimum requirements of the Telnet protocol. To make a useful program, you should extend the user interface to support some of the options that are most commonly used. You should modify the `TelnetInputStream` and `TelnetOutputStream` classes to respond appropriately to inquiries and commands relating to the options that are implemented.

You could enhance the `GlassTTY` class in a number of ways. First, you could make the screen update much more efficient. At present, any single character change on the display results in the entire 80×24 matrix being redrawn, including all the blanks at the ends of lines. This situation could be improved by keeping track of where characters have been changed and only refreshing those areas under normal conditions. Be careful to ensure that exposure is properly handled, however.

You might also add more terminal emulation features to allow direct cursor control and other capabilities. It would be sensible to implement one of the commonly used terminals, such as the VT series, so that the resulting work is as useful as possible.

Content Handling

A number of the ideas discussed for protocol handling are broadly applicable to content handling as well. As explained earlier in the chapter, the content type must be determined before getting started. Based on that information, an appropriate content handler is sought. As with protocol handlers, either a factory can be used or a specific named package can be checked. If a content handler is located, it is then responsible for receiving and decoding the data that comes to it. The results of that decoding operation must be made available to the caller in a useful form.

Content Handler Mechanisms

Content handlers are invoked by objects of the URLConnection class. When the getContent() method is called, the URLConnection determines the content type of the connection it represents; this is done via the protocol handler getContent-Type() method. Based on that type, a content handler is sought.

A similar approach to that taken for the protocol handler search is adopted. Generally, content handlers are found in a class named after the content type, in a package called sun.net.www.content. So, for example, the handler for audio/wav would be located in the class sun.net.www.content.audio.wav. Notice that the slash character (/) has been converted into a dot (.), indicating that the hierarchy of content types has been translated into a hierarchy of packages.

NOTE   Many content types—for example, application/mac-binhex40 and video/x-msvideo, which are used for HQX and AVI files, respectively—include the hyphen character and other nonalphanumeric characters. The specification says that all slash characters are converted to dots and all other nonalphanumeric characters are converted into underscore (_). This point is particularly important because the hyphen and many other nonalphanumeric characters are not legal in class names.

As with the search for a protocol handler, it is possible to install a content handler factory using the static method of the URLConnection class setContent-HandlerFactory(). If this method has been used, the content handler factory method createContentHandler() will be called with the MIME type string as its argument. If this fails, the standard package and class name search is pursued.

Content handlers must be subclasses of ContentHandler. This subclass defines a single method, getContent(), which takes a URLConnection as its argument and from that obtains the InputStream, which supplies the data to be handled.

An Example of a Content Handler

It is in the nature of a content handler that the work involved be mainly decoding the actual data passed over from the server. To produce an example that is not unduly cumbersome and overloaded with handling code that would obscure the essential point, the example presented here uses handles, which are a tiny subset of HTML.

The content type is called `text/tml`. The format of the data for `tml` is similar to HTML, except that the only tags that are understood are `<hr>` and `<br>`, which generate a horizontal rule and a newline, respectively.

Two classes make up the content handler, and a third describes a trivial test applet. The following sections describe each of these classes and how the classes work together to produce the content handler example. The source and bytecode files for this example are located on the CD-ROM in the directory `javadevhdbk\ch14`.

Defining the TmlStream Class

The `TmlStream` class takes a character stream as its input and parses it to produce a sequence of tokens. To drive the parser, the `nextToken()` method is called. This method returns an integer value that indicates whether the collected token is plain text, a token, or the end of the input.

After the next token has been assembled, and its type reported by the `next-Token()` method, calling the `tokenValue()` method returns the actual token value. This action is appropriate provided that the token type was not `ENDING`, which indicates that the end of input has been reached.

Tokens are returned as `String` objects; they are either plain text strings or the contents of a tag. Two specific tags, `<br>` and `<hr>`, are recognized by the parser. When one of these is found, it is converted into a plain text representation, either a newline or a newline followed by a string of 80 hyphens, followed by another newline. These two tokens, therefore, loosely mimic the effect of the same tokens in normal HTML. Any other token that is found is collected and then stripped of the leading and trailing `<` and `>` symbols and any spaces. Finally, the token is converted to lowercase before being returned.

While collecting characters to form a token, multiple whitespace characters are coalesced into a single-space character. So newlines, for example, are ignored and, where specifically required, must be encoded in the source by the token `<br>`. This coding is like normal HTML.

This class is not a subclass of `FilterInputStream`; it has more similarities with the `StringTokenizer` class. This dissimilarity is not a problem, since the classes that will use this class do not need to be written to use an `InputStream` as such, provided they are written correctly to use whatever API is available to them.

NOTE

The Tml Stream class is a member of the sun.net.www.content.text package simply to group it with the rest of this example; there is no specific need for this placement.

LIST 14.9   *TmlStream.java*

```
package sun.net.www.content.text;

import java.io.*;

public class TmlStream {
  public static final int  PLAIN = 0;
  public static final int  TAG   = 1;
  public static final int ENDED = -1;

  private static final String HLINE =
    "\n...................." +
    "....................\n";
  private static final String NEWLINE = "\n";

  private int lastType = PLAIN;
  private String lastString;
  private int state = PLAIN;

  BufferedReader source;
  StringBuffer buildup = new StringBuffer();


  public TmlStream(InputStream in) throws IOException {
    source = new BufferedReader(
      new InputStreamReader(in, "8859_1"));
  }

  public int nextToken() throws IOException {
    int c;
    boolean lastWasSpace = false;
    boolean completed = false;
```

```
    if (state == PLAIN) {
      do {
        c = source.read();
        if (Character.isWhitespace((char)c)) {
          if (lastWasSpace) {
            while (Character.isWhitespace((char)(c = source.read())))
              ;
            lastWasSpace = false;
          }
          else {
            c = ' ';
            lastWasSpace = true;
          }
        }
        else {
          lastWasSpace = false;
        }

        if ((c != '<') && (c != -1)) {
          buildup.append((char)c);
        }
        else {
          completed = true;
          lastType = PLAIN;
          lastString = buildup.toString();
          buildup.setLength(0);
          if (c == '<') {
            state = TAG;
          }
          else if (c == -1) {
            state = ENDED;
          }
        }
      } while (!completed);
    }
    else if (state == TAG) {
      do {
        c = source.read();
        if (Character.isWhitespace((char)c)) {
          if (lastWasSpace) {
```

```
            while (Character.isWhitespace((char)(c = source.read())))
              ;
            lastWasSpace = false;
        }
        else {
          c = ' ';
          lastWasSpace = true;
        }
      }
      else {
        lastWasSpace = false;
      }

      if (c == -1) {
        state = ENDED;
        throw new IOException("TML format error, EOF inside tag");
      }
      else if (c != '>') {
        buildup.append((char)c);
      }
      else {
        lastType = TAG; // tentative
        state = PLAIN;
        completed = true;
        lastString = buildup.toString();
        lastString = lastString.trim().toLowerCase();

        if (lastString.equals("br")) {
          lastString = NEWLINE;
          lastType = PLAIN;
        }
        else if (lastString.equals("hr")) {
          lastString = HLINE;
          lastType = PLAIN;
        }
        buildup.setLength(0);
      }
    } while (!completed);
  }
  else if (state == ENDED) {
    lastType = ENDED;
  }
```

```
      return lastType;
   }

   public String tokenValue() {
     return lastString;
   }
}
```

Defining the tml Class

The `tml` class is the actual content handler that is used to handle content of type `text/tml`. It must therefore fulfill two requirements:

- It must be a subclass of `ContentHandler`.

- It must have precisely the correct package and class name in order to be located by the default rules for content handlers. In this case, the class must be called `tml` and be located in the package `sun.net.www.content.text`.

WARNING   Although it is the convention to begin class names with a capital letter, this must not be done in this case. If you use a capital T, the class will not be recognized as a handler for the **text/tml** content type, but instead be mistaken for the **text/Tml** content type.

The behavior of the content handler is embedded in the `getContent()` method, and the data that is to be decoded is supplied by the stream encapsulated in the `URLConnection` argument to that method. In this case, the `InputStream` source is extracted from the `URLConnection` and used to construct an instance of `TmlStream` that will parse the input.

After the input streams have been set up, the `getContent()` method proceeds by collecting all the tokens into a `StringBuffer`. Tags other than `<br>` and `<hr>` are wrapped up on a line by themselves with the UNKNOWN TAG message. All plain strings, including the converted values used for `<br>` and `<hr>`, which appear as simple text, are appended to the `StringBuffer` as is.

Once the input is completely read, the contents of the `StringBuffer` are converted to a `String`, which is used to initialize a `TextArea`. This `TextArea` is then returned from the `getContent()` method.

LIST 14.10   *tml.java*

```java
package sun.net.www.content.text;

import java.io.*;
import java.net.*;
import java.awt.*;

public class tml extends ContentHandler {
  public Object getContent(URLConnection c) throws IOException {
    StringBuffer sb = new StringBuffer();
    InputStream source = c.getInputStream();
    TmlStream i = new TmlStream(source);

    int tokType;
    while ((tokType = i.nextToken()) != TmlStream.ENDED) {
      if (tokType == TmlStream.PLAIN) {
        sb.append(i.tokenValue());
      }
      else if (tokType == TmlStream.TAG) {
        System.out.println("\nUNKNOWN TAG <" + i.tokenValue() + ">");
      }
    }
    return new TextArea(sb.toString());
  }
}
```

Creating the Test Applet

The TmlTest applet tests the content handler for the text/tml content type. Notice that it does not refer directly to either of the classes that are involved in this content handling—those classes are invoked automatically without intervention by the applet.

First, the applet has to decide on the URL to fetch. If the HTML from which the applet is loaded defines a parameter url, then that value is used as a starting point; otherwise, a default of TmlTest.tml is used. The URL that is determined in this way is treated as relative to the document base from which the HTML file was loaded. This treatment allows you to provide either an absolute URL or a relative one. In either case, a URL object is constructed, and the getContent()

method is invoked on that. Notice that no intermediate URLConnection is created; creating one is possible but not necessary in this case. The URL object will handle that aspect.

The returned value from the getContent() method will, if the text/tml content handler has been invoked successfully, be a TextArea. This applet simply checks to see if the class of the returned object is an instance of the Component class; if not, it creates a label with an error message indicating the class of the object that was returned. The resulting Component is then added to the applet display in the Center region. Notice that the applet has been configured to use a BorderLayout rather than the default FlowLayout.

| **LIST 14.11** | ***TmlTest.java*** |

```
import java.applet.*;
import java.awt.*;
import java.net.*;

public class TmlTest extends Applet {
  public void init() {
    setLayout(new BorderLayout());
    String u = getParameter("url");
    if (u == null) {
      u = "TmlTest.tml";
    }
    URL url = null;
    Object o = null;
    try {
      url = new URL(getDocumentBase(), u);
      o = url.getContent();
    }
    catch (Exception e) {
      e.printStackTrace();
      throw new RuntimeException("URL trouble: " + e);
    }
    if (!(o instanceof Component)) {
      o = new Label("Can't handle content type: " +
                    o.getClass().getName());
    }
    add( (Component)o, BorderLayout.CENTER);
  }
}
```

The input file `TmlTest.tml` contains the following text:

```
hello
  there
      this
is a test<br>This should be a new line
<hr>and this should
be beneath a rule
```

When everything is running properly, this input results in the Applet Viewer display shown in Figure 14.1.

FIGURE 14.1:

The Applet Viewer showing the TmlTest applet running

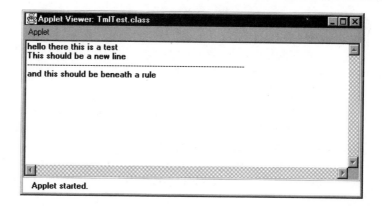

If you do not have a web server available to you, you cannot run this example. The reason is that the content type for the file `TmlTest.tml` must be specified as `text/tml`, which does not occur by recognition of the file extension, but rather by means of having a properly configured HTTP server.

> **TIP**
>
> If you do not have a web server, there are suitable ones available at no cost for evaluation. A search on the web will locate several, such as the Java Web Server or O'Reilly's web site.

If you do have a web server, you will need to copy the following files into a directory from which the server can make them available for HTTP access: `TmlTest.class`, `TmlTest.html`, and `TmlTest.tml`. Once you have located these, configure your web server to report files with the extension `.tml` as having the MIME type `text/tml` and start the server if necessary.

When the server is configured and running, start the Applet Viewer to load, via HTTP, the `TmlTest.html` file. The Applet Viewer should be started from the directory `javadevhdbk\ch14` so the `sun\net\www\content\text` subdirectory, which contains the elements of the content handler, is located in the current directory. You also need to ensure that the current directory is on your `CLASSPATH`; this is the case by default unless you explicitly set up a `CLASSPATH` value.

Server-Side Handlers

One of the opportunities that Java originally offered was for *server-side* content and protocol handlers. If a web site wanted to provide a new content type or use a specialist protocol for some reason, the expectation was that Java would allow the handlers for those services to be loaded transparently over the network when the browser needed them.

This action is still possible in principle, but as we mentioned earlier in the chapter, it is not supported under the current browsers. This section discusses the nature of this limitation and the difficulties in overcoming it. Given an understanding of the issues involved, it is possible—although not trivial—to create a browser that does handle server-side content and protocol handlers.

Dynamic Class Loading

When an applet runs in a Java browser, it can load supporting classes. When a class is needed, the class loader first searches for it on the local system to ensure the best possible response time and to maintain the integrity of the system classes so they are not usurped by imported classes that appear to have the same name. If the class is not found locally, the class loader used to load the applet proceeds to look for that class on the same system that provided the applet itself.

If a class is a member of a named package, then the URL from which the class loader attempts to load it is modified by the package name in the same way that a locally loaded class would be. For example, if an applet has been loaded from `http://www.xyz.com/interesting/myjava.class`, and that class attempts to load a class called `mysupport.math.Complex`, then the class loader will attempt to load from the URL `http://www.xyz.com/interesting/mysupport/math/ Complex.class`. This behavior appears to suggest that it would be possible to load content or protocol handlers from a server simply by placing them in the required directory structure, reflecting the package name sun.net.www.... according to the particular conditions. In fact, a number of problems arise when this is attempted.

Reviewing the Difficulties

The first difficulty with dynamic class loading is that packages starting with sun..., java..., or netscape... are protected by the security manager by default so that imported code cannot be added to them. This is done by a general mechanism. Defining two properties in the hotjava/properties file called package.restrict .access.sun and package.restrict.definition.sun, and setting the values to false will remove this restriction for the HotJava browser and Applet Viewer. Unfortunately, it also removes an important part of the security barrier that protects your system. Most notably, these changes allow an applet, or other imported code, to create and use arbitrary parts of the sun package hierarchy. One part of this, the sun.tools.debug package, would be particularly sensitive because it would potentially allow an applet to bypass all other security restrictions.

In Java 1.1 and newer, an alternative might be to redefine the property java .handler.protcol.pkgs, but this would be installation dependent. Handler loading would require that this value be set up to correspond to the configuration of the server.

Another difficulty comes up because the content and protocol handlers are not loaded by the applet; they are loaded by system classes, specifically the URL and URL-Connection classes. Whenever a class asks to use another class, the class is loaded by the same class loader that loaded the class that is making the request, unless the first class specifically requests otherwise. Here, the URL and URLConnection classes have been loaded by the system class loader, which never loads from anywhere except the local system. This means that the content and protocol handlers are only sought on the local machine.

It might appear that the way around this problem is to have an applet load the handlers. Unfortunately, this fails, too. Classes are loaded into namespaces that are controlled by the class loader that loaded them. If a content or protocol handler is loaded by an applet, it is not visible to the URL and URLConnection classes that need to use it.

Having an applet load the handlers also presents two other difficulties:

- Content and protocol handlers should be available to the browser itself, not just to the applets. It is inconvenient to have to load an applet on a page to support a particular content type used within that page. The applet would also probably be loaded too late to work properly.

- Any Java code that is not loaded by the system class loader is considered untrusted. The security manager does not operate solely on applets—any and all imported code is restricted. One of the key restrictions is that a network connection can be made only to the same host that supplied the code. Because protocol handlers must create the Socket objects that communicate with the remote host, an imported protocol handler can only connect to its originating site.

Of course, this latter difficulty does not, of itself, make the protocol handler useless, but it does continue to reduce its facility even after the other difficulties have been overcome. If the restrictions on creating sockets are not imposed completely, there is a danger of a security breach, and the browser is left wide open to attack. So the rule must not be waived.

Additional difficulties arise when using a browser that is not "pure" Java, such as Netscape Navigator or Microsoft's Internet Explorer. In such systems, the JVM is only invoked specifically to run applets and not to handle arbitrary bits of HTML. In these cases, there is clearly no immediate possibility of installing Java content or protocol handlers from remote sites.

Approaching a Solution

One approach that can be taken to make server-side handler loading a possibility is to install factories for content and protocol handlers. These allow the URL and URLConnection classes to use a more flexible approach to finding the handlers they need. To achieve this, the browser code itself must be modified because factories cannot be installed by imported code, for obvious security reasons. Instead, they must be installed once and only once by the local classes of the application.

If a factory is to be used, it must be able to communicate with the browser to determine the URL from which the current document has been loaded. Based on this, the factory can then determine the full URL from which to attempt to load any handlers required to support that particular page.

Alternatives to Server-Side Handlers

Clearly, it is not trivial to implement server-side handlers. Perhaps the biggest problem is that the result is nonstandard, which means that server-side handlers will be nothing more than an interesting academic discussion topic. This will be the case until a commercial-grade browser implements the facility and clearly documents the requirements it makes of the server.

The question remains of how the promise of Java can be fully realized. There are several answers to this:

- In a controlled environment such as a corporate intranet, the handlers can be made available along with other company-wide software simply by using file-sharing systems such as the Network File System (NFS).

- In an open environment, such as the Internet, the only solution is to embed the handling into an applet in an ad hoc way. This approach, although it lacks the elegance of the built-in content and protocol handling, can still be tidy, extensible, and reusable—provided that the handling has a good object-oriented design that considers the needs of the protocols and the applets that will use them.

- An applet can import classes to handle the content for itself, even though it cannot install the classes as a content or protocol handler for the whole system.

- The content may be provided in a form that is already supported, if necessary by using a servlet to perform the conversion.

Summary

This chapter has discussed the nature of protocols and content types. MIME was introduced as the preferred mechanism for identifying content type. Different mechanisms for handling content and protocols were discussed in the light of the organic nature of the Internet.

The mechanisms of protocol handlers and the ways in which they can be located by a browser or application needing them were introduced, along with a basic example. A second example showed the beginnings of a Telnet handler. It also described the approach to handling protocols, which require the manipulation of stream data—as distinct from those where the protocol simply requires a preliminary configuration before producing pure data.

Content handlers have been introduced, and the mechanisms for locating the handlers were discussed. An example demonstrated a severely stripped-down version of HTML being handled automatically by the Applet Viewer.

Finally, the promise and difficulties of server-side handlers were discussed, and a rudimentary server-side protocol handler mechanism was implemented on top of the standard Applet Viewer tool.

In the next chapter, we'll turn to the subject of the Java Foundation Classes (JFC) components.

PART III

The New APIs

CHAPTER

FIFTEEN

15

The JFC Swing Components

- JFC frames and menus

- JFC tabbed panes

- JFC labels and buttons

- JFC combo boxes

- JFC sliders

- JFC password fields

- JFC toolbars

The functionality of the Java Foundation Classes (JFC) includes an event propagation model, drag-and-drop support, handicapped accessibility, a wide variety of obscure specialty capabilities, and a package of components known as the Swing components or Swing Set. Even the Swing Set by itself is enormous. The javax.swing package contains 15 subordinate packages, more than 20 interfaces, and more than 75 classes. (Obviously, we won't be examining all the details here, which would require several hundred pages!)

The most important thing to remember about the Swing components is that they are just components. They're complicated, they're richly featured, and there are a lot of them, but they're just components. As a Java programmer, you already have plenty of experience using components.

This chapter introduces the following common Swing components:

JFrame	JToggleButton	JSlider
JTabbedPane	JCheckBox	JPasswordField
JTextField	JRadioButton	JToolbar
JButton	JComboBox	JTable
JLabel		

A Sampler of Swing Components

As an introduction to programming with Swing components, we will examine a single, large program. The SwingDemo application displays several types of components, organized into eight tabbed panels. The panels appear in a frame, as shown in Figure 15.1.

The first thing to observe about the SwingDemo window is that it appears to show a perfectly ordinary frame, which in turn appears to contain a perfectly ordinary text field. In fact, the frame is an instance of the JFrame class, and the text field is an instance of the JTextField class. All the familiar AWT components have corresponding JFC classes. In general, there are four differences between the AWT classes and the JFC classes:

- The JFC classes have names that begin with the letter J.

- The JFC classes typically provide more functionality than the corresponding AWT classes.

FIGURE 15.1:

The SwingDemo program

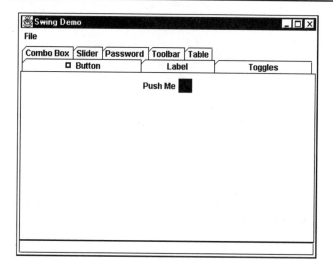

- The JFC classes reside in the javax.swing package.

- The JFC classes bypass the AWT peer mechanism.

For example, the JFC version of the java.awt.Button class is the javax.swing .JButton class. This class has no peer; a JButton interacts directly with the mouse and screen and has the same appearance and behavior on all platforms.

JFC Textfields, Frames, and Menus

The constructor for the SwingDemo program adds a JTextField to the frame. The main method and constructor are as follows:

```
public static void main(String[] args)
{
    SwingDemo that = new SwingDemo();
    that.setVisible(true);
}

public SwingDemo()
{
    super("Swing Demo");
    setSize(450, 350);
```

```
addWindowListener(new WindowAdapter() {
    public void windowClosing(WindowEvent e)
    {
        System.exit(0);
    }
});

textfield = new JTextField();
getContentPane().add(textfield, BorderLayout.SOUTH);

addMenu();
addTabbedPane();
}
```

Note that the JFrame class has one more level of containment than the AWT Frame class; a JFrame contains a subordinate container called a *content pane*, which can be obtained by calling getContentPane() on the JFrame. Child components should always be added to the content pane, rather than to the JFrame itself.

After inserting the JTextField, the constructor calls two methods that add a menu and a tabbed pane. Both methods appear in SwingDemo, just below the constructor.

The addMenu() method inserts a File menu with two choices:

The code for the addMenu() method is:

```
private void addMenu()
{
    JMenuBar mbar = new JMenuBar();
    JMenu menu = new JMenu("File");
    menu.add(new JCheckBoxMenuItem("Check Me"));
    menu.addSeparator();
    JMenuItem item = new JMenuItem("Exit");
    item.addActionListener(new ActionListener() {
        public void actionPerformed(ActionEvent e)
        {
            System.exit(0);
        }
    });
```

```
            menu.add(item);
            mbar.add(menu);
            setJMenuBar(mbar);
    }
```

This code is easy to understand, even if you don't know anything about JFC components. If you take away all the Js in the class names, you have classic AWT code. Note that the JMenuItem takes an ActionListener, just like a MenuItem. The JCheckBoxMenuItem could have been given an ItemListener, just like a CheckBox-MenuItem.

JFC Tabbed Panes

The SwingDemo constructor calls a method named addTabbedPane(). This method builds and installs a JTabbedPane. The code for addTabbedPane() appears below.

```
    private void addTabbedPane()
    {
        JTabbedPane tabbedPane = new JTabbedPane();

        tabbedPane.addTab("Button",                    // Title
                    new TabIcon(),                     // Icon
                    new ButtonPanel(textfield),        // Component
                    "Click here for Button demo");     // Tooltip

        tabbedPane.addTab("Label",
                    null,
                    new LabelPanel(),
                    "Click here for Label demo");

        tabbedPane.addTab("Toggles",
                    null,
                    new TogglePanel(textfield),
                    "Click here for Toggle demo");

        tabbedPane.addTab("Combo Box",
                    null,
                    new ComboPanel(textfield),
                    "Click here for Combo Box demo");
```

```
        tabbedPane.addTab("Slider",
                    null,
                    new SliderPanel(textfield),
                    "Click here for Slider demo");

        tabbedPane.addTab("Password",
                    null,
                    new PasswordPanel(textfield),
                    "Click here for Password Field demo");

        tabbedPane.addTab("Toolbar",
                    null,
                    new ToolbarPanel(textfield),
                    "Click here for Toolbar demo");

        tabbedPane.addTab("Table",
                    null,
                    new TablePanel(),
                    "Click here for Table demo");

        getContentPane().add(tabbedPane, BorderLayout.CENTER);
    }
```

Adding Tabs

A JTabbedPane is a kind of container that presents its contents in a tabbed-pane format. The addTab() method is overloaded. The version used here takes four arguments:

- A string that appears as the label of the tab being added
- An optional icon (null specifies that no icon should appear)
- The component that appears when the tab is selected
- A string that appears as a rollover tooltip

Adding an Icon to a Tab

In the code for the tabbed pane, only the first call to addTab() specifies an icon. The icon can be seen on the Button tab (see Figure 15.1). An icon is an instance of a class that implements the Icon interface, which has three methods:

public int getIconWidth()   Returns the width of the icon, in pixels.

public int getIconHeight()   Returns the height of the icon, in pixels.

public void paintIcon(Component c, Graphics g, int x, int y)   Paints the icon within component c, starting at (x, y), using graphics contact g.

The icon that appears on the Button tab is an instance of TabIcon, which is an inner class within the SwingDemo class:

```
class TabIcon implements Icon
{
    public int getIconWidth()   { return 16; }
    public int getIconHeight()  { return 16; }

    public void paintIcon(Component c, Graphics g, int x, int y)
    {
        g.setColor(Color.black);
        g.fillRect(x+4, y+4,
                    getIconWidth()-8, getIconHeight()-8);
        g.setColor(Color.cyan);
        g.fillRect(x+6, y+6,
                    getIconWidth()-12, getIconHeight()-12);
    }
}
```

The SwingDemo Class

The source code for the SwingDemo class follows. The complete program appears at the end of this chapter, as well as on the CD-ROM in the directory \javadevhdbk\ ch15. The main application class source is included on the CD-ROM as \javadev-hdbk\ch15\SwingDemo.java.

| **LIST 15.1** | ***SwingDemo.java*** |

```java
import javax.swing.*;
import java.awt.*;
import java.awt.event.*;

public class SwingDemo extends JFrame
{
    private JTextField      textfield;


    public static void main(String[] args)
    {
        SwingDemo that = new SwingDemo();
        that.setVisible(true);
    }

    public SwingDemo()
    {
        super("Swing Demo");
        setSize(450, 350);

        addWindowListener(new WindowAdapter() {
            public void windowClosing(WindowEvent e)
            {
                System.exit(0);
            }
        });

        textfield = new JTextField();
        getContentPane().add(textfield, BorderLayout.SOUTH);

        addMenu();
        addTabbedPane();
    }


    private void addMenu()
```

```
    {
        JMenuBar mbar = new JMenuBar();
        JMenu menu = new JMenu("File");
        menu.add(new JCheckBoxMenuItem("Check Me"));
        menu.addSeparator();
        JMenuItem item = new JMenuItem("Exit");
        item.addActionListener(new ActionListener() {
            public void actionPerformed(ActionEvent e)
            {
                System.exit(0);
            }
        });
        menu.add(item);
        mbar.add(menu);
        setJMenuBar(mbar);
    }


    private void addTabbedPane()
    {
        JTabbedPane tabbedPane = new JTabbedPane();

        tabbedPane.addTab("Button",                     // Title
                    new TabIcon(),                      // Icon
                    new ButtonPanel(textfield),         // Component
                    "Click here for Button demo");      // Help

        tabbedPane.addTab("Label",
                    null,
                    new LabelPanel(),
                    "Click here for Label demo");

        tabbedPane.addTab("Toggles",
                    null,
                    new TogglePanel(textfield),
                    "Click here for Toggle demo");

        tabbedPane.addTab("Combo Box",
                    null,
                    new ComboPanel(textfield),
                    "Click here for Combo Box demo");
```

```java
        tabbedPane.addTab("Slider",
                    null,
                    new SliderPanel(textfield),
                    "Click here for Slider demo");

        tabbedPane.addTab("Password",
                    null,
                    new PasswordPanel(textfield),
                    "Click here for Password Field demo");

        tabbedPane.addTab("Toolbar",
                    null,
                    new ToolbarPanel(textfield),
                    "Click here for Toolbar demo");

        tabbedPane.addTab("Table",
                    null,
                    new TablePanel(),
                    "Click here for Table demo");

        getContentPane().add(tabbedPane, BorderLayout.CENTER);
    }


    class TabIcon implements Icon
    {
        public int getIconWidth()   { return 16; }
        public int getIconHeight()  { return 16; }

        public void paintIcon(Component c, Graphics g, int x, int y)
        {
            g.setColor(Color.black);
            g.fillRect(x+4, y+4,
                    getIconWidth()-8, getIconHeight()-8);
            g.setColor(Color.cyan);
            g.fillRect(x+6, y+6,
                    getIconWidth()-12, getIconHeight()-12);
        }
    }
}
```

The remainder of this chapter investigates the various panes that appear within the SwingDemo program. Each pane illustrates one or more JFC components. Many of the components in the panes report status changes to the JTextField that appears at the bottom of the frame.

Improved Components

This section examines labels and several variations on the button theme: plain buttons, toggle buttons, and checkboxes. We'll take a look at the Label, Button, and Toggles panes of the SwingDemo program.

JFC Labels

The Label pane, shown in Figure 15.2, is extremely simple. It contains a single instance of the JLabel class, as you can see in the following listing.

FIGURE 15.2:

The Label pane of the SwingDemo program

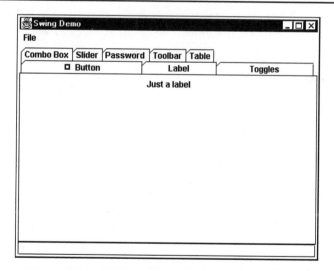

LIST 15.2   *LabelPanel.java*

```java
import javax.swing.*;

public class LabelPanel extends JPanel
{
    public LabelPanel()
    {
        add(new JLabel("Just a label"));
    }
}
```

In its simplest form, a JLabel just displays a text message. The JLabel class has facilities for adding an optional icon and for specifying the relative positions of the text and icon.

JFC Buttons

The Button pane (shown earlier in Figure 15.1) demonstrates how the JButton class provides more features than the java.awt.Button class. The source code for ButtonPanel is shown below.

LIST 15.3   *ButtonPanel.java*

```java
import javax.swing.*;
import java.awt.*;
import java.awt.event.*;


public class ButtonPanel extends JPanel
{
    private JTextField log;

    public ButtonPanel(JTextField tf)
    {
        this.log = tf;

        // Create button.
        JButton btn = new JButton("Push Me",
                             new BoxIcon(Color.blue, 2));
```

```
        // Set alternative icons.
        btn.setRolloverIcon(new BoxIcon(Color.cyan, 3));
        btn.setPressedIcon(new BoxIcon(Color.yellow, 4));

        // Set text to left of icon.
        btn.setHorizontalTextPosition(JButton.LEFT);

        // Set border.
        btn.setBorder(BorderFactory.createEtchedBorder());

        // Set listener.
        btn.addActionListener(new ActionListener() {
            public void actionPerformed(ActionEvent e)
            {
                log.setText("Button was pressed.");
            }
        });          // Visual cue: end of anonymous inner class.

        // Add button to panel.
        add(btn);
    }


class BoxIcon implements Icon
{
    private Color    color;
    private int      borderWidth;

    BoxIcon(Color color, int borderWidth)
    {
        this.color = color;
        this.borderWidth = borderWidth;
    }

    public int getIconWidth()  { return 20; }
    public int getIconHeight() { return 20; }

    public void paintIcon(Component c, Graphics g,
                          int x, int y)
    {
        g.setColor(Color.black);
        g.fillRect(x, y, getIconWidth(), getIconHeight());
        g.setColor(color);
```

```
          g.fillRect(x + borderWidth,
                     y + borderWidth,
                     getIconWidth() - 2*borderWidth,
                     getIconHeight() - 2*borderWidth);
    }
  }
}
```

The BoxIcon inner class is another implementation of the Icon interface, which was discussed earlier in the chapter. The BoxIcon constructor takes two arguments: a color and a border width.

The JButton constructor used here takes two arguments: a text string and a default icon. The default icon is blue, with a two-pixel black border. The JButton constructor call is:

```
JButton btn = new JButton("Push Me",
                          new BoxIcon(Color.blue, 2));
```

A JButton can specify alternate icons to be displayed when the JButton is in non-default states. The code at hand provides two alternate icons: one for when the cursor rolls over the button and one for when the button is pressed. The code that specifies these icons is:

```
    // Set alternate icons.
    btn.setRolloverIcon(new BoxIcon(Color.cyan, 3));
    btn.setPressedIcon(new BoxIcon(Color.yellow, 4));
```

The code specifies that the button's text should appear to the left of the icon. This is done with the following call:

```
    btn.setHorizontalTextPosition(JButton.LEFT);
```

The JButton class has several constants that allow you to set all of the possible text/icon relative locations.

The code also specifies that the button should have an etched border. The border is created with the following call:

```
    btn.setBorder(BorderFactory.createEtchedBorder());
```

The BorderFactory class has several createXXXBorder() methods for specifying various border styles.

Note the comment near the end of the constructor:

```
    // Visual cue: end of anonymous inner class.
```

Anonymous inner classes are a useful way to add a lightweight listener to a component. The syntax appears a bit strange at first. There are two ways to recognize an anonymous inner class:

- The class definition appears where you would expect an object reference. Instead of a reference, you see new *Typename*(), where *Typename* is either a class name or an interface name.

- The class definition ends with });. This combination is rarely seen in Java except at the end of the definition of an anonymous inner class.

JFC Toggles and Checkboxes

The Toggles pane, shown in Figure 15.3, displays a Toggle button, a plain checkbox, and three checkboxes organized as a radio group. The complete code for the `TogglePanel` class is shown below.

FIGURE 15.3:

The Toggles pane of the SwingDemo program

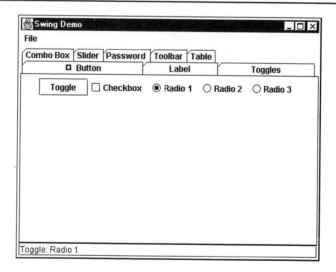

LIST 15.4   ***TogglePanel.java***

```
import java.awt.event.*;
import javax.swing.*;
```

```java
public class TogglePanel extends JPanel
{
    private JTextField      log;

    public TogglePanel(JTextField  tf)
    {
        this.log = tf;

        // Toggle button.
        JToggleButton tog = new JToggleButton("Toggle");
        ItemListener listener = new ItemListener() {
            public void itemStateChanged(ItemEvent e)
            {
                AbstractButton src = (AbstractButton)(e.getSource());
                log.setText("Toggle: " + src.getText());
            }
        };
        tog.addItemListener(listener);
        add(tog);

        // Checkbox.
        JCheckBox cbox = new JCheckBox("Checkbox");
        cbox.addItemListener(listener);
        add(cbox);

        // Radio button boxes.
        ButtonGroup btngroup = new ButtonGroup();
        for (int i=1; i<=3; i++)
        {
            JRadioButton radio = new JRadioButton("Radio " + i);
            btngroup.add(radio);
            radio.addItemListener(listener);
            add(radio);
        }
    }
}
```

JToggleButtons announce state changes by sending ItemEvents to Item-
Listeners. The Toggle button is created with the following code:

```java
// Toggle button.
JToggleButton tog = new JToggleButton("Toggle");
ItemListener listener = new ItemListener() {
```

```
public void itemStateChanged(ItemEvent e)
{
    AbstractButton src = (AbstractButton)(e.getSource());
    log.setText("Toggle: " + src.getText());
}
};
tog.addItemListener(listener);
add(tog);
```

A JCheckbox is similar to a JToggleButton, but its appearance and state change display are different. A JToggleButton looks like a button and displays its state by altering the appearance of the entire button. A JCheckbox looks like a label next to a check region and displays its state by drawing or not drawing a checkmark in the check region.

The first JCheckbox in the panel is created with the following code:

```
// Checkbox.
JCheckBox cbox = new JCheckBox("Checkbox");
cbox.addItemListener(listener);
add(cbox);
```

The three JRadioButtons on the right side of the Toggles pane are organized as a radio group. The following code creates them:

```
// Radio button boxes.
ButtonGroup btngroup = new ButtonGroup();
for (int i=1; i<=3; i++)
{
    JRadioButton radio = new JRadioButton("Radio " + i);
    btngroup.add(radio);
    radio.addItemListener(listener);
    add(radio);
}
```

New Components

The remainder of this chapter looks at four of the new JFC components that are not related to AWT components:

- A combo box, which adds functionality to the AWT Choice component

- A slider, which adds functionality to the AWT Scrollbar component

- A password field, which provides a secure way to enter text data

- A toolbar, which contains other components and supports user positioning at runtime

Each of these component types appears on its own tabbed pane in the SwingDemo application.

JFC Combo Boxes

The JComboBox class is a lot like the java.awt.Choice class. The user is prompted to select one item from a list, and the list is only visible during selection. A JCombo-Box, like a Choice, announces activity by sending ItemEvents to its ItemListeners. The main difference is that with a JComboBox, the programmer can specify the number of visible items in the list; the list will display a scrollbar if it contains more than the visible number of items.

You can set the number of visible items in a JComboBox by calling setMaximum-RowCount() after construction. Here is an example of a combo box with five visible items and a scrollbar:

The source code for the ComboPanel portion of the SwingDemo program is listed below.

LIST 15.5	*ComboPanel.java*

```
import java.awt.event.*;
import javax.swing.*;
```

```
public class ComboPanel extends JPanel
{
    private JTextField                    log;

    final static String[]        treasure = { "Gold", "Silver",
                                    "Diamonds", "Rubies", "Emeralds",
                                    "Sapphires", "Chocolate"};

    public ComboPanel(JTextField  tf)
    {
        this.log = tf;

        final JComboBox combo = new JComboBox(treasure);
        combo.setMaximumRowCount(5);
        combo.addItemListener(new ItemListener() {
            public void itemStateChanged(ItemEvent e)
            {
                log.setText("Combo: " + combo.getSelectedItem());
            }
        });
        combo.setSelectedIndex(4);
        add(combo);
        log.setText("");
    }
}
```

JFC Sliders

The JSlider class greatly enhances the functionality of the java.awt.Scrollbar class. For example, a JSlider supports both major and minor tick marks. The tick mark spacing (in pixels) can be set by calling setMajorTickSpacing(int) and set-MinorTickSpacing(int). If you set tick marks, you must explicitly enable their display by calling setPaintTicks(true).

TIP

Of course, JSlider components have extensive functionality beyond tick marks. You can learn about the features of the JSlider and the other Swing components by reading their class APIs.

When a user moves a JSlider, the JSlider sends ChangeEvents to its Change-Listeners. The source code for the SliderPanel class is listed below. The SliderPanel code produces the display shown in Figure 15.4.

FIGURE 15.4:

The JSlider component

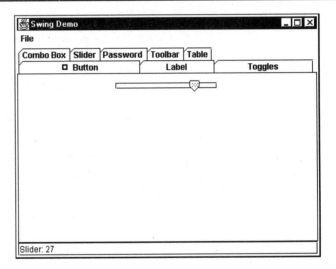

LIST 15.6   *SliderPanel.java*

```
import java.awt.event.*;
import javax.swing.*;
import javax.swing.event.*;


public class SliderPanel extends JPanel
{
    JTextField              log;
    JSlider                 slider;
```

```
public SliderPanel(JTextField  tf)
{
    this.log = tf;
    slider = new JSlider(JSlider.HORIZONTAL, -50, 50, 35);
    slider.setPaintTicks(true);
    slider.setMajorTickSpacing(10);
    add(slider);

    slider.addChangeListener(new ChangeListener() {
        public void stateChanged(ChangeEvent e)
        {
            log.setText("Slider: " + slider.getValue());
        }
    });
}
}
```

JFC Password Fields

A JPasswordField is just a JTextField that displays the same character, no matter which key the user presses. This character is called the *echo character*, and it can be set by calling the setEchoChar(char) method.

Figure 15.5 shows a JPasswordField that uses the pound character (#) for its echo character.

FIGURE 15.5:

The JPasswordField component

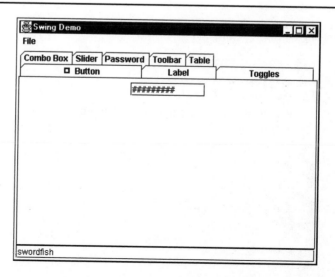

The source code for the `PasswordPanel` class is listed below.

LIST 15.7 ***PasswordPanel.java***

```java
import javax.swing.*;
import java.awt.event.*;


public class PasswordPanel extends JPanel
{
    JTextField      log;
    JPasswordField  pwf;

    public PasswordPanel(JTextField tf)
    {
        log = tf;
        pwf = new JPasswordField(10);
        pwf.setEchoChar('#');
        add(pwf);

        pwf.addKeyListener(new KeyAdapter()
        {
            public void keyReleased(KeyEvent e)
            {
                log.setText(pwf.getText());
            }
        });
    }
}
```

JFC Toolbars

A `JToolBar` is a rectangular area that can contain other components. A user can detach a `JToolBar` from the window in which it resides and place it on the Desktop as a detached window. A `JToolBar` can also be placed into another region of the window in which it originated.

Figure 15.6 shows a JFC toolbar that contains three checkboxes. Figure 15.7 shows the same toolbar after a user has detached it. Each of the checkboxes sends an `ActionEvent` to an `ActionListener`, which logs the event to the `JTextField`.

FIGURE 15.6:

The JToolBar component
with three checkboxes

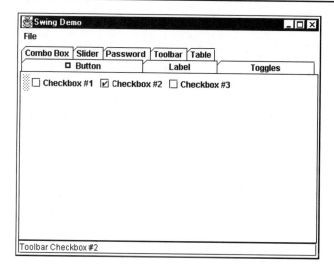

FIGURE 15.7:

A detached JToolBar
component

The code for the ToolbarPanel class appears below.

LIST 15.8   ***ToolbarPanel.java***

```java
import javax.swing.*;
import java.awt.*;

public class ToolbarPanel extends JPanel
{
    private JTextField    log;

    public ToolbarPanel(JTextField  tf)
    {
        log = tf;

        setLayout(new BorderLayout());
        JToolBar toolbar = new JToolBar();
        for (int i=1; i<4; i++)
```

```
        {
            JCheckBox cbox = new JCheckBox("Checkbox #" + i);
            toolbar.add(cbox);
            cbox.addActionListener(new ActionListener() {
                public void actionPerformed(ActionEvent e)
                {
                    JCheckBox source = (JCheckBox)(e.getSource());
                    log.setText("Toolbar " + source.getText());
                }
            });
        }

        add(toolbar, BorderLayout.NORTH);
    }
}
```

The SwingDemo Program

The following is the complete listing for the SwingDemo application.

```
import javax.swing.*;
import java.awt.*;
import java.awt.event.*;


public class SwingDemo extends JFrame
{
    private JTextField      textfield;
    private JTabbedPane     tabbedPane;


    public static void main(String[] args)
    {
        SwingDemo that = new SwingDemo();
        that.setVisible(true);
    }

    public SwingDemo()
    {
        super("Swing Demo");
```

```
        setSize(450, 350);

        // Listen for close command from title bar.
        addWindowListener(new WindowAdapter() {
            public void windowClosing(WindowEvent e)
            {
                System.exit(0);
            }
        });

        // Textfield at south is for status messages. The
        // Jcomponents use it to report events.
        textfield = new JTextField();
        getContentPane().add(textfield, BorderLayout.SOUTH);

        // Tabbed pane contains panels for the various Jcomponents.
        tabbedPane = new JTabbedPane();
        populateTabbedPane();
        getContentPane().add(tabbedPane, BorderLayout.CENTER);
    }


    private void populateTabbedPane()
    {
        tabbedPane.addTab("Button",                      // Title
                    new TabIcon(),                       // Icon
                    new ButtonPanel(textfield),          // Component
                    "Click here for Button demo");       // Tooltip

        tabbedPane.addTab("Label",
                    null,
                    new LabelPanel(),
                    "Click here for Label demo");

        tabbedPane.addTab("Toggles",
                    null,
                    new TogglePanel(textfield),
                    "Click here for Toggle demo");


        tabbedPane.addTab("Combo Box",
                    null,
                    new ComboPanel(textfield),
```

```
                              "Click here for Combo Box demo");

        tabbedPane.addTab("Sliders",
                      null,
                      new SliderPanel(textfield),
                      "Click here for Slider demo");
        tabbedPane.addTab("Password",
                      null,
                      new PasswordPanel(),
                      "Click here for Password Field demo");
        tabbedPane.addTab("Toolbar",
                      null,
                      new ToolbarPanel(),
                      "Click here for Toolbar demo");
        tabbedPane.addTab("Table",
                      null,
                      new TablePanel(),
                      "Click here for Table demo");
    }

    //
    // This icon appears on the "Button" tab.
    //
    class TabIcon implements Icon
    {
        public int getIconWidth()   { return 16; }
        public int getIconHeight()  { return 16; }

        public void paintIcon(Component c, Graphics g, int x, int y)
        {
            g.setColor(Color.black);
            g.fillRect(x+4, y+4, getIconWidth()-8, getIconHeight()-8);
            g.setColor(Color.cyan);
            g.fillRect(x+6, y+6, getIconWidth()-12, getIconHeight()-
12);
        }
    }
}
```

ButtonPanel.java

```
import javax.swing.*;
```

```java
import java.awt.*;
import java.awt.event.*;


public class ButtonPanel extends JPanel
{
    private JTextField      log;

    public ButtonPanel(JTextField tf)
    {
        this.log = tf;

        // Create button.
        JButton btn = new JButton("Push Me", new BoxIcon(Color.blue,
2));

        // Set alternative icons.
        btn.setRolloverIcon(new BoxIcon(Color.cyan, 3));
        btn.setPressedIcon(new BoxIcon(Color.yellow, 4));

        // Set text to left of icon.
        btn.setHorizontalTextPosition(JButton.LEFT);

        // Set border.
        btn.setBorder(BorderFactory.createEtchedBorder());

        // Set listener.
        btn.addActionListener(new ActionListener() {
            public void actionPerformed(ActionEvent e)
            {
                log.setText("Button was pressed.");
            }
        });          // Visual cue: end of anonymous inner class

        // Add button to panel.
        add(btn);
    }


    //
    // Inner class creates a 20x20 icon with a black
    // border. The border width and the color of the
    // interior are specified to the constructor.
```

```
//
class BoxIcon implements Icon
{
    private Color    color;
    private int      borderWidth;

    BoxIcon(Color color, int borderWidth)
    {
        this.color = color;
        this.borderWidth = borderWidth;
    }

    public int getIconWidth()  { return 20; }
    public int getIconHeight() { return 20; }

    public void paintIcon(Component c, Graphics g,
                          int x, int y)
    {
        g.setColor(Color.black);
        g.fillRect(x, y, getIconWidth(), getIconHeight());
        g.setColor(color);
        g.fillRect(x + borderWidth,
                   y + borderWidth,
                   getIconWidth() - 2*borderWidth,
                   getIconHeight() - 2*borderWidth);
    }
}
```

LabelPanel.java

```
import javax.swing.*;


public class LabelPanel extends JPanel
{
    public LabelPanel()
    {
        add(new JLabel("Just a label"));
    }
}
```

TogglePanel.java

```java
import java.awt.event.*;
import javax.swing.*;


public class TogglePanel extends JPanel
{
    private JTextField      log;

    public TogglePanel(JTextField  tf)
    {
        this.log = tf;

        // Toggle button.
        JToggleButton tog = new JToggleButton("Toggle");

        // Listener for all 3 varieties.
        ItemListener listener = new ItemListener() {
            public void itemStateChanged(ItemEvent e)
            {
                AbstractButton src = (AbstractButton)(e.getSource());
                log.setText("Toggle: " + src.getText());
            }
        };
        tog.addItemListener(listener);
        add(tog);

        // Checkbox.
        JCheckBox cbox = new JCheckBox("Checkbox");
        cbox.addItemListener(listener);
        add(cbox);

        // Radio button boxes.
        ButtonGroup btngroup = new ButtonGroup();
        for (int i=1; i<=3; i++)
        {
            JRadioButton radio = new JRadioButton("Radio " + i);
            btngroup.add(radio);
            radio.addItemListener(listener);
            add(radio);
        }
    }
}
```

ComboPanel.java

```java
import java.awt.event.*;
import javax.swing.*;


public class ComboPanel extends JPanel
{
    private JTextField          log;

    // Initialization strings.
    final static String[]       treasure = { "Gold", "Silver",
                                    "Diamonds", "Rubies", "Emeralds",
                                    "Sapphires", "Chocolate"};

    public ComboPanel(JTextField  tf)
    {
        this.log = tf;

        // Construct. Has to be final so the inner class
        // can have access.
        final JComboBox combo = new JComboBox(treasure);
        combo.setMaximumRowCount(5);

        // Combo box is like java.awt.Choice: it
        // sends ItemEvents.
        combo.addItemListener(new ItemListener() {
            public void itemStateChanged(ItemEvent e)
            {
                log.setText("Combo: " + combo.getSelectedItem());
            }
        });
        add(combo);
    }
}
```

SliderPanel.java

```java
import java.awt.*;
import javax.swing.*;
import javax.swing.event.*;
```

```java
public class SliderPanel extends JPanel
{
    private JTextField                    log;
    private JSlider                       slider;

    public SliderPanel(JTextField  tf)
    {
        this.log = tf;
        setLayout(new BorderLayout());
        slider = new JSlider(JSlider.HORIZONTAL, -50, 50, 35);
        // Draw both major and minor tick marks.
        slider.setMajorTickSpacing(20);
        slider.setMinorTickSpacing(5);
        slider.setPaintTicks(true);
        slider.setPaintLabels(true);
        add(slider, BorderLayout.NORTH);
        slider.addChangeListener(new ChangeListener() {
            public void stateChanged(ChangeEvent e)
            {
                log.setText("Value = " + slider.getValue());
            }
        });
    }
}
```

PasswordPanel.java

```java
import javax.swing.*;


public class PasswordPanel extends JPanel
{
    public PasswordPanel()
    {
        // Construct a field that is 10 chars wide.
        JPasswordField pwf = new JPasswordField(10);
        pwf.setEchoChar('#');
        add(pwf);
    }
}
```

ToolbarPanel.java

```java
import javax.swing.*;
import java.awt.*;


public class ToolbarPanel extends JPanel
{
    public ToolbarPanel()
    {
        setLayout(new BorderLayout());
        JToolBar toolbar = new JToolBar();

        // Put 3 Jcheckboxes in the toolbar.
        for (int i=1; i<4; i++)
        {
            toolbar.add(new JCheckBox("Checkbox #" + i));
        }
        add(toolbar, BorderLayout.NORTH);
    }
}
```

TablePanel.java

```java
import java.awt.event.*;
import javax.swing.*;


public class TablePanel extends JPanel
{
    public TablePanel()
    {
        String[] columnTitles =
        {
            "col1", "col2", "col3"
        };

        String[][] rows =
        {
            { "AAA", "Bbb", "Ccc" },
            { "ddd", "EeE", "FfF" },
```

```
            { "GGG", "HHH", "iii" },
            { "jjj", "KKk", "LLL" },
            { "Mmm", "NNN", "OoO" }
        };

        add(new JTable(rows, columnTitles));
    }
}
```

Summary

The JFC Swing component set is huge, and learning how to use it requires a significant investment in time and practice. However, it's worth the effort because these components are much richer and more versatile than the AWT components. The purpose of this chapter was to introduce you to a few of the basic JFC classes and show you how they worked in a demo program. For an in-depth investigation of the JFC components, refer to *Mastering Java 1.2* (published by Sybex).

The next chapter introduces another new feature that adds functionality in Java 2: the 2D API, which provides support for high-level graphics design.

CHAPTER

SIXTEEN

16

The 2D API

- The Graphics2D class

- Shapes

- Stroking

- Clipping

- Filling

- Transforming

- General paths

Java's original two-dimensional rendering facilities were a bit primitive. You could draw a line of minimal width. You could outline or fill a rectangle, an oval, or (with slightly more work) an irregular polygon. If you wanted to get fancy, you had to dabble with images. For example, if you wanted a diagonal line that was 25 pixels wide, your only hope was to do the math and create a suitable Memory-ImageSource, as described in Chapter 6. If somebody in the marketing department changed the spec to 28 pixels wide and a slightly steeper slope, you had to go back to the drawing board.

If you wanted to blend colors, use sophisticated line-join styles, or rotate your coordinate system, you found yourself in the same predicament—you had to do a lot of geometric or color-oriented coding, just to get an effect that is pretty much standard on non-Java platforms.

The JDK 1.1 functionality was simply not made to support high-level graphics design. The 2D API changes all that. This chapter introduces you to some of the basic concepts of the new API, including curves, transforms, strokes, and fills.

The subject matter of this chapter is extremely visual. The goal of this chapter is to get you familiar with the 2D rendering options that are available to you. In order to give you the best possible visual exposure to the new concepts, this chapter includes several "lab" programs. The labs let you try out a lot of options without having to go through the traditional write/compile/debug/execute/ observe cycle. The source code for these labs is listed in the text of this chapter, and you are encouraged to read the sources and understand what they do. But it is equally important to execute the programs and play with the parameters until you get a visual/kinesthetic feel for the concepts being illustrated. All of the labs are applications, and they appear on the CD-ROM in the \javadevhdbk\ch16 directory.

The Graphics2D Class and Shapes

In the JDK 1.1 model, you could draw or fill a rectangle or an oval because the Graphics class had (and still has) methods called drawRect(), fillOval(), and so on. In other words, you could draw a particular shape only if the Graphics class had a method to support that shape.

With the new 2D API, more shapes are available, and you can define your own shapes. You can draw the outline of a shape or you can fill it. You can even use a shape as a stencil. However, in order to do all this, you need to understand how to use the Graphics2D class and the Shape interface.

The Graphics2D Class

The java.awt.Graphics class has been extended. The new subclass is java.awt .Graphics2D. In Java 2, when a component's paint() method is called, the method's argument is still declared to be an instance of Graphics, but at runtime what gets passed is really an instance of the Graphics2D subclass. If you don't want the functionality of the 2D API, you can proceed as you would with JDK 1.1: Call setColor(), drawLine(), and so forth on the argument. On the other hand, if you want to take advantage of the new 2D features, you need to begin by casting the method argument to Graphics2D:

```
public void paint(Graphics g)
{
    Graphics2D g2d = (Graphics2D)g;
    // various method calls on g2d
```

Of course, all the inherited methods from the Graphics class are still available in the Graphics2D subclass. Additionally, there is extensive new functionality. In this chapter, we'll examine the following methods:

clip(Shape)	setRenderingHint(RenderingHint)
draw(Shape)	setStroke(Stroke)
fill(Shape)	shear(double, double)
rotate(double)	transform(AffineTransform)
scale(double, double)	translate(double, double)
setPaint(Paint)	

Many of these methods operate on Shapes, which are discussed in the next section.

The Shape Interface and Its Implementors

The Shape interface was introduced in JDK 1.1, but it was not used. This interface has been extensively modified for Java 2. Actually, it is very unlikely that you will ever implement the interface. Most likely, you will use one of the following implementing classes:

Arc2D   Ellipse2D

Line2D   QuadCurve2D

Rectangle2D   CubicCurve2D

RoundRectangle2D   GeneralPath

These eight classes all reside in the java.awt.geom package. The first seven classes correspond to specific curve types; the eighth, GeneralPath, represents a do-it-yourself curve that goes anywhere you want it to go. The first seven shapes are discussed in this section. GeneralPath is an extensive topic, which is covered in its own section at the end of this chapter.

NOTE   Many of the new classes introduced by the 2D API are in the java.awt package. The remainder reside in the new package java.awt.geom. If you are going to write much 2D code, you might want to get in the habit of importing java.geom.*.

In JDK 1.1, you could only use ints to specify shape parameters. With the exception of GeneralPath, all of the classes listed above require you to specify either float or double parameters. Each of the seven classes is abstract and has two inner classes, named.Float and Double. You never instantiate the abstract class; you instantiate one of the inner classes. If, for example, you want the double-precision version of Rectangle2D, you need to do something like the following:

```
double dx = 10.5;
double dy = 15.51;
double dw = 500.043;
double dh = 350.53;
Rectangle2D r2d = new Rectangle2D.Double(dx, dy, dw, dh);
```

Each of the inner classes is a subclass of its containing class. This sounds convoluted but is actually useful, because it allows the conversion performed in the last line of the code fragment above. The declarations of the outer and inner classes look like this:

```
public abstract class Rectangle2D extends RectangularShape
                                  implements Shape
{
    public static class Rectangle2D.Double extends Rectangle2D {
        ...
```

You might wonder why it is necessary to support double or float precision for parameters whose units are pixels. In JDK 1.1, there would have been no benefit. However, in Java 2 you can scale, rotate, and translate your coordinate system. You might create a space in which x ranges from -.0001 to +.0001. For such situations, you need to provide parameters with floating-point precision or, for extreme cases, double precision.

The application listed below draws a simple Rectangle2D. It can be found on the CD-ROM in \javadevhdbk\ch16\RectDemo.java.

LIST 16.1   *RectDemo.java*

```
import java.awt.*;
import java.awt.geom.*;

public class RectDemo extends Frame
{
    public static void main(String[] args)
    {
        (new RectDemo()).setVisible(true);
    }

    public RectDemo()
    {
        setSize(150, 150);
    }

    public void paint(Graphics g)
    {
        Graphics2D g2d = (Graphics2D)g;
        Rectangle2D r2d = new Rectangle2D.Float(10f, 10f, 130f, 130f);
        g2d.draw(r2d);
    }
}
```

The Line2D and Ellipse2D shapes are straightforward. The RoundRectangle2D, Arc2D, QuadCurve2D, and CubicCurve2D shapes require some explanation.

The RoundRectangle2D shape is a rectangle with rounded corners. The constructor takes the usual x/y/width/height arguments, as well as the width and height of the rounded portion of the corners. The sample code listed below draws a round rectangle at (20, 30) that is 100 pixels wide and 200 pixels high. The rounded portion of each corner is 10 pixels wide and 15 pixels high.

```
RoundRectangle2D rr =
    new RoundRectangle2D.Float(20, 30, 100, 200, 10, 15);
```

The Arc2D shape is a segment of a circle or an ellipse. The constructor for the Float inner subclass is shown below. (The Double inner subclass constructor is identical.)

```
Public Arc2D.Float(float x, float y, float wiidth, float height,
                   float arcStart, float arcExtent, int type)
```

The circle or ellipse is specified by providing the x, y, width, and height of the bounding square or rectangle. The arc itself begins at angle arcStart (measured from the right in counterclockwise degrees) and extends for arcExtent degrees. The type is one of the following:

Arc2D.CHORD   The arc is closed with a straight-line segment that connects the arc's endpoints.

Arc2D.PIE   The arc is closed with two straight-line segments that connect the arc's endpoints to the center of the circle or ellipse.

Arc2D.ARC   The arc is not closed.

The QuadCurve2D and CubicCurve2D shapes support smooth curves. A quad curve is specified by providing the curve's two endpoints and a third control point that tells the curve how to curve. A cubic curve is similar, but there are two control points. The Float subclasses have the following constructors:

```
QuadCurve2D.Float(float x0, float y0,
                  float ctrlX, float ctrlY,
                  float x1, float y1)
CubicCurve2D.Float(float x0, float y0,
                   float ctrlX0, float ctrlY0,
                   float ctrlX1, float ctrlY1,
                   float x1, float y1)
```

The Double inner classes have identical constructors, aside from the fact that the arguments are of type double.

The ShapeSampler application listed below draws a round rectangle, three kinds of arcs, a quad curve, and a cubic curve, as shown in Figure 16.1. The code appears on the CD-ROM in \javadevhdbk\ch16\ShapeSampler.java.

FIGURE 16.1:

The ShapeSampler program

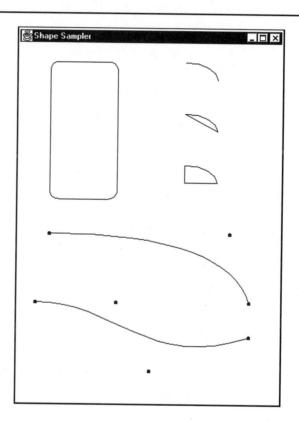

LIST 16.2	*ShapeSampler.java*

```java
import java.awt.*;
import java.awt.geom.*;


public class ShapeSampler extends Frame
```

```
{
    public static void main(String[] args)
    {
        (new ShapeSampler()).setVisible(true);
    }


    public ShapeSampler()
    {
        super("Shape Sampler");
        setSize(400, 550);
    }


    public void paint(Graphics g)
    {
        RoundRectangle2D    rrect;
        Arc2D               arc;
        QuadCurve2D         quadcurve;
        CubicCurve2D        cubcurve;

        Graphics2D g2d = (Graphics2D)g;

        rrect = new RoundRectangle2D.Float(50, 50, 100, 200, 30, 20);
        g2d.draw(rrect);

        arc = new Arc2D.Float(200, 50, 100, 50, 0, 90, Arc2D.OPEN);
        g2d.draw(arc);
        arc = new Arc2D.Float(200, 125, 100, 50, 0, 90, Arc2D.CHORD);
        g2d.draw(arc);
        arc = new Arc2D.Float(200, 200, 100, 50, 0, 90, Arc2D.PIE);
        g2d.draw(arc);

        quadcurve = new QuadCurve2D.Float(50, 300,
                                          320, 300,
                                          350, 400);
        g2d.draw(quadcurve);
        g2d.fillOval(48, 298, 5, 5);
        g2d.fillOval(318, 298, 5, 5);
        g2d.fillOval(348, 398, 5, 5);
```

```
            cubcurve = new CubicCurve2D.Float(30, 400,
                                              150, 400,
                                              200, 500,
                                              350, 450);
        g2d.fillOval(28, 398, 5, 5);
        g2d.fillOval(148, 398, 5, 5);
        g2d.fillOval(198, 498, 5, 5);
        g2d.fillOval(348, 448, 5, 5);
        g2d.draw(cubcurve);
    }
}
```

Drawing Operations

The three major operations that you can perform on a shape are drawing, filling, and clipping. You can also transform a shape, which allows you to manipulate the coordinate space of your drawing region. The basic transformations are rotation, translation, and scaling.

Stroking

In the JDK 1.1 model, the only kind of line you could draw was a solid line of infinitesimal width. With the 2D API, you can specify the line width, cap style, join style, and dash pattern.

Line style is specified in two steps:

1. Create an instance of `BasicStroke`.

2. Call `setStroke()` on the current `Graphics2D`, passing in the `BasicStroke` that you created.

There are several constructors for `BasicStroke`, offering various options for specifying or ignoring the various line qualities. The richest constructor is:

```
public BasicStroke(float width, int cap, int join, float miterLimit,
                   float dash[], float dashphase)
```

The constructor arguments have the following effects:

width   Sets the line width.

cap   Sets the cap style: BasicStroke.BUTT, BasicStroke.ROUND, or
BasicStroke.SQUARE.

join   Sets the join style: BasicStroke.BEVEL, BasicStroke.MITER, or
BasicStroke.ROUND.

miterLimit   Specifies the maximum extension of a miter join; only relevant if join is BasicStroke.MITER.

dash   Specifies an array of floats that describes the dash pattern.

dashphase   Sets the starting point within the dash array.

The StrokeLab program lets you vary the line width, caps type, and join style of
a Graphics2D. Figure 16.2 shows the program configured to use a line width of 10,
round caps, and beveled joins.

FIGURE 16.2:

The StrokeLab program

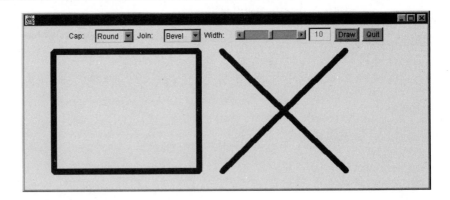

If you execute the application, you can experiment with different line widths,
caps, and joins. The code appears on the CD-ROM in \javadevhdbk\ch16\StrokeLab
.java and is listed below. The most important lines are the ones in paint() that construct a BasicStroke and then call setStroke() on the Graphics2D object:

```
BasicStroke stroke = new BasicStroke(width, cap, join);
g.setStroke(stroke);
```

LIST 16.3   StrokeLab.java

```java
import java.awt.*;
import java.awt.event.*;


public class StrokeLab extends Frame
                        implements ActionListener,
                                    AdjustmentListener
{
    private Choice              capChoice;
    private Choice              joinChoice;
    private Choice              dashCountChoice;
    private Scrollbar           widthBar;
    private TextField           widthTF;
    private Button              drawBtn;
    private Button              quitBtn;
    private StrokeCanvas        strokeCanvas;

    private final static int    WIDTH_MIN      = 0;
    private final static int    WIDTH_MAX      = 21;

    private final static String[]   CAP_TYPE_NAMES =
    {
        "Butt", "Round", "Square"
    };
    private final static int[]      CAP_TYPES =
    {
        BasicStroke.CAP_BUTT,
        BasicStroke.CAP_ROUND,
        BasicStroke.CAP_SQUARE
    };

    private final static String[]   JOIN_TYPE_NAMES =
    {
        "Bevel", "Miter", "Round"
    };
    private final static int[]      JOIN_TYPES =
    {
        BasicStroke.JOIN_BEVEL,
        BasicStroke.JOIN_MITER,
        BasicStroke.JOIN_ROUND
    };
```

```java
class WideScrollbar extends Scrollbar
{
    private int     widthPix;

    WideScrollbar(int min, int max, int widthPix)
    {
        super(Scrollbar.HORIZONTAL, 0, 1,
            WIDTH_MIN, WIDTH_MAX);
        this.widthPix = widthPix;
    }

    public Dimension getPreferredSize()
    {
        int prefHt = super.getPreferredSize().height;
        return new Dimension(widthPix, prefHt);
    }
}


public static void main(String[] args)
{
    (new StrokeLab()).setVisible(true);
}


StrokeLab()
{
    setSize(700, 300);
    Panel panel = new Panel();
    capChoice = new Choice();
    for (int i=0; i<CAP_TYPE_NAMES.length; i++)
        capChoice.addItem(CAP_TYPE_NAMES[i]);
    panel.add(new Label("Cap:"));
    panel.add(capChoice);
    joinChoice = new Choice();
    for (int i=0; i<CAP_TYPE_NAMES.length; i++)
        joinChoice.addItem(JOIN_TYPE_NAMES[i]);
    panel.add(new Label("Join:"));
    panel.add(joinChoice);
    widthBar = new WideScrollbar(WIDTH_MIN, WIDTH_MAX, 120);
```

```
        widthBar.addAdjustmentListener(this);
        widthTF = new TextField(" 0");
        widthTF.setEnabled(false);
        panel.add(new Label("Width:"));
        panel.add(widthBar);
        panel.add(widthTF);
        drawBtn = new Button("Draw");
        drawBtn.addActionListener(this);
        panel.add(drawBtn);
        quitBtn = new Button("Quit");
        quitBtn.addActionListener(this);
        panel.add(quitBtn);
        add(panel, BorderLayout.NORTH);

        strokeCanvas = new StrokeCanvas();
        add(strokeCanvas, BorderLayout.CENTER);

        addWindowListener(new WindowAdapter() {
            public void windowClosing(WindowEvent e) {
                System.exit(0);
            }
        });
    }


    public void actionPerformed(ActionEvent e)
    {
        if (e.getSource() == quitBtn)
            System.exit(0);

        strokeCanvas.repaint();
    }


    public void adjustmentValueChanged(AdjustmentEvent e)
    {
        widthTF.setText("" + widthBar.getValue());
    }
```

```
class StrokeCanvas extends Canvas
{
    public void paint(Graphics graphics)
    {
        Graphics2D g = (Graphics2D)graphics;
        g.setColor(Color.blue);
        float width = widthBar.getValue();
        int cap = CAP_TYPES[capChoice.getSelectedIndex()];
        int join = JOIN_TYPES[joinChoice.getSelectedIndex()];
        BasicStroke stroke = new BasicStroke(width, cap, join);

        g.setStroke(stroke);
        g.drawRect(50, 10, 250, 200);
        g.drawLine(340, 10, 550, 210);
        g.drawLine(340, 210, 550, 10);
    }
}
```

Filling

The 2D API offers a variety of options for filling shapes. You can still fill with solid colors, as you could in JDK 1.1, and now you can fill with a texture pattern or with a color gradient.

You tell a Graphics2D how to fill by calling its setPaint() method. The argument is of type java.awt.Paint, which is an interface. There are three classes that implement the Paint interface and are eligible to be passed into setPaint():

- java.awt.Color

- java.awt.TexturePaint

- java.awt.GradientPaint

Passing in a Color produces the same result as calling setColor(): Filling is performed with a solid color.

Passing in a TexturePaint results in a repeating fill pattern based on a buffered image. The constructor for TexturePaint is:

```
TexturePaint(BufferedImage image, Rectangle control)
```

This specifies a fill pattern based on repeating copies of image. The control rectangle specifies the portion of the image to be used and the positioning of the repeated image.

Passing a GradientPaint into setPaint() results in a smooth gradient of color. There are several constructors for GradientPaint. The general approach is to provide two control points and two colors. The first point will appear in the first color, and the second color will appear in the second color. All intermediate points will appear in a color that is a blend of the two original colors. The proportions of the original colors in the blend are derived from each point's distance from the two original control points.

The simplest GradientPaint constructor is:

```
GradientPaint(float x0, float y0, Color color0,
              float x1, float y1, Color color1)
```

The GradientLab application lets you specify the two control points and associate a color with each point. To begin, you click the mouse to define the first control point. A dialog box pops up to let you associate a color with that control point. Then you repeat the process to define the position and color of the second control point. As soon as you define the second point, the program fills in its entire area using a GradientPaint, as shown in Figure 16.3.

FIGURE 16.3:

The GradientLab program

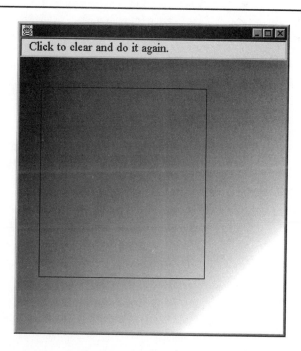

Click to clear and do it again.

The complete listing for GradientLab appears below. It also appears on the CD-ROM in \javadevhdbk\ch16\GradientLab.java.

LIST 16.4	*GradientLab.java*

```java
import java.awt.*;
import java.awt.event.*;


public class GradientLab extends Canvas
                         implements MouseListener
{
    private TextField       logTF;
    private int             nClicks;
    private int[]           xs, ys;
    private Color[]         colors;
    private ColorDialog     colorDialog;

    private final static String[]   messages =
    {
        "Click to define first point.",
        "Click to define second point.",
        "Click to fill with gradient.",
        "Click to clear and do it again."
    };


    public static void main(String[] args)
    {
        Frame frame = new Frame();
        TextField tf = new TextField();
        frame.add(tf, BorderLayout.NORTH);
        tf.setFont(new Font("Serif", Font.PLAIN, 18));
        frame.add(new GradientLab(tf), BorderLayout.CENTER);
        frame.pack();
        frame.setVisible(true);
        frame.addWindowListener(new WindowAdapter() {
            public void windowClosing(WindowEvent e)
            {
                System.exit(0);
            }
```

```
        });
    }


    GradientLab(TextField logTF)
    {
        this.logTF = logTF;
        logTF.setText(messages[0]);
        setBackground(Color.white);
        addMouseListener(this);
        xs = new int[2];
        ys = new int[2];
        colors = new Color[2];

        Component c = logTF;
        while (!(c instanceof Frame))
            c = c.getParent();
        colorDialog = new ColorDialog((Frame)c);
    }


    public Dimension getPreferredSize()
    {
        return new Dimension(400, 400);
    }


    public void mouseClicked(MouseEvent e)
    {
        if (nClicks <= 1)
        {
            xs[nClicks] = e.getX();
            ys[nClicks] = e.getY();
            colorDialog.setVisible(true);
            colors[nClicks] = colorDialog.getColor();
        }

        nClicks = ++nClicks % 4;
        logTF.setText(messages[nClicks]);
        repaint();
    }
```

```java
private void clear(Graphics g)
{
    g.setColor(Color.white);
    g.fillRect(0, 0, getSize().width, getSize().height);
}


public void paint(Graphics graphics)
{
    Graphics2D g = (Graphics2D)graphics;

    g.setColor(Color.white);
    g.fillRect(0, 0,
               getSize().width, getSize().height);

    switch(nClicks)
    {
        case 0:           // Clear
            break;

        case 1:           // 1st point
            g.setColor(Color.black);
            g.fillOval(xs[0]-5, ys[0]-5, 10, 10);
            g.setColor(colors[0]);
            g.fillOval(xs[0]-4, ys[0]-4, 8, 8);
            break;

        case 2:           // 2nd point
            g.setColor(Color.black);
            g.fillOval(xs[0]-5, ys[0]-5, 10, 10);
            g.setColor(colors[0]);
            g.fillOval(xs[0]-4, ys[0]-4, 8, 8);
            g.setColor(Color.black);
            g.fillOval(xs[1]-5, ys[1]-5, 10, 10);
            g.setColor(colors[1]);
            g.fillOval(xs[1]-4, ys[1]-4, 8, 8);
            break;

        case 3:           // 3rd point
            GradientPaint gradi = new GradientPaint(xs[0], ys[0],
                                        colors[0],
                                        xs[1], ys[1],
```

```
                                        colors[1]);
        g.setPaint(gradi);
        g.fillRect(0, 0, getSize().width, getSize().height);
        g.setColor(Color.black);
        g.drawRect(Math.min(xs[0], xs[1]),
                   Math.min(ys[0], ys[1]),
                   Math.abs(xs[0]-xs[1]),
                   Math.abs(ys[0]-ys[1]));
        break;
    }
}


public void mousePressed(MouseEvent e)   { }
public void mouseReleased(MouseEvent e)  { }
public void mouseEntered(MouseEvent e)   { }
public void mouseExited(MouseEvent e)    { }


class ColorDialog extends Dialog
                implements ActionListener, ItemListener
{
    Canvas        swatch;
    Choice        choice;
    Scrollbar[]   bars;
    TextField[]   tfs;

    final String[]  colorNames =
    {
        "Red", "Blue", "Green", "Yellow", "Orange",
        "Cyan", "Magenta", "White", "Black"
    };
    final Color[]  colors =
    {
        Color.red, Color.blue, Color.green, Color.yellow,
        Color.orange, Color.cyan, Color.magenta,
        Color.white, Color.black
    };


    ColorDialog(Frame parent)
    {
```

```
        super(parent, true);
        setSize(200, 100);
        Panel panel = new Panel();
        choice = new Choice();
        for (int i=0; i<colorNames.length; i++)
            choice.addItem(colorNames[i]);
        choice.select(8);
        choice.addItemListener(this);
        panel.add(choice);
        Button btn = new Button("Apply");
        btn.addActionListener(this);
        panel.add(btn);
        add(panel, BorderLayout.NORTH);
        swatch = new Canvas();
        swatch.setBackground(Color.black);
        add(swatch, BorderLayout.CENTER);
    }

    Color getColor() {return colors[choice.getSelectedIndex()];}

    public void itemStateChanged(ItemEvent e)
    {
        swatch.setBackground(getColor());
        swatch.repaint();
    }

    public void actionPerformed(ActionEvent e)
    {
        setVisible(false);
    }
  }
}
```

Clipping

When you use a shape as a stencil outline, the shape acts like a clipping rectangle—pixels outside the clip region are not modified by any subsequent painting operations. You specify a clip shape by calling the clip() method of the Graphics2D class, passing in the clipping shape as the method's parameter.

Figure 16.4 shows a filled rectangle with a circular clip region. The code that generated Figure 16.4 is listed below and appears on the CD-ROM in \javadevhdbk\ ch16\ClipDemo.java.

FIGURE 16.4:

Circular clip region

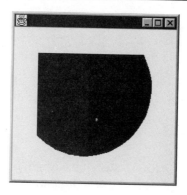

LIST 16.5   *ClipDemo.java*

```java
import java.awt.*;
import java.awt.geom.*;

public class ClipDemo extends Frame
{
    public static void main(String[] args)
    {
        (new ClipDemo()).setVisible(true);
    }

    public ClipDemo()
    {
        setSize(250, 250);
    }

    public void paint(Graphics g)
    {
        Graphics2D g2d = (Graphics2D)g;
        Ellipse2D e = new Ellipse2D.Float(10, 10, 200, 200);
        g2d.clip(e);
        g2d.fillRect(40, 60, 500, 500);
    }
}
```

Transforming

The JDK 1.1 drawing model used a rigid coordinate system. The origin was always in a component's upper-left corner; x increased to the right, and y increased downward.

The 2D API allows you to transform your coordinate space. The `Graphics2D` class has a method called `setTransform()`, which takes as its argument an instance of the `java.awt.geom.AffineTransform` class.

If you are familiar with the mathematics of coordinate transformation, you can use the `AffineTransform` constructors to create very intricate effects. The class also contains a number of static methods that make it much easier to create the following common transforms:

> **Rotation**   Keeps the origin in place but turns the axes so that they can point in arbitrary directions. (The axes remain perpendicular to each other.)
>
> **Scaling**   Changes the unit size so that, for example, a width of 100 means 100 arbitrary units rather than 100 pixels. The horizontal and vertical scales can be adjusted independently.
>
> **Translation**   Moves the origin.
>
> **Shearing**   Manipulates the axes so that they are no longer perpendicular.

The static methods of `AffineTransform` that create these transformations are:

```
getRotateInstance(double theta)
getRotateInstance(double theta, double x, double y)
getScaleInstance(double scaleX, double scaleY)
getTranslateInstance(double translateX, double translateY)
getShearInstance(double shearX, double shearY)
```

The second version of `getRotateInstance()` returns a transform that both translates and rotates.

Figures 16.5 through 16.9 show frames whose `paint()` methods all call `fillRect` (50, 50, 150, 250). Figure 16.5 shows the rectangle with no transformation. The

others show a transform applied before drawing the rectangle. The figures illustrate how transforming coordinate space changes the appearance of the rectangle. The frames were all displayed by the TransformLab application, which is listed below and is on the CD-ROM in \javadevhdbk\ch16\TransformLab.java.

FIGURE 16.5:

Rectangle without transformation

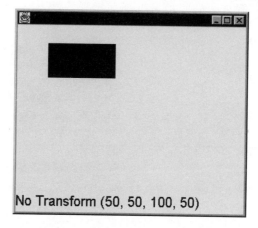

No Transform (50, 50, 100, 50)

FIGURE 16.6:

Rectangle with rotation

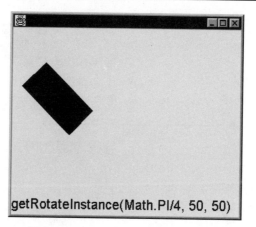

getRotateInstance(Math.PI/4, 50, 50)

FIGURE 16.7:

Rectangle with scaling

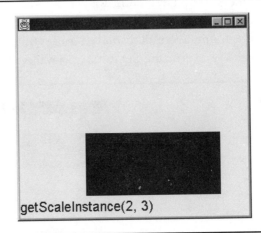

getScaleInstance(2, 3)

FIGURE 16.8:

Rectangle with translation

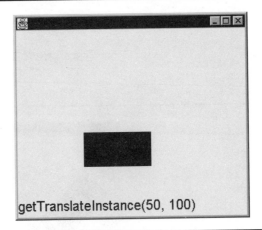

getTranslateInstance(50, 100)

FIGURE 16.9:

Rectangle with shear

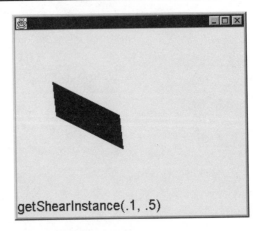

getShearInstance(.1, .5)

LIST 16.6   *TransformLab.java*

```java
import java.awt.*;
import java.awt.geom.*;


public class TransformLab extends Frame
{
    private int            nth;

    private final static String[]    info =
    {
        "No Transform (50, 50, 100, 50)",
        "getRotateInstance(Math.PI/4, 50, 50)",
        "getScaleInstance(2, 3)",
        "getTranslateInstance(50, 100)",
        "getShearInstance(.1, .5)"
    };


    public static void main(String[] args)
    {
        for (int i=0; i<info.length; i++)
            (new TransformLab(i)).setVisible(true);
    }


    public TransformLab(int nth)
    {
        this.nth = nth;
        setSize(350, 300);
        setFont(new Font("Monspaced", Font.PLAIN, 20));
        add(new Label(info[nth]), BorderLayout.SOUTH);
    }


    public void paint(Graphics g)
    {
        AffineTransform      atrans = null;

        Graphics2D g2d = (Graphics2D)g;
```

```
        switch (nth)
        {
            case 1:
                atrans = AffineTransform.getRotateInstance(Math.PI/4,
                                    50, 50);
                break;
            case 2:
                atrans = AffineTransform.getScaleInstance(2, 3);
                break;
            case 3:
                atrans =
    AffineTransform.getTranslateInstance(50, 100);
                break;
            case 4:
                atrans = AffineTransform.getShearInstance(.1, .5);
                break;
        }

        if (atrans != null)
            g2d.setTransform(atrans);

        g2d.fillRect(50, 50, 100, 50);
    }
}
```

General Paths for Your Own Curves

The shapes discussed so far are hard-coded. Each class represents a different kind of curve. When you want to draw a curve that is not represented by a standard shape, you need to use the java.awt.geom.GeneralPath class to create your own curve. After creating a GeneralPath, you can use it as you would any other shape (for example Ellipse2D or RoundRectangle2D), which means that you can draw it, fill it, or clip to it.

Specifying a Shape

The GeneralPath class has several constructors; the simplest form being the no-args constructor. After you create an instance, there are numerous methods for specifying a shape. The most common approach to specifying a shape is based on an analogy to freehand drawing. When you draw, you move your pencil to a point on your paper, you draw a straight line or a curve, and then you move to another point and repeat the process. With a GeneralPath, you use the following methods to simulate this activity:

public void moveTo(float x, float y)   Moves to the specified point.

public void lineTo(float x, float y)   Extends the curve by drawing a line segment to the specified point.

public void closePath()   Extends the curve by drawing a line segment to the point specified by the most recent moveTo() call.

The GeneralPath class has many more methods than those listed above. However, you can do a lot with just moveTo(), lineTo(), and closePath(), so we will pause here and look at some examples.

The paint() method listed below creates a GeneralPath that represents an isoceles (but not equilateral) triangle.

```
public void paint(Graphics g)
{
    Graphics2D g2d = (Graphics2D)g;
    GeneralPath path = new GeneralPath();
    path.moveTo(100, 100);
    path.lineTo(200, 100);
    path.lineTo(150, 150);
    path.closePath();
    g2d.draw(path);
}
```

NOTE   The Greek philosopher Isoceles was a contemporary of Pythagoras. He is credited with the invention of the triangle. His daughter Scalene refined the concept.

Transforming a General Path

The GeneralPath class has a transform() method, which takes as its argument an instance of AffineTransform. With this method, you can create a path that can draw a regular polygon with any desired number of sides. The next example shows how to do this.

It would be ideal if we could extend GeneralPath. The subclass could be called PolygonPath, and its constructor could be passed the desired number of sides. Unfortunately, GeneralPath is a final class, so extending it is out of the question. We will have to be content with writing a method that creates and returns an appropriate GeneralPath. The method's arguments will take the polygon's number of sides, radius, and center:

```
GeneralPath makePoly(int nSides, float radius,
                  float centerX, float centerY)  {...}
```

The method will use the moveTo() and lineTo() methods to draw the desired polygon. The geometric calculations are straightforward, provided that the polygon can be centered on the origin. This can be made to happen with the use of an AffineTransform. We have already seen transforms in the context of the Graphics2D class. The following code shows how to apply a transform to a path so that the path's origin becomes (centerX, centerY):

```
AffineTransform atrans =
  AffineTransform.getTranslateInstance(centerX, centerY);
thePath.transform(centerX, centerY);
```

Any two adjacent points of the polygon sweep out an angle of 360/nPoints degrees. It is standard to measure angles counterclockwise from the right. If the first point of the polygon is placed at zero degrees (that is, precisely to the right of the center), then the nth point sweeps out n*360/nPoints degrees. The coordinates of the point itself are easily determined. If the angle from the horizontal is theta, then x = radius*cos(theta), and y = radius*sin(theta).

The makePoly() method needs to move to the first point, draw a line to each successive point, and finally close the path. The complete method listing is shown below.

```
GeneralPath makePoly(int nSides, float radius,
                  float centerX, float centerY)
{
    GeneralPath path = new GeneralPath();

    // Move to first point.
```

```
path.moveTo(radius, 0);

// Line to remaining points.
float deltaTheta = (float)(2*Math.PI/nSides);
float theta = deltaTheta;
for (int i=1; i<nSides; i++)
{
    float x = (float)(radius * Math.cos(theta));
    float y = (float)(radius * Math.sin(theta));
    path.lineTo(x, y);

    theta += deltaTheta;
}

// Close the path.
path.closePath();

// Translate to center of polygon.
AffineTransform atrans =
  AffineTransform.getTranslateInstance(centerX, centerY);
path.transform(atrans);

return path;
}
```

Figure 16.10 shows four polygons that were drawn with paths created by the makePoly() method. The paths were created in the following paint() method:

```
public void paint(Graphics g)
{
    Graphics2D g2d = (Graphics2D)g;
    g2d.draw(makePoly( 5, 70, 100, 100));
    g2d.draw(makePoly( 6, 70, 300, 100));
    g2d.draw(makePoly( 8, 70, 100, 300));
    g2d.draw(makePoly(10, 70, 300, 300));
}
```

FIGURE 16.10:

General path for polygons

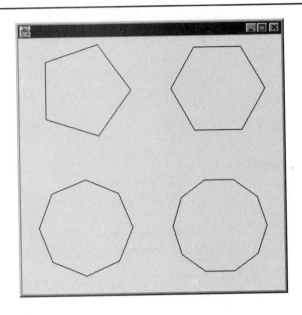

  The complete listing for the program that creates Figure 16.10 is on the CD-ROM in \javadevhdbk\ch16\Poly.java.

Drawing a Bezier Curve

A bezier curve is a smooth curve defined by two endpoints and two control points. The control points tell the curve where to go. The curve passes near the control points but generally does not pass through them. The precise effect of the control points is difficult to describe but is easily grasped intuitively if you look at enough examples. The BezLab program draws a bezier curve and allows you to drag the endpoints and control points to see the effect on the curve. Figure 16.11 shows BezLab in its initial state.

The paint() method in BezLab creates a general path and then makes two calls on that path: moveTo() and curveTo(). You are already familiar with moveTo(). The curveTo() method has the following signature:

```
public void curveTo(float control0x, float control0y, float control1x,
    float control1y, float endx, float endy)
```

The arguments specify two control points and an endpoint. The other endpoint is the current point of the general path.

FIGURE 16.11:

The BezLab program in its initial state

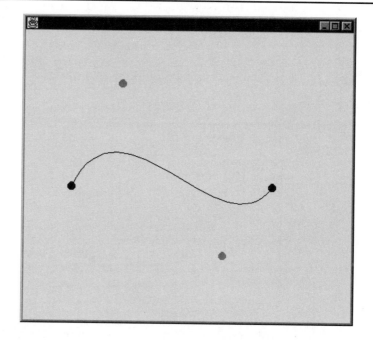

BezLab maintains two arrays that each contains four floats. The arrays are called xs and ys. The arrays contain the coordinates of the first endpoint, the first control point, the second control point, and the second endpoint. The paint() method in BezLab uses the arrays as follows:

```
public void paint(Graphics g)
{
    // Color in all points.
    for (int i=0; i<4; i++)
    {
        if (i==0 || i==3)
            g.setColor(Color.blue);
        else
            g.setColor(Color.cyan);
            g.fillOval(xs[i]-6, ys[i]-6, 12, 12);
    }
    // Draw curve.
    Graphics2D g2d = (Graphics2D)g;
    g2d.setColor(Color.black);
    GeneralPath path = new GeneralPath();
    path.moveTo(xs[0], ys[0]);
```

```
        path.curveTo(xs[1], ys[1], xs[2], ys[2], xs[3], ys[3]);
        g2d.draw(path);
    }
```

 BezLab appears on the CD-ROM in \javadevhdbk\ch16\BezLab. The complete listing follows.

LIST 16.7	***BezLab.java***

```
import java.awt.*;
import java.awt.event.*;
import java.awt.geom.*;


class BezLab extends Frame
            implements MouseListener, MouseMotionListener
{

    private int[]          xs = {  75, 150, 300, 375 };
    private int[]          ys = { 250, 100, 350, 250 };
    private int            dragIndex = NOT_DRAGGING;

    private final static int   NEIGHBORHOOD = 15;
    private final static int   NOT_DRAGGING = -1;


    public static void main(String[] args)
    {
        (new BezLab()).setVisible(true);
    }


    BezLab()
    {
        setSize(500, 450);
        addMouseListener(this);
        addMouseMotionListener(this);
        addWindowListener(new WindowAdapter() {
            public void windowClosing(WindowEvent e)
            {System.exit(0);}
        });
    }
```

```
public void paint(Graphics g)
{
    // Color in all points.
    for (int i=0; i<4; i++)
            {
        if (i==0 || i==3)
            g.setColor(Color.blue);
        else
            g.setColor(Color.cyan);
        g.fillOval(xs[i]-6, ys[i]-6, 12, 12);
            }

    // Draw curve.
    Graphics2D g2d = (Graphics2D)g;
    g2d.setColor(Color.black);
    GeneralPath path = new GeneralPath();
    path.moveTo(xs[0], ys[0]);
    path.curveTo(xs[1], ys[1], xs[2], ys[2], xs[3], ys[3]);
    g2d.draw(path);
            }


public void mousePressed(MouseEvent e)
{
    // Determine index of point being dragged.
    dragIndex = NOT_DRAGGING;
    int minDistance = Integer.MAX_VALUE;
    int indexOfClosestPoint = -1;
    for (int i=0; i<4; i++)
    {
        int deltaX = xs[i] - e.getX();
        int deltaY = ys[i] - e.getY();
        int distance =
          (int)(Math.sqrt(deltaX*deltaX + deltaY*deltaY));
        if (distance < minDistance)
        {
            minDistance = distance;
            indexOfClosestPoint = i;
        }
    }

    // Must be close enough.
    if (minDistance > NEIGHBORHOOD)
        return;
```

```
        dragIndex = indexOfClosestPoint;
    }


    public void mouseReleased(MouseEvent e)
    {
        if (dragIndex == NOT_DRAGGING)
        return;
        xs[dragIndex] = e.getX();
        ys[dragIndex] = e.getY();
        dragIndex = NOT_DRAGGING;
        repaint();
    }


    public void mouseDragged(MouseEvent e)
    {
        if (dragIndex == NOT_DRAGGING)
            return;

        xs[dragIndex] = e.getX();
        ys[dragIndex] = e.getY();
        repaint();
    }


    public void mouseClicked(MouseEvent e)    { }
    public void mouseEntered(MouseEvent e)    { }
    public void mouseExited(MouseEvent e)     { }
    public void mouseMoved(MouseEvent e)      { }
}
```

Drawing Fractals

To demonstrate a more detailed example that makes heavy use of general paths, we will develop a program called FracLabTriangle, which renders a convoluted triangle-based fractal.

NOTE

The word *fractal* was coined by Benoit Mandelbrot to describe curves that are so convoluted that their dimension exceeds two. However, the curves are definitely not three-dimensional. Mandelbrot proposed using nonintegral numbers to describe the dimensions of convoluted curves. Fractal is an abbreviation of fractional dimension.

One way to generate a fractal is to start with a simple shape such as a triangle. The shape should consist of line segments. You then apply a transformation to each line segment to turn each line segment into a strand of connected line segments, beginning where the original segment began and ending where the original segment ended. Thus, each line segment is transformed into a slightly more convoluted path. You repeat the process on the new (smaller) segments. A fractal is the result of reiterating the process infinitely many times. In practice, four or five iterations are enough to draw a very convoluted picture that does a good job of expressing the strangeness of fractals.

FracLabTriangle begins with a triangle, as shown in Figure 16.12. The transformation removes the middle third of each line segment and replaces that third with the pointy part of an equilateral triangle. The transformation is difficult to describe in words but easy to understand from a picture. Figure 16.13 shows the result of applying the transformation to each segment of the original triangle.

FIGURE 16.12:

FracLabTriangle before iteration

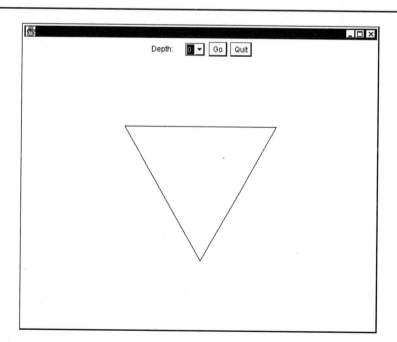

FIGURE 16.13:

FracLabTriangle after one
iteration

FIGURE 16.13:

FracLabTriangle after one
iteration

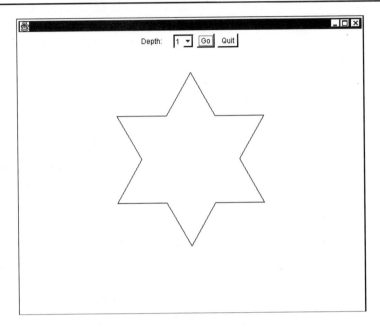

In the next step, the same transformation is applied to each of the new small line segments, resulting in Figure 16.14. After one more iteration, the shape begins to look quite convoluted, as shown in Figure 16.15. After a fourth iteration, the convolutions almost fit between the pixels, as shown in Figure 16.16.

FIGURE 16.14:

FracLabTriangle after two
iterations

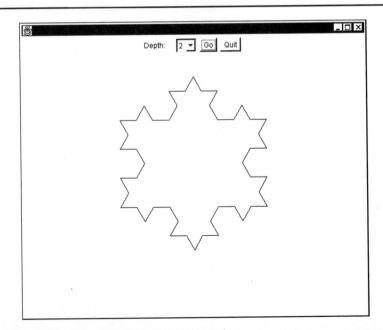

FIGURE 16.15:

FracLabTriangle after three iterations

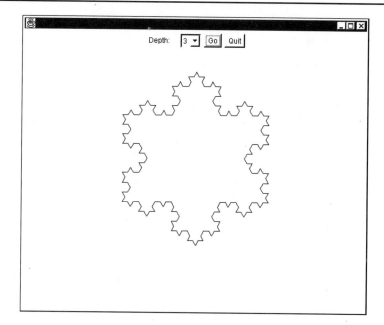

FIGURE 16.16:

FracLabTriangle after four iterations

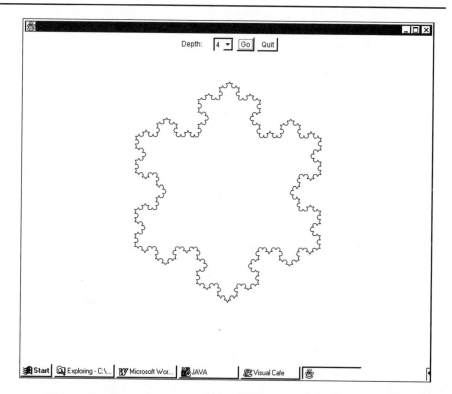

FracLabTriangle supports up to five iterations, but the fifth iteration takes a long time and produces tiny convolutions that can be appreciated only on a very large screen.

FracLabTriangle consists of four classes:

FracLabTriangle   The main application class. It extends Frame and contains a control panel.

FracCanvas   A canvas that is contained in the main frame. FracCanvas knows how to draw a fractal.

Xform   Represents a transformation. FracCanvas uses an instance of Xform as instructions on how to convert a line segment during iteration. An Xform contains some number of XformStep values.

XformStep   Represents a single piece of a transformation. Our transformation changes a line segment into four line segments, so the corresponding Xform object will contain four XformStep values.

The easiest way to understand the application is to start from the bottom, with Xform and XformStep. The Xform class encapsulates instructions on how to transform a line segment, *assuming the line segment goes from (0,0) to (1, 0)*. This is an enormous assumption. If we are allowed the assumption, the entire program becomes easy to write. (If we are not allowed the assumption, the programming is a nightmare.)

Why can we make such a radical assumption? Surely, we must be prepared to transform *any* line segment, no matter where it starts and no matter where it ends. For example, a segment might go from (14.4141, 75) to (15.5115, 76.1). We have no control over the segments we will be required to transform.

This is where the flexibility of the 2D API comes into play. The segment to be transformed cannot be moved, but the coordinate system can be transformed. We can manipulate coordinate space so that the starting point coincides with the origin and the endpoint is at (1, 0). This is accomplished in three steps:

1. Translate the coordinate origin to the starting point.

2. Scale so that the distance between the two points becomes one unit.

3. Rotate so that the endpoint is directly to the right of the starting point.

Now we only need to solve the problem of how to transform a line segment that joins the points (0, 0) and (1, 0). Figure 16.17 illustrates the transformation.

FIGURE 16.17:

The basic transformation

Before:

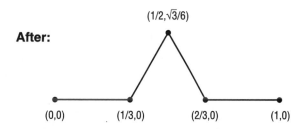

After:

Figure 16.17 shows that a line segment joining (0, 0) and (1, 0) needs to be transformed into four line segments:

- From (0, 0) to (1/3, 0)
- From (1/3, 0) to (1/2, $\sqrt{3}/6$)
- From (1/2, $\sqrt{3}/6$) to (2/3, 0)
- From (2/3, 0) to (1, 0)

Now that we can describe a transformation in words, we can develop a corresponding class. Actually, we will use two classes: Xform and XformStep. The XformStep class represents a single entry in the list above. This class only needs to encapsulate the coordinates of the next point along the strand:

```
float        x;
float        y;
```

In addition to these instance variables, the class contains a constructor, some numeric constants, and a static array of the steps that describe our transform:

```
public class XformStep
{
    private final static float        ONE_HALF  = 1f / 2f;
```

```
private final static float      ONE_THIRD = 1f / 3f;
private final static float      ROOT_3_OVER_6 =
                                    (float)(Math.sqrt(3)) / 6;

public final static XformStep[]  TRIANGLE_STEPS =
{
    new XformStep(ONE_THIRD,      0),
    new XformStep(ONE_HALF,       ROOT_3_OVER_6),
    new XformStep(2*ONE_THIRD,    0),
    new XformStep(1,              0)
};


float       x;
float       y;


public XformStep(float x, float y)
{
    this.x = x;
    this.y = y;
}
}
```

The Xform class is simply a collection of instances of XformStep. The collection is implemented as an array. There is one constructor, which takes as input an array of XformStep values:

```
public class Xform
{
    public final static Xform        TRIANGLE_XFORM =
        new Xform(XformStep.TRIANGLE_STEPS);


    public XformStep[]               steps;


    public Xform(XformStep[] steps)
    {
        this.steps = steps;
    }
}
```

Now the data representation problem is solved. The next step is to develop the FracCanvas class. The job of this class is to draw a fractal, given a set of parameters:

- The initial shape
- The transformation to apply to each line segment
- The number of iterations

The heart of FracCanvas is a method called recurse(), which has the following signature:

```
public void recurse(int depth, float x0, float y0,
                         float x1, float y1)
```

This method deals with the line segment from (x0, y0) to (x1, y1). "Dealing with" a line segment may mean simply drawing it, or it may mean expanding it by applying the transformation; it may even mean iteratively applying the transformation multiple times. The depth argument tells the method how many times to iterate. The figures shown at the beginning of this section were created with different depth arguments: Figure 16.14 shows a depth of 2, and Figure 16.16 shows a depth of 4.

As you can guess from the name, recurse() is a recursive method. If depth is 0, the method just draws a line segment that joins the two endpoints. If depth is greater than zero, the method adjusts coordinate space so that the segment goes from (0, 0) to (1, 0). The method then determines the new set of line segments (there will be four of them); for each of these segments, the recurse() method calls itself, with depth decremented by one.

The recurse() method looks like this:

```
private void recurse(int depth, float x0, float y0,
                         float x1, float y1)
{
    XformStep[]         steps;
    XformStep           step;
    int                 nPieces;
    float               x, y;
    float               nextX, nextY;
    float               range, bearing;

    // Check for bottom of recursion.
    if (depth == 0)
```

```
    {
        path.moveTo(x0, y0);
        path.lineTo(x1, y1);
        g.setStroke(thinStroke);
        g.draw(path);
        return;
    }

    // Recurse on each line segment.
    depth--;
    normalize(x0, y0, x1, y1);
    x = y = 0f;
    steps = xform.steps;
    for (int i=0; i<steps.length; i++)     // For each step ...
    {
        step = steps[i];
        nextX = step.x;
        nextY = step.y;
        recurse(depth, x, y, nextX, nextY);
        x = nextX;
        y = nextY;
    }

    // Undo temporary transformation.
    unNormalize();
}
```

The normalize() method adjusts coordinate space so that the starting point is at $(0, 0)$ and the endpoint is at $(1, 0)$. The unNormalize() method undoes the most recent normalize() call. Undoing a normalization operation is not trivial. The program maintains three stacks, called scaleStack, rotationStack, and translation-Stack. These data structures store the information that describes the various operations. Each stack is serviced by two methods.

The scale stack stores scale factors and is serviced by the scale() and unScale() methods:

```
private void scale(double scaleBy)
{
    g.scale(scaleBy, scaleBy);
    scaleStack.push(new Double(scaleBy));
}

private void unScale()
```

```
    {
        Double d = (Double)scaleStack.pop();
        double factor = 1 / d.doubleValue();
        g.scale(factor, factor);
    }
```

The rotation stack stores degrees and is serviced by the rotate() and unRotate() methods:

```
    private void rotate(double radians)
    {
        g.rotate(radians);
        rotationStack.push(new Double(radians));
    }

    private void unRotate()
    {
        Double d = (Double)rotationStack.pop();
        g.rotate(-(d.doubleValue()));
    }
```

The translation stack stores x and y translation factors and is serviced by the translate() and unTranslate() methods:

```
    private void translate(double x, double y)
    {
        g.translate(x, y);
        translationStack.push(new Double(x));
        translationStack.push(new Double(y));
    }

    private void unTranslate()
    {
        Double y = (Double)translationStack.pop();
        Double x = (Double)translationStack.pop();
        g.translate(-(x.doubleValue()), -(y.doubleValue()));
    }
```

With this infrastructure in place, it becomes easy to write the normalization method. There are two special cases that avoid numerical singularities; otherwise, the code is straightforward:

```
    private void normalize(float x0, float y0, float x1, float y1)
    {
```

```
// Translate
translate(x0, y0);                      // Translate

// Rotate
double deltaX = x1 - x0;
double deltaY = y1 - y0;
if (deltaX == 0)                        // Special case
{
    if (y0 < y1)
        rotate(Math.PI / 2);
    else
        rotate(3 * Math.PI / 2);
}
else if (deltaY == 0)                   // Special case
{
    if (x0 > x1)
        rotate(Math.PI);
    else
        rotate(0);
}
else
{
    double slope = deltaY / deltaX;
    double theta = Math.atan(slope);
    rotate(theta);
}

// Scale
double length = Math.sqrt(deltaX*deltaX + deltaY*deltaY);
scale(length);
}
```

At this point the unNormalize() method is trivial:

```
private void unNormalize()
{
    unScale();
    unRotate();
    unTranslate();
}
```

That is almost all of the FracCanvas class. There needs to be a paint() method to tie everything together. This method begins by translating the origin to the center of the canvas and scaling so that the smaller of the two dimensions (width and height) goes from –1 to +1. The code then creates an initial shape and calls recurse(). The paint() code is listed here:

```
public void paint(Graphics g1d)
{
    g = (Graphics2D)g1d;
    g.setColor(Color.blue);
    g.setStroke(new BasicStroke(0));

    scaleStack = new Stack();
    rotationStack = new Stack();
    translationStack = new Stack();
    path = new GeneralPath();
    centerAndScale2x2();

    g.setColor(Color.blue);
    for (int i=0; i<INITIAL_XS.length-1; i++)
    {
        recurse(depth, INITIAL_XS[i],   INITIAL_YS[i],
                       INITIAL_XS[i+1], INITIAL_YS[i+1]);
    }
}


public void centerAndScale2x2()
{
    // Center the origin
    Dimension size = getSize();
    translate(size.width/2, size.height/2);

    // Scale
    int mindim = Math.min(size.width, size.height);
    scale(mindim/2);
}
```

The complete listing of FracCanvas appears below, followed by FracLabTriangle. Both sources can be found on the CD-ROM, in the \javadevhdbk\ch16 directory.

LIST 16.8   *FracCanvas.java*

```java
import java.awt.*;
import java.awt.event.*;
import java.awt.geom.*;
import java.util.*;


public class FracCanvas extends Canvas
{
    private Xform              xform = Xform.TRIANGLE_XFORM;
    private int                depth = 0;
    private Stack              scaleStack;
    private Stack              rotationStack;
    private Stack              translationStack;
    private Graphics2D         g;
    private GeneralPath        path;
    private BasicStroke        thinStroke;


    //
    // These coords define the initial shape in a space with
    // origin at the center, extending from -1 to +1
    // in the smaller of the x and y dimensions.
    //
    private final static float        ROOT_ONE_THIRD =
                                          (float)(Math.sqrt(1d/3d));
    private final static float[]      INITIAL_XS =
    {
        -ROOT_ONE_THIRD, 0f, +ROOT_ONE_THIRD, -ROOT_ONE_THIRD
    };
    private final static float[]      INITIAL_YS =
    {
        -.5f, +.5f, -.5f , -.5f
    };


    public FracCanvas()
    {
        setBackground(Color.white);
        thinStroke = new BasicStroke(0);
    }
```

```java
public Dimension getPreferredSize()
{
    return new Dimension(700, 700);
}


void go(int depth)
{
    this.depth = depth;
    repaint();
}


public void paint(Graphics g1d)
{
    g = (Graphics2D)g1d;
    g.setColor(Color.blue);
    g.setStroke(new BasicStroke(0));

    scaleStack = new Stack();
    rotationStack = new Stack();
    translationStack = new Stack();
    path = new GeneralPath();
    centerAndScale2x2();

    g.setColor(Color.blue);
    for (int i=0; i<INITIAL_XS.length-1; i++)
    {
        recurse(depth, INITIAL_XS[i],   INITIAL_YS[i],
                    INITIAL_XS[i+1], INITIAL_YS[i+1]);
    }
}

private void recurse(int depth, float x0, float y0,
                                float x1, float y1)
{
    XformStep[]         steps;
    XformStep           step;
    int                 nPieces;
    float               x, y;
    float               nextX, nextY;
    float               range, bearing;
```

```
            // Check for bottom of recursion.
            if (depth == 0)
            {
                path.moveTo(x0, y0);
                path.lineTo(x1, y1);
                g.setStroke(thinStroke);
                g.draw(path);
                return;
            }

            // Recurse on each line segment.
            depth-;
            normalize(x0, y0, x1, y1);
            x = y = 0f;
            steps = xform.steps;
            for (int i=0; i<steps.length; i++)    // For each step ...
            {
                step = steps[i];
                nextX = step.x;
                nextY = step.y;
                recurse(depth, x, y, nextX, nextY);
                x = nextX;
                y = nextY;
            }

            // Undo temporary transformation.
            unNormalize();
        }


    //
    //    Translates to (x0, y0). Rotates so that (x1, x1) is
    //    to the right. Scales so that the two points are 1
    //    unit apart.
    //
    private void normalize(float x0, float y0, float x1, float y1)
    {
        // Translate
        translate(x0, y0);                      // Translate

        // Rotate
        double deltaX = x1 - x0;
        double deltaY = y1 - y0;
        if (deltaX == 0)                        // Special case
```

```
        {
            if (y0 < y1)
                rotate(Math.PI / 2);
            else
                rotate(3 * Math.PI / 2);
        }
        else if (deltaY == 0)              // Special case
        {
            if (x0 > x1)
                rotate(Math.PI);
            else
                rotate(0);
        }
        else
        {
            double slope = deltaY / deltaX;
            double theta = Math.atan(slope);
            rotate(theta);
        }

        // Scale
        double length = Math.sqrt(deltaX*deltaX + deltaY*deltaY);
        scale(length);
    }


    private void unNormalize()
    {
        unScale();
        unRotate();
        unTranslate();
    }


    private void scale(double scaleBy)
    {
        g.scale(scaleBy, scaleBy);
        scaleStack.push(new Double(scaleBy));
    }


    private void rotate(double radians)
    {
        g.rotate(radians);
```

```
        rotationStack.push(new Double(radians));
    }

    private void translate(double x, double y)
    {
        g.translate(x, y);
        translationStack.push(new Double(x));
        translationStack.push(new Double(y));
    }


    private void unScale()
    {
        Double d = (Double)scaleStack.pop();
        double factor = 1 / d.doubleValue();
        g.scale(factor, factor);
    }


    private void unRotate()
    {
        Double d = (Double)rotationStack.pop();
        g.rotate(-(d.doubleValue()));
    }


    private void unTranslate()
    {
        Double y = (Double)translationStack.pop();
        Double x = (Double)translationStack.pop();
        g.translate(-(x.doubleValue()), -(y.doubleValue()));
    }


    //
    //    Scale a graphics context so that the origin is at the center
    //    and the smaller dimension is from -1 to +1.
    //
    public void centerAndScale2x2()
    {
        // Center the origin
        Dimension size = getSize();
        translate(size.width/2, size.height/2);
```

```
                    // Scale
                    int mindim = Math.min(size.width, size.height);
                    scale(mindim/2);
            }
      }
```

Extending the Triangular Fractal

The triangular fractal is just one of a large family of curves. In theory, you can create a fractal by starting with any initial shape and applying any transformation.

 The CD-ROM contains an advanced version of the FracLabTriangle application. The advanced application is called simply FracLab, and it resides in its own subdirectory because it has its own versions of the support classes. It is similar to FracLab, but its GUI has a Choice component to allow you to choose other fractals.

The FracLab version presents the triangle fractal, as well as two other fractals. Both new shapes start with a square, as shown in Figure 16.18.

FIGURE 16.18:

The FracLab program starting with a square

The program has two transformations that can operate on this shape. The Box transformation indents each line segment. This transformation is illustrated in Figure 16.19. Figure 16.20 shows the result of applying the transformation four times.

FIGURE 16.19:

FracLab's Box transformation

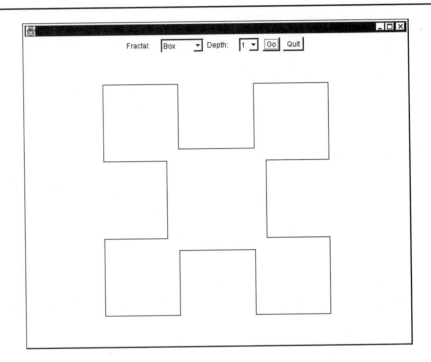

A more sophisticated transformation can be applied to the initial square shape. The new transformation still indents each line segment. In addition, an "island" is drawn within the indentation. Figure 16.21 shows the transformation, which is called the Coast transformation. Figure 16.22 shows the result of applying the Coast transformation four times.

FIGURE 16.20:

FracLab's Box transformation
after four iterations

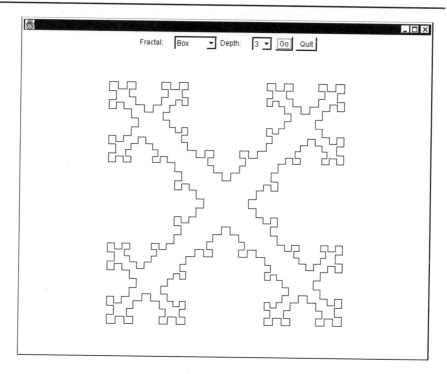

FIGURE 16.21:

FracLab's Coast
transformation

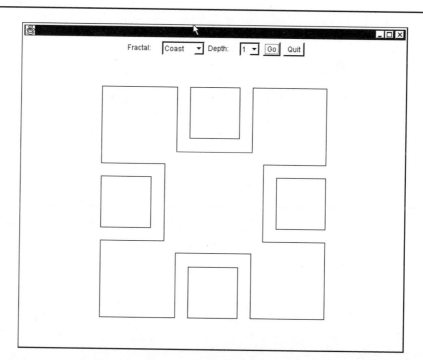

FIGURE 16.22:

FracLab's Coast
transformation after
four iterations

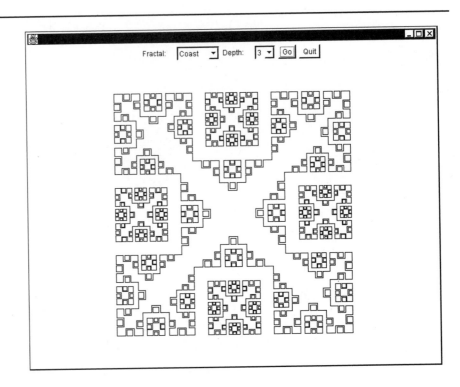

Summary

In this chapter, you learned how to use the 2D API to expand Java's traditional two-dimensional drawing facilities. You began by exploring the Graphics2D class. Then you learned about the Shapes abstract superclass and the various subclasses that extend it. In particular, you learned about the GeneralPath class, which is used when the other subclasses don't support the type of drawing that you want to perform. You learned about the three major operations that you can perform on a Shape: drawing, filling, and clipping.

You also learned about transformations, which allow you to manipulate the coordinate space of your drawing region. The basic transformations are rotation, translation, and scaling. Finally, you looked at a detailed fractal case study that made extensive use of the 2D API.

In the next chapter, you'll learn about the Java Beans API, which is designed to promote software reusability.

CHAPTER

SEVENTEEN

17

Java Beans

- Java Bean introspection

- Java Bean properties

- Java Bean events

- Java Bean customization

- Java Bean persistence

- The Beans Development Kit and the BeanBox

As a Java application developer, you know that designing complex object-oriented software is both expensive and revision-intensive. The programmer must carefully consider class relationships, object interactions, and timing. The challenge becomes more acute in a multithreaded environment, where timing is a somewhat fuzzier issue. One solution to these problems is to develop a set of classes whose relationships and timings are determined abstractly, proven over several uses, then applied to the problem at hand. These kinds of solutions are called *design patterns*, and they arise from another important principle: There is no need to solve the same problem twice.

Virtuous design is a fine thing, but in business it must have a tangible benefit, and for years that perceived benefit has been software reuse. Looking at broad problem sets as application domains, developers might design their high-level application code as a framework. A *framework* is something "heavier," more elaborate, and more case-specific than a design pattern, but it is also general enough to apply to many problems in one domain (for example, graphics-based action games). The objective is to leverage the investment of time, money, and testing across successive development efforts, meaning subsequent projects realize a faster time to market.

The Java Beans API is one such framework and is the subject of this chapter. We'll begin with an introduction to the Beans API, its component model, and its implementation. Then we'll discuss Bean properties, events, and customization in detail. Finally, we'll cover the use of the Beans Development Kit.

An Introduction to the Beans API

The Beans API describes the abstract relationships and interactions among key classes and the means to produce different objects that will behave consistently with all objects and associated tools relying on the same specification. The purpose of the API is to bring the goal of writing reusable Java code down to the component level, so that users of components have the assurance Beans will work together regardless of who made them. The Beans specification also describes conventional techniques for writing modular, lightweight code that is suitable for use in an application container with other Beans and with components built on other platforms, such as ActiveX/COM.

In much the same way that CAD engineering relies on standard parts to design machines quickly and at a known cost, the vision of a component-based software economy means dividing the work among creators, designers, and assemblers. Each agent contributes to the application by focusing on one stage of the overall building process. Figure 17.1 illustrates a conventional view of the relationship among these stages.

FIGURE 17.1:

A hypothetical Bean development model

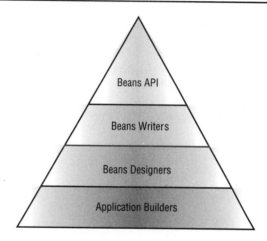

Some suppliers produce a repository of general-purpose Beans from scratch. Each Bean encapsulates a coherent set of functions, along with some exposed controls that permit modification. Component designers select some of these components to customize and marry together, possibly to make more complex Beans or applets. Finally, application designers, charged with satisfying user-interface and other presentation requirements, choose and assemble major components to produce the final application document.

Given a variety of spell checkers available as Beans, for example, a component-built word processor should be able to include industry-specific lexicons (such as legal or medical) or even alternate languages. The developer simply needs to get the appropriate Bean from a supplier and build it into the application through a GUI-based builder tool. Another approach might allow mixing and matching of Bean-based software products in an application suite container. Perhaps one such container license qualifies how many application Beans it can integrate, leaving both the variety and number of application services to be determined by the user. The broad-minded vendor thus gets into the business of providing a large base of modular components.

No matter how component development might ultimately be deployed, Java's cross-platform flexibility makes a compelling case for doing it with Beans. The widespread availability of Windows on the desktop makes COM (Component Object Model) a persuasive model as well. One question we need to answer, if we deem Beans the preferred choice for building components, is how to work with ActiveX/COM controls.

The Component Model and Beans Implementation

The framework of the Java Beans API is based on a model for services that is generally accepted, ensuring that Beans are not conceptually different from other kinds of components. The services model includes five categories:

- Properties
- Publishing and discovery
- Customization
- Persistence
- Intercommunication

Each of these categories is discussed in the following sections.

Properties

Properties are the data and services a component makes available for editing. Any public class data that can be changed or read through setXXX() and getXXX() methods is an example of a Bean property.

A component should optionally be able to send updates to other components when a property state is altered. This delivery mechanism is intended as a convenience to the designer who wishes to coordinate a common property of several components, such as background color.

Publishing and Discovery

Publishing and discovery describe how a component's internal composition is determined and which elements will be available for modification at design time. Inspection includes data, methods, constructors, and with Beans, any special naming conventions or syntax that signal a component-specific attribute.

In Java, this publishing and discovery facility is called *reflection* (`java.lang .reflect`), and it is a general tool for decomposing any object. The `java.beans` package includes a class called the `Introspector` that uses reflection to operate on Bean instances, then applies some recognition rules for exposing properties, enabling property-sheet style updates, and overriding reflection if the developer wishes.

NOTE   The `Introspector`'s ability to override reflection lets the programmer "rewrite" the Bean's appearance. A separate `BeanInfo` class is required, which is discussed later in this chapter.

Customization

Customization refers to changing the presentation of properties or services a component publishes, or optionally providing a component designer with a special GUI that simplifies complex property changes. A customizer can aid the designer by flagging other properties that require attention after a change elsewhere or by executing related alterations automatically. Most Bean development will likely take place in one of several available builder tools, so the Bean writer can use customization to ensure a common look-and-feel to the designer.

Persistence

Persistence gives the designer and application builder a way to save component modifications to a new, self-contained component; alternatively, it supports the application builder's means for connecting multiple components together and creating an applet or application. Beans leverage object serialization as implemented in `java.io` for the base utility. Again, a developer can write new components from existing ones by hand or use a tool that automates the work.

Intercommunication

Finally, some *intercommunication* model is needed for components to pass and receive information. This convention ensures that one component can talk to any other component, so far as the target component is "interested" in outside events, and that the behavior is common across all environments. This requires a model that is abstract and event-driven in design. A major impetus for changing the AWT event model in the JDK 1.1 release was Bean development support, which uses an update or callback strategy to allow for maximum flexibility.

Like any subclass of java.awt.Component, a source Bean broadcasts updates of its state to a known "delegate" (a listener interface). A target Bean may register interest in implementing the delegate and registering itself with the source.

Bean Resources

The fundamental Beans-related resources are located in java.lang.Class and three packages: java.lang.reflect, java.lang.beancontext, and java .lang.beans. Each of these packages is discussed in the following sections.

TIP   Look for the latest announcements of new specifications and products on Sun's official Beans web site, http://java.sun.com/beans.

The reflect Package

The java.lang.reflect package supports reflection for all Java objects. The classes Constructor, Field, and Method each implement the Member interface, which declares methods for determining the name, scope, and declaring class of an implementing type.

The following are two new classes in the Java 2 release:

AccessibleObject   Provides an access flag that can be used to disable reflection. AccessibleObject is a parent class of Constructor, Field, and Method.

ReflectPermission   Extends java.security.BasicPermission. This class allows each Bean element to be "named" as a resource, and access restrictions can be applied to each resource. This behavior is analogous to file permissions in Unix.

The beancontext Package

The java.lang.beancontext package, new in Java 2, provides containment services, called *contexts*, which make it possible to nest and control Beans in a hierarchical structure. Containment behavior with respect to nesting is similar to GUI containers. With a scheme for Bean-specific containers in place, it should be easier for the designer or assembler to combine Beans and provide external control ports, allowing the context to provide administrative control for all contained Beans.

The containment services facility stems from the Beans Runtime Containment and Services Protocol, one of three major services in the Java 2 Beans API. Drag-and-drop and the Java Activation Framework (currently under review) are the other two main services implemented in Java 2.

The beans Package

The `java.lang.beans` package contributes some services for runtime Bean execution, but it primarily establishes the contract all visual builder tools must implement to support design-time work. Services include methods for incorporating customizers in a builder tool, property editing and update notification, and a set of descriptor classes used for supplementing or overriding reflection data. Two new interfaces support integrating Beans into a context:

> `AppletInitializer`   Provides controls for an applet Bean that operates within a context, or nested structure.

> `DesignMode`   A parent interface to `java.beans.BeanContext` that specifies how a context notifies its nested Bean members when editing changes occur.

Reflection, Introspection, and Naming

Java's reflection mechanism can be used on any runtime object. `java.lang.Class` includes methods that return objects of type `Constructor`, `Field`, and `Method`, each of which is defined in `java.lang.reflect`. Decomposing a class is easy, as demonstrated by the `RectangleFields` application, which prints out the name of each `Field` object in `java.awt.Rectangle`. This program is shown below and is included on the CD-ROM in the directory `\javadevhdbk\ch17\RectangleFields.java`.

LIST 17.1	*RectangleFields.java*

```
import java.awt.Rectangle;
import java.lang.reflect.Field;

public class RectangleFields
{
    public static void main(String args[])
    {
        // try{} provides an enclosing scope; declare variables out
```

```
        // here so we only enclose exception-bound operations
        Class rectClass = null;
        Field rectField[] = null;

        try
        {
            // Load class Rectangle so we can reflect its contents,
            // and retrieve all Fields specific to the class
            rectClass = Class.forName("java.awt.Rectangle");
            rectField = rectClass.getDeclaredFields();
        }
        // getDeclaredFields() throws this
        catch(SecurityException se)
        {
          System.out.println("Access to Rectangle fields denied");
        }
        // Class.forName() throws this
        catch(ClassNotFoundException cnfe)
        {
          System.out.println("Didn't find the Rectangle class");
        }

        // Print toString() of each element to stdout
        System.out.println("Fields in Rectangle are:");
        for (int i = 0; i < rectField.length; i++)
        {
          System.out.println(rectField[i].toString());
        }
    }
}
```

Here's the output:

```
Fields in Rectangle are:
public int java.awt.Rectangle.x
public int java.awt.Rectangle.y
public int java.awt.Rectangle.width
public int java.awt.Rectangle.height
private static final long java.awt.Rectangle.serialVersionUID
```

TIP
To print **Rectangle**'s **Method** objects instead, substitute **Method** for **Field** references in the **RectangeFields.java** code, or better yet, just add them in and start creating a full-service decomposition tool. Note that the output of **Method** objects is more than a page long.

This application illustrates one step the **Introspector** takes in analyzing a Bean. The Bean writer alerts the **Introspector** to properties, along with other important characteristics, by adhering to a method signature pattern, or naming convention, that the **Introspector** recognizes. These naming conventions are listed in the Beans specification document, and they include property updates, event handling, customization, and techniques for modifying the results of reflection. Each of these aspects of Beans is described in this chapter.

The **Introspector** takes things a few steps further than **RectangleFields**. The **Introspector** walks a Bean's entire class hierarchy; if a child class overrides a parent member, the **Introspector** follows the rules of inheritance as expected. This means that the Bean's property sheet can fill up with values that were inherited but not intended for presentation as properties. Some builder tools provide a means for automatically hiding these unwanted properties. However, the BeanBox, which is the reference tool that is part of the Beans Development Kit (BDK), does not filter out parent properties. (The BeanBox is discussed later in this chapter.)

TIP
Some texts that discuss Beans, including the Java Software specification, use the term *design patterns* instead of *naming conventions*. Some object-oriented programming purists may find this term misleading with respect to the **Introspector**, and it is avoided in this chapter.

Bean Properties

The **Introspector** derives a Bean property from any set*XXX*() and get*XXX*() method pair that follow conventional encapsulation techniques. The **BeanField** class supplies accessor and mutator methods for the members message and messageFlag:

```
public class BeanField extends java.awt.TextField
{
    String message = "Write your message here";
    boolean messageFlag = false;

    // Constructor
    public BeanField()
    {
        super(message);
    }

    // Support for String property "message
    public String getMessage()
    {
        return message;
    }

    public void setMessage(String newMessage)
    {
        message = newMessage;
    }

    // Support for boolean property messageChanged,
    // encapsulates messageFlag boolean
    public boolean isMessageChanged()
    {
        return messageFlag;
    }

    public void setMessageChanged(boolean newState)
    {
        messageFlag = newState;
    }
}
```

All that's required to designate a property is a getXXX()/setXXX() method pair. In the case of a boolean property, isMessageChanged() and getMessage-Changed() are a special-case syntax that may be more useful than get and set, but this syntax is not required. The general description for producing a read-write property is as follows:

```
public void set<Property> (<PropertyType> value) {…}
public <PropertyType> get<Property>() {…}

public void set<Property>(boolean value){…}
public boolean is<Property> () {…}
```

Two other naming conventions are used to identify array-based (indexed) properties. The first convention recognizes a property that passes the array as a whole:

```
public <PropertyType>[] get<Property>(){}
public void set<Property>(<PropertyType>[] value){}
```

The second signature applies to indexed properties that pass a single element:

```
public <PropertyType> get<Property>(int index){}
public void set<Property>(int index, <PropertyType> value){}
```

Read-only and write-only properties are described as having only a get*XXX*() or set*XXX*() method, respectively. Finding a meaningful use for a write-only property is problematic, but read-only properties are a simple way to pass reference-only information to anyone using with a Bean, as in this example:

```
…
public String getWarning()
{
        return "This Bean is not threadsafe in this revision."
}
```

The Introspector sees a get*XXX*()/set*XXX*() method pair as a simple property, in which changes in value concern only the local Bean. It also recognizes two other property types, called *bound* and *constrained*, by their use of an event-style naming convention in the Bean code. The bound and constrained property types are described shortly.

Properties and Data Types

In the BeanField class shown at the beginning of this section, using a String type for the variable message and its get*XXX*()/set*XXX*() methods is convenient and produces clearer code, but it is not required. If message were an array of type char or private in scope and no other changes were made, this code would work equally well. Properties are not required to maintain a type-specific relationship to the data they represent. Thus, the scope and encapsulation rules of Bean data are no different from those for any other class data. This is the expected approach in terms of good object design, but there are drawbacks as well as benefits to doing it this way.

It is easier to subclass a Bean if properties do not have to be type-specific, because knowledge of an object's internal state types is irrelevant. They can be shown as properties by whatever types are meaningful at design time, and the subclass can simply provide wrapper methods to the parent class methods and add code. In some cases, it also may be more useful to offer access to several internal data types through a single property, as illustrated in the following example:

```java
public class TrafficLightBean extends Canvas implements Serializable
{
    // Light states are true/false; code must support state
    // checking to ensure one light is on at a time
    private boolean stop = true;
    private boolean wait = false;
    private boolean go = false;
    private Color currentLight = Color.red;

    ...
    // Support for Color property "lightState"
    // represented by three booleans: stop, wait, and go
    public java.awt.Color getLightState()
    {
        return currentLight;
    }

    public void setLightState(Color newState)
    {
        if (newState == getLightState()) return;
        if newState == Color.green
        {
            stop = false;
            wait = false;
            go = true;
        }
        // and so on for red and yellow lights...
        ...
```

```
        currentLight = newState;
    }
    // code for displaying and painting the object …
}
```

In this example, TrafficLightBean's three possible states are stored as unrelated boolean values. The getLightState() and setLightState() methods present one property to the designer; the set method silently handles the details of setting all three values through a single change.

NOTE   In this example, setLightState() does not check the new Color value for validity (to see if it is green, yellow, or red). Invalid changes to a property are often handled best by throwing an exception, as will be shown in an example using this same class, presented later in this chapter.

Since no semantic or logical relationship is enforced between a Bean's data and its properties, it's good practice to document which methods establish properties, along with the variable names and data types they represent. The flexibility of separating a property from the type it encapsulates means simple errors, like typos or case mismatches, can create a lot of confusion. If the code compiles but the Introspector does not create a property as you expected, you should check the spelling and capitalization of the method pair.

TIP   One philosophical goal behind the Beans framework is to encourage designers to experiment and connect Beans together in unexpected ways. Tolerating some amount of property mismatching among Bean properties is therefore expected. One way to avoid this problem with a Bean whose property ranges are unusually restrictive is to create a new data type and a custom editor property for it, so that it does not appear to invite casual testing. For example, in our traffic light program, we might want a property editor that allows the user to choose red, green, or yellow only. A Choice component type, rather than a palette-style editor, would be a better fit.

Bound Properties

A property that *binds* its changes to another Bean's property fires a change update, which the target accepts automatically. There can be as many targets as there are available Beans, so changes in a "control" Bean could be used to automatically update all related Beans, simplifying the designer's work of coordinating state behavior in an application.

A source Bean property binds its changes to a target Bean's property through a reference to PropertyChangeSupport. The source Bean adds and removes target Bean properties to its update notification list through PropertyChangeSupport's registration model. The binding Bean uses this notification list to call listeners through firePropertyChange(), which is called from the set*XXX*() method of the binding property. The firePropertyChange() argument list includes the property name and both old and new property values, which must be passed as object references. The following code fragment typifies the necessary code pieces:

```java
import java.io.Serializable;
import java.awt.event.*;
import java.beans.*

public class Billboard extends Panel implements Serializable
{
  private String message;   // Billboard text
  private int duration;     // Hours sold to current sponsor

  private PropertyChangeSupport propBind =
      new PropertyChangeSupport(this);

  // "Wrapper" methods to register listeners; the Introspector
  // recognizes this syntax once the Bean is instantiated
  public void addPropertyChangeListener(PropertyChangeListener pcl)
  {
    propBind.addPropertyChangeListener(pcl);
  }

  public void removePropertyChangeListener (PropertyChangeListener
                                            pcl)
  {
    propBind.removePropertyChangeListener(pcl);
  }

  // Support for String property "message"
  public String getMessage()
  {
    return message;
  }
```

```
      // setMessage() supports property binding
      public void setMessage(String newMessage)
      {
        String oldMessage = message;
        message = newMessage;
        propBind.firePropertyChange("message", oldMessage, newMessage);
      }

      // Support for integer property "duration"
      public int getDuration()
      {
        return duration;
      }

      // setDuration() supports property binding
      public void setDuration(int newTime)
      {
        int oldTime = duration;
        duration = newTime;
        // Primitive types can't be passed in property updates
        Integer oldDuration = new Integer(oldTime);
        Integer newDuration = new Integer(newTime);
        propBind.firePropertyChange("duration", oldDuration,
                                    newDuration);
      }
      ...
    }
```

The Billboard Bean requires one PropertyChangeSupport reference for all binding properties. The firePropertyChange() method passes the property name as a literal String, all lowercase, followed by the old and new property values. (Passing the property literal in all lowercase characters ensures that a test of the property won't fail for lack of proper capitalization.) The Beans specification offers no direct rationale for passing the old value in a bound property change, but it does serve a purpose. The firePropertyChange() argument list conforms to the list for fireVetoableChange(), which handles constrained property updates. Maintaining a common argument list for both cleans up the code, makes it easier to change a property update from bound to constrained or vice versa, and allows the Beans framework to support one signature for all property-based message passing.

NOTE   The target Bean requires no code to support binding. When one property is bound
to another in a builder tool, a hookup class is written and compiled automatically.
This mediating logic is called an *adapter*, and is discussed in the "Beans Events"
section later in this chapter.

Constrained Properties

Constrained properties work similarly to bound properties, but they permit target properties to reject updates. Conditional updating can be more complex than automatic binding, because it raises a series of questions about how targets are updated and how property values among several Beans are coordinated.

Constrained properties use a notification scheme that allows the target to reject updates. Supporting constrained properties can grow increasingly complex where property updates are propagated to many other Beans. In particular, serial or daisy-chained conditional updates are worth avoiding unless there is a compelling reason for using them. In any case, it's a good idea to plan constrained property behavior carefully to avoid application design problems.

Given multiple targets of a single update, it's possible that some will accept the change; other targets may reject it, and rejection may occur under different conditions. An update might be rejected because the new value is illegal or invalid (a new int value, interpreted as a radius in pixels, exceeds the screen's boundaries), or merely inappropriate (a new foreground color might match the current background color, causing the component to wash on repaint()).

With constrained property changes, it is also important to consider whether the source Bean property blindly accepts all incoming change requests. Assume a constrained property invalidates some new data it receives. In this case, simplicity suggests it should throw the sender an exception and cancel firing the change to its targets. If the source accepts the value and updates interested targets, but one or more of them reject the change, it may be simplest—but not desired—to change the source property and its targets back to the original value. The requirements for behavior are open-ended. The step-by-step plan presented here assumes the simplest case, in which all constrained properties strive to remain the same.

NOTE   A typical "what-if" question in classroom settings concerns targets that accept an update but reject attempts to revert to the old value. One possible scenario is that an application Bean accepts an update to its revision number property but rejects a subsequent license key property change. The old license key can't enable the current software revision, rendering the application useless. In such cases, it may be much simpler to devise another approach to the update scheme (a "bundled" update, for example), rather than write elaborate case logic to roll back from any of a series of related property changes.

The conventional strategy for a constrained property update is as follows:

- The source Bean implements `PropertyChangeListener`.

- Within the Bean's `propertyChange()` method, the source property's `setXXX()` method is called inside a `try{}` block; the `setXXX()` method declares that it throws `PropertyVetoException` to enforce this.

- The constrained property's `setXXX()` method throws a `PropertyVeto-Exception` if the new data is invalid.

- If the proposed change is valid, `fireVetoableChange()` is called on all listeners.

- If any target throws an exception indicating a rejected change, the `setXXX()` method exits, leaving the original value intact.

- Otherwise, the new value replaces the old value.

- The change is fired to bound property listeners, if supported.

TIP   Implementing `PropertyChangeListener` is a source Bean's protection against unwanted changes from a Bean that attempts to bind its changes. This approach can also be used to remind a curious designer what the boundaries of the value are.

Target beans that accept updates conditionally implement `VetoableChange-Listener`. This interface supplies one method:

`vetoableChange(PropertyChangeEvent e)`   Throws a `PropertyVeto-Exception` if the new value does not meet the target property's criteria.

A fully constrained update cycle means the hosting Bean maintains a reference to VetoableChangeSupport and provides wrapper methods to add and remove VetoableChangeListener.

The syntax is the same as with PropertyChangeSupport. The following code fragment illustrates the minimum code required to support a constrained property:

```java
public class LicenseServer implements Serializable
{
    private String encryptedKey;
    VetoableChangeSupport vcs = new VetoableChangeSupport(this);

    // "Wrapper" methods for VetoableChangeSupport
    // to alert the Introspector
    public void addVetoableChangeListener(VetoableChangeListener
                                          vcl)
    {
      vcs.addVetoableChangeListener(vcl);
    }

    public void removeVetoableChangeListener(VetoableChangeListener
                                             vcl)
    {
      vcs.removeVetoableChangeListener(vcl);
    }

    // Support for the constrained property "key"
    public String getKey()
    {
      return encryptedKey;
    }

    public void setKey(String newKey)
    {
        vcs.fireVetoableChange("key", encryptedKey, newKey);

        // If the target does not throw an exception,
        // accept the new value locally
        encryptedKey = newKey;
    }
}
```

The following example elaborates on the TrafficLight Bean example shown earlier. The context of this illustration is a rudimentary traffic-simulation program. In this model, a light may change to red at any time but must reject a change to green if the current state is yellow, indicating the expected update should have been red. In a simple Bean simulation, we might have a Traffic-Sensor Bean that binds its changes to lightState. We want to ensure that Traffic-LightBean has the final say:

```java
import java.awt.*;
import java.awt.event.*;
import java.beans.*;
import java.io.*;

public class TrafficLightBean
extends Canvas
implements Serializable, ActionListener, PropertyChangeListener
{
  // Each light state is true/false; code must support state
  // checking to ensure one light is on ("true") at a time.
  private boolean stop = true;
  private boolean wait = false;
  private boolean go = false;
  private Color currentLight = Color.red;

  private PropertyChangeSupport pcs =
      new PropertyChangeSupport(this);
  private VetoableChangeSupport vcs =
      new VetoableChangeSupport(this);

  // Listener registration for bound properties
  public void addPropertyChangeListener(PropertyChangeListener
                                        pcl)
  {
    pcs.addPropertyChangeListener(pcl);
  }

  public void removePropertyChangeListener(PropertyChangeListener
                                           pcl)
  {
    pcs.removePropertyChangeListener(pcl);
  }
```

```java
// Listener registration for constrained properties
public void addVetoableChangeListener(VetoableChangeListener
                                      vcl)
{
  vcs.addVetoableChangeListener(vcl);
}

public void removeVetoableChangeListener(VetoableChangeListener
                                         vcl)
{
  vcs.removeVetoableChangeListener(vcl);
}

// Support for Color property "lightState"
// represented by booleans stop, wait, and go
public Color getLightState()
{
  return currentLight;
}

public void setLightState(Color newState)
    throws PropertyVetoException
{
  // Ignore same-state signaling
  if (newState.equals(getLightState())) return;

  // Validate newState
  // Cannot change to green if we are expecting red
  if (newState.equals(Color.green))
  {
    // "==" operator is safe because we guarantee the use
    // of static Color members internally
    if (getLightState() == Color.yellow)
    {
      throw new PropertyVetoException();
    }

    // newState is valid.  Send value to vetoable targets.
    vcs.fireVetoableChange("lightstate", newState, currentLight);
```

```
            // No one vetoed if we got this far, so change values
            stop = false;
            wait = false;
            go = true;
            Color oldLight = currentLight;
            currentLight = newState;

            // Fire the update to bound properties
            pcs.firePropertyChange("lightstate", newState, oldState);
        }

        // Include changes to red and yellow states here…
        …
    }

    // Implement PropertyChangeListener here
    // Check opposing lights have changed to red
    public void propertyChange(PropertyChangeEvent pce)
    {
        if (pce.getPropertyName().equals("lightstate")
        {
            Color change = (Color)pce.getNewValue();
            try
            {
                setLightState(change);
            }
            catch(PropertyVetoException pve){ }
        }
    }
    // Code to display and paint the object goes here…
}
```

It's worth noting that we run into several obstacles with a property whose data type is different from its underlying class member. To make things easier, we ended up using the member currentLight. Other approaches include making one property for the boolean members stop, wait, and go, then yoking them together through a customizer or specialized editor, or just doing away with them, which may not be practical in production code.

Bean Events

The Beans API's bound and constrained property change mechanisms are simple extensions of Java's event model. `PropertyChangeSupport` and `VetoableChange-Support` each deliver an event object—an instance of `PropertyChangeEvent`—that contains information about the event. This information includes the name of the property that changed, the old value, and the new one. The event is delivered to any registered listener. For bound and constrained properties, listeners are added in a builder tool when the Bean containing the binding or constrained property "points to" or specifies the target Bean as a recipient of a property update.

In practice, this process looks and feels quite different from building a Java GUI. An AWT component that wants to listen implements a listener interface. The interface carries the event type that the source component uses to signal an event. The first component registers itself as a listener to the source event by creating a reference to the source type and calling the source's add*XXX*`Listener()` method. The target then receives event updates by declaring itself to conform to the interface type. In this scenario, the programmer is used to thinking of the target as the active agent.

The difference lies in what the builder tool does to support the connection of any two compatible Beans that might be chosen. A programmer knows a `Frame` must implement an `ActionListener` to receive an `ActionEvent` from a `Button`. In a Beans builder tool, the only prerequisite is that Bean A fires an event that Bean B supports in the argument list of one or more methods. It's the builder tool's job to write the code necessary to complete the connection. Furthermore, Beans aren't even required to extend a `java.awt.Component` or use one of the provided `Event` types. A Bean writer therefore must peel back the event model to apply the structure that is normally assumed in building a standard GUI.

Bean event-handling can be generalized to four main objects:

- An event source
- An event target
- The event object itself
- An event delegate, or listener interface

Each of these objects is discussed in the following sections.

Bean Event Sources

A Bean event source fires events, allows other Beans to register or unregister interest in its events, and maintains a data structure of listeners to maintain at event-notification time. The naming convention for all event sources is the same:

```
public void add<XXXListener>(<XXXListener> listenTarget){}
public void remove<XXXListener>(<XXXListener> listenTarget){}
```

The *XXX* portion specifies the listener interface that the source uses to route a fired event to its target. The target must have at least one method with an argument list that includes an object of the same type declared by the listener interface's declared method. There are few other requirements of a Bean as an event source. A Bean may store registered listeners in any way it sees fit (a Vector is the conventional choice), and it may update its current listeners in any order, as long as each listener is notified.

It's assumed that a Bean event source will want to allow any number of listeners to register; this default behavior is termed *multicast*. In order to establish a source that accepts only one listener (*unicast*), the naming convention changes slightly:

```
public void addXXXListener(XXXListener listenTarget) throws
java.util.TooManyListenersException{}
public void removeXXXListener(XXXListener listenTarget){}
```

WARNING   In practice, a multicast source could also be set up as an *n*-cast source, where *n* establishes the number of possible listeners. Using TooManyListenersException in conjunction with an *n*-cast strategy, however, is not supported, even if its name suggests a broader use than "no more than one listener." Using this exception other than for unicast delivery may cause no harm, but it violates the specification's defined use, meaning a builder tool could misinterpret nonstandard usage.

To follow the event model properly, an event source must construct an event object and send a copy of it to each registered target. The event object bears the responsibility of requiring the event source to identify itself, as detailed in the next section.

Bean Event Objects

When subclassing an AWT component, a number of coding chores and design decisions are avoided by inheriting an AWT component's existing event structure and behavior. But when the programmer requires a Bean event source that is best built from scratch, the easiest place to start is by determining what kinds of event objects it will use.

New event types hook into the AWT event-handling scheme by subclassing java.util.EventObject. All subclasses of EventObject require the object that constructs it (the event source) to be included in the constructor's argument list. Any data of particular importance that the event source wishes to provide can also be added to the constructor's argument list and supplemented in the event object code by a get*XXX*() method for easy access.

Let's say we want to build a simple Bean that sends its instance name and a message whenever it is acted upon. We'll think of this external action as a kind of event we want to record in a running log. We'll call the Bean a Node and call its logging information a NodeAlertEvent. The code for this example follows and is included on the CD-ROM in the directories \javadevhdbk\ch17\NodeAlert-Event.java, NodeListener.java, and Node.java.

LIST 17.2   *NodeAlertEvent.java*

```java
import java.util.*;

public class NodeAlertEvent
extends EventObject
{
    private String name;
    private String message;

    // Event construction is performed by another object, which
    // passes itself as an argument
    public NodeAlertEvent(Object source, String newName, String msg)
    {
        super(source);
        name = newName;
        message = msg;
    }

    public String getName()
    {
        return name;
    }
```

```
    public String getMessage()
    {
        return message;
    }
}
```

The source passed to the constructor is sent to EventObject's class through a call to super(), which ultimately hooks the local object into the event-handling structure. Typically, source's only intended function is to support constructing EventObject; name and message are exposed in the argument list as a matter of convenience.

Now that NodeAlertEvent is built, we can build the listener interface that will carry instances of it on behalf of the event source.

LIST 17.3   *NodeListener.java*

```
public interface NodeListener
{
    public void nodeAlert(NodeAlertEvent nae);
}
```

When it is time to fire an event update to all listeners, Node simply uses a reference of type NodeListener to typecast each of Node's listeners, and then call that object's nodeAlert() implementation. The following listing shows the event source class in full detail.

LIST 17.4   *Node.java*

```
import java.awt.event.*;
import java.awt.*;
import java.io.*;
import java.util.*;

public class Node
extends Panel
implements Serializable, ActionListener
{
    private static int totalNodes;    // Tracks all nodes created
    private int counter;              // Instance number of node
```

```java
private String nodename;
private String messageType;
private int currentAlert;
private Button pressMe;
private Label system, message;
private Vector vec;                    // Stores listeners

private Color [] alertColor = { Color.white,
                                Color.pink,
                                Color.yellow,
                                Color.magenta,
                                Color.orange,
                                Color.red,
                                Color.darkGray,
                                Color.blue };

private String [] alertName = { "White",
                                "Pink",
                                "Yellow",
                                "Magenta",
                                "Orange",
                                "Red",
                                "Dark Gray",
                                "Blue" };

/* Constructor */
public Node()
{
   setLayout(new BorderLayout());
   totalNodes++;
   counter = totalNodes;
   currentAlert = 0;
   nodename = "Node" + counter;
   messageType = "Default Alert";
   pressMe = new Button("Send message");
   system = new Label(nodename, Label.CENTER);
   message = new Label(messageType, Label.CENTER);

   pressMe.addActionListener(this);
   add(system, "North");
   add(message, "Center");
```

```
    add(pressMe, "South");
    setSize(100,100);
}

/*
 * ActionListener for button pressMe
 */
public void actionPerformed(ActionEvent ae)
{
    int level = currentAlert % alertName.length;
    nodename = "Node" + counter;
    message.setText(alertName[level]);
    message.setBackground(alertColor[level]);
    repaint();
    notifyNodeAlertEvent();
    currentAlert++;
}

/*
 * Registration support for Node listeners
 */
public void addNodeListener(NodeListener nl)
{
    // Check for double registration
    if (vec.contains(nl)) return;
    vec.addElement(nl);
}

public void removeNodeListener(NodeListener nl)
{
    if (vec.contains(nl))
    {
        vec.removeElement(nl);
    }
}

/*
 * Called by actionPerformed()
 * Updates listeners first-come, first-serve
 */
protected void notifyNodeAlertEvent()
```

```
{
   NodeAlertEvent nae = null;
   nae = new NodeAlertEvent(this, nodename, messageType);
   Vector fireVec = (Vector)vec.clone();

   for (int i = 0; i < fireVec.size(); i++)
   {
      NodeListener target = null;
      target = (NodeListener)fireVec.elementAt(i);
      target.nodeAlert(nae);
   }
}

/*
 * Support for properties:
 *    Property nodename -> String nodename
 *    Property alertType -> String messageType
 */

public void setNodename(String newName)
{
   String oldName = nodename;
   nodename = newName;
   system.setText(nodename);
}

public String getNodename()
{
   return nodename;
}

public void setAlertType(String newMessage)
{
   String oldMessage = messageType;
   messageType = newMessage;
   message.setText(messageType);
}

public String getAlertType()
{
   return messageType;
}
}
```

Notice that we've included a graphic appearance to the Bean. We have a responsibility to maintain state as well as broadcast changes, and that responsibility is slightly different for simple, bound, and constrained property models. In this simple model, we "advertised" local-only changes by placing the code within the actionPerformed() method. This code will nonetheless look familiar if you read the discussion of bound and constrained property changes earlier in this chapter. There are no support features to encapsulate, as we did with PropertyChange-Support and VetoableChangeSupport. Providing them locally is not much extra work, but we may want to move property change code into the appropriate setXXX() method.

Bean Event Targets and Adapters

Event targets have only one requirement: They must support a method that includes the appropriate EventObject subclass in its argument list. The name of the target method is irrelevant, but in order to accommodate event types outside the java.awt.event package, the target Bean must know about them in advance. From the point of view of a Bean target, the most effective source strategy is to stick with standard AWT event types whenever possible. If the target then subclasses Component, it inherits several ways to receive events.

Target Beans do not need to implement listener interfaces for whatever kind of event is passed their way. Connecting source and target Beans together is accomplished by a builder tool that generates and compiles an "event hookup" on the fly. The hookup acts as a proxy, implementing the interface used by the source when it sends notifications and calling the target method through that interface's declared method.

The following hookup, or adapter class source code, was generated automatically by the BDK BeanBox. We connected one demo Bean, BlueButton, to another demo Bean, called Juggler, by way of an ActionEvent. Juggler contains the method stopJuggling(), which takes an ActionEvent, so that its animation can be stopped at any time using a button control. Once we confirmed the connection (you'll see an example later in this chapter), the BeanBox wrote the following:

```
// Automatically generated event hookup file.

package tmp.sunw.beanbox;
import sunw.demo.juggler.Juggler;
import java.awt.event.ActionListener;
import java.awt.event.ActionEvent;
```

```
public class ___Hookup_1504cd72aa implements
java.awt.event.ActionListener, java.io.Serializable {

    public void setTarget(sunw.demo.juggler.Juggler t) {
        target = t;
    }

    public void actionPerformed(java.awt.event.ActionEvent arg0){
        target.stopJuggling(arg0);
    }

    private sunw.demo.juggler.Juggler target;
}
```

Multiplexing and Demultiplexing

A builder tool can automatically write simple adapters that intercept and mediate event information between source and target Beans. It's also possible to code adapter classes by hand and extend them beyond hooking up property updates or generic events to perform other types of middleman services.

NOTE   Adapter classes, as discussed here, may bring to mind the various adapter classes in the `java.awt.event` package. Each of those classes implements a corresponding interface by providing null method bodies. The programmer who frequently uses the listener interfaces in this package can save a little time and typing by extending adapter classes and overriding just the necessary methods. These types of adapter classes do not have much in common with the adapter Bean strategy discussed here.

Adapter classes can also be coded to handle multiple kinds of relationships between source and target Beans, where a hookup may be inefficient or impossible because the desired target does not know about the source Bean's event types. In this sense, any class that can listen to an event source and forward information to a target is called an *adapter*. If the class forwards information from one source to many targets, it is called a *multiplexing* adapter; conversely, if the class channels multiple sources to a single target, it is a *demultiplexing* adapter.

An ambitious adapter can become complex very quickly. The following example, a class called NodeMux, is intended as a very terse introduction.

NodeMux demultiplexes event updates from any number of Node instances that might be deployed. To keep things simple, NodeMux collects the information itself in a textfield. The code for this example is included on the CD-ROM in the directory \javadevhdbk\ch17\NodeMux.java.

LIST 17.5   *NodeMux.java*

```java
import java.awt.*;

public class NodeMux
extends Panel
implements NodeListener, Serializable
{
  private String nodeMessage;
  private String nodeName;
  private TextArea reports = new TextArea(10,40);

  public NodeMux()
  {
    add(reports);
  }

  public void nodeAlert(NodeAlertEvent nae)
  {
    synchronized(this)
    {
      nodeName = nae.getName();
      nodeMessage = nae.getMessage();
      reports.append(nodename + " reports " + nodeMessage + "\n");
    }
  }
}
```

Introspection and the BeanInfo Interface

By default, the Introspector reads an instantiated Bean's contents by applying reflection to it. Once it has the Bean's raw data, its public methods and data members, for the most part, it can apply the naming conventions mentioned throughout this chapter to identify properties and events. The results are available through the getBeanInfo() method, which returns a reference to the BeanInfo interface. This interface supports eight methods, each of which represents a category of information the Introspector captures:

getAddtionalBeanInfo()   Returns any additional BeanInfo objects that pertain to the Bean, such as the BeanInfo of a parent class.

getBeanDescriptor()   Returns the names of the Bean class and its associated Customizer class, if any.

getDefaultEventIndex()   Declares which event in the EventDescriptor array is selected by default.

getDefaultPropertyIndex()   Declares which property in the Property-Descriptor array is selected by default.

getEventSetDescriptors()   Lists the event types that a Bean knows how to fire.

getIcon()   Allows the Bean writer to associate a 16×16 or 32×32 GIF file with a Bean for display in a builder tool.

getMethodDescriptors()   Lists the public methods of the Bean.

getPropertyDescriptors()   Lists properties associated with the Bean.

In general, Descriptor-style methods allow the programmer to elaborate on the information for each Descriptor type. The Index-style method calls permit the setting of a default value in the index.

A Bean writer may wish to reject some or all of the reflection information a Bean returns. For example, the goal may be to replace it with information about properties or events that is more concise, more descriptive, or simply more suitable to a particular user. Another possibility is that reflection may be ignored completely.

Any Bean class may optionally provide an associated class for the purpose of limiting or changing reflection data. This class must be named after the Bean class itself plus the suffix BeanInfo, and it must implement either the BeanInfo interface or a subclass such as SimpleBeanInfo. When a Bean is instantiated, the Introspector attempts to locate an associated BeanInfo class. If it finds one, the Introspector takes the information the BeanInfo file provides and accepts it in favor of applying reflection. If any of these implemented methods return null, reflection is applied as a backup.

The fastest way to ignore all reflection information is to extend SimpleBean-Info, which implements BeanInfo but returns non-null values that "deny" the existence of various reflected data. This class is more commonly used to reduce the chore of declaring every method in the BeanInfo interface just to override one or two of them.

 The example below, NodeBeanInfo, calls getBeanDescriptor only so that a customizer can be associated with the class. The code for this example is included on the CD-ROM in the directory \javadevhdbk\ch17\NodeBeanInfo.java.

LIST 17.6	*NodeBeanInfo.java*

```java
import java.beans.*;

public class NodeBeanInfo extends SimpleBeanInfo
{
  // Make sure the customizer gets noticed
  public BeanDescriptor getBeanDescriptor()
  {
    BeanDescriptor addOn = new BeanDescriptor
                        (Node.class,NodeCustomizer.class);
    return addOn;
  }
}
```

Bean Customization

In a manner roughly similar to the way that a BeanInfo class intervenes in the reflection of a Bean, customizers allow Beans to create their own GUIs for configuring the Bean or coordinating complex property changes that would otherwise be difficult to achieve in a builder tool's standard property editor facility. All customizers extend Panel and implement the Customizer interface.

There are three methods to support, two of which require the customizer to register and unregister property update listeners. Supporting these methods is a reminder to fire property changes as often as the GUI itself requires repainting. The third method, setObject(), retrieves the Object Bean to be customized. This method must be called only once, and it must be called before the customizable component is added to an AWT container, or the Object reference may enter a confused state.

The following example, NodeCustomizer, illustrates a simple GUI that could easily be enhanced as desired. The code for this example is included on the CD-ROM in the directory \javadevhdbk\ch17\NodeCustomizer.java. Once the hook is set up through a BeanDescriptor in NodeBeanInfo, implementation of the customizer is straightforward.

LIST 17.7   *NodeCustomizer.java*

```java
import java.awt.*;
import java.awt.event.*;
import java.beans.*;

public class NodeCustomizer
extends Panel
implements Customizer, KeyListener
{
  private PropertyChangeSupport pcs =
      new PropertyChangeSupport(this);
  private Node node;
  private TextField labelField;

  public NodeCustomizer()
  {
    setLayout(null);
  }

  public void setObject(Object obj)
  {
    node = (Node)obj;
    Label t1 = new Label("Node Name:", Label.CENTER);
    add(t1);
    t1.setBounds(10, 5, 60, 30);
```

```
            labelField = new TextField(node.getLabel(), 20);
            add(labelField);
            labelField.setBounds(80, 5, 100, 30);
            labelField.addKeyListener(this);
        }

        public void keyReleased(KeyEvent e)
        {
            String txt = labelField.getText();
            target.setLabel(txt);
            // just force a refresh
            support.firePropertyChange("", null, null);
        }

        public void keyTyped(KeyEvent e) {}
        public void keyPressed(KeyEvent e) {}

        public void addPropertyChangeListener(PropertyChangeListener
                                                pcl)
        {
            pcs.addPropertyChangeListener(pcl);
        }

        public void removePropertyChangeListener(PropertyChangeListener
                                                pcl)
        {
            pcs.removePropertyChangeListener(pcl);
        }
    }
```

Bean Persistence

In order for a Bean to conform to the goals of a generic component model, we must be able to save any Bean's state data to a stream. Implementing java.io .Serializable expedites the lion's share of work. The Serializable interface tags the implementing class, enabling the JVM's internal algorithm for rolling out any object of that type. (See Chapter 12 for a detailed discussion of the `Serializable` interface.)

Certain classes, like `java.awt.Image`, are not supported by `Serializable`; others, like `java.lang.Thread`, have no meaningful persistent state. The programmer maintains the burden of finding an alternate means of achieving persistence if it cannot be ignored. In the case of an `Image`, including the graphic separately in a JAR file may be the simplest solution. Other data, like threads, should be marked `transient`.

NOTE   If otherwise `Serializable` data cannot be saved in its current state, such as an account number in clear text, use the `Externalizable` interface. This interface's `readExternal()` and `writeExternal()` methods require the programmer to hand-serialize data, so the code can be bulky and tedious for complex objects. The source code for `ExternalizableButton`, which comes with the BDK, illustrates the work required.

Builder tools are expected to provide a menu-based choice for saving a new Bean to serialized form as a .ser file. They should also automate the creation of a JAR file for any new Bean. A JAR file is the required storage model for Beans that load into a builder tool such as the BeanBox.

Building a Bean JAR file from scratch is simple. Using the `jar` utility provided with the JDK, you simply archive into a single file all classes associated with a Bean, along with a manifest that lists the included classes and whether or not they are actual Beans. The BeanBox attempts to load into the toolbox palette any class that is declared as a Bean in the JAR manifest. Here is the manifest, called `manifest.tmp`, for the `Node` Bean, along with all the supplementary classes that have been included throughout this chapter.

```
Manifest-Version: 1.0

Name: Node.class
Java-Bean: True

Name: NodeBeanInfo.class
Java-Bean: False

Name: NodeCustomizer.class
Java-Bean: False
```

```
Name: NodeMux.class
Java-Bean: True

Name: NodeAlertEvent.class
Java-Bean: False

Name: NodeListener.class
Java-Bean: False
```

The jar utility's argument switches largely conform to the Unix tar command. The following line will create node.jar. Once written, it can be transferred to the BDK's jars directory, where the BeanBox looks for all JAR files by default:

```
$ jar cfm node.jar manifest.tmp Node*.class
$ copy node.jar …\Bdk\jars\node.jar
```

The Beans Development Kit (BDK)

Builder tools that support Beans are rapidly growing more sophisticated, incorporating more and larger component libraries and introducing features that further expedite Bean development. Because the core API is so simple, commercial vendors are free to implement any visual paradigm they think will attract customers, and the differences among the available interfaces can be quite dramatic.

The BDK distributed by Java Software, the recently adopted name of the former JavaSoft, is not intended as a commercial product but rather as a reference tool. Much like the JDK, the relevant API documentation is accompanied by a variety of demo Beans, and source code is available for both the API and the demos.

The BeanBox

The core tool of the BDK is the BeanBox, a no-frills test container analogous to the Applet Viewer distributed with the JDK. The BeanBox operates in two modes: enabled design mode (the BeanBox, a toolbox palette, and a property sheet are displayed) or disabled (just the BeanBox is displayed). Functions supported include the following:

- Adding Beans to the test container
- Resizing and moving Beans

- Modifying Bean states through their property sheets
- Hooking Beans together through property changes or events
- Saving a single component in serialized form (.ser file)
- Making an applet with the current contents
- Loading a new JAR file

The BeanBox is started through a shell script (run.sh) on Solaris platforms and by a batch file (run.bat) on Windows machines. With the BeanBox running and design mode enabled, you can click a Bean listing in the toolbox, move the cursor to a point within the BeanBox, and click again to create an instance of the Bean. Figure 17.2 shows the BeanBox up and running, with an instance of the Juggler and Molecule Beans already deployed. The Juggler Bean is currently selected, which prompts the property sheet to display its modifiable values.

FIGURE 17.2:

The BeanBox with Juggler and Molecule Beans displayed

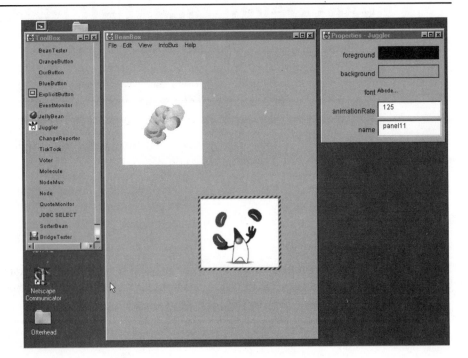

Figure 17.3 shows the BDK property editor window displaying the property list for the OurButton demo Bean. There are seven properties displayed in four different editor interfaces: Textfields are used for label and font size; choice boxes are deployed for large font and debug; and a Canvas subclass represents the Color values foreground and background. Each subeditor is a type of PropertyEditor that is selected according to the data type used by the method pair the Introspector finds. The font property has a special FontEditor interface that pops up when a font is selected.

FIGURE 17.3:

Property sheet for
OurButton Bean

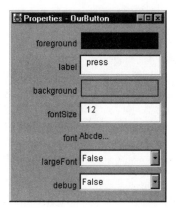

Demo Beans

The demo Beans that are shipped with the BDK and are designed to illustrate the features available through the Beans API or to highlight how a small application or applet can be easily modularized as a Bean. Each of these demo Beans is described here.

NOTE   The source code for each demo Bean is shipped with the BDK. In the most recent revisions of the BDK, there are some organizational differences between the Beans available in the BeanBox tool palette and the names of the source files. For example, all four Button-based Beans reside in a single buttons folder. You may end up looking around a little to find the desired source. The corresponding .MK or .GMK file will have the path, or you can start browsing at BDK\demo\sunw\demo.

BeanBox   A reference tool for rudimentary Bean deployment and experimenting. Deemed a "correct" implementation of the Java Beans specification, it is available for certifying a new Bean's conformance to the API. BeanBox is a subclass of Panel, so multiple instances can be recursively embedded.

OurButton   Described in the source code as a "lightweight AWT component." OurButton directly subclasses java.awt.Component. It has no way of constructing and binding to a ButtonPeer on the local platform (which is why it's called *lightweight*). It doesn't inherit java.awt.Button, so it must supply its own event-handling code and bind properties from scratch. It is a useful model for creating any new Component subclass as a Bean.

ExplicitButton   Subclasses OurButton, but adds no members, methods, or interfaces, so their visual appearance is identical. The difference is in ExplicitButton's BeanInfo and Customizer classes. ExplicitButtonBeanInfo allows only four properties to be available for modification: foreground, background, label, and font. The fontSize, largeFont, and debug properties are omitted. ExplicitButtonCustomizer offers a lean, "proof-of-concept" GUI as a basis for comparison to the BeanBox standard property editor.

OrangeButton   A hand-coded variation of ExplicitButton that has its background set to Color.orange. The change is saved to a file through object serialization and is made into a JAR file for builder tool loading. OrangeButtonWriter.java, located in BDK\demo\sunw\demo\buttons, handles the property in about 17 lines of code; archiving is done through the make file, as with the other demo Beans.

BlueButton   Similar to OrangeButton in function, BlueButton uses an instance of ExternalizableButton, a subclass of ExplicitButton. ExternalizableButton itself is not presented as a stand-alone demo Bean. It is a support class that implements the java.io.Externalizable interface. All details of saving an externalized instance to and restoring from a file must be handled atomically by the local class, using writeExternal() and readExternal() method calls.

EventMonitor   Provides a TextArea to capture the full details of the events it receives. Several properties are available to tailor the event output and change EventMonitor's display size. The event detail is verbose, so you should use a lot of window space to cut down on scrolling.

JellyBean   A visually plain component that draws a jellybean, but also supports a bound property, color, and a constrained one, priceInCents. When the JellyBean Bean binds its color to another Bean, the update is automatic. However, priceInCents may be rejected by the target Bean.

Juggler   A threaded animation applet Bean. It provides two methods, startJuggling() and stopJuggling(), which take ActionEvent objects as arguments. The Bean's juggling behavior can be tied to any subclass of java.awt.Button component. The source code is a useful reference for writing a threadsafe applet that permits event-driven user control.

ChangeReporter   One of a few simple testing Beans included in the demos. It accepts PropertyChangeEvent objects of any type and writes the stored property name with its new value. This Bean subclasses java.awt.TextField and supports several editable properties, including number of columns displayed and caret position.

TickTock   Fires a PropertyChangeEvent every five seconds by default. Because it does not extend an AWT component, it has no runtime appearance, and it can be rendered invisible in design mode as well. Both its interval and seconds properties are bound properties.

Voter   Behaves as a catchall constrained property target. It displays its current veto state as a "Yes" or "No" in its label. When its property veto-All is set to No, Voter rejects all change requests. When it is set to Yes, it accepts them.

Molecule   Displays a 3-D model for one of six available molecules. You may rotate any model using the mouse. Each molecule model is specified in a data file that lists each atom of the molecule, along with its coordinate position. (You might notice that the data for the water molecule is very rough.) A MoleculeEditor class lists the available molecules through a Choice component. Controlling rotation is also possible by connecting a button to Molecule's rotateX() and rotateY() methods.

QuoteMonitor   An example of RMI (Remote Method Invocation) applied to a Bean. QuoteMonitor will contact an RMI server to retrieve a stock quote. The easiest way to see this Bean at work is by starting the Quote-ServerApp through the make file in Bdk\demo.

TIP

Windows 95/98 or NT users can relocate to the Bdk\demo directory, bring up a DOS prompt, and type **start nmake −f quote.mk run** prior to loading Quote-Monitor in the BeanBox. Solaris users can **execute gnumake −f quote.gmk run &** from the same directory. Loading the Bean with no quote server running pops up a dialog box with these same instructions.

JDBC Select   Connects to a database and issues a SQL select statement. For a complete look at how a customizer file can simplify handling of multiple properties, load JDBC Select in the BeanBox and select Customize from the Edit menu. The source code file, SelectCustomizer.java, is located in Bdk\demo\sunw\demo\select.

SorterBean   A variation of the demo sorting applet that ships with the JDK. A single sorting graphic is displayed, but you may choose which sorting algorithm to use through the property editor. The interface provided for changing the property algorithm is text-oriented, however, so you must know the names of each available algorithm, which are BubbleSort, BidirBubbleSort, and QSort.

BridgeTester   Provides hooks for up to four different event firings and a monitor display to list values as they are passed by a PropertyChangeEvent. The display shows the current value for String and each primitive, excluding char.

Transitional   A prototype for writing Beans based on the JDK 1.02 event model. To change this Bean's color property, simply click the Bean display. A Transitional Bean has no support for callback events, so it cannot receive updates from the property editor. Attempting to do so in the BeanBox generates a warning message about Transitional Beans. The message is printed to the window from which the BeanBox was launched.

A Sample Hookup

The following sequence illustrates a typical event hookup in the BeanBox. In this example, we use the Molecule Bean and tie its x-axis and y-axis rotation behavior to an ExplicitButton instance. The screen progression begins with the two buttons in place and already labeled through the property sheet, as shown in Figure 17.4. The Molecule Bean is available but not receiving event firings from either button.

FIGURE 17.4:

BeanBox ready for event hookups

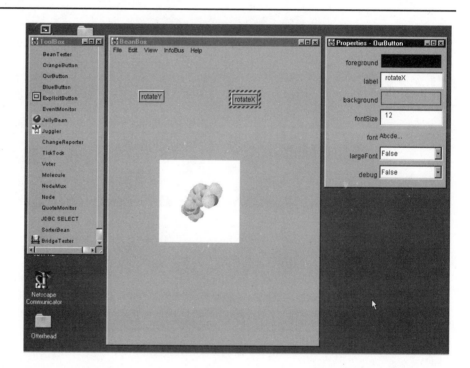

To connect an ExplicitButton to the Molecule, we first specify the event we want to use to establish a link. With the rotateX ExplicitButton selected, we follow the menu path to Edit ➤ Events ➤ button push ➤ actionPerformed, as shown in Figure 17.5. This menu choice specifies which event we want passed when we complete our connection.

FIGURE 17.5:

Selecting an actionPerformed event

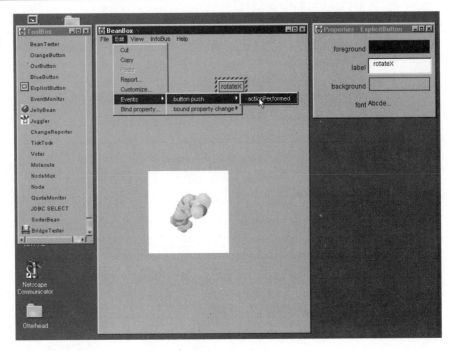

TIP

It's worth noting that the BeanBox won't tell us in advance if `Molecule` has a method that takes an `ActionEvent`. We would simply have to experiment if we didn't have the source code or other information. As a rule, it's a good idea to create Beans that accept a common event type, at least as a testing port if nothing else.

After we select the event from the menu, the BeanBox provides our `rotateX` button with a line for completing the link between the source and target Bean. There is a distinction between the display area of the component and its border area that we must take note of. We want to complete the link on the target's border area, taking care not to accidentally trigger the component's behavior with a misplaced mouse click. The event "lead" is shown in Figure 17.6.

When we click the event line at `Molecule`'s border area, an EventTargetDialog window, shown in Figure 17.7, appears with a list of methods that accept the event we are firing. Naturally, clear method naming is important to assist the designer in making meaningful choices. The third choice in this list is the method `rotateX()`, which is what we choose. BeanBox writes and compiles an adapter class to link the source event and target method together. We test the hookup by clicking our rotateX button and observing Molecule's display. The hookup source code is available for inspection at \Bdk\beanbox\tmp\sunw\beanbox\.

FIGURE 17.6:

ExplicitButton rotateX with an event line to Molecule

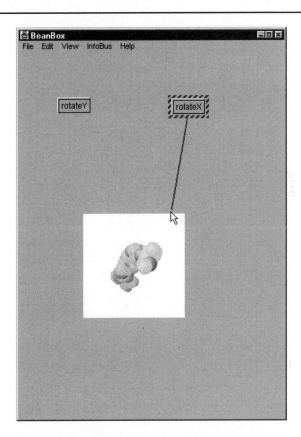

FIGURE 17.7:

The EventTargetDialog box, populated by Molecule

Summary

As you've learned in this chapter, the Java Beans component model is a compelling model for building cross-platform, lightweight subapplications in lieu of monolithic applications. The next "killer app" may not be an application at all, but a series of components that allow the designer to forge unexpected combinations into innovative products. The next big step in reusable software could well be components whose usefulness far exceeds their original design.

In the next and final chapter, we'll address a topic that is of great importance to Java application developers, security.

CHAPTER

EIGHTEEN

18

Security

- Java's security mechanisms

- Java's security configuration

- Java's authorization and permissions

- Access Control Lists

- Guidelines for creating secure programs

- Java's cryptographic APIs

Java has been designed with security in mind. From the design of the source language to the fundamental design of the bytecode language and JVM, security requirements are everywhere.

JDK 1.1 added API functionality for user security features, such as signatures and signing of JAR archives. With the advent of Java 2, security has been opened up to the control of the user or system administrator. You can change or extend security policy without making changes to program sources. You also can control the trust allocated to imported classes in a fine-grained, feature-by-feature fashion, depending on either the origin of the class file, or the signatures it carries. Most important, the fine-grained mechanisms allow you to grant a single privilege (for example, to read and write the `C:\Windows\Temp\scratch.dat` file) to imported code, without allowing that code access to any other file or other sensitive part of your system.

This chapter discusses all aspects of Java security, beginning with security concepts and terminology. We also cover the JVM security mechanisms (sometimes called the *three-pronged approach*), the new security policy mechanisms, keys and certificates, signing archives, and the APIs such as `MessageDigest` and `Signature`.

Security Concepts

The fundamental purpose of all computer security is to control access to resources. These resources being protected might be items of data, I/O devices such as modems, or access to the CPU itself. Here, we will first look at the components that make up a securable system, and then explore how a system can control access to its resources.

Components of a Securable System

If you are to keep control of the resources of a machine or network, you must first have a clear plan that tells which resources are being protected and which accesses to them are legitimate. This is called your *security policy*. The following sections describe the elements that you need to consider when developing your security policy.

Who Are You?

Any use of a computer resource is initiated by a human (or perhaps a category, or group, of humans). Therefore, the first requirement when implementing computer security is the ability to determine with confidence the identity of that human.

There are two aspects to this problem of determining identity. First, the human must have a unique identifier in the computer system and must use that identifier when gaining access to the system. This is called *identification*.

In an ideal world, no one would lie about their identity (or anything else), but in the real world, and especially a real world connected by the Internet, such deception is practiced regularly. The next aspect of any computer security system is therefore *authentication*. This is the process of attempting to prove that the human is indeed who he or she claims to be. Conventionally, authentication is achieved by means of a password, but stronger mechanisms exist. The strongest authentication mechanism you are most likely to come across is a *smart card*. As long as the card is physically protected—and ensuring that protection might not be trivial—it is much harder for an impostor to pretend to be you.

Sometimes, you need to associate your identity with a document or file (often in Java, this is a JAR file containing classes), even though you will not be physically present when the files are used. To achieve this, a mechanism called a digital signature is commonly used. A *digital signature* (or just *signature* if the context is clearly electronic) is a validation code that is associated with a file in such a way that anyone can check that the signature is correct, but only one person can generate it. In this way, it effectively proves that an individual put the signature on the file. Digital signatures are discussed in more detail later in this chapter.

In a system that provides identification, authentication, and digital signatures as means of identifying an individual, actions that are performed can be associated with that individual. This can be essential in, for example, electronic commerce, where the security system can be used to prove to the reasonable satisfaction of a legal body that the individual did indeed knowingly take part in the transaction. Such a concept of proof-of-involvement is normally called *nonrepudiation*.

What Do You Want?

Once an individual has been identified and authenticated, some degree of access will be granted to the system's facilities. Some sort of database records which rights of access each individual should be granted. The granting of certain permissions, or access to certain facilities, is known as *authorization*.

Clearly, there is little point in identifying an individual and keeping a database of the facilities that individual should have access to unless there is some mechanism built into the system that prevents access to unauthorized resources. This mechanism is commonly referred to as *resource control*. This is the foundation stone of the rest of the system. Without resource control, the data structures that are used for identification, authentication, authorization, and so forth could be modified freely, and hence the whole security system would fail.

Did Someone Touch This?

Two particular reasons for controlling the access of individuals to resources are to protect data from unauthorized tampering and to preserve the secrecy of private data. These functions are primarily the responsibility of the authorization and resource control aspects of the system, but additional mechanisms may be used to strengthen this protection.

There are ways to keep a code that is representative of the contents of a file but uses only a few bytes of storage. If the file contents are changed, the code value will no longer match. If the codes are stored separately from the files that they describe, then you will be able to tell if damage has occurred. Some of the common codes are called checksums, cyclic redundancy checks (CRCs), or message digests, depending on the mathematics they use to calculate values. In terms of sensitivity and reliability, the checksum is the weakest and the message digest is the strongest. Mechanisms of this sort can be used to detect both accidental and deliberate damage to data in any form, such as data stored in a file or data transmitted over a network. These types of checks collectively provide *data integrity*.

It's None of Your Business!

If the strongest protection of data against unauthorized knowledge is required, then some form of encryption should be used. *Encryption* involves hiding data using some sort of mathematical alteration scheme that is easy to reverse by the intended reader, but very difficult to reverse by anyone else.

NOTE　　Encryption, sometimes also referred to as *enciphering*, is different from *encoding*, which is the term usually applied to standard (and not secret) ways to represent data. For example, the ASCII and EBCDIC standards for representing characters using numbers are referred to as forms of encoding.

Encryption usually uses a publicly known algorithm for changing the plain-text (the original data) into the cipher-text (the secret form) and back again. The secrecy comes from the use of special numbers, called *keys*, which are used to modify the way that the encryption process proceeds. If secrecy is to be maintained, then some degree of secrecy must be applied to the keys.

Encryption mechanisms generally fall into two categories. In one case, a single key is used (or two keys that have a simple relationship that allows one to be derived easily from the other), so that essentially the same key is used for encryption and decryption. Therefore, anyone who is equipped to encrypt data is equally well equipped to decrypt it. Such a scheme is known as a *secret-key* or a *symmetric* cipher.

In symmetric cryptography, the hard part is that the key itself must be kept hidden from everyone except the two people who are authorized to take part in the conversation. Since one party will create the key, transmitting the key to the other party in a secure fashion is a vital and nontrivial operation.

In the other category of encryption, different keys are used to encrypt and decrypt the data. Of course, there is a mathematical relationship between the two keys, but the computation required to derive one from the other is sufficiently difficult (would take so long) that it is considered impossible to perform. One key can be made public while the other is kept secret by the originator of the pair. If anyone wants to send a message to the originator of the key pair, he or she can encipher that message using the key that was published. This well-known key is commonly called the *public key*. The resulting message can be decrypted only by using the other key, which was retained by the originator of the pair. This is known as the *private key*. Such a scheme is known as *public-key cryptography* or *asymmetric cryptography*.

If a message is enciphered using the private key, then it can be deciphered by anyone, since the corresponding public key is well known. This does not provide for secrecy of the data, but the successful deciphering effectively proves that the message was created using the corresponding private key. If you know that the private key is held *only* by a particular individual, then you know that that person created the message. This is the basis of digital signatures.

Who Did That?

Things might go wrong despite the best efforts to maintain the system security. In such circumstances, it is helpful if some log exists that describes the actions that have been performed on the system. Keeping such a log is called *auditing*. Auditing is often performed for accounting and billing purposes, but it can be of value in helping to clear up when a security breach (whether malicious or accidental) has occurred.

Auditing can take up a lot of space, so it is generally impractical to keep logs as a hard copy. Usually, a disk file is used. Even so, the disk requirements can become huge. Another problem with disk files is that it is often possible for a malicious attacker to delete or modify the files in order to hide his or her tracks. Despite these reservations, a security-sensitive site should audit carefully and should check the logs regularly.

> **NOTE**   Auditing can be well worth the extra overhead. Clifford Stoll, in his book *The Cuckoo's Egg* (Pocket Books, 1995; ISBN: 0671726889), describes, in the style of a great spy novel, the true story of an international malicious attacker who was caught because of a 15-cent discrepancy between two different auditing mechanisms.

Now that we have outlined the components that make up a securable system, we will look at how it is possible to build a system that controls access to its resources. This implements the resource-control feature described earlier. Keep in mind the fundamental role that resource control plays in the system security: If resource control fails, the databases that implement identification, authentication, and other controls can be corrupted.

Operating System Controls

In a conventional machine language, the instruction set can provide direct access to any part of memory and any part of the I/O system. Multiuser systems include special hardware that can restrict accesses to memory and I/O while the system is running. When the operating system switches between processes as part of its scheduling operations, it also reconfigures this special hardware to prevent one process from having any access to the memory of another process. This control mechanism is often referred to as the memory management unit (MMU).

The MMU itself is part of the I/O system, and the entire I/O space is normally inaccessible to ordinary user processes. Access to I/O, and hence to the MMU, is usually permitted to only a special pseudo-user that can be recognized automatically by the hardware. This pseudo-user represents the operating system itself and is often called *Kernel mode*.

Memory Management Defenses

Kernel mode is typically entered when a software interrupt is executed. Because software interrupts normally jump to code via pointers in a special area of memory, and memory can be protected against improper modification by the MMU, we have a self-consistent security mechanism. This mechanism protects the memory of one process from accidental or malicious access by another and has the potential to control all access to I/O devices such as disks, terminals, modems, and so on. Figure 18.1 illustrates how these rules for a defensive circle protect the system against attack or program error.

FIGURE 18.1:

The defensive circle of
memory management

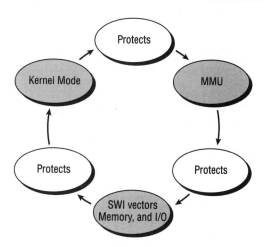

This approach has been a standard part of operating system design theory for at least 20 years, and most modern operating systems provide something along these lines. The scheme has two significant weaknesses in the context of Java programs:

- It doesn't even try to protect the memory of a process from misuse by that same process.

- The protection of both I/O devices and memory is wholly inadequate in the light of Java's ability to download executable code from untrusted, and potentially hostile, sources.

Let's take a moment to consider what these two weaknesses mean to programmers.

Holes in the Line of Defense

If a process has unrestricted access to its own memory space, then the contents of memory can be viewed in any way that suits the executing program. In many ways, this is powerful, allowing compact use of memory and all sorts of little tricks intended to enhance performance (and we all know that performance-enhancing tricks are the traditional machismo of programmers). Unfortunately, it also means that programming mistakes can often go unnoticed until they have destroyed most of the program and its data, and hidden their own tracks in the bargain. Such mistakes are often called *pointer errors* and can be very difficult to track down.

In a Java runtime system, the process's own memory is effectively inaccessible until specifically requested. When memory is requested, the process must state its purpose—for example, "I'd like space for an int" or "I'd like space for a string." After the memory has been requested and its intended use has been stated, the system is able to ensure that all subsequent accesses to that memory are appropriate—for example, access to the int space is either a read or write of an int value. This "typesafe" operation has two major benefits:

- It protects the programmer against a great many bugs (and hence, a great deal of embarrassment) that often arise in conventional systems.

- It is a fundamental part of Java's security mechanisms (as you will see in the next section).

In any system that allows downloadable code, there is the possibility that code might be badly written or malicious. Java takes steps to protect the memory and I/O of the system not just based on the identity of the user who initiated the process, but also based on the origin of the code that the process is executing. The next section describes how Java protects memory against pointer errors and the system as a whole against the actions of untrusted code. These mechanisms form the basis of all Java security.

Java's Security Foundations

So far in this chapter, we have looked at traditional memory management and considered some ways that Java's downloadable content capability requires more powerful control mechanisms if a system is to remain secure. The essential goal of Java system security is to be able to control the capabilities of individual sections of code as they execute. Commonly, a piece of code will be denied certain privileges if that code originated from an untrusted source.

Convention has it that there are three parts to Java's defense mechanisms: the bytecode verifier, class loaders, and the security manager. These three terms succinctly describe the three key elements of Java's runtime defenses, but there is one static feature upon which the bytecode verifier in particular depends: the design of the JVM instruction set itself. The following sections discuss what these four terms mean and how these components form a securable system.

The JVM Instruction Set

There is one major difference between Java as a platform and the other execution platforms upon which the whole of the Java security story rests. This is the design of the JVM instruction set. The first difference is that unlike almost any other machine language, the JVM instruction set does not address memory directly and, regardless of the underlying machine architecture, has no I/O instructions. The second difference is that every instruction is strongly typed; that is, the number of arguments and the type of each are unambiguously defined. This applies even to method calls.

If the JVM instruction set does not address memory directly, then how does it access data? The answer is that JVM instructions refer to memory in a symbolic way. For example, suppose that we have a reference to an object. That reference might or might not be an actual memory address in the conventional sense, but we do not know if that is so—and even if it is, that knowledge has no value. If we want to read an int field from an object, we execute an instruction like this:

```
getfield #4 <Field int x>
```

This reads an int value from a field of the object referred to by the top stack entry. The field is described by entry number four in the symbol table. The fourth entry of the symbol table describes an int called x. Because of the symbolic nature of this instruction, it is possible to check if the described field actually is an `int` value. If it is not, then the instruction can be rejected.

This idea of strongly typed instructions is used to allow modeling of any Java code, so that a certain degree of correctness may be proved or disproved for that code. This is the job of the bytecode verifier, which we will consider next.

The Bytecode Verifier

When a class is first loaded, it is subjected to a number of checks. The first of these validate...the format of the class file and the symbol table that is contained within the class file. Provided that these checks are successful, the bytecode verifier is invoked next.

The bytecode verifier checks the flow of each method, instruction by instruction, with a view to proving the type-correctness of the method. For each method, the verifier starts by assuming that the method is invoked with the correct arguments. It then checks that each instruction in turn starts with the correct data types at the top of the stack and ends by providing the correct stack frame for the next instruction. This check covers all instructions, including method calls. It is possible to check the method calls since the class file carries full type information for method arguments and return values. The checks must also verify that all branch instructions are executed at points where the stack is correct for the instruction at the target of the branch.

Sometimes, an instruction might refer to a field in another class that is not yet loaded. Rather than compel the loading of the other class, the verifier typically defers the checking of such instructions to the point where the instruction is first executed. In this way, if the code is never executed, the other class might never need to be loaded, but the checks are still completed before the code can run.

In addition to checking that all instructions (including method calls) are executed with the correct argument types, the verifier also checks that the accesses themselves are legal, thus enforcing the access-control mechanisms `private`, `protected`, and default access.

This bytecode verification process depends on the design of the bytecode itself. It is possible to check that every instruction is executed with the data of the correct type on the stack because every instruction is fully typed. Separate instructions are provided for each type. For example, there are instructions for reading `int`, `long`, `float`, and `double` values.

Given that the bytecode verification process, along with the design of the bytecode language, proves the type-correctness and access-correctness of each method, it is possible to enforce other, higher-level checks. These checks are conventionally enforced by the security manager. Although that single class has been replaced by a system of several classes in Java 2, the term *security manager* still adequately describes this system.

The Security Manager

The security manager system builds upon the foundation provided by bytecode verification. Given that all methods are known to be executed with the correct argument types, the security manager's role is to check that individual calls to use protected resources, such as files, are acceptable at runtime. To make these decisions, the security manager has information about the calling stack frames, the actual arguments to the call, and the security policy that the user has configured.

The most fundamental job that the security manager must perform involves the loading of native libraries. As mentioned earlier, the bytecode language cannot express direct memory or I/O operations. Such machine control is left to libraries written in the underlying machine's language—libraries containing native methods.

Before any method can execute a native method, the enclosing class must link that library. This is done using the call System.loadLibrary() or System.load(). Note that it is not sufficient for the library to be loaded into the JVM; it is also necessary for the symbol table of the calling class to be linked to the library. The load call invokes the security manager. If the security manager decides that the call is inappropriate, it throws an exception and the loading is not performed. Typically, the security manager will reject a call to load a library if the requesting class is not local to the system.

Given that direct access to native methods is protected, it is necessary to protect indirect access to those methods. This is also the responsibility of the security manager system. First, the library classes must be coded carefully to ensure that the security manager is always invoked before the native method can be called. This is done by the following approach:

- All native methods should be declared as private, so that access to them is restricted to other methods in the same class.

- A limited set of nonprivate entry points should be provided.

- The entry points should check the arguments for validity and check with the security manager for permission to execute the body of the functionality. If these checks are successful, then the native is invoked; otherwise, an exception is thrown from the security manager.

To help in deciding if a call should be permitted, the security manager has access to the stack frames of the calling thread. It can use the stack frame information to determine the class involved in each method call all the way up to the starting method of the thread. From the class, it can determine the origin of the code. Typically, local code is trusted more highly than code loaded from a remote site, and code signed by a trusted entity is trusted more highly than unsigned code.

For example, suppose a call is made to try to create a FileOutputStream. If a SecurityManager is installed in the JVM, then the constructor for FileOutput-Stream calls the checkWrite() method of the SecurityManager object. This typically checks the call stack to find out if any nonlocal code is involved in the call hierarchy; if not, it allows the FileOutputStream to be created. If, on the other hand, nonlocal code is involved, then the checkWrite() method checks with some kind of policy database to determine if the particular file that is to be created is allowed. An attempt to write to a file in the temporary directory might be permitted, even though an attempt to write to another file would have been rejected.

Class Loaders

The remaining part of Java's security foundation is the class loader. So far, we have described a system that uses the design of the bytecode language to produce a verifiably typesafe system. The fact that programs are typesafe can be used to support a runtime checking mechanism that ensures that calls to potentially sensitive resources are made by properly authorized code with acceptable arguments. These mechanisms—verification and security management—both support and are supported by the class loader system.

The only way to load a class into the JVM is via the defineClass() final protected native methods, which are declared in the abstract base class java.lang .ClassLoader. This method ensures that the verification system is called properly, and hence is part of the typesafety mechanism.

The class loader is also responsible for performing some other checks that form part of the system security. The verification mechanisms ensure that access to a protected method is restricted to members of the same package and to subclasses, so we can be confident that access to the `defineClass()` method is restricted. The security management system allows runtime control of the execution of sensitive methods. The construction of a class loader, access to certain special package hierarchies (such as `sun.*`), and the ability to define new package members in some package hierarchies (such as `java.*`) are restricted by the security manager, provided that the class loader makes the effort to check.

The following are responsibilities of the class loader that impact system security:

- Ensure that the class is properly named. Multiple or leading dots (for example: `.myutils.Bezier` or `myutils..netscape.cache.Bezier`) must be rejected since they might force local loading of a class from a location other than the proper class path.

- Ensure that local classes are loaded in preference to remote ones. This might cause a name clash, but it ensures that foreign code cannot usurp local code.

- Ensure that classes, once loaded, are cached. If a loaded class is not cached and its presence recorded, it might be loaded twice, which would result in duplication of the static variables and possibly make some instances of the class unable to access their own `private` variables.

- Maintain separate namespaces for classes loaded by different class loaders. A namespace is like a prefix to the package name and arranges that identically named classes loaded by different class loaders are treated as different classes. This behavior is especially important for applets.

In JDK 1.0 and 1.1 systems, you needed to create a class loader if you wanted special loading behavior, such as loading from a network. Furthermore, the responsibilities listed above were left to you to implement. With Java 2, the framework has been greatly improved.

First, if you do choose to implement a new class loader, you only need to subclass the `java.security.SecureClassLoader` and implement a single method `findLocalClass()`. The `findLocalClass()` method is not particularly security sensitive; it only needs to perform the actual loading of the bytecode file.

More important, it is now possible to provide virtually all the functionality you might require from a special class loader simply by implementing a special protocol handler. This protocol handler can be used by the existing `java.net.URLClassLoader`, and you no longer risk jeopardizing your system's security. Class loading is explained in Chapter 1, and creating protocol handlers is discussed in Chapter 14.

A Quick Recap

This section has covered a lot of ideas, so it's probably a good idea to collect the vital ones together for a quick recap:

- The foundation of Java's security is the design of the bytecode language. This allows the type-correctness of a program to be proven before it is run.

- The bytecode verifier implements the typesafety proofs.

- The bytecode verifier is run as part of the process of installing a new class into the JVM. The typesafety mechanisms themselves are used to control access to the crucial (ClassLoader) code that performs this installation.

- Given that executing programs are typesafe, arguments are always of the expected type and improper memory or I/O access is impossible.

- Since bytecode cannot perform direct memory or I/O accesses, native methods are the only access to system resources. Native methods are constructed to be private. (This is a general requirement if security is to be maintained; the language itself permits nonprivate native methods.)

- Based on the accessibility modifiers, the typesafety mechanisms control access to native methods. Because private native methods are the only access to system resources and can be accessed only by other methods in the same class, accessible gatekeeper methods can use the argument lists and calling stack frame of a request to decide whether or not to permit a requested access. This decision making forms the security manager feature of Java.

- The typesafety system is able to prevent any class from loading classes unless that class is a subclass of ClassLoader, and the security manager can prevent any untrusted code from creating any instance of a subclass of ClassLoader.

- Since the class loader that loads a class forms part of the namespace of the class, the typesafety mechanism can always identify foreign code properly.

- The class loader mechanism uses the security manager system to protect particularly sensitive packages, such as sun.* and java.*, for additional safety.

- The security argument that is formed by the bytecode verifier, security manager, and class loaders is a self-consistent but circular one. If any one part of the system is breached, the whole system fails.

WARNING

The security mechanisms depend on the integrity of the files in the original JVM distribution. Adding new classes to CLASSPATH, replacing any classes in the distribution, modifying native libraries, and changing any of the executable programs (especially the JVM) involve a risk to your system's security. Java cannot protect you or itself against any of the other routes by which malicious damage can occur. These routes include malicious executables sent via FTP, floppy disks with viruses, word processor files containing macros, other forms of active content, attacks against your browser, attacks against other Internet services such as e-mail, and so forth.

We have now described the basis of Java's security mechanisms. These features provide the enhanced program robustness and reliability that comes from being able to check that method arguments are in the proper range for a call, and they also form the foundation for all the remaining security APIs. Java 2 introduces a much more flexible mechanism for controlling access to resources by remote code than was provided for earlier releases. The next section discusses this new system.

Authorization and Permissions

Java controls access to machine resources based more on the source of a class file than on the identity of individuals. Decisions about access to the machine resources are generally made from the starting premise that the human who is operating the machine is entitled to perform any action that the underlying operating system will permit, and therefore Java doesn't need to worry about limiting the operations. Instead, the access-control mechanisms are directed at limiting the capabilities of pieces of code that have come from remote sources. The fundamental issues still apply—the code must be identified, authenticated, and granted access to resources accordingly. The Access Control List API, which provides a framework for resource control, is described later in this chapter.

Here, we will first see how the Java 2 approach to security compares with earlier JDK versions, and then explore the components of the new security system.

NOTE
Java is quite capable of performing identification and authentication of users. It includes an API as a work-in-progress to provide the mechanism for controlling access to arbitrary users. However, this is not the familiar mode for Java operation. You would not expect to have to log in to your browser, although you might have to log in to a remote web site. Similarly, you would not expect to have to log in to your own Java programs.

The Java 2 Approach

In JDK releases 1.0 and 1.1, the resource-control mechanism was relatively simple. All remote code was identifiable and all requests for resource access were passed through a single object of the SecurityManager class. These calls were either permitted or denied based on the origin of the code in the calling stack frames. Local code would be trusted; remote code would generally be untrusted. Remote code could be identifed by the fact that the class loader used to load it was non-null. You could identify the class loader used to load a class by issuing a statement like this:

```
ClassLoader loader = this.getClass().getClassLoader();
```

This determines the class loader used to load the class that defines the object this.

This mechanism was simple and easy to understand, but relatively hard to modify. To implement any change to the security policy, such as to trust classes that originated from one particular server, you needed to write and install a whole new SecurityManager class. This was not particularly difficult, but since it was security-critical code, you had to pay close attention to what you were doing. Furthermore, many system features in Java make extensive use of system resources, and as such there were many calls to the SecurityManager that were not easy to understand.

Another significant difficulty with the JDK 1.0 and 1.1 SecurityManager approach was that it was difficult to extend. The SecurityManager object would be installed in the system by calling the method System.setSecurityManager(), and this could be used only once. If you tried to install two security managers, they didn't nest or act in parallel—the second attempt caused a security exception.

To understand the problem, consider this scenario: You and a colleague are creating new libraries that provide access to special resources (these might be special hardware, such as scanners or modems and the like, or might be databases that should be kept for trusted code only). To add security checks to protect your code, you both create a special subclass of SecurityManager that adds an extra check method to protect your facility. Now, if an end user wants to protect both your systems, that user cannot install both security managers. Instead, the user must take the source for these and merge them together to produce a single SecurityManager class that provides for both new facilities.

The Java 2 security system is much more flexible. It is possible to reconfigure the security policy without writing any code. Java 2 provides a configuration file that contains text, which you can edit by hand. Additionally, the Java 2 approach has the following advantages:

- All classes outside the JDK installation directory are subjected to permission checks, not just those loaded from remote sites. You can still give your local classes any capability they require, but you need to do so explicitly.

- It is possible to define the control mechanisms for new resources in a way that can be fully integrated with the system.

- Multiple independent new resources do not interfere with each other.

- You can use the text file for configuration of new resources exactly as you do for configuring the built-in ones.

In the next sections, we will look at the components of the Java 2 security system.

NOTE   The new security policy does not prevent the use of custom SecurityManager objects if you already have them. If you install such an object, it will work just as it did in the older JDK versions. This is because the new control mechanisms are implemented via a new SecurityManager object. This means that if you install your SecurityManager, you will lose most of the new functionality and some of the flexibility. In most cases, it is relatively easy to take the policy of a custom SecurityManager and reimplement it using the new mechanism.

Permissions

The fundamental unit of the new security system is a base class called java.security .Permission. Instances of specific subclasses of this class are used to represent permission to perform particular operations. For example, the java.io.File-Permission class is used to describe permission to access a file or files. Typically, a

`Permission` instance is created with two textual arguments. The first is called the *name* and the second is called the *action*. In fact, the titles of these arguments are only suggestions, but in the particular case of a `FilePermission`, they are accurate descriptions. For example, suppose that a `FilePermission` is created like this:

```
FilePermission fp = new FilePermission("/etc/passwd", "read");
```

This describes the permission to read the file /etc/passwd.

Simply creating the `Permission` object does not grant permission, however. When a privileged operation is attempted, a database of permissions is checked against the origin of the requesting code. If a matching one can be found, then the operation is permitted. We will look at this in more detail shortly.

Permissions can be created with wildcards. For example, you can create a `FilePermission` that describes all files in a particular directory or all files in a particular tree. Some permissions can have wildcards applied to their action parts. It is important to appreciate that this behavior, while conventional, is implemented by the individual `Permission` subclasses, so you must check the documentation to determine if it is available in any particular case. Similarly, if you create new `Permission` classes, you must code the wildcard behavior, if any, yourself. As an example, if you wanted to describe permission to read any file or directory under /tmp, you would create a permission like this:

```
FilePermission fp = new FilePermission("/tmp/-", "read");
```

We will look at creating `Permission` classes later in this chapter.

The Policy File

We have pointed out that the mere existence of a particular `Permission` does not grant that permission; for that to happen, the `Permission` must be in a particular database. As an application programmer, you do not normally write code to create or maintain this database of permissions, since there is code built into the runtime system that does this before any application is started. In fact, the database that contains the `Permission` objects, which is known as the *policy*, is loaded from a text file. A file called java.security, located in a subdirectory jre\lib\security under the base directory of the Java installation, contains an entry, which is normally:

```
policy.java=java.policy
```

This entry causes the security policy to be loaded from a file called java.policy in the same jre\lib\security directory. Additionally, permissions are loaded into the policy from a file called .java.policy stored in the individual user's home directory.

Clearly, this is only relevant on a multiuser system. In a Windows system, this information is taken from the user.home property.

Granting Permissions

The policy file contains a series of grant statements. Each of these contains a list of permissions that should be granted to code in a particular protection domain. The concept of a *protection domain* describes all classes loaded from the same source and signed by the same signers. A grant statement looks like this:

```
grant signedBy "myfriend",  codeBase "http://friendly.com/" {
  permission java.io.FilePermission "/tmp/*", "read";
};
```

This entry indicates that code that is signed by an entity known to me as myfriend, which was loaded from anywhere beneath the base URL http://friendly.com/, is to be granted permission to read any file in the /tmp directory. Code from other locations or code that is not signed by myfriend will not be granted this privilege unless some other grant block says so.

You can specify multiple signers by using a comma-separated list of entity names, but this requires that the code be signed by *all* the named entities, not just any one from the list. If you wish to express that the trust is to be granted if the code is signed by any one of the signers in a list, then you must use multiple grant blocks with duplicated contents.

Multiple permission lines may be included in each grant block, in which case all the listed permissions will be granted to code satisfying the requirements of signature and origin.

You can grant trust to unsigned code from a particular location, to signed code from any location, or even to unsigned code from any location, simply by leaving out either or both of the signedBy and codebase fields. For example, the default statement, which is present in the java.policy file as distributed, simply says:

```
grant {
  ...
```

The default grant statement contains entries that grant limited access to system properties, mimicking the restricted permissions of untrusted code in JDK versions 1.0 and 1.1.

It is important to realize that this default entry, and the limited permissions it grants, now applies to all code on your CLASSPATH. In Java 2, unrestricted permissions are granted by default only to classes in the core JDK distribution. You will notice that the policy file contains an entry explicitly granting `AllPermission` to classes loaded from the `lib\ext` directory under Java's installation path. It is easy enough, of course, to extend permissions to a particular path, but you do need to do so explicitly.

Using Variables

You can use properties, such as `user.home`, in the policy file if you wish. For example, there is a default entry that grants full permissions to any classes loaded from the `lib\ext` directory under the distribution directory. The `grant` entry for this is:

```
grant codeBase "file:${java.home}/lib/ext/" {
```

This capability may be disabled by modifying the `java.security` file. In that file, find the line:

```
policy.expandProperties=true
```

Set it to `false`.

Using the Policy Tool

Although it is relatively easy to edit the policy file by hand, it is perhaps a little daunting for "ordinary users" who are not familiar with system administration or programming. Because of this, Java 2 provides a GUI-based tool, called the Policy Tool, to assist in editing policy files.

Figure 18.2 shows the Policy Tool main window after a particular policy file has been opened. Notice that for each `grant` statement, there is one entry in the list.

FIGURE 18.2:

The Policy Tool main window

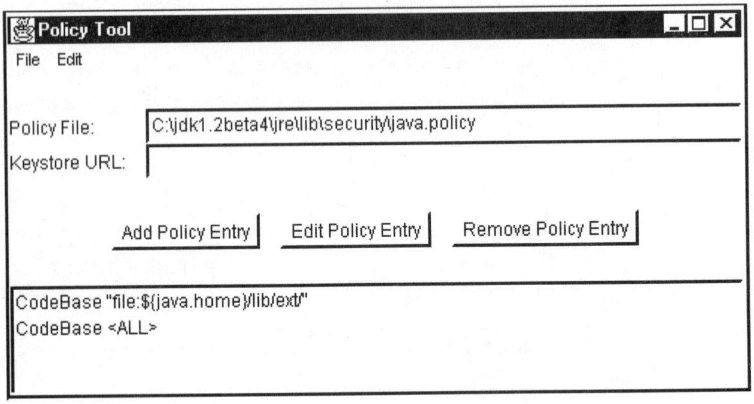

The Policy Tool works as follows:

- To add a new grant statement, click the Add Policy Entry button. This pops up a dialog box inviting you to enter the signers and codebase for the new grant statement, as shown in Figure 18.3.

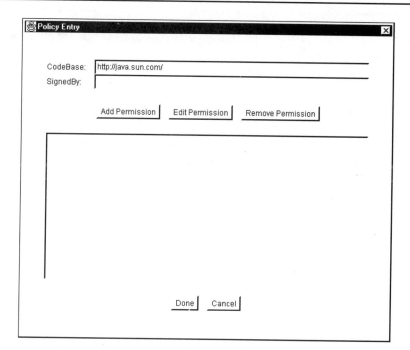

- After you select an existing grant entry in the main window, you can view the associated permissions by clicking the Edit Policy Entry button. This brings up the window shown in Figure 18.4, which is also the starting point for editing the permission list.

- To add a new permission, click the Add button. This brings up the dialog box shown in Figure 18.5. This dialog box has four fields:

  Permission   This is for the class of the permission to be granted. The choice box lists the built-in ones for ease of operation.

  Name   This is for the name of the permission. Recall that in the case of a FilePermission, this describes the file or directory node to which access is to be granted.

Actions   This describes the action associated with the permission. For files, this might be Read or Read,write.

Signed By   This refers to a part of the policy file and allows you to specify that the permission class itself (or rather the JAR it is loaded from) must be signed.

FIGURE 18.4:

The permission list for a grant statement

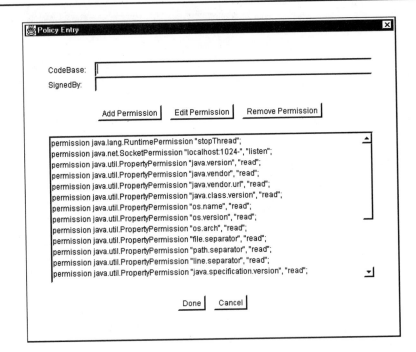

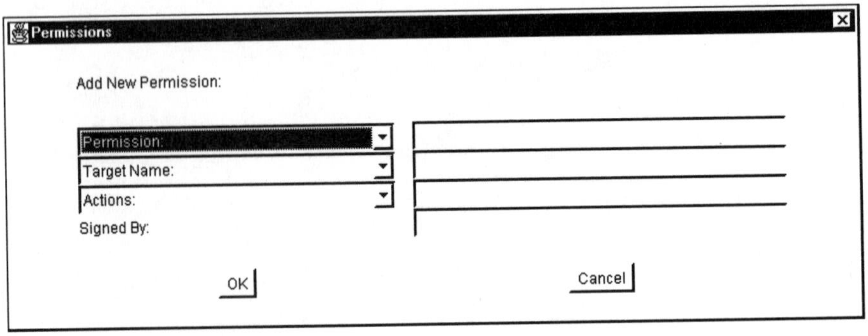

FIGURE 18.5:

Adding a permission to a grant statement

The idea of signing the Permission class warrants a little discussion. Permission classes themselves take a part in the decision to grant or deny access to the resources they describe, so a deliberately corrupted Permission class could readily breach the security system. The signedBy entry in the permission record allows you to require that the validity of the Permission class is checked too, and it is vital for any permission classes that are not loaded locally.

WARNING   It's a wise precaution to add the signedBy entry even for your local permissions. But remember that if you cannot protect your JVM distribution from hackers, then Java cannot protect you either. Do not allow signed local permissions to give you a false sense that you can ignore the routine security administration of your machine.

We have made several references to entities that have signed code. So far, we have not looked at how an identity is named. Identifying code sources is addressed next.

Code Source Identification

The new security policy mechanisms used in Java 2 revolve around the idea that code from a particular server or code that is identified by a particular digital signature may be granted additional permissions. The signing entity is identified by an alias, such as myfriend in the policy file example discussed earlier in the chapter. If you want to use a particular alias in the policy file, the alias name and associated public key must be installed in a local database. This database, like the policy database, is defined in the file lib/security/java.security. The default entry is:

```
keystore=sun.security.tools.JavaKeyStore
```

This entry describes the fully qualified class name of the implementation of key storage that is to be used by the system. The sun.security.tools.JavaKeyStore class and its supporting classes implement the permanent storage of keys in a file called .keystore, which is kept in the user's home directory.

We will look at key management (using the keytool utility and certificates) in a moment, but there are two peripheral issues to discuss first. One issue is the security of the keystore file itself. This file is used to store keys against the aliases to which they relate, and those aliases are used to grant permissions to imported code. Clearly, this file must be protected carefully; otherwise, it might be possible for someone to install a modified key against an alias to which you have allocated a great deal of trust. If this happened, your trust would be misplaced. Of course, this is the same issue that we've addressed before: You must protect your base JDK system in order for it to protect you. Because the `keystore` file must be protected, it is encrypted, and each operation upon it requires the use of a password. Additionally, separate passwords can be applied to each key in the store.

What Is a Certificate?

Public key cryptography, and with it, digital signature systems, depend on one party creating a related pair of keys and keeping one secret while the other is distributed freely to any interested recipient. From this starting point, one of two things can occur: The public key can be used to encrypt a message that can be decrypted only by the holder of the private key, or the private key can be used to encrypt a message that can be decrypted by anyone who has the public key, but could only have been created by the holder of the private key that is paired with the public one. This latter scenario is how digital signatures work.

If you receive a message that decrypts successfully using a particular public key, what do you know about the origin of the message? Well, you know that it was created by the holder of the private key that matches the public key you hold. However, that itself does not tell you who the holder of the private key is. If you are to be sure of who originated the message, you need to have confidence about who holds the private key. For this to happen, you need to receive the public key in a way that makes you confident about its origin. This requirement might be satisfied if you meet the person face to face and he or she gives you the public key in person. Similarly, perhaps with a different degree of certainty, the requirement might be satisfied if you receive notification via registered mail or courier, or perhaps if you telephone the person and ask. In many cases, however, such mechanisms are unduly cumbersome for managing hundreds of keys. You need a better way.

Now suppose that you get a single public key from someone named Trent. You take all the precautions you think reasonably necessary to ensure the key's validity. This allows you to identify with confidence messages sent to you by Trent. Now imagine that Trent sends you a message with information about the public key of someone else, named Alice. Trent assures you that he is sure that the key is valid, and he tells you what he did to ensure this validity. Now, if (and only if) you trust Trent to be honest about what he tells you, and you also feel that the actions he took to ensure that the key really belonged to Alice were good enough, then you can trust the public key that Trent sent you, because the message that contained Alice's key was signed by Trent.

Continued on next page

Messages that contain the public key of a third party and are signed by a trusted interme- diary (Trent in our example) are called *certificates*. The trusted intermediary is called a *cer- tification authority*, and the process by which the certification authority decides if a key is genuinely the property of a particular third party is described by the *certification service practices* statement. Each certification authority should issue such a statement, and you should consider if it is good enough for your purposes before you trust certificates from any particular certification authority.

Finally, the public key of a certification authority is generally distributed in the form of a certificate, signed by the certification authority itself, and is called a *root certificate*. The signature attached to a root certificate serves only to maintain the format of the certifi- cate; it does not attest to the validity of that root certificate. You must be sure that you obtain valid root certificates and take adequate steps to authenticate them. This has an important corollary: You must take care over the origin of your web browser.

It has become conventional for web browser software to come with root certificates for many authorities preinstalled. This is convenient if, and only if, you can still be sure about the authenticity of those certificates. Imagine that you obtain your browser preinstalled from a hardware vendor, from an unfamiliar FTP site, or on a floppy disk from someone at work. If you use an uncertain distribution channel, you cannot be sure that the root cer- tificates that are installed are all valid.

Using the keytool Utility

The keytool utility is a command-line tool that manages keys using certificates. keytool has two main jobs:

- Create private and public key pairs for you to use.
- Store certificates from other entities against an alias of your choosing.

Creating Keys   To create a pair of keys for your own use, use the -genkey option of keytool. You will be prompted for the keystore password and your per- sonal details. The keystore password is used to protect the keystore as a whole. However, keep in mind that you must still protect the keystore file because the encryption used is relatively weak (this is necessary for it to be exportable from the U.S.). The personal information covers your name, organization, and geo- graphical location. You can leave any or all of this as "Unknown" while you are experimenting, but you will need to provide most of the information when you create a certificate for actual use.

After you have entered the requested information and confirmed that it is correct, keytool seems to pause for a few moments. During this time, it is generating a public and private key pair for you and storing them in the form of a certificate. This certificate is signed, but it is signed by yourself. As such, the signature is not really useful; it simply indicates that the certificate has not been accidentally corrupted and maintains the normal certificate format. If you want the certificate to be of general value, you must get it signed by one or more certification authorities. For a certification authority signature, you must first create a certificate-signing request, as described next.

NOTE   By default, keytool creates key pairs for use with DSA signatures. If you want keys for other algorithms, such as DES encryption, use the -keyalg option to specify this. Be aware that key generation for encryption algorithms is not supplied with the JDK outside the U.S. because of export restrictions.

Creating a Certificate-Signing Request   For your own certificate to be generally useful, you will probably want it to be signed by one of the well-known certification authorities, such as Verisign. To achieve this, you must generate a certificate-signing request and send the request to the certification authority. You use the -csr option of keytool to generate a certificate-signing request. The resulting text output looks similar to this:

```
---BEGIN NEW CERTIFICATE REQUEST---
MIICfjCCAjsCAQAweTELMAkGA1UEBhMCROIxEjAQBgNVBAgTCUJlcmtzaGlyZTESMBAG
V29raW5naGFtMRgwFgYDVQQKEw9QdXJwbGUgQ3VwIEx0ZC4xEDAOBgNVBAsTB1Vua25v
BgNVBAMTDVNpbW9uIFJvYmVydHMwggG3MIIBLAYHKoZIzjgEATCCAR8CgYEA/X9TgR11
Luzk5/YRt1I870QAwx4/gLZRJmlFXUAiUftZPY1Y+r/F9bow9subVWzXgTuAHTRv8mZg
n5/oBHsQIsJPu6nX/rfGG/g7V+fGqKYVDwT7g/bTxR7DAjVUE1oWkTL2dfOuK2HXKu/y
AccCFQCXYFCPFSMLzLKSuYKi64QL8Fgc9QKBgQD34aCF1ps93su8q1w2uFe5eZSvu/o6
PQeCZ1FZV4661FlP5nEHEIGAtEkWcSPoTCgWE7fPCTKMyKbhPBZ6i1R8jSjgo64eK7Om
+iE1YvH7YnoBJDvMpPG+qFGQiaiD3+Fa5Z8GkotmXoB7VSVkAUw7/s9JKgOBhAACgYBY
/BpOao6FM6fVagcBaIW0fa8F5hyclfXe2TLVY2SYA8X2vsO3/CQYS/+zNbC9l3XBQbj2
v9p4/t5tz4EmLjLjDuugK8ri8UUTkOu8CdU+o5tBSENfdBVQOr1tYx5gBVb41gHk+AYI
X6WwM5opxqAAMAsGByqGSM44BAMFAAMwADAtAhQXNjE8Ryarg9iGnpwZvSCl2ze1BAIV
JzbzPy5UYRIoISIlhWHI
---END NEW CERTIFICATE REQUEST---
```

Although it looks strange, the certificate-signing request contains only 7-bit ASCII characters, so it can be sent by e-mail (or by any other convenient method) to the certification authority, who will then sign it. Well, to be more accurate, the certification authority will consider your request, take your money, go through the procedures for validating that you are who you claim to be and that the certificate-signing request is truly yours. Then it will return a signed certificate to you. Since this is all rather tedious and expensive, while experimenting, you might prefer to use a demonstration certificate (available from most certification authorities at no charge). This is the same as an ordinary certificate, but it has a shorter expiration date and is signed by a different certification-authority signature so that it will not be trusted by accident.

After you receive your signed certificate, you should import it, as explained next.

Importing a Certificate   If someone sends you a certificate, you will need to install it into your keystore so that you can use it later. This is done using the -import option. Each certificate is stored with an alias, which is the shorthand name by which you refer to the certificate, for example, in a policy file. If you do not specify an alias, then the keytool utility assumes that you are referring to the default alias, which is mykey. To import a new certificate, you must provide an alias that is different from the default alias.

The first certificate you should import is a certification authority certificate that will be referred to by other certificates. When you receive a signed certificate back from the certification authority, you should install it over your original one. This is done by using the -import option, and you must have installed the certification authority's own certificate first. Save your new certificate in a file, for example, \temp\newcert, then issue the command:

```
keytool -import -file \temp\newcert
```

After this command, your alias will refer to the certification authority-signed certificate rather than the self signed one.

WARNING   There is a difficulty with using most certification authority-signed certificates with the standard distribution of Java 2. Almost all the certification authorities use the RSA/SHA standard for signing the certificates that they issue. The JDK, as distributed, can handle only DSA signatures. Before you can install a signed certificate from any of the popular certification authorities, you must obtain a new security provider package that supports RSA signing. An example of such a provider is the Cryptix package available from http://www.systemics.com/docs/cryptix/.

Sending Your Certificate to Others   Your certificate is not directly useful to you. It is of value when other people have copies of it. To obtain the distribution format of your certificate, use the -export option of keytool. This generates more 7-bit ASCII output in a style similar to that of the certificate-signing request. You send this output to your friends, colleagues, or anyone else, perhaps publishing it on your web page. They can then install this in their own key databases and use it to validate your messages or to send you encrypted messages, depending on the key type that is embedded in the certificate.

Handling Multiple Certificates   You may want to have certificates of your own from more than one certification authority. To do this, you must have multiple copies of your own key information. keytool actually keeps an alias name associated with every key certificate it stores, and so far, that alias has been the default, which is mykey.

If you want to store more than one certificate—and you will need to do so to store other people's certificates—you must use different aliases for them. You can specify the alias to which any particular keytool operation relates by using the option -alias <alias>. All the commands we've looked at so far work as if they included the text -alias mykey on the command line.

To create a second copy of your own key information (both the public and private parts), use the -keyclone option. For this, you should specify a new alias that will be used to refer to the newly created copy of your certificate. This is done using the -dest <newalias> argument.

Signing and Verifying JAR Files

The capability to sign JAR files was introduced with JDK 1.1. This is particularly important in Java 2, since it forms one of the two bases for identifying the origin of a class and hence allocation of trust. Signing a JAR file and manually verifying the signatures on a JAR file are both performed using the tool jarsigner in Java 2 (JDK 1.1 used the tool javakey).

Signing a JAR File   Signing a JAR file is quite simple, provided that you have a private key in your keystore (achieved using the -genkey option of keytool, as described earlier). Simply issue a command of this form:

```
jarsigner <archive.jar> <alias>
```

Substitute the name of your JAR archive for <*archive.jar*> and your alias, for example mykey, in place of <*alias*>. When you issue this command, the jarsigner program will prompt you for the password that protects your keystore and, if appropriate, for the password that protects your alias entry. Be sure to specify an alias that has a private key associated with it, because you cannot sign with public keys. This means that you can only sign with your own keys.

Verifying a JAR File   Generally, the signatures on a JAR archive are read and verified by a class loader when the class is used by an application or applet. However, if you want to, you can validate signatures manually. This is also done using the jarsigner tool. Simply issue a command of this form:

```
jarsigner -verify -verbose <archive.jar>
```

The output will list the files in the archive. The left column in the file list will include an *m*, *s*, and/or *k* to indicate the status of the file, as follows:

- A letter *m* indicates whether the file is listed in the manifest. Any file, except for files in the META-INF directory itself, will be in the manifest if it was added using the jar program, but might not be if added with another program, such as a variant of ZIP.

- A letter *s* indicates that a file is signed.

- A letter *k* tells you that the signature matched a certificate in your keystore.

Note that a signature can be verified (letter *s*) without necessarily being a signature in which you have placed trust (letter *k*).

The final output of the jarsigner -verify -verbose <*archive.jar*> command is usually the message "jar verified." This message indicates that the archive is intact and has not been corrupted.

If you omit the -verbose option from the jarsigner -verify command, you will get only the "jar verified" message, which tells you that signatures were found and intact but gives no indication about trust you have placed in them. That is, the message does not indicate whether or not a matching key is found in the store; it just tells you that the JAR has not been corrupted.

Provided that you use the -verbose option, you can also add the -ids option. This causes the important details of each signature, such as the signer's name and the alias in your keystore, to be output with each file.

Sealing Packages in JAR Files

JAR files allow you to specify that a package they contain may not be added to by classes from other JARs. This is an important capability if you are delivering a potentially security-sensitive archive. In this case, you should seal the packages as well as sign the JAR file for the greatest protection. Note that, by default, an archive is not sealed.

The manifest file (`META-INF/MANIFEST.MF`) specifies sealing in one of two ways. You can indicate that all the packages in the JAR file are sealed with this entry:

```
Archive-Sealed: true
```

Alternatively, you can indicate that a seal applies to a specific package like this:

```
Name: mywork/utils/
Package-Sealed: true
```

This tag can also be used in reverse. If an entire archive is sealed with `Archive-Sealed: true`, then you can release the seal on one particular package by using this approach, but specifying `Package-Sealed: false` instead.

To put entries into the manifest file, create a template manifest file (`manifest.tmp`) that contains the entries you wish to specify, like this:

```
Archive-Sealed: true

Name: mywork/utils/
Package-Sealed: false
```

Notice the blank line that separates entries in the file.

To use this as part of the manifest for a JAR archive you create, issue a `jar` command line of this form:

```
jar cmf manifest.tmp <outfile.jar> <files_to_archive...>
```

The `m` and `f` options indicate the use of an overriding manifest file and the explicit output filename. The order of these options needs to match the order in which you provide the actual names of these files in the argument list.

Security System Extensions

We've talked about how the new Java 2 security model allows you a great deal of flexibility over the security that applies to your own system. One of the most important features of this new security model, however, is its extensibility.

In the JDK 1.1 security model, the security policy was represented by a `Security-Manager` object, and the system prevented the installation of more than one of these objects. This was intended to ensure that security policy could not be inadvertently modified after it had been installed. However, the inability to create multiple `SecurityManager` objects also presented a potentially serious obstacle.

Imagine that you have created a new native library that brings a particular facility, such as a serial port or a smart card reader, into a Java system. If you created such a library, you also would want to provide the means to control its security. To do this, you would need to create a new `SecurityManager` with an additional check method. Unfortunately, of course, most browsers have their own `SecurityManager`, and you can't install both of them.

In the Java 2 security model, if you have a new library that needs to check for a particular permission, you can do this easily. First, you create a new `Permission` class and document it. The end users of your library can now refer to this new permission in their policy files without needing to alter the rest of the system. Second, when you write your library code, you make inquiries of the `AccessController` to determine if permission is granted for any particular operation.

When you implement a new `Permission` class, the bulk of the work goes into the `implies()` method. This is the method that the access-control system queries when a decision must be made. The system works like this:

- The access-control system maintains a database that is effectively an in-memory copy of the policy file. This database is a collection of `Permission` objects that represent what is allowed.

- When a library method is about to perform a sensitive operation, it creates a new instance of a `Permission` that represents what it wishes to do—we'll call this a *request*.

- This request is passed into the access controller, which then calls the `implies()` method of the `Permission` to see if the request should be granted.

The idea is simple enough. If, for example, you have a `FilePermission` in your policy that indicates that read/write access is granted for files in the directory \temp, and a request is issued to read the file \temp\banana, the request should be granted. However, the `Permission` that describes the request ("\temp\banana", "read") does not exactly match the `Permission` that is in the policy ("\temp*", "read,write"); it is the responsibility of the `implies()` method to ensure that this is handled correctly.

In fact, you usually do not need to do any significant work when you create a new `Permission` class, since the supplied ones are often good enough. The `BasicPermission` class implements an `implies()` method that checks for wildcards in the name of the `Permission`, although it ignores the action. The fact that `BasicPermission` ignores its action argument need not be a problem, since you can embed an equivalent to the action part in the `Permission` name and use wildcards to resolve the situation. Hence, instead of having the permission `"banana"`, `"peel"`, you would grant the permission `"banana.peel"` with no action. You simply need to create a new `final` subclass and provide the appropriate constructors, since these are not inherited. You'll see an example of creating a `Permission` class in the next section.

You might think there isn't even any need to create a subclass—couldn't you just use the `BasicPermission` class directly? Well, yes, you probably could, but by subclassing it, you reduce the chance of a naming conflict messing up your protection. Suppose that you have two systems that both want security from the `BasicPermission` class, but the names or action lists have similar contents. You could end up with `Permission` objects in the database that grant permission to both facilities by mistake. Furthermore, you should ensure that individual `Permission` classes that are actually used are marked as `final`. This is important to ensure that the behavior of the `implies()` method cannot be usurped.

An Example Using Permissions

Let's look at a simple example of using the `Permission` classes to extend the security system. We will pretend that we have a smart card that provides management of keys, certificates, and medical records. The example uses the following files:

- `SmartCard.java` is the library class that represents our smart card's API.

- `SmartCardPermission.java` contains the `Permission` subclass that is used to control access to `SmartCard`.

- `SmartUser.java` is a simple test program that attempts to use the features of a `SmartCard` object.

 The source for these three files follows. On the CD-ROM, the source files for this example are in two different directories. Two files—`SmartCard.java` and `SmartUser.java`—are located in the directory javadevhdbk\ch18. The `SmartCardPermission.java` file is located in the subdirectory smart\security, which reflects its package name.

LIST 18.1   *SmartCard.java*

```java
import java.io.*;
import java.security.*;
import java.util.*;
import smart.security.*;

public class SmartCard {
  private Hashtable keypairs = new Hashtable();
  private Hashtable certificates = new Hashtable();
  private String medicalNotes;
  private String emergencyInfo;

  public SmartCard() {
    keypairs.put("mine", "1234,5678");
    certificates.put("his", "2345");
    medicalNotes =
      "Checkup 1/1/95, all well. Shots up to date 2/2/97";
    emergencyInfo =
      "Likes Jelly Beans in a crisis";
  }

  public Object getKeypair(String keyname) {
    SmartCardPermission p =
      new SmartCardPermission("key.read");
    AccessController.checkPermission(p);
    // if checkPermission didn't throw an exception,
    // permission was granted, so if we got here,
    // we're ok to proceed
    return keypairs.get(keyname);
  }

  public void setKeypair(String keyname, Object key) {
    SmartCardPermission p =
      new SmartCardPermission("key.write");
    AccessController.checkPermission(p);
    keypairs.put(keyname, key);
  }

  public Object getCertificate(String name) {
    SmartCardPermission p =
      new SmartCardPermission("certificate.read");
```

```
      AccessController.checkPermission(p);
      return certificates.get(name);
    }

    public void setCertificate(String name,
      Object certificate) {
      SmartCardPermission p =
        new SmartCardPermission("certificate.write");
      AccessController.checkPermission(p);
      keypairs.put(name, certificate);
    }

    public String getMedicalNotes() {
      SmartCardPermission p =
        new SmartCardPermission("medical.notes.read");
      AccessController.checkPermission(p);
      return medicalNotes;
    }

    public String getEmergencyNotes() {
      SmartCardPermission p =
        new SmartCardPermission("medical.emergency.read");
      AccessController.checkPermission(p);
      return emergencyInfo;
    }
}
```

LIST 18.2   *SmartCardPermission.java*

```
package smart.security;

import java.security.*;

public final class SmartCardPermission extends BasicPermission {
  public SmartCardPermission(String name, String action) {
    super(name, action);
  }

  public SmartCardPermission(String name) {
    super(name);
  }
}
```

LIST 18.3   *SmartUser.java*

```java
import java.security.*;

public class SmartUser {
  public static void main(String args[]) {
    SmartCard s = new SmartCard();
    try {
      System.out.println("keys are: " + s.getKeypair("mine"));
    }
    catch (SecurityException ex) {
      System.out.println("Permission to read keys refused");
    }
    try {
      s.setKeypair("another", "abcd,efgh");
      System.out.println("wrote a keypair");
    }
    catch (SecurityException ex) {
      System.out.println("Permission to write a key refused");
    }
    try {
      s.setCertificate("whose", "new123");
      System.out.println("wrote a certificate");
    }
    catch (SecurityException ex) {
      System.out.println(
        "Permission to write a certificate refused");
    }
    try {
      System.out.println(
        "got certificate: " + s.getCertificate("his"));
    }
    catch (SecurityException ex) {
      System.out.println(
        "Permission to read a certificate refused");
    }
    try {
      System.out.println(
        "Medical notes are: " + s.getMedicalNotes());
    }
    catch (SecurityException ex) {
      System.out.println(
        "Permission to read medical notes refused");
```

```
      }
      try {
        System.out.println(
          "Emergency notes are: " + s.getEmergencyNotes());
      }
      catch (SecurityException ex) {
        System.out.println(
          "Permission to read emergency notes refused");
      }
    }
  }
```

Running the Program without Permissions

You will want to run the example several times, experimenting with different security policies. First run it without granting any permissions. Select the directory javadevhdbk\ch18 on the CD-ROM and issue a command of this form:

> **java SmartUser**

You will see the following output:

```
Permission to read keys refused
Permission to write a key refused
Permission to write a certificate refused
Permission to read a certificate refused
Permission to read medical notes refused
Permission to read emergency notes refused
```

This indicates that the code in the class SmartUser was indeed denied any privileges over the SmartCard software. This is because of the new rule that privileges are only granted to code in the base JDK installation by default.

Granting Permissions

Next, try granting some permissions. First, locate the file that contains your policy. On Windows or any single-user system, edit the file jre\lib\security\java .policy located under the JDK installation directory. You can use a text editor or the Policy Tool. Add a line like the one shown below to the block that starts grant { (the block that grants permissions to unsigned foreign code):

```
permission smart.security.SmartCardPermission "*";
```

Notice that this uses a wildcard for the name, but the action part of the permission is ignored. If you run the program now, you should see this output:

```
keys are: 1234,5678
wrote a keypair
wrote a certificate
got certificate: 2345
Medical notes are: Checkup 1/1/95, all well. Shots up to date 2/2/97
Emergency notes are: Likes Jelly Beans in a crisis
```

This indicates that all the permissions were indeed granted.

Although it is potentially useful to grant all permissions in this way, you'll probably want to be a little more selective in most cases. Edit the policy file again and comment out the line you just added (do this with either /* ... */ or // style comments). Now add this line:

```
permission smart.security.SmartCardPermission "certificate.read";
```

When you run the program this time, you should see that all the permissions are denied except for reading the certificate value.

You can use a wildcard in just one part of the permission arguments. Put these entries, one at a time into your policy file and run the program with each:

```
permission smart.security.SmartCardPermission "medical.*";
permission smart.security.SmartCardPermission "medical.emergency.*";
  rmission smart.security.SmartCardPermission "key.*";
```

Allocating Trust to a JAR

The next experiment for you to try is the allocation of trust to a signed JAR file. Copy the archive called Smart.jar from the CD-ROM on to your hard drive. Add the JAR, in its location on your hard drive, to your CLASSPATH. For example, if you placed the file in the directory C:\TEMP, you would issue this command on a Windows system:

```
set CLASSPATH=%CLASSPATH%;C:\TEMP\Smart.jar
```

Edit your java.policy file to remove all SmartCardPermission references and run the SmartUser program from the JAR file to satisfy yourself that permission is not granted.

Next, add an entry like this to the policy file:

```
grant codebase "file:/C:/TEMP/Smart.jar" {
  permission smart.security.SmartCardPermission "medical.*";
};
```

Satisfy yourself that you are able to run the program, and that full permissions are granted.

Now let's add a signature to the JAR file. Make sure that you have a public and private key pair. If you already have an appropriate entry in your keystore, you can skip this step. Otherwise, issue this command:

```
keytool -genkey
```

Then answer the questions that follow about your personal details. If you issue the command exactly as shown here, you will end up with a key pair associated with the alias "mykey". The rest of these instructions assume that alias. If you have a different alias in your keystore, modify the commands you issue accordingly.

Once you have a key pair in the keystore database, you can sign your copy of the JAR file. Issue the following command and provide the keystore password when prompted:

```
jarsigner c:\TEMP\Smart.jar mykey
```

Now that you have a signed archive, you can investigate allocating trust to that signature. First, bring up the policy file in an editor again. Delete any entries that refer to the smart.security.SmartCardPermission. Now add a single entry to the end of the file, like this:

```
grant signedBy "mykey" {
    permission smart.security.SmartCardPermission "*", "*";
};
```

Save the file and run the program again. This time, you should see that all permissions are granted. This is because the archive was signed, and the signature matched the public key in your keystore against the alias mykey.

Understanding the SmartCardPermission and SmartCard Classes

The most important class to understand in this example is SmartCardPermission .java. It is also the simplest class. All it does is to subclass BasicPermission, changing its name and restoring the two variations of constructor that are defined for the parent class. The idea is to demonstrate that the BasicPermission class defines a permission that is entirely usable for many circumstances, including those that need a rudimentary wildcard-handling mechanism.

So that the SmartCardPermission class can be exercised, the file SmartCard.java contains a trivial database that simulates some of the features of a real smart card. Each of the methods defined in the SmartCard class checks if it should proceed by first constructing a new instance of SmartCardPermission that describes the operation that is being requested and then calling the AccessController.checkPermission() method. If the checkPermission() method simply returns, then permission is granted and the requested operation (read keys or whatever) is completed. However, sometimes the checkPermission() method throws an exception. This behavior indicates that the permission is denied. If an exception is thrown by checkPermission(), then the requesting method in the SmartCard class simply abandons the effort by allowing the exception to propagate to its caller in turn.

Prevention of Checks on Callers

We have seen that the general rule of the security model is that the trust placed in a method call is determined by the least trusted class in the call hierarchy. Sometimes a trusted class needs to perform a restricted operation, such as reading a file containing font information, as a legitimate part of performing a nonrestricted operation, such as drawing text, on behalf of untrusted callers. In the normal course of events, such a scenario would be rejected, because the aggregate trust level of the call stack would be inadequate for reading files. However, it is reasonable that the trusted class might do this, provided that it is coded carefully so that only the proper files can be read and that the information in them cannot be leaked in any potentially dangerous way to the caller.

If you are writing a trusted class that provides an unrestricted facility but uses restricted facilities to achieve its goal, you can avoid checks on callers by using a mechanism in the AccessController class. This is AccessController.doPrivileged(). When you write code using this method, you should be careful to ensure that the privileged services you use are protected from the calling classes, and that any potentially sensitive information your class obtains in this way cannot be leaked out.

Using the method is relatively easy. You encapsulate your request for a restricted service in the public Object run() method of a class that implements the interface java.security. Because the normal security controls are effectively switched off between these calls, it is very important that you keep the number of operations in that run() method to an absolute minimum. Often, you will need to make only a single method call inside the run() method. The resulting code (using an anonymous inner class for clarity) looks like this:

```
AccessController.doPrivileged(
  new PrivilegedAction() {
    public Object run() {
      // sensitive operation
      return null;
    }
  }
);
```

Calling doPrivileged() does not entirely shut off the security checks. What it actually does is simply to stop the tests from considering the privilege of any callers above the current method in the stack. This does not grant any privilege to the class that calls the doPrivileged() method, nor does it allow the privilege of that method to be passed down into other method calls in other classes. All it does is to prevent the checks from going up the stack to the callers of this method.

Often, you will need to pass data into the PrivilegedAction.run() method. This can be done by creating a non-anonymous class to implement the Privileged-Action interface and using its constructors to pass in arguments. However, it is probably easiest to use an anonymous inner class and arrange for it to have access to the necessary data via variables in the enclosing method. This can be done by making those variables final. If a variable cannot be made final because of multiple assignments to it, then simply copy its value into another variable that is marked final, like this:

```
int value = 99; // this variable is subject to changes
  // lots of work, including use of "value"
final int valueCopy = value;
AccessController.doPrivileged(
  new PrivilegedAction() {
    public Object run() {
      // sensitive operation
      int something = valueCopy; // or other use of "valueCopy"
      return null;
    }
  }
);
```

The Object return from the run() method may be ignored, as in the examples just shown, or it can carry a returned value from inside the doPrivileged() call.

Clearly, primitive return values must be wrapped in an appropriate class type; for example, an `int` return would be carried in an `Integer` object.

User Authentication

The mechanisms provided by the `SecurityManager` system, mainly through the `AccessController`, are aimed at controlling the resource access of classes based on their origin. Of course, in many real programs, it is the identity of the user that determines if a particular operation is permitted.

In many cases, a user's access to resources can be handled by the underlying operating system. For example, on a multiuser system, Java might be willing to permit my code to create a `FileInputStream` object, but the underlying operating system might reject the request on the basis that I do not have read permission for that file. Sometimes, however, a Java program needs to make decisions of this sort. This is particularly true of servers that make a facility available over the network. In these cases, the process owner, which is the basis on which the operating system will permit or reject a resource access, does not reflect the identity of the requesting person.

To provide a solution in this scenario, we need the following elements:

- Identification of the user

- Authentication of the identity

- Resource containment

Java's APIs do not directly provide for the first two of these elements, but there is an API that provides a framework for the implementation of resource containment. This is the Access Control List API.

Access Control Lists

The Access Control List (ACL) API provides a basic framework for a system that determines if a resource access should be granted to a requester. The elements of the ACL API that are defined in the core Java packages are only interface specifications; no implementation is available. However, there is a sample implementation that is provided with Sun's JDK. Note that this implementation is implemented by classes in the sun.* package hierarchy, and therefore you cannot rely on it being present in any particular distribution. Nonetheless, the sun.* ACL implementation allows us to investigate the behavior of a typical ACL implementation in practice.

Five interfaces are defined in the java.security.acl package: Acl, AclEntry, Group, Owner, and Permission. One additional interface is used by the ACL API, which is java.security.Principal. Concrete classes implementing these interfaces are used at runtime to build a data structure that describes a security policy.

For each resource you wish to control, you need a separate Acl object. An Acl object has a list of AclEntry objects, each of which has a polarity and is associated with a Principal. The polarity indicates if this AclEntry is granting or denying permissions. The Principal describes who or what the permissions relate to—typically, either a single person or a group.

For each resource that is to be controlled, you create an Acl object. For each distinct Principal, you can add an AclEntry listing permissions to be granted and an AclEntry listing permissions to be denied. Each Permission represents an action that might be performed on the resource. This structure is shown in Figure 18.6.

FIGURE 18.6:

Access Control List structure

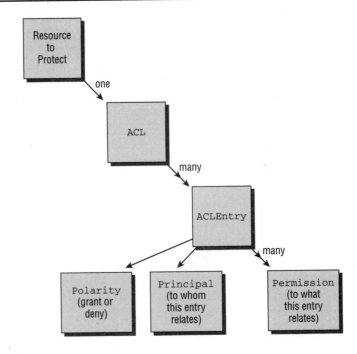

For each `Principal`, there can be zero or one negative `AclEntry` denying permissions, and zero or one positive `AclEntry` granting permissions. A permission is not granted unless there is a positive entry, so it might seem odd that the `AclEntry` can be negative. The reason is that a `Principal` might represent a group, where a group is itself a collection of `Principal` objects. It is possible for several `AclEntry` objects to relate to the same single `Principal` object if that single `Principal` is a member of several groups.

ACL Rules

Now we have the possibility of both granting and denying entries for the same permission for the same target `Principal`, so how is this conflict resolved? The rules are as follows:

- Individually specified permissions override group specified ones.
- If individual permissions both grant and deny, then they are scrapped.
- If group permissions both grant and deny, then they are scrapped.

To determine if a permission should be granted, these are the steps that are taken:

1. Find the individual `Permission` objects for this `Principal`.
2. If a positive entry exists but a negative entry does not, grant the permission.
3. Otherwise, if a negative entry exists but a positive entry does not, deny the permission.
4. Otherwise, locate all the `Permission` objects in `AclEntry` objects that relate to groups of which the `Principal` is a member.
5. If there are positive entries but not negative ones, grant the permission
6. Otherwise, deny the permission.

Notice that conflicting or absent individual entries pass the argument to the group, while group permissions can only grant a permission if only positive entries exist. If negative group entries cancel positive group entries, the fallback position is that the permission is denied.

Clearly, conflicting individual entries should be regarded as an administrative error; however, it is quite reasonable to expect such conflicts in group entries since an individual can properly belong to more than one group.

Ownership

The calls that add entries to an Acl require two parameters. The second of these is the AclEntry that is to be added, but the first is a Principal referred to as an owner. An owner is specified when the Acl is first created, and more owners can be added later if required.

The methods addOwner() and deleteOwner() take two arguments. The first is a reference to an existing owner, and the second is a reference to another owner to be added or removed. These methods are defined by an interface called Owner, which is extended by the Acl interface.

NOTE   The Owner interface is rather curiously named. The name Ownable would seem much more fitting, since it is an interface that describes the capabilities of an object that can be possessed by a Principal, rather than the Principal that possesses the object.

An Example Using Authentication

Since the java.security.acl package contains only interfaces, without any concrete classes, we must look elsewhere for implementations of this strategy. It turns out that there are implementations delivered with Sun's JDK since version 1.1. However, these implementations are in the sun.security.acl; therefore, it is not possible to use them in a program that seeks to be 100% pure Java. Despite this, these Acl implementations are very easy to use, and a short example is warranted.

Our example is called TryAcl, and its listing follows. The source and bytecode files for this example are included on the CD-ROM in the directory javadev-hdbk\ch18.

LIST 18.4   *TryAcl.java*

```java
import java.util.*;
import java.security.*;
import java.security.acl.*;
import sun.security.acl.*;

public class TryAcl {

  public static void main(String argv[]) {
    Principal principal = new PrincipalImpl("Individual");
    Principal owner = new PrincipalImpl("Owner");

    Group group = new GroupImpl("Group");
    group.addMember(principal);

    java.security.acl.Permission read =
      new PermissionImpl("Read");
    java.security.acl.Permission write =
      new PermissionImpl("Write");

    Acl acl = new AclImpl(owner, "acl");

    AclEntry principalGrantEntry =
      new AclEntryImpl(principal);
    AclEntry principalDenyEntry = new AclEntryImpl(principal);
    principalDenyEntry.setNegativePermissions();
    AclEntry groupGrantEntry = new AclEntryImpl(group);
    AclEntry groupDenyEntry = new AclEntryImpl(group);
    groupDenyEntry.setNegativePermissions();

    try {
      acl.addEntry(owner, principalGrantEntry);
      acl.addEntry(owner, principalDenyEntry);
      acl.addEntry(owner, groupGrantEntry);
      acl.addEntry(owner, groupDenyEntry);
    }
    catch (NotOwnerException ex) {
      System.out.println("owner isn't an owner of this ACL");
      System.exit(1);
    }
```

```java
      System.out.print("With empty entries: ");
      System.out.print("Read permission is ");
      if (!acl.checkPermission(principal, read)) {
        System.out.print("not ");
      }
      System.out.println("granted.");

      groupGrantEntry.addPermission(read);
      System.out.print("With group grant: ");
      System.out.print("Read permission is ");
      if (!acl.checkPermission(principal, read)) {
        System.out.print("not ");
      }
      System.out.println("granted.");

      principalDenyEntry.addPermission(read);
      System.out.print("With individual deny: ");
      System.out.print("Read permission is ");
      if (!acl.checkPermission(principal, read)) {
        System.out.print("not ");
      }
      System.out.println("granted.");

      principalGrantEntry.addPermission(read);
      System.out.print("With individual grant: ");
      System.out.print("Read permission is ");
      if (!acl.checkPermission(principal, read)) {
        System.out.print("not ");
      }
      System.out.println("granted.");

      groupDenyEntry.addPermission(read);
      System.out.print("With group deny: ");
      System.out.print("Read permission is ");
      if (!acl.checkPermission(principal, read)) {
        System.out.print("not ");
      }
      System.out.println("granted.");
    }
  }
```

Running the TryAcl Program

To run the program, simply select the directory javadevhdbk\ch18 on the CD-ROM and issue the command:

java TryAcl

This will result in the following output:

```
C:> java TryAcl
With empty entries: Read permission is not granted.
With group grant: Read permission is granted.
With individual deny: Read permission is not granted.
With individual grant: Read permission is granted.
With group deny: Read permission is not granted.
```

Notice how the permissions for group and individual entries merge, and satisfy yourself that you understand how the conflicting entries are handled.

In the first case, no permissions have been added, so the effect is that the permission is denied. When a groupGrantEntry is added, and in the absence of any overriding individual entry or conflicting group entry, permission is granted. Immediately, an individual denial is added. This overrides the group permission, and permission is revoked. After a conflicting individual grant entry is added, the individual entries are ignored and the groupGrantEntry becomes effective again, so the permission is granted. Finally, adding a groupDenyEntry after the individual entries have canceled each other out results in the group entries also being canceled, and the permission is again revoked.

The bulk of the code relates to building the data structures that the Acl object works with. The various constructors of *xxx*Impl objects actually build the Acl, AclEntry, Principal, Group, and Permission objects. As the program adds each Permission to an AclEntry, it prints a message that includes the result of the test acl.checkPermission(principal, read). The two arguments to this call are the Principal object for which the permission is being checked and the Permission object that describes what action the Principal wishes to take.

Understanding the Implementation Details

A number of significant implementation details are handled in this example. These concern duplicate names, non-Java classes, and ACL structures.

Duplicate Names   First, notice that the `Permission` objects in use here are `java.security.acl.Permission`, not `java.security.Permission`. The same name, `Permission`, occurs in both the `java.security.acl` and `java.security` packages, and we need both packages since `Principal` is defined in `java.security`. In this example, we handle this by qualifying the name `Permission` whenever it arises. Another approach would be to import the one you need explicitly, using the line:

```
import java.security.acl.Permission;
```

rather than:

```
import java.security.acl.*;
```

Which approach you choose for your own applications is a matter of stylistic preference.

Non-Java Classes   Another point to emphasize is that the objects here are being created from classes in the `sun.security.acl` package, which may not be freely distributed, so the program cannot be 100% pure Java. Since there are no implementations of the `java.security.acl` interfaces in the core packages, this is a difficult problem to resolve. Probably the best approach is to create a utility class that has static factory methods that create the various implementation objects. This way, changes in the implementation can be accommodated relatively easily.

A second enhancement would be to use properties to define the implementation classes or package that should be used by the factory. Since you will need to invoke constructors that take arguments, you will need to use the reflection facilities to construct the instances.

It is clearly inappropriate for a real program to define the permissions and principals in code. Instead, some sort of file-based mechanism should be used. Ideally, the mechanism should refer to the identity databases of the underlying machine, but that approach risks becoming platform dependent. To maintain portability, you will need to provide careful encapsulation into implementation classes.

ACL Structures   It is crucial to appreciate that the ACL structures are not able to enforce access control by themselves. Their effectiveness depends on a number of support features that you must provide in your program. Most important, you must ensure that all access to the resource to be protected is granted only after the `Acl` object has been checked. This is easiest to implement if the resource is accessed through a single method that includes the `checkPermission()` method call.

The ACL facilities relate only to the decision-making part of access control; they are not involved in identifying or authenticating the principals upon which their decisions are based. This is important—you cannot have a meaningful ACL implementation unless you first find a sensible way to identify the individuals and groups that will be controlled.

Guidelines for Safer Coding

It is worth spending some time considering how design features and style might affect the security of Java systems that incorporate your code. The following are some suggestions for writing code for secure programs, with explanations of the logic behind each suggestion. It is important that you understand the reasoning, since there will undoubtedly be occasions where other features of a particular project will make a suggestion meaningless, or at least less meaningful. It is up to you to decide which coding practices best suit your own situation.

Private Variables

It is a general principle of pure object orientation that the state of an object—that is, its member variables—are accessible only by the methods of the class itself. For reasons of efficiency, most object-oriented languages allow you to permit some level of access to those state variables from nonmember methods.

When you code Java classes, it is a sound starting point to make all of your member variables `private`. This means that you might need to provide accessor and possibly mutator methods to allow the use of those variables from outside, and hence your program will run slower. So why is this a good idea? Well, in many cases, an ill-conceived change to a member variable can damage the internal consistency of an object, and this will result in a program bug that is possibly difficult to track down. If all access is forced to go through member methods, then you are able to enforce the restrictions that need to apply. Furthermore, if there are side effects to the change, you can ensure that they are properly implemented.

To understand the side effects and how making variables `private` can help, imagine you have created a class called Box, which represents the x, y, width, and height values of a rectangle on some arbitrary coordinate space. You decide to allow `public` access to these four variables.

Later, someone else decides to use your Box class as the base class on which to construct a new class called VirtualScreen. The VirtualScreen class represents a rectangular area of a display device, like a window. When the position or size of that window is to be changed, the display must be updated, and other objects may need to be asked to redraw themselves (exposure callbacks) or a backing storage array that maintains a copy of the contents of the VirtualScreen might need to be resized. All of these are *side effects*.

Now suppose the variables are generally accessible from outside the Box class. That means that anyone can alter the value of the variables by assignment. If that happens, nothing will make the side effects happen, and VirtualScreen will eventually become corrupted. On the other hand, if the variables are private, they can be accessed only via methods like setX(), setWidth(), and so forth. A direct consequence of this is that you can ensure that the necessary side effects of modifying the size or position are applied.

Notice that by making the variables private, rather than allowing them to be protected or default access, you have maintained the tightest control over any side effects. If a subclass of VirtualScreen is to be written, it must modify the variables (as was the case for VirtualScreen itself) by calling super.setX() and so forth. This prevents the subclasses of VirtualScreen from forgetting or bypassing the side effects and perhaps equally important, it protects the code against classes not in the hierarchy.

Of course, these comments simply reiterate what object-oriented design has stressed from the start. In effect, code is only robust and reusable if it is impossible for it to be misused. The only way to check against misuse is to code those checks into methods and ensure that all access is forced to go through those methods.

You might reasonably ask, "But doesn't making all variables private make the program horribly slow?" Well it might, but there are some factors to consider:

- In many cases, because of the nature of Java bytecode and the bytecode verifier, it is quite easy to perform optimizations that translate simple accessor or mutator methods into direct variable access. This means that private variables with accessor methods can sometimes be as fast as direct variable access while still being easy to maintain.

- If you decide that indirect access to a private variable is in fact responsible for your program's poor performance, you can change a variable's access from private without even needing to recompile, let alone modify, any other code. On the other hand, changes that reduce accessibility can cause nightmares to implement.

- It is probably generally true that both you and your clients would do better having a program that works but is slow rather than having a program that doesn't run correctly because of some hard-to-find bug.

WARNING   Never assume that you know the cause of a program's slow execution unless you have proof from a profiler. Many overzealous programmer hours have been spent in the past optimizing loops so they execute 100 times faster than before, only to discover that the loop just optimized took only 100 milliseconds to execute, and that the 20 minutes that makes the program unusable is actually in some other part of the code entirely.

A final comment is that a `private` variable is, by definition a more secure variable. Although we've focused on code reliability, robustness, and reusability, keep in mind that if it is possible to misuse a variable by accident, then it is certainly possible to misuse it maliciously.

Precondition and Postcondition Tests

Preventing direct access to the state of your objects ensures that the only way that other code interacts with your objects is through methods. Often, a method will have restrictions on the conditions under which it can work properly. For example, a method that calculates the square root of a number and returns a `double` can work only if its argument is nonnegative. You might code a method that takes a string argument but requires that the length of that string must be less than a certain amount. You could have a method that cannot be used unless the object as a whole is in some particular state—for example, properly initialized.

You can, and should, add checks that test if these conditions, which are generally known as *preconditions*, are met when your methods are called. If you find that a precondition is not met, you should throw some subclass of `RuntimeException`. You will notice that many of the methods in the standard Java classes throw this type of exception.

Throwing RuntimeException

It is important to distinguish improper use of a method from a method call that fails for some other reason, such as "not found." A precondition check should fail if the program is actually incorrect. For example, calling a square root method with a negative value is a program bug. The problem might occur for several reasons: The design failed to recognize the possibility and therefore failed to provide an alternative execution path, the design failed to recognize the need to use complex numbers in this part of the program, or there is an implementation bug and the number should not have been negative in the first place. A similar argument would apply if an array index goes out of bounds (unless you are deliberately waiting for the exception because you chose not to count the loop iterations)—an attempt to access an invalid array subscript indicates a bug in the program, and a RuntimeException is the proper response.

Where a precondition fails, throwing a RuntimeException, rather than any other type of exception, is appropriate since the language does not require you to handle these with try/catch blocks nor to declare if your method throws them. When you are developing an application, you want to get program bugs out in the open as quickly as possible and as near to their point of origin as possible. It would be a mistake to provide handler code that tries to handle and recover from a design error. You also do not want to clutter up your source code with handlers that will never be executed if the program works properly. Throwing a RuntimeException at least ensures that the checks are per method rather than per method invocation. There are therefore fewer of them.

Sometimes it is possible to determine if a method has worked correctly. To be fair, this often involves performing the whole calculation over again by some other algorithm. However, if you seek the best reliability, you can add another calculation and add a check at the end of the method to ensure that both results agree. Tests of this type are called *postcondition* tests. As with a precondition, if a postcondition fails, you should throw a RuntimeException and take the opportunity to fix the bug that has been exposed as early as possible.

Creating Conditional Compilations

You may be thinking that all these extra tests at the start and end of your methods will slow your program down to a crawl. This might well be true, but again there are ways to keep the execution time under control.

Although Java does not have a preprocessor in the same way that C and C++ do, you can still create conditional compilation. If you declare an initialized static final boolean and use that in an if() condition, the compiler will remove the subordinate block entirely from the output bytecode if the value of the variable is false. Consider this class skeleton:

```
public class ConditionalCode {
  public static final boolean DO_CHECKS = true;
  ...
  /**
    * end must be larger than start
    */
  public void someMethod(int start, int end) {
    if (DO_CHECKS) {
      if (end <= start) {
        throw new InvalidArgumentException(
          "end must be larger than start");
      }
    }
    ...
  }
}
```

Note that for the conditional compilation effect to occur, you must recompile the class when you change the value of the constant. If this is inconvenient during development, instead of making the variable a compile-time constant, you can initialize it from a property, like this:

```
public static final boolean DO_CHECKS =
  Boolean.getBoolean("ConditionalCode.debug");
```

Now if you invoke the code like this:

```
java -DConditionalCode.debug=true ConditionalCode <arguments>
```

you can switch checks on and off from the command line. This is particularly useful if you have debug messages rather than condition checks. When the code nears release, you can change the declarations to compile-time constants and gain the benefit of reduced class size that results from conditional compilation as distinguished from conditional execution.

If you want to switch on or off all the checks in a group of related classes at the same time, you can declare the boolean constant in an interface, like this:

```
public interface Check {
  public static final boolean DO_CHECKS = false;
}
```

```
public class ConditionalCode implements Check {
  /**
    * end must be larger than start
    */
  public void someMethod(int start, int end) {
    if (DO_CHECKS) {
      ...
```

Such an approach gives less control over individual class behavior, but you will need to change only one source file to switch the conditional behavior on or off. Just don't forget that you *must* still recompile all the affected classes!

Final Methods and Classes

If you write a method that encapsulates security-sensitive behavior, you should consider making it final. Recall that a final method cannot be overridden in a subclass, and hence prevents the possibility of your class being subverted by a subclass that tries to bypass your code's behavior in some way.

Several of the sensitive classes in the Java distribution make use of final methods; most noticeably, in the ClassLoader class, the defineClass() method is final. This is the method that actually installs a class into the JVM, and there can be no legitimate reason for trying to modify its behavior.

Sometimes simply preventing an individual method from being overridden is not enough. You might feel that the entire class must be protected against any overriding at all. In this case, you should make the class final. This not only ensures that is it impossible to modify any individual method by overriding, but it also prevents any other kind of corruption, such as incorporating new methods or constructors. The Permission classes discussed earlier in this chapter are examples of final classes.

Gatekeeper Methods

If you are providing a security-sensitive method, particularly any native method, restrict the accessibility of the method as much as possible by making it private. Then provide a gatekeeper method through which the functionality of the sensitive method may be accessed. A gatekeeper method is an accessible method—commonly but not necessarily public—that imposes validity checks upon the arguments of the call and performs security checks on the caller before calling the security-sensitive method.

Interposing a gatekeeper method is especially important where native methods are concerned. It is a great deal easier and more reliable to perform checks on arguments in Java than in most of the languages that might be used to create a native method. In particular, Java ensures type correctness and prevents stack overflows by rogue arguments. Oversized character arrays, however, are a common way to corrupt functions written in C or C++.

Native Methods

Even with a gatekeeper method, you still need to code native methods with care. A poorly written native method might be persuaded to perform improper actions even with legitimate arguments. None of Java's checks can be imposed on the native code; Java checks can be used only on the bytecode that calls the native code.

The safest approach is to keep native methods to a minimum. Where you do need to create native methods, keep them as small and simple as possible. Use Java code to perform as much of the work as possible, either before or after the native method itself.

The single most important point here is that your native methods should be kept private. If they are not, then more often than not there will be some way to subvert their behavior that makes it possible to damage system security, even though the methods probably look safe at first sight.

Inner Classes

If you use inner classes in a security-sensitive context, you must be very careful. If an inner class makes any access to a private member of its enclosing class, then the compiler will quietly make methods to facilitate this. The methods the compiler creates are default access, and they could be picked up using either guesswork or reflection. Once located, the method can be used by any package member to access the private member.

These uninvited methods need to be created by the compiler because the JVM does not actually understand inner classes as such, so the inner and outer classes are no more related than any other pair of classes in the same package. The generated methods are the only workable way that an inner class can be granted access to private members in the enclosing scope.

Ideally, you should not allow any inner class to have any access to members of an enclosing class if those members are private for security reasons or if they might be used as leverage against your security. However, if circumstances dictate that such an approach is really the only practical choice available to you, there are some things you can do to provide protection.

One approach is to seal the package containing your class and inner class, which will effectively disallow any additional classes being added to your class, especially if combined with the signing of your classes. We'll talk more about signing and sealing packages shortly.

Another approach is to deliberately create access methods similar to those that the compiler would have constructed. Use these methods instead of directly accessing the private member. To make this approach secure, you also need to create a new Permission class and use the AccessController to protect the use of the methods. Depending on the particular nature of the private members you are protecting, you might only need to check to ensure that no imported code is permitted to call your methods, you might want to ensure that only classes from the same code source are successful, or you might even insist that only the single inner class for which access was intended succeeds. Such checks should be encoded in the implies() method of the Permission subclass you create. You also might need to create an instance of SecurityManager and call the getClassContext() method to obtain an array of the calling classes currently on the stack.

Method Restrictions

"That which is not explicitly permitted is denied" is a general mantra for all security systems, and it is definitely the correct approach. When you are coding some functionality, you should give some thought to the purpose of that functionality. Once you have decided why you are creating the method, decide who the legitimate callers are and what range of use they need to put the method to. Then aim to restrict the method's use to those callers and to argument lists that support that use.

Allowing more use of a method than you can see an immediate need for is a compelling idea that seems to offer greater possibilities for reuse, and certainly many methods do need to be `public`. However, if there is any chance that the method might be employed to subvert security, then more care is necessary. Only allow use for which you can see a clear need, and satisfy yourself that the method cannot be misused.

> **NOTE** All too often in the past, designers have left useful features or side effects in their programs, only to discover that these have been exploited as security holes later. This happened with the debug facility in early versions of `sendmail`, the traditional Unix e-mail delivery program, and appears to be a fundamental design feature with Active-X.

If you find later that you have been unduly restrictive with a method, it is a simple matter to make it more accessible or to permit a greater range of arguments. On the other hand, making a change to reduce accessibility or outlaw previously accepted argument ranges might be very difficult to implement.

Signed and Sealed Packages

If you create security-sensitive classes, you will usually need to create a `Permission` class to support them. To reduce the risk of the classes being subverted in transit, it's also a good idea to sign the JAR file that you deliver them in and to seal the package that contains them.

Signing the JAR will allow the recipients of your package to validate that they have received your code, rather than someone else's similarly named code. Sealing the package allows you to prevent other classes from being downloaded into the same package space, and hence allows you to place some confidence in the protection of package-accessibility methods (that is, methods with default accessibility).

> **NOTE** Since Java's beginnings, the packages `java.*`, `sun.*`, and `netscape.*` have been protected by the applet class loader and the security managers. However, the ability of a JAR to indicate that the package it defines is sealed is a new and valuable feature in Java 2.

Cryptographic APIs

A framework that provides an interface to cryptographic functionality was introduced with JDK 1.1. Due to U.S. export controls, this framework is split into two separate parts:

- An exportable part, which is in the core Java APIs, called the Java Cryptography Architecture (JCA). The JCA provides for digital signatures, message digests, and key pair generators.

- A restricted part, called the Java Cryptography Extension (JCE). The JCE provides encrypted streams.

The framework provided by the JCA and JCE is extensible. Like many other parts of the Java system, they use factory methods and interfaces (and abstract classes) to allow new implementations to be plugged into the system without requiring changes to client source code.

> **NOTE** There are implementations of encryption algorithms that have been either created outside the U.S. or granted export licenses from the U.S. Furthermore, it is reasonable to assume that efforts are being made to obtain an export license for at least some part of the JCE, implementing "weak" algorithms or, more precisely, using weak keys. Here, we will consider only the facilities of the JavaSoft-originated frameworks and not discuss the nonstandard facilities.

First, we will look at the use of the cryptographic APIs. Then we will explore how the framework can be extended to allow you to write new algorithm implementations and incorporate them into the Java runtime system.

The Signature System

Digital signatures use asymmetric encryption to provide a degree of confidence that someone has had sight of a message. The idea works like this:

- Alice generates a pair of keys for asymmetric encryption.

- One of these keys is passed to Bob by some means. (This means is important, and we'll come back to it later in the chapter.)

- Alice has a message she wants to send to Bob, and she wants Bob to know that she has seen this message. She encrypts the message with the private key that only she knows, and then sends it to Bob.

- Bob finds that the message was successfully decrypted using the other key that Alice gave him. This shows that the message had been encrypted by the key that is a pair with the one he got from Alice, and hence that Alice did the encryption.

Actually, what normally happens is slightly different from this, but the principle is the same. In most signature systems, Alice does not encrypt the message. Instead, she generates a message digest, which is like a checksum but cryptographically difficult to forge, and then encrypts that digest value. The resulting smaller data block is appended to the end of the message. Validation then consists of calculating the digest value of the message body to decrypt the signature block; if the two values match, the message was properly signed.

Although the mathematics of signature validation are probably sound enough, it is crucial to appreciate that all the mathematics demonstrate is that the message was encrypted with the other key of the pair. Consider the case of Bob and Alice. Bob needs to be certain that Alice did in fact originate the key pair—that he received the public key of the pair that Alice generated rather than some other public key that was substituted by a third party. He also needs to be sure that Alice has kept her private key private.

The key distribution problem is generally solved using certificates, but this does not address the possibility that Alice might have given her private key away. For example, she could have given it someone else for convenience, such as to a friend when she went on vacation, or by accident—perhaps some hacker literally stole her key from her computer files.

Calculating a Signature Value

Let's consider how you can write code that creates signatures. First, we will assume that your code has already got a private key to use for the signing operation and an array of bytes that contains the data to be signed. This code fragment considers the variable privateKey to contain the reference to the signing key and the variable data to be a reference to an array of bytes that contain the message data:

```
1. Signature s = Signature.getInstance("SHA");
2. s.initSign(privateKey);
```

```
3. s.update(data);
4. byte [] signatureValue = s.sign();
```

Simple isn't it? Line 1 uses the factory method getInstance() to obtain a Signature object that will calculate SHA signatures. Line 2 initializes that Signature object using the private key. Line 3 uses the update() method to run the data block through the signature calculations. You can call the update() method as many times as you need so that all the data to be signed is passed through the calculations.

In fact, there are three variations of update() methods: one takes a single byte, one takes a whole array of bytes, and the third takes an array of bytes along with a starting offset and length. These three update() methods are comparable with the read() methods of an InputStream.

The final operation after all the data has been processed is to calculate the signature value itself. This occurs in line 4, when the sign() method is called. The sign() method returns an array of bytes that are the signature value. This value is appended to the message so that the recipient can validate the signature. The sign() method returns an X509 coded signature block.

Validating a Signature Value

When you receive a message with a signature block, you will want to validate that signature. Consider an example where the public key is referred to via the variable publicKey, the message data is in an array referred to by the variable data, and the signature is in an array referred to by the variable signature. Validation is done like this:

```
 1. Signature s = Signature.getInstance("SHA");
 2. s.initVerify(publicKey);
 3. s.update(data);
 4. try {
 5.    if (!s.verify(signature)) {
 6.      System.out.println("Signature did not verify!");
 7.    }
 8.    else {
 9.      System.out.println("Signature verified OK");
10.    }
11. }
12. catch (SignatureException se) {
13.    System.out.println("Signature format trouble -" +
14.      " signature not verified");
15. }
```

You probably notice a correspondence with the code used to create the signature. First, we obtain a Signature object exactly as before. In line 2, we initialize it, but this time we initialize it for verification rather than for signing, which involves providing the public key rather than the private one. The update() method, with all its variations, is the same in line 3. Finally, the verification is done by the method verify(), which returns true if the verification is successful, returns false if it is unsuccessful, or throws a SignatureException in case of other troubles. For example, a SignatureException would be thrown if verify() was called on a Signature object that was initialized using initSign() instead of initVerify() or if the signature was in the wrong format.

Although the handling of signature calculations is really quite simple, the examples we've just looked at have ignored the problem of obtaining keys to use for the signing and verification operations. The next section addresses the topic of keys.

Key Storage Facilities

Java 2 includes an abstract base class called java.security.KeyStore that provides definitions for all the methods needed to access an arbitrary key storage mechanism. Actually, it represents a certificate store, and certificates are used to represent keys, but the effect is the same.

As explained earlier, the file lib/security/java.security under the Java installation directory includes the following entry:

```
keystore=sun.security.tools.JavaKeyStore
```

This defines the implementation class to be used for the key storage facilities; that is, the sun.security.tools.JavaKeyStore class is a subclass of java.security.KeyStore, which provides the default implementation of key storage. The idea should be familiar to you by now: There is a factory method in the base class that allows a program to use the keystore mechanism that is installed locally without needing to reconfigure the program code. You might want to use a different key storage mechanism if you have a means of storing keys on a smart card, for example.

Let's take a look at the code you need to load a private and public key pair for use with signing and verifying operations. In this code fragment, three string variables are assumed to be declared and initialized elsewhere: storePass is the password for the keystore, keyPass is the individual password for the private key, and me is the alias name of the key pair to be recovered.

```
1. KeyStore ks = KeyStore.getInstance();
```

```
 2. String ksfName = System.getProperty("keystore");
 3. File ksFile = null;
 4. if (ksfName == null) {
 5.    ksfName = System.getProperty("user.home");
 6.    if (ksfName == null) {
 7.       ksfName = System.getProperty("user.dir");
 8.    }
 9.    ksFile = new File(ksfName, ".keystore");
10. }
11. else {
12.    ksFile = new File(ksfName);
13. }
14. FileInputStream in = new FileInputStream(ksFile);
15. ks.load(in, storePass.toCharArray());
16. PrivateKey pk = (PrivateKey)(ks.getKey(me, keyPass));
17. PublicKey pk = ks.getCertificate(me).getPublicKey();
```

In this code, line 1 uses the KeyStore.getInstance() factory method to create an instance of the keystore implementation that is specified in the file lib/security/ java.security. Lines 2 to 13 determine what file contains the keystore itself, which normally should be a file called .keystore located in the user's home directory. This code allows the use of a property to override the location. Also, if no property is specified and the user's home directory returns null, then the code falls back to looking for the .keystore file in the current directory.

When the filename has been determined, the file is opened as an input stream in line 14, and the contents of the file are read into the keystore in line 15. Notice that the ks.load() method in line 15 takes the keystore password, in the form of a char array rather than a String, as its second argument.

Finally, the keys themselves are loaded. Line 16 loads the private key and must provide, as the second argument to the getPrivateKey() method call, the password that protects that key. If no particular password was provided when the key was generated using keytool, then by default, keytool gave it the same password that is used to protect the entire keystore. (Using keytool is discussed earlier in the chapter.)

In line 17, the public key is loaded. Notice that the public key is loaded from the certificate, while the private key was loaded directly from the keystore. Certificates exist to distribute public keys, not private ones. So, the private key is kept by the keystore and the public key is kept by the certificate, which is in turn kept by the keystore.

An Example Using Keys and a Signature

The code fragments shown so far do not form complete examples that you can run. So, let's take a moment to put this all together and create a working program that collects keys from the keystore and can sign or verify a file using those keys.

 The source of the example is shown below and is also included on the CD-ROM in the directory javadevhdbk\ch18.

LIST 18.5	*Signer.java*

```java
import java.security.*;
import java.io.*;

public class Signer {
  KeyStore ks;
  Signature sig;

  public static void main(String args[]) throws Throwable {
    if ((args.length == 0) || (args[0].startsWith("-h"))) {
      System.out.println(
        "Usage: java Signer <textfile> <sigfile>" +
        " <alias> <storepass> [<keypass>]\n" +
        "Properties signature.algorithm, signer.verifyonly" +
        " and keystore recognized");
      System.exit(0);
    }
    FileInputStream toSign = new FileInputStream(args[0]);
    File sigFile = new File(args[1]);
    String myAlias = args[2];
    String storePassword = args[3];
    String keyPassword = (args.length > 4) ?
      args[4] : storePassword;
    String algorithm =
      System.getProperty("signature.algorithm", "DSA");
    Signer that = new Signer(algorithm, storePassword);
    if (!Boolean.getBoolean("signer.verifyonly")) {
      that.sign(toSign, sigFile, keyPassword, myAlias);
    }
    else {
      toSign = new FileInputStream(args[0]);
      System.out.println("The signature does " +
```

```
        (that.verify(toSign, sigFile, myAlias) ? "" : "not ") +
        "verify correctly.");
   }
 }

 public Signer(String algorithm, String storePass)
  throws GeneralSecurityException, IOException {
   ks = KeyStore.getInstance("JKS");
   String ksfName = System.getProperty("keystore");
   File ksFile = null;
   if (ksfName == null) {
     ksfName = System.getProperty("user.home");
     if (ksfName == null) {
       ksfName = System.getProperty("user.dir");
     }
     ksFile = new File(ksfName, ".keystore");
   }
   else {
     ksFile = new File(ksfName);
   }
   FileInputStream in = new FileInputStream(ksFile);
   ks.load(in, storePass.toCharArray());
      sig = Signature.getInstance(algorithm);
 }

 public void sign(InputStream source, File sigfile,
   String keyPass, String me)
   throws GeneralSecurityException, IOException{

   Key pk = ks.getKey(me, keyPass.toCharArray());
   if (!(pk instanceof PrivateKey)) {
     System.err.println("I need a Private key for this operation");
     System.exit(1);
   }
   sig.initSign((PrivateKey)pk);

   byte [] buffer = new byte[source.available() + 100];
   int count = 0;
   while ((count = source.read(buffer)) > 0) {
     sig.update(buffer, 0, count);
   }
   source.close();
```

```
byte [] signatureBlock = sig.sign();
  FileOutputStream out = new FileOutputStream(sigfile);
  out.write(signatureBlock);
  out.close();
}

public boolean verify(InputStream signed,
  File sigfile, String me)
  throws GeneralSecurityException, IOException{
    PublicKey pk = ks.getCertificate(me).getPublicKey();
  sig.initVerify(pk);

  byte [] buffer = new byte[signed.available() + 100];
  int count = 0;
  while ((count = signed.read(buffer)) > 0) {
    sig.update(buffer, 0, count);
  }
  signed.close();

  FileInputStream sigin = new FileInputStream(sigfile);
  byte [] signatureBlock = new byte[sigin.available()];
  sigin.read(signatureBlock);
  sigin.close();

  return sig.verify(signatureBlock);
  }
}
```

Running the Signer Program

To run the program, you need to have created a private and public key pair in your system's keystore file. The keys should be of an algorithm type that supports signing. Typically, this will be DSA, which happens to be the default for the keytool program. If you need to create your keys, issue a command like this:

```
keytool -genkey -alias myself -keyalg DSA
```

This will prompt you to enter the keystore password and the personal details that identify the alias myself. A typical operation looks like this:

```
C:\work> keytool -genkey -alias myself -keyalg DSA
Enter keystore password:  obvious
```

```
What is your first and last name?
  [Unknown]:  Simon Roberts
What is the name of your organizational unit?
  [Unknown]:
What is the name of your organization?
  [Unknown]:  Purple Cup Ltd.
What is the name of your City or Locality?
  [Unknown]:  Superior
What is the name of your State or Province?
  [Unknown]:  Colorado
What is the two-letter country code for this unit?
  [Unknown]:  US
Is <CN=Simon Roberts, OU=Unknown, O=Purple Cup Ltd., L=Superior,
    S=Colorado, C=US> correct?
  [no]:  y

Enter key password for <myself>
        (RETURN if same as keystore password):
C:\work>
```

After you have a public and private key pair for the alias myself in your keystore, you can generate a signature for a file. Obtain a test file—any file will do—and issue a command of this form:

java Signer *<inputfile> <sigfile> <alias> <storepass>*

The program reads the .keystore database using the password provided as *<storepass>*, extracts the key pair for the *<alias>* given, and uses the private key to generate a signature block for the contents of *<inputfile>*. That signature is written out to the file *<sigfile>*.

If you modify the command line to look like this:

java -Dsigner.verifyonly=true Signer *<inputfile> <sigfile> <alias>*
<storepass>

and the file *<sigfile>* already exists, then the program skips the signature-generation phase and simply attempts to verify the signature that is already provided. If you modify either the input file or the signature file with an editor, or delete your key pair using the -delete option of the keytool command, you will find that the signature block no longer verifies.

Handling the Keys and the Signature

You should recognize the significant parts of the program from the earlier discussions on signing and key handling. There are three key parts: loading the keys from the keystore, calculating the signature, and verifying the signature.

The constructor for the Signer class obtains a KeyStore object and loads it from the file. The code for this is almost exactly the same as was shown in the fragment describing loading a keystore. In addition, the constructor creates a Signature object. The KeyStore and Signature objects are held in instance variables ks and sig.

The sign() method uses the provided KeyStore and Signature objects to obtain the private key, then reads and generates a signature for the specified file. There are two slight differences between this code and the sample fragments listed earlier:

- This code is organized differently. Here, we do not create a Signature object because that has already been done. Similarly, we simply extract a private key since the keystore has already been set up.

- The update() method of the Signature object is called in a loop. This ensures that the whole file is read, even if it is read if multiple chunks (this would normally happen, given the use of the available() method, only if the input file was a stream of some kind, such as the keyboard).

The verify() method is similar in organization to the sign() method. It starts by extracting the appropriate public key from the certificate for the alias requested, then reads the input file, possibly in multiple chunks. Finally, it reads the signature file and verifies that the signature is correct using the sig.verify() method.

TIP The example is fully functional as is, but its value would be greater if the signature was read and written using either hexadecimal or the Base 64 encoding format. This is because 8-bit binary is not suitable for use over e-mail links.

Message Digests

Message digests are similar to checksums or cyclic redundancy checks in that they represent the contents of a message with a relatively short number. The idea is that if two people calculate the digest value of the same message, they will get the same result. However, if the message is changed—even slightly—on its way from one to the other, then the digest values calculated on the two versions will be radically different. Another important property of a message digest is that it is impractical to deliberately arrange for the message to have a particular digest value by making changes to a particular message.

Message Digest Security Cautions

So what do message digests give us? Well, suppose that someone sends you a message along with the digest value of that message. When you receive the message, you calculate the digest and find that the value matches the one that you received with the message. This tells you to a high degree of confidence that the message is the same message for which the digest was calculated. But does this tell you that the message has not been tampered with? Well, no—it tells you that the message did not suffer any accidental damage. If the message and the digest arrive by the same route, then any malicious modification cannot be detected, since all the attacker needs to do is to calculate the digest that is appropriate to the altered message and substitute that in the same way that the message was changed.

This might make it appear that a message digest is a relatively useless concept in cryptography. That would not be true. The important point that you need to grasp is that the digest itself doesn't tell you anything unless you are confident the digest is uncorrupted. You can gain confidence about this in several ways. For example, if multiple copies of the digest are sent to you by independent means—such as by courier, telephone, fax, e-mail, or a web site—the chances of the malicious interceptor being able to change all those versions are very slight. If the digests that you receive by these means all match, and they also match the digest that you calculate for your message, then you can be confident that the message is unchanged.

Such a complex mechanism for distributing a digest is generally unacceptably impractical, and fortunately, unnecessary. The normal way that a digest is used is as part of a digital signature. Since public key cryptography is computationally intensive, and hence slow, it is usual to sign a document by encrypting the message digest rather than the document itself. Since the digest is smaller—typically, 512 to 1024 bits in length—the encryption is much faster than it would be for an entire message. However, since it is impractical to find a substitute message that generates the same digest as the original, the signature is still acceptably safe.

Calculating Message Digest Values

Let's take a look at how you can use the APIs provided in the java.security package to calculate message digest values for data. Consider the following example, called Digester.java, which is also on the CD-ROM in the directory javadevhdbk\ch18.

LIST 18.6   *Digester.java*

```java
import java.io.*;
import java.security.*;
import java.math.*;

public class Digester {
  public static void main(String args[]) throws Throwable {
    FileInputStream in = new FileInputStream(args[0]);
    String algorithm = System.getProperty(
      "digester.algorithm", "SHA");
    OutputStream os = System.out;
    if (args.length == 2) {
      os = new FileOutputStream(args[1]);
    }
    PrintWriter out = new PrintWriter(os);

    MessageDigest md = MessageDigest.getInstance(algorithm);
    byte [] buffer = new byte[in.available() + 100];
    int count = 0;
    while ((count = in.read(buffer)) > 0) {
      md.update(buffer, 0, count);
    }
    byte [] digest = md.digest();

    BigInteger bi = new BigInteger(digest);
    out.println(bi.toString(16));
    out.close();
  }
}
```

Running the Digester Program

To run the program, select that directory and issue a command of this form:

java Digester *<message>*

Substitute the path and filename of a sample message file for *<message>*. The program calculates the SHA-1 digest value of the input and prints the result as a hexadecimal number to its output. If you run the program several times, or run it on unaltered copies of the same file, you should always get the same digest value. However, if you change the file even by a single bit, you should see that the resulting digest value is radically changed.

Although the program calculates SHA-1 digest values by default, you can ask for other algorithms if they are installed in your system. JDK 1.1 and 1.2 are distributed with the MD5 algorithm installed, so you can try this if you wish. To invoke a different algorithm, set the value of the property digester.algorithm to the required text when running the program, like this:

java -Ddigester.algorithm=MD5 Digester message.txt

One important point to note is that the output value from this program is written in signed hexadecimal. Most systems that present digest values to users, such as e-mail, generally do so using the Base 64 notation. Therefore, if you calculate the digest value of an e-mail message, you will not see the same characters as the e-mail itself reports.

In the case of e-mail, there are two further complications:

- You need to be careful to select the correct boundaries for the message upon which you calculate the digest. E-mail headers are excluded from the digest calculation.

- E-mail digests are calculated on what is called the *canonical form* of the message. The canonical form refers to a particular way of representing the message that does not vary between platforms—in particular, that line endings are represented by carriage-return, line-feed pairs.

Outputting the Digest Value

The program starts by opening the input file for which a digest is to be calculated. It proceeds to choose the digest algorithm to use by checking if a system property is defined that overrides the default. Next, an output channel is selected. This channel can be the system output or a file specified on the command line. Either way, the output is encapsulated in a `PrintWriter` to allow the use of the `println()` method.

Once the channels are opened, a `MessageDigest` object of the correct algorithm is obtained using the factory method `MessageDigest.getInstance()`. Calculation of the digest is performed simply by calling the `update()` method as many times as necessary to ensure that all the data bytes have been processed. Finally, the `digest()` method is called to complete the calculation and return the result as an array of bytes. The entire calculation could have been performed using the `digest(byte[])` method if we could be sure that the data would arrive in a single block.

The digest value is output in signed hexadecimal simply by creating a `java.math.BigInteger` object from the byte array and using the `toString(int)` method to request output in hexadecimal.

> **NOTE**
>
> Because the calculation of message digests is so simple in the Java APIs, this code has little value beyond that of an example. For this reason, it has not been encapsulated into a form that would be particularly suitable for reuse beyond cut-and-paste operations.

Security Providers

We have seen that the use of the cryptographic APIs is fairly simple, and in part this is due to the architecture of the cryptographic framework. This architecture allows alternative implementations of the individual cryptographic functions to be installed easily by the user or system administrator and makes it possible for programs that use cryptographic functions to make use of these new facilities transparently.

The basis of this extensibility is encapsulated in a simple class called `java.security.Provider`. The `Provider` class is really just a lookup mechanism that provides information about the classes that provide the implementations of individual cryptographic functions. As a whole, the package has a name, version number, and description, which are also handled by the Provider object.

Let's consider the specific example of adding a new message digest algorithm. So that we don't clutter up the demonstration of creating and installing a new provider, and to avoid export control issues for this book, we'll implement a trivial algorithm: the checksum. Although a checksum is not a cryptographic algorithm in any sense, it serves to calculate a repeatable value on a block of data, and as such holds a place in the framework of code that we will produce.

Using Engine Classes

Although the Provider object is the central point of the implementation of a suite of cryptographic algorithms, none of the algorithm code is located there. Rather, each algorithm is implemented in what is called an *engine class* or *Service Provider Interface* (SPI) class. The engine classes in Java 2 are abstract superclasses of the individual cryptographic classes. So there is a MessageDigestSpi class that we need to implement to produce our new provider package.

In the case of the message digest system, these are the methods of the Message-DigestSpi class:

```
clone()
engineDigest()
engineDigest(byte[], int, int)
engineGetDigestLength()
engineReset()
engineUpdate(byte)
engineUpdate(byte[], int, int)
```

There are really five distinct functions here: update, digest, reset, get length, and clone. They are used as follows:

- The engineUpdate() methods are where the actual algorithm must be provided.

- The engineDigest() methods are called to complete the calculation and return the result.

- The engineReset() method should reset the calculation to the start, as if no input had been provided.

- The `engineGetDigestLength()` method is used to return the number of bytes in the byte array that is returned by the `engineDigest()` methods.

- Finally, you should implement the `clone()` method in an engine class if you want to be able to duplicate a particular digest part way through. If you implement the `clone()` method, you should also mark your engine class with the flag interface `implements Cloneable`.

For most engines, the method `engineGetDigestLength()` will return a constant value or a value that is determined when the individual instance is created. This would be the case if the digest algorithm allowed for variable-length results. The `engineReset()` method is usually just a case of setting the variables that hold the state of the calculation to zero or whatever their starting value should be. These methods are relatively obvious. The update and digest methods might warrant a closer look, however.

There are two `engineUpdate()` methods. One simply takes a byte and should update the current digest calculation using that value. The second takes an array of bytes along with an offset and length that indicate what part of the array should be used. It is possible to implement either of these methods in terms of the other, but a well-founded principle demands that all data-transfer operations be done in the largest block possible so that you do not pointlessly throw away efficiency. Based on this principle, you should generally implement the array handling version first, and then implement the single-byte handling version independently or as a call to the array handling version, like this:

```
// array handling method has the algorithm code in it
public void engineUpdate(byte [] buffer, int offset, int length) {
  // calculate updates for subarray
}

// byte handling method calls array handling method
public void engineUpdate(byte b) {
  // create an array with b as the only element
  byte [] buf = { b };
  engineUpdate(buf, 0, 1);
}
```

Adopting this approach ensures that large updates will be done relatively efficiently by a single call to the array handling method and without multiple calls to the byte handling method. It also avoids the duplication of code—and resulting maintenance nightmare—that would occur if the byte handling method also had all the code to implement the algorithm in question.

The MessageDigestSpi class also has two engineDigest() methods. One of these takes no arguments. The other takes an array of bytes and two int values. The primary purpose of both is to complete the digest calculation and return the result. The version that takes no arguments creates an array of bytes and returns this as the result. The other takes an array of bytes as an argument, along with an offset and byte-count limit. Provided that it fits in the byte-count limit, the result is placed in the caller-supplied array at the offset specified. Be careful to recognize that the array in this case is for output data, not input. This version of the engineDigest() method returns the number of bytes written into the array as an int. Again, it is possible to implement either of these methods in terms of each other. If you wish to implement the zero-argument version in terms of the three-argument version, you can do so like this:

```
public byte [] engineDigest() {
  byte [] rv = new byte[engineGetDigestLength()];
  engineDigest(rv, 0, rv.length);
  return rv;
}
```

Alternatively, you can implement the three-argument version in terms of the zero-argument version like this:

```
public int engineDigest(byte [] buffer, int off, int len) {
  int realLength = engineGetDigestLength();
  if (len < realLength) {
    throw new RuntimeException(
      "Insufficient space provided for digest");
  }
  System.arraycopy(
    engineDigest(), 0, buffer, off, realLength);
  return realLength;
}
```

It is up to you which way you approach this question. You can implement the three-argument version and call that from the zero-argument version or the other way around. However, there are two points to consider:

• If you implement both individually, you will have the usual maintenance nightmares when you want to fix a bug or extend the algorithm. You will also end up with twice as much code.

- Commonly, you will be working with instances of java.math.BigInteger when performing these calculations. Although that class can easily provide you with the bytes it contains, it can do so only directly by returning an array to you. This behavior is most readily compatible with implementing the zero-argument engineDigest() method directly and implementing the three-argument version by calling the zero-argument version.

Using the Provider Class

Now that we have considered the requirements of the MessageDigestSpi class, let's take a look at the use of the Provider class before we go on to fully implement the checksum algorithm in a provider of our own. As mentioned earlier, the Provider class is not involved in implementing the cryptographic algorithm but is simply concerned with making the algorithm implementation classes available.

In fact, the Provider class extends java.util.Properties, which in turn extends the java.util.Hashtable class. The Hashtable and Properties classes are used to store key-value pairs; in a sense, they are container objects that are good at doing lookup operations on one of the two fields they contain. This lookup capability is used by the Provider class to associate an algorithm name with an implementation class name.

For example, we will implement a message digest algorithm, which we will call SUM, and we will do it using an engine class purplecup.SumEngine. To make this information available to the security class management system, we create a Provider object that contains MessageDigest.SUM and purplecup.SumEngine as a key and value pair. If our provider offers other capabilities, such as algorithms for signatures or other digest algorithms, then each capability will be represented by another key-value pair.

Although the value part of the key-value pair in a provider is simply a fully qualified class name, the key part warrants an additional comment. The key is made up of two parts. First, there is the category of algorithm that is being implemented, such as MessageDigest or Signature. Immediately following the algorithm category there should be a period (.), and immediately after that there should be an algorithm name.

TIP   Algorithm names need to be standardized. In an attempt to ensure this, Java-Soft has documented the names of all common algorithms and specified a (slightly empirical) mechanism for determining names for new algorithms. These names and mechanisms are detailed in Appendix A of the document "Java Cryptography Architecture, API Specification & Reference," which is normally distributed as part of the Java 2 documentation set in a file called `docs/guide/security/CryptoSpec.html`.

The `Provider` class, in addition to documenting the association between algorithms and implementation classes, also documents the entire provider. When you define a provider, you specify the name, version number, and a description of the package as a whole.

Installing a Security Provider

Before you can use a new security provider package, you need to install it into your system. There are two ways to achieve this: a runtime way that makes the provider available to individual applications or a system configuration way that makes the provider transparently available to any application.

To install a provider for use with a particular application, you add code of this form to the startup of that program:

```
java.security.Security.addProvider(new MyProvider());
```

or

```
java.security.Security.insertProviderAt(new MyProvider(), 1);
```

Both of these methods are checked by the security management system and are denied to any untrusted code by default. The first installs the provider at the bottom of the priority table. The second form allows you to install the provider at a specified place in the priority table—in this case, the top. Note that indexes in the priority table start at one rather than at zero.

The priority table warrants some explanation: Because multiple providers can be installed simultaneously, and they might provide some of the same algorithms, there needs to be a mechanism to determine which provider to use in preference to others that can offer the requested algorithm. This is done by associating a priority order with the providers, so that requests for an algorithm are normally fulfilled using the highest priority provider possible.

> **TIP**
>
> It is possible to request a specific provider when making a `getInstance()` request by using an overloaded `getInstance()` method that takes two string objects as its arguments. The first argument represents the algorithm name, and the second represents the requested provider name. If you use this approach, you should consider making a second request that doesn't specify a provider if the first fails. This approach avoids the risk of making the program dependent upon the installation of a particular provider. Better still, try to arrange that this kind of configuration be tunable using properties so that system administrators can update the program without you needing to recompile any code.

Static installation of a provider is also quite easy. Under your Java installation directory, there is a directory called `lib`. In that directory, there is another directory called `security`, and in that directory, there is a file called `java.security`. In the Sun JDK, the `java.security` file contains a line like this:

```
security.provider.1=sun.security.provider.Sun
```

This line indicates that the highest priority (indeed only) security provider class in the normal JDK distribution is supplied in the class `sun.security.provider.Sun`.

To add another provider to your system, simply edit this file and insert a new line that indicates the class name and priority of your provider, for example:

```
security.provider.2=purplecup.SecurityProvider
```

Well, we've talked about this for long enough. Now we can examine a complete example.

A Security Provider Example

A security provider requires a minimum of two classes. You need to implement an algorithm as a subclass of one of the Service Provider Interface (Spi) classes, and a you need a `Provider` class to describe the implementation class. Our example actually uses three separate classes—`SumEngine.java`, `SecurityProvider.java`, and `TestSum.java`—since the main program we use to test the provider suite is located in a class by itself. The source listings for these classes follow, and they are also included on the CD-ROM in the directory `javadevhdbk\ch18`.

LIST 18.7   *SumEngine.java*

```java
package purplecup;

import java.security.*;
import java.math.*;

public class SumEn(***gine extends MessageDigestSpi implements Clone-
able {
  private int val;
  private static final int BYTE_COUNT = 4;

  public byte [] engineDigest() {
    BigInteger b = BigInteger.valueOf((long)val);
    return b.toByteArray();
  }

  public int engineDigest(byte [] buffer, int off, int len) {
    if (len < BYTE_COUNT) {
      throw new RuntimeException(
        "Insufficient space provided for digest");
    }
    System.arraycopy(
      engineDigest(), 0, buffer, off, BYTE_COUNT);
    return BYTE_COUNT;
  }


  public int engineGetDigestLength() {
    return BYTE_COUNT;
  }

  public void engineReset() {
    val = 0;
  }

  public void engineUpdate(byte[] data, int off, int count ) {
    int end = off + count;
    for (int i = off; i < end; i++) {
      val += data[i];
    }
  }
```

```java
    public void engineUpdate(byte b) {
      // create an array with b as the only element
      byte [] buf = { b };
      engineUpdate(buf, 0, 1);
    }
}
```

LIST 18.8   *SecurityProvider.java*

```java
package purplecup;

import java.security.*;

public class SecurityProvider extends Provider {
  public SecurityProvider() {
    super("PurpleCup", 0.9,
      "Checksum example of a provider." +
      " Not cryptographicaly useful");
    put("MessageDigest.SUM", "purplecup.SumEngine");
    // more algorithms simply need more put() calls
  }
}
```

LIST 18.9   *TestSum.java*

```java
import java.security.*;
import java.io.*;
import java.math.*;

public class TestSum {
  public static void main(String args[]) throws Throwable {
    if (Boolean.getBoolean("install")) {
      System.out.println("Installing the provider");
      Security.addProvider(new purplecup.SecurityProvider());
}
    FileInputStream in = new FileInputStream(args[0]);
    byte [] data = new byte[in.available()];
    in.read(data);
    in.close();
```

```
    MessageDigest d = MessageDigest.getInstance("SUM");
    d.update(data);
    byte [] sum = d.digest();

    BigInteger bi = new BigInteger(sum);
    System.out.println("Checksum is: " + bi.toString(16));
  }
 }
```

We will run the program in three ways: without installing the provider and then with two techniques for installing the provider.

Without the Provider   Issue a command of this form:

java TestSum *<message>*

This should fail, because SUM is not recognized. You will see a message like this:

```
java TestSum message.txt
java.security.NoSuchAlgorithmException: algorithm SUM not available.
      at java.security.Security.getEngineClassName(Security.java:286)
      at java.security.Security.getEngineClassName(Security.java:307)
      at java.security.Security.getImpl(Security.java:483)
      at java.security.MessageDigest.getInstance
  (MessageDigest.java:128)
      at TestSum.main(TestSum.java:16)
```

Temporary Provider Installation   Next, let's run the program so that it installs the provider on a temporary basis. We can do this by issuing a modified command, like this:

java -Dinstall=true TestSum *<message>*

Notice the addition of -Dinstall=true to this command. Setting the property install to true causes the program to install the provider into the current JVM instance, and hence allows the rest of the program, and the checksum calculation, to proceed. You should see two output messages like this:

```
Installing the provider
Checksum is: 13da
```

The actual checksum you get will depend upon the message file you supply.

System Installation   Finally, we will install the provider as part of your system. To do this, edit the file `lib\security\java.security` located under your main Java installation directory. Find the line:

```
security.provider.1=sun.security.provider.Sun
```

This line is about 40 to 50 lines from the top. Just below that line, add this line:

```
security.provider.2=purplecup.SecurityProvider
```

This line causes the security system to try to load a provider from the class `purplecup.SecurityProvider`. To load the class successfully, the `purplecup` subdirectory that contains the `SecurityProvider.class` file must be on the CLASSPATH. Provided that you have the current directory on your CLASSPATH and are running in the `javadevhdbk\ch18` directory of the CD-ROM, this will be the case.

Once you have made the changes to the `java.security` file, run the program again (without the `-Dinstall=true` setting), like this:

java TestSum *<message>*

The output should consist of only one line that indicates the checksum value. The first line that was output when you used the `-Dinstall=true` setting (`Installing the provider`) has not been issued. This demonstrates that the provider was picked up as part of the default system security configuration.

Now remove the provider by undoing the changes you made to your `java.security` file.

WARNING   Although this provider is harmless and doesn't even try to provide any algorithms that you might want to use in security-sensitive operations, you should remove this configuration line from your system when you have completed this investigation. As a matter of principle, you should keep all security-related files as tidy as possible.

Outputting the Checksum Value   Running the `TestSum.main()` method first checks if the property `install` is defined as `true`. If it is, then it calls the method `Security.addProvider()` to install the provider on a per-JVM basis. Note that it will not be installed over the top of a similarly named, previously installed provider. This is to ensure that it cannot subvert a previously installed provider. Next, a `FileInputStream` is opened using the first argument of the program as the filename. This entire file is read into an array in one pass. Note that the approach of using the `available()` method is not suited to reading from standard input or other streams that are not connected to files.

Once the data bytes are ready, we call the `MessageDigest.getInstance()` method to request a checksum digest, then the `update()` and `digest()` methods to obtain the checksum. If the provider is installed, this should work.

Finally, the checksum value is output in hexadecimal using a `java.math.BigInteger` to perform the conversion.

Understanding the SecurityProvider Class   The `purplecup.SecurityProvider` class has three essential features:

- It is a subclass of `java.security.Provider`. This is necessary if the security system is to recognize it as a valid provider.

- The constructor calls the superclass constructor and passes three arguments to it: the provider name, version number, and comments field. This information can be extracted by a client program and perhaps displayed to a user for acceptance before using the provider, or the version number could be checked to ensure a certain minimum revision level.

- It places into its own `hashtable` key-value pairs that describe the algorithms it implements and the classes that implement the engines for those algorithms. So, in this case the `put()` method adds the key `MessageDigest.SUM` and the value `purplecup.SumEngine`.

Understanding the Engine Class   The third part of this program's set is the engine class itself. In this example, our provider provides a single algorithm, so there is only a single engine class. In a commercial provider, you would commonly find more than one algorithm, so there would be multiple engine classes and multiple `put()` method calls in the `Provider` class itself.

Because this is an engine for a message digest algorithm, the class must subclass the `MessageDigestSpi` abstract base class. This requires it to implement the methods discussed earlier in the chapter (in the "Using Engine Classes" section):

```
engineDigest()
engineDigest(byte[], int, int)
engineGetDigestLength()
engineReset()
```

```
engineUpdate(byte)
engineUpdate(byte[], int, int)
```

These methods are quite simple because the checksum algorithm is simple. An ongoing value of checksum is maintained in the variable val, and this is updated by the engineUpdate() methods. The engineDigest() methods simply use the Big-Integer class to convert the checksum in the variable val into an array of bytes. This is neither the fastest nor most memory efficient way to achieve this conversion, but it is simple to read and hard to program incorrectly. The supporting methods engineGetDigestLength() and engineReset() simply return a constant value (4, which is the number of bytes in an int) and set the current sum value to 0, respectively.

The last observation to be made about this particular engine class is that it declares implements Cloneable. This gives permission for the object to be cloned. If the clone() method is called on a SumEngine object, the Object.clone() method will be used along with a simple bit for bit-copy results. Such a copy is entirely appropriate in this example because there is only one instance data field and that is of a primitive type. If you create more complex engine classes, you will need to give a little more thought to implementing the Cloneable interface. In particular, you will probably need to provide a clone() method of your own and call super.clone() to perform a basic bit copy before performing some additional modifications to the resulting copied object.

> **NOTE** The checksum algorithm is not a cryptographic algorithm. Therefore, you should treat this code only as a template to be used when creating your own providers.

Ciphers

As mentioned earlier in the chapter, the encryption software is supplied separately as a kit called the JCE (Java Cryptography Extensions). This separation is necessary because the U.S. export regulations (speaking rather broadly) prevent U.S. citizens and companies from supplying encryption software outside North America.

The JCE APIs are kept in the javax.* package hierarchy instead of the core java.* hierarchy. These APIs consist broadly of two parts: Cipher objects and Key*xxx* classes.

The provisions for `Cipher` objects are in a similar context to that used for `Signature` and `MessageDigest` objects. A `Cipher` can be obtained using one of the `Cipher.getInstance()` static methods. Then the object can be initialized with a key, set into either encrypt or decrypt mode, and used to encode or decode blocks of data. An alternative mode of operation is available using the `CipherInputStream` and `CipherOutputStream` classes, which encapsulate a `Cipher` object and a stream for convenient use.

To support the `Cipher` class, two classes are provided that handle keys: the `KeyGenerator` and `KeyAgreement` classes. Again, static `getInstance()` methods work with the registered providers to locate an implementation that provides for the algorithm you request. The `KeyGenerator` class is used to create keys in isolation—typically, those used for symmetric encryption. You must then find a secure way to get the resulting key to the other end of your encrypted channel. This is commonly done using an asymmetric (public key) algorithm. Keys for such algorithms often require the agreement of both parties, which the `KeyAgreement` class supports.

Socket Factories and SSL

The JCE for Java 2 not only supplies a framework for arbitrary encryption protocols but also provides an implementation of SSL (Secure Sockets Layer). As with the rest of the JCE, the packages are located in the `javax.*` hierarchy. In this case, there is a special hierarchy—`javax.net.ssl.`—that contains most, but not all, of the relevant classes.

Socket Factory Classes   To facilitate the use of different types of sockets with the minimum of changes to a program, JCE provides socket factories. Two classes exist in the package `javax.net`: `ServerSocketFactory` and `SocketFactory`. These classes include static `getDefault()` methods that allow an application to obtain the default socket factory object for the host platform.

`ServerSocketFactory` has three methods called `createServerSocket()`. `SocketFactory` has four variations of the `createSocket()` method. These overloaded methods allow for different control over the created sockets, in the same way that simple `java.net.Socket` and `java.net.ServerSocket` constructors are available in a variety of forms.

SSL Factory Classes   The SSL classes include two socket factories in the javax.net.ssl packages: SSLServerSocketFactory and SSLSocketFactory.

Setting up an SSL connection requires some handshaking between the server and client machines, and this handshaking requires some information. SSL is designed to provide for user identification and authentication, and hence nonrepudiation, data integrity, and privacy via encryption. To do this, SSL uses certificates and private/public key pairs of the same kind as discussed earlier.

It should not surprise you to learn that the SSL factories need to perform more work than the default socket types before they can create a socket or server socket. The initialization of an SSL socket or server socket requires the user to be identified and authenticated, and requires the private key and certificate for the user. So that this tedious and repetitive configuration process does not need to be part of each application program's source code, a framework allows the necessary extras to be invoked from outside the application.

The two key parts of SSL configuration are called login and authentication. These are provided for SSL as separate classes and are non-Java packages that vary between implementations. The idea is simply that you start the login program with the Java interpreter and provide as arguments the name of the authenticator class, your application class, and finally the arguments to your application.

The Java interpreter runs the login class main() method, which loads the authenticator class and uses it to validate the user, typically via a username and password. Once the user has been validated, the appropriate key and certificate are loaded from persistent storage and made available (perhaps via static class members or singleton objects) to the SSL factory classes. Finally, the argument list is modified so that only the real arguments for your program exist, your class is loaded, and the main() method is invoked with the modified argument list. This invocation is achieved using reflection. The process goes like this:

1. You issue a command of this form:

   ```
   java LoginProg AuthSystem MyCode myargs1 myargs2
   ```

2. The LoginProg main() method starts and loads the AuthSystem class.

3. The AuthSystem class identifies and authenticates the user.

4. The keys and certificates for the authenticated user are loaded so they are available to the SSL factory methods.

5. The MyCode class is loaded.

6. A String array containing only "myargs1" and "myargs2" is copied from the original argument list.

7. The main() method of MyCode is invoked using the new array as argument. Reflection does the work for this.

Export Control Issues

Although the JCE cannot generally be exported beyond North America, the technology for strong encryption is freely available in the rest of the world. In fact, there is a library of packages exactly mimicking the JCE that has been developed entirely outside the U.S. This library is available for both commercial and noncommercial use free of charge (subject to some terms, which are little more than proper acknowledgment of the authors' efforts).

> **TIP**
>
> The Cryptix libraries include implementations of major cryptographic algorithms, including DES, 3DES, RSA, and IDEA. IDEA was originally developed outside the U.S. and is cited in *Applied Cryptography: Protocols, Algorithms, and Source Code in C* by Bruce Schneier (John Wiley & Sons, 1995) as probably the strongest algorithm available today. The Cryptix library suite is available from `http://www.systemics.com/docs/cryptix/`.

Summary

This chapter has covered a great deal of material; the following list will remind you of the key points covered:

• Security concepts and terminology include identification, authentication, digital signature, nonrepudiation, authorization, resource control, data integrity, encryption (symmetric and asymmetric), and auditing.

• There is a plan for Java security, from the very foundations of the JVM. This plan has been subjected to enormous public scrutiny.

- The three features—the bytecode language design and the verifier, the `ClassLoader`, and the `SecurityManager`—form a defensive circle where each part helps protect the others.

- Authorization mechanisms in Java 2 include the policy file, permissions, keys and certificates, and signing JAR archives.

- The access-control APIs in Java 2 all hinge around the `AccessController` `.checkPermission()` method, but include the `beginPrivileged()` and `end-Privileged()` methods.

- The ACL APIs can be used as a framework for an access-control system. An implementation of these is provided in the `sun.security.acl` non-core package in Sun JDKs.

- Approaches to safer coding include using `private` variables, precondition/postcondition tests, `final` methods and classes, gatekeeper methods, and sealed packages. In a nutshell, these are all elements of encapsulation.

- The cryptographic APIs include provisions for handling the keystore and writing and installing cryptography providers.

If this chapter has done its job, you will now understand the security facilities of Java, appreciate at least some part of why Java is a platform (not just a language), and be able to compare Java's security facilities with other systems. Perhaps more important, you will be able to write security-sensitive code with competence and use the cryptographic APIs to implement complex cryptographic facilities like digital signatures.

APPENDIX

Frequently Asked Questions

This appendix presents some of the more frequently asked questions that arise when programmers get past the basics of Java and start tackling some real programming tasks. It also contains answers to questions that programmers might not realize they need to ask.

The questions are organized under the general headings:

- Language and compiler
- AWT
- Security

Language and Compiler

Why Doesn't Java Have a Preprocessor?

Because Java borrows so much from C and C++, it might seem surprising that there is no preprocessor. The *preprocessor* is a feature of C and C++ that allows you to create macros for use in the program. The preprocessor is commonly used to define literal constants so that, for example, a program can refer to MAX_ARGS instead of 1024. The preprocessor is also used to provide conditional compilation, which is typically used to code platform-specific variations in traditional programming languages. Both of these effects can be achieved in other ways; see "How Can I Declare a Constant?" and "How Can I Achieve Conditional Compilation?" in this appendix for more information.

The most important reason the preprocessor was left out is that it is so easy to misuse. The preprocessor allows arbitrarily complex macros to be created, and these macros can be used to change the nature of the language. For example, you could define the words BEGIN and END to be used in place of curly braces to indicate blocks. Often, reading a piece of C code involves substantial effort to work out what special macros are in effect in a particular source file and, consequently, what the code really means. The designers decided that the advantages a preprocessor would have offered were greatly outweighed by the disadvantages, and so it was left out.

How Can I Declare a Constant?

Constants of primitive types are simply defined by creating variables with the modifiers static and final applied to them. Therefore, the declaration:

```
public static final boolean DEBUG = true;
```

would cause DEBUG to be a constant of type boolean, accessible from any other class as *Xxxx*.DEBUG, where *Xxxx* is the enclosing class name and there is no need for an instance of its enclosing variable.

This approach actually has a significant advantage over the preprocessor approach. Because the constant declaration is strongly typed, the compiler can check its use properly. As an aside, programmers who like to use the enum mechanism of C++ also have the advantage that, unlike enum, constants can also be String objects.

I've Tried to Declare a Constant, but I Can Still Change the Value—What's Wrong?

The Java language specification allows the modifiers static and final to be in the declaration of a class instance, like this:

```
public static final StringBuffer sb = new StringBuffer("Fickle");
```

However, this declaration does not actually define a constant StringBuffer object. The static modifier affects the declaration and works as expected in this case. Unfortunately, the final modifier affects the *value* of the variable, and the problem lies in the meaning of value as applied to variables of nonprimitive types.

For variables that refer to class instances, the value is actually the reference value (typically a memory pointer), so the final modifier prevents the reference from being changed. In other words, the variable can never refer to any other object, but the object itself can still be changed.

I Thought Method Arguments Were Passed by Value— Why Is My Method Changing the Value in the Caller?

Method arguments are passed by value in Java, but as outlined in the previous answer, the value of a variable of any object type is actually a reference. Consider a method call like this:

```
Date d = new Date();
    :
```

```
nextMonth(d);
System.out.println("The date now reads " + d);
   :
public void nextMonth(Date locald)
   locald.setMonth(locald.getMonth() + 1);
}
```

The usual semantics of pass by value would mean that the modifications to locald made in the nextMonth() method would be lost when the method returns, and the printed message would show today's date. However, although in the nextMonth() method locald is a private copy of the value of d, the value of d is a *reference* and not the object to which d refers. Hence, the call to locald.setMonth() actually modifies the same object as is referred to by d in the caller.

I Thought Objects Were Passed by Reference into Methods —Why Can't I Change the Value?

Consider this example code fragment:

```
Date d = new Date();
   :
nextMonth(d);
System.out.println("The date now reads " + d);
   :
public void nextMonth(Date locald)
   locald = new Date(locald.getYear(),
                     locald.getMonth(),
                     locald.getDate());
   locald.setMonth(locald.getMonth() + 1);
}
```

You might mistakenly expect this code to behave the same as the example in the previous answer. In this example, at the entry to the nextMonth() method, locald refers to the same Date object as in the caller. However, this is not the same as pass by reference. Java always passes method arguments by value, so locald is not the same variable as d; it is a copy of its value. Changing the object to which locald refers does not affect either the value of d or the object to which d refers. This arrangement of memory is shown in Figure 1.

Another possibility to consider is that a number of classes in Java describe *immutable* objects—objects that, once created, have a constant value. These include the String class and the wrappers for the primitive data types, such as the Boolean, Integer, and Double classes.

FIGURE 1:

Values and references in a
method call

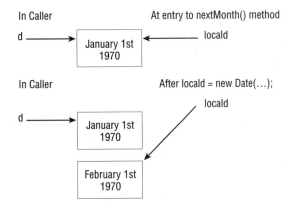

How Can I Achieve Conditional Compilation?

Conditional compilation provides a way of writing a single source file with parts
that are compiled or not compiled under the influence of constants. For example,
consider this block of C code, which uses the C preprocessor to achieve conditional compilation:

```
#if defined(DEBUG)
   printf("Value so far is %d", value);
#endif
```

If the DEBUG constant is defined, but without regard to its value, this code would
be compiled as a single printf() function call. On the other hand, if DEBUG has not
been defined, then no code is output for the printf() call.

It turns out that Java can provide conditional compilation as a result of compiler optimizations and the final mechanism for constants. Consider these fragments of code, taken from the Suite.java example described in Chapter 5.

```
public static final TRACE = true;
        :
      if (TRACE) {
         System.out.println("checking " + s);
      }
```

In this example, if the definition of TRACE is changed to false, the compiler will
not generate any code for the conditional block because it is impossible for the
conditional block ever to be executed. So although this appears to be a runtime
condition, it is in fact optimized into conditional compilation.

Why Do I Have to Handle Some Exceptions but the Compiler Overlooks Others?

The Java compiler is rather fussy about exception handling. In general, if an exception can occur in a region of code, it is either handled by the try/catch mechanism or the method as a whole is declared with a throws clause to advise the caller that the exception might be passed up.

In fact, this rule applies to exceptions that are subclasses of the Exception class but is waived for exceptions that are subclasses of either the RuntimeException class or the Error class.

Why Is There a Distinction among Exception, Error, and RuntimeException Classes?

The Error class is used for significant system difficulties, such as running out of memory. There are two general features common to the causes of errors. First, the causes of errors are severe, making it difficult to recover from such problems. For example, writing a handler to recover from running out of memory can be very tiresome. Unless such a handler is carefully designed, the first thing it needs to do is allocate some memory to work with. Given the nature of the original problem, such an attempt at memory allocation will fail. The second feature of the causes of errors is that they are not program errors—bugs—but rather are environmental difficulties, such as insufficient memory or missing library components, at execution time.

Runtime exceptions, of which the NullPointerException is a well-known example, arise specifically from programming problems. One type of programming problem might be a design error, such as when a particular condition was not anticipated and handled, or it might be an implementation bug. The essence of the RuntimeException is that a *correct* program never generates one; therefore, the source should not be cluttered with handler code for this exception.

All other exceptions can legitimately occur under potentially recoverable conditions in a correct program. Typical examples of these sorts of conditions are disks missing from drives or disconnected network cables. Because these exceptions occur under legitimate working conditions, the Java compiler insists that any code that might throw such an exception must either handle it or explicitly declare that the exception is to be passed to the caller of this method.

What Are Runtime Exceptions Really About?

Because runtime exceptions represent programming errors, they are ideal for expressing preconditions and postconditions. A *precondition* is a testable condition that must hold immediately before the invocation of a method, such as limiting the range of valid arguments. A *postcondition* is guaranteed to be true at the method's exit.

A method that calculates the square root of a number might have a precondition that the number is not negative. Its postcondition is that the returned value, when multiplied by itself, gives—within the accuracy limits of the calculation system—the original number. By programming checks for these conditions, and throwing a runtime exception where the tests fail, it is possible to significantly improve the reliability of the resulting code. This improvement occurs because bugs are brought out into the open sooner and hence fixed earlier.

Not all methods have readily expressed postconditions, but a great many are written with either implied or explicit preconditions. These might be obvious consequences of the method semantics, such as the square root example, or they might be more arbitrary, implementation-specific ones, such as "the total number of characters in all the argument strings must not exceed 128." In either case, testing the precondition at the method entry and throwing a `RuntimeException` if the condition is not met will ensure that misuse of the method, either by an accidental bug or a failure to read (or write) the documentation, will be caught immediately when the program is run, not months later when the customer is making mission-critical use of your software.

What Is an Inner Class and How Can I Use One?

Inner classes are a language feature added with the transition to JDK 1.1 that allows the definition of a class to be contained within another class. Before this addition, classes could only be defined as members of a package, and their visibility was defined either as public or default access.

An inner class can be defined like this:

```
class BigAndComplicated {
  class SmallSupport {
    // variables
    // and methods as usual
  };
```

```
    // variables, including instances of SmallSupport
    // and methods
}
```

The visibility of the SmallSupport class is restricted to the BigAndComplicated class. This does not mean, however, that SmallSupport objects cannot exist or cannot be used outside a BigAndComplicated object; it is only the visibility of the definition that is restricted. A class can return an instance of an inner class, which is an important use for an inner class. If an inner class implements some public interface, such as the Enumeration interface, it can be much tidier than having the whole outer class implement that interface.

In fact, the inner class can be anonymous. Consider this example, which is on the CD-ROM in the directory javadevhdbk/app/Inner.java:

LIST 1   *Inner.java*

```java
import java.util.*;

public class Inner {
  String s = "Hello";

  public Enumeration listem() {
    return new Enumeration () {
    int x;
      public boolean hasMoreElements() {
        return x < s.length();
      }
      public Object nextElement() {
        return new Character(s.charAt(x++));
      }
    };
  }
  public static void main(String args[]) {
    Inner that = new Inner();
    Enumeration e = that.listem();
    while (e.hasMoreElements()) {
      System.out.print(
        ((Character)(e.nextElement())).charValue());
    }
    System.out.println("\nDone");
  }
}
```

Here, the `listem()` method returns an `Enumeration` object. The object it actually returns is an instance of an unnamed inner class (remember that `Enumeration` is an interface, not a class name). The syntax used implies that an unnamed class that implements the `Enumeration` interface has been defined. A particularly useful feature of the inner class is that it has access to the variables of the enclosing class. In fact, it has access to the enclosing instance variables. In effect (and in implementation, too), the instance of the inner class is given a copy of the `this` reference of the object that created it. These mechanisms allow the inner class defined here to access the `String` variable s.

Inside the inner class, additional methods and instance variables may be declared. In this example, a variable x is used as a counter to track the next character from the string that should be returned when the `nextElement()` method is invoked. Note that if an inner class is defined inside a method, it will have access to the local variables, including the argument list, of that method if, and only if, those variables are marked `final`.

You could reasonably ask why this strategy is better than having the outer class declare that it implements the `Enumeration` interface. The main reason is that in using the inner class approach, it is possible to define another method in the `BigAndComplicated` class, which returns another, different, `Enumeration` object. Additionally, this type of approach can simplify maintenance by improving the clarity of the code.

What Is Reflection and How Can I Use It?

The `java.lang.reflect` package allows you to examine the class definition of an object at runtime. It allows you to extract a full definition of the accessible API for the object's class, listing the constructors, methods, and variables. Reflection also allows you to access the variables and invoke the methods.

 The `Reflector.java` example demonstrates reflection. It allows you to load and run a class or to examine the constructors, fields, and methods that make up a class. The source for this example is located on the CD-ROM in the directory `javadevhdbk/app/Reflector.java`, and the corresponding bytecode is in the file `Reflector.class`.

LIST 2   *Reflector.java*

```
import java.io.*;
import java.util.*;
import java.lang.reflect.*;
```

```java
import java.awt.*;
import java.awt.event.*;
import java.applet.*;

public class Reflector extends Applet {
  private static final String runText = "Run";
  private static final String examineText = "Examine";

  private Panel topRow = new Panel();
  private Button run = new Button(runText);
  private Button examine = new Button(examineText);
  private TextField classname = new TextField(40);
  private TextArea response = new TextArea(30, 60);

  public Reflector() {
    setLayout(new BorderLayout());

    topRow.add(classname);
    topRow.add(run);
    topRow.add(examine);
    add(topRow, BorderLayout.NORTH);

    response.setEditable(false);
    add(response, BorderLayout.CENTER);

    run.addActionListener(
      new ActionListener() {
        public void actionPerformed(ActionEvent ev) {
          execute(classname.getText());
        }
      }
    );

    classname.addActionListener(
      new ActionListener() {
        public void actionPerformed(ActionEvent ev) {
          execute(classname.getText());
        }
      }
    );

    examine.addActionListener(
```

```
      new ActionListener() {
        public void actionPerformed(ActionEvent ev) {
          examine(classname.getText());
        }
      }
  );
}

public static void main(String args[]) {
  Reflector that = new Reflector();
  MortalFrame f = new MortalFrame("Reflector");
  f.add(that, BorderLayout.CENTER);
  f.pack();
  f.setVisible(true);
}

public void execute(String cmdline) {
  String command = null;
  StringTokenizer tok = new StringTokenizer(cmdline, " \t");
  if (tok.hasMoreTokens()) {
    command = tok.nextToken();
  }
  else {
    return;
  }
  // collect arguments
  Vector v = new Vector();
  while (tok.hasMoreElements()) {
    v.addElement(tok.nextElement());
  }
  String [] invokeArgs = new String[v.size()];
  for (int i = 0; i < v.size(); i++) {
    invokeArgs[i] = (String)(v.elementAt(i));
  }

  Class toRun = null;
  Object objectToRun = null;
  try {
    toRun = Class.forName(command);
    objectToRun = toRun.newInstance();

    if (objectToRun instanceof Applet) {
```

```
          MortalFrame f = new MortalFrame("Applet " + command);
          Applet a = (Applet)objectToRun;
          f.setVisible(true);
          f.add(a, BorderLayout.CENTER);
          a.init();
          a.start();
          f.setSize(200, 200);
        }
      else {
        Class [] mainParamTypes = new Class[1];
        mainParamTypes[0] = invokeArgs.getClass();
        boolean success = false;
        Object [] invokeParam = new Object[1];
        invokeParam[0] = invokeArgs;
        Method mainMethod = toRun.getMethod("main", mainParamTypes);

        mainMethod.invoke(null, invokeParam);
      }
    }
    catch (InvocationTargetException ite) {
      response.setText("Exception in application:\n" +
                        ite.getTargetException());
    }
    catch (Exception e) {
      response.setText("Unexpected exception :\n" + e);
    }
  }

  public void examine(String command) {
    Class toSnoop = null;
    int i = command.indexOf(' ');
    if (i != -1) {
      command = command.substring(0, i);
    }
    try {
      toSnoop = Class.forName(command);
      Constructor [] constructors = null;
      Field [] fields = null;
      Method [] methods = null;
      constructors = toSnoop.getConstructors();
      fields = toSnoop.getDeclaredFields();
```

```java
        methods = toSnoop.getDeclaredMethods();

        response.setText("Constructors:\n");
        for (i = 0; i < constructors.length; i++) {
          response.append(constructors[i] + "\n");
        }

        response.append("\nFields:\n");
        for (i = 0; i < fields.length; i++) {
          response.append(fields[i] + "\n");
        }

        response.append("\nMethods:\n");
        for (i = 0; i < methods.length; i++) {
          response.append(methods[i] + "\n");
        }
      }
      catch (ClassNotFoundException cnfe) {
        response.setText("Class not found");
      }
    }
}

class MortalFrame extends Frame {
  private static int count;

  public MortalFrame(String title) {
    super(title);
    count++;
    addWindowListener(
      new WindowAdapter() {
        public void windowClosing(WindowEvent ev) {
          setVisible(false);
          dispose();
          if (count == 0) {
            System.exit(0);
          }
        }
      }
    );
  }
}
```

The example runs as an application. The program launches a window like the one in Figure 2.

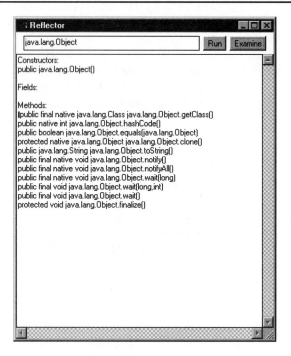

Enter the name of a class into the textfield and click the Examine button. A list of the constructors, fields, and methods of the class is placed in the text area. The fully qualified name of any class on the CLASSPATH is acceptable, so you can enter java.lang.String or any class in the local directory.

To run a Java application from the Reflector class, type the name of the class into the textfield, followed by any arguments it requires. Then click the Run button. If the class specified is an Applet class, it is invoked as such. To support the applet, a separate window is launched, and the applet is started within that window. If the class is not an Applet class but has a main() method, then that method will be invoked and the arguments provided will be passed to it.

When either the Examine or Run button is clicked, the action() method is called. This method determines which button was clicked and calls either the execute() or examine() method as appropriate. Both the execute() and examine() methods start by obtaining the defining Class object for the specified class by using the Class.forName() static method.

The execute() method then creates an instance of the class by invoking the newInstance() method on the defining Class object. The instanceof operator is used to test the object that is returned from the newInstance() method to determine if it is an applet. If it is an applet, then a frame is created, the applet is added to the frame, and the init() and start() methods of the applet are called. (This same behavior is used in the MinAppletViewer example in Chapter 10.) If the newly created object is not an applet, then the Reflect package is used to check for and invoke the main() method.

The Reflect package defines a number of classes, including the Method, Field, and Constructor classes. Instances of these classes describe methods, fields, and constructors of a class, respectively. Using instances of these classes, along with instances of the classes they represent, methods and constructors can be invoked and field values can be manipulated. To invoke a method, the following steps are necessary:

1. Obtain a reference to the object for which the method is to be invoked. In other words, to use reflection to invoke x.method(), you first must have the reference x. This reference is unnecessary if you want to invoke a constructor or static method.

2. Obtain the Class object that defines this class by applying the getClass() method to an instance or, as is the case in this example, by applying the Class.forName() static method, which loads a class when given its name.

3. Once a Class object has been obtained, four methods allow you to obtain Method objects from that class. The getMethods() method returns an array of Method objects that define all public methods available in this class, including inherited ones. The getMethod() method takes arguments that specify a particular name and argument list. It then returns a Method object describing the single specified method, if it exists. Two similar methods— getDeclaredMethods() and getDeclaredMethod()—extract methods of any accessibility but do not return inherited methods, only those declared at this class level.

4. Given an instance of the Method class, the method that that instance describes can be invoked using the invoke() method. The invoke() method takes two arguments. The first is a reference to the object that provides the context for the method call. Inside the method, this first reference will become the this object. The second argument is an array of Object objects that define the parameters to be passed into the invoked method. If the method to be invoked is static, then the first argument may be null.

5. When the method returns, its return value is passed back as the return value from the `invoke()` method. If a primitive type is returned, it is wrapped up in an appropriate object. For example, an `int` is wrapped in an `Integer` object, and a `short` in a `Short` object. If an exception is thrown, then an `InvocationTargetException` is created with the original exception wrapped up inside. The `InvocationTargetException` is then thrown from the `invoke()` method.

In this case, `main()` is static, so no object is needed to invoke the method. In fact, one was obtained previously anyway to allow the `instanceof` operator to be used to see if the method was an applet. The class could have been so checked using the `getClasses()` method of the `Class` class, which would have avoided the need to create an instance that would be redundant if the class turned out not to be an applet.

In the `Reflector` example, the `Method` object that defines the `main()` method is obtained from the defining class using the `getMethod()` method. Strictly, the program should verify that the method found is declared as `public static void`, but for the sake of simplicity, this is overlooked.

The method is invoked using an array of `String` objects as its argument. Notice that the definition of the `invoke()` method requires that it takes an array of `Object` objects, and the elements of this array are intended to represent the elements of the argument list. The `main()` method requires one argument, and so the `Object` array should have one element. The single argument to the `main()` method is an array of `String` that has been constructed using the contents of the textfield and that is placed as the first and only item in the `invokeargs` array.

The `examine()` method first extracts the class name from the start of the textfield, which simply involves checking for any spaces that separate a class name from arguments intended for a `main()` method. Once the class name has been established, the `Class.forName()` static method is used to obtain a `Class` object describing the requested class. The `getConstructors()`, `getDeclaredMethods()`, and `getDeclared-Fields()` methods are called on the resulting `Class` object. These methods return arrays of objects that describe constructors, methods, and fields respectively. The `examine()` method proceeds by iterating these arrays in turn, extracting the textual representation of each element of the array and appending it to the text area. The textual representations returned by the implied `toString()` method call (which results from the application of the + operator) return strings that represent the original declarations.

A variety of facilities can be used on a `Constructor`, `Method`, or `Field` object once it has been obtained in the above manner. For methods, the modifiers, parameter types, return type, and exceptions can all be extracted. For constructors, the modifiers, parameter types, and exception types can be extracted. For fields, the modifiers and types of the field may be extracted.

Methods can be invoked using the `invoke()` method with two arguments. The first argument is the object that is to be `this` in the method call. The second argument is an array of `Object` instances. The elements of the array form the parameters of the method call. Dynamic method lookup is performed to determine the correct overriding version of the method to use.

Constructors can be invoked using the `newInstance()` method with one argument. The `Class` class has provided a `newInstance()` method with zero arguments, but the `Constructor` class allows any constructor to be invoked with whatever arguments are appropriate.

The value of a field can be read and modified as required. A number of methods allow access to fields of primitive types. For fields of object type, it will normally be necessary to make further use of the reflection facilities in order to manipulate the data.

Note that the facilities of the `java.lang.reflect` package are tightly controlled by the security manager. Applets cannot generally use the introspection facilities just described, and even applications are subject to the language rules governing field access. It is not, for example, possible to use reflection to read private fields.

What Does *Deprecated* Mean in Documentation?

Deprecated is a javadoc comment that a class author can add to the source code. javadoc then advertises this comment in the resulting HTML documentation. It indicates that a particular class, method, or field should not be used for new developments. It is usually accompanied by additional information that details the new mechanism for obtaining the functionality using nondeprecated features.

Deprecated features might be removed altogether from future releases of a package, so the warnings issued by the compiler should not be taken lightly.

What Does clone() Do?

The `clone()` method is declared in the `Object` class and is therefore inherited into every subclass. It creates a duplicate of an object using a shallow copy. *Shallow copy* means that the bit patterns of your original object are duplicated, so if any of the member variables of your object are themselves references, then the objects that are referred to are *not* duplicated. The alternative form of behavior is called a deep copy. A *deep copy* copies only the primitive variables of an object and actually calls itself recursively to replicate any object instances that are part of the object. A deep copy is more difficult because the programmer needs to ensure that the recursion stops eventually. This problem is most noticeable in self-referential data structures, such as a circular linked list.

Because the clone() method is defined in the Object class, it is available in all other classes. Also, because it is a member of the Object class, you will not normally find it listed in the documentation because the javadoc tool only makes entries for methods actually defined in a particular class.

In some circumstances, the shallow copy behavior of the clone() method might be inappropriate. Consider a class that defines a member variable serialNumber. Cloning such an object should really give it a new serial number value; if it hasn't, the semantics of the object will have been damaged. In such a circumstance, over-riding the clone() method will allow you to control the behavior so that it is suitable to your class.

Despite clone() being defined in the Object class, you cannot call it for every object. There are two reasons for this limitation. First, the Object clone() method is declared as protected, so it is inaccessible from some objects. If you define your own clone() method for a class, you can make it public (an example of this is in Chapter 3). Second, the clone() method requires that the object it copies implements the Cloneable interface, which means that unless the writer of a class intended that you should be able to clone an instance, the attempt will fail, throwing a CloneNotSupportedException.

You might wonder why clone() is defined in the Object class if the designers did not intend it to be freely usable in all subclasses. The reason is that clone() gets inside your object and copies memory directly with native code that does a block copy of memory. Of course, you can't do that in normal Java code because it requires arbitrary pointer manipulation. The designers had to provide the mechanism at a central point and allow you to decide whether you wanted it to be enabled for your particular class.

The Cloner.java example demonstrates the salient points of using clone(). This example is on the CD-ROM in the directory javadevhdbk\app\Cloner.java.

LIST 3   *Cloner.java*

```java
public class Cloner implements Cloneable{
  private int serial;
  private boolean isValid;
  private StringBuffer name;
  private static int lastSerial = 0;

  public Cloner(String name) {
    synchronized(this.getClass()) {
      serial = lastSerial++;
    }
    this.name = new StringBuffer(name);
    isValid = true;
  }

  protected Object oldClone() {
    Cloner newOne = null;
    try {
      newOne = (Cloner)(super.clone());
    }
    catch (CloneNotSupportedException e) {
      e.printStackTrace();
    }
    return newOne;
  }

  protected Object clone() {
    Cloner newOne = null;
    try {
      newOne = (Cloner)(super.clone());
      synchronized (this.getClass()) {
        newOne.serial = lastSerial++;
      }
    }
    catch (CloneNotSupportedException e) {
      e.printStackTrace();
    }
    return newOne;
  }
```

```
protected Object newClone() {
  Cloner newOne = null;
  try {
    newOne = (Cloner)(super.clone());
    synchronized (this.getClass()) {
      newOne.serial = lastSerial++;
    }
    newOne.name = new StringBuffer(newOne.name.toString());
  }
  catch (CloneNotSupportedException e) {
    e.printStackTrace();
  }
  return newOne;
}

public String toString() {
  return "[" + getClass().getName() +
    ",serial=" + serial +
    "," + (isValid ? "" : "in") + "valid" +
    "," + name + "]";
}

public static void main(String args[]) {
  Cloner a = new Cloner("fred");
  Cloner b = new Cloner("jim");
  Cloner c = (Cloner)(a.clone());
  Cloner d = (Cloner)(b.oldClone());
  Cloner e = (Cloner)(a.newClone());
  System.out.println("Cloner a is " + a);
  System.out.println("Cloner b is " + b);
  System.out.println("Cloner c is " + c);
  System.out.println("Cloner d is " + d);
  System.out.println("Cloner e is " + e);

  a.name.append("erick");
  System.out.println("Cloner a is " + a);
  System.out.println("Cloner c is " + c);
  System.out.println("Cloner e is " + e);
}
}
```

When you run the program, you will see this output:

```
Cloner a is [Cloner,serial=0,valid,fred]
Cloner b is [Cloner,serial=1,valid,jim]
Cloner c is [Cloner,serial=2,valid,fred]
Cloner d is [Cloner,serial=1,valid,jim]
Cloner e is [Cloner,serial=3,valid,fred]
Cloner a is [Cloner,serial=0,valid,frederick]
Cloner c is [Cloner,serial=2,valid,frederick]
Cloner e is [Cloner,serial=3,valid,fred]
```

Each Cloner instance has the three variables serial, isValid, and name. The main() method creates two of these objects with the arguments fred and jim. The program then copies these two objects using the methods clone(), oldClone(), and newClone().

The oldClone() method simply invokes super.clone(), which results in the duplicated serial number that you see between the objects b and d, both of which report serial number 1 in the output.

The clone() method corrects this error by reassigning the value of serial immediately after the copy. Therefore, the values of serial between objects a, c, and e are distinct and correctly allocated.

Next, the main() method appends the string erick to the string buffer name of the object a and prints out the values of a, c, and e. The name strings of these are reported as frederick, frederick, and fred, respectively, which indicates that the clone() method was a shallow copy because the name object was not duplicated but is shared. By contrast, the newClone() method created a new name object that is unaffected by modifications to the old object.

What Does equals() Do?

It is important to understand that there is nothing special about equals(). The intention behind this method is to provide a "deep comparison," as opposed to the "shallow comparison" of the == operator. When == is applied to two objects, it compares two object references (essentially pointers) and determines whether they refer to the same piece of memory. The idea of the equals() method is that it should inspect the instance variables of the two objects and determine whether the instance variables are equal. It could be argued that *equals* is not the best possible name; *matches* or *sameAs* might convey the idea a bit better.

There is an unfortunate misconception among some Java programmers that equals() works on the same level as clone(); that is, it makes a mysterious system-level call to do a bit-by-bit comparison of the two objects. This is not the case. The equals() method is inherited by all classes from Object, and each class is responsible for its own implementation.

There is no guarantee that equals() will be implemented for all JDK classes. If a class does not explicitly state in its API that it implements an equals(), then it will use whatever version it inherits from its superclass. This version will accurately compare the superclass portions of its two objects but will ignore the subclass portions. A return value of false can be trusted in this case, but a return value of true only means that the objects match each other to a certain extent.

Programmers who are designing utility classes that will be used by other developers should generally provide an equals() method for each class. Doing so could greatly ease the debugging cycle in the same way that providing a useful toString() method simplifies life.

If a class contains a reference to an object of another class, it must be decided whether equals() should do a shallow or a deep comparison on the reference. If the class contains an object-type instance variable called ref, should the implementation be equals(Object that) check this.ref == that.ref (shallow comparison), or should it call this.ref.equals(that.ref)? The correct decision depends entirely on the nature of the class, and the only guideline is that the implementation should be clearly documented.

Any implementation of equals() should begin by calling the inherited version to check the superclass portions of the two objects being compared. The code fragment below shows how to do this:

```
public boolean equals(Object that)
{
    if (super.equals(that) == false)
        return false;

        ...

}
```

It is important to realize that the implementation of equals() in the Object class simply uses pointer comparison; that is, its effect is identical to ==. Because of this, you should avoid calling super.equals() if the resulting method would be the Object.equals() method.

The argument to equals() is declared to be of type Object; in other words, it can be any nonprimitive. For the equals() methods in other classes to be overriding—rather than overloading—methods, it is essential that the argument must always be declared as Object. Furthermore, the language specification requires that equals() should return false if called on to compare two objects that are not of the same class. An implementation of equals() should therefore start by checking the class of the argument before checking any variables. For example, the SomeClass class might do the following:

```java
public boolean equals(Object that)
{
    if (!(that.getClass()== this.getClass()))
        return false;
    if (super.equals(that) == false)
        return false;
        ...
}
```

This precaution also ensures that the equals() method is commutative; that is, it ensures that the result of a.equals(b) will always be the same as the result of b.equals(a), regardless of the classes of a and b.

Is There Anything Special about toString()?

This method is slightly special; toString() is used in Java's overload of the + operator for string concatenation.

When the Java compiler detects that either operand of the + operator is a string, it converts the other operand to a string, uses a string buffer to concatenate the strings, and converts the final string buffer back to a string. A primitive operand is converted to a string by calling the static String method valueOf() on the primitive. An object is converted to a string by calling the object's toString() method.

Consider the following line of code, which assumes that i is an int and thing is an object:

```java
String s = "abc" + i + thing;
```

The Java compiler would treat this line as an abbreviation for:

```java
String s = ((new StringBuffer("abc"))
            .append(String.valueOf(i))
            .append(thing.toString())).toString();
```

This simple example shows why it is a very good thing that the designers of Java permitted a single instance of operator overloading to creep into the language.

Be cautious when using the + operator to convert operands to strings simply for convenience. Consider the expressions `"hello " + 1 + 2 + 3` and `1 + 2 + 3 + " hello"`. In the first case, the left-to-right associativity of the + operator means that the value of the whole expression is the string `"hello 123"`, but for the second case the result is `"6 hello"`.

Why Can't I Override a Method to Make It Less Accessible?

In Java's view of objected-oriented programming, you are allowed to keep a reference to an object in a variable, provided the type of the variable is appropriate for the object. Suppose you have an `Employee` class and a `Manager` class that extends `Employee`. You can refer to an object of the `Manager` class using either a variable of the `Manager` type or of the `Employee` type because a `Manager` *is an* `Employee` but has extra or modified features. So any operation that can properly be applied to an `Employee` can be applied to a `Manager`, too. This allows you to use an `Employee` variable to refer to a `Manager` object. For instance:

```
Employee [] staff = new Employee[10];
staff[0] = new Manager();
```

Now any operations on `staff[0]` are actually working on a `Manager` object.

Imagine then what would happen if a method, say, `getJobDescription()`, was defined public for an `Employee` but private for a `Manager`. The compiler could not reject the construction `staff[0].getJobDescription()`, nor could the bytecode verifier, but the access would be theoretically illegal. This difficulty precludes you from making methods of a derived class more private when overriding the parent class definition.

Variables *can* be declared with the same name in both a parent and derived class and with less accessibility in the derived class. However, in this case, the new variable does not override the old one. Instead, it shadows it. *Shadowing* is distinct from overriding and means that dynamic binding does not occur with variables, and the compiler makes a decision about which of the two variables you are referring to at compilation time based on the type of the reference.

What Does import Really Do?

The `import` statement sometimes causes a bit of confusion. In fact, it simply provides a context for shortened class names. For example, the class name `java.awt.Button` is commonly referred to simply as `Button`, which is permitted if the statement `import java.awt.*;` has been issued. The import statement does not change a class name, nor does it change the contents or size of the `.class` output file.

So why might you use an explicit `import` rather than the wildcard form? If you are a Java instructor, you might get into this habit as a deliberate way to learn the detailed contents of each package. If you need to import classes from multiple packages, but some of the classes in those packages have common names, then you might simply import the ones you actually need.

AWT

How Can I Use Unicode Characters?

Although Java uses Unicode internally to represent characters, its keyboard and screen capabilities are constrained by the host platform. Java does not come with a set of special fonts and a fancy input tool to allow the entry of characters not normally supported by the platform (at least, not at the time of this book's writing).

What Java does give you, along with the platform-independent internal representation, is the ability to perform appropriate conversions between the internal Unicode and external local format. For example, if your computer is a PC that is set up to run with the code page 863 character set, supporting French Canadian, then characters that are typed at the keyboard will be translated into Unicode as they are read by Java. Similarly, on output, the Unicode characters will be translated back to local form.

Sometimes, you will need to read or write characters using a character encoding different from that used by your own machine. This situation could arise if you are making a network connection or using a file prepared on some other machine. Under these conditions, you can explicitly control the translation that is used by creating `InputStreamReader` and `OutputStreamWriter` objects and explicitly specifying an encoding standard rather than accepting the default.

A command-line tool, called native2ascii, is provided with the JDK. This tool uses the Unicode escape conventions of Java to convert files between a local character representation and plain ASCII. The documentation for this tool also lists the various encoding formats that can be used.

More details of these mechanisms may be found in Chapters 5 and 9, which cover portability issues and file I/O and streams, respectively.

Why Does My Component Ignore the Size I Specify?

Setting a size for an AWT component—using either constructor arguments or the setSize() or setBounds() method—is ineffective if the component is subject to the control of a layout manager. Most layout managers expect to control the position and size of the components in their domain. If you do not want a component size changed by the layout manager, you can either avoid using a layout manager or you can use a layout manager that does not concern itself with size but only with position. In either case, you probably want to avoid losing the facilities of the layout manager with respect to other components in the layout. To ensure that these facilities are preserved, place the component in question in a panel of its own and set the layout manager of that panel to be a FlowLayout object.

It is possible to set a container to use no layout manager, but if more than one component is involved, it is generally unwise because you will need to position them all with explicit code, and the result is likely to be platform dependent. A better approach is to write a LayoutManager class of your own that imposes the layout policy you require. Examples of this approach are given in Chapter 4.

Why Does My Text Component Ignore the Width I Specify?

The width argument to the TextField and TextArea class constructors specify a preferred size in terms of the average character width. Assuming you are sure the component is not being controlled by a layout manager (see the previous answer), the problem probably relates to the font used in your text component.

Most fonts are proportionally spaced or of variable widths, which means that it is not possible to have one width that displays a precise number of characters without considering what the characters are. Lowercase characters are generally narrower than their uppercase equivalents. The preferred width of the component is taken in terms of the average width specified as part of the font definition.

If you really need to display a precise number of characters across a text component, then you will have to use a monospaced font such as Courier.

Security

I Run a Corporate Intranet and My Applets Need File System Access—How Can I Retain Protection Against Outside Applets?

Sign them!

In JDK 1.0.*x*, a Java class—whether an applet, application, or supporting class—was granted privileges based on the class loader that had obtained that bytecode for the class. The *primordial* class loader is the built-in class loader that only loads classes from the CLASSPATH value and only from the local file system. If a class had been loaded by the primordial class loader, then it was granted full privilege on that basis. Alternatively, if a class was not loaded by the primordial class loader, it was considered to be foreign. By default, the security manager prevented foreign code from doing anything that was considered sensitive, such as reading or writing files. It was possible to turn off this protection, but the situation was all or nothing; if you trusted any foreign code at all, you had to trust all foreign code entirely. Clearly, this is not an acceptable situation in an intranet environment, even if it is not connected to the Internet, because it allows imported applets unrestrained access to important corporate data and facilities.

In an intranet, you will generally have a library of corporate-standard utility programs located on central servers. These will appear to be foreign code to Java, but you probably do want to grant them trusted privileges, such as access to file systems.

Using digital signatures and the jarsigner tool, which are part of Java 2 (javakey was used at 1.1), you can mark classes in a JAR archive as trusted, regardless of their origin or the class loader that fetched them. This procedure is called *signing* the class. Typically, you might sign classes you have written, and you might sign code supplied to you from a source you trust. However, you almost certainly should not sign anything imported from other sources unless you have the source code, you have checked the source, you compiled the sources yourself, and there is a clearly stated reason why the class requires privilege to achieve its proper job.

Full details of how to sign archives and how to grant privilege based on those signatures are in Chapter 18.

INDEX

Note to the Reader: Throughout this index **boldfaced** page numbers indicate primary discussions of a topic. *Italicized* page numbers indicate illustrations.

SYMBOLS

A

C

F

G

K

M

N

O

P

V

W

X

Y

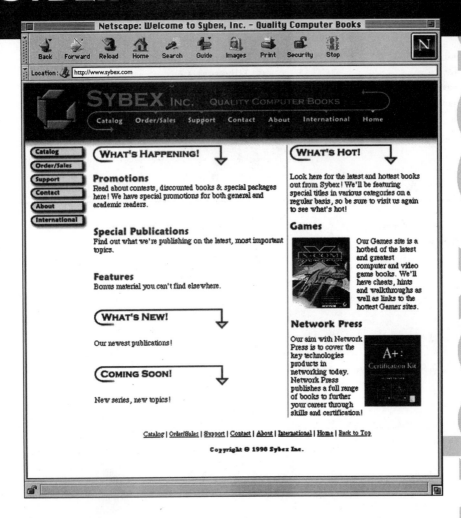